Environmental Economics:
A Reader

Environmental Economics: A Reader

Edited by
Anil Markandya and
Julie Richardson

St. Martin's Press   **New York**

First published in the United States of America in 1992

Printed in Great Britain by Biddles Ltd., Guildford and King's Lynn

ISBN 0–312–09476–0 (hardback)
    0–312–09477–9 (paperback)

Library of Congress Cataloging-in-Publication Data

Environmental economics: a reader / edited by Anil Markandya and
    Julie Richardson
      p. cm.
    ISBN 0–312–09476–0. — ISBN 0–312–09477–9 (pbk.)
    1. Environmental policy—Economic aspects.   2. Economic
development—Environmental aspects.   I Markandya, Anil, 1945–
II, Richardson, Julie.
HC79.E5E5772 1993
363.7—dc20   92-36048
                                                              CIP

Contents

Contents

Acknowledgements

The publishers would like to thank the authors and copyright holders of the following chapters for permission to reprint them in this volume:

Ch 1 from *Environmental Quality in a Growing Economy,* ed H Jarrett, copyright © by Resources for the Future; ch 2 from *Journal of Environmental Economics and Management,* Dec 1987, copyright © 1987 by Academic Press Inc; ch 3 from JH Dales, *Pollution, Property and Prices,* University of Toronto Press 1968, copyright © University of Toronto Press; ch 4 from *Science* vol 162, 1968, copyright © 1968 by the American Association for the Advancement of Science; ch 5 from *American Economic Review,* vol 57, 1967, and ch 16 from vol 79, 1982, both copyright © American Economic Association; ch 6 from *Economic Inquiry,* vol 24, 1987; ch 7 from *Quarterly Journal of Economics,* vol 102, 1987 by permission of The MIT Press, Cambridge Massachusetts, copyright © The MIT Press; ch 8 from *Transactions of the American Fisheries Society,* vol 116, 1987, reprinted by permission of the author; ch 9 from *Land Economics,* vol 59, 1983, reprinted by permission of the University of Wisconsin Press, copyright © The University of Wisconsin Press; ch 10 from *Journal of Risk and Uncertainty,* vol 1, 1988, reprinted by permission of Kluwer Academic Publishers; ch 11 from *Journal of Environmental Economics and Management,* vol 15, 1988, copyright © 1988 by Academic Press Inc; ch 13 from *American Journal of Agricultural Economics,* vol 69, 1987, and ch 17 from vol 61, 1979, both reprinted by permission of The American Agricultural Economics Association; ch 14 from *Southern Economic Journal,* vol 52, 1985, reprinted by permission of The Southern Economic Association; ch 15 from *Review of Economics and Statistics,* vol LXVIII, 1986, copyright 1986 by the President and Fellows of Harvard College; ch 18 from *Swedish Journal of Economics,* vol 73, no 1, 1971, reprinted by permission of the authors; ch 19 from *Journal of Public Economics,* vol 5, 1976, © North-Holland Publishing Company, reprinted by permission of Elsevier Science Publishers; ch 20 from *Statistical and Mathematical Aspects of Pollution Problems,* ed JW Pratt 1974, reprinted by permission of Marcel Dekker Inc; ch 21 and ch 24 both from *Oxford Review of Economic Policy,* vol 6, 1990 by permission of Oxford University Press, copyright © Oxford University Press and *Oxford Review of Economic Policy* 1990; ch 23 from Environmental Department Working Paper no 19, 1989, reprinted by permission of The World Bank; ch 24 reprinted by permission of the author; ch 25 from World Resources Institute 1989, reprinted by permission of the World Resources Institute; ch 26 from *Millenium Journal of International Studies,* 1991; ch 28 from Overseas Development Administration, 1991, reprinted by kind permission of the Overseas Development Administration.

The economics of the environment: an introduction

Anil Markandya and Julie Richardson

INTRODUCTION

The subject of environmental economics is in its early to mid twenties; about as old as most of the undergraduates and young postgraduates who may be reading this book. As with most ideas in economics, it followed rather than led; being a response to the concerns of many people about their deteriorating environment, and a reaction to the prevailing economic and social orthodoxy of the post-war period that limitless economic growth was possible. Economics, believing it had 'conquered' the problem of unemployment in the 1950s and 1960s, turned its attention to the mysteries of economic growth, asking what would a long term equilibrium look like; and whether it would be stable or whether the economy would, in the long term, be subject to fluctuations and instability. In the tremendous intellectual effort that went into understanding growth one fact was sadly ignored; that some of the inputs essential to the production process were limited in supply. Ever increasing population and rising per capita income could not be accommodated with the earth's limited natural resources. Using a word that has become fashionable more recently, the question of the **sustainability** of the growth process was not properly addressed.

It was not just an abstract concern with the long run that motivated the interest in the environment. As people became richer, they found that the supply of produced goods such as cars and refrigerators was increasing compared to that of clean air, or a quiet neighbourhood or open parkland, or unpolluted water. These environmental goods were becoming relatively scarce, but the demand for them was rising as real incomes rose. Since many of these goods were also ones that could not naturally be increased in supply from the efforts of the private sector (for a variety of reasons that are discussed below), there was a role for public sector regulation. Institutions such as the Environmental Protection Agency in the US were founded with a mandate to protect the environment. But in doing so the essential questions of how much to protect it, or what should be paid in protecting it, or what methods to use in protecting it had to be answered.

The foundations for providing the answers lay in the economic theory of welfare economics, and in particular in the theory of external effects or externalities. Students familiar with elementary economics will recognize these terms. Those who are not familiar should know that welfare economics is concerned with questions of economic justice, of how resources should be allocated in society so that individual and social welfare is maximised. Externalities are items such as noise or polluted air, which have an effect on a person's welfare, but whose level is determined without properly taking account of that welfare effect.

In professional terms, many of the theoretical questions arising from external

7

effects had been sorted out as long ago as the 1930s, by economists such as Pigou. Hence, even when the social problems arising from environmental degradation became critical, the more professionally ambitious economists did not turn their attention to them. It was felt that environmental economics was nothing more than externalities dressed up in their Sunday best. All that was needed was the imposition of the right tax and all would be well. However, it has not been that simple and, as environmental regulation has become increasingly important and as fresh problems have emerged, such as the threat to the global environment in the form of climate change, many branches of economic analysis have been needed. As with other areas such as labour and education, a sub-discipline of environmental economics has emerged.

This book is a selected set of readings covering a very wide range of material and an enormous literature on environmental economics. It has had to be very selective and doubtless many classic papers left out will raise environmental eyebrows somewhere. Where the omissions are obvious we will try and offer an explanation; in other cases we can only plead *de gustibus*. One broad area that has been excluded is that of natural resource economics – the theory and practice of the use of resources such as oil, materials, forests and fish. A proper treatment of these topics would need a book of its own. Instead this set of readings concentrates on the general principles that arise in managing the ambient environment, and how those principles can be translated into practice.

The readings are divided into five parts. The first is an **introduction to the broad issues of environment in an economic setting.** The second is concerned with **translating the value of environmental goods and services into the common unit of money,** so that they can be compared with each other and with other non-environmental goods. Valuation has played a central role in environmental economics and is the area that we have covered most extensively. The third section looks at the **principles determining the regulation of the environment.** The question of which instruments should be used, and what are pros and cons of alternatives such as taxes or direct controls have been much debated both at a theoretical and an empirical level. The fourth section gives a flavour of a relatively new field, that of **environment and development.** The belief that environmental concerns were a rich country's preserve, and that tackling poverty was the paramount concern of developing countries remained the conventional wisdom for much of the 1960s and 1970s. The change came about in the 1980s, when the key role of the natural resource base in the very process of development led some economists to emphasize the protection of environmental resources in the development plans of such countries, and to seek the goal of **sustainable development.** Finally the last section looks at **the global environmental problems** by which all countries, rich and poor, are affected. The challenges posed by these problems lead us into uncharted waters, where international cooperation has to determine policy and where the conflict between what is attainable and would be efficient may be very strong.

BASIC CONCEPTS: THE ECONOMY AND THE ENVIRONMENT

We begin the readings with a classic article by Boulding: *The economics of the coming spaceship Earth.* It represents a radical piece of thinking at a time (mid 1960s) when growth theory was in its prime, and it poses a compelling analogy between the laws of thermodynamics and those of economics. The first law translates into saying that the waste generated as a result of the cumulative production and consumption must be present somewhere in the physical system. The capacity of that system to absorb waste must therefore be taken into account when planning economic activity. Of course, to the extent that we recycle waste, the pressure on the assimilative capacity is reduced but, according to the second law of thermodynamics, increasing entropy means that complete recycling can never be achieved. In a provocative way, Boulding draws a number of lessons from these laws for economics.

The second article, by Daly, *The economic growth debate: what some economists have learnt but many have not,* is a careful and reflective piece asking what are the real limits to economic growth? In the early 1970s there was debate about the limits to growth in which some economists proceeded to show that as the earth's mineral resources ran out, economic activity would be reduced and could even lead to a catastrophic economic decline. But such projections were naïve and did not take enough account of substitutes or technological developments. Resources do not simply 'run out'; they are progressively depleted, and as they become scarce more effort is put into economizing on them and in finding substitutes. Daly's article looks at the limits to growth in a more sophisticated way, examining the social and physical constraints.

The next two articles in the first section deal with the question of property rights. The excerpt from Dales' book, *Pollution, Property and Prices,* explains clearly what is meant by a property right, and why common property, or property with insufficiently defined rights of use and exchange can suffer from misuse. He makes the obvious but telling point that animals that are owned, such as cows or pigs never suffer from problems of extinction but those such as whales with ill-defined rights can be threatened with extinction. The subsequent and final article in this section is the classic short paper by Hardin, *The tragedy of the commons.* The tone is rather pessimistic – a 'tragedy' being defined as the inevitable working of a process – and concludes that the solution to the overriding problem of our time – overpopulation – is not 'technical' but rather moral. The moral dimension arises in his view from the need to restrict the use of common resources. Economists might disagree with whether methods for restricting such resources fall in the moral or economic domain, but the examples and the discussion are both instructive and thought-provoking.

VALUATION METHODS AND APPLICATIONS
In our opinion some of the most exciting work in the field of environmental economics has been on the valuation of environmental costs and benefits. Valuation is important both for investment decisions involving environmental impacts, and for the regulation of the environment. At the same time it is difficult to put money values on things such as clean air, or a fine view. For commodities that are traded we can use market prices, but for items that influence welfare but which do not pass through markets, prices do not exist. That does not mean, of course, that they do not have a value, or that the value cannot be translated into money terms and compared to other things that are valued. A range of techniques has been developed for valuing environmental goods and services, and examples of them are reviewed in this section. Before looking at the articles in detail it is worth noting that the environmental literature distinguishes between use and non-use values. Use values are derived from the welfare that the particular environmental commodity provides through its services, now or in the future.

Examples include a quiet environment, a fine view, or a wildlife park. Not that 'use' in this sense does not imply physical contact with the environment; it could be use through seeing a movie about the park, or enjoying an article in a newspaper about a pristine environment.

Non-use values are more complex to analyse. They derive from the welfare that members of the present generation may obtain because they know that future generations will enjoy a clean environment. This is referred to as bequest value. In addition some economists have argued that there is welfare to be obtained from the **very existence of a commodity.** This existence value has nothing to do with use **in any form,** direct or indirect. There is some controversy about existence values, particularly how they fit into a utilitarian framework, and how they can be translated into money values. If it is argued, as some 'deep ecologists' do, that existence value relates to the intrinsic worth of something irrespective of what human beings think of it, then it is difficult to reconcile that with values derived from the sorts of utility or welfare models that economists use. In the first paper in this section, Krutilla's *Conservation reconsidered,* these different types of value are discussed with many examples from the conservation literature. Krutilla wrestles with the notion of existence value as related to the bequest motive, but also suggests that it may arise from 'an exclusive sentimental basis'.

The second article in this section, Plummer and Hartman's, *Option value: a general approach,* is an attempt to bring together results on this difficult question. The basic notion of option value arises from that fact that individuals may be willing to pay a certain sum today for the future use of a commodity but, in the presence of uncertainty, that willingness to pay will differ from the average value attached to that commodity, the reason for the difference arising from the uncertainty itself. This is best illustrated by an example. Suppose that a playground that you frequented as a child was going to be converted into a parking lot. In order to prevent the development, you were asked what your willingness to pay to prevent the development would be. Assuming you are too old to use it yourself, you imagine that your children would use it in a few years' time. The amount you would pay today for them to have the right to use the park is the **option price.** However, it is uncertain that they will in fact use it. You might have moved from the neighbourhood, or better playgrounds might exist. For each possible combination for future scenarios there will be value attached to the use of the playground. The expected value is the sum of these values, with weights equal to the probabilities attached to them.

The difference between the option price and the expected value *ex post* is the **option value** and the central questions are (a) is this value positive and (b) how large is it? The presumption that it is positive can be misplaced, as the Plummer and Hartman article shows. The paper by Brookshire, Eubanks and Randall, *Estimating option prices and existence values for wildlife resources,* discusses the conceptual and empirical issues that arise in trying to measure these values.

A major source of controversy that arises in valuing environmental impacts is the difference between a willingness to pay measure and a willingness to accept compensation measure. Economic valuation is anthropogenic (i.e. based on human values), and individualistic (i.e. based on personal preferences). The theory of value defines the value attached to a given amount of something as the willingness to pay (WTP) for that amount, or the willingness to accept payment (WTA) if that amount is taken away. The 'currency' in which the payment is

Introduction

measured is normally assumed to be money but it need not be – it could be anything that has an exchange value. It is also important to note that both WTP and WTA are defined in terms of the individual's current circumstances – i.e. taking account of his income, wealth and other prices that s/he faces. According to economic theory of consumer demand the difference between these two measures should not be large, any discrepancy being attributable to the real income effect associated with the change in the amount of the good consumed. However, empirical studies find large differences in some cases. Is the theory wrong or are the questions posed in such a way that the answers are not truthful in all cases? It is probably a bit of both. The paper by Coursey, Hovis and Schulze, *The disparity between willingness to accept and willingness to pay measures of value,* reviews the issues that arise and examines theories of value derived from the psychological literature, in which individual aversion to a loss is stronger than attraction to an equivalent gain. As these theories have some empirical support, it suggests that the value attached to a programme or project that leads to a loss of amenity might be greater than that attached to an equivalent gain.

Methods for valuing environmental goods have been classified as: (a) asking direct questions about WTP and WTA for the good in question; (b) finding a relationship between the demand for the good and the demand for/consumption of complementary goods and (c) measuring the physical impact and valuing it directly. The first method is referred to as contingent valuation (CV) and has been the subject of intensive debate in recent years. The essential issue is, how accurate is the method when there is no actual payment taking place? One might expect individuals to be untruthful if they thought it was in their interest, but in practice this source of error (or bias) turns out not to be that large. Other sources of bias are those arising from the hypothetical nature of the question, what information is made available and what the method of payment is assumed to be. The paper by Hoehn, *Contingent valuation in fisheries management: the design of satisfactory contingent valuation formats,* does a remarkable job of describing the issues in a short and succinct article. It has little to do with fish but it provides an excellent survey of the main problems that arise in this method.

The next two papers are applications of the method. Brookshire, Eubanks and Randall in *Estimating option prices and existence values for wildlife resources,* use CV to value grizzly bear and bighorn sheep wildlife resources in Wyoming. It is also an example of the valuation of options prices directly, wihout having to go into option value, and the difficulties associated with that concept. In general if option price can be measured it is the preferable concept. The paper by Gerking, De Haan and Schulze, *The marginal value of job safety: a contingent valuation study,* is an example of the application of the CV method to the valuation of job risk. This may seem to have little to do with the environment, but what is being valued is the WTP for a reduced risk of death, or the WTA of a small increase in that risk. The estimated values can then be used to value changes in the environmental risks of death arising from factors such as air or water pollution, although the validity of transferring values from one situation to the other have been debated (see Pearce and Markandya (1989)). In any event the Gerking et al. paper is a good example of the application of the CV method to value risks, using the most recent econometric techniques for analysing the answers, and looking at the difference between WTP and WTA in this context.

Methods of environmental valuation based on complementary markets look at the actual expenditures that individuals make in avoiding unpleasant environmental impacts, or in experiencing desirable ones. The commonest class of models in this area is the one that looks at the relationship between land and property values and environmental impacts. These 'hedonic' models have been extensively studied, both from a theoretical and empirical perspective. A second class of models are those that look at time and money spent in going to places where a desirable environment may be experienced. These are referred to as travel cost models. Excerpts of the paper by Markandya, *The value of the environment: a state of the art survey,* provide an overview of the theoretical issues that arise in the applications of the models, as well as others that are discussed in this section. They also indicate where these methods of valuation have been used in developing countries, something that was, until recently, believed to be too difficult to do, owing to the lack of data and properly functioning markets.

An example of the hedonic price estimation approach that offers a clear exposition of the method is the paper by Murdoch and Thayer, *Hedonic price estimation of variable urban air quality,* which shows that the correct measurement of environmental quality is a key factor in the successful application of this method.

Two papers have been included on the travel cost method. The first is the one by Bockstael, Strand and Hanemann, *Time and the recreational demand model,* in which the theory of incorporating time costs into recreational demand models is set out in a comprehensive way. It also provides an interesting empirical illustration of the model that is proposed in the article. The second, by Kerry Smith and Desvousges, *The generalised travel cost model and water quality benefits: a reconsideration,* provides a state of the art survey of the 'second generation' models that have been used to value environmental benefits from travel cost and site attribute data. The conclusion that the benefit estimates are sensitive to the modelling and estimation assumptions is discouraging because there is no objective method by which many relevant decisions can be made. Judgment plays an important part and the derived figures will also have a large element of uncertainty.

The last method of valuation considered is one that relies on scientific data linking environmental impacts with an economic value. It may seem surprising but the methods considered so far do not attempt to link damage and the environmental variables in a physical way. So, for example, if there is a relationship between air pollution and house prices, it is assumed that the individuals concerned have valued the damage that the pollution would do to health, plus any other impacts such as visibility, and have balanced the damage against the costs of avertive action, such as paying more to live in an area where the pollution impact is less. Clearly this model will only work if the information about the impacts is good, and if the markets function well. If either of these assumptions is not valid it is necessary to value the damage directly. In the earlier models, this was done by estimating a 'dose response function' which linked measures of pollution to physical measures of damage such as number of excess deaths, or increased symptom days. A value for each physical measure of damage was then used to arrive at an estimate of the damage caused. However, these simple models failed to take account of individual responses to avert undesirable impacts. It is possible, for example, that a simple dose response relationship would pick up no observed link between pollution and health damage simply because individuals were spending money on drugs to prevent any undesirable effects. The paper by Gerking and Stanley, *An economic analysis of air pollution and health: the case of St. Louis,* is one of the first to look at the broader health function in which individuals are producers of good health and in which they adjust their expenditure on medical care in response to air pollution changes.

Where more than one method of valuing the environment is available, it is natural to ask how the answers from the one relate to the other. Since there is no 'objective' way of assessing the estimated environmental costs (if there were we would not need to use these indirect techniques), such comparisons also provide a check on the plausibility of the figures obtained. A great deal has been done on comparing the estimates from different methods applied to the same problem. The paper by Brookshire, Thayer, Schulze and D'Arge, *Valuing public goods: a comparison of survey and hedonic approaches,* is one of these. It is particularly interesting because it derives a theoretical result that the hedonic damage estimate should be greater than the CV based estimate. Data from the Los Angeles area are carefully examined and found to support this proposition, as well as indicating that the two sets of estimates are broadly consistent.

Another study that compares the estimates from different methods is the paper by Bishop and Heberlein, *Measuring values of extramarket goods: are indirect measures biased?* This is a classic study which looks at hypothetical CV estimates for goose hunting permits in Wisconsin against actual payments for the same permits and against a travel cost model of the benefits. The results were encouraging in that the hypothetical valuation, the actual payments and the travel cost estimates were broadly consistent.

INSTRUMENTS FOR ENVIRONMENTAL CONTROL AND APPLICATIONS

In the 1920s Pigou proposed a system of pollution charges or taxes to correct for environmental externalities. This theoretically ideal Pigovian tax achieves an optimal level of externality where the marginal costs of pollution abatement are equated to the marginal pollution damage costs. In reality, however, there is no real world charge that comes close to this optimal level; instead policy makers are more concerned with achieving acceptable levels of environmental externalities.

Since Pigou, a substantial literature has accumulated discussing both the need for government intervention in the control of externalities and the various policy options and instruments available to policy makers. The seminal paper by Coase (1960) has inspired a large literature questioning whether there is in fact any need for government intervention at all. The original hypothesis was that there was no necessity for full-scale regulatory activity and in fact policy makers should encourage the inherent tendency for private maket bargains in the externality to be struck between the polluter(s) and sufferer(s). In theory, a process of private bargaining would lead the economy to the social optimum, *independently* of the initial allocation of property rights. Although very powerful, the market bargaining argument is generally over-rated, and in fact a number of reasons why governments cannot rely on this laissez-faire prescription have been identified. These range from inherent difficulties in identifying the affected parties to the potentially prohibitive transactions costs of the bargaining process.

The criticisms and shortcomings of the private bargaining solution therefore identify a need for government intervention. The current debate focuses on the form that intervention should take and in particular on the *choice between direct regulations and economic or market based instruments.* Generally, economists have favoured the use of economic instruments on the grounds of cost efficiency and technological dynamism but their enthusiasm is not universally reflected and has met resistance from industry, governments and the general public. In the past, most countries have relied primarily on a command and control type of approach but increasingly many countries are also using economic instruments to supplement direct regulations. This trend is revealed in a recent OECD survey (OECD 1989) which identifies 150 applications of economic instruments being applied in the fourteen member countries surveyed.

The ongoing debate about the correct choice or mix of policy instruments shows quite clearly that no single instrument can be said to be uniquely superior. *Ceteris paribus*, the cost efficiency characteristic of market based instruments is very powerful. But later writers have stressed that the efficiency advantages can be undermined and that the case for fixed quantity standards is strengthened when other factors are taken into account. In this volume, we consider how uncertainty may influence the choice between price and quantity based instruments. The pioneering work in this area is Weitzman's essay, *Prices vs quantities,* (1974) and the broader generalisation by Roberts and Spence in *Effluent charges and licences under uncertainty,* which has been included in this set of readings. Several writers have also highlighted the perverse outcomes that may result when the assumption of well-behaved damage costs and profit functions is violated. Of particular importance is the article by Starrett and Zeckhauser, *Treating external diseconomies – markets or taxes* which examines the implications of *non-convexity* for market bargaining solutions and environmental policy.

Policy instruments for environmental control

Policy makers have an array of instruments at their disposal to control environmental externalities which are summarised in Table 1.

Table 1 Policy instruments for environmental policies

Economic instruments	
Redefining property rights	Tradable Emission Permits; liability insurance legislation.
Tax/charge systems	Effluent charges, user charges, product charges and administrative charges.
Subsidies	Financial aid in installing new technology; subsidies to environmental R&D expenditure.
Deposit-refund systems	Combines charges and subsidies so as to provide incentives to return pollutants for recycling.
Regulation	
Standards	Effluent, ambient and technology standards.
Resource use quotas	Emission quotas, harvesting quotas; by allowing quotas to be traded among market agents, the quota system would be transformed to a system of tradeable permits.

Source: OECD (1989)

These instruments can be broadly classified into direct regulations, also known as the 'command and control' strategies; and economic instruments which make use of the market mechanism and price incentives. The most common form of control is the setting of fixed standards which may be framed in terms of effluent emissions, ambient concentrations or technological specifications. Standard setting also requires the establishment of a monitoring agency which has the power to impose penalties for non-adherence. This system of control is particularly attractive to legislators as it involves minimum upset to the status quo and is generally perceived to be fairer and hence more politically viable. However, economists and leading environmental groups have stressed that the same environmental quality standards can also be achieved by using charges or marketable permits but at a lower total cost. This very important result is due to Baumol and Oates, *The use of standards and prices for protection of the environment,* and it still remains the most powerful argument in favour of the use of market based instruments to regulate environmental externalities.

The relative efficiency of market based instruments

The main market based instruments to control environmental externalities are Pigovian taxes and emission permits or quotas which are freely tradeable. An optimal pollution tax or charge obliges the polluter to pay the full cost of the environmental services they consume and will be set equal to marginal damage costs at the optimal externality load. The idea of pollution permits was first introduced by Dales (op. cit.) and is based on a system of emission permits or quotas which are issued to polluters. These permits are freely tradeable, and in principle can be bought and sold on a permit at the going market price. The pollution standard is therefore determined by the supply of pollution permits which can easily be adjusted.

Faced with emission charges or the price of emission credits (which under Pareto optimality conditions will be equalised), the cost-minimising firm will seek ways to reduce pollution – either via output reductions, investments in clean-up activities or new technologies. The incentive to reduce pollution emissions will continue until the marginal abatement costs are equal to the credit price or emission charge. Abatement costs are likely to differ across firms but, so long as all firms seek to minimise costs, the final outcome will ensure that marginal abatement costs are equalised across firms. This is precisely the condition for cost effectiveness as originally formulated by Baumol and Oates (1971). In addition, market based instruments provide continuing incentives for polluters to search for cost minimising ways of abating pollution and in this sense are technologically dynamic.

Given the theoretical attractiveness of market based instruments and opportunities for practical implementation via the pricing and standards procedure, governments have been remarkably slow to integrate them into their environmental control package. Certainly, there has been considerable resistance on the part of industry, but perhaps the potential cost savings are insufficient to outweigh the transitional costs. These issues have been investigated by Tietenberg in *Economic instruments for environmental regulation.* According to the theory, the potential cost savings are typically very large and certainly are sufficient to justify the trouble of moving away from the status quo. But in practice, the experience of pollution permit trading in the United States reveals that the theoretical models have led to unrealistically high expectations of realisable net savings. Tietenberg analyses the discrepancy and concludes that the production technology does not display the smooth Marshallian cost curves which enable easy switching between production processes. In reality, existing sources cannot instantaneously retrofit the new cleaner technologies and therefore their ex-post control options are considerably more constrained than theory would suggest. In addition, the US example prohibits certain types of trade which would have been permissable under the standard model. But overall, Tietenberg

15

concludes that the emission trading program in the US has improved upon the command and control program that proceeded it.

The air pollution emission trading program in the US is the only example of its kind. In Europe and Japan, the concept of emission charges is more popular. The OECD has recently identified eighty applications in fourteen member states, largely in the area of water, waste and noise pollution. But, the majority of these charges have been used far less ambitiously than most economists would prescribe. Most charges have been levied at a relatively low level and hence do not provide sufficient price incentives to encourage polluters to reduce discharges to the socially optimal level. In fact the motivation for such charges is to raise revenue rather than to convey a set of price incentives to polluters. The revenue is often used for environmental projects and in some cases is returned to the polluting agents in the form of subsidies to encourage installation of cleaner technologies, or for environmental research and development. Charges of this type are known as distributive pollution charges and should be clearly distinguished from incentive pollution charges which have Pigovian optimality properties. The introduction of genuine incentive charging has been slow, not because of failure to appreciate their theoretical cost-effectiveness but rather due to industrial and political resistance. Pure incentive charging raises important questions about infringement of established property rights and the interpretation of the 'polluter pays principle'.

Polluter pays principle and property rights

In the early 1970s the OECD formulated the Polluter Pays Principle which states that 'the polluter should bear the expenses of carrying out the (pollution prevention and control) measures decided by public authorities to ensure that the environment is in an acceptable state' (OECD 1972). However, this statement is ambiguous as it is unclear whether the polluter should also be responsible for the pollution damage that their emissions still cause when the environment has reached an 'acceptable state'. To clarify the situation, a later statement was issued by the OECD which reads, 'if a country decides that, above and beyond the costs of controlling pollution, the polluters should compensate the polluted for damage which would result from residual pollution, this measure is not contrary to the PPP, but the PPP does not make this additional measure obligatory' (OECD 1975).

In practice, no country has attempted to implement the extended polluter pays principle due to fierce resistance from industry to any proposals for pure incentive charging on the full amount of the effluent load.

Effects of uncertainty and irreversibility in the choice of policy instrument

In the discussion so far there has been an implicit assumption that the marginal abatement and marginal damage functions can be estimated with accuracy and hence the socially optimum level of externality is known. In reality this information is not available, and hence the regulator must quantify its uncertainty about abatement and damage costs in the form of subjective probabilities. The implementation of an environmental policy based on an inaccurate estimate of the optimal level of externality will result in social deadweight losses. These losses will depend on the relative slopes of the underlying damage and cost functions and will differ according to whether price or quantity control mechanisms are used. Roberts and Spence in *Effluent charges and licenses under uncertainty* compare the ex-post deadweight losses associated with effluent charges and marketable licenses in the presence of uncertainty. They note that:

effluent charges bring about too little cleanup when cleanup costs turn out to be higher than expected, and they induce excessive cleanup when the costs of cleanup turn out to be too low. Licenses have the opposite failing. Since the level of cleanup is predetermined, it will be too high when cleanup costs are high and too low when costs are low.

Hence, when abatement costs are uncertain, effluent charges and licence outcomes deviate from the optimum in opposite directions. Which kind of imperfection is preferable depends on the curvature of the damage function. According to Roberts and Spence, if the expected damage function is linear, then the effluent charge is the preferable instrument. Conversely, if marginal damages increase sharply with effluent load, then a licence scheme is relatively more attractive.

These results are a generalisation of the earlier work by Weitzman, in his essay 'Prices and Quantities'. Introducing uncertainty makes the decision between price and quantity controls less straightforward. The efficiency advantages of price instruments will not necessarily be sufficient to outweigh the social deadweight losses associated with selecting the wrong output level. Both Roberts and Spence, and Weitzman conclude that a mixed price-quantity scheme would be an attractive alternative in many situations as each can protect against the failings of the other.

Impact of non-convexity in the production function
The usual policy prescription for externalities implicitly assumes that the marginal external cost and marginal profit functions are 'well behaved' such that a unique and stable equilibrium can be secured. But sometimes the externalities are not of the convenient type and in certain cases the externality itself can generate non-convexity in the production possibility curve. Starrett and Zeckhauser in *Treating external diseconomies – markets or taxes* examine the implications of non-convexity for environmental policy and indicate how such an anomaly might manifest itself in the real world. To illustrate how non-convexity might occur, they use the example of wandering cattle that trample the neighbour farmer's crops. To satisfy the normal assumption of full convexity the marginal damage function must be increasing over the relevant range. But what if the addition of a fifth cow to the herd induces the neighbouring farmer to discontinue business? Beyond four cows profits are identically zero and the profit function is not convex. In this case, the externality itself has generated non-convexity in the production possibility set.

The presence of non-convexity over the relevant output range has far-reaching implications for the design of environmental policy. The above analysis suggests that using marginal losses may understate the true damage costs and will lead to less stringent environmental controls. For example, firms that have already been forced out of business due to the non-convexity characteristic will not be counted at all in the damage estimate, and those that have already absorbed the bulk of their potential damage from pollution will only be registering negligible and declining marginal losses in the later stages. Under these circumstances a non-optimal equilibrium may be established with relatively low taxes and high pollution levels.

ENVIRONMENT AND SUSTAINABLE DEVELOPMENT
An extensive and rich literature applying environmental economics to the

developing world has emerged over the last five years. The main issues revolve around the concept of *sustainable development* and the constraints to its global realisation. In this set of readings, we highlight the importance of poverty and population pressure; inherent market failures such as insecure tenure rights and the absence of markets for natural resource services; and finally government policy failure as the root causes of environmental degradation in many developing countries.

The concept of sustainable development

The literature on sustainable development is already vast and continues to grow. Over the past twenty-five years we have witnessed two distinguishable environmental revolutions. The first, in the late 1960s and early 1970s, stressed that the environmental capacity would be the ultimate 'limit to growth' acting as the binding constraint on traditional economic policies aimed at raising real incomes. By the 1980s the focus of the debate had shifted, emphasising the potential complementarity between growth and environmental improvement. The essence of the new thinking was how to identify the means to grow in an environmentally benign way. This new revolution provides the foundations of the concept of sustainable development. The term has become a popular catch phrase and as Pearce, Markandya and Barbier (1989) point out 'it is difficult to be against "sustainable development"'. It sounds like something we should all approve of, like 'motherhood and apple pie'. The concept is usually associated with the Brundtland Commission Report in 1987; but the true origins can be traced back to the 'World Conservation Strategy: Living Resource Conservation for Sustainable Development' (IUCN 1980). The second World Conservation Strategy builds on the ideas developed in the original report but recognises a more central role for economics. The concept of 'economic sustainability' is introduced in the form of the requirement to pass on to future generations a non-declining stock of capital assets, including environmental assets, to ensure inter-generational equity.

It was the Brundtland Commission publication *Our Common Future* in 1987 that really put the concept of sustainable development on the international agenda and highlighted its applicability to the environmental problems in the developing world. The report recognises that in most developing countries there is a greater dependence on natural resources and the environment as an input into production and economic growth. Essentially, development and the environment are complements; it is not economic growth per se that is to be rejected but there is a need to search for alternative development strategies and technologies based on sustaining and expanding the environmental resource base. In the words of the Brundtland Commission:

> There has been a growing realisation in national governments and multilateral institutions that it is impossible to separate economic development issues from environmental issues; many forms of development erode the environmental resources upon which they must be based, and environmental degradation can undermine economic development. (Brundtland Commission, 1987, p. 3)

The report reflects the importance of economic efficiency in achieving the goals of sustainable development but also stresses that the benefits of development must be distributed equitably. Social equity both within and across generations is a fundamental goal and prerequisite to achieve sustainable development. In this context poverty is seen as a major cause and effect of global environmental problems and that attempts to deal with environmental problems will be thwarted unless a broader perspective that encompasses the factors underlying world poverty and international inequity is adopted.

The most widely quoted definition of sustainable development is 'to ensure that (development) meets the needs of the present without compromising the ability of future generations to meet their needs.' (Brundtland Commission, 1987, p. 8). It is a popular phrase which appeals to all, but what does it really mean and how can the concept be operationalised?

Markandya has written extensively on the topic of sustainable development. In his paper, *Criteria for sustainable agricultural development*, he suggests a set of working rules or targets covering equity, resilience and efficiency as a first step in making the concept operational in the agricultural sector. In working toward these sustainability targets, three broad areas of action are identified – those of valuation, regulation and monitoring. The array of valuation techniques and their empirical applications to the environmental sector have been discussed earlier. These estimates can then be utilised as an input into project appraisal and investment analysis; and environmental policy decisions on pricing, taxation and other regulatory instruments as discussed.

The third area, that of *environmental accounting* or monitoring is also fundamental to the pursuit of a policy of sustainable development. Markandya and others stress the need to develop a set of sustainability indicators that can be used to evaluate performance. But much of the information required to do this, such as data on the stocks and service flows related to environmental assets, is not routinely collected or analysed. The current system of national income accounting reflects the emphasis on the Keynesian aggregates of consumption, savings, investment and government expenditures, all of which are carefully defined and used to analyze the performance of the economic system. Emphasis on these economic variables has led to a dangerous asymmetry and inconsistency in the way we think about the value of natural resources which has been institutionalised in the national accounting system. The fundamental definition of sustainable income requires that information be gathered on natural resource stocks and service flows. Robert Repetto et al. in *Wasting assets: natural resources in the national income accounts* explore these issues showing how the 'difference in the treatment of natural resources provides false signals to policy makers and reinforces the false dichotomy between the economic and the environment that leads policy makers to ignore or destroy the latter in the name of economic development'.

Although the anomaly is now widely accepted there is less consensus on how it should be corrected. The Expert Committee of the UN Statistical Office have encouraged the use of satellite accounts which show estimates of natural resource balance sheets and depreciation but which are displayed alongside the traditional accounts in ancillary tables. In other words, although the UN supports the adoption of physical accounts as developed by Leontief (1970) and others, it does not recommend the full integration of natural resources into the core national accounts. This further step requires monetary valuation of the stocks and flows related to natural resources which are inherently difficult to estimate. Repetto considers the pros and cons of both the physical and monetary approaches but notes that few countries have implemented the UN recommendations. Consequently, GDP still remains the prime measure of economic performance in the vast majority of countries. Failure to integrate natural resources in the national accounting framework fuels the widely held belief that rapid rates of economic growth can be achieved and sustained by exploiting the natural resource base.

POVERTY, POPULATION PRESSURE AND THE ENVIRONMENT LINKAGE

The Brundtland Report and later writers have identified poverty as one of the major constraints in achieving the goals of sustainable development. In most developing countries, the poorest segments of the population occupy the least resilient and most threatened environmental areas. They have the least capability to respond to exogenous shocks such as drought or a collapse in commodity prices and consequently their survival response may result in actions which degrade the environment. For example, they may forgo investments and intensify farming on existing lands reaping short term benefits but reducing production potential in the long term. Alternatively, the response may involve the farming of more marginal and ecologically fragile areas and the clearance of surrounding forest areas for timber, agriculture and livestock grazing.

But the linkages between environmental degradation and poverty are not so simple. It is not necessarily the case that poor farmers in their search for food, would convert forests to farms, grow food on steep slopes and degrade marginal farmland. Alternative responses also include the expansion of output in ecologically fragile areas using ecologically sound practices such as terracing or agroforestry; in other cases, farmers might leave the land and search for non-farm employment either in rural areas or via migration to the cities. These alternative responses to exogenous shocks lead observers to conclude that 'impoverishment by itself does not cause environmental degradation. Much depends on the coping strategies of the poor, which depends on availability of options, cultural factors and policies by governments, local and national' (Warford and Pearce, forthcoming).

If the state of poverty can exist without environmental degradation, then the interesting question is what causes environmental degradation and the exogenous shocks that force smallholders to adopt unsustainable farming practices. Jagannathan (1989) investigates some of the underlying causal factors behind observed changes in natural resource use and gives us a number of reasons to doubt the direct poverty-environment link. His insights are based on empirical studies in Indonesia and Nigeria in which intertemporal changes in the natural resource base are compared with economic and demographic information from socio-economic data over the ten year period 1976–1986. Overall, he concludes:

> In both West Java and Nigeria, major observable changes in the physical system since the 1970s such as, conversion of tree crop farms to food crop farms, clearing the bush for farming, disappearance of forest reserves and the expansion of human settlements, could be traced back to stimuli from economic incentives, rather than to just poverty-induced exactions. The economic stimuli have been influenced by several factors: the structure of product and factor markets, policies that encouraged private investments in agriculture, and the size and direction of public investments'. (Jagannathan 1989, p. 28)

Introduction

Most importantly, the changes in land use have been a rational response to changing economic opportunities as defined by public policies and institutional reforms. Hence, although environmental degradation could be observed in the study areas it could most often be traced back to government policy intervention or market failure; there were few cases where it was directly caused by poverty. Foy and Daly in *Allocation, distribution and scale as determinants of environmental degradation* take these arguments one step further. In addition to government and market failures that affect allocations in the natural resource sector, they also stress the importance of inequitable resource distributions and population pressure as root causes of environmental degradation.

THE ROOT CAUSES OF ENVIRONMENTAL DEGRADATION

The poverty-environment debate focuses on the reaction of the poor to exogenous shocks and changes in the overall incentive structure. However, to gain an overall understanding of the forces leading to environmental degradation requires an overview of changes in the incentive structure for the poor and non-poor alike. Theodore Panayatou in his thorough and enlightening analysis of *The economics of environmental degradation: problems, causes and responses* observes that there are few problems that are common to all countries as environmental degradation. Certainly, countries may differ in level of development, degree of indebtedness and extent of absolute and relative poverty, but they are often united by their common failure to achieve sustainable natural resource management. Indeed, it is striking that rapidly growing Southeast Asia has similar environmental problems as stagnating sub-Saharan Africa or heavily indebted Latin America. These observations indicate that it is misguided to single out international debt or poverty as unique, unidirectional causal factors of environmental degradation. In fact, economic stagnation, financial distress, poverty and environmental degradation are all symptoms of more fundamental government policy and market failures. According to Panayatou:

> A combination of policy and market failures causes disassociation between scarcity and price, benefits and costs, rights and responsibilities, actions and consequences. . . . The end result is an incentive structure which induces people to maximise their profits by appropriating other people's resources and shifting their own costs onto others, rather than by economising on scarce resources and investing in enhancing their productivity. (Panayatou 1990)

In most cases, the root causes of these failures can be traced back to government policy (government policy failure) and the nature of the markets for natural resources (market failure). He draws heavily on the recent experiences of a broad spectrum of developing countries in Asia, Africa and South America to illustrate these linkages and concludes that the combination of government policy and inherent market failures are as detrimental to sustainable natural resource management as they are to economic growth.

INTERNATIONAL AND GLOBAL ENVIRONMENTAL PROBLEMS

The discussion so far has been limited to environmental problems and policy responses within national boundaries. But there is no reason that environmental externalities should respect the physical boundaries drawn by sovereign states.

The current threat from greenhouse gases, CFCs and acid rain bear witness to this fact. In the absence of a multinational governing body to control such transboundary or global pollutants, the solution must be found in cooperative voluntary agreements. This is where the real challenge of international environmental policy lies and which has been addressed in Mäler's paper *International environmental problems*. This paper draws heavily on his earlier work but broadens the discussion to include other global environmental threats including climatic change and loss of biodiversity.

Mäler distinguishes between unilateral, regional reciprocal and global environmental externalities. A classical example of a unidirectional externality would be the pollution of the River Rhine in Europe, in which upstream polluting countries cause damage to downstream suffering countries. A regional reciprocal externality occurs when a group of countries is both the source and victim of an environmental problem. Acid rain in Europe is the most obvious example. Finally, we have the case of global environmental problems which refer to the pollution of the global commons having consequences for the vast majority of countries. The global commons are open access resources that are shared by all countries including the atmosphere, the stratosphere and the oceans. Examples of global common externalities include global warming, ozone depletion and loss of biological diversity. International agreements and conventions on environmental protection have been taken at various levels and with varying degrees of success. However, most of the agreements specify emission reduction deadlines which occur well into the 1990s and beyond and consequently have not yet been put to the test.

Mäler illustrates with the 'Acid Rain Game' how, in the absence of cooperative agreements, countries will emit more pollutants into the atmosphere than is socially efficient. Each country will extend its use of the common property resource as far as it is domestically beneficial, without regard to the consequences for the other users. In the case of acid rain, if a country is not bound by an international agreement, it will emit sulphur to the point where the marginal abatement cost equals the marginal damage cost caused by domestic emissions. A collection of countries acting in such a self interested manner will lead to a non-cooperative Nash equilibrium which does not correspond to a collectively rational outcome. The acid rain game model shows how cooperative agreements between countries can lead to a collectively rational outcome and a corresponding Pareto improvement.

In theory cooperative agreements are highly desirable. However, the practical design of international agreements encounters a number of fundamental problems which must be borne in mind. Firstly, the global target has to be determined on the basis of uncertain information both in terms of scientific predictions and the economic valuation of the costs and benefits of pollution control. The sustainability principle has secured a place in recent international negotiations on environmental change. For example, the ozone convention is effectively a zero depletion policy and hence is equivalent to a constant natural capital stock target. Likewise, current negotiations on greenhouse gas emissions are heading this way. However, many neoclassical economists would reject global targets based on sustainability criteria alone since they imply that reductions in the natural capital stock cannot be contemplated regardless of the benefits of reductions. Pearce in *Economics and the global environmental challenge* shows how the sustainability and traditional neoclassical approaches can be reconciled

Introduction

for many environmental problems of a global nature. In particular, a cautious approach should be adopted regarding environmental resources that háve features of non-substitutability and irreversibility. Once the global target has been specified, there is the problem of how to achieve this target in a cost minimising way. In particular, how are emission reduction targets to be shared given that both abatement and damage costs will differ across countries. Global targets specified in terms of equi-proportional emission reductions appear attractive on equity grounds but will incur greater efficiency losses than an agreement based on cost minimising objectives. This problem will be more acute the greater the differences in marginal abatement and damage costs across countries. Finally, the agreement must be designed in such a way as to offer incentives to induce parties to sign and stick to the agreement. For example, an incentive structure can be integrated into the initial allocation of emission rights. Alternatively, the revenues from emission taxes may be used to fund resource transfers to induce countries with high abatement costs or low damage cost to join the agreement. The importance of establishing a special resource fund was recognised at the London meeting on protecting the ozone layer in which a fund of US$ 240 million was set up to help developing countries adjust to the CFC phase out.

Once the global target has been specified, international policy makers have an array of policy tools at their disposal which broadly can be classified as 'command and control' or 'market based' instruments. Command and control policies are based on fixed pollution standards that must be met by all polluters independent of relative abatement and damage costs. Market based instruments include pollution taxes and marketable permits which both make use of market signals in allocating the cost burden across polluters. Pearce highlights the relevance of applying market based instruments to global environmental issues. In particular he shows how the tax and permit systems can be designed to achieve both cost efficiency and provide incentives for cooperation across nation states.

So far our discussions have focused on physical externalities crossing nation boundaries or polluting the global commons. However, there are many interesting examples of global environmental interdependencies that are not based on such physical interactions. In particular, there are many examples of environmental services that are provided by some countries but from which the whole global community reaps benefits. Many of these services are of a public good nature and are usually provided free of charge due to the absence of mechanisms to appropriate their full economic value on international markets. Take for example biodiversity which is a public good. Biodiversity refers to the variety and variability of all animals, plants and micro-organisms and its value lies in the informational value contained in a more diverse range of genes, species and ecosystems. Maintenance of biodiversity is an environmental problem of global significance and of growing urgency as species extinction rates are currently estimated at approximately 10,000 to 20,000 per year (Wilson 1988).

The contribution of economics to the biodiversity debate is still in its infancy. Flint in *Biological diversity and developing countries* lays out the main economic issues highlighting the inherently difficult problems in placing an economic value on preserving biodiversity and tracing the root causes of biodiversity loss back to a combination of market and government policy failure. The preservation of natural habitats and the maintenance of biodiversity will require the establishment of mechanisms to appropriate the full economic value from this informational service. Swanson (1991) has indicated a number of possible routes to enable developing countries to realise this informational value. One possibility is the creation of patent rights in genetic information. The United States is already experimenting in this area with its patency protection of unique uses of biological information. Secondly, there may be potential for the establishment of international research laboratories in areas offering unique biological information. The main users of such a service would undoubtedly be the pharmaceutical and chemical industries which currently free ride on the informational service. Finally, the establishment of national parks, accompanied by investments in infrastructure for tourism, is a more widely acknowledged route both to maintain biodiversity and to realise its value through the established market demand for tourism.

REFERENCES

Coase, R. (1960), 'The Problem of Social Cost', *Journal of Law and Economics,* October.
ECE (1989), *Joint Task Force on Environment and Economics,* Geneva.
IUCN (1980), *World Conservation Strategy: Living Resource Conservation for Sustainable Development,* IUCN.
Leontief, W. (1970), 'Environmental Repercussions and the Economic Structure: An Input-Output Approach', *The Review of Economics and Statistics II.*
OECD (1972), *Annex to the Recommendation on Guiding Principles Concerning International Economic Aspects of Environmental Policies,* OECD, Paris.
OECD (1975), *The Polluter Pays Principle: Definition, Analysis, Implementation,* OECD, Paris.
OECD (1989), *Economic Instruments for Environmental Protection,* Paris.
Pearce, D.W. and A. Markandya (1989), *Environmental Policy Benefits: Monetary Valuation,* OECD, Paris.
Pearce, D.W., A. Markandya and E. Barbier (1989), *Blueprint for a Green Economy,* Earthscan.
Swanson T. (1991), 'Conserving Biological Diversity' in Pearce, D.W. (ed.) (1991), *Blueprint 2,* Earthscan.
Warford, J. and D.W. Pearce (forthcoming), *Environment and Economic Development.*
Weitzman, M. (1974), 'Prices vs Quantities', *Review of Economic Studies,* Vol. 41.
Wilson, E. (ed.) (1988), *Biodiversity,* National Academy Press, Washington DC.
World Commission on Environment and Development (1987), *Our Common Future,* Oxford University Press, Oxford.

PART 1

Basic concepts: the economy and the environment

PART I

Chapter 1

The economics of the coming spaceship Earth

Kenneth E. Boulding

We are now in the middle of a long process of transition in the nature of the image which man has of himself and his environment. Primitive men, and to a large extent also men of the early civilizations, imagined themselves to be living on a virtually illimitable plane. There was almost always somewhere beyond the known limits of human habitation, and over a very large part of the time that man has been on earth, there has been something like a frontier. That is, there was always some place else to go when things got too difficult, either by reason of the deterioration of the natural environment or a deterioration of the social structure in places where people happened to live. The image of the frontier is probably one of the oldest images of mankind, and it is not surprising that we find it hard to get rid of.

Gradually, however, man has been accustoming himself to the notion of the spherical earth and a closed sphere of human activity. A few unusual spirits among the ancient Greeks perceived that the earth was a sphere. It was only with the circumnavigations and the geographical explorations of the fifteenth and sixteenth centuries, however, that the fact that the earth was a sphere became at all widely known and accepted. Even in the nineteenth century, the commonest map was Mercator's projection, which visualizes the earth as an illimitable cylinder, essentially a plane wrapped around the globe, and it was not until the Second World War and the development of the air age that the global nature of the planet really entered the popular imagination. Even now we are very far from having made the moral, political, and psychological adjustments which are implied in this transition from the illimitable plane to the closed sphere.

Economists in particular, for the most part, have failed to come to grips with the ultimate consequences of the transition from the open to the closed earth. One hesitates to use the terms "open" and "closed" in this connection, as they have been used with so many different shades of meaning. Nevertheless, it is hard to find equivalents. The open system, indeed, has some similarities to the open system of von Bertalanffy,[1] in that it implies that some kind of structure is maintained in the midst of a throughput from inputs to outputs. In a closed system, the outputs of all parts of the system are linked to the inputs of other parts. There are no inputs from outside and no outputs to the outside; indeed, there is no outside at all. Closed systems, in fact, are very rare in human experience, in fact almost by definition unknowable, for if there are genuinely closed systems around us, we have no way of getting information into them or out of them; and hence if they are really closed, we would be quite unaware of their existence. We can only find out about a closed system if we participate in it. Some isolated primitive societies may have approximated to this, but even these had to take inputs from the environment and give outputs to it. All living organisms, including man himself, are open systems. They have to receive inputs in the shape of air, food, water, and give off outputs in the form of effluvia and excrement. Deprivation of input of air, even for a few minutes, is fatal. Deprivation of the ability to obtain any input or to dispose of any output is fatal in a relatively short time. All human societies have likewise been open systems. They receive inputs from the earth, the atmosphere, and the waters, and they give outputs into these reservoirs; they also produce inputs internally in the shape of babies and outputs in the shape of corpses. Given a capacity to draw upon inputs and to get rid of outputs, an open system of this kind can persist indefinitely.

There are some systems – such as the biological phenotype, for instance the human body – which cannot maintain themselves indefinitely by inputs and outputs because of the phenomenon of ageing. This process is very little understood. It occurs, evidently, because there are some outputs which cannot be replaced by any known input. There is not the same necessity for ageing in organizations and in societies, although an analogous phenomenon may take place. The structure and composition of an organization or society, however, can be maintained by inputs of fresh personnel from birth and education as the existing personnel ages and eventually dies. Here we have an interesting example of a system which seems to maintain itself by the self-generation of inputs and in this sense is moving toward closure. The input of people (that is, babies) is also an output of people (that is, parents).

Systems may be open or closed in respect to a number of classes of inputs and outputs. Three important classes are matter, energy, and information. The present world economy is open in regard to all three. We can think of the world economy or "econosphere" as a subset of the "world set," which is the set of all objects of possible discourse in the world. We then think of the state of the econosphere at any one moment as being the total capital stock, that is, the set of all objects, people, organizations, and so on, which are interesting from the point of view of the system of exchange. This total stock of capital is clearly an open system in the sense that it has inputs and outputs, inputs being production which adds to the capital stock, outputs being consumption which subtracts from it. From a material point of view, we see objects passing from the noneconomic into the economic set in the process of production, and we similarly see products passing out of the economic set as their value becomes zero. Thus we see the econosphere as a material process involving the discovery and mining of fossil fuels, ores, etc., and at the other end a process by which the effluents of the system are passed out into noneconomic reservoirs – for instance, the atmosphere and the oceans – which are not appropriated and do not enter into the exchange system.

From the point of view of the energy system, the econosphere involves inputs of available energy in the form, say, of water power, fossil fuels, or sunlight, which are necessary in order to create the material throughput and to move matter from the noneconomic set into the economic set or even out of it again; and energy itself is given off by the system in a less available form, mostly in the form of heat. These inputs of available energy must come either from the sun (the energy supplied by other stars being assumed to be negligible) or it may come from the earth itself, either through its internal heat or through its energy of rotation or other motions, which generate, for instance, the energy of the tides. Agriculture, a few solar machines, and water power use the current available energy income. In advanced societies this is supplemented very extensively by the use of fossil fuels, which represent, as it were, a capital stock of stored-up sunshine. Because of this capital stock of energy, we have been able to maintain an energy input into the system, particularly over the last two centuries, much larger than we would have been able to do with existing techniques if we had had to rely on the current input of available energy from the sun or the earth itself. This supplementary input, however, is by its very nature exhaustible.

The inputs and outputs of information are more subtle and harder to trace, but also represent an open system, related to, but not wholly dependent on, the transformations of matter and energy. By far the larger amount of information and knowledge is self-generated by the human society, though a certain amount of information comes into the sociosphere in the form of light from the universe outside. The information that comes from the universe has certainly affected man's image of himself and of his environment, as we can easily visualize if we suppose that we lived on a planet with a total cloud-cover that kept out all information from the exterior universe. It is only in very recent times, of course, that the information coming in from the universe has been captured and coded into the form of a complex image of what the universe is like outside the earth; but even in primitive times, man's perception of the heavenly bodies has always profoundly affected his image of earth and of himself. It is the information generated within the planet, however, and particularly that generated by man himself, which forms by far the larger part of the information system. We can think of the stock of knowledge, or as Teilhard de Chardin called it, the "noosphere," and consider this as an open system, losing knowledge through ageing and death and gaining it through birth and education and the ordinary experience of life.

From the human point of view, knowledge, or information, is by far the most important of the three systems. Matter only acquires significance and only enters the sociosphere or the econosphere insofar as it becomes an object of human knowledge. We can think of capital, indeed, as frozen knowledge or knowledge imposed on the material world in the form of improbable arrangements. A machine, for instance, originates in the mind of man, and both its construction and its use involve information processes imposed on the material world by man himself. The cumulation of knowledge, that is, the excess of its production over its consumption, is the key to human development of all kinds, especially to economic development. We can see this preeminence of knowledge very clearly in the experiences of countries where the material capital has been destroyed by a war, as in Japan and Germany. The knowledge of the people was not destroyed, and it did not take long, therefore, certainly not more than ten years, for most of the material capital to be reestablished again. In a country such as Indonesia, however, where this knowledge did not exist, the material capital did not come into being either. By "knowledge" here I mean, of course, the whole cognitive structure, which includes valuations and motivations as well as images of the factual world.

The concept of entropy, used in a somewhat loose sense, can be applied to all three of these open systems. In material systems, we can distinguish between entropic processes, which take concentrated materials and diffuse them through the oceans or over the earth's surface or into the atmosphere, and antientropic processes, which take diffuse materials and concentrate them. Material entropy can be taken as a measure of the uniformity of the distribution of elements and, more uncertainly, compounds and other structures on the earth's surface. There is, fortunately, no law of increasing material entropy, as there is in the corresponding case of energy, as it is quite possible to concentrate diffused materials if energy inputs are allowed. Thus the processes for fixation of nitrogen from the air, processes for the extraction of magnesium or other elements from the sea, and processes for the desalinization of sea water are antientropic in the material sense, though the reduction of material entropy has to be paid for by inputs of energy and also inputs of information, or at least a stock of information in the system. In regard to matter, therefore, a closed system is conceivable, that is, a system in which there is neither increase nor decrease in material entropy. In such a system all outputs from consumption would constantly be recycled to become inputs for production, as for instance, nitrogen in the nitrogen cycle of the natural ecosystem.

In the energy system there is, unfortunately, no escape from the grim second law of thermodynamics; and if there were no energy inputs into the earth, any evolutionary or developmental process would be impossible. The large energy inputs which we have obtained from fossil fuels are strictly temporary. Even the most optimistic predictions expect the easily available supply of fossil fuels to be exhausted in a mere matter of centuries at present rates of use. If the rest of the world were to rise to American standards of power consumption, and still more if world population continues to increase, the exhaustion of fossil fuels would be even more rapid. The development of nuclear energy has improved this picture, but has fundamentally altered it, at least in present technologies, for fissionable material is still relatively scarce. If we should achieve the economic use of energy through fusion, of course, a much larger source of energy materials would be available, which would expand the time horizons of supplementary energy input into an open social system by perhaps tens to hundreds of thousands of years. Failing this, however, the time is not very far distant, historically speaking, from the sun, even though with increased knowledge this could be used much more effectively than in the past. Up to now, certainly, we have not got very far with the technology of using current solar energy, but the possibility of substantial improvements in the future is certainly high. It may be, indeed, that the biological revolution which is just beginning will produce a solution to this problem, as we develop artificial organisms which are capable of much more efficient transformation of solar energy into easily available forms than any that we now have. As Richard Meier has suggested, we may run our machines in the future with methane-producing algae.[2]

The question of whether there is anything corresponding to entropy in the information system is a puzzling one, though of great interest. There are certainly many examples of social systems and cultures which have lost knowledge, especially in transition from one generation to the next, and in which the culture has therefore degenerated. One only has to look at the folk culture of Appalachian migrants to American cities to see a culture which started out as a fairly rich European folk culture in Elizabethan times and which seems to have lost skills, adaptability, folk tales, songs, and almost everything that goes up to make richness and complexity in a culture, in the course of about ten generations. The American Indians on reservations provide another example of such degradation of the information and knowledge system. On the other hand, over a great part of human history, the growth of knowledge in the earth as a whole seems to have been almost continuous, even though there have been times of relatively slow growth and times of rapid growth. As it is knowledge of certain kinds that produces the growth of knowledge in general, we have here a very subtle and complicated system, and it is hard to put one's finger on the particular elements in a culture which make knowledge grow more or less rapidly, or even which make it decline. One of the great puzzles in this connection, for instance, is why the takeoff into science, which represents an "acceleration," or an increase in the rate of growth of knowledge in European society in the sixteenth century, did not take place in China, which at that time (about 1600) was unquestionably ahead of Europe, and one would think even more ready for the breakthrough. This is perhaps the most crucial question in the theory of social development, yet we must confess that it is very little understood. Perhaps the most significant factor in this connection is the existence of "slack" in the culture, which permits a divergence from established patterns and activity which is not merely devoted to reproducing the existing society but is devoted to changing it. China was perhaps too well organized and had too little slack in its society to produce the kind of acceleration which we find in the somewhat poorer and less well organized but more diverse societies of Europe.

The closed earth of the future requires economic principles which are somewhat different from those of the open earth of the past. For the sake of picturesqueness, I am tempted to call the open economy the "cowboy economy," the cowboy being symbolic of the illimitable plains and also associated with reckless, exploitative, romantic, and violent behavior, which is characteristic of open societies. The closed economy of the future might similarly be called the "spaceman" economy, in which the earth has become a single spaceship, without unlimited reservoirs of anything, either for extraction or for pollution, and in which, therefore, man must find his place in a cyclical ecological system which is capable of continuous reproduction of material form even though it cannot escape having inputs of energy. The difference between the two types of economy becomes most apparent in the attitude towards consumption. In the cowboy economy, consumption is regarded as a good thing and production likewise; and the success of the economy is measured by the amount of the throughput from the "factors of production," a part of which, at any rate, is extracted from the reservoirs of raw materials and noneconomic objects, and another part of which is output into the reservoirs of pollution. If there are infinite reservoirs from which material can be obtained and into which effluvia can be deposited, then the throughout is at least a plausible measure of the success of the economy. The Gross National Product is a rough measure of this total throughput. It should be possible, however, to distinguish that part of the GNP which is derived from exhaustible and that which is derived from reproducible resources, as well as that part of consumption which represents effluvia and that which represents input into the productive system again. Nobody, as far as I know, has ever attempted to break down the GNP in this way, although it would be an interesting and extremely important exercise, which is unfortunately beyond the scope of this paper.

By contrast, in the spaceman economy, throughout is by no means a desideratum, and is indeed to be regarded as something to be minimized rather than maximized. The essential measure of the success of the economy is not production and consumption at all, but the nature, extent, quality, and complexity of the total capital stock, including in this the state of the human bodies and minds included in the system. In the spaceman economy, what we are primarily concerned with is stock maintenance, and any technological change which results in the maintenance of a given total stock with a lessened throughput (that is, less production and consumption) is clearly a gain. This idea that both production and consumption are bad things rather than good things is very strange to economists, who have been obsessed with the income-flow concepts to the exclusion, almost, of capital-stock concepts.

There are actually some very tricky and unsolved problems involved in the questions as to whether human welfare or well-being is to be regarded as a stock or a flow. Something of both these elements seems actually to be involved in it, and as far as I know there have been practically no studies directed towards identifying these two dimensions of human satisfaction. Is it, for instance, eating that is a good thing, or is it being well fed? Does economic welfare involve having nice clothes, fine houses, good equipment, and so on, or is to be measured by the depreciation and the wearing out of these things? I am inclined myself to regard the stock concept as most fundamental, that is, to think of being well fed as more important than eating, and to think even of so-called services as essentially involving the restoration of a depleting psychic capital. Thus I have argued that we go to a concert in order to restore a psychic condition which might be called "just having gone to a concert," which, once established, tends to depreciate. When it depreciates beyond a certain point, we go to another concert in order to restore it. If it depreciates rapidly, we go to a lot of concerts; if it depreciates slowly, we go to a few. On this view, similarly, we eat primarily to restore bodily homeostasis, that is, to maintain a condition of being well fed, and so on. On this view, there is nothing desirable in consumption at all. The less consumption we can maintain a given state with, the better off we are. If we had clothes that did not wear out, houses that did not depreciate, and even if we could maintain our bodily condition without eating, we would clearly be much better off.

It is this last consideration, perhaps, which makes one pause. Would we, for instance, really want an operation that would enable us to restore all our bodily tissues by intravenous feeding while we slept? Is there not, that is to say, a certain virtue in throughput itself, in activity itself, in production and consumption itself, in raising food and in eating it? It would certainly be rash to exclude this possibility. Further interesting problems are raised by the demand for variety. We certainly do not want a constant state to be maintained; we want fluctuations in the state. Otherwise there would be no demand for variety in food, for variety in scene, as in travel, for variety in social contact, and so on. The demand for variety can, of course, be costly, and sometimes it seems to be too costly to be tolerated or at least legitimated, as in the case of marital partners, where the maintenance of a homeostatic state in the family is usually regarded as much more desirable than the variety and excessive throughput of the libertine. There are problems here which the economics profession has neglected with astonishing singlemindedness. My own attempts to call attention to some of them, for instance, in two articles, as far as I can judge, produced no response whatever; and economists continue to think and act as if production, consumption, throughput, and the GNP were the sufficient and adequate measure of economic success.

It may be said, of course, why worry about all this when the spaceman economy is still a good way off (at least beyond the lifetimes of any now living), so let us eat, drink, spend, extract and pollute, and be as merry as we can, and let posterity worry about the spaceship earth. It is always a little hard to find a convincing answer to the man who says "What has posterity ever done for me?" and the conservationist has always had to fall back on rather vague ethical principles postulating identity of the individual with some human community or society which extends not only back into the past but forward into the future. Unless the individual identifies with some community of this kind, conservation is obviously "irrational." Why should we not maximize the welfare of this generation at the cost of posterity? *"Après nous, le déluge"* has been the motto of not insignificant numbers of human societies. The only answer to this, as far as I can see, is to point out that the welfare of the individual depends on the extent to which he can identify himself with others, and that the most satisfactory individual identity is that which identifies not only with a community in space but also with a community extending over time from the past into the future. If this kind of identity is recognized as desirable, then posterity has a voice, even if it does not have a vote; and in a sense, if its voice can influence votes, it has votes too. This whole problem is linked up with the much larger one of the determinants of the morale, legitimacy, and "nerve" of a society, and there is a great deal of historical evidence to suggest that a society which loses its identity with posterity and which loses its positive image of the future loses also its capacity to deal with present problems, and soon falls apart.[4]

Even if we concede that posterity is relevant to our present problems, we still face the question of time-discounting and the closely related question of uncertainty-discounting. It is a well-known phenomenon that individuals discount the future, even in their own lives. The very existence of a positive rate of interest may be taken as at least strong supporting evidence of this hypothesis. If we discount our own future, it is certainly not unreasonable to discount posterity's future even more, even if we do give posterity a vote. If we discount this at five percent per annum, posterity's vote or dollar halves every fourteen years as we look into the future, and after even a mere hundred years it is pretty small – only about one-and-a-half cents on the dollar. If we add another five percent for uncertainty, even the vote of our grandchildren reduces almost to insignificance. We can argue, of course, that the ethical thing to do is not to discount the future at all, that time-discounting is mainly the result of myopia and perspective, and hence is an illusion which the moral man should not tolerate. It is a very popular illusion, however, and one that must certainly be taken into consideration in the formulation of policies. It explains, perhaps, why conservationist policies almost have to be sold under some other excuse which seems more urgent, and why, indeed, necessities which are visualized as urgent, such as defense, always seem to hold priority over those which involve the future.

All these considerations add some credence to the point of view which says that we should not worry about the spaceman economy at all, and that we should just go on increasing the GNP and indeed the Gross World Product, or GWP, in the expectation that the problems of the future can be left to the future, that when scarcities arise, whether this is of raw materials or of pollutable reservoirs, the needs of the then present will determine the solutions of the then present, and there is no use giving ourselves ulcers by worrying about problems that we really do not have to solve. There is even high ethical authority for this point of view in the New Testament, which advocates that we should take no thought for tomorrow and let the dead bury their dead. There has always been something rather refreshing in the view that we should live like the birds, and perhaps posterity is for the birds in more senses than one; so perhaps we should all call it a day and go out and pollute something cheerfully. As an old taker of thought for the morrow, however, I cannot quite accept this solution; and I would argue, furthermore, that tomorrow is not only very close, but in many respects it is already here. The shadow of the future spaceship, indeed, is already falling over our spendthrift merriment. Oddly enough, it seems to be in pollution rather than in exhaustion that the problem is first becoming salient. Los Angeles has run out of air, Lake Erie has become a cesspool, the oceans are getting full of lead and DDT, and the atmosphere may become man's major problem in another generation, at the rate at which we are filling it up with gunk. It is, of course, true that at least on a microscale, things have been worse at times in the past. The cities of today, with all their foul air and polluted waterways, are probably not as bad as the filthy cities of the pretechnical age. Nevertheless, that fouling of the nest which has been typical of man's activity in the past on a local scale now seems to be extending to the whole world society; and one certainly cannot view with equanimity the present rate of pollution of any of the natural reservoirs, whether the atmosphere, the lakes, or even the oceans.

I would argue strongly also that our obsession with production and consumption to the exclusion of the "state" aspects of human welfare distorts the process of technological change in a most undesirable way. We are all familiar, of course, with the wastes involved in planned obsolescence, in competitive advertising, and in poor quality of consumer goods. These problems may not be so important as the "view with alarm" school indicates, and indeed the evidence at many points is conflicting. New materials especially seem to edge towards the side of improved durability, such as, for instance, neolite soles for footwear, nylon socks, wash and wear shirts, and so on. The case of household equipment and automobiles is a little less clear. Housing and building construction generally almost certainly has declined in durability since the Middle Ages, but this decline also reflects a change in tastes towards flexibility and fashion and a need for novelty, so that it is not easy to assess. What is clear is that no serious attempt has been made to assess the impact over the whole of economic life of changes in durability, that is, in the ratio of capital in the widest possible sense to income. I suspect that we have underestimated, even in our spendthrift society, the gains from increased durability, and that this might very well be one of the places where the price system needs correction through government-sponsored research and development. The problems which the spaceship Earth is going to present, therefore, are not all in the future by any means, and a strong case can be made for paying much more attention to them in the present than we now do.

It may be complained that the considerations I have been putting forth relate only to the very long run, and they do not much concern our immediate problems. There may be some justice in this criticism, and my main excuse is that other writers have dealt adequately with the more immediate problems of deterioration in the quality of the environment. It is true, for instance, that many of the immediate problems of pollution of the atmosphere or of bodies of water arise because of the failure of the price system, and many of them could be solved by corrective taxation. If people had to pay the losses due to the nuisances which they create, a good deal more resources would go into the prevention of nuisances. These arguments involving external economies and diseconomies are familiar to economists and there is no need to recapitulate them. The law of torts is quite inadequate to provide for the correction of the price system which is required, simply because where damages are widespread and their incidence on any particular person is small, the ordinary remedies of the civil law are quite inadequate and inappropriate. There needs, therefore, to be special legislation to cover these cases, and though such legislation seems hard to get in practice, mainly because of the widespread and small personal incidence of the injuries, the technical problems involved are not insuperable. If we were to adopt in principle a law for tax penalties for social damages, with an apparatus for making assessments under it, a very large proportion of current pollution and deterioration of the environment would be prevented. There are tricky problems of equity involved, particularly where old established nuisances create a kind of "right by purchase" to perpetuate themselves, but these are problems again which a few rather arbitrary decisions can bring to some kind of solution.

The problems which I have been raising in this paper are of larger scale and perhaps much harder to solve than the more practical and immediate problems of the above paragraph. Our success in dealing with the larger problems, however, is not unrelated to the development of skill in the solution of the more immediate and perhaps less difficult problems. One can hope, therefore, that as a succession of mounting crises, especially in pollution, arouse public opinion and mobilize support for the solution of the immediate problems, a learning process will be set in motion which will eventually lead to an appreciation of and perhaps solutions for the larger ones. My neglect of the immediate problems, therefore, is in no way intended to deny their importance, for unless we make at least a beginning on a process for solving the immediate problems we will not have much chance of solving the larger ones. On the other hand, it may also be true that a long-run vision, as it were, of the deep crisis which faces mankind may predispose people to taking more interest in the immediate problems and to devote more effort for their solution. This may sound like a rather modest optimism, but perhaps a modest optimism is better than no optimism at all.

REFERENCES
1. Ludwig von Bertalanffy, *Problems of Life* (New York: John Wiley and Sons, 1952).
2. Richard L. Meier, *Science and Economic Development* (New York: John Wiley and Sons, 1956).
3. Kenneth E. Boulding, "The Consumption Concept in Economic Theory," *American Economic Review*, 35:2 (May 1945), pp. 1–14; and "Income or Welfare?," *Review of Economic Studies*, 17 (1949–50), pp. 77–86.
4. Fred L. Polak, *The Image of the Future*, Vols. I and II, translated by Elise Boulding (New York: Sythoff, Leyden and Oceana, 1961).

Chapter 2

The economic growth debate: what some economists have learned but many have not

Herman E. Daly

INTRODUCTION

One thing economists should have learned from the economic growth debate is the importance of defining the term "growth." By "growth" I mean quantitative increase in the scale of the physical dimensions of the economy; i.e., the rate of flow of matter and energy through the economy (from the environment as raw material and back to the environment as waste), and the stock of human bodies and artifacts. By "development" I mean the qualitative improvement in the structure, design, and composition of physical stocks and flows, that result from greater knowledge, both of technique *and of purpose*. Simply put, growth is quantitative increase in physical dimensions; development is qualitative improvement in non-physical characteristics. An economy can therefore develop without growing, just as the planet Earth has developed (evolved) without growing. Neoclassical growth models notwithstanding, there is good evidence that neither the Earth's surface nor the flux of solar energy grows at a rate equal to the rate of interest! In fact they seem not to grow at all. Yet qualitative evolution occurred and continues to occur.

Two general classes of limits to "growth" in the above-defined sense can be further distinguished: biophysical limits and ethicosocial limits. In both cases it is growth, not development, that is limited. There may or may not exist limits to development, but that is another topic. Standard neoclassical economics was built on the assumption that the economy is far from both limits; i.e., that it is always biophysically possible and ethicosocially desirable for aggregate product to grow. As Abramowitz[1] put it, echoing Pigou: "Economists have relied, however, on a practical judgment, namely, that a change in economic welfare implies a change in total welfare in the same direction if not in the same degree". This practical judgment ceases to be true as the economy approaches either or both limits. The gain in economic welfare could easily be more than offset by a loss of natural ecosystem services provoked by the extra production, or by a deterioration in the moral quality of society induced by the widespread use of a meretricious "good". Perfect internalization of all externalities would presumably make economic welfare coextensive with total welfare, so the economist might save appearances by appealing to the ever better internalization of ever more pervasive externalities. However, this is reminiscent of adding epicycles, or more perhaps of Archimedes' boast that he could move the earth if only he had a fulcrum and a long enough lever.

Consider a somewhat far-fetched but apt analogy. Neoclassical economics, like classical physics, is a special case that assumes that we are far from limits – far from the limiting speed of light or the limiting smallness of an elementary particle in the case of physics – and far from the limiting carrying capacity of the environment, and the limiting satiety of consumers' wants, in the case of economics. Just as in physics so too in economics: the classical economic theories do not work well in regions close to limits. A more general theory is needed to embrace both "normal" and limiting cases. In economics the need is especially great because economic growth means that the close-to-the limits case more and more becomes the norm. The nearer we are to limits the less can we assume that economic welfare and total welfare move in the same direction. Rather we must learn to define and explicitly account for the other sources of welfare that growth inhibits and erodes when it presses against limits. The economics of an empty world with hungry people is different from the economics of a full world, even when many do not yet have the full stomachs, full houses, and full garages of the "advanced" minority.

Let us now consider in more detail the two categories of limits to growth, and the nature of the welfare losses that come about when each limit is stressed by growth.

BIOPHYSICAL LIMITS

Three interrelated conditions – finitude, entropy, and complex ecological interdependence – combine to form the fundamental biophysical limits to growth.

The economy, in its physical dimensions, is an open subsystem of a larger, but finite, ecosystem which is both the supplier of low entropy raw materials and the absorber of its high entropy wastes. The growth of the economic subsystem is limited by the size of the overall system, by its dependence on the overall system as a source of low-entropy inputs and as a sink for high-entropy waste outputs, and by the intricate ecological connections which are more easily disrupted as the scale of the economic subsystem grows relative to the total ecosystem. Moreover, these three basic limits interact. Finitude would not be so limiting if everything could be recycled, but entropy prevents complete recycling. The entropy law would not be so limiting if environmental sources of low entropy and sinks for high entropy were infinite, but both are finite. The fact that both are finite plus the entropy law, means that the ordered structures of the economic subsystem are maintained at the expense of creating a more than offsetting amount of disorder in the rest of the system. If the part of the system that pays the entropy bill is the sun (as in traditional peasant economies) then we need not worry. But if the disorder is imposed mainly on parts of the terrestrial ecosystem (as in a modern industrial economy) then we need to pay attention. This disordering (depletion and pollution) of the ecosystem interferes with the life support services rendered to the economy by other species and by natural biogeochemical cycles. The loss of these services should surely be counted as a cost of growth, to be weighed against benefits at the margin. But our national accounts, by which economic growth is measured, emphatically do not do this. Instead, the defensive expenditures we are obliged to make to protect ourselves from the loss of these natural services are added in GNP, which is invariably taken as an index of welfare, in spite of cautionary footnotes. There is, strangely enough, no comparable accounting of national costs.

Finite time, as both a physical coordinate and an experienced dimension of existence, must be counted as a limit along with finite space. Production, consumption, regeneration, recycling, etc., all take time, and what is possible on one time frame may be absolutely impossible on another. As Linder[18] has shown, the relative price of time in terms of goods has been increasing thanks to the increasing productivity of labor time, with the consequence that we attempt to raise the marginal return on non-work time to equal the higher return on work time, and succeed mainly in congesting the temporal dimension of existence as surely as we congest the spatial dimensions. Consequently total welfare may decline as economic welfare increases.

The question of time also causes much confusion about the relevance of the entropy law as a limit. Consider the following quote from Danish economist Mogens Boserup:

> I am told that [the sun] is huge enough to last for a few billion years which is far beyond the conceivable duration of the species *homo sapiens*. Therefore, the entropy story, entertaining or thrilling as it may be, is irrelevant, in the precise sense that nothing follows from it for human action and policy, today or in any future about which we can sensibly talk and plan.

There are three time frames worth distinguishing. First, the extremely long run concept of entropy as the ultimate equilibrium state, the final "heat death" or chaos. Second, the immediate, moment-to-moment concept of entropy as a directional process or "time's arrow" and a gradient down which all physical processes ride. Third, the medium run period of one generation or one average lifetime, say 25–75 years over which solar low-entropy remains essentially constant, while the terrestrial sources of low entropy, upon which industrial civilization is based, may become significantly depleted. Let us agree with Boserup that the first meaning is irrelevant. I do not know of anyone who ever claimed otherwise, and Boserup cites no examples. The relevance of the second meaning to economics, however, is as elementary and pervasive as the difference between a lump of coal and a pile of ashes, between raw material and waste material (Georgescu-Roegen[13]). If the qualitative difference between equal quantities of raw material and waste material is not relevant to economics, then what is? And entropy is the measure of that qualitative difference. Recognition of the third time frame would have kept Boserup from missing the point that industrial growth is limited by the stock of terrestrial low entropy rather than by the stock of solar low entropy, which is superabundant but is itself irrelevant because solar energy is flow-limited; i.e., its total amount may be practically unlimited, but its flow-rate of arrival to earth is strictly limited, and so far remains beyond our control. But even if we were able to increase the flow of solar energy to earth we would be foolish to do it since the constant solar flux is the basis of the fixed biophysical budget on which all species live, and to which they have adapted by co-evolution over millions of years. A significant change in the solar flux would result in a wholesale invalidation of eons of adaptation.

Human beings must also ultimately live within that constant long-run biophysical budget, even though economic expansion can temporarily be financed by draw-down of terrestrial stocks of minerals, and takeover of the "place in the sun," or habitats, of other species. These somewhat loaded but very descriptive terms, "draw-down" and "takeover," were introduced by Catton[7].

The economic growth debate

Growth (as opposed to development) is largely based on draw-down and takeover. Clearly these two processes ultimately reach biophysical limits, but, as will be argued in the next section, ethicosocial limits are probably more binding.

Economists seem to have learned about the first law of thermodynamics (conservation of matter-energy) and the limits it imposes. Production functions are now sometimes required to respect a materials balance constraint (Kneese, Ayres, and d'Arge[16]). But the limits to growth stemming from the second law of thermodynamics (entropy law) are not yet widely understood by economists (Ayres[2], Daly[8], Georgescu-Roegen[13]). Probably many economists have dismissed the relevance of the entropy law because of the association of the term with a group of energy ecologists who advocate an erroneous energy theory of value (Daly[10]), or with certain loose analogical uses frequently made of the entropy concept in fields far from physics. It is therefore worth stating as emphatically as possible that the use of the concept of entropy here, following Georgescu-Roegen, has nothing to do with any energy theory of value, nor is it an economic analog to the physical concept. Rather it is the physical concept itself and its relevance to economics is that of a constraint on market valuation, not a substitute for it.

Respect for the first law goes back at least to Marshall[19] who noted that:

> Man cannot create material things . . . His efforts and sacrifices result in changing the form or arrangement of matter to adapt it better for the satisfaction of his wants . . . as his production of material products is really nothing more than a rearrangement of matter which gives it new utilities, so his consumption of them is nothing more than a disarrangement of matter which diminishes or destroys its utilities.

If we stop here, as most economists do, without considering the implications of the second law, then we get a very incomplete and misleading picture. We just keep rearranging and disarranging indestructible building blocks. Nothing is used up. This picture of continuously recycling building blocks fits perfectly with the basic vision of the economic process as a circular flow. Matter and energy – like money – just keep going around in an isolated system with no inlets and no outlets. Since the circular flow model of the textbooks has no points of contact with anything outside itself, the environment cannot possibly constrain economic growth, or influence the economy in any way whatsoever!

However, there also exists a second law of thermodynamics, the implications of which modify this picture fundamentally. Since the rearrangement of matter is the central physical fact about the economic process, we must ask what determines the capacity to rearrange matter? Is that capacity conserved, like matter-energy itself, or is it used up? Is all matter equally capable of being rearranged? The answers to these questions are provided by the second law, as follows. The capacity to rearrange matter is variously called "free," "available," or "low-entropy" energy, and is irrevocably used up. Structured, concentrated (low entropy) matter is easier to rearrange (i.e., uses up less available energy) than is the case for unstructured, dissipated (high entropy) matter. In effecting these rearrangements available energy is degraded into unavailable energy, which, as the name suggests, can no longer be used to rearrange matter. In reality there is no circular flow of matter-energy within an isolated system – no perpetual motion! Instead there is a one-way, linear entropic flow (throughput) from the

39

environment (depletion) through the economy (production and depreciation), and back to the environment (pollution). Abstract money (exchange value) may flow in a circle, but the flow of concrete matter-energy through the economy is ultimately linear. To apply conclusions derived from a model of the circular flow of money to issues dominated by the linear throughput of matter-energy is a classic of the fallacy of misplaced concreteness. The circular flow of money can indeed grow forever, just as monetary debt can grow at compound interest forever. But real wealth and income always have physical dimensions and consequently can grow exponentially only for a limited time. Biophysical limits are real.

One may grant that biophysical limits are real but still doubt that they are near. What evidence is there that we are near enough the limits to carrying capacity to have to correct our classical far-from-the-limits economic theories? There is an abundance of evidence for whoever will look. The "Global 2000 Report to the President" concludes that,

> At present and projected growth rates, the world's population would reach 10 billion by 2030 and would approach 30 billion by the end of the twenty-first century. These levels correspond closely to the estimates by the U.S. National Academy of Sciences of the maximum carrying capacity of the entire earth.

In case that estimate seems comfortably vague and far off the "Global 2000 Report" also tells us that, "If present trends continue, the world in 2000 will be more crowded, more polluted, less stable ecologically, and more vulnerable to disruption than the world we live in now."

Evidence that global per capita production of the basic renewable resource systems (forests, fisheries, croplands, and grasslands) have all peaked and begun to decline has been presented by Brown[6]. Even the present declining levels of productivity were reached only with the aid of large fossil fuel subsidies. As this subsidy is withdrawn there will be an acceleration in the rate of productivity decline of renewable systems.

Reduction in number of species is occurring at record rates, mainly as a result of habitat takeover (Ehrlich and Ehrlich[12]). A twenty percent reduction in total number of species is projected by the year 2000.

There is no more "frontier," no more empty continents, no more infinite sources and sinks. There is just the "high frontier" of outer space, which, as far as we know, is more barren than any terrestrial desert and vastly more expensive to get to. The idea that biophysical limits to growth are near as well as real is not just the fabrication of "doomsayers."

ETHICOSOCIAL LIMITS

Even while growth is still biophysically possible other factors may limit its desirability. Four ethicosocial propositions limiting the desirability of growth will be discussed:

(1) The desirability of growth financed by drawdown is limited by the cost imposed on future generations.

(2) The desirability of growth financed by takeover is limited by the extinction or reduction in number of sentient sub-human species whose habitat disappears.

(3) The desirability of aggregate growth is limited by self-cancelling effects on welfare.
(4) The desirability of growth is limited by the corrosive effects on moral standards of the very attitudes that foster growth, such as glorification of self-interest and a scientistic-technocratic world view.

Let us consider each of these propositions in more detail.

Limits to draw-down

Growth supported by drawdown of geological or ecological capital is limited by moral obligation to future generations who will have neither the minerals nor biological gene pool that were depleted for the benefit of the present generation. Clearly, the basic needs of the present always should take precedence over the basic needs of the future, since unless the former are satisfied there will not be a future generation. But should the extravagant luxuries of the present take precedence over the basic needs of the future? Surely the basic answer is no, although we may disagree on just where to draw the line. But at some point the claim of the future for petroleum to fashion plows to grow food outweighs the claim of the present to use that petroleum to fly a few people across the Atlantic a few hours faster in a Concorde airplane. Now that is certainly a moral judgment, and economists avoid such judgments by appealing to the market where everyone's preferences count, weighted by their incomes. This assumes that all moral values are expressable in terms of individual behavior without regard to collective or community action, and that the income weights are acceptable. But even this evasion will not work for the case in point because future generations cannot bid in present markets. Somehow the present must restrain its own consumption on the basis of moral concern for the future.

Moral concern for the future can be individualistically or socially expressed. Page[21] has elaborated two interpretations, one individualistic and one collectivistic, of how the interests of future generations may be reflected in the present value formula commonly used to discount future costs and benefits. The individualistic interpretation Page labels "selfish altruism," which means that the utility in the present value formula refers to the utility of the present generation only, but the present individuals derive some utility from contemplating the welfare of future people. Therefore the present is willing to make sacrifices for the future, but applies a discount factor. Consequently the contemplated welfare of people in the distant future counts less in the welfare of the present than does the contemplated welfare of nearer future generations. Future welfare is in effect discounted by present individuals to arrive at an "equivalent" in terms of present welfare. In the collectivist interpretation, or "disinterested fairness" as Page calls it, the present generation as a whole collectively restrains its consumption in the interests of the future by putting itself in the future's place; i.e., by imagining an intergenerational distribution that would be regarded as fair by a convention of representatives of each generation who did not know in advance the place of their generation in the temporal sequence. This Rawlsian "veil of ignorance" leads to an egalitarian consumption rule. This rule is put into effect by discounting at the rate of increase of productivity, rather than by the time preference rate of the first generation, as in the selfish altruism case.

The disinterested fairness interpretation embodies an objective value of fairness in the sense of a general, operationally defined principle. The individualistic interpretation is based on subjective relativism – nothing need be agreed on by anyone (except the underlying philosophy of subjective relativism itself!). In the disinterested fairness approach present draw-down and the growth therefrom is limited by the objective value of fairness. In the selfish altruism approach (standard present value maximization) draw-down is limited only by the subjective preferences of the present generation. The hypothetical disinterested fairness approach represents an ethically based collective limit to drawdown. The actual selfish altruism approach may or may not exercise a restraint on drawdown, depending on the balance of individual subjective preferences and on the relative weights placed on them by the distribution of income. Of course these preferences may include some values that the individuals acting on them regard as objectively right. But the point is that such values still receive no more weight than someone else's velleities. Willingness to pay is the ultimate criterion.

This argument can be cast in traditional terms. Since future people cannot bid in present markets, the market is of necessity temporally parochial, and tends to undervalue depletable resources. A spatial analog would be the undervaluation of offshore oil leases that would result if only the residents of Cocodrie, Louisiana were allowed to bid! Or to put it in even more conventional neoclassical terms, fair valuation depends on a fair distribution of endowments, or market power. But intertemporally the future's endowment is endogenously determined by the present's actions, so fair endowments cannot be assumed exogenously, before market interactions. To highlight the difficulty in yet another way, consider that "allocation" refers to division of resources among alternative uses, for a given set of people with a given distribution of endowments. Different generations are different sets of people, so it is clear that a concept of "intergenerational allocation" will have to sin against the standard neoclassical distinction between allocation and distribution.

Provision for future people is partly a public good, and becomes more so the farther into the future one looks. One reason why individuals seldom worry about their descendents beyond grandchildren is that it makes less and less sense with each generation to consider any descendant as "yours". One's grandchild is the grandchild of four people in one's own generation, one's greatgrandchild has eight such great grandparents, and one's nth generation descendant has 2^n co-progenitors in the present generation. Because of sexual reproduction future people are a social product, not an individual product, and whatever responsibility we feel for them (beyond, say, great grandchildren) must be put into effect through collective measures rather than through individualistic market behavior (Daly[9]).

In sum, obligations to future generations provide a moral limit to the rate of drawdown, and indirectly to the rate of growth. How stringent this obligation is can be debated. My own view is that present claims should dominate future claims only up to some level of resource use that is sufficient for a good life for a population that is sustainable at that level. The notions of "sufficiency" and "sustainability" unfortunately were banished from modern growth economics, because they are dialectical, i.e., partially overlapping with their "other" and not subject to precise analytical definition. However, by that criterion we must also eliminate the concepts of "money" and "national product," and be content to remain silent on all important issues.

Limits to takeover

Economic growth requires space for increasing stocks of artifacts and people, and for increasing sources of raw material and increasing sinks for waste materials. Other species also require space, their "place in the sun." The fact that other species provide life-support services to the human species gives them instrumental value to us. This instrumental limit was considered in the previous section on biophysical limits under the heading of "ecological complexity and interdependence." Another limit to takeover derives from the intrinsic value of other species; i.e., counting them as sentient (though probably not self-conscious) beings which experience pleasure and pain, and whose "utility" should be counted in global welfare economics, even though it does not give rise to maximizing market behavior. To deny that sub-human creatures experience pleasure and pain is not only arbitrary but also contrary to all evidence of our evolutionary connection with them. In addition to sub-human utility many would consider "super-human utility" as well; i.e., the value God places on His creation and His purposes for it, which may be more subtle and inscrutable than simply maximizing present value for the current generation of entrepreneurs.

The idea that the pleasure and pain of sub-human species should receive some weight greater than zero appealed to Bentham[3], from whom economics adopted its basic utilitarian philosophy. Bentham argued that the interests of inferior animals has been improperly neglected. "The question is not," says Bentham, "Can they *reason*? Nor, can they *talk*? But, can they *suffer*?" Although some ecological egalitarians object to the term "sub-human" species, I make no apology for it because (aside from the fact that the sub-human species could not understand my apology) I take it as axiomatic that a person is worth more than a rabbit – that "a man is worth many sparrows." And yet a corollary of the latter proposition is that a sparrow's worth cannot be zero. How many sparrows are worth a man? No one knows, though I'm sure some clever econometrician will not shrink from the task of inputting implicit shadow prices to sparrows, probably based on the market price of the insect repellent that could be saved if there were one more sparrow around to eat the insects. But even if this absurdity were accomplished it would only be an estimate of instrumental value, not intrinsic value.

Moral claims for the intrinsic worth of sub-human species should exert some limit on takeover, although it is extremely difficult to say how much (Birch and Cobb[4]). The idea that the market already accomplishes this limit ("whoever wants to conserve whales can go buy himself one with his own money and keep it!") is plainly ludicrous. Preservation of sub-human species, like provision for the distant future, is a public good that must be served by collective action. Clarification of this limit is a major philosophical task, but if we wait for a definitive answer before imposing some limits on takeover, then the question will be rendered moot by extinctions which are now occurring at an extremely rapid rate compared to past ages. Of course we already impose some limits in the form of national parks and wildlife refuges. But these are both insufficient and under constant threat of takeover.

Takeover of the habitat and consequent extinction of another species is an irreversible act and therefore represents a draw-down of ecological capital and thus entails a cost to future generations as well. Therefore the considerations of the previous section are relevant here. In fact the drawdown element is even more serious for renewables than for non-renewables, since the depletion of renewables represents a loss in perpetuity. An extra barrel of oil used today represents only a one-time sacrifice by some future generation. Extinction of a gene pool represents a loss to all future generations.

Limits from the self-cancelling effects of aggregate growth

The Easterlin Paradox has caused a number of economists to question the assumption that aggregate economic growth increases social welfare, even in the absence of drawdown takeover, and biophysical limits. In a now classic article Easterlin[11] presented evidence on the association between self-rated happiness and income. The "paradox" is this: in a given country at a given time one finds a positive correlation between income and happiness. A larger percentage of rich people rated themselves as "very happy" than did poor people – just as everyone would expect. But for different countries with very different income levels the differences in reported happiness are small. Likewise for a single country experiencing growth there is no rise in self-rated happiness (i.e., the fractions reporting themselves as happy or unhappy) in spite of substantial increase in average income.

How to explain the paradox? Abramowitz[1], following Easterlin, has offered several explanations. The most obvious is a variation on the relative income hypothesis. As J.S. Mill put it, "Men do not desire to be rich, but to be richer than other men." Or in John Ruskin's words, "The force of the guinea you have in your pocket depends wholly on the fault of a guinea in your neighbor's pocket." Taken literally economists might have good reason for objecting to Ruskin's statement. However, it is quite reasonable to argue that happiness, at least at the current margin in rich countries, is a function of relative income, not absolute income. Since everyone's relative income cannot increase, aggregate growth has self-cancelling effects on welfare. Self-cancellation occurs in two ways. First, if everyone's income goes up by $x\%$ then all relative positions are unchanged and there is complete cancelling at the intra-personal level; i.e., no one feels better or worse off. Second, if some peoples' relative income goes up then that of others must go down. In this event we have an inter-personal cancelling which we might expect to be rather complete since the struggle over relative shares is a zero sum game. The only way growth could make anyone happier is to make someone else less happy. If one is an egalitarian he might argue that making the poor better off is worth the price of making the rich worse off, so that growth which benefits the poor is not subject to total cancelling out. This is certainly a logical possibility, but in the real world what grows is the reinvested surplus which is controlled by the rich for the primary benefit of the rich. The poor get the "trickle down," as it is so aptly called.

The basic social question raised by the relative income answer to the Easterlin Paradox is, Why grow? Or to put the question more sharply, why grow beyond the level where absolute needs have been met and where growth is therefore dedicated to satisfying relative needs at the margin?

In this context it is worth recalling Keynes'[15] comment on the distinction between absolute and relative needs, and the self-cancelling nature of the latter.

> Now it is true that the needs of human beings may seem to be insatiable. But they fall into two classes – those which are absolute in the sense that we feel them whatever the situation of our fellow human beings may be, and those which are relative in the sense that we feel them only if their satisfaction lifts

us above, makes us feel superior to our fellows. Needs of the second class, those which satisfy the desire for superiority, may indeed be insatiable: for the higher the general level, the higher still are they. But this is not so true of the absolute needs – a point may soon be reached, much sooner perhaps than we are all of us aware of, when these needs are satisfied in the sense that we prefer to devote our further energies to non-economic purposes.

Another resolution of the Easterlin Paradox focuses on change in income level rather than the level of income itself as the determinant of happiness. Once one is accustomed to an income level life becomes a routine matter of dealing with marginal frustrations imposed by the habitual budget constraint. Happiness is the temporary adjustment to a higher level of income. Unhappiness is the reverse. Since higher income groups probably contain a relatively large percentage of people whose incomes have recently risen, while low income groups contain a relatively large proportion of people whose incomes have recently fallen, we get the result that higher income people are, on the average, happier than lower income people, even though it is change, not level, of income that is determining happiness. Instead of the relative income hypothesis the analog here is the permanent vs. transitory income hypothesis. The consequence of this view is, as Abramowitz points out, that, "other things being equal we should have to grow *faster* in order to be happier, and we should have to keep on growing just to stay in the same place. Is it any wonder people feel caught in a rat race?" (Abramowitz[1]).

Hirsh[14] and Linder[18] have emphasized the rising relative price of space (position) and time, respectively, as self-cancelling factors in growth. Hirsh emphasizes the self-cancelling effects of increasing competition for a limited number of "positional goods"; i.e., best locations, chairmanships, etc. He illustrates the self-cancelling by analogy to spectators at a football game who are all brought to their feet by a spectacular play. With everyone now standing on tiptoe and craning his neck, the aggregate result is that no one has any better view than when all were seated. Previously a high school degree was a good qualification for most jobs. Then the same jobs began to require a B.A. degree, and then an M.A., an M.B.A., or a Ph.D. Does this "upgrading" mean that more is being accomplished, or that we are all just standing on tiptoe to achieve the same benefits we previously enjoyed while everyone was sitting down?

Linder has pointed out that the increasing productivity of labor time means that an hour of time is worth more in terms of goods. In other words as goods become relatively cheaper compared to time, then time must become relatively expensive in terms of goods. Increasing goods-affluence implies increasing time-scarcity, at least in terms of the substitution effect of the increase in the relative price of time. The income effect works in the opposite direction, but seems to be much weaker than the substitution effect. So as we become goods-rich we also become time-poor, and can afford fewer time-intensive activities such as personal care of the aged, the sick, and of children, as well as domestic service. The self-cancelling feature is evident if we reflect that: "The average man, no matter how rich he becomes, can never command the services of more than one other average man – even if he spends his entire income to buy it" (Abramowitz, 1979).

In sum, it would appear that aggregate growth just shifts the burden of scarcity on to time and relative position, which at the margin are constraints that are no less irksome than the previous ones of greater goods scarcity with lower levels of positional goods competition and time scarcity.

Another possible explanation of the Easterlin Paradox is that satisfaction derived from work has become increasingly negative, or less positive, as growth has increased, so that increased happiness from more goods has been offset by the increasing irksomeness of routinized, specialized work.

Finally, since neither Easterlin nor anyone else can measure absolute levels of happiness, it is always possible to maintain that the average American today really is much happier absolutely than his counterpart of thirty years ago, and that the average Swede is much happier than the average Italian, regardless of the constancy of the percentages in each category of self-evaluated happiness. No one can prove or disprove such a claim, but I think that most of us simply do not believe it.

The implication of these self-cancelling effects is that growth is less important for human welfare than we have heretofore thought. Consequently, other competing goals should rise relatively in the scale of social priorities. Future generations, sub-human species, community, and whatever else has been sacrificed in the name of growth, should henceforth be less sacrificed simply because growth is less productive of general happiness than used to be the case when marginal income was dedicated mainly to the satisfaction of absolute wants rather than relative wants.

Depletion of moral capital as a limit to growth

Hirsh[14] argues that: "Morality of the minimum order necessary for the functioning of a market system was assumed, nearly always implicitly, to be a kind of permanent free good, a natural resource of a nondepleting kind". Elaborating on the relation of Adam Smith's "Theory of Moral Sentiments" to his "Wealth of Nations," Hirsh points out that for Smith men could safely be trusted not to harm the community in pursuing their own self interest not only because of the invisible hand of competition, but also because of built-in restraints on individual behavior derived from shared morals, religion, custom, and education. The problem that Hirsh sees is that, "continuation of the growth process itself rests on certain preconditions that its own success has jeopardized through its indivdiualistic ethos. Economic growth undermines its social foundations."

The undermining of moral restraint has sources on both the demand and supply sides of the market for commodities. E.J. Mishan (1980) has noted that "a society in which 'anything goes' is ipso facto, a society in which anything sells." A corollary is that self-restraint or abstinence in the interests of any higher claims than immediate gratification by consumption is bad for sales, therefore bad for production, employment, tax receipts and everything else. The growth economy cannot grow unless it can sell. The idea that something should not be bought because it is frivolous, degrading, tawdry, or immoral is subversive to the growth imperative. On the supply side the success of science-based technology has fostered the pseudo religion of "scientism," i.e., the elevation of the deterministic, materialistic, mechanistic, and reductionistic research program of science to the status of an ultimate World View. Undeniably the methodological approach of scientific materialism has led to great increases in our technological prowess. Its practical success argues for its promotion from working hypothesis or research program to World View. But a World View of scientific materialism leaves no room for purpose, for good and evil, for better and worse states of the world. It erodes morality in general and moral restraint in economic life in particular. As power has increased, purpose has shrunk.

The baleful consequence of this fragmenting of the moral order, which we are depleting just as surely as we are wrecking the ecological order, is, as Mishan[20] points out, that, "effective argument [about policy] becomes impossible if there is no longer a common set of ultimate values or beliefs to which appeal can be made in the endeavor to persuade others." Just as all research in the physical sciences must dogmatically assume the existence of objective order in the physical world, so must research in the policy sciences dogmatically assume the existence of objective value in the moral world. Policy must be aimed at moving the world toward a better state of affairs or else it is senseless. If "better" and "worse" have no objective meaning, then policy can only be arbitrary and capricious. C.S. Lewis[17] forcefully stated this fundamental truth, "A dogmatic belief in objective value is necessary to the very idea of a rule which is not tyranny or an obedience which is not slavery." Likewise, Mishan claims that, "a moral consensus that is to be enduring and effective is the product of a belief only in its divine origin." In other words, an enduring ethic must be more than a social convention. It must have some objective transcendental authority. All attempts to treat moral value as entirely a part of nature to be manipulated and programmed by psychology or genetics only ends in a logical circularity. Moral value cannot be reduced to or explained as a mere result of genetic chance and environmental necessity, without at the same time losing its authority. Even if we knew how to remake moral values as human artifacts, we must still have a criterion for deciding which values should be emphasized and which stifled in the new order. But if that necessary criterion is itself an artifact of humanly manipulated chance and selection, then it too is a candidate for being remade. There is nowhere to stand.

Once the word gets out (and it already has) that majority has no basis other than random chance and natural selection under impermanent environmental conditions, then it too will have about as much authority as the Easter Bunny. In sum, the attitudes of scientific materialism and cultural relativism actively undercut belief in a transcendental basis for ethical value, which undercuts moral consensus, which undercuts the minimum moral restraint on self-interest presupposed by Adam Smith and most of his followers.

Writers of theistic persuasion, such as Lewis and Mishan, or writers of moralistic tendency of indeterminate religious persuasion such as Hirsh, are not the only ones to insist on this dilemma. E.O. Wilson[22], sociobiologist and scientific materialist par excellence, has clearly stated the same logical problem in the form of two dilemmas.

The first dilemma is that:

> The species lacks any goal external to its own biological nature . . . .
> Traditional religious beliefs have been eroded, not so much by humiliating disproofs of their mythologies as by the growing awareness that beliefs are really enabling mechanisms for survival. Religions, like other human institutions, evolve so as to enhance the prestige and influence of their practitioners.

Wilson further recognizes that, "the danger implicit in the first dilemma is the rapid dissolution of transcendental goals toward which societies can organize their energies."

Wilson is a scientific materialist and does not himself believe in "transcendental goals," but he recognizes their important survival value in providing social cohesion, even if "illusory." Rather than base our society on "transcendental illusions," Wilson wants to "Search for a new morality based upon a more truthful definition of man, [to] dissect the machinery of the mind and retrace its evolutionary history". But honesty and logic lead Wilson to recognize a second dilemma:

> Which is the choice that must be made among ethical premises in man's biological nature . . . we must consciously choose among the alternative emotional guides we have inherited.
> . . . at the center of the second dilemma is found a circularity: we are forced to choose among the elements of human nature by reference to value systems which these same elements created in an evolutionary age now long vanished.

In other words, our inherited value systems are a product of random mutation and natural selection by the environment of the hunter-gatherer, and are not likely to be well adapted to the environment of atomic power and genetic engineering. But the difficulty is even more basic: neither moral value nor rational thought can be trusted if it is fully explainable by arational and amoral causes. Random mutation and natural selection by an evolving environment, as currently understood, are arational and amoral events, and although they can certainly explain much, they cannot possibly explain rational and moral thought itself. Otherwise the theory of evolution itself would be merely a product of genetic chance and environmental selection, and would in the long run stand or fall not by its legitimate claim to be in large part true, but by its survival value. But Wilson admits that its survival value is low, indeed negative, because it must undercut a belief in transcendental value, which, right or wrong, does have high survival value in providing a basis for social cohesion (the first dilemma). If there is no objective transcendental value to appeal to in argument then persuasion is impossible and conflicts of interest become more violent. Furthermore, reason itself cannot accept the view that it is fully explainable by arational events without immediately losing all authority. If one's thoughts are caused by arational events in a purely mechanical world (no matter over how long a time period), then why take any of them seriously, including the thought that thoughts have arational causes?

Wilson has struggled with the same issue that bothered Mishan and Lewis, both cited earlier. I have emphasized Wilson's treatment in order to underline the fact that the dilemma is a logical one and exists for scientific materialists as much as for theists.

It is well to recall the connection of this apparent digression with the theme of economic growth. The forces propelling economic growth are simultaneously eroding the moral foundations of the very social order which gives purpose and direction to that growth. On the demand side of the market the glorification of self-interest and the pursuit of "infinite wants" leads to a weakening of moral distinctions between luxury and necessity. Moral limits constraining demand for junk are inconvenient in a growth economy, because growth increases when junk sells. So the growth economy fosters the erosion of the values upon which it depends, such as honesty, sobriety, trust, etc. On the supply side the "infinite" power of science-based technology is thought to be capable of overcoming all biophysical limits. But even if this erroneous proposition were true the very world view of scientism leads to the debunking of any notion of trascendental value and to undercutting the moral basis of the social cohesion presupposed by a market society. As internal moral restraint is eroded then external police power is substituted, and the latter requires real resources taken from other uses to substitute for the depletion of the "free public good" of moral restraint based on shared values.

At a minimum the problem of sustainability requires maintaining intact the moral knowledge or ethical capital inherited from the past. In fact, sustainability really requires an increase in knowledge, both of technique and of purpose, sufficient to offset, insofar as possible, the inevitable degradation of our physical world.

REFERENCES

1. Abramowitz, M. "Economic growth and its discontents", in *Economics and Human Welfare* (Michael Boskin, Ed.), Academic Press, New York (1979).
2. Ayres, R.U. and I. Nair (1984) "Thermodynamics and Economics," in *Physics Today,* November.
3. Bentham, J. *An Introduction to the Principles of Morals and Legislation,* University of London (1970).
4. Birch, C. and J. Cobb, *The Liberation of Life,* Cambridge University Press, Cambridge, England (1981).
5. Boserup, M. "Are there depletable resources?" in *Economic Growth and Resources* (Christopher Bliss and Mogens Boserup, Eds.), St. Martin's, New York (1980).
6. Brown, L.R. *Building a Sustainable Society,* Norton, New York, (1981).
7. Catton, W. *Overshoot,* Univ. of Illinois Press (1980).
8. Daly, H.E. *Steady-State Economics,* Freeman, San Francisco (1977).
9. Daly, H.E. "Chicago school individualism versus sexual reproduction: A critique of Becker and Tomes", *J. Econom. Issues* (March 1982).
10. Daly, H.E. "Thermodynamic and Economic Concepts as Related to Resource-Use Policies: Comment," *Land Econom.* (August 1986).
11. Easterlin, R.A. "Does economic growth improve the human lot?" in *Nations and Households in Economic Growth* (P.A. David and R.M. Weber, Eds.), Academic Press, New York (1974).
12. Ehrlich, P. and A. Ehrlich, *Extinction: The Causes and Consequence of the Disappearance of Species,* Random House, New York (1981).
13. Georgescu-Roegen, N. *The Entropy Law and the Economic Process,* Harvard Univ. Press, Cambridge, MA (1971).
14. Hirsh, F. *Social Limits to Growth,* Harvard Univ. Press, Cambridge, MA (1976).
15. Keynes, J.M. *Essays in Persuasion,* Norton, New York (1963).
16. Kneese, A.V., R.V. Ayres, and R. d'Arge. *Economics and the Environment: A Materials Balance Approach,* Resources for the Future, Washington, D.C. (1970).
17. Lewis, C.S. *The Abolition of Man,* Macmillan, New York (1965).
18. Linder, S.B. *The Harried Leisure Class,* Columbia Univ. Press, New York (1970).
19. Marshall, A. *Principles of Economics,* 9th ed., Macmillan, New York (1961).
20. Mishan, E.J. "The growth of affluence and the decline of welfare", in *Economics, Ecology, Ethics"* (H.E. Daly, Ed.), Freeman, San Francisco (1980).
21. Page, T. *Conservation and Economic Efficiency,* Johns Hopkins Univ. Press, Baltimore (1977).
22. Wilson, E.O. *On Human Nature,* Harvard Univ. Press, Cambridge, MA (1978).

Chapter 3
The property interface

J.H. Dales

"Interface" is current academic slang for "boundary." It is along physical interfaces, when air meets water, or water meets land, or prairie meets woodland, that many of the most mysterious and exciting phenomena of the physical and biological world occur. Similarly in social science. The dividing line between work and leisure forms an interface between economics and sociology; behavioural studies at this margin throw considerable light on social attitudes on the one hand and economic performance on the other. And every observer of politics knows how important the "floating vote" is, how behaviour along the margins between voters and non-voters, and between party A supporters and party B supporters, affects the outcomes of elections.

"Property rights" form interfaces between law and several social sciences, especially economics, political science, and sociology. It is with property rights as the dividing line between law and economics that we shall be chiefly concerned, and our first task is to survey this boundary from both sides of the fence.

In everyday conversation we usually speak of "property" rather than "property rights," but the contraction is misleading if it tends to make us think of property as *things* rather than as *rights,* or of ownership as outright rather than circumscribed. The concepts of property and ownership are created by, defined by, and therefore limited by, a society's system of law. When you own a car, you own a set of legally defined rights to use the vehicle in certain ways and not in others; you may not use it as a personal weapon, for example, nor may you leave it unattended beside a fire hydrant. Among the most important rights you do have are the right to prevent others from using the vehicle, except with your permission and on your terms, and the right to divest yourself of your ownership rights in the vehicle by selling them to someone else. We may say, then, that ownership always consists of (1) a set of rights to use property in certain ways (and a set of negative rights or prohibitions, that prevent its use in other ways); (2) a right to prevent others from exercising those rights, or to set the terms on which others may exercise them; and (3) a right to sell your property rights.

What economics deals with is the buying and selling, or leasing, or using, of property rights. It could hardly be otherwise. You can only buy, sell, lease, rent, lend, or borrow things that are owned; and the only things that are owned are property rights. The prices of the things you buy and sell are prices for property rights to those things.

We can see immediately, then, the interaction that is constantly going on at the interface between law and economics. Consider further the example of automobile ownership. If property rights change so that automobiles cannot be driven unless they are equipped with exhaust-control devices the price of automobiles is likely to rise; if property rights are changed so that automobiles may not be used in cities, the price of cars is likely to fall. On the other hand, if the price of cars rises or falls, so that people own fewer or more of them, there will be social and political pressures on the legal system to change the prescription of property rights in automobiles – to change the law about where they may be driven, how fast they may be driven, where and when they may be parked, and so on. There is always, then, an interface where the law of automobile ownership and the economics of automobile ownership meet, but the boundary may be shifted by a change in either the legal or the economic aspect of the situation. So long as such shifts are small and gradual the interface remains relatively peaceful. But if a major change occurs in either the law or the economics of automobile ownership, the shift in the boundary may be large and abrupt; the legal and economic aspects of the situation tend to become disjointed, and the interface then becomes seriously disturbed. This may be as good a way as any of describing the emergence of a new social problem or set of social problems. But before we attempt to analyse such problems, we must pursue the concept of property rights somewhat further.

MORE PROPERTY RIGHTS

We have discussed property rights to physical objects. The concept can be easily extended to such things as money, stocks, and bonds. These documents have no particular uses in themselves, but they give their owners certain rights; these rights are exclusive – others can be prevented from using them – and they are transferable. In our society, too, individuals may be said to have property rights to their own labour: a person can use his time for any legal purpose; he has exclusive rights to the fruits, monetary or otherwise, of his efforts; and he can sell his services (and often use them as security for borrowing). In the "extended family" system that is found in several African societies people do *not* have full property rights to their labour since one's distant relatives have a customary right to share in one's earnings; the lack of exclusive property rights to income naturally results in some unusual features of the labour market in extended family societies.

It is when we come to various forms of public property that the concept of property rights becomes rather more tenuous – and yet, paradoxically, even more enlightening. A publicly owned building is very much like a privately owned building; the government can use it for whatever purpose it wishes, can prevent others from using it, and can sell or rent it. A public road system is a rather different matter; since it is built for public use (not, like a government building, solely for the use of government employees) there is no question of exclusive use, and in practice there is only very limited transferability of the asset. Thus while a government "owns" a road system, and can set general rules about its use, its ownership is clearly of a very special kind, reflecting the special public nature of the asset.

We also say that a government "owns" the air and water systems within its jurisdiction. Air and water create special problems partly because they are "natural" assets – unlike roads, they are not man-made and the quantity of them cannot be altered – and partly because they are mobile, "flowing" resources that move around from one area to another. About the only things in this world that are not owned in any sense are the high seas and their animal inhabitants. We shall call these special types of property – roads, water, air, public parks and so on – *common property*. The term covers all property that is both owned in common (or unowned as in the case of oceans) and used in common; and it is to a study of common property that I now turn.

Before I do so, however, I want to try to avoid a possible misconception. I have been talking about property rights and not "private property." That sadly overworked and ill-defined phrase, "private property," has become an ideological concept that I want nothing to do with. I think that in some cases property rights should be vested in individuals; in other cases in groups of individuals, such as firms; and in some cases in governments. Different types of situations, it is reasonable to suppose, call for different forms of ownership. But in any event: no ideology! No "private property"! Just "property rights," by whomever exercised.

COMMON PROPERTY, RESTRICTED AND UNRESTRICTED

The first question to ask is why some property is owned in common. If we think of the history of this continent we remember that at one time virtually all the land was owned by some government. The land, however, was sold off to private owners, except for some public domain that the government wished to keep for its own use, and for the land in far northern areas in Canada that no private party wished to buy. On the other hand, many road systems were at one time privately owned toll roads, and these have all been brought under common ownership. What makes it easy to arrange for full property rights to land, and thus for private ownership of land, is that land is easily divisible (you can buy a few square yards or a few square miles) and not mobile (by means of fences, exclusivity of use can be enforced at a reasonable cost). Roads are land, of course, and the existence of common property in road systems is therefore a matter of choice; people have made a collective decision that it is more convenient to build and operate roads in common than to have private owners run the "road industry."

Air and water (except for a few non-navigable streams), however, seem to be owned in common because there is no alternative. There is no feasible way of separating a cubic yard, or an acre, of water from other cubic yards or acres; there is therefore no way of ensuring exclusive use; fences simply don't work. (Major drainage basins provide for a physical separation of waters up to the point where they enter oceans. These large units might be bought privately by one owner; but even if a private buyer came forward, society would undoubtedly decide that it would be undesirable to put all the water in a major drainage basin under the control of a private monopolist.) Thus it seems to be the physical characteristics of air and water, the fact that they are fluids and are naturally mobile over the face of the earth, that make it inevitable that they be owned in common or "vested in the right of" some government as the constitutional lawyers put it.

The nominal owner of a common property asset (i.e., some government) has, of course, an undoubted right to lay down rules for the use of the property. Rules for the use of man-made common property, such as parks or roads, are usually promulgated by the owner; as is nearly always true of stationary property – the French, with reason, refer to real estate as *immeubles* – enforcement of rules about use is practicable at reasonable cost. Where specific rules about the use of common property are laid down, we can call it "restricted" common property. Until recently, however, most governments have *not* made rules about the use of air or water. Implicitly, the government policy or rule has been that anyone could use air and water for whatever purpose he wished, without charge, permission, or hindrance. Such property we shall refer to as unrestricted common property.

In the past most people, at least in Canada, would no doubt have agreed that air and water resources were so vast that no rule about their use was needed. That day has now passed. But even if it be agreed that some regulation of use would be beneficial, we must still ask if the desired rules would be enforceable at reasonable cost. A "no-policy" policy makes sense if the cost of enforcing a positive policy is greater than its benefits. The costs of enforcing a policy fall, however, with improvement in administrative techniques, including such administrative hardware as computers and automatic monitoring devices. Such improvements therefore involve the possibility that rules about the use of common property resources that were impracticable in the past may be practicable now. Moreover, as larger and larger populations press against our fixed resources of air and water, the benefits to be gained by rules regulating their use increase, while enforcement costs are likely to become more easily bearable as they are spread over larger populations. These considerations suggest why our political scientists and our lawyers ought to be on a continuous look-out both for new legislative methods and for old ones that become newly practicable, in order to help control the use of our two most important common property resources, air and water.

The economic effect of making common property available for use on a no-rule basis, so that it may be freely used by anyone for any purpose at any time, is crystal clear. Common property will be over-used relative to both private property and to public property that *is* subject to charges for its use or to rules about its use; and if the unrestricted common property resource is depletable, over-use will in time lead to its depletion and therefore to the destruction of the property.

There is an old saying that "everyone's property is no one's property," the inference being that no one looks after it, that everyone over-uses it, and that the property therefore deteriorates. History bears out the truth of this saying in many sad ways. Property that is freely available to all is unowned except in a purely formal, constitutional, sense, and lack of effective ownership is almost always the source of much mischief. The inefficiency of medieval farming resulted in large part from the fact that ownership rights were usually poorly defined; in particular, the commons were unowned (i.e., owned by everybody – and nobody), and common pastures were so overstocked that their productivity fell to the vanishing point. Not until ownership concepts had evolved to a point where something like a modern view of property rights in land became accepted was it possible to use the land efficiently and increase agricultural output.

Another example: The sad list of animal species that have been extinguished by man's predation results purely from the fact that property rights in these animals did not exist, perhaps because they could not have been enforced if they had been established, but in any event because they did not exist. If animals are sought after they are valuable, and if they are owned those who seek them will have to pay their owners for the right to kill or capture them. Owners will charge a high enough price for the right to kill their animals that some stock of animals will always remain; you don't have to be an economist to know that it doesn't pay to kill the goose that lays the golden egg. No domestic animal has ever been threatened with extinction simply because domestic animals are owned. Nobody owned the buffalo or the passenger pigeon; and in recent years whales and kangaroos have been sadly victimized by the absence of ownership. If in the past Canadian governments had said of trees, as they said of buffaloes and passenger pigeons, that they belonged to everybody and everybody could cut them down free of charge, we may be sure that there would be no lumber industry or pulp and paper industry in Canada today.

With the rise of the automobile, the treating of road systems as unrestricted common property has accentuated congestion problems and public toll-roads may be the best way of relieving them. At any rate cities are beginning to learn

that freeways seldom make for free-flowing traffic, and that the building of
freeways soon increases traffic to the point where more freeways have to be built.
Medieval men who witnessed the overstocking of unrestricted common pastures
would understand automobile congestion on unrestricted common roads.
(Knowing that common pasturing led to the deterioration of the livestock as well
as of the pasture, they might also observe with interest the deterioration of the
automobile stock resulting from, say, a hundred-car pile-up on a California
freeway.)

Air and water in this country, and in most other countries, have been treated
as unrestricted common property; so long as they are so treated air and water
pollution will increase and the physical condition of our air and water assets will
continue to deteriorate. Moreover, as has already been pointed out, we can
manufacture more roads, but we cannot manufacture more air or water; all we
can do is to use existing supplies as wisely as possible. It is time, I believe, that we
took air and water out of the category of unrestricted common property, and
began to establish some specific rules about their use or, to put it another way, to
establish something more sophisticated in the way of property rights to their use
than the rule that "anything goes." That rule may have been quite sensible in the
past, when the demands made by human populations on the services of air and
water were very small compared to the volumes of these assets; the benefits of
controlling use would probably have been small and the costs of enforcing
restrictions would no doubt have been large. All I am arguing is that growth in
population, production, and urbanization inexorably changes the balance of the
benefit cost analysis against the policy of doing nothing and in favour of some
positive policy. But to say that is not to say or in any way to imply that it is an easy
matter to choose a *wise* positive policy, or to establish wise new property rights to
the use of air and water.

SOCIAL PROBLEMS

Like benefit-cost analysis, an analysis based on property rights provides a way of
looking at pollution problems (and other social problems); but unlike the
economic analysis, which is confined to the study of solutions that have been
proposed, the legal analysis often generates proposals for solutions to social
problems. In this section, I propose to look at, and comment on, a few examples
of the relationships between property rights and social problems. Two points
should be kept in mind throughout. First, there is no perfect legal solution to
social problems, any more than there is a perfect economic solution. Second, a
given legal definition of property rights in an asset has not only economic
consequences (as we have seen in the previous section of this chapter) but also
social and political consequences; there are interfaces between law and sociology
and law and political scence, as well as between law and economics.

Consider, first, a frivolous example. You are driving in a city after a heavy rain,
and inadvertently drive through a large puddle of water so fast that you
thoroughly drench some unfortunate pedestrian who happened to be in the wrong
place at the wrong time. When you notice through your rear-view mirror that the
victim is taking down your licence number, you stop and, after a brief
conversation, pay him $10, shake hands, and go on your way.

This problem, then, was settled expeditiously and with a minimum of social
friction. The reason is that the legal situation was clear and known to both parties.
Ownership of an automobile did not confer the right to dirty other peoples'

clothing, and ownership of clothing did confer the right not to have it dirtied by inattentive motorists; and neither party was interested in having a judge tell them what they both knew. The law might, of course, have said the reverse – that pedestrians had to look out for splashing motorists, rather than saying that motorists had an obligation to avoid splashing pedestrians. Had this been the case, there would have been no more social friction, but the economic outcome would have been different; the cost of the incident would have been borne by the pedestrian rather than the motorist. If the law had not been clear, there would have been bad feelings, there might have been a court case, and the economic outcome would have been unpredictable. There is much to be said for definiteness especially where the law is concerned.

Notice, too, that the existing law about splashing problems imposes the cost of injury on the active party, the motorist, rather than the passive pedestrian. The probable rationale for this policy is not the *social* view that the pedestrian is more important than the motorist, but the *technological* consideration that motorists can more easily avoid splashing pedestrians than pedestrians can avoid being splashed by motorists, and the *economic* consideration that it is cheaper to persuade motorists that it does not pay to splash pedestrians than to protect pedestrians by building a six-foot wall along the interface between sidewalks and roads. As a pedestrian, a motorist, and a taxpayer, I think the present law is very sensible.

Imagine, now, that you own a factory in Toronto and that you have been dumping your untreated factory wastes into Lake Ontario for forty years. Until recently not a single person complained of your practices and you are breaking no law by continuing to do what you have always done. Yet in the last couple of years it seems that you have become a villainous polluter, a heartless despoiler of nature, and a sneak thief robbing the children of Toronto of their natural right to swim in Lake Ontario; the press is after your scalp and trying to put the government on you; even your best friends seem to think that "something ought to be done about pollution." You object to such rough treatment, and reply that your lawyers advise that you have as much right to dump your garbage in Lake Ontario as any kid has to swim in it. You are probably right, legally, but you are in for a lot of trouble with your public relations.

Two comments suffice. Unrestricted common property rights are bound to lead to all sorts of social, political, and economic friction, especially as population pressure increases, because, in the nature of the case, individuals have no legal rights with respect to the property when its government owner follows a policy of "anything goes." Notice, too, that such a policy, though apparently neutral as between conflicting interests, in fact always favours one party against the other. Technologically, swimmers cannot harm the polluters, but the polluters can harm the swimmers; when property rights are undefined those who wish to use the property in ways that deteriorate it will inevitably triumph every time over those who wish to use it in ways that do not deteriorate it. Economically and socially the question is always which set of interests *should* prevail, or rather what sort of accommodation should be made among the various interests concerned. The question is always, and inescapably, the great question of social justice.

Questions of social justice can be answered in many ways. Consider carefully the following example of an actual solution to water pollution problems in Britain. For this example, which I find utterly fascinating, I am indebted to Douglas Clarke who has recently described it in the following words.

The island of Great Britain is moist and verdant, and blessed with innumerable cool streams that once were all haunts of trout and salmon. Most of them still are, even though they now flow through an industrialized countryside. The total poundage of fine game fish taken would put any accessible part of Canada to shame. We are so used to the idea that the waters of any industrial area are a write-off, so far as quality angling is concerned, that one cannot help but be curious as to how all that fishing is maintained.

It is not because they do not have to watch out for pollution. There is an organization called the Anglers' Cooperative Association which has been in existence for nineteen years, which has taken over the watch dog functions formerly left to individuals. It is an interesting organization. It has a fluctuating and rather small list of members and subscribers, barely enough to keep an office open, but it is able to call on some powerful help, especially legal. It has investigated nearly 700 pollution cases since it started and very rarely does it fail to get abatement or damages, as the case requires. These anglers have behind them a simple fact. Every fishery in Britain, except for those in public reservoirs, belongs to some private owner. Many of them have changed hands at high prices and action is always entered on behalf of somebody who has suffered real damage. It has been that way from ancient times. Over here the fishing belongs to everybody – and thus to nobody. The A.C.A. exists merely to take action where individuals may not act themselves.

Two cases from some time back well explain why the Derwent, which flows through the industrial city of Derby, still has its trout. Action was entered against the city because its effluent was harmful to trout, and the city, through its legal representatives, claimed in the highest court in the land that it was completely unreasonable to expect them to maintain the standards of a trout stream. The A.C.A., incidentally, acted on behalf of the "Pride of Derby Angling Club," which leased the fishery from the titled gentleman who owned it. The law lords said that the city had no more right to put its muck in the river than the citizens had to put theirs on the property of their neighbours. About the same time, and for the same city and river, an injunction was obtained against British Electric, a public corporation. All they had been doing was to run warm water directly into the river. Trout like it cool. The A.C.A. also deals with such – to us – trivia as mud running into a stream from a new road grade, or a ditch. It doesn't have to and the anglers are willing to go to court. This is actually a good example of a common form of pollution which we accept but which is quite unnecessary and not hard to avoid.

What it amounts to is that you can have good fishing, which means good water, in a river in a populated British countryside if you make it your business to have it. It is not only Britain. We get an anglers' magazine from Germany and there are lovely illustrations showing good fishing on the Ruhr river, of which you may have heard, and on the Binnen, or inner, Alster, . . . in the industrial part of Hamburg. . . .

I will be the first to admit that there are geological and climatic differences between Ontario and western Europe which have influenced the impact of European settlement on our area, so that some of our streams have, inevitably, a less constant flow and a warmer temperature than they used to have. Within these limitations, however, we ask ourselves why we have to sacrifice water quality still further by deliberate pollution.

Some time ago the A.C.A. analyzed their comparatively few failures. In some cases the polluter could not be identified. In some other cases the polluter was insolvent, hence no damages. They call this failure. However, and this underlines the comparison between them and us, the most important single cause of failure was when the anglers who suffered from the pollution had no concrete evidence of interest, such as a valid lease, and had only tacit consent or a gentleman's agreement with the owner, who refused to become involved in the action. That sounds familiar. We, as individuals, fish the waters that we all own, collectively. As individuals we have sustained no damages at law. Collectively – as owners – well, forget it. In Britain, when a truck involved in an accident spills chemicals into a stream, the public liability insurance pays for the fish, for all the costs of clean-up and restocking, and for the loss of use and enjoyment during the period between kill and restoration because property damage has been done. Who looks after us?

Officially we have tried to do by statute what the British have done by the Common Law, but never, apparently, have we really meant what we said. Our first legislation, in 1865, had its teeth pulled in 1868. It is interesting that one simply cannot conceive of a judgment or an injunction obtained through legal action by the A.C.A. being set aside. Part of the explanation may be social. The A.C.A. has the Duke of Edinburgh for Patron. Apparently it is quite all right for him to be honorary keeper of a watch dog that has sunk its teeth into government corporations such as British Electric and the Coal Board, municipalities big and small, industries and private individuals, without fear or favour. I notice that His Grace the Duke of Devonshire is President, and there are two more dukes among the vice-presidents, (that is over ten per cent of the total number of non-royal dukes), as well as two additional peers, [and] a couple of knights. . . .

There are many worthwhile comments to be made about this passage, but let me mention only a few of them. Note, first, that the solution results from a particular set of property rights (based in this case on Common Law) that are enforced by the courts, and that the property rights seem to be in the fish, or the fishing, not the water; there is no administrative agency that is concerned either with the fish or the water. Second, the solution may seem simple but in fact it isn't; Mr Clarke is careful to suggest that the workability of the system may depend in important ways on such apparently irrelevant factors as the English climate, English history, and the particular social status enjoyed by the English nobility.

Third, there is no way of knowing whether the solution is a "good" one or not. At one level of analysis it can be argued that the solution favours the fishermen over industrials and municipalities who have to bear the costs either of disposing of their wastes in such a way as to avoid polluting the rivers of buying up the fishing rights to a river and then using it for waste disposal purposes; and there seems no obvious reason why the shoe should not be on the other foot – why polluters should not own property rights in the waste disposal capability of the river, in which case the fishermen, if they wanted to fish, would have to buy out the polluters' rights. Note, however, that if the government "owner" of the river follows a policy of "anything goes" neither party can buy out the other because neither has anything to sell! Under a system of unrestricted common property, groups that have opposing interests in the use of the property cannot negotiate because they have nothing to negotiate with; all they can do is yell interminably at each other.

In my opinion, however, it is often misleading to think of pollution problems in terms of groups rather than in terms of the society as a whole. In the present example fishermen no doubt live in cities and buy manufactured products, and industrialists and residents of cities no doubt sometimes go fishing. The groups are, in fact, all mixed up together. And it is not true that fishermen pay nothing for their good fishing; they pay higher prices for manufactured goods and higher municipal taxes than pay would pay if the law favoured polluters and if fishing were not so good. Similarly, polluters get better fishing for their higher expenditures on waste disposal. From an over-all, social point of view the whole British population in effect buys good quality fishing (and other water-based recreation) by paying higher taxes and higher prices for goods; in Ontario, we have in effect accepted water pollution in return for cheaper goods and lower taxes. Which is the better policy? A silly question deserves a silly answer: whichever policy is preferred is better.

Mr Clarke makes it quite clear that he prefers the British solution, or something like it. So do I. It would help if we could let our provincial member of parliament know roughly where each of us stands on the question of better quality air and water versus higher taxes and higher costs of goods. But it wouldn't help very much. The important question is *how much* "better quality environment" we would be willing to buy at different "prices" in terms of higher taxes and higher costs of goods, and most of us are not sure about this. As was suggested in the last chapter, the only way to answer the question may be to have the politicians start charging us for better quality air and water and then keep "upping the ante" until we say "Enough! No more!"

The trouble is that when we call a halt about half of us will think we are already spending too much to improve the environment, and about half of us will want to spend more; therefore very few of us will be very happy with the outcome. In some cases there is nothing more that can be done. In many other cases, however, there *is* a better solution; we have in fact often adopted it, but it is only recently that Professor Mishan, an economist, has generalized the argument that underlies it. The point is that it is often possible to avoid the sort of fifty-fifty compromise that we have been discussing. Take the question of smoking on a train, for example. If all passengers, half of whom are smokers, are required to come to a single decision, they may decide to allow smoking or not to allow smoking (in which case half of them are going to be unhappy all of the time) or they may decide to allow smoking during half the journey (in which case all of them will be unhappy half of the time). The sensible solution in this case is to provide what Mishan calls "separate facilities," i.e., to provide both smoking cars and no-smoking cars; everyone should then be happy all of the time. This solution, of course, is not applicable in a single-cabin vehicle such as a bus; "separate facilities" may not always be practicable. Zoning laws in cities are another common example of the "separate facilities" type of solution.

Is this solution applicable to pollution problems? Not perfectly, certainly, but to some considerable extent. Although air and water move around they do not mix thoroughly; over a large area such as Ontario it is certainly practicable to provide for different air and water qualities in different regions. When pollution matters come under municipal control different municipalities, or groups of municipalities, are likely to provide different quality environments. Under provincial control, the same variety is possible if the provincial authorities choose to follow some variation of the "separate facilities" or "zoning" principle. This principle will not always be applicable, and may not always be desirable. It is, however, always worth considering, if only because it offers some possibility of meeting a variety of demands and opinions with a variety of solutions. Instead of giving property rights in water use to polluters *or* fishermen, it may be thought desirable to assign the rights to fishermen in one area and to polluters in another.

SUMMARY

This chapter has tried to suggest that legal definitions of property rights lie at the heart of social decision-making and problem-solving. Property rights are clearly antecedent to economics, since it is property rights that define the economist's "goods and services," and we have seen, particularly in the discussion of unrestricted common property, how property rights affect individual and social behaviour. A study of property rights gives us no magic key for the solution of social problems, but it does lead to suggestions for solutions that are refreshingly different from those offered by economists and other social scientists.

The main substantive conclusion I wish to draw from this chapter is that to treat air and water as unrestricted common property is socially indefensible. A policy of "anything goes" is defensible if the cost of enforcing a positive policy exceeds the benefits to be gained from it. This may be true now of polar ice, and it may have been true in the past of air and water, although I doubt it; English courts have apparently long enforced property rights in fishing, and in the process have enforced one solution to the problem of water pollution. In any event, it is perfectly clear on both theoretical and historical grounds that, as population grows, unrestricted common property will be over-used and deteriorate physically to the point of uselessness. On the assumption that we don't want that to happen to our air and water, it is high time that we began to devise some new forms of property rights, not to air and water, but to the *use* of air and water. In Ontario, during the last dozen years, we have begun to move in that direction, at least to the extent of changing the status of air and water from unrestricted to restricted common property. But the field for new ideas and social experimentation is still wide open.

Chapter 4
The tragedy of the commons

Garrett Hardin

The population problem has no technical solution; it requires a fundamental extension in morality.

Garrett Hardin

At the end of a thoughtful article on the future of nuclear war, Wiesner and York[1] concluded that: "Both sides in the arms race are . . . confronted by the dilemma of steadily increasing military power and steadily decreasing national security. *It is our considered professional judgment that this dilemma has no technical solution.* If the great powers continue to look for solutions in the area of science and technology only, the result will be to worsen the situation."

I would like to focus your attention not on the subject of the article (national security in a nuclear world) but on the kind of conclusion they reached, namely that there is no technical solution to the problem. An implicit and almost universal assumption of discussions published in professional and semipopular scientific journals is that the problem under discussion has a technical solution. A technical solution may be defined as one that requires a change only in the techniques of the natural sciences, demanding little or nothing in the way of change in human values or ideas of morality.

In our day (though not in earlier times) technical solutions are always welcome. Because of previous failures in prophecy, it takes courage to assert that a desired technical solution is not possible. Wiesner and York exhibited this courage; publishing in a science journal, they insisted that the solution to the problem was not to be found in the natural sciences. They cautiously qualified their statement with the phrase, "It is our considered professional judgment . . . .". Whether they were right or not is not the concern of the present article. Rather, the concern here is with the important concept of a class of human problems which can be called "no technical solution problems," and, more specifically, with the identification and discussion of one of these.

It is easy to show that the class is not a null class. Recall the game of tick-tack-toe. Consider the problem, "How can I win the game of tick-tack-toe?" It is well known that I cannot, if I assume (in keeping with the conventions of game theory) that my opponent understands the game perfectly. Put another way, there is no "technical solution" to the problem. I can win only by giving a radical meaning to the word "win"· I can hit my opponent over the head; or I can drug him; or I can falsify the record. Every way in which I "win" involves, in some sense, an abandonment of the game, as we intuitively understand it. (I can also, of course, openly abandon the game – refuse to play it. This is what most adults do.)

The class of "No technical solution problems" has members. My thesis is that the "population problem," as conventionally conceived, is a member of this class. How it is conventionally conceived needs some comment. It is fair to say that most people who anguish over the population problem are trying to find a way to avoid the evils of overpopulation without relinquishing any of the privileges they now enjoy. They think that farming the seas or developing new strains of wheat will solve the problem – technologically. I try to show here that the solution they seek cannot be found. The population problem cannot be solved in a technical way, any more than can the problem of winning the game of tick-tack-toe.

Population, as Malthus said, naturally tends to grow "geometrically," or, as we would now say, exponentially. In a finite world this means that the per capita share of the world's goods must steadily decrease. Is ours a finite world?

A fair defense can be put forward for the view that the world is infinite; or that we do not know that it is not. But, in terms of the practical problems that we must face in the next few generations with the foreseeable technology, it is clear that we will greatly increase human misery if we do not, during the immediate future, assume that the world available to the terrestrial human population is finite. "Space" is no escape.[2]

A finite world can support only a finite population; therefore, population growth must eventually equal zero. (The case of perpetual wide fluctuations above and below zero is a trivial variant that need not be discussed.) When this condition is met, what will be the situation of mankind? Specifically, can Bentham's goal of "the greatest good for the greatest number" be realized?

No – for two reasons, each sufficient by itself. The first is a theoretical one. It is not mathematically possible to maximize for two (or more) variables at the same time. This was clearly stated by von Neumann and Morgenstern,[3] but the principle is implicit in the theory of partial differential equations, dating back at least to D'Alembert (1717–1783).

The second reason springs directly from biological facts. To live, any organism must have a source of energy (for example, food). This energy is utilized for two purposes: mere maintenance and work. For man, maintenance of life requires about 1600 kilo-calories a day ("maintenance calories"). Anything that he does over and above merely staying alive will be defined as work, and is supported by "work calories" which he takes in. Work calories are used not only for what we call work in common speech; they are also required for all forms of enjoyment, from swimming and automobile racing to playing music and writing poetry. If our goal is to maximize population it is obvious what we must do: We must make the work calories per person approach as close to zero as possible. No gourmet meals, no vacations, no sports, no music, no literature, no art . . . I think that everyone will grant, without argument or proof that maximizing population does not maximize goods. Bentham's goal is impossible.

In reaching this conclusion I have made the usual assumption that it is the acquisition of energy that is the problem. The appearance of atomic energy has led some to question this assumption. However, given an infinite source of energy, population growth still produces an inescapable problem. The problem of the acquisition of energy is replaced by the problem of its dissipation, as J.H. Fremlin has so wittily shown.[4] The arithmetic signs in the analysis are, as it were, reversed; but Bentham's goal is still unobtainable.

The optimum population is, then, less than the maximum. The difficulty of defining the optimum is enormous; so far as I know, no one has seriously tackled this problem. Reaching an acceptable and stable solution will surely require more than one generation of hard analytical work – and much persuasion.

We want the maximum good per person; but what is good? To one person it is wilderness, to another it is ski lodges for thousands. To one it is estuaries to nourish ducks for hunters to shoot; to another it is factory land. Comparing one good with another is, we usually way, impossible because goods are incommensurable. Incommensurables cannot be compared.

Theoretically this may be true; but in real life incommensurables *are* commensurable. Only a criterion of judgment and a system of weighting are needed. In nature the criterion is survival. Is it better for a species to be small and hideable, or large and powerful? Natural selection commensurates the incommensurables. The compromise achieved depends on a natural weighting of the values of the variables.

Man must imitate this process. There is no doubt that in fact he already does, but unconsciously. It is when the hidden decisions are made explicit that the arguments begin. The problem for the years ahead is to work out an acceptable theory of weighting. Synergistic effects, nonlinear variation, and difficulties in discounting the future make the intellectual problem difficult, but not (in principle) insoluble.

Has any cultural group solved this practical problem at the present time, even on an intuitive level? One simple fact proves that none has: there is no prosperous population in the world today that has, and has had for some time, a growth rate of zero. Any people that has intuitively identified its optimum point will soon reach it, after which its growth rate becomes and remains zero.

Of course, a positive growth rate might be taken as evidence that a population is below its optimum. However, by any reasonable standards, the most rapidly growing populations on earth today are (in general) the most miserable. This association (which need not be invariable) casts doubt on the optimistic assumption that the positive growth rate of a population is evidence that it has yet to reach its optimum.

We can make little progress in working toward optimum population size until we explicitly exorcize the spirit of Adam Smith in the field of practical demography. In economic affairs, *The Wealth of Nations* (1776) popularized the "invisible hand," the idea that an individual who "intends only his own gain," is, as it were, "led by an invisible hand to promote . . . the public interest".[5] Adam Smith did not assert that this was invariably true and perhaps neither did any of his followers. But he contributed to a dominant tendency of thought that has ever since interfered with positive action based on rational analysis, namely, the tendency to assume that decisions reached individually will, in fact, be the best decisions for an entire society. If this assumption is correct it justifies the continuance of our present policy of laissez-faire in reproduction. If it is correct we can assume that men will control their individual fecundity so as to produce the optimum population. If the assumption is not correct, we need to reexamine our individual freedoms to see which ones are defensible.

Tragedy of freedom in a commons

The rebuttal to the invisible hand in population control is to be found in a scenario first sketched in a little-known pamphlet[6] in 1833 by a mathematical amateur named William Forster Lloyd (1794–1852). We may well call it "the tragedy of the commons," using the word "tragedy" as the philosopher Whitehead used it:[7] "The essence of dramatic tragedy is not unhappiness. It resides in the solemnity of the remorseless working of things." He then goes on to say, "This inevitableness of destiny can only be illustrated in terms of human life by incidents which in fact involve unhappiness. For it is only by them that the futility of escape can be made evident in the drama."

The tragedy of the commons develops in this way. Picture a pasture open to all. It is to be expected that each herdsman will try to keep as many cattle as possible on the commons. Such an arrangement may work reasonably satisfactorily for centuries because tribal wars, poaching, and disease keep the numbers of both man and beast well below the carrying capacity of the land. Finally, however, comes the day of reckoning, that is, the day when the long-desired goal of social stability becomes a reality. At this point, the inherent logic of the commons remorselessly generates tragedy.

As a rational being, each herdsman seeks to maximize his gain. Explicitly or implicitly, more or less consciously, he asks, "What is the utility *to me* of adding one more animal to my herd?" This utility has one negative and one positive component.

1. The positive component is a function of the increment of one animal. Since the herdsman receives all the proceeds from the sale of the additional animal, the positive utility is nearly +1.
2. The negative component is a function of the additional overgrazing created by one more animal. Since, however, the effects of overgrazing are shared by all the herdsmen, the negative utility for any particular decision-making herdsman is only a fraction of −1.

Adding together the component partial utilities, the rational herdsman concludes that the only sensible course for him to pursue is to add another animal to his herd. And another; and another . . . But this is the conclusion reached by each and every rational herdsman sharing a commons. Therein is the tragedy. Each man is locked into a system that compels him to increase his herd without limit – in a world that is limited. Ruin is the destination toward which all men rush, each pursuing his own best interest in a society that believes in the freedom of the commons. Freedom in a commons brings ruin to all.

Some would say that this is a platitude. Would that it were! In a sense, it was learned thousands of years ago, but natural selection favors the forces of psychological denial.[8] The individual benefits as an individual from his ability to deny the truth even though society as a whole, of which he is a part, suffers. Education can counteract the natural tendency to do the wrong thing, but the inexorable succession of generations requires that the basis for this knowledge be constantly refreshed.

A simple incident that occurred a few years ago in Leominster, Massachusetts, shows how perishable the knowledge is. During the Christmas shopping season the parking meters downtown were covered with plastic bags that bore tags reading: "Do not open until Christmas. Free parking courtesy of the mayor and city council," In other words, facing the prospect of an increased demand for already scarce space, the city fathers reinstituted the system of the commons. (Cynically, we suspect that they gained more votes than they lost by this retrogressive act.)

In an approximate way, the logic of the commons has been understood for a long time, perhaps since the discovery of agriculture or the invention of private property in real estate. But it is understood mostly only in special cases which are not sufficiently generalized. Even at this late date, cattlemen leasing national land on the western ranges demonstrate no more than an ambivalent understanding, in constantly pressuring federal authorities to increase the head count to the point where over-grazing produces erosion and weed-dominance. Likewise, the oceans of the world continue to suffer from the survival of the philosophy of the commons. Maritime nations still respond automatically to the shibboleth of the "freedom of the seas." Professing to believe in the "inexhaustible resources of the oceans," they bring species after species of fish and whales closer to extinction.[9]

The National Parks present another instance of the working out of the tragedy of the commons. At present, they are open to all, without limit. The parks themselves are limited in extent – there is only one Yosemite Valley – whereas population seems to grow without limit. The values that visitors seek in the parks are steadily eroded. Plainly, we must soon cease to treat the parks as commons or they will be of no value to anyone.

What shall we do? We have several options. We might sell them off as private property. We might keep them as public property, but allocate the right to enter them. The allocation might be on the basis of wealth, by the use of an auction system. It might be on the basis of merit, as defined by some agreed-upon standards. It might be by lottery. Or it might be on a first-come, first-served basis, administered to long queues. These, I think, are all the reasonable possibilities. They are all objectionable. But we must choose – or acquiesce in the destruction of the commons that we call our National Parks.

POLLUTION

In a reverse way, the tragedy of the commons reappears in problems of pollution. Here it is not a question of taking something out of the commons, but of putting something in – sewage, or chemical, radioactive, and heat wastes into water; noxious and dangerous fumes into the air; and distracting and unpleasant advertising signs into the line of sight. The calculations of utility are much the same as before. The rational man finds that his share of the cost of the wastes he discharges into the commons is less than the cost of purifying his wastes before releasing them. Since this is true for everyone, we are locked into a system of "fouling our own nest," so long as we behave only as independent, rational, free-enterprisers.

The tragedy of the commons as a food basket is averted by private property, or something formally like it. But the air and waters surrounding us cannot readily be fenced, and so the tragedy of the commons as a cesspool must be prevented by different means, by coercive laws or taxing devices that make it cheaper for the polluter to treat his pollutants than to discharge them untreated. We have not progressed as far with the solution of this problem as we have with the first. Indeed, our particular concept of private property, which deters us from exhausting the positive resources of the earth, favors pollution. The owner of a factory on the bank of a stream – whose property extends to the middle of the stream – often has difficulty seeing why it is not his natural right to muddy the waters flowing past his door. The law, always behind the times, requires elaborate stitching and fitting to adapt it to this newly perceived aspect of the commons.

The pollution problem is a consequence of population. It did not much matter how a lonely American frontiersman disposed of his waste. "Flowing water purifies itself every 10 miles," my grandfather used to say, and the myth was near enough to the truth when he was a boy, for there were not too many people. But as population became denser, the natural chemical and biological recycling process became overloaded, calling for a redefinition of property rights.

HOW TO LEGISLATE TEMPERANCE?

Analysis of the pollution problem as a function of population density uncovers a not generally recognized principle of morality, namely: *the morality of an act is a function of the state of the system at the time it is performed.*[10] Using the commons as a cesspool does not harm the general public under frontier conditions, because there is no public; the same behaviour in a metropolis is unbearable. A hundred and fifty years ago a plainsman could kill an American bison, cut out only the tongue for his dinner, and discard the rest of the animal. He was not in any important sense being wasteful. Today, with only a few thousand bison left, we would be appalled at such behaviour.

In passing, it is worth noting that the morality of an act cannot be determined from a photograph. One does not know whether a man killing an elephant or setting fire to the grassland is harming others until one knows the total system in which his act appears. "One picture is worth a thousand words," said an ancient Chinese; but it may take 10,000 words to validate it. It is as tempting to ecologists as it is to reformers in general to try to persuade others by way of the photographic shortcut. But the essense of an argument cannot be photographed: it must be presented rationally – in words.

That morality is system-sensitive escaped the attention of most codifiers of ethics in the past. "Thou shalt not . . ." is the form of traditional ethical directives which make no allowance for particular circumstances. The laws of our society follow the pattern of ancient ethics, and therefore are poorly suited to governing a complex, crowded, changeable world. Our epicyclic solution is to augment statutory law with administrative law. Since it is practically impossible to spell out all the conditions under which it is safe to burn trash in the back yard or to run an automobile without smog-control, by law we delegate the details to bureaus. The result is administrative law, which is rightly feared for an ancient reason – *Quis custodiet ipsos custodes?* – "Who shall watch the watchers themselves?" John Adams said that we must have "a government of laws and not men." Bureau administrators, trying to evaluate the morality of acts in the total system, are singularly liable to corruption, producing a government by men, not laws.

Prohibition is easy to legislate (though not necessarily to enforce); but how do we legislate temperance? Experience indicates that it can be accomplished best through the mediation of administrative law. We limit possibilities unnecessarily if we suppose that the sentiment of *Quis custodiet* denies us the use of administrative law. We should rather retain the phrase as a perpetual reminder of fearful dangers we cannot avoid. The great challenge facing us now is to invent the corrective feedbacks that are needed to keep custodians honest. We must find ways to legitimate the needed authority of both the custodians and the corrective feedbacks.

FREEDOM TO BREED IS INTOLERABLE

The tragedy of the commons is involved in population problems in another way. In a world governed solely by the principle of "dog eat dog" – if indeed there ever was such a world – how many children a family had would not be a matter of public concern. Parents who bred too exuberantly would leave fewer descendants, not more, because they would be unable to care adequately for their children. David Lack and others have found that such a negative feedback demonstrably controls the fecundity of birds.[11] But men are not birds, and have not acted like them for millenniums, at least.

65

If each human family were dependent only on its own resources; *if* the children of improvident parents starved to death; *if*, thus, overbreeding brought its own "punishment" to the germ line – *then* there would be no public interest in controlling the breeding of families. But our society is deeply committed to the welfare state,[12] and hence is confronted with another aspect of the tragedy of the commons.

In a welfare state, how shall we deal with the family, the religion, the race, or the class (or indeed any distinguishable and cohesive group) that adopts overbreeding as a policy to secure its own aggrandizement?[13] To couple the concept of freedom to breed with the belief that everyone born has an equal right to the commons is to lock the world into a tragic course of action.

Unfortunately this is just the course of action that is being pursued by the United Nations. In late 1967, some 30 nations agreed to the following:[14]

The Universal Declaration of Human Rights describes the family as the natural and fundamental unit of society. It follows that any choice and decision with regard to the size of the family must irrevocably rest with the family itself, and cannot be made by anyone else.

It is painful to have to deny categorically the validity of this right; denying it, one feels as uncomfortable as a resident of Salem, Massachusetts, who denied the reality of witches in the 17th century. At the present time, in liberal quarters something like a taboo acts to inhibit criticism of the United Nations. There is a feeling that the United Nations is "our last and best hope," that we shouldn't find fault with it; we shouldn't play into the hands of the archconservatives. However, let us not forget what Robert Louis Stevenson said: "The truth that is suppressed by friends is the readiest weapon of the enemy." If we love the truth we must openly deny the validity of the Universal Declaration of Human Rights, even though it is promoted by the United Nations. We should also join with Kingsley Davis[15] in attempting to get planned Parenthood-World Population to see the error of its ways in embracing the same tragic ideal.

CONSCIENCE IS SELF-ELIMINATING

It is a mistake to think that we can control the breeding of mankind in the long run by an appeal to conscience. Charles Galton Darwin made this point when he spoke on the centennial of the publication of his grandfather's great book. The argument is straightforward and Darwinian.

People vary. Confronted with appeals to limit breeding, some people will undoubtedly respond to the plea more than others. Those who have more children will produce a larger fraction of the next generation than those with more susceptible consciences. The difference will be accentuated, generation by generation.

In C. G. Darwin's words: "It may well be that it would take hundreds of generations for the progenitive instinct to develop in this way, but if it should do so, nature would have taken her revenge, and the variety *Homo contracipiens* would become extinct and would be replaced by the variety *Homo progenitivus*".[16]

The argument assumes that conscience or the desire for children (no matter which) is hereditary – but heridiatry only in the most general formal sense. The result will be the same whether the attitude is transmitted through germ cells, or exosomatically, to use A. J. Lotka's term. (If one denies the latter possibility as well as the former, then what's the point of education?) The argument has here been stated in the context of the population problem, but it applies equally well to any instance in which society appeals to an individual exploiting a commons to restrain himself for the general good – by means of his conscience. To make such an appeal is to set up a selective system that works toward the elimination of conscience from the race.

PATHOGENIC EFFECTS OF CONSCIENCE

The long-term disadvantage of an appeal to conscience should be enough to condemn it; but has serious short-term disadvantages as well. If we ask a man who is exploiting a commons to desist "in the name of conscience," what are we saying to him? What does he hear? – not only at the moment but also in the wee small hours of the night when, half asleep, he remembers not merely the words we used but also the nonverbal communication cues we gave him unawares? Sooner or later, consciously or subconsciously, he senses that he has received two communications, and that they are contradictory: (i) (intended communication) "If you don't do as we ask, we will openly condemn you for not acting like a responsible citizen"; (ii) (the unintended communication) "If you *do* behave as we ask, we will secretly condemn you for a simpleton who can be shamed into standing aside while the rest of us exploit the commons."

Everyman then is caught in what Bateson has called a "double bind." Bateson and his co-workers have made a plausible case for viewing the double bind as an important causative factor in the genesis of schizophrenia.[17] The double bind may not always be so damaging, but it always endangers the mental health of anyone to whom it is applied. "A bad conscience," said Nietzsche, "is a kind of illness."

To conjure up a conscience in others is tempting to anyone who wishes to extend his control beyond the legal limits. Leaders at the highest level succumb to this temptation. Has any President during the past generation failed to call on labor unions to moderate voluntarily their demands for higher wages, or to steel companies to honor voluntary guidelines on prices? I can recall none. The rhetoric used on such occasions is designed to produce feelings of guilt in noncooperators.

For centuries it was assumed without proof that guilt was a valuable, perhaps even an indispensable, ingredient of the civilized life. Now, in this post-Freudian world, we doubt it.

Paul Goodman speaks from the modern point of view when he says: "No good has ever come from feeling guilty, neither intelligence, policy, nor compassion. The guilty do not pay attention to the object but only to themselves, and not even to their own interests, which might make sense, but to their anxieties".[18]

One does not have to be a professional psychiatrist to see the consequences of anxiety. We in the Western world are just emerging from a dreadful two-centuries-long Dark Ages of Eros that was sustained partly by prohibition laws, but perhaps more effectively by the anxiety-generating mechanisms of education. Alex Confort has told the story well in *The Anxiety Makers;*[19] it is not a pretty one.

Since proof is difficult, we may even concede that the results of anxiety may sometimes, from certain points of view, be desirable. The larger question we should ask is whether, as a matter of policy, we should ever encourage the use of a technique the tendency (if not the intention) of which is psychologically pathogenic. We hear much talk these days of responsible parenthood; the coupled words are incorporated into the titles of some organizations devoted to birth control. Some people have proposed massive propaganda campaigns to instill responsibility into the nation's (or the world's) breeders. But what is the meaning of the word responsibility in this context? Is it not merely a synonym for the word conscience? When we use the word responsibility in the absence of substantial sanctions are we not trying to browbeat a free man in a commons into acting against his own interest? Responsibility is a verbal counterfeit for a substantial *quid pro quo*. It is an attempt to get something for nothing.

If the word responsibility is to be used at all, I suggest that it be in the sense Charles Frankel uses it.[20] "Responsibility," says this philosopher, "is the product of definite social arrangements." Notice that Frankel calls for social arrangements – not propaganda.

MUTUAL COERCION MUTUALLY AGREED UPON

The social arrangements that produce responsibility are arrangements that create coercion, of some sort. Consider bank-robbing. The man who takes money from a bank acts as if the bank were a commons. How do we prevent such action? Certainly not by trying to control his behaviour solely by a verbal appeal to his sense of responsibility. Rather than rely on propaganda we follow Frankel's lead and insist that a bank is not a commons; we seek the definite social arrangements that will keep it from becoming a commons. That we thereby infringe on the freedom of would-be robbers we neither deny nor regret.

The morality of bank-robbing is particularly easy to understand because we accept complete prohibition of this activity. We are willing to say "Thou shalt not rob banks," without providing for exceptions. But temperance also can be created by coercion. Taxing is a good coercive device. To keep downtown shoppers temperate in their use of parking space we introduce parking meters for short periods, and traffic fines for longer ones. We need not actually forbid a citizen to park as long as he wants to; we need merely make it increasingly expensive for him to do so. Not prohibition, but carefully biased options are what we offer him. A Madison Avenue man might call this persuasion; I prefer the greater candor of the word coercion.

Coercion is a dirty word to most liberals now, but it need not forever be so. As with the four-letter words, its dirtiness can be cleansed away by exposure to the light, by saying it over and over without apology or embarrassment. To many, the word coercion implies arbitrary decisions of distant and irresponsible bureaucrats; but this is not a necessary part of its meaning. The only kind of coercion I recommend is mutual coercion, mutually agreed upon by the majority of the people affected.

To say that we mutually agree to coercion is not to say that we are required to enjoy it, or even to pretend we enjoy it. Who enjoys taxes? We all grumble about them. But we accept compulsory taxes because we recognize that voluntary taxes would favor the conscienceless. We institute and (grumblingly) support taxes and other coercive devices to escape the horror of the commons.

An alternative to the commons need not be perfectly just to be preferable. With real estate and other material goods, the alternative we have chosen is the institution of private property coupled with legal inheritance. Is this system perfectly just? As a genetically trained biologist I deny that it is. It seems to me that, if there are to be differences in individual inheritance, legal possession should be perfectly correlated with biological inheritance – that those who are biologically more fit to be the custodians of property and power should legally inherit more. But genetic recombination continually makes a mockery of the doctrine of "like father, like son" implicit in our laws of legal inheritance. An idiot can inherit millions, and a trust fund can keep his estate intact. We must admit that our legal system of private property plus inheritance is unjust – but we put up with it because we are not convinced, at the moment, that anyone has invented a better system. The alternative of the commons is too horrifying to contemplate. Injustice is preferable to total ruin.

It is one of the peculiarities of the warfare between reform and the status quo that it is thoughtlessly governed by a double standard. Whenever a reform measure is proposed it is often defeated when its opponents triumphantly discover a flaw in it. As Kingsley Davis has pointed out,[21] worshippers of the status quo sometimes imply that no reform is possible without unanimous agreement, an implication contrary to historical fact. As nearly as I can make out, automatic rejection of proposed reforms is based on one of two unconscious assumptions: (i) that the status quo is perfect; or (ii) that the choice we face is between reform and no action; if the proposed reform is imperfect, we presumably should take no action at all, while we wait for a perfect proposal.

But we can never do nothing. That which we have done for thousands of years is also action. It also produces evils. Once we are aware that the status quo is action, we can then compare its discoverable advantages and disadvantages with the predicted advantages and disadvantages of the proposed reform, discounting as best we can for our lack of experience. On the basis of such a comparison, we can make a rational decision which will not involve the unworkable assumption that only perfect systems are tolerable.

RECOGNITION OF NECESSITY

Perhaps the simplest summary of this analysis of man's population problems is this: the commons, if justifiable at all, is justifiable only under conditions of low-population density. As the human population has increased, the commons has had to be abandoned in one aspect after another.

First we abandoned the commons in food gathering, enclosing farm land and restricting pastures and hunting and fishing areas. These restrictions are still not complete throughout the world.

Somewhat later we saw that the commons as a place for waste disposal would also have to be abandoned. Restrictions on the disposal of domestic sewage are widely accepted in the Western world; we are still struggling to close the commons to pollution by automobiles, factories, insecticide sprayers, fertilizing operations, and atomic energy installations.

In a still more embryonic state is our recognition of the evils of the commons in matters of pleasure. There is almost no restriction on the propagation of sound waves in the public medium. The shopping public is assaulted with mindless music, without its consent. Our government is paying out billions of dollars to create supersonic transport which will disturb 50,000 people for every one person who is whisked from coast to coast 3 hours faster. Advertisers muddy the airwaves of radio and television and pollute the view of travelers. We are a long way from outlawing the commons in matters of pleasure. Is this because our Puritan inheritance makes us view pleasure as something of a sin, and pain (that is, the pollution of advertising) as the sign of virtue?

Every new closure of the commons involves the infringement of somebody's personal liberty. Infringements made in the distant past are accepted because no contemporary complains of a loss. It is the newly proposed infringements that we vigorously oppose; cries of "rights" and "freedom" fill the air. But what does "freedom" mean? When men mutually agreed to pass laws against robbing, mankind became more free, not less so. Individuals locked into the logic of the commons are free only to bring on universal ruin: once they see the necessity of mutual coercion, they become free to pursue other goals. I believe it was Hegel who said, "Freedom is the recognition of necessity."

The most important aspect of necessity that we must now recognize, is the necessity of abandoning the commons in breeding. No technical solution can rescue us from the misery of overpopulation. Freedom to breed will bring ruin to all. At the moment, to avoid hard decisions many of us are tempted to propagandize for conscience and responsible parenthood. The temptation must be resisted, because an appeal to independently acting consciences selects for the disappearance of all conscience in the long run, and an increase in anxiety in the short.

The only way we can preserve and nurture other and more precious freedoms is by relinquishing the freedom to breed, and that very soon. "Freedom is the recognition of necessity" – and it is the role of education to reveal to all the necessity of abandoning the freedom to breed. Only so, can we put an end to this aspect of the tragedy of the commons.

NOTES

1. J. B. Wiesner and H. F. York, *Sci. Amer.* 211 (No. 4), 27 (1964).
2. G. Hardin, *J. Hered.* 50, 68 (1959); S. von Hoernor, *Science* 137, 18 (1962).
3. J. von Neumann and O. Morgenstern, *Theory of Games and Economic Behaviour* (Princeton Univ. Press, Princeton, N.J., 1947), p. 11.
4. J. H. Fremlin, *New Sci.,* No. 415 (1964), p. 285.
5. A. Smith, *The Wealth of Nations* (Modern Library, New York, 1937), p. 423.
6. W. F. Lloyd, *Two Lectures on the Checks to Population* (Oxford Univ. Press, Oxford, England, 1833), reprinted (in part) in *Population, Evolution, and Birth Control,* G. Hardin, Ed. (Freeman, San Francisco, 1964), p. 37.
7. A. N. Whitehead, *Science and the Modern World* (Mentor, New York, 1948), p. 17.
8. G. Hardin, Ed. *Population, Evolution, and Birth Control* (Freeman, San Francisco, 1964), p. 56.
9. S. McVay, *Sci. Amer.* 216 (No. 9), 13 (1966).
10. J. Fletcher, *Situation Ethics* (Westminster, Philadelphia, 1966).
11. D. Lack, *The Natural Regulation of Animal Numbers* (Clarendon Press, Oxford, 1954).
12. H. Girvetz, *From Wealth to Welfare* (Stanford Univ. Press, Stanford, Calif., 1950).
13. G. Hardin, *Perspec. Biol. Med.* 6, 366 (1963).
14. U. Thant, *Int. Planned Parenthood News,* No. 168 (February 1968), p. 3.
15. K. Davis, *Science* 158, 730 (1967).
16. S. Tax, Ed., *Evolution after Darwin* (Univ. of Chicago Press, Chicago, 1960), vol. 2, p. 469).
17. G. Bateson, D. D. Jackson, J. Haley, J. Weakland, *Behav. Sci.* 1, 251 (1956).
18. P. Goodman, *New York Rev. Books* 10 (8), 22 (23 May 1968).
19. A. Comfort, *The Anxiety Makers* (Nelson, London, 1967).
20. C. Frankel, *The Case for Modern Man* (Harper, New York, 1955), p. 203.
21. J. D. Roslansky, *Genetics and the Future of Man* (Appleton-Century-Crofts, New York, 1966), p. 177.

PART 2

Valuation methods and applications

Chapter 5
Conservation reconsidered

John V. Krutilla

> *It is the clear duty of Government, which is the trustee for unborn generations as well as for its present citizens, to watch over, and if need be, by legislative enactment, to defend, the exhaustible natural resources of the country from rash and reckless spoliation. How far it should itself, either out of taxes, or out of State loans, or by the device of guaranteed interest, press resources into undertakings from which the business community, if left to itself, would hold aloof, is a more difficult problem. Plainly, if we assume adequate competence on the part of governments, there is a valid case for some artificial encouragement to investment, particularly to investments the return from which will only begin to appear after the lapse of many years.*
>
> A. C. Pigou

Conservation of natural resources has meant different things to different people. But to the economist from the time of Pigou, who first took notice of the economics of conservation [10, p. 27ff], until quite recently, the central concerns have been associated with the question of the optimal intertemporal utilization of the fixed natural resource stocks. The gnawing anxiety provoked by the Malthusian thesis of natural resource scarcity was in no way allayed by the rates of consumption of natural resource stocks during two world wars occurring between the first and fourth editions of Pigou's famous work. In the United States, a presidential commission, reviewing the materials situation following World War II, concluded that an end had come to the historic decline in the cost of natural resource commodities [12, pp. 13–14]. This conclusion reinforced the concern of many that the resource base ultimately would be depleted.

More recently, on the other hand, a systematic analysis of the trends in prices of natural resource commodities did not reveal any permanent interruption in the decline relative to commodities and services in general [11]. Moreover, a rather ambitious attempt to test rigorously the thesis of natural resource scarcity suggested instead that technological progress had compensated quite adequately for the depletion of the higher quality natural resource stocks [1]. Further, given the present state of the arts, future advances need not be fortuitous occurrences; rather the rate of advance can be influenced by investment in research and development. Indeed, those who take an optimistic view would hold that the modern industrial economy is winning its independence from the traditional natural resources sector to a remarkable degree. Ultimately, the raw material inputs to industrial production may be only mass and energy [1, p. 238].[1]

While such optimistic conclusions were being reached, they were nevertheless accompanied by a caveat that, while we may expect production of goods and services to increase without interruption, the level of living may not necessarily be improved. More specifically, Barnett and Morse concluded that the quality of the

73

physical environment – the landscape, water, and atmospheric quality – was deteriorating.

These conclusions suggest that on the one hand the traditional concerns of conservation economics – the husbanding of natural resource stocks for the use of future generations – may now be outmoded by advances in technology. On the other hand, the central issue seems to be the problem of providing for the present and future the amenities associated with unspoiled natural environments, for which the market fails to make adequate provision. While this appears to be the implication of recent research,[2] and is certainly consistent with recent public policy in regard to preserving natural environments, the traditional economic rationale for conservation does not address itself to this issue directly. The use of Pigou's social time preference may serve only to hasten the conversion of natural environments into low-yield capital investments.[4] On what basis, then, can we make decisions when we confront a choice entailing action which will have an irreversible adverse consequence for rare phenomena of nature? I investigate this question below.

Let us consider an area with some unique attribute of nature – a geomorphologic feature such as the Grand Canyon, a threatened species, or an entire ecosystem or biotic community essential to the survival of the threatened species.[5] Let us assume further that the area can be used for certain recreation and/or scientific activities which would be compatible with the preservation of the natural environment, or for extractive activities such as logging or hydraulic mining, which would have adverse consequences for scenic landscapes and wildlife habitat.

A private resource owner would consider the discounted net income stream from the alternative uses and select the use which would hold prospects for the highest present net value. If the use which promises the highest present net value is incompatible with preserving the environment in its natural state, does it necessarily follow that the market will allocate the resources efficiently? There are several reasons why private and social returns in this case are likely to diverge significantly.

Consider the problem first in its static aspects. By assumption, the resources used in a manner compatible with preserving the natural environment have no close substitutes; on the other hand, alternative sources of supply of natural resource commodities are available.[6] Under the circumstances and given the practical obstacles to perfectly discriminating pricing, the private resource owner would not be able to appropriate in gate receipts the entire social value of the resources when used in a manner compatible with preserving the natural state. Thus the present values of his expected net revenues are not comparable as between the competing uses in evaluating the efficiency of the resource allocation.

Aside from the practical problem of implementing a perfectly discriminating pricing policy, it is not clear even on theoretic grounds that a comparison of the total area under the demand curve on the one hand and market receipts on the other will yield an unambiguous answer to the allocative question. When the existence of a grand scenic wonder or a unique and fragile ecosystem is involved, its preservation and continued availability are a significant part of the real income of many individuals.[7] Under the conditions postulated, the area under the demand curve, which represents a maximum willingness to pay, may be significantly less than the minimum which would be required to compensate such individuals were they to be deprived in perpetuity of the opportunity to continue enjoying the natural phenomenon in question. Accordingly, it is conceivable that the potential losers cannot influence the decision in their favor by their aggregate willingness to pay, yet the resource owner may not be able to compensate the losers out of the receipts from the alternative use of the resource. In such cases – and they are more likely encountered in this area – it is impossible to determine whether the market allocation is efficient or inefficient.

Another reason for questioning the allocative efficiency of the market for the case in hand has been recognized only more recently. This involves the notion of *option demand* [14]. This demand is characterized as a willingness to pay for retaining an option to use an area or facility that would be difficult or impossible to replace and for which no close substitute is available. Moreover, such a demand may exist even though there is no current intention to use the area or facility in question and the option may never be exercised. If an option value exists for rare or unique occurrences of nature, but there is no means by which a private resource owner can appropriate this value, the resulting resource allocation may be questioned.

Because options are traded on the market in connection with other economic values, one may ask why no market has developed where option value exists for the preservation of natural environments.[8] We need to consider briefly the nature of the value in question and the marketability of the option.

From a purely scientific viewpoint, much is yet to be learned in the earth and life sciences; preservation of the objects of study may be defended on these grounds, given the serendipity value of basic research. We know also that the natural biota represents our reservoir of germ plasm, which has economic value. For example, modern agriculture in advanced countries represents cultivation figuratively in a hot-house environment in which crops are protected against disease, pests, and drought by a variety of agricultural practices. The energy released from some of the genetic characteristics no longer required for survival under cultivated conditions is redirected toward greater productivity. Yet because of the instability introduced with progressive reduction of biological diversity, a need occasionally arises for the reintroduction of some genetic characteristics lost in the past from domestic strains. It is from the natural biota that these can be obtained.

The value of botanical specimens for medicinal purposes also has been long, if not widely, recognized. Approximately half of the new drugs currently being developed are obtained from botanical specimens.[9] There is a traffic in medicinal plants which approximates a third of a billion dollars annually. Cortisone, digitalis, and heparin are among the better known of the myriad drugs which are derived from natural vegetation or zoological sources. Since only a relatively small part of the potential medicinal value of biological specimens has yet been realized, preserving the opportunity to examine all species among the natural biota for this purpose is a matter of considerable importance.

The option value may have been only a sentimental basis in some instances. Consider the rallying to preserve the historical relic, "Old Ironsides."[10] There are many persons who obtain satisfaction from mere knowledge that part of wilderness North America remains even though they would be appalled by the prospect of being exposed to it. Subscriptions to the World Wildlife Fund are of the same character. The funds are employed predominantly in an effort to save exotic species in remote areas of the world which few subscribers to the Fund ever hope to see. An option demand may exist therefore not only among persons currently and prospectively active in the market for the object of the demand, but among others who place a value on the mere existence of biological and/or geomorphological variety and its widespread distribution.[11]

If a genuine value for retaining an option in these respects exists, why has not a market developed? To some extent, and for certain purposes, it has. Where a small natural area in some locality in the United States is threatened, the property is often purchased by Nature Conservancy,[12] a private organization which raises funds through voluntary subscriptions.[13] But this market is grossly imperfect. First, the risk for private investors associated with absence of knowledge as to whether a particular ecosystem has special characteristics not widely shared by others is enormous.[14] Moreover, to the extent that the natural environment will support basic scientific research which often has unanticipated practical results, the serendipity value may not be appropriable by those paying to preserve the options. But perhaps of greatest significance is that the preservation of the grand scenic wonders, threatened species, and the like involves comparatively large land tracts which are not of merely local interest. Thus, all of the problems of organizing a market for public goods arise. Potential purchasers of options may be expected to bide time in the expectation that others will meet the necessary cost, thus eliminating cost to themselves. Since the mere existence or preservation of the natural environment in question satisfies the demand, those who do not subscribe cannot be excluded except by the failure to enroll sufficient subscribers for its preservation.

Perhaps of equal significance to the presumption of market failure are some dynamic characteristics of the problem suggested by recent research. First, consider the consumption aspects of the problem. Davidson, Adams, and Seneca have recently advanced some interesting notions regarding the formation of demand that may be particularly relevant to our problem [5, p. 186].

> When facilities are not readily available, skills will not be developed and, consequently, there may be little desire to participate in these activities. If facilities are made available, opportunities to acquire skill increase, and user demand tends to rise rapidly over time as individuals learn to enjoy these activities. Thus, participation in and enjoyment of water recreational activities by the present generation will stimulate future demand without diminishing the supply presently available. Learning-by-doing, to the extent it increases future demand, suggests an interaction between present and future demand functions, which will result in a public good externality, as present demand enters into the utility function of future users.

While this quotation refers to water-based recreation, it is likely to be more persuasive in connection with some other resource-based recreation activity. Its relevance for wilderness preservation is obvious. When we consider the remote backcountry landscape, or the wilderness scene as the object of experience and enjoyment, we recognize that utility from the experience depends predominantly upon the prior acquisition of technical skill and specialized knowledge. This, of course, must come from experience initially with less arduous or demanding activities. The more the present population is initiated into activities requiring similar but less advanced skills (e.g., car camping), the better prepared the future population will be to participate in the more exacting activities. Given the phenomenal rise of car camping, if this activity will spawn a disproportionate number of future back-packers, canoe cruisers, cross-country skiers, etc., the greater will be the induced demand for wild, primitive, and wilderness-related opportunities for indulging such interest. Admittedly, we know little about the demand for outdoor experiences which depend on unique phenomena of nature – its formation, stability, and probable course of development. These are important questions for research, results of which will have significant policy implications.

In regard to the production aspects of the "new conservation," we need to examine the implications of technological progress a little further. Earlier I suggested that the advances of technology have compensated for the depletion of the richer mineral deposits and, in a sense, for the superior stands of timber and tracts of arable land. On the other hand, there is likely to be an asymmetry in the implications of technological progress for the production of goods and services from the natural resource base, and the production of natural phenomena which give rise to utility without undergoing fabrication or other processing.[15] In fact, it is improbable that technology will advance to the point at which the grand geomorphologic wonders could be replicated, or extinct species resurrected. Nor is it obvious that fabricated replicas, were they even possible, would have a value equivalent to that of the originals. To a lesser extent, the landscape can be manufactured in a pleasing way with artistry and the larger earth-moving equipment of today's construction technology. Open pit mines may be refilled and the surroundings rehabilitated in a way to approximate the original conditions. But even here the undertaking cannot be accomplished without the cooperation of nature over a substantial period of time depending on the growth rate of the vegetal cover and the requirements of the native habitat.[16] Accordingly, while the supply of fabricated goods and commercial services may be capable of continuous expansion from a given resource base by reason of scientific discovery and mastery of technique, the supply of natural phenomena is virtually inelastic. That is, we may preserve the natural environment which remains to provide amenities of this sort for the future, but there are significant limitations on reproducing it in the future should we fail to preserve it.

If we consider the asymmetric implications of technology, we can conceive of a transformation function having along its vertical axis amenities derived directly from association with the natural environment and fabricated goods along the horizontal axis. Advances in technology would stretch the transformation function's terminus along the horizontal axis but not appreciably along the vertical. Accordingly, if we simply take the effect of technological progress over time, considering tastes as constant, the marginal trade-off between manufactured and natural amenities will progressively favor the latter. Natural environments will represent irreplaceable assets of appreciating value with the passage of time.

If we consider technology as constant, but consider a change in tastes progressively favoring amenities of the natural environment due to the learn-by-doing phenomenon, natural environments will similarly for this reason represent assets of appreciating value. If both influences are operative (changes in technology with asymmetric implications, and tastes), the appreciating value of natural environments will be compounded.

This leads to a final point which, while a static consideration, tends to have its real significance in conjunction with the effects of parametric shifts in tastes and technology. We are coming to realize that consumption-saving behavior is motivated by a desire to leave one's heirs an estate as well as by the utility to be obtained from consumption.[17] A bequest of maximum value would require an appropriate mix of public and private assets, and, equally, the appropriate mix of opportunities to enjoy amenities experienced directly from association with the natural environment along with readily producible goods. But the option to enjoy the grand scenic wonders for the bulk of the population depends upon their provision as public goods.

Several observations have been made which may now be summarized. The first is that, unlike resource allocation questions dealt with in conventional economic problems, there is a family of problems associated with the natural environment which involves the irreproducibility of unique phenomena of nature – or the irreversibility of some consequence inimical to human welfare. Second, it appears that the utility to individuals of direct association with natural environments may be increasing while the supply is not readily subject to enlargement by man. Third, the real cost of refraining from converting our remaining rare natural environments may not be very great. Moreover, with the continued advance in technology, more substitutes for conventional natural resources will be found for the industrial and agricultural sectors, liberating production from dependence on conventional sources of raw materials. Finally, if consumption-saving behavior is motivated also by the desire to leave an estate, some portion of the estate would need to be in assets which yield collective consumption goods of appreciating future value. For all these reasons we are confronted with a problem not conventionally met in resource economics. The problem is of the following nature.

At any point in time characterized by a level of technology which is less advanced than at some future date, the conversion of the natural environment into industrially produced private goods has proceeded further than it would have with the more advanced future technology. Moreover, with the apparent increasing appreciation of direct contact with natural environments, the conversion will have proceeded further, for this reason as well, than it would have were the future composition of tastes to have prevailed. Given the irreversibility of converted natural environments, however, it will not be possible to achieve a level of well-being in the future that would have been possible had the conversion of natural environments been retarded. That this should be of concern to members of the present generation may be attributable to the bequest motivation in private economic behavior as much as to a sense of public responsibility.[18]

Accordingly, our problem is akin to the dynamic programming problem which requires a present action (which may violate conventional benefit-cost criteria) to be compatible with the attainment of future states of affairs. But we know little about the value that the instrumental variables may take. We have virtually no knowledge about the possible magnitude of the option demand. And we still have much to learn about the determinants of the growth in demand for outdoor recreation and about the quantitative significance of the asymmetry in the implications of technological advances for producing industrial goods on the one hand and natural environments on the other. Obviously, a great deal of research in these areas is necessary before we can hope to apply formal decision criteria comparable to current benefit-cost criteria. Fully useful results may be very long in coming; what then is a sensible way to proceed in the interim?

First, we need to consider what we need as a minimum reserve to avoid potentially grossly adverse consequences for human welfare. We may regard this as our scientific preserve of research materials required for advances in the life and earth sciences. While no careful evaluation of the size of this reserve has been undertaken by scientists, an educated guess has put the need in connection with terrestrial communities at about ten million acres for North America [4, p. 128]. Reservation of this amount of land – but a small fraction of one per cent of the total relevant area – is not likely to affect appreciably the supply or costs of material inputs to the manufacturing or agricultural sectors.

The size of the scientific preserve required for aquatic environments is still unknown. Only after there is developed an adequate system of classification of aquatic communities will it be possible to identify distinct environments, recognize the needed reservations, and, then, estimate the opportunity costs. Classification and identification of aquatic environments demand early research attention by natural scientists.

Finally, one might hope that the reservations for scientific purposes would also support the bulk of the outdoor recreation demands, or that substantial additional reservations for recreational purposes could be justified by the demand and implicit opportunity costs. Reservations for recreation, as well as for biotic communities, should include special or rare environments which can support esoteric tastes as well as the more common ones. This is a matter of some importance because outdoor recreation opportunities will be provided in large part by public bodies, and within the public sector there is a tendency to provide a homogenized recreation commodity oriented toward a common denominator. There is need to recognize, and make provision for, the widest range of outdoor recreation tastes, just as a well-functioning market would do. We need a policy and a mechanism to ensure that all natural areas peculiarly suited for specialized recreation uses receive consideration for such uses. A policy of this kind would be consistent both with maintaining the greatest biological diversity for scientific research and educational purposes and with providing the widest choice for consumers of outdoor recreation.

NOTES

1. The conclusions were based on data relevant to the U.S. economy. While they may be pertinent to Western Europe also, all of my subsequent observations are restricted to the United States.
2. For example, see [7].
3. It must be acknowledged that with sufficient patience and perception nearly all of the arguments for preserving unique phenomena of nature can be found in the classic on conservation economics by Ciriacy-Wantrup [3].
4. An example of this was the recent threat to the Grand Canyon by the proposed Bridge and Marble Canyon dams. Scott makes a similar point with reference to natural resource commodities [13].
5. Uniqueness need not be absolute for the following arguments to hold. It may be, like Dupuit's bridge, a good with no adequate substitutes in the "natural" market area of its principal clientele, while possibly being replicated in other market areas to which the clientele in question has no access for all practical purposes.
6. The asymmetry in the relation posited is realistic. The historic decline in cost of natural resource commodities relative to commodities in general suggests that the production and exchange of the former occur under fairly competitive conditions. On the other hand, increasing congestion at parks, such as Yellowstone, Yosemite, and Grand Canyon, suggests there are no adequate substitutes for these rare natural environments.

7. These would be the spiritual descendants of John Muir, the present members of the Sierra Club, the Wilderness Society, National Wildlife Federation, Audubon Society and others to whom the loss of a species or the disfigurement of a scenic area causes acute distress and a sense of genuine relative impoverishment.
8. For a somewhat differently developed argument, see [6].
9. For an interesting account of the use of plants for medicinal purposes, see [8].
10. The presumption in favor of option value is applicable also to historic and cultural features; rare works of art, perhaps, being the most prominent of this class.
11. The phenomenon discussed may have an exclusive sentimental basis, but if we consider the "bequest motivation" in economic behavior, discussed below, it may be explained by an interest in preserving an option for one's heirs to view or use the object in question.
12. Not to be confused with a public agency of the same name in the United Kingdom.
13. Subscriptions to the World Wildlife Fund, the Wilderness Society, National Parks Association, etc. may be similar, but, of course, much of the effect these organizations have on the preservation of natural areas stems not from purchasing options, but from influencing public programs.
14. The problem here is in part like a national lottery in which there exists a very small chance for a very large gain. Unlike a lottery, rather large sums at very large risk typically would be required.
15. I owe this point to a related observation, to my knowledge first made by Ciriacy-Wantrup [3, p. 47].
16. That is, giving rise to option value for members of the present population.
17. See [2]; also [9].
18. The rationale above differs from that of Stephen Marglin which is perhaps the most rigorous one relying on a sense of public responsibility and externalities to justify explicit provision for future generations. In this case also, my concern is with providing *collective consumption goods for the present and future*, whereas the traditional concern in conservation economics has been with provision of *private intermediate goods for the future*.

REFERENCES

1. Barnett, H.J. and C. Morse, *Scarcity and Growth: The Economics of Natural Resource Availability*. Baltimore 1963.
2. Chase, S.B. Jr., *Asset Prices in Economic Analysis*. Berkeley 1963.
3. Ciriacy-Wantrup, S.V. *Resources Conservation*. Berkeley 1952.
4. Darling, F. and J.P. Milton, ed., *Future Environments of North America, Transformation of a Continent*. Garden City, N.Y. 1966.
5. Davidson, P., F.G. Adams, and Seneca, "The Social Value of Water Recreation Facilities Resulting from an Improvement in Water Quality: The Delaware Estuary," in A.V. Kneese and S.C. Smith, ed., *Water Research*, Baltimore 1966.
6. Kahn, A.E. "The Tyranny of Small Decisions: Market Failures, Imperfections, and the Limits of Economics," *Kyklos*, 1966, 19 (1), 23–47.
7. Kneese, A.V. *The Economics of Regional Water Quality Management*. Baltimore 1964.
8. Kreig, M.B. *Green Medicine: The Search for Plants that Heal*. New York 1964.
9. Modigliani F. and R. Brumberg, "Utility Analysis and the Consumption Function: An Interpretation of Cross-Section Data." in K.K. Kuri-hara, ed., *Post-Keynesian Economics*, New Brunswick 1954.
10. Pigou, A.C. *The Economics of Welfare*. 4th ed., London 1952.
11. Potter N. and F.T. Christy, Jr., *Trends in Natural Resources Commodities: Statistics of Prices, Output, Consumption, Foreign Trade, and Employment in the United States, 1870–1957*. Baltimore 1962.
12. The President's Materials Policy Commission, *Resources for Freedom, Foundation for Growth and Security*, Vol. I. Washington 1952.
13. Scott, A.D. *Natural Resources: The Economics of Conservation*. Toronto 1955.
14. Weisbrod, B.A. "Collective Consumption Services of Individual Consumption Goods," *Quart. Jour. Econ.*, Aug. 1964, 77, 71–77.

Chapter 6
Option value: a general approach

Mark L. Plummer and Richard C. Hartman

This article examines a potential bias if expected consumer surplus is used to measure the benefits of a price change under uncertainty. This bias, which is called option value, may be positive or negative. A general framework is developed for analyzing the determinants of the sign of option value, and this framework is applied to three types of uncertainty: income uncertainty, quality uncertainty, and uncertainty over consumer tastes. In the first two cases, option value has a determinate sign; however, in the last case, option value may be positive, negative, or zero in an unpredictable fashion.

In a world of certainty, measurement of the consumer benefits of a price change is, at least in theory, straightforward. The compensating variation is an appropriate measure of a consumer's willingness to pay for a price change; the equivalent variation is an appropriate measure of a consumer's willingness to relinquish the current price in exchange for a new price.

The problem of measuring the consumer benefits of a price change is not so straightforward in a world of uncertainty. Other authors, most recently Graham [1981], have debated the appropriateness of different measures when uncertainty is present. In this article, we explore the relation between two possible measures, each of which may be appropriate under different circumstances. The first measure is simple: the expected value of the compensating variation of the price change, or expected consumer surplus. The second measure is called a consumer's "option price." This is the maximum constant amount a consumer is willing to pay across states of the world for the price change. Thus, while consumer surplus may vary across states of the world, option price is constant.

Earlier, Burton Weisbrod [1964] argued that, when demand is uncertain, the expected value of consumer surplus will underestimate the constant maximum payment the consumer is willing to make across states of the world. Weisbrod argued that option price measures both the value of retaining an option to consume a good and the expected value of actually consuming the good;[1] expected consumer surplus measures only the latter of these two values. The difference between option price and expected consumer surplus, or option value, is therefore positive.[2]

Since Weisbrod's article, several authors have analyzed the relation between expected consumer surplus and option price or, more simply, the sign of option value. Their results have been mixed: option value has been shown to be negative, positive, zero, and ambiguous at different points in its history.[3] The variation in these results is disturbing. Graham [1981] suggests that option price is the proper measure of the consumer benefits of a price change under uncertainty as long as

81

contingent claims markets do not exist. Expected consumer surplus, however, may be easier to estimate if the source of the consumer uncertainty is known and if, say, there are historical data on consumer demand. Using such information, the expected consumer surplus of a price change under uncertainty could be estimated. The sign of option value, then, is important for determining a potential bias in the use of such an estimate in place of option price.

This conclusion is supported in part by the empirical results cited in Fisher and Raucher [1984]. There, the authors conclude that the non-use benefits of improved water quality, some of which may consist of consumers' option value, are at least half as great as direct use benefits.[4] This suggests that, at least in one area, the sign of option value is an important public policy concern.

In this article, we present a general approach to option value. A given state of the world is represented by a unique level of a state variable, T. This state variable may be income, a price, the quality of a good, or even "tastes." Using this approach, we argue that the sign of option value is the same as the sign of the correlation between consumer surplus and the marginal utility of income across states of the world.[5] With this general result, the sign of option value then can be determined for many particular forms of uncertainty.

We also argue that the problem of determining the sign of option value changes in a fundamental way when one goes from a model with two states of the world to a model with three or more states. This raises questions about the generality of the results produced by models with only two states and, as we argue below, poses some problems in analyzing the sign of option value if uncertainty is over tastes.

The article is divided into three sections. Section I formally analyzes the relation between expected consumer surplus and option price. In this section we present a simple theorem about the sign of option value and discuss the intuition behind the theorem. In section II, we apply this theorem to three types of uncertainty. These three types of uncertainty are income uncertainty, quality uncertainty, and uncertainty about preferences or tastes. The final section draws some conclusions about the option value controversy.

THE SIGN OF OPTION VALUE

Let $U(M,P,T)$ be a consumer's indirect utility function, where M is income, P is the price of the good in question, and T is a single variable that represents the state of the world.[6] In the analysis to follow, T can be any parameter that might enter the indirect utility function except the price, P, of the good whose price change is being evaluated. (The price change being evaluated is not itself random.) T could, for example, be the price of some other good, a parameter representing quality or tastes, or even income. For notational simplicity, we do not recognize explicitly the prices of other goods because they are not changing and do not enter the analysis unless, of course, T represents such a price.

Suppose now we are interested in evaluating a change in P from P_0 to P_1 with $P_1 < P_0$. The compensating variation measure of consumer surplus, S, is defined implicitly by

(1) $$U(M,P_0,T) = U(M - S,P_1,T).$$

Let $S(T)$ be the solution to equation (1). Because T is random, so is S, and we denote its expected value by $\overline{S}$.

Option price, OP, is defined by

(2) $$EU(M,P_0,T) = EU(M - OP,P_1,T)$$

where the expectation is taken over the distribution of T. By taking expectations on both sides of equation (1) we note that

(3) $$EU(M - S(T),P_1,T) = EU(M - OP,P_1,T).$$

Finally, option value, OV, is the difference between option price and expected consumer surplus, or $OV = OP - \bar{S}$.

We now argue that the sign of option value depends on the correlation between S and the marginal utility of income, U_M, across states of the world. (We use subscripts to denote partial differentiation.) We first give some assumptions that are sufficient to produce a determinate sign for option value. We then present a theorem on the sign of option value, relate the theorem to the correlation between S and U_M, and discuss the intuitive argument behind the theorem. In the rest of the text, we suppress the price argument, P, in the indirect utility function.

We first make the assumption that the individual is risk averse in the sense that $U_{MM} < 0$ everywhere. When income (wealth) is uncertain, this is the standard definition of risk aversion. We adopt it here even though parameters other than income may be uncertain. In addition, we make the following two assumptions.

Assumption 1: $S(T)$ is a strictly monotonic function of T, i.e., it is either strictly increasing or strictly decreasing.

Assumption 2: $U_M(M - OP,T)$ and $U_M(M - S(T),T)$ are both either strictly increasing in T or strictly decreasing in T over all relevant T, i.e., the derivatives $dU_M(M - OP,T)/dT$ and $dU_M(M - S(T),T)/dT$ have the same, constant sign.[7]

With these assumptions we prove the following:

Theorem

Under the assumptions given above, the sign of option value satisfies:

(4) $$\text{sgn}(OV) = \text{sgn}(dS/dT)\,\text{sgn}(dU_M/dT).$$

A formal proof is given in Appendix A [of the original article] where we also discuss the importance and the implications of the two assumptions.

Now, if S and U_M are either both increasing or both decreasing in the random variable T, they themselves are random variables that are positively correlated. If one is increasing in T while the other is decreasing, they are negatively correlated. Thus, so long as the marginal utility of income and consumer surplus vary monotonically across states of the world, the sign of option value is the same as the sign of their correlation.

The intuition behind the theorem is straightforward.[8] Suppose a consumer is offered the opportunity to purchase a good at a price lower than the current one, but that the consumer's demand for the good is uncertain at present. The consumer is offered two methods of purchasing the price decrease. Under the first method, the consumer agrees to pay the additional consumer surplus generated by the price change for the state of the world that is realized. Under the second method, the consumer agrees to pay a single amount, the expected consumer surplus $\bar{S}$, regardless of the realized state.

The consumer will choose the payment method that leaves the consumer with a higher level of expected utility.[9] This choice, in turn, reveals the sign of option value. If the consumer prefers the first method of payment, it must be that $EU(M - S(T),T) > EU(M - \bar{S},T)$. By equation (3), we therefore have $EU(M - OP,T) > EU(M - \bar{S},T)$, which implies $OP < \bar{S}$ or that option value is negative. If the consumer prefers the second method, similar reasoning suggests that option value is positive.

The consumer's choice of a payment method depends on the correlation between the marginal utility of income and the consumer surplus of the price change. Because the two payment methods have the same expected payment $(\bar{S})$, their effects on the consumer's expected wealth are the same. There is a second effect, however, which must be considered. The expected utility of a risk-averse individual generally is changed when income is redistributed between states of the world. A payment of $\bar{S}$ in each state takes a constant amount from a consumer's income in each state and so essentially lacks any redistribution effect, but a payment of $S(T)$, which varies across states, does have such an effect.

If $S(T)$ is positively correlated with the marginal utility of income, greater-than-average payments would be made in states of the world where the marginal utility of income is relatively high (a "poor" state); similarly, less-than-average payments would be made in states where the marginal utility of income is relatively low (a "rich" state). When $S(T)$ and $U_M(T)$ are positively correlated, then the payment of $S(T)$ in the realized state has the expectation of taking relatively more from the "poor" states and relatively less from the "rich" states.

On the other hand, a constant payment method would take the same amount from each state. The effect of the first payment method is to lower a consumer's expected utility below the level achieved with the second payment method. Hence, a consumer would choose the constant payment method, making option value positive.

In this view, option value is the premium (if positive) or discount (if negative) a consumer is willing to pay or accept if payment for the price change is made on an *ex ante* basis rather than on an *ex post* basis. This conclusion, of course, is relevant to any opportunity that increases consumer surplus under uncertainty. In public policy matters, there is some debate concerning the appropriate view to take in evaluating uncertain benefits of a government project: *ex ante* or *ex post*.[10] Our theorem implies that the resolution of this debate may have an important impact on the estimation of a project's benefits because, as long as option value is not zero, the level estimated will be a function of whether the benefits are evaluated before or after the uncertainty is resolved.

The theorem above, then, has potential implications for different instances where the benefits of an action or opportunity must be evaluated under uncertainty. The importance and implications of the assumptions underlying the theorem are discussed in Appendix A [of the original article]. We note that these assumptions are not trivial: they are not met for all types of uncertainty and for all types of utility functions. It may be possible, however, to guarantee that the two assumptions are satisfied when the state variable, T, takes a particular form and certain restrictions on behaviour are assumed. We now turn to an examination of three particular forms of uncertainty.

APPLICATIONS

In this section we first examine the sign of option value when the consumer's income at the time the price change will occur is uncertain. The second type of uncertainty we consider is uncertainty about the "quality" of a good. Finally, we examine a more general type of uncertainty: state-dependent preferences or "taste-uncertainty." In each of these cases, we derive an explicit formula for the sign of option value using equation (4), and determine whether assumptions 1 and 2 are met. Throughout this section, we assume that the consumer faces a proposed price change for a good, X, from P_0 to P_1 with $P_0 > P_1$.

Income uncertainty

Let income, M, be uncertain at the point in time when the proposed price change will occur. If T corresponds to M, we can drop T from the indirect utility function and our assumption of risk aversion implies that $dU_M(M - OP)/dM < 0$.

For a risk averse individual facing income uncertainty, the sign of option value, as shown by equation (4), is opposite the sign of dS/dM. Moreover, it is easily shown that the sign of dS/dM is the same as the sign of X_M^o, where X^o is the demand for X.[11] Thus, the sign of option value is opposite the sign of X_M^o. When income is uncertain, option value is negative for a normal good.

To ensure that assumption 1 is met, we need only assume that X^o is strictly normal or strictly inferior over the range of possible incomes. Assumption 2 is also met for this type of uncertainty. To see this, note that implicit differentiation of equation (1) gives $dS/dM < 1$, so that $dU_M(M - S(M))/dM = (1 - dS/dM)U_{MM} < 0$. Thus, both $U_M(M - OP)$ and $U_M(M - S(M))$ are strictly decreasing in M.

Quality uncertainty

Although income uncertainty produces a determinate sign for option value, it is rarely the type of uncertainty that is appropriate for the option value problem. More often, authors have assumed that preferences are state-dependent: in other words, that tastes are uncertain. In the next section, we consider taste-uncertainty in a general form; in this section, we present an alternative and rather specific way of characterizing this type of uncertainty.

Consider, for example, a hiker planning a trip to Mt. Rainier National Park. The hiker's income likely will affect the hiker's valuation of such a trip, as will the prices of gasoline, hiking boots, and so on. *Non-monetary* factors will also affect the hiker's valuation: the amount of rainfall or sunshine on the day of the trip, the extent to which the site is crowded, the level of the snowpack, and so forth. These other, non-monetary factors are part of what can be called the *quality* of the hiking trip. In general, we define the "quality" of a good as the levels of any attributes that are unpriced but measurable in some objective way.

Let Q be the level of the quality of good X, and suppose Q is uncertain before purchase. A potential change in the price of X will have uncertain benefits. We can apply equation (4) to determine the sign of option value for this quality uncertainty:

$$(5) \qquad \text{sgn}(OV) = \text{sgn}(dS/dQ)\, \text{sgn}(dU_M/dQ).$$

Suppose Q affects only the marginal utility of X (in the direct utility function). For example, the level of the snowpack in Mt. Rainier National Park most likely does not affect the hiker's marginal utility of sailing on Puget Sound. For this special case, we establish the following in Appendix B [of the original article]:

$$(6) \qquad \text{sgn}(dS/dQ) = \text{sgn}(X_Q^o)$$

$$(7) \qquad \text{sgn}(dU_M/dQ) = \text{sgn}(X_Q^o)\, \text{sgn}(X_M^o)$$

Substituting from these equations into equation (4) and using the fact that $(\text{sgn}(X_Q^o))^2$ is positive, we have

$$(8) \qquad \text{sgn}(OV) = \text{sgn}(X_M^o).$$

This result is the opposite of that obtained for income uncertainty, but the two results are perfectly compatible.

For normal goods in the case of income uncertainty, consumer surplus and the marginal utility of income have a negative covariance. This is because of the way each is related to income: an increase in income increases consumer surplus (for a normal good) and decreases the marginal utility of income (for risk-averse individuals).

For quality uncertainty, consumer surplus and the marginal utility of income have a positive covariance for a normal good. When quality increases, consumer surplus increases as long as an increase in quality increases the market demand for X. Given this relationship between Q and X^o, an increase in quality also increases the marginal utility of income as long as X is a normal good. Intuitively, this is because when quality increases, a dollar can buy the same amount of a more highly valued good (a higher quality X). If an increase in quality decreases the demand for X, consumer surplus decreases and so does the marginal utility of income. Thus, for a normal good, there is a positive covariance and option value is positive.

We now check whether the assumptions underlying the theorem are satisfied. Clearly, if Q affects only the marginal utility of X, then $S(Q)$ and $U_M(M - OP, Q)$ are strictly monotonic as long as X_Q^o is strictly positive or strictly negative over the range of possible quality, and as long as X^o is strictly normal or strictly inferior over the same range. In addition, $dU_M(M - OP, Q)/dQ$ and $dU_M(M - S(Q), Q)/dQ$ have the same sign if X^o is normal. Indeed, we have

$$(9) \qquad dU_M(M - OP, Q)/dQ = U_{MQ}(M - OP, Q)$$

and

$$(10) \qquad dU_M(M - S(Q), Q)/dQ = U_{MQ}(M - S(Q), Q) - (dS/dQ)U_{MM}.$$

From equations (7) and (6), we know about

$$(11) \qquad \text{sgn}(U_{MQ}) = \text{sgn}(X_Q^o)\,\text{sgn}(X_M^o)$$

and

$$(12) \qquad -\text{sgn}((dS/dQ)U_{MM}) = \text{sgn}(X_Q^o)$$

because $U_{MM} < 0$. Therefore, as long as $X_M^o > 0$,

$$(13) \qquad \text{sgn}(dU_M(M - S(Q), Q)/dQ) = \text{sgn}(X_Q^o)$$
$$= \text{sgn}(dU_M(M - OP, Q)/dQ),$$

which satisfies our second assumption.

Taste uncertainty

As we have noted above, many authors have analyzed the sign of option value using the assumption that tastes are uncertain. For example, Schmalensee [1972] posits two states of the world, one in which the consumer has a "strong desire" to visit Yellowstone Park, and one state in which the consumer has "no desire" to make the visit. Graham [1981] also uses an example with two states of the world, where the construction of a dam is being considered and years are either "wet" or "dry".

In both cases, the authors characterize uncertainty as involving "tastes," rather than as variation in income, prices, or quality. When the uncertainty is over these latter types of factors, certain restrictions on behavior will ensure that assumptions 1 and 2 are satisfied. Moreover, in most cases these restrictions are testable in that they involve potentially observable behavior. If the uncertainty is over tastes, however, there is an inherent drawback: tastes are generally unobservable. Thus, there are very few grounds for restricting behaviour in any but arbitrary ways, and it is generally not possible to test whether the assumptions of our theorem (or any other theorem) are met.

There is one case where taste uncertainty usually will produce a determinate sign for option value. When there are only two states of the world, or only two possible values of T, $S(T)$ and $U_M(T)$ are always monotonic (ignoring the case where $S(T)$ and $U_M(T)$ are equal across states of the world).[12] With three or more states of the world, however, there is no guarantee that $S(T)$ and $U_M(T)$ are monotonic functions. Previous authors who have examined taste uncertainty using a two state model usually have obtained a determinate sign for option value. Unfortunately, these results may vanish as soon as the model includes more than two possible states.

Consider an example where there are four states of the world. Suppose that consumer surplus increases across states of the world $(S(1) < S(2) < S(3) < S(4))$ but that the marginal utility of income is first increasing $(U_M(1) < U_M(2))$ and then decreasing $(U_M(3) < U_M(4))$. If the probability that $T \geq 3$ is zero, the assumptions that $S(T)$ and $U_M(T)$ are monotonic are satisfied and our theorem shows that option value is positive. Similarly, if the probability that $T \leq 2$ is zero, option value is negative.

If all four states have a non-zero probability, our assumptions are not met and option value, in general, will be ambiguous. Suppose the probability of each state is 1/4. In states 1 and 4, the marginal utility of income is relatively low, but state 1 involves a payment of $S(1) < \bar{S}$ and in state 4, $S(4) < \bar{S}$. In states 2 and 3, the marginal utility of income is relatively high, but the payments involved are again less-than-average (state 2) and greater-than-average (state 3). Hence, a consumer surplus payment method, relative to a constant payment of $\bar{S}$, takes from both a "rich" state (4) and a "poor" state (3) and gives to both types of states.

Therefore, if $S(T)$ and $U_M(T)$ are not both monotonic, option value may be positive or negative, depending on the probability distribution. Across states 1 and 2, $S(T)$ and $U_M(T)$ are positively correlated; across states 3 and 4, they are negatively correlated. When states 1 and 2 are relatively more likely, the positive correlation may "outweigh" the negative correlation and, if so, option value is positive. When states 3 and 4 are more likely, the opposite may occur and option value is likely to be negative. This implies that, for the same individual, option value can be positive or negative, depending on the probability distribution rather than just on the changes in consumer surplus and the marginal utility of income across states of the world.

In a completely general characterization, with n possible states of the world or a continuous distribution, "tastes" can change in an endless variety of ways. Similarly, models that use state-dependent preferences generally are simple with only two states of the world but intractable with more than two states. Hence, characterizing uncertainty as involving tastes or preferences in a general form seems incapable of producing a determinate sign for option value if there are more than two possible states of the world.

CONCLUSIONS

The concept of option value originated with the insight of Weisbrod that a price change under uncertainty presents a measurement problem different from the classic consumer surplus problem. With the theorem above, we can now, in many cases, put a determinate sign on option value.

The intuition behind the theorem, however, makes one point clear: "option value" has very little to do with the value of an option. Instead, if a price change is proposed under uncertainty, option value is a measure of the premium or discount a consumer is willing to pay or accept to purchase the price change by making a constant payment of $\overline{S}$ rather than a payment of $S(T)$ in each state of the world. Although both methods have the same effect on expected wealth, the variation in $S(T)$ may provide the consumer with additional benefits or harm (relative to the constant payment of S) because the payment varies as the marginal utility of income varies.

In essence, option value is a measure of the value of one institution for diversifying risk relative to another.[13] The ideal institution, of course, would be a perfect contingent claims market. Absent this, and faced with a choice between two payment methods with the same expected dollar value, a risk-averse individual will choose that method which has greater success in diversifying the risk faced by the consumer.

This reasoning is very different from that originally envisioned by Weisbrod. Nevertheless, the concept of option value is relevant when option price is the appropriate measure of consumer benefits and when expected consumer surplus is easier to measure. Thus, whereas the current option value debate has moved far beyond Weisbrod's original argument, we are still concerned with the basic issue raised in that article: To what extent are (expected) consumer benefits imperfectly measured when uncertainty is present?

Most recent authors who have examined this issue empirically have concluded that the possible bias is significant.[14] The implications of the theorem above, however, should interject a note of caution into future empirical research. Option value need not be positive, as Weisbrod's original argument suggested. If the benefits of retaining an option to consume a good under uncertainty are to be evaluated, the sign of option value can be predicted, dependent on the source of demand uncertainty and on consumer preferences.

Consider, for example, a project that maintains access to a recreation area. If uncertainty about the demand for the area arises because of uncertain quality (e.g., crowding, wildlife, or weather), then we predict option value to be positive, as long as recreation is a normal good. If, however, the demand is uncertain because of uncertainty over consumers' tastes, little can be said *a priori* about the sign of option value. Indeed, with more than two states, uncertainty over tastes yields no obvious predictions for the sign of option value. Moreover, it seems overly restrictive to assume only two states of the world (a consumer uses or does not use the area) as this essentially denies the ability to increase or decrease marginally the consumption of recreation.

Thus, empirical analysis of option value should begin with a careful model of demand uncertainty and consumer preferences. As we have shown above, for at least two sources of uncertainty – income and quality – option value has a determinate sign. Without such a model, the hunt for option value lacks a clear check of its theoretical validity. Although empirical estimation of its magnitude is in itself important, without a prediction of the sign of option value we lack the ability to compare our empirical results with our theory and so support our demonstration that option value has a solid grounding in economic theory.

NOTES

1. The actual nature of the good in question will affect these values in a broad manner. If a consumer faces the possible loss of a market of a unique consumption opportunity, such as a nearby recreation site, the consumer may value the option to consume even if current consumption is zero. Similarly, there may be a value in retaining an option to consume a single seller's product if sellers' products are differentiated or if sellers enjoy some market power. On the other hand, if the possible loss involves, say, only a single shoemaker in a perfectly competitive market for shoes, retaining such an option would have no value because the consumer surplus for an individual sheomaker's product is zero in such a market.
2. Weisbrod [1964] used the term "option value" to refer to what is now called "option price." The terminology that is used currently, which distinguishes between option price and option value, was developed in Krutilla, et al., [1972]. This definition of option value must be distinguished from the "quasi-option value" developed by Arrow and Fisher [1974] and Henry [1974]. Quasi-option value reflects the adjustment that should be made to "expected benefits" to reflect the loss of options in situations where an irreversible decision is made and where the future will reveal additional relevant information. Hanemann [1984a] provides a thorough examination of quasi-option value. Hanemann [1984b] investigates a relationship between quasi-option value and option value, and argues that even though the two notions deal with different aspects of decision making under uncertainty, attempts to express quasi-option value in money terms give rise to a problem analogous to that involved in determining whether option price or expected consumer surplus is the appropriate welfare measure.
3. See Bishop [1982] and Smith [1983] for recent summaries of this literature.
4. Fisher and Raucher [1984] review six published studies that estimate use and non-use benefits of improved water quality. They also report the results of two recent EPA studies which examined the Monongahela and Potomac Rivers.
5. Chavas and Bishop (unpublished) make a similar point but their analysis is very different from the one provided here. The analysis in Cook and Graham [1977] leads to a similar relation between this correlation and a measurement bias but in a different context. Cook and Graham use a two state model to investigate the value of what they call an "irreplaceable" commodity. If there is some probability, p, that such a commodity will be lost, Cook and Graham show that the amount of insurance a consumer will purchase against such a loss is related to the value of a reduction in p. The amount of insurance, however, may understate or overstate this value. The direction of this bias can be shown to be related to the correlation between the value of the irreplaceable commodity and the marginal utility of income across the two states of the world ("commodity is lost" and "commodity is not lost"). (Cook and Graham do not make an explicit note of this relation.) Smith [1984] shows how the Cook and Graham analysis can be used to establish an upper bound for the size of option value when there are two states of the world and certain other assumptions are made. See Smith [1984], especially p. 293.
6. The variable T may be either continuous or discrete. Throughout the paper, we treat T as if it is a continuous variable with a probability distribution that may be either continuous or discrete. This allows us to express much of our argument in terms of derivatives rather than discrete changes. The assumption that T is a continuous variable can be relaxed without changing the results of the paper. See also note 7. The assumption that T is a single variable cannot be relaxed without the possibility that our results will change.
7. If T is a variable without a natural ordering, such as "tastes," the ordering of states of the world becomes arbitrary. Clearly monotonicity will not be invariant to different

orderings. In this case, suppose there are N states of the world and that there is an ordering such that $S(T) < S(T+1)$ for $T = 1, \ldots, N - 1$. Then our assumptions are that, for the same ordering and for U_M evaluated at *either* $M - OP$ or $M - S(T)$, $U_M(T) < U_M(T+1)$ or $U_M(T) < U_M(T+1)$ for $T = 1, \ldots, N - 1$.

8. William Strang should be credited for developing this intuitive explanation for the case of income uncertainty.
9. At first glance, it may appear that a constant payment would always be preferred to a variable payment because the latter apparently is "riskier" than the former. This reasoning is incorrect: the uncertainty is over the random variable T and the choice of a constant payment method does not resolve this uncertainty. Instead, as we show in the text, a variable payment may counteract or exacerbate the effects of the variation in T. The occurrence of one or the other of these two possibilities determines the sign of option value.
10. For example, see Ulph [1982] for a review and analysis of *ex ante* versus *ex post* viewpoints in the valuation of life.
11. See Hartman and Plummer [1981].
12. It is, of course, possible that although, say, $U_M(M - OP,1) > U_M(M - OP,2)$, that $U_M(M - S(1),1) < U_M(M - S(2),2)$. In such a case, option value may be ambiguous even though $S(T)$, $U_M(M - OP,T)$, and $U_M(M - S(T),T)$ are monotonic functions. Nevertheless, we feel it is important to point out that *one* of two assumptions sufficient to produce a determinate sign for option value is always satisfied in a two-state model.
13. Smith and Desvousges [1984] provide a more general discussion of the effects of different institutions on the valuation of an opportunity under uncertainty. They develop a model where a consumer may be exposed to a hazardous substance and analyze the consumer's valuation of a reduction in the probability of exposure. They demonstrate that this value depends on the availability of institutions capable of diversifying risk.
14. See Fisher and Raucher [1984].

REFERENCES

Arrow, K.J., and Fisher, A.C. "Environmental Preservation, Uncertainty, and Irreversability." *Quarterly Journal of Economics,* May 1974, 313–19.

Bishop, R.C. "Option Value: An Exposition and Extension." *Land Economics,* February 1982, 1–15.

Chavas, J., and R.C. Bishop. "Ex-Ante Consumer Welfare Evaluation in Cost-Benefit Analysis." unpublished.

Cook, P.J., and D.A. Graham. "The Demand for Insurance and Protection: The Case of Irreplaceable Commodities." *Quarterly Journal of Economics,* February 1977, 143–56.

Fisher, A., and R. Raucher. "Intrinsic Benefits of Improved Water Quality: Conceptual and Empirical Perspectives," in *Advances in Applied Micro-Economics,* Vol. 3, edited by V.K. Smith and A.D. Witte. Greenwich, Conn.: JAI Press, forthcoming.

Graham, D.A. "Cost-Benefit Analysis under Uncertainty." *American Economic Review,* September 1981, 715–725.

Hanemann, W.M. "Information and the Concept of Option Value." University of California, Berkeley, Division of Agricultural and Resource Economics, Working Paper No. 228, 1984a.

—— "On Reconciling Different Concepts of Option Value." unpublished, 1984b.

Hartman, R.C., and M.L. Plummer. "Option Value under Income and Price Uncertainty." Discussion Paper No. 81–15, Department of Economics, University of Washington, December 1981.

Henry, C. "Option Values in the Economics of Irreplaceable Assets." *Review of Economic Studies,* 1974, 89–104.

Krutilla, J.V., C.J. Cicchetti, A.M. Freeman, III, and C.S. Russell. "Observations on the Economics of Irreplaceable Assets," in A.V. Kneese and B.T. Bower, eds., *Environmental Quality Analysis: Theory and Method in the Social Sciences.* Baltimore, 1972.

Option value

Schmalense, R. "Option Demand and Consumer's Surplus: Valuing Price Changes under Uncertainty." *American Economic Review,* December 1972, 813–24.

Smith, V.K. "A Bound for Option Value." *Land Economics,* August 1984, 292–6.

—— "Option Value: A Conceptual Overview." *Southern Economic Journal,* January 1982, 654–68.

—— and W.H. Desvousges. "The Valuation of Risk Reductions Associated with Regulatory Policies." unpublished, 1984.

Ulph, A. "The Role of Ex Ante and Ex Post Decisions in the Valuation of Life." *Journal of Public Economics,* August 1982, 265–76.

Weisbrod, Burton A. "Collective Consumption Services of Individual Consumption Goods." *Quarterly Journal of Economics,* August 1964, 71–7.

Chapter 7

The disparity between willingness to accept and willingness to pay measures of value

Don L. Coursey, John L. Hovis and William D. Schulze

INTRODUCTION

Psychologists have long argued that people are much more averse to a loss than attracted to an equivalent gain. This behaviour, termed loss aversion, has been formalized by Kahneman and Tversky [1979] in their reformulation of expected utility theory, prospect theory. In prospect theory the utility function is replaced by a value function that evaluates changes in income from the current level. Increases in income are weighted by a relatively small marginal utility. Decreases in income are weighted by a much larger marginal utility. In effect, the value function implies that a kink in the relationship between utility and income occurs at the initial income or reference point and that the slope of the utility function for losses in income is steeper than it is for gains.

In a recent paper Knetsch and Sinden [1984] report a series of experiments that demonstrate the existence of a large disparity between willingness to accept (WTA) and willingness to pay (WTP) measures of value. They argue that the psychological theory of loss aversion explains this difference. Economic theory would suggest that individuals who exhibit a large disparity between WTA and WTP are perhaps underperceiving the value of gains or overperceiving the value of losses, are behaving in an irrational manner, and will consequently achieve a lower level of well-being than if they behaved in a true utility-maximizing manner. This would, in contrast to loss aversion, usually imply near equal values for WTA and WTP (see Willig [1976]). Further documentation of a larger than expected disparity between WTA and WTP has been obtained in surveys asking for the value of a variety of public goods. For example, Cummings, Brookshire, and Schulze [1986] document six cases in which survey values for commodities ranging from hunting permits to cleaner air show disparities from about three to one up to ten to one in the ratio of WTA to WTP. Given the serious challenge to economic theory presented by both the Knetsch and Sinden results and the survey research mentioned above, it is important to note that recent research in experimental economics suggests several modifications to the experimental design used by Knetsch and Sinden. This paper reports on an experiment that incorporates these modifications and that we believe considerably attenuates the disparity between WTA and WTP at least after individuals have accumulated market-like experience. However, for commodities such as public goods that are

92

not traded in markets, loss aversion may still have serious implications for welfare economics.

The first concern with respect to the Knetsch and Sinden experiments is the use of lottery tickets as the "commodity" to be valued. Their objective is to determine whether an inexplicably large difference between willingness to accept and willingness to pay (sell) measures of value exists. The hypothesis they are implicitly testing is that changing the frame or context of the decision from a choice to sell to a choice to purchase will itself have a large impact on values. However, by introducing uncertainty into their experimental design, a second source of potentially irrational behavior may be introduced into the analysis. It has been demonstrated repeatedly in economic laboratory experiments that initial choices made under uncertainty do not conform to the predictions of the expected utility model (see, for example, Knez, Smith, and Williams [1985]). More specifically, Grether and Plott [1979] have documented the phenomenon of "preference reversal" for the case in which individuals face a choice between two lotteries. Preference reversal can be illustrated as follows: Lottery A has a high probability of a low monetary reward; Lottery B has a lower probability of a higher monetary reward. Grether and Plott demonstrate convincingly that the same individual will often choose Lottery A over Lottery B but assign a higher monetary value to B than to A. Preferences, as determined by the pattern of choice, are reversed when expressed in monetary terms. Ideally, a test of the existence of a disparity between WTA and WTP measures of value would, at least initially, be conducted under certainty.

The second concern with the Knetsch and Sinden experimental design is the failure to use an institution that allows for learning. None of the Knetsch and Sinden experiments utilize repeated learning trials for individuals to familiarize themselves with the market institution employed. "One shot" experiments like the ones utilized by Knetsch and Sinden almost never produce behavior consistent with economic theory. A large body of the experimental economics literature has been focused on the comparison and development of *special* solicitation institutions (market-like mechanisms) that are *demand revealing* [Smith, 1977; Cox, Roberson, and Smith, 1982]. One such mechanism is the Vickrey or competitive auction [Vickrey, 1961, 1976]. It is such a mechanism that we employ (in contrast to the Knetsch-Sinden experiment) to obtain values for WTA and WTP that might be interpreted as mature market values.

The Vickrey auction is a modification of the traditional sealed bid auction, where incentives for demand (or supply) revelation are restored. In a Vickrey auction eliciting WTA, to use the sample sealed bids for a public construction project, the lowest bid wins, but the winner receives as payment for doing the work an amount equal to the second (or next to) lowest bid. If a Vickrey auction were used to elicit WTP at an art sale, all bids would be sealed, the highest bid would win, but the winner would pay an amount equal to the second highest bid. Since individuals in Vickrey auctions do not pay or receive what they bid, incentives for false (strategic bids) are not present. In experimental situations the Vickrey market institution performs well in revealing individual demand. However, an important observation to be drawn from experimental economics is that individuals participating in a Vickrey auction do not initially reveal "true" values. On a purely theoretical economic basis, they "should" realize that this is their dominant strategy. However, a number of trial iterations are required to allow individuals the opportunity to learn that revealing "true" values is their best strategy [Coppinger, Smith, and Titus, 1980; Cox, Roberson, and Smith, 1982].

The importance of learning and experience in laboratory markets cannot be overemphasized. Studies such as those reported in Knetsch and Sinden have concentrated on inconsistencies in *individual* responses to questions solicited *outside* of *market* situations. But, as noted by Knez, Smith, and Williams [1985], "If individuals modify their opinions and their decisions in light of this [market] experience, these effects will not be reflected in the instruments that have been used in 'framing' studies . . . Most (but not all) experimental markets show some learning effects over time with equilibrium behavior quite different from start-up behavior." We show below that although individual opening bids in a Vickrey auction show a large disparity between WTA and WTP, consistent with the results of Knetsch and Sinden, ending bids submitted after a series of learning trials are similar. Thus, the market-like learning experience of the Vickrey auction causes the disparity reported by Knetsch and Sinden to be greatly reduced. One interpretation of this result is that as individuals evaluate the consequences of their decisions over a series of iterative trial auctions, they more fully learn both their "true" preferences and that full demand revelation is their dominant strategy. Since much economic activity takes place in organized markets, this result suggests that economic theory is most likely adequate to explain behavior as long as individuals have the opportunity to "learn to be rational" through market experience. In other words, economic theory is correct in predicting that WTA and WTP will usually be close in a mature market setting [Willig, 1976]. However, a large disparity may well persist outside of markets or where inexperienced market decisions are made.

EXPERIMENTAL DESIGN

The first difficulty in developing an experimental design to explore divergences between WTA and WTP is the choice of a commodity for sale and purchase by subjects. The commodity must be unfamiliar to the subjects to avoid preconceived notions of value that could bias the results and to allow a large potential disparity between WTA and WTP to exist. Experimental economists, under conditions of certainty, have traditionally used "induced values." The commodity in induced-value experiments can simply be a coupon that can be redeemed at the end of the experiment by the subject for its face value in cash. Thus, the value to the subject of the commodity is controlled by the experimenter. It is precisely this framework in which the strong demand-revealing nature of the Vickrey auction has been demonstrated. However, this controlled value framework does not plausibly allow for a divergence between WTA and WTP to exist for subjects. Thus, a commodity with an initially unknown value to the subjects must be used.

The commodity chosen for use in the experiment is a bitter-unpleasant taste experience. Psychologists have traditionally used sucrose octa-acetate (SOA) in taste experiments because it is the only known laboratory substance that is bitter and yet nontoxic. SOA is safe (breaking down into sugar and vinegar in the body) but very unpleasant [Green, 1941; Linegar, 1943]. In the WTA experiments, subjects are offered payment to taste SOA. In the WTP experiments subjects offer to pay to avoid tasting SOA. Tasting involves the subject holding a one-ounce cup of a concentrated SOA solution in the mouth for 20 seconds. The SOA taste experience was carefully described both verbally by the experimenter and in the written instruction package each subject received at the start of the experiment.

Four groups of eight full-time students recruited from undergraduate business classes at the University of Wyoming participated in the WTA experiments, and four similar groups of eight students participated in the WTP experiments. No subject participated in more than one experiment. The first part (Part I) of each experiment consisted of asking each of eight subjects either how much hypothetically they must be paid to taste SOA (WTA experiments) or how much hypothetically they would pay to avoid testing SOA (WTP experiments). The bids produced in the first part of the experiment are termed purely hypothetical (H) bids because individuals had not yet tasted the SOA liquid.

The second part of the experiment (Part II) involved three steps. In the first step individuals tasted a few sample drops of the SOA solution. In the second step individuals were again asked for the WTA or WTP bids to taste a full one-ounce cup of SOA. We refer to these values as semi-hypothetical (SH) bids. In the third step the experimental monitor attempted to lower (raise) the WTA (WTP) bids in 25 cent increments. The process was initiated from the level of the individual's semi-hypothetical bid. As soon as an individual refused to further lower (raise) his bid, the monitor recorded the final bid as the individual's semi-hypothetical iterated (SHI) bid. All subjects were addressed on a one-to-one basis. This procedure was designed both to give individuals some limited experience with the commodity and to determine how closely hypothetical values might correspond to final auction values. The procedure for obtaining hypothetical values closely follows the survey mechanism proposed by Randall et al. [1974].

In the third part of the experiment (Part III) the eight individuals in a group participated in a Vickrey auction designed to elicit individual competitive bids. Four one-ounce cups of the SOA solution were auctioned to the group of eight individuals. For brevity only the structure of the WTP auction is described below. The WTA auction was conducted in a mirror-like manner.

Each individual in the WTP auction was given a $10 credit to use in the auction (no credit was given in the WTA auction). During each trial each individual first submitted his or her bid to avoid tasting one cup of the SOA solution. Bids were then collected by the monitor and rank ordered from highest to lowest. The fifth highest bid was then reported back to the eight subjects as the reigning price. The four individuals with bids higher than the reigning price were then able to determine that they had "won" the auction implying that they could pay the reigning price (not their own bid) to avoid tasting SOA. The losers paid nothing but had to taste the SOA solution if the trial was final. To determine whether the trial was final, unanimity was required among the winners. Only if no winner objected, was the trial considered final. Further, the first four trials were nonbinding in that even if no winner objected, another trial was conducted. Trials 5 and on could produce a potentially binding outcome. The experiment ended either with no objections among winners, in which case four individuals paid to avoid tasting SOA and four individuals had to taste the SOA; or in the case where an objection remained after ten trials, all parties had to taste the SOA solution. Both the unanimity requirement and the nonbinding practice trials have been shown to be helpful in promoting learning and, as a result, in revealing true values in induced value experiments [Smith, Williams, Bratton, and Vannoni, 1982; Smith, 1982; Coursey and Smith, 1984; Miller and Plott, 1983]. In particular, the unanimity requirement allows a "winner" who has made a mistake to reject the outcome and force another auction trial.

EXPERIMENTAL RESULTS

A summary of the results from the four willingness to accept and the four willingness to pay experiments is reported in Figure 7.1. Each point plotted in the two diagrams represents an average bid of the eight subjects who participated in a single experiment. Plotted are Part I hypothetical bids, Part II semi-hypothetical bids and iterated semi-hypothetical bids, and Part III trial-by-trial outcomes. Figure 7.2 reports the same data found in Figure 7.1, but averages are taken across all individuals in both sets of experiments. Part III average trial-by-trial outcomes are reported for the first four trials and, since different experiments concluded on different trials, for the ending trial.

A one-tailed rank-sum test utilizing average data obtained from the eight experiments was conducted at the 99 percent confidence level in order to compare willingness to accept and willingness to pay measurements obtained in the three parts of our experiment. This test was used because bids obtained in the experiment are not normally distributed. Applying the rank sum test, we reject the hypothesis that willingness to accept and willingness to pay measurements obtained in Part I's totally hypothetical setting are equal. That is, points α and α' in Figure 7.2 are statistically different. This statistical difference extends to Part II's semi-hypothetical bids β and β'. After the iterative bidding process was conducted, willingness to accept (pay) bids decreased (increased) as expected $(\gamma < \beta, \gamma' > \beta')$, but final iterative bids γ and γ' remain statistically different. *Only after completion of the auction process* can we accept the hypothesis that willingness to accept and willingness to pay measurements ω and ω' are equivalent.

We also used the rank-sum test to consider whether there was a difference between methods used to collect willingness to accept and willingness to pay bids. We cannot reject the hypothesis that any of the three traditional survey methods used to obtain hypothetical values reported for Parts I and II yield different average willingness to accept or willingness to pay bids. That is, α, β, and γ are statistically equivalent, and α', β', and γ' are statistically equivalent. After the auction process was conducted, final willingness to accept bids did collapse to a lower value ω. However, a corresponding phenomenon did not occur in the willingness to pay experiments. A statistically significant rise in willingness to pay bids did not occur with the exception of the single experiment WTP2. Thus, competitive pressures do not appear to hold with an equal force in the willingness to accept (supply) and the willingness to pay (demand) auctions. The reported evidence strongly suggests that subjects do decrease their requested payments required to consume the SOA solution. This result does not extend unequivocally or symmetrically to the willingness to pay auction environment.

SUMMARY AND CONCLUSIONS

First, note that as one moves from left to right across Figure 7.2, WTA and WTP move in opposite directions through each and every phase of the experiment. The hypothetical WTA and WTP results (expressed as average values across individuals) are initially far apart (points α and α', respectively). This result is consistent with the existing literature supporting a large disparity between WTA and WTP obtained in the field survey approach for valuing goods (see, for example, Hammack and Brown [1974]; Bishop and Heberlein [1979]; and Rowe et al. [1980]). It is, of course, this literature that motivated the Knetsch and Sinden experiments. Surprisingly, actual experience with the commodity (tasting SOA) drives hypothetical WTA and WTP farther apart (points β and β').

The disparity between WTA and WTP

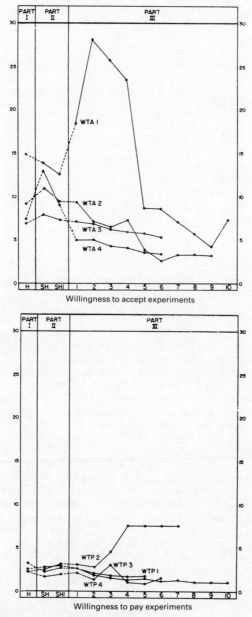

Willingness to accept experiments

Willingness to pay experiments

Figure 7.1 Average single experiment responses.
Each point represents average of the eight individuals who participated in a single experiment.

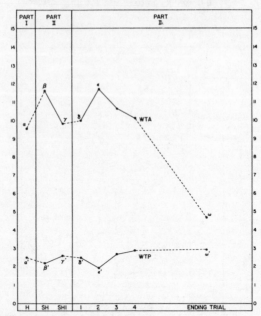

Figure 7.2 Overall average experimental responses
Each point represents overall average of the thirty-two individuals who participated in each of the WTA and WTP experiments.

Iterative bidding causes WTA and WTP to converge (points γ and γ'). Obviously, this suggests that the iterative procedure may be of some use in obtaining hypothetical values. As the Vickrey auction begins (points δ and δ'), opening bids for WTA and WTP are similar to, but further apart than, the iterated hypothetical bids. In the second auction trial (ϵ and ϵ') WTA and WTP diverge. This may be the result of some individuals in the experiment attempting to employ dynamic trial strategy not addressed in the static Vickrey models. Another explanation for this early divergence may, as Knetsch and Sinden suggest, be cognitive dissonance. Individuals may on the WTA side be engaged in "wishful thinking" as to how much they "ought" to be paid to taste a bitter substance. In any case, in early trials individuals may not initially understand that the best strategy is to reveal "true" values, but ultimately WTA and WTP converge strongly (points ω and ω'). This convergence is, however, strongly asymmetrical in that the WTA measure of value "collapses" downward under the competitive market-like experience of the auction, while WTP trial values show only a modest and statistically insignificant upward movement. This suggests that if cognitive dissonance is at work, it does not largely apply on the WTP side but rather may be induced by the prospect of receiving money on the WTA side.

Final auction measures of WTA (point ω) and WTP (point ω') are statistically similar. However, although hypothetical WTA (say, that from point γ) is not statistically similar to WTA obtained in the auction (point ω), hypothetical willingness to pay (say, point γ') is statistically similar to WTP obtained from the auction (point ω').

98

These results suggest three conclusions. First, hypothetical measures of value obtained using WTA are likely to be biased upwards from values obtained from a market-like auction. Psychological factors may well explain this bias.

Second, hypothetical measures of value obtained using WTP may correspond more closely than hypothetical WTA measures to market values. Psychological factors do not appear to influence hypothetical WTP to the degree present for WTA. Framing effects may thus be reduced by use of hypothetical WTP measures of value.

Third, given the demand-revealing nature of and learning experiences in the Vickrey auction, values for WTA and WTP tend to converge in a mature setting. This result is consistent with economic theory and suggests that the divergence obtained in early trials of the experiment for WTA and WTP may result mainly from lack of a market experience. To wit, if the initial divergence in WTA and WTP measures is due to cognitive dissonance as some psychologists suggest, individuals may well learn to become more rational under the pressure of a competitive market. However, as Knetsch and Sinden have demonstrated, psychological arguments may be of great value in explaining behavior that occurs with limited market experience.

REFERENCES

Bishop, R.C., and T.A. Heberlein, "Measuring Values of Extra-Market Goods: Are Indirect Measures Biased?" *American Journal of Agricultural Economics,* VI (December 1979), 916–30.

Coppinger, V.M., V.L. Smith, and J.A. Titus, "Incentives and Behavior in English, Dutch and Sealed-Bid Auctions," *Economic Inquiry,* XVIII (January 1980), 1–22.

Coursey, D.L., and V.L. Smith, "Experimental Tests of an Allocation Mechanism for Private, Public or Externality Goods," *Scandinavian Journal of Economics,* LXXXVI (1984), 468–84.

Cox, J.L., B. Roberson, and V.L. Smith, "Theory and Behavior of Single Price Auctions," V.L. Smith, ed., *Research in Experimental Economics,* II (Greenwich, CT: JAI Press, 1982).

Cummings, R.G., D.S. Brookshire, and W.D. Schulze, eds., *Valuing Environmental Goods: As Assessment of the Contingent Valuation Method* (Totowa, NJ: Rowman & Allanheld, 1986).

Green, M.W. "Sucrose Octa-Acetate as a Possible Bitter Stomachic," *Bulletin of the National Formulary Committee of the American Pharmaceutical Association,* X (1941), 131–33.

Grether, D.M., and C.R. Plott, "Economic Theory of Choice and the Preference Reversal Phenomenon," *American Economic Review,* LXIX (1979), 623–38.

Hammack and Brown, *Waterfowl and Wetlands: Toward Bioeconomic Analysis* (Baltimore, MD: The John Hopkins University Press, 1974).

Kahneman, D., and A. Tversky, "Prospect Theory: An Analysis of Decision Under Risk," *Econometrica,* XLVII. (March 1979), 263–91.

Knetsch, J.L., and J.A. Sinden, "Willingness to Pay and Compensation Demanded: Experimental Evidence of an Unexpected Disparity in Measure of Value," this *Journal* XCIX (August 1984), 507–21.

Knez, P., V.L. Smith, and A. Williams, "Individual Rationality, Market Rationality, and Value Estimation," *American Economic Review,* LXXV (March 1985), 397–402.

Linegar, C.R., "Acute and Chronic Studies on Sucrose Octa-Acetate by the Oral Method," *Bulletin of the National Formulary Committee of the American Pharmaceutical Association,* XI (1943), 59–63.

Miller, G., and C. Plott, "Revenue Generating Properties of Sealed-Bid Auctions," in V.L. Smith, ed., *Research in Experimental Economics,* III (Greenwich, CT: JAI Press, 1983).

Randall, A., B. Ives, and C. Eastman, "Bidding Games for Valuation of Aesthetic Environmental Improvements," *Journal of Environmental Economics and Management,* I (1974), 132–49.

Rowe, R., R. d'Arge, and D. Brookshire, "An Experiment on the Economic Value of Visibility," *Journal of Environmental Economics and Management,* VII (1980), 1–19.

Smith, V.L. "The Principal of Unanimity and Voluntary Consent in Social Choice," *Journal of Political Economy,* LXXXV (1977), 1125–39.

——, A.W. Williams, W.K. Bratton, and M.G. Vannoni, "Competitive Market Institutions: Double Auctions vs. Sealed Bid-Offer Auctions," *American Economic Review,* LXXII (March–May, 1982), 58–77.

Vickrey, W., "Counterspeculation, Auctions and Competitive Sealed Tenders," *Journal of Finance,* XVI (March 1961), 8–37.

——, "Auctions, Markets, and Optimal Allocation," in Y. Amihud, *Bidding and Auctioning for Procurement and Allocation* (New York, NY: University Press, 1976).

Willig, R.D. "Consumers' Surplus without Apology," *American Economic Review,* LXVI (September 1976), 589–97.

Chapter 8

Contingent valuation in fisheries management: the design of satisfactory contingent valuation formats

John P. Hoehn

Fishery resources produce a wide range of recreational, commercial, and aesthetic goods. Fisheries management guides the production of these goods and allocates them to different uses. These production and allocation decisions involve difficult trade-offs that are induced by the scarcity of both natural and fiscal resources. For instance, resource scarcity would force a management agency to make trade-offs across resources directed to fisheries rehabilitation and resources directed to fisheries enhancement. Resource scarcity also forces an agency to decide how to distribute resources across the often conflicting demands of recreational, commercial, and aesthetic interests.

Economic information assists in quantifying the trade-offs that individuals are willing to make across different resource services (Brown 1984). Commercial resource values quantify trade-offs in the commercial sector. Commercial values are readily measured by market prices, quantities, and ordinary statistical methods of demand-and-supply analysis.

Measurement of recreational and aesthetic values is more elusive. Markets for recreational services are typically incomplete or nonexistent. Adequate assessment of these latter values presents a challenge to both economics and fisheries management agencies. Failure to assess recreational and aesthetic values results in a biased picture of management trade-offs.

Three sets of techniques are used for measuring the values of services not explicitly priced by markets. The hedonic technique measures the value of resource services that are obtained through the purchase of some market good (Freeman 1979). The travel cost technique measures values using the travel costs that individuals incur to access a resource service (Freeman 1979). Finally, contingent valuation elicits values directly from the individuals who are potentially affected by a change in management policy (Randall *et al.* 1974; Brookshire and Crocker 1981).

Three characteristics make contingent valuation particularly useful in measuring resource values. First, it is flexible enough to value a wide range of policy impacts; an analyst is not limited to historical variations in resource services and markets (Brookshire and Crocker 1981). Second, with adequate research design, contingent value data are entirely comparable to the value results obtained with other valuation techniques (Schulze *et al.* 1981; Cummings *et al.*

1986; Smith *et al.* 1986). Finally, when rigorous hypothesis tests are possible, outcomes are consistent with the validity of contingent value data (Brookshire *et al.* 1982; Randall *et al.* 1983; Hoehn, in press).

The purpose of this paper is to identify the features of reliable contingent valuation formats. The first section of the paper outlines five important elements of a contingent valuation format. The second section examines the relationship of these elements to potential sources of error in contingent value outcomes. The third section discusses a conceptual framework that can be used to control valuation errors. The final section suggests five key features of reliable contingent valuation formats.

CONTINGENT VALUATION FORMATS
A contingent valuation of policy change is typically implemented in a survey sample setting. The objective of the contingent valuation format is to set up an exchange situation in which an individual may price policy impacts. A contingent valuation format poses a conditional choice: "If a policy were to change environmental services from an initial s^0 to a subsequent s^1 at a cost of $\$x$, would you accept or reject the policy change?" The conditional choice context is adaptable to virtually any set of policy impacts that can be communicated to respondents and to value concepts such as option price, option value, and existence value.

The design of a contingent valuation format involves a choice of five elements: (1) presentation medium, (2) description of policy impacts, (3) method of provision, (4) method of payment, and (5) value elicitation. Each element may be modified to fit a particular valuation context. Each element constitutes a potential source of error in the elicited valuations. To enhance the accuracy of value responses, format elements should be formulated in a way that is consistent with the policy being valued.

The presentation medium is the mode of communication between the research and a respondent. The most common presentation medium is the personal interview. In this form, a sample of households potentially affected by a policy change is drawn and the heads of those households are contacted. Questionnaires usually contain an extensive verbal narrative to describe the policy change. Self-directed formats have also been used in mail surveys (Bishop and Heberlein 1979; Randall *et al.* 1985).

The description of policy impacts is the respondent's only direct source of information about the issue at hand. If the description is incomplete, misleading, or inconsistent with actual alternatives, misleading valuations may be produced. A respondent's comprehension is likely to be enhanced if descriptions are oriented toward perceived elements of the environment. Verbal description is usually supplemented with photographs, diagrams, or tables. The challenge is to develop a policy description that is both technically accurate and intelligible in terms of routine experience.

The method of provision is the way in which a policy change would actually be implemented. If the investigator suggests that a particular agency would implement a policy, the value response could be colored by the respondent's attitude toward the agency. To avoid this agency-specific effect, contingent valuation questionnaires tend to avoid references to specific agencies and refer, if necessary, to a nonspecific regional or local program (Tolley *et al.* 1984; Randall *et al.* 1985). With this type of format, the emphasis is placed on the feasibility of policy change rather than on a specific agency of change.

The method of payment is the means by which the costs or savings arising from a policy are passed to the affected members of the public. Examples are surcharges, sales taxes, and user fees. In early valuation experiments, it appeared that specific payment vehicles had to be posed to make the exercise real and credible (Randall *et al.* 1974), but valuation results proved difficult to interpret if all respondents were not equally susceptible to the payment vehicle. More recent experiments have stressed the lump sum "cost" of policy change – perhaps in the form of generally higher taxes and prices – and have avoided references to specific payment vehicles (Tolley *et al.* 1984; Randall *et al.* 1985).

The value elicitation section is the element of a format that actually obtains the value data from respondents. Though the narrative of a value elicitation section is usually rather brief, its development involves rather subtle and difficult choices. In developing this section, an investigator must (1) clarify the entitlements or property rights implicit in a policy change and (2) select a procedure for eliciting values.

The entitlements implicit in a policy determine whether a valuation should be based on willingness to pay or willingness to accept compensation. If respondents are entitled to the initial policy situation, a Hicksian compensating format is appropriate. A Hicksian compensating format obtains willingness to pay for policies that improve on an initial situation and willingness to accept compensation for policies that make respondents worse off. If respondents are not entitled to the initial policy situation, a Hicksian equivalent format is appropriate. A Hicksian equivalent format forces respondents to pay to avoid a policy change that would make them worse off and asks their willingness to accept compensation to forego a change that would make them better off (Brookshire *et al.* 1980).

When policy entitlements are unclear, an investigation may incorporate the compensating and equivalent forms into single format or into different subsamples. For instance, for a policy that would reduce the quality of a fishery, a questionnaire may elicit both a willingness to accept compensation and a willingness to pay to prevent the reduction.

Procedures for actually eliciting value data vary along three dimensions. Specific elicitation procedures are developed by selecting features from each of these three dimensions.

The first dimension is the form of a value response. The response may be (1) an actual statement of maximum willingness to pay or minimum willingness to accept compensation or (2) a respondent's acceptance or rejection response to a fixed pairing of policy impacts and cost. The accept–reject responses are relatively easy to elicit from respondents and can be analyzed by the methods of Hanemann (1984) and Seller *et al.* 1985).

Second, values may be elicited (1) as a single response or (2) in an iterated procedure which bases subsequent valuation questions on preceding responses. Iterative procedures are described by Randall *et al.* (1974) and may encourage a respondent to undertake a more complete consideration of policy.

Third, a starting point for valuation may be posed by the questionnaire or elicited directly from the respondent. However, value responses are occasionally influenced by poorly constructed questionnaires that pose starting points (Boyle *et al.* 1985). If starting points are posed by the questionnaire, multiple-regression analysis should be used to determine whether starting-point effects are present in the value data (see Thayer 1981; Boyle *et al.* 1985).

POTENTIAL SOURCES OF ERROR

Researchers have proposed several ways to catalog potential sources of error in the contingent valuation. One can find references to four rather loosely defined sets of effects: (1) the hypothetical context of contingent valuation, (2) the information conveyed by the format to respondents, (3) strategic behavior by respondents as they try to affect policy outcomes, and (4) larger than anticipated differences in the value outcomes of willingness to pay and willingness to accept formats (Rowe et al. 1980; Schulze et al. 1981; Rowe and Chestnut 1983; Cummings et al. 1986). Evidence regarding these effects is reviewed in this section.

Hypothetical context

Hypothetical effects may arise as individuals evaluate the gains and losses that are posed by a prospective policy (Brookshire and Crocker 1981). Bishop and Heberlein (1979) compared contingent and simulated markets and found that contingent valuation gave smaller willingness to pay and larger willingness to accept values than the simulated markets. However, later research by Bishop and Heberlein (1986) questioned the strength of their earlier conclusion. In a broad review of the psychological literature, Cummings et al. (1986) found evidence of significantly different outcomes between actual and hypothetical payment situations.

There appear to be three possible reasons for hypothetical effects in contingent valuation. First, the choice context described by the contingent valuation questionnaire may fail to correspond to the actual choice context. This problem of context correspondence is widely recognized by social psychologists (Ajzen and Fishbein 1977). This source of error can be avoided by recognizing that contingent values are conditioned on the structure of the contingent valuation format and by developing formats that accurately describe intended policies.

A second source of hypothetical error arises in communicating complex policy information to a respondent. The format's description of policy may be accurate, but errors in the respondent's perception and comprehension may occur. Policy impacts are often complex and unfamiliar. The time constraints of an interview restrict repetition and review. Given these constraints, flawed perception or comprehension may result in a flawed valuation of the proposed change.

Third, the contingent valuation setting may allow too little time for respondents to complete their decision processes. Research by Smith (1980), Pommerehne et al. (1982), and Coursey et al. (1987) underscores the correlation between time and improved decisions. The time constraints of a typical contingent valuation interview may cut short a respondent's decision processes and introduce errors into the value response.

Information bias

Information bias may arise as individuals formulate an expectation of policy impacts subject to the information conveyed by a contingent valuation format (Rowe et al. 1980). In a general sense, information effects overlap the problem of context correspondence discussed with respect to hypothetical effects (Cummings et al. 1986). However, as used in the contingent valuation literature, information bias tends to refer to the effects of procedural elements of the contingent format, such as starting points, that are not necessarily a feature of the proposed policy.

Careful design, pretesting, and analysis can at least detect, if not eliminate, the impact of information bias. For instance, starting-point effects may stem in part from respondent fatigue due to a lengthy questionnaire or a lengthy sequence of iterative valuations (Rowe *et al.* 1980). Pretesting of the questionnaire can detect formats that are sensitive to these effects and appropriate modifications can be made. If starting-point effects are not detected until the final analysis, the sensitivity of the value results to these effects should be examined. With auxiliary assumptions, it may be possible to measure the size of starting-point effects and estimate an unbiased valuation (Thayer 1981).

Payment vehicles such as sales taxes and user fees have also been identified as sources of information bias (Rowe *et al.* 1980; Cummings *et al.* 1986). It seems more appropriate, however, to view payment vehicles not as biasing factors but as potentially important features of a policy change. Rowe *et al.* (1980), Daubert and Young (1981), and Greenly *et al.* (1981) found significant differences in valuations associated with different payment vehicles, though Brookshire *et al.* (1980, 1982) found no significant effects. Recent format designs avoid the use of specific payment vehicles (Tolley *et al.* 1984; Randall *et al.* 1985).

Strategic effects
Strategic effects stem from an individual's attempt "to influence the outcome or results of the [evaluation] by not revealing a true valuation" (Rowe *et al.* 1980). Strategic behavior in public decision making has been recognized at least since the eighteenth century (Hume 1888). Recent research, however, shows that it is possible to control the incentives for truth-telling through an appropriate design of the decision-making context (Clarke 1971; Groves 1973; Green and Laffont 1977; Groves and Ledyard 1977).

Evidence of strategic effects in contingent valuation is unexpectedly weak. Bohm (1972), Scherr and Babb (1975), and Schneider and Pommerehne (1981) found little experimental evidence of pronounced strategic behavior. Smith (1980) tested the strength of strategic effects against a set of incentives designed to encourage a truthful statement of values; his results suggest that even weak incentives for truth-telling may be enough to counter the prospect of strategic behavior. Brookshire *et al.* (1976) and Rowe *et al.* (1980) found no evidence of strong strategic behavior in their contingent valuation experiments.

The absence of strong strategic effects in contingent valuation may be more problematic than their presence. The lack of strategic response may indicate that the respondent views the entire experiment as rather academic and remote from actual policy processes (Brookshire *et al.* 1976). Confidence in contingent valuation would be stronger if the operative incentives were clearer.

Willingness to pay or accept compensation
Hammack and Brown (1974), Bishop and Heberlein (1979), Gordon and Knetsch (1979), Brookshire *et al.* (1980), Rowe *et al.* (1980), and Knetsch and Sinden (1985) all reported differences between willingness to pay and willingness to accept compensation that were much greater than would have been predicted by existing theory as developed by Willig (1976) and Randall and Stoll (1980). The cause of such divergences remains unclear. Recent experiments by Coursey *et al.* (1987) suggest that the divergence may be due to a respondent's incomplete decision processes: measures of willingness to pay and willingness to accept diverged at the outset of an iterative bidding process but reconverged with successive iterations.

IMPROVED FORMAT DESIGN

Improved design of contingent valuation formats requires a systematic understanding of contingent behavior. An explanatory model would encompass the potential sources of error and suggest their likely effect on valuations. The predicted relationships could then be used to assess the adequacy of contingent value data in economic analyses and to guide the design of improved contingent valuation formats.

Recent research by Alan Randall and me (Hoehn and Randall 1987) suggests the possibility of a systematic explanation of contingent behaviour. Our basic approach is to adapt the standard economic choice model of perfect information and instant optimization (Ferguson and Gould 1975) to the constraints of the contingent valuation context. Our analysis encompasses the primary potential sources of error identified in the last section: errors in communication, time-constrained decision processes, and incentives in value statement. In this section, I outline the structure of our model.

Contingent behavior and value outcomes

The typical contingent valuation context confronts an individual with the problems of value formulation and value statement. The value formulation problem arises to the extent that an individual is unfamiliar with a prospective policy change. Value formulation encompasses two potential sources of error: errors in communication as a respondent assimilates new information and errors in the time-constrained decision or search process. The value statement problem encompasses strategic behavior. Our analysis indicates that errors in both value formulation and value statement may have an impact on value outcomes.

The impact of value formulation depends upon whether the valuation procedure is posed in a Hicksian compensating or a Hicksian equivalent format. For simplicity, I discuss the impact of value formulation in terms of willingness to pay.

In a Hicksian compensating format, an individual seeks to determine the maximum amount of income that he or she is willing to pay in order to get the prospective policy change. Communication errors introduce uncertainty into the respondent's perception of this change, which causes a risk-averse respondent to formulate a lower valuation than he or she would for a clearly understood policy. In addition, due to an incomplete decision process, the respondent fails to identify maximum willingness to pay and instead identifies something less than the maximum. Both communication error and the incomplete decision process imply that the valuation formulated in a Hicksian compensating format, denoted fHC, is something less than the ideal Hicksian measure, HC.

The formulated compensating measure fHC is a function of the time and effort spent in decision making. As the amount of effort allocated to the formulation process increases, fHC tends to increase (it does not decrease) toward HC. Eventually, if sufficient time and effort are allocated to the decision process, fHC approximates HC.

A format designed to elicit a Hicksian equivalent valuation forces the respondent to determine the maximum amount of income that he or she is willing to pay in order to avoid the prospective policy change. The Hicksian equivalent format forces a respondent (1) to forecast his or her personal level of well-being under the prospective policy and (2) to determine his or her maximum willingness to pay to avoid that level of well-being. The forecasting problem tends to push the formulated value measure fHE upward while the payment formulation problem tends to push fHE downward. As a result, fHE may be greater than, less than, or equal to the ideal equivalent value measure HE.

The impact of additional time and effort on fHE is not clear. Whether fHE increases or decreases depends on the amount of time and effort allocated to forecasting the postchange level of well-being versus the amount of time allocated to payment formulation.

Once fHC or fHE is formulated, the respondent faces the choice of whether or not to actually report the formulated valuation. If it is in his or her long-term best interest to respond truthfully to the valuation question, the respondent states fHC or fHE, whichever is relevant. However, an individual may perceive more immediate incentives to distort fHC or fHE and instead report a substitute measure, sHC or sHE.

Our model suggests that two, often implicit, elements of the contingent valuation context determine the immediate structure of incentives: (1) the implementation rule and (2) the payment rule. The implementation rule defines the relationship between an individual's value response and the likelihood that the project will be implemented. The payment rule describes an individual's payment in the event that a prospective policy is actually implemented.

Three incentive structures are particularly relevant to contingent valuation. In the first incentive structure, a respondent believes (1) that the prospective policy will be implemented if benefits exceed costs and (2) that, in the event of implementation, payment will be proportional to the respondent's stated valuation. The respondent weighs the probable personal benefits of implementation against the probable personal costs. The result is a compromise between stating the full fHC or fHE and stating nothing. The compromise implies that the respondent states something less than the full formulated valuation: $sHC \leq fHC$; $sHE \leq fHE$.

The second incentive structure involves a respondent who supposes that (1) the prospective policy will be implemented if benefits exceed costs and (2) that his or her payment is the average cost of project implementation. With this set of incentives, a respondent who behaves strategically would try to shift the stated sample mean valuation toward his or her own formulation. A risk-neutral respondent who believes his or her formulated valuation is equal to the sample mean valuation states sHC equal to fHC and sHE equal to fHE. A risk-averse individual with the same belief states something less than his or her formulated valuation. An individual who suspects that his or her formulated valuation deviates from the sample mean valuation reports sHC or sHE to exaggerate that deviation. Such behavior tends to increase the variance of the stated valuations but leaves the sample mean unaffected. On average, $sHC \leq fHC$; $sHE \leq fHE$.

In the third case, the respondent assumes that (1) the prospective policy will be implemented if a majority of individuals responds favorably to a impact-payment pair and (2) that his or her payment will be equal to the described per-person costs of implementation. With this fixed-cost referendum, an individual can do no better than respond "accept" to a payment that is less than fHC or fHE and respond "reject" to a payment that is greater than fHC or fHE. Given an iterated schedule of prospective costs, an individual would accept all policy-payment pairs until the prospective payment exceeds fHC or fHE. In this manner, the individual identifies the stated valuations $sHC = fHC$; $sHE = fHE$.

The net effect of value formulation and value statement differs across the

Hicksian compensating and equivalent formats. In a Hicksian compensating format, value formulation and value statement lead to an understatement of the ideal compensating value measures: $sHC \leq fHC \leq HC$. Benefit measures elicited in terms of stated willingness to pay $sWTP^c$ do not overstate the ideal WTP^c. Costs measured in terms of stated willingness to accept $sWTA^c$ ($= -sHC$) do not understate the ideal cost measure WTA^c. A compensating format does not overstate the net benefits of policy change since $(sWTP^c - sWTA^c) \leq (WTP^c - WTA^c)$.

The net effect of value formulation and value statement on the stated Hicksian equivalent measures is less clear. Though the likely incentives suggest an understatement of fHE, the value formulation process itself leads to an ambiguous relation between fHE and HE.

Empirical evidence

The analytical results are consistent with a range of existing empirical evidence. The model also appears to "explain" empirical anomalies such as the initial divergence of willingness to pay and willingness to accept compensation. In this section, I discuss the analytical results as empirical hypotheses. These hypotheses can be used to understand existing data and to direct further research.

The model suggests the respondents learn about their preferences as more time and effort are allocated to value formulation. This learning process implies that the stated compensating value sHC does not decrease with more time and effort. This result is consistent with Randall *et al.* (1985) and Coursey *et al.* (1987).

Willingness to pay and willingness to accept compensation diverge unless respondents have prior experience in valuing the proposed policy change. This hypothesis follows because extant theory suggests that $WTP^c \leq WTA^c$ and our model implies that $sWTP^c < WTP^c$ and $sWTA^c \geq WTA^c$. Within our model, value formulation and value statement drive an additional wedge between willingness to pay and willingness to accept. This divergence is consistent with the empirical evidence discussed above.

Willingness to pay and willingness to accept tend to converge as more time and effort are given to valuation. The model predicts that $sWTP^c$ tends to increase and $sWTA^c$ tends to decrease with more time and effort. This prediction is consistent with the recent results of Coursey *et al.* (1987).

Results of an accept–reject, fixed-cost elicitation procedure dominate the outcomes of a "How much are you willing to pay?" format. This hypothesis follows since the structure of the accept-reject format simulates the incentives of the fixed-cost referendum. This hypothesis is consistent with the empirical findings of Tolley *et al.* (1984). This hypothesis may also help to explain the relative immunity of contingent valuation to strategic behavior. With referenda and their informal equivalent, opinion polls, a common feature of public decision making in the United States, respondents may simply assume that the referendum incentives are relevant to contingent valuation. This ingrained response would support the generally weak existing evidence of strategic behavior.

Finally, an iterated accept–reject, fixed-cost elicitation procedure results in stated valuations that are closer to the true valuation HC and that dominate the valuations of any other payment rule. An iterative process encourages the respondent to take more time and effort with value formulation. The accept–reject, fixed-cost procedure implies sHC equal to fHC. This hypothesis is consistent with the tentative evidence of Sorg (1982).

FEATURES OF RELIABLE FORMATS

Contingent valuation encompasses a large class of alternative format designs. These format designs do not all perform equally well. However, from the preceding discussion, it is clear the performance of contingent valuation can be controlled. In this section, I suggest five conclusions regarding format design.

First, valuation results obtained with a Hicksian compensating format, sHC, are more conservative than the ideal compensating measures, HC. A compensating format does not overstate the net benefits of policy change. Used in benefit–cost analysis, the stated compensating measures may not be ideal but they are pragmatically useful. Stated compensating values correctly identify detrimental policies as having net benefits less than zero. Policy changes that are truly beneficial are likely to show net benefits greater than zero. In a policy setting with many competing proposals, stated value information can be used to weed out detrimental policies and narrow the focus of public decisions to the few most beneficial policy alternatives.

Second, Hicksian equivalent formats appear to yield generally unreliable value results. Further research may indicate cases where the degree or sign of the error is clear. In the meantime, Hicksian compensating formats give the most satisfactory value outcomes.

Third, the implicit implementation rule and payment rules determine the incentives for value statement. The theoretical evidence suggests than an accept–reject, fixed-cost elicitation procedure yields the best value estimates. The accept–reject procedure reduces the possibility that a benefit–cost analysis would reject a truly beneficial policy.

Fourth, an iterated accept–reject procedure is likely to increase the amount of time devoted to value formulation and, in a Hicksian compensating format, yield value estimates that are closest to the ideal measures.

Finally, format design should be reviewed with respect to four features: (1) the description of policy that is conveyed to a respondent, (2) the implicit implementation rule, (3) the implicit payment rule, and (4) the complexity of the valuation problem. A change in one of these features is likely to shift the stated valuations. Increased complexity may require more time and effort on the part of the respondent. Tables, graphs, or computer-assisted formats may speed the assimilation of information and assist in repetition and review.

REFERENCES

Ajzen, I., and M. Fishbein (1977) Attitude-behaviors relation: a theoretical analysis and review of empirical research. *Psychological Bulletin* **84**: 888–918.

Bishop, R.C., and T.A. Heberlein (1979) Measuring values of extramarket goods: are indirect measures biased? American Journal of Agricultural Economics **64**: 927–930.

Bishop, R.C., and T.A. Heberlein (1986) Does contingent valuation work? Pages 123–147 *in* R.G. Cummings, D.S. Brookshire, and W.D. Schulze. Valuing environmental goods: an assessment of the contingent valuation method. Rowman and Allanheld. Totowa, New Jersey.

Bohm, P. (1972) Estimating demand for public goods: an experiment. European Economic Review 3: 111–130.

Boyle, K.J., R.C. Bishop and N. Bouwes (1985) Starting point bias in contingent valuation bidding games. Land Economics **61**: 187–194.

Brookshire, D.S. and T.D. Crocker (1981) The advantages of contingent valuation methods for benefit cost analysis. Public Choice **36**: 235–252.

Brookshire, D.S., B. Ives, and W.D. Schulze (1976) The valuation of aesthetic preferences. *Journal of Environmental Economics and Management* 3: 325–346.

Brookshire, D.S., A. Randall, and J.R. Stoll (1980) Valuing increments and decrements in natural resource service flows. *American Journal of Agricultural Economics* **62**: 478–488.

Brookshire, D.S., M.A. Thayer, W.D. Schulze, and R.C. d'Arge (1982) Valuing public goods: a comparison of survey and hedonic approaches. *American Economic Review* **72**: 165–176.

Brown, T.C. (1984) The concept of value in resource allocation. *Land Economics* **60**: 231–246.

Clarke, E.H. (1971) Multipart pricing of public goods. Public Choice **11**: 17–33.

Coursey, D.L., J.J. Hovis, and W.D. Schulze (1987) On the supposed disparity between willingness to accept and willingness to pay measures of value. *Quarterly Journal of Economics* **102**: 679–690.

Cummings, R.G., D.S. Brookshire and W.D. Schulze (1986) Valuing environmental goods: an assessment of the contingent valuation method. Rowman and Allanheld, Totowa, New Jersey.

Daubert, J.T. and R.A. Young (1981) Recreational demands for maintaining instream flows: a contingent valuation approach. *American Journal of Agricultural Economics* **63**: 666–676.

Ferguson, C.E. and J.P. Gould (1975) Microeconomic theory. Irwin, Homewood, Illinois.

Freeman, A.M. (1979) The benefits of environmental improvement. Johns Hopkins University Press, Baltimore, Maryland.

Gordon, I.M., and J.L. Knetsch (1979) Consumers' surplus measures and the evaluation of resources. *Land Economics* **55**: 1–10.

Green, J.R. and J.J. Laffont (1977) Incentives in public decision-making. North-Holland, Amsterdam.

Greenly, D.A., R.C. Walsh, and R.A. Young (1981) Option value: empirical evidence from a case study of recreation and water quality. *Quarterly Journal of Economics* **95**: 657–673.

Groves, T. (1973) Incentives teams. *Econometrica* **41**: 617–663.

Groves, T., and J. Ledyard (1977) Optimal allocation of public goods: a solution to the 'free rider' problem. *Econometrica* **45**: 783–809.

Hammack, J., and G.M. Brown (1974) Waterfowl and wetlands: toward bioeconomic analysis. Johns Hopkins University Press, Baltimore, Maryland.

Hanemann, M.W. (1984) Welfare evaluation in contingent valuation experiments with discrete responses. *American Journal of Agricultural Economics* **66**: 332–341.

Hoehn, J. In press. Contingent valuation and the prospect of a satisfactory benefit cost indicator. *In* R.L. Johnson and G.V. Johnson. editors. Economic valuation of natural resources: issues, theory, and applications. Westview Press. Boulder, Colorado.

Hoehn, J.P., and A. Randall (1987) A satisfactory benefit cost indicator from contingent valuation. *Journal of Environmental Economics and Management* **14**: 226–247.

Hume, D.A. (1888) Treatise on human nature, Oxford University Press, Oxford.

Knetsch, J., and J.A. Sinden (1985) Willingness to pay and compensation demanded: experimental evidence from an unexpected disparity in measures of value. *Quarterly Journal of Economics* **100**: 507–521.

Pommerehne, W.W., F. Schneider, and P. Zweifel (1982) Economic theory of choice and the preference reversal phenomenon: a reexamination. *American Economic Review* **72**: 569–574.

Randall, A., G.C. Blomquist, J.P. Hoehn, and J.R. Stoll (1985) National aggregate benefits of air and water pollution control. University of Kentucky, Report prepared under United States Environmental Protection Agency cooperative agreement CR881-056-01-0. Lexington.

Randall, A., J.P. Hoehn, and D.S. Brookshire (1983) Contingent valuation surveys for evaluating environmental assets. *Natural Resources Journal* **23**: 645–648.

Randall, A., B. Ives, and C. Eastman (1974) Bidding games for valuation of aesthetic environmental improvements. *Journal of Environmental Economics and Management* **1**: 132–149.

Contingent valuation

Randall, A., and J.R. Stoll (1980) Consumer's surplus in commodity space. *American Economic Review* **70**: 449–455.

Rowe, R.D., and L.G. Chestnut (1983) Valuing environmental commodities: revisited. *Land Economics* **59**: 404–410.

Rowe, R.D., R.C. d'Arge, and D.S. Brookshire (1980) An experiment on the value of visibility. *Journal of Environmental Economics and Management* **7**: 1–19.

Scherr, B.A., and E.M. Babb (1975) Pricing public goods: an experiment with two proposed pricing systems. *Public Choice* **23**: 35–53.

Schneider, F., and W.W. Pommerehne (1981) Free riding and collective action: an experiment in public microeconomics. *Quarterly Journal of Economics* **95**: 689–704.

Schulze, W.D., R.C. d'Arge and D.S. Brookshire (1981) Valuing environmental commodities: some recent experiments. *Land Economics* **57**: 151–172.

Seller, C., J.R. Stoll, and J.P. Chavas (1985) Validation of empirical measures of welfare change: a comparison of nonmarket techniques. *Land Economics* **61**: 156–175.

Smith, V.K., W.H. Desvousges and A. Fisher (1986) A comparison of direct and indirect methods for estimating environmental benefits. *American Journal of Agricultural Economics* **68**: 280–290.

Smith, V.L. (1980) Experiments with a decentralized mechanism for public goods decisions. *American Economic Review* **70**: 584–599.

Sorg, C. (1982) Valuing increments and decrements of wildlife resources: further evidence. Master's thesis, University of Wyoming, Laramie.

Thayer, M.A. (1981) Contingent valuation techniques for assessing environmental impacts: further evidence. *Journal of Environmental Economics and Management* **8**: 27–44.

Tolley, G.A., and eight coauthors (1984) Establishing and valuing the effects of improved visibility in the eastern United States. University of Chicago. Report prepared under United States Environmental Protection Agency cooperative agreement CR807-076-01-1. Chicago.

Willig, R.D. (1976) Consumers' surplus without apology. *American Economic Review* **66**: 589–597.

Chapter 9
Estimating option prices and existence values for wildlife resources

David S. Brookshire, Larry S. Eubanks and Alan Randall

INTRODUCTION

The benefit-cost analyst has traditionally focused on the use values of natural environments. However, other values should be counted as part of the total value of a natural resource or environment. In particular, Weisbrod (1964) set forth option value for natural environments, and Krutilla (1967) has suggested values for natural environments. Although the suggestions of Weisbrod and Krutilla have prompted much discussion in the literature regarding the theoretical nature of such values, little research has been directed toward empirical estimation (see Long 1967; Cicchetti and Freeman 1971; Schmalensee 1972; Bohm 1975; and Greenley *et al.* 1981). Much of this literature has been summarized and reviewed in Bishop (1982).

An approach to valuing nonmarketed commodities, referred to as the contingent valuation approach, has been developed which can be successfully utilized in estimating values associated with retaining the option to future use and existence of a natural environment. Regardless of the theoretical arguments that option value will be positive, negative, or zero, option price (option value plus expected consumer surplus) is the appropriate value to measure increments or decrements of a natural environment. A straightforward application of the contingent valuation approach can be used to estimate both option price and existence value. However, the existing literature from Long (1967) through Schmalensee (1972, 1975) and Bohm (1975) to Bishop (1982) is obsessed with the problem of double-counting. In evaluating the losses that would result from, for example, converting a valued recreational environment to some alternative use incompatible with recreation, the procedure of adding the expected consumer's surplus from projected future use (in the "no conversion" alternative) to the aggregate option price of uncertain future users would introduce a double-counting error.

This problem does not arise in quite the same form in the context of our empirical study. Our situations involved valuing increments in supply (not threatened decrements). In such cases, it is entirely appropriate to value the "with project" stream of recreation services by summing the value of expected future use at the current level of provision and the aggregate option price of the proposed increment in provision.[1] Thus, double-counting is not so grave a threat in evaluating programs that propose increments, rather than decrements, in availability of some resource.

This perhaps helps place the double-counting problem in perspective. Double-

112

counting is seldom an elusive, abstract theoretical problem. It is more nearly a pragmatic concern, and its avoidance most commonly requires the consistent application of rather simple logic.

This paper explores the analytical structure of option price and existence value and develops a modification of the contingent valuation approach to estimate option price and existence value for specific natural resources whose future supply is uncertain. Further, the contingent valuation approach enables estimates of individual discount rates to be derived for nonmarketed goods. Estimating individual discount rates results from considering time horizons in the analysis. Currently little is empirically known about individual discount rates for non-marketed goods.

The empirical analysis explores the case of grizzly bear and bighorn sheep wildlife resources in Wyoming. Both wildlife populations have been threatened by human activity and therefore provide an excellent case for an empirical attempt to estimate option price and existence values.

OPTION PRICE AND EXISTENCE VALUES FOR WILDLIFE RESOURCES

This section will present a framework to describe the relationship between option price, expected consumer's surplus, and option value. We will be brief since Bishop has recently summarized the relevant literature (1982). Originally discussed by Cichetti and Freeman (1971), a key difference exists in this presentation in that we will show that option value is positive for risk averse individuals when future availability of the resource is uncertain.[2] Further, the relationship between option price and the probability of future availability can be shown to be expressed as a concave functional relationship for a risk averse individual. Finally, the nature of existence value will be discussed.

An individual consumer – assumed to be a grizzly-bear hunter – is confronted with the possibility that the grizzly-bear population will be unavailable for use in the future.[3] Suppose also the grizzly-bear hunter could purchase the option to hunt grizzly bear in the future. Included with the option to future hunting is a statement of the price that must be paid for the hunting activity itself.

Option value (OV) is defined as the difference between option price (OP) and expected consumer's surplus (CS) where consumer's surplus is either the Hicksian compensated or equivalent variation measure. Option price is the maximum amount the grizzly-bear hunter would pay to keep the right to hunt grizzly bear in the future at a fixed set of prices.

Assume the hunter's income is Y_o and the following indifference relationships hold: $U_2 > U_2^* > U_1 > U_1^*$. Given that the hunter does not purchase the option, the hunter can attain an indifference level U_2 if the grizzly-bear population is available, whereas if the grizzly-bear population is not supplied, the hunter only attains U_1. Assuming the hunter purchases the option at a price OP_2, the available income is decreased and the hunter's budget line would then be shifted inward. In this case, if the grizzly-bear population is available, the hunter attains utility level U_2^*, or U_1^* if the population is not available.

Using the following notation:

$P(S/O) \equiv$ probability of supply given the option is purchased;
$P(NS/O) \equiv$ probability of not being supplied given the option is purchased;
$P(S/NO) \equiv$ probability of supply given the option is not purchased;
$P(NS/NO) \equiv$ probability of not being supplied given the option is not purchased;

the grizzly-bear hunter's expected utility if the option is not purchased can be written as

$$\overline{U}_{NO} = (P(S/NO) \cdot U_2 + P(NS/NO) \cdot U_1) \tag{1}$$

The expected utility if the option is purchased is written

$$\overline{U}_O = (P(S/O) \cdot U_2^* + P(NS/O) \cdot U_1^*) \tag{2}$$

The maximum amount the grizzly-bear hunter would pay for the option would be the value that makes the expected utilities from the two possible decisions equal, i.e., $U_O = U_{NO}$. To illustrate the determination of option value, the following assumptions are made: (1) $P(S/NO) = 1/2$; (2) $P(NS/NO) = 1/2$; and (3) $P(S/O) = 1$. Given these assumptions the maximum amount the hunter would pay for the option to hunt grizzly bear in the future would be the value which makes

$$U_2^* = 1/2(U_2 + U_1) \tag{3}$$

In order to compare this value with the expected consumer's surplus (measured as compensating variation) which could be written $P(NS/NO) \cdot OP_1 = 1/2 \, OP_1$, let us examine a Friedman-Savage type diagram such as Figure 1, which shows the relationship between utility (U) and income (Y). The grizzly-bear hunter represented by Figure 9.1 is a risk averter since the expected utility function is concave. U_2^* is the mid-point on the utility axis between U_1 and U_2, and the income level associated with U_2^* is $Y_o - OP_2$, where OP_2 is the option price. Clearly, OP_2 is greater than expected consumer's surplus which is $1/2 \, OP_1$. This individual is indifferent between paying OP_2 to assure U_2^* with certainty and paying nothing and having an equal probability of attaining U_1 or U_2. The difference between OP_2 and $1/2 \, OP_1$ is option value.

Option value is a risk aversion premium and will be positive where the future availability of a natural resource is uncertain, even assuming certainty in demand. Thus, if the individual has risk neutral preferences, option price and expected consumer's surplus will be equal, while for a risk taker, expected consumer's surplus will exceed option price and option value will be negative. Finally, Figure 9.1 suggests that for a risk averse individual, the relationship between option price and the probability of future availability can be expressed as an increasing concave function, while for a risk taker the relationship would be expressed by an increasing convex function.

There are two reasons for emphasizing supply uncertainty. First, demand uncertainty creates ambiguity with respect to the sign of option value.[4] Second, without the presence of supply uncertainty the relevance of the option value concept for the application of benefit-cost analysis to increments and decrements of natural environments is nonexistent. Why would there be a willingness to pay for the option to future use of a natural environment if future availability of the environment is certain? There would be no risk aversion premium, even for the uncertain demander if the services of the natural environment are certainly available in the future. Thus, our interest lies in the probability of future supply in relation to the magnitude of option price.

The above discussion has not addressed the concept of existence value because it is not directly applicable. Existence value refers to the willingness to pay for the

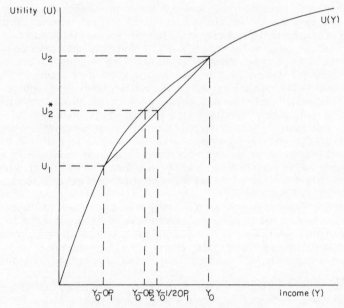

Figure 9.1 Option value for risk averter.

existence or preservation of natural resources (e.g., Grand Canyon, Grand Tetons, grizzly bears, or blue whales).[5] Some individuals may derive satisfaction from knowing that certain species and natural environments exist and therefore may be willing to pay for the preservation of such natural resources. Thus individuals having existence values may not even demand the generation of use values associated with such natural environments. Existence value then would be a pure public good since consumption activities associated with existence value are both nonrival and nonexclusive. The fact that existence value is a public good[6] explains lack of market provision for such values, in general, and the need to develop methods to empirically derive such values.[7]

EXPERIMENTAL DESIGN

The probability of future availability of a natural resource is an essential element for the concepts of option value, option price, and existence value. For empirical purposes in estimating option price, resources whose future availability is, in fact, uncertain and whose continued existence is in question must be chosen. Two wildlife populations that meet this condition have been selected for analysis: grizzly bear and bighorn sheep in Wyoming.

The grizzly-bear population in Wyoming has been steadily declining, due to the growing encroachment by humans on grizzly-bear habitat resulting from energy development, general population increases, and increases in recreational demands. The passage of the Endangered Species Act Amendments of 1973 resulted in the suspension of grizzly-bear hunting in Wyoming in 1975. Therefore, there is now little probability of future availability of a grizzly-bear population for

115

hunting; in fact, given the suspension of hunting, the probability of future availability may even be zero. However, a zero probability assumption is not necessary, only that the moratorium on hunting suggests a likelihood that the existence of the grizzly population in the future is severely threatened.

Historically, bighorn sheep habitat and populations also have declined in Wyoming. At one time, virtually all of Wyoming supported populations of bighorn sheep.[8] However, bighorn sheep populations have declined to such an extent that the Wyoming Game and Fish Department only allows approximately 350 hunting permits to be issued each year, in order to pursue the state's objective of managing the bighorn sheep resource on a sustained yield basis.

The collection of the necessary information to estimate option price and existence value involves the same considerations as valuing other nonmarket goods. Bohm draws the analogy by saying: "Thus, from a practical viewpoint, estimating option price does not add any new dimensions to the measurement problem that always exists for cases where an estimate of the consumer's surplus is required" (1975, p. 736).

Techniques recently developed for valuing nonmarket goods can be applied to the estimation of option price and existence value. A summary of this work including discussions of potential biases and issues of replication can be found in Schulze *et al.* (1981). A theoretical comparison and empirical cross check between contingent valuation and hedonic techniques can be found in Brookshire *et al.* (1982).

In the survey technique, a series of contingent markets are established. Initially, the respondent is presented with information pertaining to the current availability and the quality of the good under question. In some cases, it is necessary to present an institutional setting relevant to the contingent market but distinctly different from the actual current setting. From either the current or relevant institutional setting, a series of contingent markets are presented. Valuation of the good is obtained in each of these markets. A mechanism of payment is also specified for eliciting the bid. (See Brookshire *et al.* 1980, for a complete discussion of the contingent approach.)

The expected probability of future license availability is the "good" which individual respondents are bidding upon in the case of hunter option prices. For example, if the probability of license availability is a 25% chance of future availability, then the individual's bid will represent a Hicksian compensated measure of welfare associated with this chance of future license availability.[9]

We know of one previously published research effort attempting to estimate option and existence values (Greenley *et al.* 1981). A number of essential differences between our approach and the approach taken in that study must be pointed out. Greenley *et al.* (1981) utilized a survey instrument in which there is no explicit mechanism by which those who do not purchase the option to future preserved use of the natural environment are excluded from future use if the preserved natural environment is available. While Greenley *et al.* (1981) discuss "option values", it appears they measure some type of option price. Further serious questions in terms of potential free riders are raised by the survey. The approach reported here uses a contingent market in which an explicit exclusion mechanism is incorporated. Also, Greenley *et al.* (1981) did not examine empirically the influence of demand or supply uncertainty on the magnitude of the estimated values, while this paper does. As has been discussed, supply uncertainty is of critical importance. Finally, Greenley *et al.* utilized a dichotomous choice regarding the potential availability of a natural resource (1981). The difficulty is that an all-or-nothing approach is difficult to relate to preservation versus development choices.

The survey instrument employed to collect information for determining option price and existence value follows the basic contingent market structure. The respondent received information as to the causes of decreasing habitat and the notion of expanding current habitat. The respondent was informed that under existing conditions, the probability of any individual obtaining a hunting license in a year was 10% for bighorn sheep and zero for grizzly bear. Since Wyoming Game and Fish already excluded hunters from grizzly-bear and bighorn-sheep hunting, a similar mechanism was designed for those who did not wish to purchase the option for hunting.[10] Thus, a contingent market was established in that new hunting areas were proposed which would be made available for hunting either 5 or 15 years in the future.[11] However, an individual respondent was confronted with only one time horizon. Exclusion from the market was prescribed since payment beginning now and continuing every year was necessary to qualify the respondent to enter a drawing for licenses in the future. Thus free-riding was impossible in this context. Finally, the method of payment was specified as a "grizzly bear (bighorn sheep) stamp."[12] Each individual who participated in this program would pay a fixed annual amount and would enjoy the benefits of the program starting either 5 or 15 years hence and continuing into the future. Individuals did not get to choose which program they participated in. Those who did not pay were to be excluded from the benefits of the proposed purchase program. Thus a straightforward "How much are you willing to pay annually?" was set forth to the respondent for a specified time horizon at 4 probability levels.

Finally, the respondent was queried as to whether, if a license were obtained, he would definitely or only possibly hunt the species in question. This explored potential alternative levels of certainty of demand that the respondent attached to hunting if a license were obtained (i.e., either 1 or < 1), and allows an analysis of the influence of uncertain demand on the stated option price.

A second possible response to the survey instrument enabled collection of data for estimating existence value and observer option price. Early in the survey, the instrument identified those respondents who would never want to hunt the animal in question. A respondent who was certain not to be a hunter may still be willing to pay for the existence of grizzly bear or bighorn sheep or for the option to observe grizzly bear or bighorn sheep in the future. Therefore, the nonhunter was directed to answer a set of questions concerned with payments to preserve grizzly bear or bighorn sheep. In addition, this section of the survey inquired as to whether the individual expected to ever observe the species in question. If observation was expected, the bid has been interpreted as observer option price; if not, as existence value.

Since a respondent is presented with a contingent market that produces a given option in either 5 or 15 years, the numerical magnitudes of the response to the willingness-to-pay questions will represent the annualized value of the present-value benefit stream associated with a given option, assuming the individual must make an annual payment. This can be expressed with the following equations for the 5- and 15-year samples:

$$\hat{B}_5 = f(r) \sum_{t=5}^{T} \frac{B_t}{(1+r)^t} \qquad [4]$$

$$\hat{B}_{15} = f(r) \sum_{t=15}^{T} \frac{B_t}{(1 + r)^t} \qquad [5]$$

where

B_t = the annual benefits to the individual associated with a given option;
$\hat{B}_5$ = the annualized value associated with the 5-year sample;
$\hat{B}_{15}$ = the annualized value associated with the 15-year sample;
r = the respondent's discount rate;
$f(r)$ = an annualization formula;
t = the time period ($t = 0, 1, \ldots, T$), where 0 denotes the current period and T
the final planning period.

Since the respondent is being queried as to his willingness to pay for an increase in a valued good, the individual would be willing to pay, at most, B_t, which is the maximum annual value to the individual of obtaining a given option.[13] This implies that $\hat{B}_5$ and $\hat{B}_{15}$ represent annual payments for future benefits which are equal to the annualized value of the stream of expected future benefits.

Solving [4] and [5] for B_t and r and then dividing equation [4] by equation [5] and factoring out B_t yields:

$$\hat{B}_5 \sum_{t=15}^{T} \frac{1}{(1 + r)^t} = \hat{B}_{15} \sum_{t=5}^{T} \frac{1}{(1 + r)^t} \qquad [6]$$

This expression can be used to infer an estimate of the discount rate, r, used by the respondent in making the bid, assuming that individual preferences are identical and utilizing the mean values of the sample bids in each of the samples as estimates for $\hat{B}_5$ and $\hat{B}_{15}$. With an estimate of r, the annual benefit to the individual associated with a given option (B_t) can be estimated.

A necessary assumption is choosing the value used for T, the planning horizon. Different values for T will influence the estimated value of the discount rate. However, the estimated discount rate will converge towards a maximum as T increases. It was presumed $T = \infty$ since the contingent market structure was addressing the question of expanding current habitat and maintaining the expansion for all future hunting. This will make the estimate of r an upper bound, which, of course, must be kept in mind when interpreting the results. Assuming the planning horizon is infinite, equation [6] can be rewritten as:[14]

$$\hat{B}_5 (1 + r)^5 = \hat{B}_{15} (1 + r)^{15} \qquad [7]$$

Expression [7] will be used in the discount rate estimation reported below. This will bias the estimates by providing an upper bound to the estimated discount rate.[15]

EMPIRICAL ANALYSIS

Table 9.1 summarizes the estimated mean values and standard errors for the option prices related to the alternative probabilities of future supply associated with certain or uncertain hunting demand.[16] There are several influences on the pattern of these estimated option prices that are interesting.

Estimating option prices and existence values

The most obvious influence on the pattern of bids would be from the alternative probabilities of future supply of the wildlife resource for hunting. A priori expectations would be that an individual would be willing to pay a greater amount of money for the option to hunt grizzly bear or bighorn sheep in the future as the promised probability of future availability of the resource increases. One would expect that a plot of the relationship between supply probability and mean bid would represent an increasing function. Such a pattern is, in fact, present in the data. Mean bids for the option to hunt grizzly bear or bighorn sheep in the future do increase as the probability of future availability increases. The magnitude of the bids reported in Table 9.1 from the lowest value of $9.70 for certain grizzly-bear hunters in the 15-year sample to $29.16 for uncertain bighorn sheep hunters in the 15-year sample.

Uncertainty in demand may also influence the pattern of bids. The influence of demand uncertainty can be examined by comparing uncertain with certain bids for each time horizon, i.e., 5 or 15 years. A priori, the certain demand bids are expected to exceed the uncertain demand bids, given the time horizon. Given a probability of supply, uncertain demand implies a greater degree of uncertainty and therefore a smaller willingness to pay for a specified option than would be the case if demand were certain. In other words, a specified probability of future availability should be of more value to the certain demander than to the uncertain demander. However, this pattern is not generally reflected by the estimated bids. Only in the case of the 5-year sample for grizzly-bear hunters do the certain bids exceed the uncertain bids. Furthermore, in all cases the estimated means are statistically different at the 99% level of significance.

The time horizon over which the option prices are estimated can also be expected to influence the pattern of bids. Equations [4] and [5] suggest that the estimated option price associated with the 5-year time horizon ($\hat{B}_5$) should exceed the option price for the 15-year time horizon ($\hat{B}_{15}$). If individuals respond with the annualized value of their present value benefit streams, then, in general, the estimated option price for the 5-year contingent markets will exceed the estimated option price in the 15-year contingent markets. This expected time-related pattern of bids is reflected in the data with respect to the certain bids in both the grizzly-bear and bighorn-sheep cases. However, this pattern is not generally reflected in the uncertain bids. In only 3 of 16 possible comparisons of uncertain bids do the 5-year time horizon bids exceed the 15-year time horizon bids, and for two of those cases the estimated means are not statistically different.[17] It is unclear why the expected time influence would be observed in the case of certain demand and not in the case of uncertain demand.

Since this sample of data was obtained by a mail survey, the potential for self-selection bias may exist and contribute to unexpected response patterns.[18] Although the potential respondents were randomly selected, the actual returned responses may be nonrandom. That is, an individual's choice of whether to respond or not is a function of the importance to the individual of hunting grizzly bear or bighorn sheep in the future. If so, then uncertain demanders might be less likely to respond than certain demanders, and that uncertain demanders with a greater willingness to pay for a given probability of supply are more likely to respond than uncertain demanders with a smaller willingness to pay. This would result in the distribution of uncertain bids being skewed upwards. This possibility may explain both the unexpected pattern of time influences as well as the earlier pattern of certain and uncertain demands.

Table 9.1 Mean bids ($) and standard errors of the option bids for certain and uncertain hunters.

Probability of future availability	Grizzly bear				Bighorn sheep			
	Certain		Uncertain		Certain		Uncertain	
	B_5 (5 years)	B_{15} (15 years)	B_5 (5 years)	B_{15} (15 years)	B_5 (5 years)	B_{15} (15 years)	B_5 (5 years)	B_{15} (15 years)
90%	21.50* (3.05) (247)	15.50 (2.06) (252)	16.90 (2.92) (65)	25.90 (6.16) (47)	22.90 (2.10) (342)	17.50 (.179) (300)	27.00 (5.26) (54)	29.16 (6.92) (44)
75%	19.00 (2.84) (245)	14.05 (1.96) (250)	14.12 (2.44) (65)	21.70 (5.38) (47)	19.86 (1.81) (342)	15.44 (1.63) (300)	25.69 (5.24) (54)	24.83 (5.80) (44)
50%	15.10 (2.52) (245)	11.40 (1.78) (250)	12.08 (2.22) (65)	19.47 (5.23) (47)	16.53 (1.59) (342)	13.34 (1.54) (300)	23.47 (5.19) (54)	20.52 (5.41) (44)
25%	12.30 (2.42) (245)	9.70 (1.70) (250)	10.00 (2.22) (63)	17.87 (5.17) (47)	13.26 (1.46) (341)	11.18 (1.46) (296)	16.65 (3.96) (53)	16.26 (4.85) (44)

* Mean bid, standard errors of the means and the sample size, respectively.

Estimating option prices and existence values

Also a priori expectations regarding the nature of demand uncertainty might be incorrect due to insufficient knowledge. Schmalensee (1972) has shown that assumptions regarding comparability of utility when demand is certain versus when demand is uncertain will influence whether option value is positive, negative, or zero. Perhaps we cannot know the actual relationship without empirical observation, and the empirical results here may suggest this. Further, if an individual is uncertain concerning future demand regarding the exercise of the option to hunt if obtained, then a longer time horizon is possibly of value. That is, they value the longer decision horizon in formulating plans and decisions. Such an influence might offset the influence of discounting postulated by equations [4] and [5] on the previous page, even to an extent that the uncertain bid for the 15-year sample could be larger than the uncertain bid for the 5-year sample. Unfortunately, it is impossible to point to a single explanation for the unexpected bid patterns.

One final observation should be made concerning the estimated option prices reported. In Section 2 it was assumed that an individual hunter had risk averse preferences, and such preferences should be reflected by a functional relationship between option price and supply uncertainty that is increasing but at a decreasing rate (see Krutilla *et al.* 1972). The curves derived from this data do not generally suggest such a relationship. On the contrary, the plotted relationship between estimated option price and supply probability seem to suggest risk-taking preferences. Certainly such a result was unexpected, but there should be no cause for concern. After all, the assumption of risk aversion is necessary for positive option *value* interpreted as a risk aversion premium, given certain preferences. If individuals are risk takers instead, then option value would be negative, given certain preferences. Of course, for assumptions to be useful they should be confirmed by empirical experience. The empirical results presented here suggest that the latter case is a serious possibility. In any case, option price is the appropriate value for estimation, regardless of preferences.

Returning to the time influence on the certain bids, the discussion of equations [4]–[7] implies discount rates can be estimated. Table 9.2 presents estimated discount rates by the time pattern of certain bids. Equation [7] is used to derive these estimates. Discount rates for the uncertain bids have not been reported due to the unexplained bid patterns just discussed. Table 9.2 presents the results of estimating the implied discount rates associated with the certain and uncertain option bids using expression [7]. The estimated range of discount rates for the certain option bids for grizzly bear and bighorn sheep is .98% to 3.35% for the alternative future supply probability levels.

Table 9.2 Estimated discount rates for certain grizzly bear and bighorn sheep hunters.

Probability of future availability	Grizzly bear	Bighorn sheep
90%	3.35%	2.70%
75%	3.05%	2.55%
50%	2.83%	2.18%
25%	2.43%	.98%

The estimated discount rates for the certain hunters can be used to estimate the annual benefit, B_t, associated with each option. B_t is estimated with either of the following two expressions, assuming $T = \infty$.

$$\hat{B}_t = \hat{B}_5 (1 + r)^5, \qquad t = 5, \ldots, \infty \qquad [8]$$

$$\hat{B}_t = \hat{B}_{15} (1 + r)^{15}, \qquad t = 15, \ldots, \infty \qquad [9]$$

Table 9.3 presents the estimated annual benefits indicating a declining pattern as the probability of future availability declines. For the 90% availability the annual value for bighorn sheep is estimated to be about \$26.10 to \$13.70 for the 25% availability.

Table 9.3 Estimated annual net benefits (B_t) to the certain demanders of each of the options.

Probability of future availability	Grizzly bear	Bighorn sheep
90%	\$25.40	\$26.10
75%	\$22.00	\$22.50
50%	\$17.30	\$18.40
25%	\$13.90	\$13.90

Many factors that would influence the magnitude of the option price have been examined. To distinguish the effects on the bids, the following variables are introduced into an OLS linear regression: (1) the certainty level of hunting in the event of obtaining a license, (2) the time horizon for obtaining a license, (3) individual's income level, (4) probability of obtaining a license, and (5) the individual's age. The results are presented in Table 9.4. Both individual bid curves and mean bid curves were estimated.

Examining the individual bid curve results first, both the bighorn and grizzly bear equations are significant at the .01 confidence level. For the individual grizzly bear expression the coefficients for age, income, and chance levels of obtaining a license are significant at the .01 confidence level and the coefficient for certainty (i.e., will definitely hunt or not) is significant at the .10 confidence level. The individual bid equation for bighorn sheep results in the coefficients for the time horizon for obtaining a license, the probability of obtaining a license and the individual's age being significant at the .01 confidence level. A series of analyses of variance tests on the different variables was conducted. However, the results were not significant. Further, an array of other socioeconomic variables (i.e., marital status, education level, rural or nonrural, and length of residence in Wyoming) were tested and found not to be significant. Finally, a test of mean values for the certain and uncertain hunters were conducted in order to determine if any socioeconomic differences existed between the two samples groups. We failed to reject in all cases the null hypothesis that the mean values were the same for the certain and uncertain hunters.

Estimating option prices and existence values

Table 9.4 Estimated bid equations.

Dependent variable	Estimated coefficients[1]						R² N (# obs) F values[7]	Standard error Mean squared error
	Intercept	Certain[2]	Years[3]	Income[4]	Chance[5]	Age[6]		
Individual bid for grizzly bear	12.77 (3.43)**	5.08 (2.09)***	-.23 (.15)	.0002 (.00006)**	13.85 (3.02)**	-.19 (.06)**	.03 1743 9.37	31.23 975.43
Individual bid for bighorn sheep	23.59 (3.31)**	-.38 (2.15)	-.46 (.14)**	.00008 (.00006)	-.27 (2.89)***	.03 (.06)**	30.82 1858 11.91	949.78
Mean bid for grizzly bear	24.27 (4.10)**	1.79 (1.73)	.02 (.17)	.0003 (.00007)**	14.05 (3.47)**	-.55 (.06)**	.39 184 22.93	11.65 135.62
Mean bid for bighorn sheep	22.78 (4.44)**	.87 (1.89)	.11 (.19)	-.00007** (.00008)	10.40 (3.82)**	-.35 (.06)**	.18 188 7.95	12.96 168.08

[1] Standard errors are reported in parentheses.
[2] Given the individual's bid, a value of 0 if he definitely would hunt if a license were obtained, and value of 11 uncertain.
[3] A value of 5 if the time horizon for obtaining a license was 5 years, or 15 if the time horizon were 15 years.
[4] The income for an individual in the individual bid equations or the mean income of the class the individual falls in for the mean bid equations.
[5] Represents the probability of obtaining a license: 90%, 75%, 50% and 25%.
[6] The age for an individual in the individual bid equations or the mean age of the class the individual falls in for the mean bid equations.
[7] All equations are significant at the .01 level of confidence.
 ** Denotes significance at the .01 level of confidence.
 *** Denotes significance at the .10 level of confidence.

123

In order to estimate the mean bid relationship, the sample was divided into four income categories:

Income category	Income range ($/year)	Mean income ($/year)
1	0–11,999	6,000
2	12,000–19,999	16,000
3	20,000–26,999	23,000
4	27,000 and above	———

That is, the data set was partitioned first by the above income classes and then further by whether the individual was certain or not (0 if definitely would hunt, 1 if uncertain). The rationale for estimating a mean bid curve follows that of Bradford (1970) and Brookshire *et al.* (1980). Both mean bid equations were significant at the .01 confidence level. The coefficients for income, chance of obtaining a license, and the age variables are significant at the .01 confidence level for the mean bighorn sheep equation. For the mean bid grizzly-bear equation the coefficient for chance of obtaining a license and age variables are significant at the .01 confidence level.

The bid equations in Table 9.4 represent an attempt to understand influences on the bid. Of special interest is that in only the individual bid equation for bighorn sheep is the coefficient significant for the variable depicting the time horizon in obtaining the license. A priori we would expect the time horizon to play a prominent role in the determination of the bid. Additionally, whether the individual would or would not hunt and income levels also would be expected to influence the bid. However, this does not appear to be the case. In contrast, the chance of obtaining a license, as well as the individual's age, do consistently influence the bid. Future research might explore these points.

Turning now to existence value, Table 9.5 presents means and standard errors for the existence value bids and the observer option price bids. These bids are consistent with expectations in that all the 5-year bids exceed the 15-year bids. With respect to the relative magnitudes between those respondents who feel that they will probably see one of these animals in its natural habitat and those who think they will not, no a priori expectations are made. The mean bids for observer option prices are in the range of $20 for both grizzly bear and bighorn sheep, regardless of the time element. The estimated existence values show more variation, with $24.00 mean existence value for grizzly bear in the 5-year sample compared with $15.20 in the 15-year sample, while the bighorn sheep results are significantly lower, $7.40 and $6.90, respectively. The estimated discount rates associated with the grizzly-bear and bighorn-sheep preservation bids range from .35% to 4.68% respectively, assuming again that $T = \infty$.

CONCLUDING COMMENTS

It is now agreed that option price represents the largest sure payment that will be made to secure an option for future use (Bishop 1982; Graham 1981). Thus, of the various sure payment concepts – option price, option value, and expected consumer's surplus – option price is the appropriate one for evaluation of future use benefits.[19] To state it another way, in cases where expected surplus differs from option price, the proper valuation concept is option price.

Table 9.5 Mean existence value bids and observer option bids.

	Grizzly bear			Bighorn sheep		
	5 year	Discount rates	15 year	5 year rates	Discount	15 year
Mean observer option bid	$21.80 (2.6)[1] N=223[2]	r=.4%	$21.00 (2.9) N=205	$23.00 (2.2) N=302	r=2.5%	$18.00 (1.7) N=265
Mean existence bid	$24.00 (5.0) N=153	r=4.7%	$15.20 (3.1) N=170	$ 7.40 (2.1) N=110	r=.6%	$ 6.90 (1.7) N=108

[1] Standard error
[2] Sample size

Since price-revealing options markets are seldom operational, the analyst often faces something of a dilemma: Is it best to project future use from past use patterns, thus generating an estimate of expected surplus to serve as an approximation for option price (as Schmalensee 1975, suggests)? Or, is it best to estimate option price using some form of contingent market in an experimental or survey context (as Bohm 1975, suggests)? Taking Schmalensee's approach would expose one to the unreliability of future use projections. In addition, it would leave one uncertain as to the sign as well as the magnitude of the error introduced by substituting expected surplus for option price, in the case where future demand is uncertain. Where only supply is uncertain, we can be assured that $OP \geq ES$ for all but the risk takers, but uncertainty as to the magnitude of the difference remains. Taking Bohm's approach would expose one to questions about the reliability of those contingent markets that are not strictly incentive-compatible. With regard to these questions the evidence is incomplete and somewhat mixed (see, for example, Bishop and Heberlein 1979, and Brookshire et al. 1982).

In this study, we took the latter approach, estimating option price in a contingent market. The focus was on uncertainty of supply: specifically, we estimated willingness to pay (i.e., the compensating measure of value) for programs that would increase the certainty of supply of game populations, but never entirely eliminate supply uncertainty. The primary focus was on option price for hunting opportunities, but other values were also estimated: observer option price for certain nonhunters and existence values for certain nonobservers.

Our study demonstrates the feasibility of conceptually sound empirical estimation of nonuser values, using contingent markets. There is some, but nevertheless incomplete, evidence that these contingent markets performed reliably: estimated prices were of plausible magnitude, as were the inferred marginal time-preference rates of respondents, and individual willingness to pay exhibited and the expected relationships with respondent's income and age, the promised probability of supply and the waiting period until the supply was made available. On the other hand, some unexpected results were obtained for uncertain demanders of hunting opportunities. It remains unresolved as to whether these apparent anomalies can be attributed to problems with contingent markets, relatively small samples, or self-selection bias, which especially afflicts voluntary-response mail surveys. Finally, we have no evidence in the form of cross-technique comparisons of the kind reported in other contexts by Bishop and Heberlein (1979) and Brookshire et al. (1982).

In retrospect, we feel a guarded optimism about the use of contingent markets to estimate option prices. If we were to concede that the estimates generated in such markets are necessarily indicative rather than reasonably precise (and the empirical evidence on this point is still sketchy), we would nevertheless argue that indicative estimates of the conceptually valid measure of uncertain future use values represent a useful contribution to the information base for natural resource allocation decisions.

NOTES

1. Double-counting would, of course, occur if the value of projected future use at the proposed level of provision was added to the aggregate option price of the proposed increment. But, it is unlikely that the analyst would fall into this trap, since it would involve two conscious attempts to generate estimates for the proposed level of provision. One would surely become aware of the redundancy!

2. Given that Schmalensee (1972) has utilized a definition of risk aversion not generally used in standard microeconomic textbooks, it is appropriate to emphasize that we are following the standard treatment. That is, a risk averse individual has a concave expected

Estimating option prices and existence values

utility function (see, for example, Varian 1978, p. 108). Of course, regardless of the terminology, it should be noted that option value will be positive for the case discussed here if the expected utility function is concave.

3. Use of wildlife resources can be consumptive (i.e., hunting/harvesting activities) and nonconsumptive (i.e., photographic/observation). Thus, an option value may arise for either use due to spillover impacts from many non-wildlife-related human consumption and production activities, creating uncertain supply conditions. See Bishop for an additional discussion on supply uncertainty (1982).

4. Also, Schmalensee has noted that the ambiguity in the sign of option value depends on the relationship between utility mappings when the natural resource is demanded and when it is not (1972). Perhaps the impression has been left, therefore, that option value cannot be theoretically defended in general. On the other hand, examining supply uncertainty suggests that the concept of option value is meaningful.

5. Krutilla and Fisher (1975) have discussed existence value by referring to individuals who have such values as "vicarious consumers."

6. There are some private nonprofit activities that are providing for existence values, for example, Save the Blue Whale Fund and the Nature Conservancy. However, the free-rider problem suggests that even when private activities provide for public goods, they will generally be underprovided and the revealed values will therefore inaccurately reflect the social value of such goods.

7. Existence, in the case at hand, pertains to a regional or subregional phenomenon.

8. The initial cause of the decline of bighorn sheep was disease. However, the populations did not reestablish themselves. Thus some of the original habitat can be viewed as lost due to man's increasing presence.

9. In the terminology used by Schmalensee (1972), this bid would be an estimate of the "compensating option price," which is associated with a .25 probability of future supply.

10. Approximately 3,000 bighorn-sheep and grizzly-bear survey instruments were mailed to Wyoming resident elk, deer, and antelope hunters. Information pertaining to activity values associated with these animals was also obtained. The sample was drawn randomly from a list of hunting-license holders. Coupled with a follow-up mailing, approximately 25–30% of the survey instruments were returned.

11. This assumption of availability in 5 or 15 years complicates the analysis as will be seen in the following section. However, in order to make the contingent market realistic, such an assumption appears to be necessary. Respondents could not be expected to believe that making a payment this year would result in a substantially larger number of grizzly bear, for example, next year.

12. This follows the very successful duck stamp program for purchasing and preserving wetlands in the United States.

13. It is assumed that B_t is zero for years 1 through 5 and 15, respectively, and positive thereafter.

14. This expression results from annualizing the present value of the benefit stream to perpetuity which can be written for the 5-year sample as:

$$B_5 = \frac{B_t/r}{(1 + r)^5}$$

15. It might also be argued that hunters may have interdependent utility functions, which have the utility functions of their children influencing their own utility functions. In such a case, part of a hunter's option bid may include a value for keeping open the option of his descendants as well. This would then imply a planning horizon long enough that the assumption of an infinite horizon would not bias the estimates to any "large" extent. This issue, however, was not specifically addressed in the survey.

16. An anomaly of the results is that 39% and 28% of the certain demanders of grizzly-bear and bighorn-sheep bids, respectively, were zero. While for the uncertain demanders only .01% and .03% were zero bids. The zero bids were not eliminated from the analysis.

17. Note that in all the other comparisons of option price, between the 5-year sample means and the 15-year sample means, whether for the certain or uncertain cases, the means are statistically different at the 99% confidence level.
18. See J.J. Heckman (1979) for a discussion of self-selection bias and its implications for estimation of behavioral relationships in economics.
19. In an interesting recent analysis, Graham (1981) introduces the possibility that some pattern of contingent payments may exist that generates greater aggregate willingness to pay.

REFERENCES

Bishop, R.C., and Heberlein, T.A. (1979) "Measuring Values of Extra-Market Goods: Are Indirect Measures Biased?" *American Journal of Agricultural Economics* **61** (Dec.): 926–30.
—— (1982) "Option Value: An Exposition and Extension." *Land Economics* **58** (Feb.): 1–15.
Bohm, P. (1975) "Option Demand and Consumer's Surplus: Comment." *American Economic Review* **65** (Sept.): 733–36.
Bradford, D.F. (1970) "Benefit-Cost Analysis and Demand Curves for Public Goods." *Kyklos* **23**: 775–91.
Brookshire, D., Randall, A., and Stoll, J. (1980) "Valuing Increments and Decrements in Natural Resource Service Flows." *American Journal of Agricultural Economics* **63** (Aug.).
——, Thayer, M., Schulze, W., and d'Arge, R. (1982) "Valuing Public Goods: A Comparison of the Survey and Hedonic Approaches." *American Economic Review* **72** (Mar.): 165–77.
Cicchetti, C.J., and Freeman, A.M., III. (1971) "Option Demand and Consumer Surplus: Further Comment." *Quarterly Journal of Economics* **85**: 528–39.
Endangered Species Act of 1973. (1973) Public Law 93–250 in *United States Statutes at Large, 93rd Congress, 1st Session* **87**: 884–903.
Graham, D.A. (1981) "Cost-Benefit Analysis under Uncertainty." *American Economic Review* **71**: 715–25.
Greenley, D.A., Walsh, R.G., and Young, R.A. (1981) "Option Value: Empirical Evidence from a Case Study of Recreation and Water Quality." *Quarterly Journal of Economics* **96** (Nov.): 657–73.
Heckmann, J.J. (1979) "Sample Selection Bias as a Specification Error." *Econometrica* **47** (Jan.): 153–61.
Krutilla, J.V. (1967) "Conservation Reconsidered." *American Economic Review* **57** (Sept.): 777–86.
——, Cicchetti, C.J., Freeman, A.M., III; and Russell, C.S. (1972) "Observations on the Economics of Irreplaceable Assets." In *Environmental Quality Analysis: Theory and Method in Social Science,* eds. A.V. Kneese and B.T. Bower.
——, and Fisher, A.C. (1975) *The Economics of Natural Environments.* Baltimore: The Johns Hopkins University Press.
Long, M.F. (1967) "Collective Consumption Services of Individual Consumption Goods: Comment." *Quarterly Journal of Economics* **81(2)**: 351–52.
Schmalensee, R. (1972) "Option Demand and Consumer's Surplus: Valuing Price Changes under Uncertainty." *American Economic Review* **62**: 813–24.
—— (1975) "Option Demand and Consumer's Surplus: Reply." *American Economic Review* 65(4) (Sept.): 737–9.
Schulze, W., d'Arge, R. and Brookshire, D. (1981) "Valuing Environmental Commodities: Some Recent Experiments." *Land Economics* **57** (May): 151–72.
Varian, H.R. (1978) *Microeconomic Analysis.* New York: W.W. Norton and Company, Inc.
Weisbrod, B.A. (1964) "Collective-Consumption Services of Individual-Consumption Goods." *Quarterly Journal of Economics* **78** (Aug.): 471–77.

Chapter 10

The marginal value of job safety: a contingent valuation study

Shelby Gerking, Menno De Haan and William Schulze

Marginal value of safety estimates from labor market data generally have been obtained using empirical hedonic wage models. As discussed more fully in reviews by Smith (1979), Marin and Psacharopoulos (1982), Dickens (1984), and Dillingham (1985), these estimates are marked by wide divergence and conspicuous anomalies. Reasons cited for this outcome include problems of measuring fatal and nonfatal job-related accident risks, failure to adequately control for human capital and workplace characteristics, and differential bargaining strength of unionized workers. While the importance of such factors should not be minimized, exclusive focus on them draws attention away from another serious issue. Gegax, Gerking, and Schulze (1987) argue that there are many types of jobs in which fatal accident risks do not enter the production function. In this situation, the marginal product of risk is zero, no hedonic gradient exists, and the value of alterations in safety must be assessed in settings other than the labor market and/or using alternatives to the hedonic price method.

This article estimates the marginal value of safety by directly asking respondents in a national random-sample mail survey about their willingness to substitute money for changes in job-related fatal accident risks. Two versions of this approach, referred to as contingent valuation, are considered: respondents stated either willingness to pay for a specified reduction in job-related fatal accident risks, or additional compensation required to willingly accept an increase in such risks. Thus, worker preferences for safety are directly measured, in contrast to the hedonic price method which focuses on the locus of tangency points between worker indifference curves and firm isoprofit curves in the wage–risk plane. Viscusi and O'Connor (1984) previously elicited willingness to accept contingent values for nonfatal job accident risks in their study of chemical workers. The present study apparently is the first to obtain in a labor market context (1) contingent values for fatal risks, and (2) willingness to pay, as contrasted with willingness to accept, values to avoid those risks. Numerous contingent valuation studies, however, recently have been conducted in related settings such as traffic safety (Jones-Lee, Hammerton, and Philips, 1985), water quality (Desvousges, Smith, and Fisher, 1987) and exposure to toxic wastes (Smith and Desvousges, 1987). Cummings, Brookshire, and Schulze (1986) critically evaluate uses of contingent valuation in environmental benefit assessment.

The following discussion also considers three aspects of the contingent valuation data to sharpen interpretation of the marginal value of safety estimates. First, contingent values are obtained for small changes in risks of job-related fatal accidents *perceived* by respondents. Measurement of perceived risk is a central issue in computing marginal value of safety estimates – one that has failed, with few exceptions (see, for example, Viscusi and O'Connor, 1984), to receive sufficient attention in existing literature. Psychologists have long argued that the cognitive process used to form risk beliefs is complex and often leads to perceptions that are inconsistent with objective measures of risk (Kahneman and Tversky, 1979, 1984; Lichtenstein et al., 1978) Second, relationships are analyzed between respondents' marginal safety values and their income and socioeconomic/demographic characteristics (e.g., race, gender, union membership status, education). Parallel analyses often are undertaken in hedonic wage–risk studies (see, for example, Thaler and Rosen, 1976; Viscusi, 1978; Olson, 1981; and Worrall and Butler, 1983). Yet, the present study provides a unique opportunity to examine these interactions from the standpoint of worker preferences alone. Third, relationships are analyzed between marginal safety values and initial levels of risk faced. In contrast to Smith and Desvousges (1987), results presented below show a significant positive association between these two variables.

The remainder of the article is divided into three sections. Section 1 discusses the mail survey data. Section 2 analyzes contingent values in detail and shows their relationship to other variables measured in the mail survey. Implications and conclusions are drawn out in section 3.

MAIL SURVEY DATA

Empirical work in this study uses data collected by national mail survey during summer, 1984. Implementation of the mail survey closely followed Dillman's (1978) total design method. For example, care was taken in preparing cover letters and survey materials sent to respondents. Postcard reminders were sent eight days after the initial mailing. A replacement questionnaire and cover letter was sent to everyone who had not responded within three weeks. A more complete description of the survey methodology, questionnaire pretesting, and copies of all materials can be found in Gegax et al. (1985).

Survey materials were sent to (1) a simple random sample of 3000 U.S. households, and (2) 3000 additional households randomly selected from 105 counties that have disproportionately large concentrations of high-risk industries. In the second component, the sample included an equal number of households (750) from the northeast, northcentral, south, and west regions of the U.S.[1] Of 6000 questionnaires mailed, 749 (12.5%) were returned as undeliverable and 2103 were returned in completed form. Thus, the net response rate was about 40%.

Although the response rate was reasonably good in the light of length and complexity of the questionnaire, it does raise questions about possible biases in the resulting sample. A general problem with mail surveys is that better-educated, higher-income individuals tend to respond with greater frequency than other groups. The present survey is no exception. Dickie and Gerking (1988), who use these data to test for interregional wage equality, note that in a restricted sample of full-time workers very similar to the one analyzed in section 2, 6.8% did not complete high school, as compared with 16.5% of employed civilians aged 25 or older in the U.S. Also, 43.9% of workers were employed as managers or professionals as compared with 26.4% in the general U.S. population. Therefore, a cost of using the mail survey approach may be an undersampling of low-human-capital-low-income workers. If job safety is a normal good, then workers in high-risk jobs may be underrepresented in the present sample.

Three types of information were obtained from the head of each responding household. First, the survey developed two measures of each household head's perceived risk of a fatal accident at work. With respect to the first measure, respondents were shown a list of 13 major causes of death at work (e.g., motor vehicle accident, electrocution, gun shot, explosion) and asked to rank the likelihood of each occurring to them on an ordinal integer scale with 1 labeled "Could Never Happen" and 5 labeled "Most Likely to Happen." This exercise encouraged respondents to review various sources of accidental death risk on their own job and to evaluate which, if any, of these sources posed a credible threat. The variable RISK1 then was computed for each respondent by averaging his rankings across sources of perceived job-related fatality risk. Immediately after providing information needed for RISK1, respondents were shown an illustration of a ladder (see Figure 10.1) with ten equally spaced steps. For reasons elaborated below, each step denoted the number of annual job-related fatal accidents per 4000 workers. Seven example occupations were placed on the ladder according to their average levels of job-related risk of death ranging from relatively safe jobs such as schoolteachers to more dangerous jobs such as lumberjacks. Respondents then specified the step number, which defined the variable RISK2, that most closely described their risk of job-related accidental death. It is worth emphasizing that both RISK1 and RISK2 measure *perceived* risks of accidental death on the job and may be viewed as disaggregated versions of the DANGER variable used by Viscusi (1979).

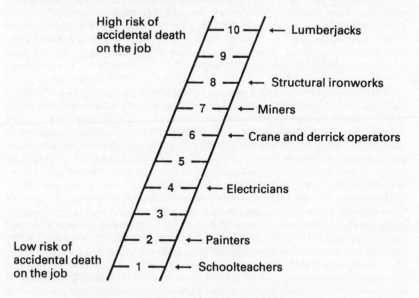

Figure 10.1 Risk ladder shown to survey respondents.

131

Procedures used to construct RISK2 are worth further elaboration. The risk ladder scale and six of the seven example occupations are based on data presented in Thaler and Rosen (1976, p. 288). These data measure extra deaths per 100,000 policy years of life insurance underwriting experience after subtracting expected deaths by age and occupation based on sample records and standard life tables. For example, in the Thaler and Rosen sample, lumbermen had 256 extra deaths per 100,000 policy years (or approximately ten extra deaths per 4000 policy years). Consequently, this example occupation was placed on the tenth rung of the risk ladder. Similar calculations were made for structural ironworkers, miners, cranemen and derrickmen, electricians, and painters, and these occupations were approximately placed on the ladder. Schoolteachers, an occupational group not considered by Thaler and Rosen, were arbitrarily assigned to the first rung of the ladder.

The mean of RISK2 in the sample analyzed in the following section is 2.64. Thus, the average perceived risk of death was less than one in 2000. This comparatively large figure may be partly an outcome of using the Thaler and Rosen data to calibrate the risk ladder. Marin and Psacharopoulos (1982) point out that if occupational and nonoccupational death risks are positively correlated, then the Thaler and Rosen data would overestimate occupational death risks. Also, the comparatively high mean value may indicate that respondents overperceived fatal accident risks. Bureau of Labor Statistics (U.S. Department of Labor, 1986) data on actual fatal accidents by industry indicate death probabilities on the order of one worker in 5000 to 10,000 per year. Reinforcing the point on overperception of risk is the fact that, as previously noted, high-income, high-human-capital individuals are overrepresented in the sample, implying an underrepresentation of workers in high-risk jobs.

The second type of information collected pertains to the contingent valuation analysis. Half of the surveys asked how large an increase in annual wages would induce respondents to voluntarily work at the same job if risk of accidental death were one step higher on the ladder than where they placed their initial assessment. The other half of the surveys asked how large a decrease in annual wages respondents willingly would forego if their job-related risk of death were moved one step lower on the ladder. Thus, the former question asks for willingness to accept, the latter asks for willingness to pay, and both make use of the ladder used to construct RISK2. For the contingent valuation questions, then, respondents had to assess for themselves how much incremental risk was involved in a one-step move on the ladder. The only subjective way they would have to understand this change in risk would be to *imagine* the threats involved to workers in the various example jobs used on the ladder. Therefore, the quality of marginal value of safety estimates obtained from the survey depends critically on an understanding of the change in risk presented.[2]

To answer the valuation question, respondents marked one of 37 boxes denoting dollar amounts ranging from $0 to more than $6000 that most closely approximated willingness to pay or willingness to accept for a one-step movement on the risk ladder. However, individuals receiving the willingness-to-pay version whose initial job risk assessment was placed on the first rung of the ladder, and individuals receiving the willingness-to-accept version whose initial job risk assessment was placed on the tenth rung, were unable to make this one-step move. As a consequence, these willingness-to-pay respondents were instructed to bid on movement from the second to the first rung and willingness-to-accept respondents were asked how much money they would require to induce them to move from rung nine to rung ten. Of the willingness-to-pay respondents included in the final data set (the composition of which is discussed below), 50.9% placed their initial level of job risk on the first rung of the ladder – a result that indicates that the range of risks depicted may have been too narrow. Correspondingly, 1.2% of the willingness-to-accept respondents placed their initial risk level on the tenth rung of the ladder.

Third, the survey also measures respondents' human capital, workplace, and socioeconomic characteristics. Key variables used in this study are (1) years of schooling, (2) whether head is a union member, (3) years of age, (4) race, (5) gender, and (6) annual labor earnings. More precise definitions of variables used in the analysis are presented in Table 10.1 in section 2.

As previously indicated, completed questionnaires were received from 2103 respondents. For several reasons, however, not all of this information could be used in the analysis. Responses from 872 retired or unemployed individuals were excluded, since the job risk and labor earnings questions did not apply to them. Additionally, responses from 32 individuals who did not answer the contingent valuation questions were dropped. Also excluded were 338 individuals who did not supply key information related to contingent values, such as labor earnings and initial level of job risk faced. These restrictions reduced the original number of respondents to a sample size of 861 observations.

ANALYZING CONTINGENT VALUES

Mean contingent valuation bids for a one-step move on the risk ladder are $665 for the willingness-to-pay questionnaires and $1705 for the willingness-to-accept version. Multiplying these values by 4000 yields marginal value of safety estimates of $2.66 million and $6.82 million for two subsamples. Both values are significantly greater than zero using a t-test. Thus, the contingent values should not be automatically dismissed as purely random or ill-considered responses to a hypothetical question. Also, the distribution of both willingness-to-pay and willingness-to-accept responses are positively skewed with medians less than means. Partially responsible for this outcome is the comparatively large number of zero bids: 47.4% of the willingness-to-pay contingent values were zero and the corresponding figure for willingness-to-accept contingent values was 23.2%. This clustering of bids at zero may reflect the previously mentioned narrow range of risks shown on the ladder. Alternatively, it may mean that some workers do not bother to calculate small positive bids and simply report zero instead. A decision to edit or deny the value of small risk reductions in certain situations is in fact a rational response to the innumerable risks which are present in daily life. Only some risks can receive attention given limited resources. Thus, the many zero bids likely reflect a prior decision by respondents to edit their own job-related risks.

Notice that the mean willingness-to-accept estimate of the marginal value of safety exceeds that obtained using the willingness-to-pay approach by a factor of approximately 2.5. This finding is similar to results reported by Knetsch and Sinden (1984), Brookshire and Coursey (1987), Coursey, Hovis, and Schulze (1987), and Viscusi, Magat, and Huber (1987) showing that willingness-to-accept contingent values are larger than those obtained in a willingness-to-pay framework. Additionally, it is consistent with the observation that people are reluctant to accept involuntary risks. Since labor markets are voluntary institutions, it may well be the case that hedonic studies of wages and risk reveal willingness-to-pay values.

Table 10.1 Two-limit Tobit estimates from two subsamples: dependent variable is the contingent valuation bid.

Explanatory variable	Definition	Subsample estimates			
		Willingness to pay		Willingness to accept	
CONSTANT		-2570.28 (-2.469)	-788.66 (-0.955)	448.63 (0.386)	2218.71 (2.065)
EARN	Labor earnings from respondent's main job in 1983	0.0217 (2.885)	0.0272 (3.055)	0.0228 (2.982)	0.0249 (3.249)
RISK1	Perceived risk of job-related fatal accidents from 13 causes	630.38 (2.462)	—	690.36 (2.850)	—
LOWRISK	1 if RISK 1 is less than or equal to its mean value; 0 otherwise	—	-783.99 (-2.228)	—	-597.51 (-1.708)
RACE	1 if white; 0 otherwise	-1257.20 (-2.212)	-1281.24 (-2.269)	-546.04 (-0.656)	-612.92 (-0.739)
AGE	Years of age	22.35 (1.602)	22.72 (1.621)	-13.98 (-0.909)	-17.19 (-1.103)
GENDER	1 if male; 0 if female	-387.33 (-0.880)	-357.61 (-0.826)	419.58 (0.678)	513.69 (0.823)
SCHOOL1	1 if formal schooling ended with completion of high school (or vocational program), or before; 0 otherwise	739.96 (1.624)	693.55 (1.498)	-496.59 (-1.009)	-402.67 (-0.810)
SCHOOL2	1 if formal schooling ended with some college or completion of bachelor's degree; 0 otherwise	676.47 (1.725)	657.22 (1.683)	-533.48 (-1.205)	-426.75 (-0.967)
SCHOOL3	1 if formal schooling ended post-graduate training or completion of post-graduate degree; 0 otherwise				
UNION	1 if respondent is a union member; 0 otherwise	-3.46 (-0.011)	43.98 (0.139)	-314.014 (-.815)	-179.13 (-0.462)
STEP1	1 if RISK2 equals 1; 0 otherwise	486.22 (1.382)	458.99 (1.261)	—	—
SUMMARY STATISTICS					
Standard error		2643.17	2649.50	3293.64	3311.28
Log of likelihood		-2570.28	-2031.70	-2471.00	-2472.90
Number of observations		444	444	417	417

Marginal value of job safety

The contingent valuation willingness-to-pay estimate ($2.66 million) is close to Viscusi's (1978) widely cited $3.4 million estimate (in 1984 dollars) and lies within Dillingham's (1985) "best-guess" range of marginal safety values ($1.3–$2.7 million in 1984 dollars) based on his analysis of labor market studies. Thus, the contingent valuation willingness-to-pay estimate of the marginal value of safety is not implausible in light of results from previous labor market studies.

Further analysis of both willingness-to-pay and willingness-to-accept contingent values reveals interesting relationships with other variables. This analysis was undertaken by estimating the effects of explanatory variables including annual labor earnings, race, gender, age, union membership, schooling, and initial level of risk faced in the contingent valuation bid to move one step on the risk ladder. Estimates of this relationship were obtained using a two-limit tobit procedure because of the large proportion of zero bids and the truncation of the bid distribution at $6000. All observations in each subsample are used in the regression analysis.

Use of all observations represents a departure from practices often followed in contingent valuation studies in which attempts are made to eliminate protest and/ or outlier bids prior to statistical analysis. As noted by Smith and Desvousges (1987), protest bids can be defined as zero bids given by respondents for reasons *other than* as a reflection of the value of alteration in risk or as in indication of budget limitations. Outlier bids, on the other hand, can be defined as influential or implausible bids and identified using both statistical and nonstatistical procedures. Both types of troublesome bids, however, are more easily defined than identified, and methods used to determine which bids to ignore are arbitrary. For example, Rowe and Chestnut (1987) suggest throwing out bids that violate pre-specified consistency checks based on income or the cost of obtaining by other means the good for which the bid was obtained. Jones-Lee, Hammerton, and Philips (1985) trimmed bid distributions by removing upper tail responses that displayed discontinuity in terms of order of magnitude in relation to other responses. Also, Smith and Desvousges analyze only positive bids using Heckman's (1979) two-step estimator to correct for the sample selection effects that result from dropping the zero bids. This latter approach may well eliminate some valid bids that simply happen to be zero, and does not identify outlier bids. In any case, rather than resort to bid elimination procedures that would end up being difficult to defend, all usable observations were included in the data set.[3]

Table 10.1 presents two-limit tobit estimates from the willingness-to-pay and willingness-to-accept subsamples. The dependent variable in each regression is the contingent valuation bid to move one rung up, in the case of willingness to accept, or down, in the case of willingness to pay, on the risk ladder. The *t*-statistics are shown in parentheses beneath the coefficient estimates, and summary statistics provided at the bottom of the table indicate that the null hypothesis of no relationship between the dependent variables and all explanatory variables would be rejected at conventional significance levels. Also, previously promised definitions of explanatory variables are given in the second column.

Most of these variable definitions are straightforward; however, RISK1 and STEP1 require further elaboration. RISK1 was created by adding the ordinal 1-to-5 rankings of perceived likelihood of death from each major accidental cause and dividing by number of causes considered (13). STEP1 reflects whether a willingness-to-pay respondent initially placed his job on the first rung of the risk ladder. Recall that because these respondents could not then move down a step, they were asked to bid on a move from the second rung to the first. A variable corresponding to STEP1 was not included in the willingness-to-accept regressions because only 1.2% of respondents in this subsample placed their initial level of risk on the tenth rung of the risk ladder.

Results presented in Table 10.1 use RISK1 rather than RISK2. RISK2 performed poorly in all regressions (both for willingness-to-pay and willingness-to-accept subsamples) in which it was included. Coefficients of RISK2 (not presented) occasionally were negative and seldom had t-statistics exceeding .50 in absolute value. As discussed more fully below, coefficients of RISK1 are positive and significant at conventional levels. The Pearson correlation between RISK1 and RISK2 is approximately .46 in each of the two subsamples. One explanation for the difference in performance of these two variables is that the question on which RISK1 is based provided respondents with more perceptual cues or reminders of risk than did the risk ladder. In other words, they found it easier to subjectively assess the chance of occurrence of specific causes of accidental death than to place their job on a risk ladder in comparison with seven example occupations. A second explanation may be that the small number of rungs on the risk ladder prevented precise coefficient estimation. Yet the risk ladder still may have aided respondents in thinking through how much a unit change in risk is worth to them.

Estimates presented in Table 10.1 show effects of earnings, perceived initial risk levels, race, age, gender, union membership status, and schooling on willingness-to-pay and willingness-to-accept contingent valuation bids for a small change in job safety. The first willingness-to-pay regression (see column 3 of Table 10.1) shows strong positive relationships between the contingent valuation bid and EARN and RISK1. Thus, higher bids were obtained from respondents with higher levels of 1983 labor earnings and who perceived greater likelihoods of accidental death on their jobs. The positive coefficient of EARN was expected given the presumption that a reduction in the probability of a job-related fatal accident is a normal good. Additionally, the positive coefficient of RISK1 suggests that respondent indifference curves are upward sloping in the money–risk plane. This result sharply contrasts with the negative association between option price bids and baseline risk levels found by Smith and Desvousges (1987). Moreover, it supports theoretical analyses of Jones-Lee (1974) and Weinstein, Shepard, and Pliskin (1980) which demonstrate that under plausible assumptions, individuals would be willing to pay larger amounts to avoid a unit of risk reduction, the higher the initial level of risk faced.

The relationship between willingness to pay and perceived initial risk levels is further analyzed in the regression shown in the fourth column of Table 10.1. There is only one difference in specification between this regression and the one shown in column 3: RISK1 has been dropped and the dummy variable LOWRISK has been added. As indicated in the table, LOWRISK measures whether RISK1 is less than its mean value of 2.23. Thus, the negative coefficient of LOWRISK indicates that respondents facing below-average perceived risk levels are willing to pay less for a one-step movement down the risk ladder than are respondents facing above-average perceived risk levels. This finding is consistent with contingent valuation willingness-to-pay results in the Jones-Lee, Hammerton, and Philips (1985) study suggesting that willingness to pay to avoid risk of death in a traffic safety context is an increasing, concave function of risk reduction.

Marginal value of job safety

Returning to the column 3 regression, other results of interest are that willingness to pay to avoid job-related fatal accident risks tends to be larger for older workers. The coefficient of AGE, however, with t-statistic of approximately 1.60, is not significantly different from zero at the 10% level using a two-tail test. Yet, this positive coefficient does provide weak evidence that workers may become increasingly averse to job-related fatal accidents as they age. Additionally, the coefficient of UNION has a particularly small t-statistic of $-$0.011. Thus, preferences of union members for job safety are not different from those of nonunion members – a result that at first may be surprising in light of most previous labor market studies. Viscusi (1978), Dickens (1984), Olson (1981), and Worrall and Butler (1983), for example, note significant wage premiums earned by union members who work at riskier jobs and zero (even occasionally negative) wage premiums for nonunion members who work at riskier jobs.[4]

One explanation for these results may be that unions alter the wage–risk tradeoff even though union members' preferences for risk do not differ from those of nonunion members. This alteration in the wage–risk relationship may reflect a mechanism through which unions capture their economic rents. Another possible explanation may lie in differences in risk perceptions between union and non-union workers. As demonstrated by Viscusi (1983), unions play a key role in collecting and disseminating job-related risk information, thus increasing their members' awareness of safety hazards. Moreover, unionized jobs may be riskier than jobs in the nonunion sector. In the mail survey data, unionized workers perceived somewhat greater levels of risk on their jobs than did nonunionized workers. Averages of RISK1 and RISK2 were 2.44 and 3.30 for unionized workers and 2.11 and 2.23 respectively, for nonunion members. More jobs in the nonunion sector, therefore, may have low odds of a fatal accident and for a larger share of these jobs, fatal accident risks may not enter the production function. Thus, the marginal product of increased job-related fatal accidents is zero and no hedonic wage–risk gradient exists. Yet, as reflected in the insignificant coefficient of UNION, there may be little difference between union and nonunion worker preferences to avoid fatal accident hazards while on the job.

The coefficient of RACE is negative and significant at the 5% level using a two-tail test, indicating that nonwhites are willing to pay more for safety than are whites. Additionally, the positive, but barely significant, coefficients of SCHOOL1 and SCHOOL2 suggest that willingness to pay for safety decreases with formal education levels (note that SCHOOL3 is the omitted schooling dummy) and the small t-statistic on the coefficient of GENDER indicates no difference in preferences for safety between males and females. Although results for these socioeconomic characteristics are not totally implausible, they may occur, in part, because of confounding with the perceived risk measure. Nonwhites and individuals with lower levels of schooling may work at riskier jobs than do more highly educated whites. Thus, the negative coefficient of RACE and the positive coefficients of SCHOOL1 and SCHOOL2 simply may reflect effects of perceived risk on contingent valuation willingness to pay bids. Finally, the positive coefficient of STEP1 is significantly different from zero only at the 20% level using a two-tail test. Thus, workers who rated their initial level of job safety on the lowest rung of the risk ladder do not appear to have a strong tendency to give different contingent valuation willingness-to-pay bids than other workers.

Willingness-to-accept contingent valuation estimates, shown in the fifth and sixth columns of Table 10.1, are similar to those for willingness to pay in two

S. Gerking, M. De Haan, W. Schulze

respects. First, coefficients of EARN and RISK1 are positive with t-statistics of 2.85 or greater. Also, the coefficient of LOWRISK (see column 6) is negative and significant at the 10% level using a two-tail test, thus providing additional evidence that indifference curves increase at an increasing rate in the money-risk plane. Second, coefficients of UNION and GENDER are not significantly different from zero at conventional levels, again implying that preferences for safety do not differ between union and nonunion workers or between males and females. Key differences between the willingness-to-pay and willingness-to-accept regressions are that, in the latter, coefficients of RACE, SCHOOL1, and SCHOOL2 have small t-statistics. Additionally, the constant terms in the willingness-to-accept regressions are larger, thus reflecting the larger mean bid obtained when using this method as compared with willingness to pay. Using a X^2 test, the null hypothesis of no difference between the coefficients in the willingness-to-pay and willingness-to-accept regressions is rejected at the 1% level.

CONCLUSIONS

This article has presented marginal value of safety estimates obtained in a labor market context using the contingent valuation method. This method has the virtue of focusing directly on how workers substitute job risk for money. Data collected from a national random sample mail survey were used to measure both willingness-to-accept and willingness-to-pay values to avoid job-related fatal accident risks. Thus, the analysis is similar to that in Viscusi and O'Connor (1984) who measured the willingness of chemical workers to accept small increases in nonfatal job-related risk. Yet this study is the first to examine (1) contingent values for job-related fatal accidents, and (2) willingness to pay for increased job safety. The distinction between willingness-to-accept and willingness-to-pay values is important because, on average, the former are about 2.5 times the latter. Moreover, the average willingness-to-pay estimate of $2.66 million is roughly consistent with marginal value of safety estimates obtained by applying the hedonic price method to unionized and/or blue-collar workers.

A key feature of mail survey data is the measurement of perceived job-related fatal accident risks. Psychologists have argued that risk beliefs may be inconsistent with objective measures of risk. Measurement of these beliefs, however, has received little attention to date in the safety literature except for the previously cited article by Viscusi and O'Connor. In any case, the relationship between contingent values, perceived risk and other variables is analyzed using a two-limit tobit procedure. Contingent values increase at an increasing rate with initial levels of perceived job-related fatal risk, a result that stands in contrast to findings of Smith and Desvousges (1987) in their study of toxic waste exposure hazards. Additionally, contingent values are unaffected by union membership status. Large differences between marginal safety values of union and nonunion workers represent a major source of controversy in the hedonic labor market safety literature. Thus, the present study suggests that nonunion workers have similar preferences for safety as do union workers and that for public policy purposes, marginal value of safety estimates obtained for one group can be applied to the other.

ACKNOWLEDGEMENTS

This research was partially supported by the U.S. Environmental Protection

Agency under cooperative assistance agreements CR-811077-01-0 and CR-812054-01-1. However, the article does not necessarily reflect the views of the sponsoring organization. We thank Kip Viscusi, David Brookshire, and Don Coursey for numerous helpful suggestions on earlier drafts and Karen Radosevich, George Cutts, Chari Pepin, Mark Dickie, and Doug Gegax for excellent research assistance.

NOTES

1. Difference between means tests were performed for each variable measured in the two subsamples. None of these tests rejected the null hypothesis of no difference at the 5% level. Surprisingly, percentages of respondents in one-digit occupation and industry classifications were not significantly different between the two subsamples even though the latter characteristics were a basis for selecting counties with disproportionately high levels of employment in high-risk industries. As a consequence, the methods used here to identify potential respondents in risky jobs were judged to be ineffective. Yet, empirical work was simplified because unweighted data from the two subsamples simply could be pooled.
2. The situation for hedonic studies of wages and job safety is in reality quite similar in that workers must base their actual risk-motivated behavior on subjective assessments of job risks. These subjective assessments are based on perceptual cues or reminders of risk in the workplace (loud noises, fences, hardhats, warning signs, etc.) as well as on experience (especially recent experience) with specific sources of danger. Thus, both contingent valuation and hedonic labor market studies are based on workers' perceptions of risk either based on information presented in the survey instrument or on available information presented in and around the workplace, respectively.
3. In preliminary work, the Smith and Desvousges adaptation of Heckman's two-step estimator was applied to both the willingness-to-pay and willingness-to-accept subsamples. However, ordinary least-squares coefficient estimates in the second step to explain the positive contingent valuation bids proved to be highly dependent on the variables selected for inclusion in the first-step probit regression. As a consequence, this approach was not pursued further.
4. Note that Dillingham and Smith (1984) found little support for this conclusion in their analysis of May, 1979 Current Population Survey data.

REFERENCES

Brookshire, David S. & Coursey, Don L. Measuring the Value of a Public Good: An Empirical Comparison of Elicitation Procedures. *American Economic Review* (Vol. 77, No. 4, 1987), pp 554–566.

Coursey, Don L., Hovis, John J., & Schulze, William D. The Disparity Between Willingness to Accept and Willingness to Pay Measures of Value. *Quarterly Journal of Economics* (Vol. 102, No. 2, 1987), pp 679–690.

Cummings, Ronald G., Brookshire, David S., & Schulze, William D. *Valuing Environmental Goods: An Assessment of the Contingent Valuation Method.* Totowa, NJ: Rowman & Allanheld Publishers, 1986.

Desvousges, William H., Smith, V. Kerry, & Fisher, Ann. Option Price Estimates for Water Quality Improvements: A Contingent Valuation Study for the Monongahela River. *Journal of Environmental Economics and Management* (Vol. 14, No. 3, 1987), pp 248–267.

Dickens, William T. Differences Between Risk Premiums in Union and Nonunion Wages and the Case for Occupational Safety Regulation. *American Economic Review* (Vol. 74, No. 2, 1984), pp 320–323.

Dickie, Mark & Gerking, Shelby. Interregional Wage Differentials: An Equilibrium Perspective. *Journal of Regional Science* (1988), forthcoming.

Dillingham, Alan E. The Influence of Risk Variable Definition on Value-of-Life Estimates. *Economic Inquiry* (Vol. 23, No. 2, 1985), pp 277–294.

Dillingham, Alan E. & Smith, Robert S. Union Effects on the Valuation of Fatal Risk. *Industrial Relations Research Association.* Proceedings of the Thirty-Sixth Annual Meeting, December 28–30, 1983, San Francisco, (1984), pp 270–277.

Dillmann, Donald A. *Mail and Telephone Surveys: The Total Design Method,* New York: Wiley-Interscience, 1978.

Gegax, Douglas, Gerking, Shelby, & Schulze, William. Perceived Risk and the Marginal Value of Safety. Manuscript, Department of Economics, University of Wyoming, Laramie, WY, 1987.

Gegax, Douglas et al. Valuing Safety: Two Approaches. Volume IV in: *Experimental Methods for Assessing Environmental Benefits.* Washington, DC: U.S. Environmental Protection Agency, 1985.

Heckman, James J. Sample Selection Bias as a Specification Error. *Econometrica* (Vol. 47, No. 1, 1979), pp 153–161.

Jones-Lee, Michael W. The Value of Changes in the Probability of Death or Injury. *Journal of Political Economy* (Vol. 82, 1974), pp 835–849.

Jones-Lee, M.W., Hammerton, M., & Philips, P.R. The Value of Safety: Results of a National Sample Survey. *The Economic Journal* (Vol. 95, No. 377, 1985), pp 49–72.

Kahneman, Daniel & Tversky, Amos. Prospect Theory: An Analysis of Decision Under Risk. *Econometrica* (Vol. 47, No. 2, 1979), pp 263–291.

Kahneman, Daniel & Tversky, Amos. Choices, Values, and Frames. *American Psychologist* (Vol. 39, No. 4, 1984), pp 341–350.

Knetsch, Jack L. & Sinden, J.A. Willingness to Pay and Compensation Demanded: Experimental Evidence of an Unexpected Disparity in Measures of Value. *The Quarterly Journal of Economics* (Vol. 99, No. 3, 1984), pp 507–521.

Lichtenstein, S. et al. Judged Frequency of Lethal Events. *Journal of Experimental Psychology: Human Learning and Memory* (Vol. 4, No. 6, 1978), pp 551–578.

Marin, Alan & Psacharopoulos, George. The Reward for Risk in the Labor Market: Evidence from the United Kingdom and a Reconciliation with Other Studies. *Journal of Political Economy* (Vol. 90, No. 4, 1982), pp 827–853.

Olson, Craig A. An Analysis of Wage Differentials Received by Workers on Dangerous Jobs. *Journal of Human Resources* (Vol. 16, No. 2, 1981), pp 167–185.

Rowe, Robert D. & Chestnut, Lauraine G. Valuing Changes in Morbidity: WTP Versus COI Measures. Manuscript, Energy and Resource Consultants, Inc., Boulder, CO, 1987.

Smith, V., Kerry & Desvousges, William H. An Empirical Analysis of the Economic Value of Risk Changes. *Journal of Political Economy* (Vol. 95, No. 1, 1987), pp 89–114.

Smith, Robert S. Compensating Wage Differentials and Public Policy: A Review. *Industrial and Labor Relations Review* (Vol. 32, No. 3, 1979), pp 339–352.

Thaler, Richard & Rosen, Sherwin. The Value of Saving a Life: Evidence from the Labor Market. In: Nestor E. Terleckyj, ed., *Household Production and Consumption.* New York: Columbia University Press for NBER. 1976.

Viscusi, W. Kip. Labor Market Valuations of Life and Limb: Empirical Evidence and Policy Implications. *Public Policy* (Vol. 26, No. 3, 1978), pp 359–386.

Viscusi, W. Kip. *Employment Hazards: An Investigation of Market Performance.* Cambridge, MA: Harvard University Press, 1979.

Viscusi, W. Kip. *Risk By Choice: Regulating Health and Safety in the Workplace.* Cambridge, MA: Harvard University Press, 1983.

Viscusi, W. Kip & O'Connor, Charles J. Adaptive Responses to Chemical Labelling: Are Workers Bayesian Decision Makers? *American Economic Review* (Vol. 74, No. 5, 1984), pp 942–956.

Viscusi, W. Kip, Magat, Wesley, & Huber, Joel. An Investigation of the Rationality of Consumer Valuations of Multiple Health Risks, *Rand Journal of Economics* (Vol. 18, No. 4. 1987).

Weinstein, Milton C., Shepard, Donald S., & Pliskin, Joseph S. The Economic Value of Changing Mortality Probabilities: A Decision-Theoretic Approach. *Quarterly Journal of Economics* (Vol. 94, No. 2, 1980), pp 373–396.

Worrall, John D. & Butler, Richard J. Health Conditions and Job Hazards: Union and Nonunion Jobs. *Journal of Labor Research* (Vol. 4, No. 4, 1983), pp 339–347.

U.S. Department of Labor, Bureau of Labor Statistics. *Occupational Injuries and Illnesses in the U.S., By Industry, 1984.* Bulletin 2259. Washington, DC: U.S. Government Printing Office, 1986.

Chapter 11

The value of the environment: a state of the art survey

Anil Markandya

VALUATION METHODS
The approaches to the economic measurement of environmental benefits can be broadly classified as:

(a) those based on direct and indirect market information, such as property values, wage rates; expenditure on related goods etc.;

(b) those based on stated preferences in the absence of markets, as expressed through questionnaires or through public or charitable contributions;

(c) those based on dose-response data linking environmental changes to pollutants.

In *all* cases the purpose is to elicit individual values, as expressed in terms of willingness to pay for an environmental improvement, or willingness to accept compensation for an environmental deterioration. However, in the first two, where market information is sought, or where stated preferences are sought in the absence of markets, the link between willingness to pay or accept payment and the measured value is much clearer than it is in the third case, where the method relies much more on scientific and engineering data. The remainder of this paper describes each of the techniques and discusses the main problems that arise in implementing them.

MARKET BASED METHODS: HEDONIC PRICE APPROACHES
The hedonic price approach looks for a market in which goods or factors of production (especially labour services) are bought and sold, and observes that environmental factors are frequently attributes of those goods or factors. Thus, a fine view or the level of air quality is an attribute or feature of a house, a risky environment may be features of certain jobs, and so on. It has long been recognized that the value of a piece of land is related to the stream of benefits to be derived from that land. Agricultural output and shelter are the most obvious of such benefits, but access to the workplace, to commercial amenities and to environmental facilities such as parks; and the environmental quality of the neighbourhood in which the land is located are also important benefits which accrue to the person who has the right to use a particular piece of land. The property value approach to the measurement of benefit estimation is based on this simple underlying assumption. Given that different locations have varied environmental attributes, such variations will result in differences in property values. With the use of appropriate statistical techniques the hedonic approach attempts to (a) *identify* how much of a property differential is due to a particular environmental difference between properties and (b) *infer* how much people are

Value of the environment

willing to pay for an improvement in the environmental quality that they face and what the social value of the improvement is. Both the identification and the inference activities involve a number of issues which are discussed in some detail below[1].

The identification of a property price effect due to a difference in pollution levels is usually done by means of a *multiple regression* technique in which data are taken either on a small number of similar residential properties over a period of years (time series), or on a larger number of diverse properties at a point in time (cross section), or on both (pooled data). In practice almost all property value studies have used cross-section data, as controlling for other influences over time is much more difficult. In doing the exercise what one is seeking to identify is the curve AB of Figure 11.1 below. This is the relationship between the level of the environmental attribute z, and the price of the related market property. It reflects the results of a market equilibrium between households who wish to purchase a property with a certain level of the attribute z and property developers and owners who supply dwellings at different attribute levels. This 'equilibrium' is represented in terms of a set of points of tangency between the individuals' bid curves and the suppliers' supply, or offer, curves for housing with different levels of z. For any change in the attribute, say from z_1 to z_2 the household's willingness to pay for the improvement would be the distance as in Figure 11.1. However, the estimated hedonic method, using the results of the econometric estimation described above, would result in an over-estimation of the benefits of an improvement, or an underestimation of the cost of a deterioration[2].

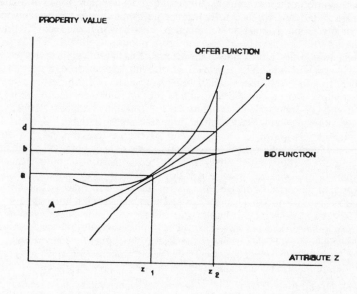

Figure 11.1 Hedonic prices, bid and offer functions.

Having established that the method, applied as described above, would result in an overestimation of the benefit, the questions that follow are: (a) how serious is the overestimate and (b) can it be corrected by adapting the method in one way or another? As far as the magnitude of the bias is concerned, economists have carried out simulation exercises where the utility function representing consumer preferences is specified explicitly, as are the details of the supply of properties with attribute z. One of these has concluded that the hedonic estimate of benefits could be *as much as two to three times the true willingness to pay for the benefit*[3]. In another study[4], two situations were compared; one in which a vacant piece of urban land is to be developed (the 'Greenfield Case') and the other in which an existing site is to be improved (the 'Brownfield Case'). In the first case the without-project alternative would be to have squatter settlements, whereas in the second case the without-project situation would be to have no change from the status quo. The study reports that the overstatement of benefits in the Greenfield case is much smaller than in the Brownfield case. For example, if the with-project value is twice the without-project value, the overstatement in the Greenfield case is less than 50%, whereas in the Brownfield case it is over 100%.

These simulation results are interesting and useful but they also have their limitations. The complexities of the real situations cannot be replicated in models with simple utility functions and land markets. Thus, it is also important to look at the results of actual hedonic price studies and compare them to those obtained by other methods on the same data. A few such comparisons have been done for developed countries by Brookshire and others and show that, whereas in one study the hedonic estimate was around three times that obtained by questionnaire approach, in another it was actually *less* than the questionnaire-based estimate[5]. There is no clear evidence, therefore, from actual empirical studies, to show that the hedonic estimate is consistently much higher than that obtained by other methods.

The second question posed above was whether this bias could be corrected. In his original article Rosen had recognized the difficulty, and proposed a two-stage procedure, in which the prices of attribute z obtained from the estimation as described above were then used to estimate the bid functions. There are a few studies in the US that carry out this two stage estimation procedure[6]. However, the estimation problems raised in doing so are formidable, though not insurmountable. In particular it is difficult to ensure that the bid and offer functions are identifiable from the equilibrium price data as obtained in the first stage estimation. These issues have been examined in great detail in previous survey papers[7]. In general their conclusion is that the two-stage estimation procedure can be carried out, with the use of advanced techniques and skilled econometricians and not on a routine basis. There is nothing that has changed in the last few years to disagree with this conclusion.

There are other difficulties with using the hedonic method. It can really only be applied when households are *aware* of the costs or benefits of the environmental attribute; and when they are *able* to adjust their residential locations to choose whatever combination of attributes they want. The analyst has to ensure these conditions are satisfied before employing the technique. Once applied, there are many detailed decisions that have to be made. A primary one is whether to use rental or property price data. Rental price data are theoretically the better, but in practice the rental market is less perfect in some countries. One advantage of using rental data is that property prices reflect not only current levels of the attribute but future expected levels as well. Thus they may not give a clear idea of what the willingness to pay for current levels is[8].

In the econometric estimation, there are the usual issues of choice of functional form, choice of variables, etc. The choice of functional form can result in significant differences in the estimated benefits, even when the statistical tests cannot distinguish between the forms (i.e. both forms are considered acceptable). The accepted 'best' practice here is to use the Box–Cox transformation, allowing the form to be determined by the data. Once the equation has been estimated, for example in log-linear form, one needs to get back to the original variables to obtain the hedonic prices in money terms. But there is a bias involved in the transformation. Taking the example cited above, if the impact of z on the log of the price is estimated, taking the antilog of the coefficient will give the impact of z on the *median* price, not the mean price, which is what is desired. There are bias correction methods available, but these are not always applied[9].

Often the hedonic effect of interest is not a continuous variable but a dichotomous one – e.g. either a house has sewerage connection or it does not. When there are such variables as explanatory factors, care has to be taken in interpreting the coefficients. There are methods developed for calculating the relative change in the price but again these are not always carefully applied[10].

What can one conclude about the use of hedonic price methods from all this? In practice, only the first-stage estimation is usually carried out and the results used to obtain rough values for the impact of the attribute in question. It is probably not worthwhile asking for the second stage to be attempted at this point – the data and other sources of error are too great for the additional effort in this direction to be worthwhile. Some of the other improvements in estimation procedure – the use of flexible functional forms, employing proper transformation procedures and, most important of all, including as many of the relevant variables as possible – are certainly worth undertaking. But in all this discussion it is important to keep the issues in perspective. Virtually *all* estimation methods, including those identifying simple demand and supply curves, which are frequently used in deriving and estimating benefits outside the environmental context, would, if subjected to the sort of scrutiny that has been applied here, be found wanting in many respects. The desire and the need to improve estimation methods should not lead one into throwing the baby out with the bath water. Benefit estimation is not, and probably never will be, an exact science. For *many* applications even obtaining an order of magnitude of the benefits or costs is worthwhile. Hedonic methods, applied judiciously, where they are valid on grounds of functioning markets and well informed consumers, have an important role to play, especially where large projects are involved and when the data collection costs can be justified.

Applications of this method have been successfully carried out in developed countries, to estimate the costs of air and noise pollution, and of changes in amenities. However, their use in developing countries has been more limited; valuation of the benefits of sites and services is among the main applications to be found. Only now are the studies of the costs of air pollution using hedonic methods being undertaken in countries such as Korea, Thailand and Mexico. In the agricultural sector, they have a potential usefulness in assessing the capitalized benefits through agricultural land of changes in facilities such as irrigation or accessibility to markets but no major applications have been found. Hence their use is expanding in the developing country context and more experience can be expected to be gained in connection with the resource-related projects in the near future.

MARKET BASED METHODS: CONTINGENT VALUATION

The contingent valuation method (CVM) uses a direct approach – it basically asks people what they are willing to pay for a benefit, and/or what they are willing to receive by way of compensation to tolerate a cost. What is sought are the personal valuations of the respondent for increases or decreases in the quantity of some good, contingent upon a hypothetical market. Respondents say what is the maximum they would be willing to pay (WTP) for an environmental improvement or the minimum they would be willing to accept (WTA) for a decline in environmental quality *if* a market existed for the good in question. Alternatively, they might be asked whether they are willing to pay or willing to accept a particular figure. A contingent market is taken to include not just the good itself (an improved view, better water quality, etc.), but also the institutional context in which it would be provided, and the way in which it would be financed.

The aim of the CVM is to elicit valuations – or 'bids' which are close to those that would be revealed if an actual market existed. The hypothetical market – the questioner, questionnaire and respondent – must therefore be as close as possible to a real market. The respondent must, for example, be familiar with the good in question. If the good is improved scenic visibility, this might be achieved by showing the respondent photographs of the view with and without particular levels of pollution or, if the good is an improvement in water quality, he must appreciate in terms that are familiar to him, what this means. The design of a contingent valuation is now a professional activity, in which several points of design and implementation have been stressed.

The first issue is what form the survey should take. Should it be a personal interview, a mail survey or a telephone interview? The personal interview is the most common and favoured method although it can be quite expensive. Mail surveys have, however, also been used with some success in the US[11]. The second is the way in which the change will be carried out. Will it be the responsibility of a particular agency, and how will it be paid for? These factors could influence the answers received. Third is the method by which the WTP or WTA is measured. There are three broad methods that have been used. The first is a simple question: what is your maximum WTP or minimum WTA? The second is the use of an iterated procedure, where the interviewer starts with a given figure and asks whether the WTP is equal to or more or less than that. If it is more he increases the figure and if it is less he decreases it, carrying on until the desired answer is reached. This method falls under the title of bidding games. Finally, there is a simple presentation of impact and WTP or WTA and the respondent is simply asked whether he or she is willing to pay that sum, or willing to accept that sum. The answer, yes or no, is recorded and no further question is asked. Naturally this method yields less information but it can be analysed using discrete data techniques and is less prone to the kinds of biases discussed below.

Since the use of contingent valuation methods was introduced in the early 1970s, a lot of work has been done to identify biases or sources of error in the estimates. These have been classified in the following categories: hypothetical context bias, information bias, strategic bias, and policy or vehicle of payment bias[12].

Hypothetical bias is said to arise for the simple reason that the situation being

146

described is hypothetical and the WTP or WTA figures are not actually paid or received. In an attempt to measure this, economists have compared the results of contingent valuation answers with those from experiments where actual payments were to be made or received. The earliest of these involved the issue of hunting permits and later ones consisted of experimental situations involving actual and hypothetical payments for accepting or not having to drink an unpleasant tasting liquid. The results showed that, whereas for WTP the results of the actual and hypothetical experiments were quite close, for WTA they were different by an amount that was statistically significant. Furthermore, there was a difference between WTP and WTA figures that was larger than would be justified on theoretical grounds. This distinction between WTP and WTA will be returned to later[13].

For carefully-designed studies hypothetical bias can be kept within acceptable bounds for measuring WTP if certain conditions, which can be broadly described as the 'reference operating conditions', are satisfied. First, the choices presented must be as close as possible to actual choices, including the policies that are being followed. Second, complex information regarding the choices has to be passed on carefully, in terms that are comprehensible to the respondent and without too strict a time constraint. Third, the respondent has to have enough time to formulate his or her response. Recent research has indicated the importance of all these factors[14].

Information bias arises for reasons very similar to hypothetical bias but the term is used in the contingent valuation literature to refer to biases arising from the format design rather than those arising from the context of the actual choices involved. Biases are found to arise, for example, in bidding games based on the initial bid proposed – the so-called starting point bias. The final response achieved has been found to be influenced by that starting point. This can be avoided by checking for a relationship between the two during the pretesting of the questionnaire, and adjusting the design accordingly. Pretesting the questionnaire is, of course, an essential feature of any contingent valuation exercise. Another source of information bias is said to arise because the responses are sensitive to the method of payment for the improvement that is proposed – e.g. surcharges, utility fees, taxes, etc.; and to the agency that is identified as carrying out the improvements. It is not clear, however, whether these differences are really 'biases' or represent meaningful divergencies reflecting the fact that WTP *is* contingent on how the payments are to be made. Recent studies of contingent valuation have, however, tended to avoid reference to specific payment vehicles[15].

Much of the bias associated with format design can be eliminated by using the discrete 'accept–reject' format which, according to recent evidence, gives the best value estimates. With such a procedure there is no need to undertake a bidding procedure or any other iterated procedure where subsequent questions are based on previous ones. It seems that this is very much the direction in which contingent valuation is going, although it places the same burden on defining the problem fully and clearly for the respondent and giving him or her enough time to formulate a response.

Finally there is the issue of *strategic bias*. This is said to arise from the individual's desire to influence the outcome of the study, for his or her personal benefit. Economists have long believed that strategic bias was a serious impediment to the use of survey and questionnaire methods, but the empirical evidence does not support this. Moreover, there are now design methods available that provide incentives for truth telling. Experiments using these methods have revealed that even with quite weak incentives for truth telling, one can overcome the presence of strategic behaviour. Thus this issue does not remain a problem in well designed studies[16].

The final methodological issue that remains is that of the discrepancy between WTP and WTA. The empirical evidence strongly indicates that answers to questions about willingness to accept compensation for a loss of amenity yield much higher answers than questions about the willingness to pay to retain the same amenity once it is there. On the basis of economic theory the differences between the two should not be that large. Given the general tendency for WTP to be more consistent and plausible, researchers have tended to use them rather than WTA figures, even when the situation being valued involved a loss of amenity (the question would then be posed as what are you willing to pay to prevent the loss).

The reasons why WTA and WTP differ as much as they do are not fully understood. One explanation is based on the assumption that WTA questions need more time to be properly understood and assimilated. Some experiments have shown that, in an iterative bidding process, the two differed considerably, but that they come closer together in successive iterations. Others, however, have argued that the differences are meaningful and indicate that a person needs more in the way of compensation for what he is going to lose than he is willing to pay for what he might get – because what matters is not the final set of goods and services that a person has, but the *changes* in the set relative to some reference point. That reference point is often the *status quo* and losses from it have a higher value than gains of equal magnitude to it. This approach, which is based on psychological prospect theory, has been put forward as, an explanation of the discrepancy between WTP and WTA[17].

The implications of accepting the differences as real are that one should not use the lower WTP figures when valuing a loss in environmental benefit. This in turn would lead to higher values for conservation projects. At present the debate is unresolved and the tendency remains to use WTP. One reason for this is purely practical. Although WTA figures are higher, they are also more varied, with some individuals stating extremely high WTAs (in the millions of dollars), and others stating that no sum would compensate them for the loss. Unless one wishes to give such individuals the right effectively to veto any change, it is hard to see how WTA can be practically applied for losses of amenity.

In the empirical evaluation, a very large part of the literature on CVM is taken up with discussion about its 'accuracy'. Accuracy is not easy to define. Since the basic aim of CVM is to elicit 'real' values, a bid will be accurate if it coincides (within reason) with one that would result if an actual market existed. But since actual markets do not exist *ex hypothesi* (otherwise there would be no reason to use the technique), accuracy must be tested by seeing that:

- the resulting bid is similar to that achieved by other techniques based on surrogate markets (house price approach, wage studies, etc.);
- the resulting bid is similar to one achieved by introducing the kinds of incentives that exist in real markets to reveal preference.

Some comments have already been made on the relationship between hedonic estimates and those of CVM and other methods. A comparison between CVM and methods such as the travel cost, or the use of dose-response techniques reveals that, in most cases, there is broad consistency between these methods. Consistency is taken here to mean that the estimates are generally within plus or minus 100 per cent of each other[18]. That may seem to be a large range but, in the context of the general uncertainties surrounding such estimation, it should be regarded as providing useful information to the decision-maker. One suspects that if the application of CVM and the alternative method were scrutinised more closely, one could reduce this range even more.

CVM has been used extensively to elicit values of improvements in water quality, the benefits of less air pollution, and the option and existence values of species and sites. Values for the latter have been found to be very large in studies conducted in the United States, Germany and the Scandinavian countries, and on the valuation of natural resources located in developing countries by the residents of developed countries. Thus willingness to pay for the conservation of rain forests, through CVM and other methods, has been estimated at as much as $8 per adult in the United States. There is some controversy about such estimates regarding whether they take enough account of the aggregation problem referred to earlier in this paper (i.e. that such figures cannot be added to CVM and other estimates of WTP for conservation because the respondent is not assuming that he has to pay for all these items) but they are nevertheless indicative of a large conservation existence value.

Until recently, the use of such techniques in developing countries was believed to be very difficult, if not impossible, due to the sophistication of the 'as if' experiments involved. However, some recent work has been carried out on the valuation of water, sewerage and tourism benefits at the IDB (in several Latin American countries) and on water supply at the World Bank in Brazil, India, Nigeria, Pakistan, Tanzania and Zimbabwe. The World Bank studies were specially designed to investigate the possibility of using contingent valuation in developing countries and the program showed that the technique can indeed be effectively employed in that context[19].

What can one conclude about CV methods? The technique, which suffered from a credibility problem for many years, has now reached a state of maturity that should enable it to overcome that problem. One of its strong advantages is its versatility – it can, in principle, be used in all circumstances. The professional consensus is that CVM *can* provide reasonable and interesting data on benefits or costs, but that the studies have to be conducted with great care, and the respondent has to be very familiar with the subject matter of the valuation. The views on the relevance of this method are therefore changing fast and it is quite likely that its use will extend to other areas in the valuation of environmental benefits in developing countries.

MARKET BASED METHODS: TRAVEL COST APPROACHES

Travel cost models are based on an extension of the theory of consumer demand in which special attention is paid to the value of time and the choice of site visits. They are used to value the benefits of improvements in recreational facilities in parks, or the values of cultural sites that are visited by people from many different locations. Numerous applications exist for the US, and some for Europe and Australia. In developing countries, some models are being used to estimate benefits from tourism development in countries with game parks (such as Kenya), or special trekking areas (such as Nepal). Another area of applications has been to value benefits of fuelwood supply (or the supply of replacements such as kerosene), where households 'pay' for the fuelwood by spending time collecting it (as was recently done in Zimbabwe).

The essential issues regarding benefit estimation in travel cost models can be viewed in Figures 11.2 and 11.3. One assumes that there is a demand for the services of a particular site, which are contingent on the attributes of that site, and of other sites offering similar services. An example may be visits to beaches, or to a game park. The alternatives will depend on who is making the visits. For local residents the alternatives are other sites in the vicinity. For foreign tourists there will be other sites in the country, and conceivably in other countries offering similar packages of facilities. In all these cases the objective is to estimate the relevant demand curves, and then value the increase in welfare as a result of the project, which is expected to result in a shift in the demand curve and perhaps in a change in the price. The 'price' referred to here is not something that can be measured just in terms of what one has to pay to enter the site. There may be no such payment, and in any case that payment is only a small part of the total cost. The other items that make up the price are the time taken to get to the site, and the costs of getting there. An important part of the travel cost method is the estimation of that price. The increase in welfare in Figure 11.2, as a result of an improvement in the quality of the site, is given *approximately* by the shaded area. The reason why it is only approximate is discussed later.

In developing countries one is also interested in using this method to estimate points on a demand curve for a commodity such as water or fuelwood. For many people such commodities are delivered and the consumer pays for the delivery as well as the commodity. But others have to collect the commodity, in which case there may be no money charge once it has been collected. The collection time can be quite significant a part of the person's total time available, and has an opportunity cost that can be measured. That opportunity cost gives the implicit price of the commodity and can be used to value, for example, the introduction of delivery systems, which convert a time cost to a money cost. In Figure 11.3 the benefits of the introduction of such a system at a price P1 are shown in the shaded area.

The theory and practice of estimating the demand curves as shown in Figure 11.2 has been developed considerably since the 1960s, when the first serious estimates were carried out[20]. Broadly speaking the issues can be divided into those relating to the estimation methods and those relating to the welfare implications of the estimated equations – i.e. how can one obtain an estimate of the benefits or costs associated with any given change once the demand curves have been estimated? Each of these are considered below.

EMPIRICAL ISSUES

Whichever method is used to estimate the demand for site services, one of the key questions is what value should be attached to time. Several studies show that the estimated parameters, as well as the estimated benefits of any changes, are highly sensitive to the assumed value of time[21]. It is usual to take between a quarter and a half of the average wage as the appropriate value, with a third being the most common fraction used. Given the sensitivity of the results to this parameter it is important to evaluate the case for a given figure carefully, taking account of the circumstances that are relevant to the application in question. An underestimation of the time costs results in demand being estimated as more

Value of the environment

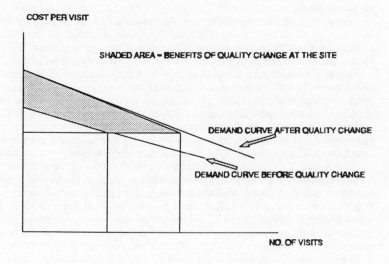

Figure 11.2 Benefit estimation from travel cost models.

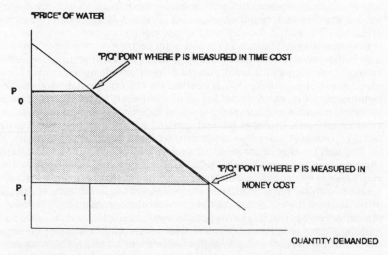

Figure 11.3 Benefit estimation using travel cost models.

sensitive to money costs than it really is, which would have an effect on the measured welfare.

The models used for the estimation of recreational benefits (which have been the main application of travel cost models) can be classified into two groups – continuous variable specifications and discrete variable specifications. In the former the number of visits to a site are treated as the dependent variable, with household characteristics as explanatory variables. This is of course extremely demanding of data, as one needs to know who visited the site, where they came from and what their personal circumstances were. In addition there are the problems of how to treat different lengths of visit, and how to deal with the fact that those who do visit are only a fraction of the set of potential visitors. Ideally one should estimate both the number of visits and length of each visit simultaneously but this is difficult to do. Ignoring the length of each visit would result in a bias, if for example those who came from far away spend considerably longer at the site. Then their cost per unit of time spent would be lower than was estimated assuming equal time, and the resulting demand curve would be steeper than the true one. An EPA study examined the bias resulting from this issue and found that ignoring the time spent on the site resulted in an overestimation of the number of visits. But the effect was small and the impact on the slope of the estimated demand curve was negligible. Hence the issue did not emerge as of great importance[22].

More serious, however, is the bias resulting from the fact that the estimated demand equation is based on data from households that have made a visit and ignores those that did not make one. This so-called truncation bias results in the estimated demand curve in Figure 11.2 being flatter than the true demand curve and therefore the change in surplus being larger than the true change. Methods are available to correct the bias resulting from truncation, which are not particularly data-hungry and when applied result in noticeably different estimates of the benefits. Thus it is important to make this correction[23].

Having estimated the demand function for a site, how does one then find the shift in that function as result of change in the site attributes? Ideally one should estimate the demand for all relevant sites simultaneously, including as explanatory factors the attributes of the sites, such as quality of the water, facilities available, etc. But this is impossible to do in practice. One alternative approach has been to estimate the demand for each site separately, including as an explanatory variable the cost and attributes of the 'next best site'. However, this is arbitrary and not very satisfactory. The most promising procedure used so far has been to estimate the demand for each site separately as a function of the characteristics of the household, and then examine how the demand parameters vary *across sites* according to the attributes of the sites. For example, in each demand equation one would have a coefficient relating the number of visits to the price. That coefficient would vary across sites and one might find, for example, that an increase in dissolved oxygen would raise the value of that coefficient. In terms of Figure 11.2, this would be equivalent to saying that an improvement in water quality shifts the slope of the demand curve, making it steeper. This information can then be used to estimate the benefits[24], as has been done in the US but it is clearly extremely demanding in terms of data.

When there are many sites and the choice between them is determined on competitive grounds by consumers, the continuous variable models are probably not the most suitable ones, and it would be better to turn to the discrete choice alternatives. The random utility model (RUM) is especially suited to the task of identifying the choice among substitute sites. In one of its most popular forms it generates the multinomial logit equation, which defines the probability that a particular site will be visited, as function of the attributes of that and other sites, and the characteristics of the household. One of its limitations, however, is that it cannot then explain the *frequency* of visits to a site (i.e. how many times the person visits a site in a season). This can be overcome by attaching to the multinomial equation a *single continuous demand equation for trips to all sites*. The other serious limitation of the simple multinomial form is its assumption that the relative chances of any two sites being chosen are independent of all other sites (the so-called independence of irrelevant alternatives). This will be violated when choices are made in a sequential order. For example, one might decide either to go to a beach in region A or go to a game park in region B. Once that decision has been made, the next one would be to choose among the beaches or game parks. This is referred to as the nested multinomial logit and has been used in the recreational literature[25]. Again data requirements are quite formidable, however, and it is unlikely that they will be satisfied in most developing country contexts, although it is becoming generally acknowledged that the combination of the RUM and the single demand equation is probably the best in terms of estimating demand for recreational sites.

WELFARE ISSUES

Having estimated the demand for each site either in continuous or discrete or discrete *cum* continuous terms, the next question is how to use that information to estimate the benefits of changes in environmental quality. In the continuous case one needs first to estimate the shift in the demand curve and then try and estimate the shaded area in Figure 11.2. However, there are some problems associated with doing that. These are not easy to explain in a non-technical way, but essentially they arise because the benefits of a quality improvement as measured by the shaded area in that figure are only an approximation to the true benefits, which should be measured on a related but different demand curve (the compensated demand curve). Normally the errors involved in using the empirical demand curve as it is estimated from the data are small, but in the case of quality changes, that can no longer be guaranteed. Hence one should go back to the underlying utility function on which the demand functions are based. But this is not always possible, as the latter are not specified, especially with the quality variables included[26]. Theoretically this is an issue, but how important it is has not yet been clearly established.

In the discrete models, the measurement of the benefits has to be based on the random utility model. As its name suggests, it assumes that the individual's utility is a random function of income and consumption. The welfare measure is then based on finding the income change that compensates the individual for the change in the environmental quality, taking the average or expected utility in each case. This method has now been developed and applied in recreation model benefit estimation and can be used to estimate the benefits of introducing new sites as well as eliminating existing ones, something that cannot be done with the continuous models alone[27].

What can one say in conclusion about travel cost models? The first point to note is that, in the context of developed countries, the most important applications of the method are with regard to recreational benefits, whereas in developing countries they are in the estimation of the demand for products such as water and fuelwood. For this purpose, much the most critical issue is the valuation of time. There are some general guidelines available for this in standard textbooks, but each case is special and the local circumstances must be taken into account. However, recreational benefits are becoming important even in developing countries, especially those where there is an important tourist trade. For these, investments in improvements in quality and infrastructure need to be valued and some of the models that have evolved in the US could be of use. In particular the random utility model could be used to estimate demand by site without too much difficulty, as long as the data can be collected, which should be feasible. The more ambitious system-wide estimation of site benefits as carried out in the US, however, must be considered to be virtually impossible to replicate in any of the borrower countries.

DOSE-RESPONSE BASED VALUATION PROCEDURES
Sometimes benefit estimation methods do not seek to measure the revealed preferences for the environmental good in question. Instead, they calculate a 'dose-response' relationship between pollution and some effect, and only then is some measure of the economic value of that effect applied. Examples of dose-response relationships include the effect of pollution on health; the effect of pollution on the physical depreciation of material assets such as metals and buildings; the effect of pollution on aquatic ecosystems, and the effect of soil erosion on agricultural yields.

In general the indirect valuation approach is always applicable to environmental problems. That is, if there is some damage and it is linked to a cause, the relationship between that cause and effect is a dose-response linkage. Once the dose response relationship is established, indirect approaches then utilize valuations which are applied to the 'responses'. For example, consider the linkage between water pollution and health. Then, once the health effects are established, a value of life and/or of illness is applied. The procedure can be summarized as follows:

(i) Estimate a physical damage function of the form
   $R = R(P, \text{other variables})$
   where R is the physical damage (the response), P is the pollution;
(ii) Calculate the coefficient of R on P through (typically) statistical regression analysis – i.e. calculate $\Delta R/\Delta P$ (where Δ means 'change in');
(iii) Calculate the change in pollution due to environmental policy – i.e. calculate ΔP;
(iv) Calculate $V.\Delta P.(\Delta R/\Delta P) = V.\Delta R = \Delta D$, where ΔD is the 'damage avoided' by the environmental policy and is thus equal to the benefits of that policy.

Indirect procedures do not *easily* constitute a method of finding willingness to pay (WTP) for the environmental benefit (or the willingness to accept (WTA) compensation for environmental damage suffered). For example, one might find that a certain program of soil conservation would reduce erosion by a certain amount and result in increased yields of existing crops of an amount that can also be estimated and valued using existing prices. However, there is no guarantee that the farmers would actually be willing to pay that amount for the benefits. The reason is that, with the new soil conditions, the pattern of crops grown would change, as would the prices they fetch and farmers would want to take account of these changes. In another example, suppose that a disease eradication program reduced the incidence of malaria, so that the number of work days lost could be measured. An estimate of the benefit based on valuing those days in terms of the average wage (which has been used in this context) would not provide an accurate estimate of the benefits because individuals' willingness to pay of the reduced risk will depend on how they value risk, as well as how they value the discomfort and inconvenience of contracting malaria. These may bear no relation to the wage costs of the expected number of days lost.

The essential point here is that the step from the dose-response estimation to the valuation is not as simplistic as is often assumed. In fact what is often needed is to link the dose-response estimates of the damage to a behavioral model of the demand for the products that are affected. In some of the more sophisticated studies using dose-response relationships this has been done, but in general it has not[28]. Often, the data simply do not permit the estimation of the more refined model, in which case even the simpler models can be very useful providing their limitations are realised and the kinds of biases they are likely to generate are allowed for.

The dose response tends to be used particularly for two reasons. The first is when it is thought that people are unaware of the effects that pollution causes. The second is when eliciting preferences by any one of the direct methods is not possible for reasons of data, or lack of 'market sophistication' in the population, or both. The second reason applies especially in developing countries, where price and expenditure data are generally poor and where, at least until now, the use of contingent valuation techniques has been limited because it is believed that the answers would suffer from strategic, hypothetical and operational biases.

Where environmental benefit estimation has been undertaken in developing countries, it has overwhelmingly been of this form. In the international donor agencies, there are several examples of dose-response estimation methods, especially related to agriculture. A few general points worth noting from these are:

(a) environmental costs and benefits are estimated mainly for changes in agriculture output following land use and land management programmes. However, the dose-response relationships on which these are based are often quite crude. Furthermore, as has been discussed above, there is often no allowance for the fact that individuals adapt to changes in their environment. Thus, for example, if soil conditions are expected to improve as a result of a project, farmers will change to different inputs and grow different corps than they did in poorer soil conditions. Not allowing for such changes, and assuming that the same inputs and output mixes will prevail would result in an underestimate of the benefits of such changes. This is because the changes themselves are likely to generate further benefits;
(b) many environmental impacts are not valued in these exercises. The reasons for this range from a lack of data to an unwillingness to use the appropriate techniques. The former include benefits such as increased crop residues and the spillover effects of projects and health benefits from public health programs. The latter include benefits of conservation *per se*.

A. Markandya

VALUATION OF MORTALITY IMPACTS

One of the most important areas where environmental impacts occur is that of human health. Changes in air and water quality lead to changes in the incidence of diseases, the impairment of activities and changes in life expectancy. Valuing these impacts requires one to establish a link between the pollution and a measure of health status; for example between increases in SO_2 and increases in probability of death. However, the next step, that of valuing the change in health status can vary considerably. At one extreme are comprehensive models of individual behavior, in which individuals optimize their responses to environmental changes through a combination of measures – relocation, increased expenditures on avertive behavior, increased medication, etc. At the other are models that ignore individual responses and look instead at measures of lost production, increased cost of treatment, etc. In between are models that try to infer WTP on the basis of responses to similar risks in other situations (e.g. the hedonic wage method). This section reviews these methods and assesses their relevance and applicability in the developing country context.

Before discussing alternative methods of mortality valuation, it is important to address the criticisms of studies that place money values on changes in morbidity and mortality, especially the latter. These argue that, human life being sacred, it is beyond (or outside the scope of) monetary valuation. Hence attempts to do the latter are carrying benefit estimation too far. While one can understand the reasons for these criticisms, their focus is misplaced. What one is valuing in studies of mortality and morbidity is not a certain person's willingness to pay to avoid dying sooner, or suffering a longer period of illness, but an increase in the risk of this happening. Looked at in this way, it is apparent that individuals freely undertake actions which increase their risk of death or illness, because they derive income or utility from the associated actions. Participating in a risky sport, or working in a risky environment, or travelling by a risky mode of transport are all examples.

Some confusion in this regard in caused by the fact that the economists frequently speak of the 'value of life'. this is best shown by means of an example. Suppose the probability of death is reduced form 0.0002 to 0.0001 (i.e. by one in ten thousand). If the average willingness to pay for this reduction is $10, then the average value of life for that group is defined as $10/10^{-5}$ or $1,000,000. This is not what any one individual is willing to pay to avoid death. Rather it is a summary way of expressing, in one number, a WTP and a change in probability. In this form it can also be transported to other situations, unfortunately not always correctly. For example, one might have a situation where there was a change in probability of death from 0.01 to 0.02 (i.e. an increase of one in a hundred). If a population of 1000 people were affected, the WTP for the change could be calculated as

$$\$0.01 \times 1.000,000 \times 1000 = \$100,000,000$$

However, such a calculation presupposes that (a) the figure of $1,000,000 is applicable to this different group, (b) a probability change of one in a hundred, from a level of one in a hundred is simply 100 times the impact of a probability change of one in ten thousand, from a level of two in ten thousand.

There is a considerable literature which argues that value of life studies cannot be transported from one group to another, and that reaction for changes in probabilities do not obey the simple law from above. Hence care needs to be taken in carrying out either of these manoeuvres.

In mortality studies, two approaches have been adopted to valuing changes in risk. The first which goes back a long time[29], calculates the present value of gross earnings of the individual over his remaining lifetime and multiplies that by the charge in risk[30]. This approach has been widely used to estimate benefits in developed countries but in recent years it has been subject to much criticism. The reason is that it ignores individual own preferences, or the WTP for the reduction in risk. Another is that it places a low value on the lives of the elderly (low productivity) and children (coming too far in the future[31]). Thus using this method of valuation will underallocate resources for programs that benefit these groups.

In ignoring willingness to pay, recent research shows that this method generally underestimates the benefits of a reduction in the visit of mortality. However the amount by which it underestimates it is unclear, or too model-specific to be able to be used as a general guide[32].

Although the alternative approach – i.e. that of valuing WTP is theoretically more satisfactory, it too has several difficulties associated with it. Two of the techniques discussed earlier in this chapter have been used to value changes in the WTP or WTA of the risk of death. The first is the hedonic-wage approach, where differences in wages are explained using the hedonic method, with one of the variables being the occupational mortality rate. Such studies face many technical difficulties[33], but they do generate plausible values for the risk coefficient, and thereby for a WTA-based value of life. The other is the use of CVM methods, where individuals respond to questionnaires as discussed earlier. There is a substantial literature on the use of the CVM approval in this context which cannot be summarised here[34]. However, the main issues that arise from both hedonic and CVM studies can be addressed. These are:

- how far do individual perceptions of risk match the objective probabilities, and where the two differ, which should one take?
- is the response to risk, as shown in hedonic wage studies, relevant to the response to risk as it would arise in an environmental context?
- what is the relevance of actual expenditure on goods that reduce environmental risk?
- what are the effects of a latency period on the WTP for an increased risk of death? In other words, how would the WTP for something which affects the current probability of dying compare to the WTP for something which will affect death probabilities in 20 years? and
- what account, if any, should be taken of the WTP of others for the change in note of death?

Each of these is addressed below.

The relationship between subjective probabilities of mortality and the relative frequencies, as obtained from empirical data, varies considerably. Recent studies indicate that

(i) on labor markets, perceived probabilities tend to be higher than actual ones, perhaps by as much as 50%[35].
(ii) there is a tendency to overestimate low probabilities of death (e.g. radiation risks) and overestimate probabilities with higher frequencies[36].
(iii) individuals distinguish between the probability of death as applied to a population, and their own probability of death, which they underestimate (it-can't-happen-to-me phenomenon)[37].

There is a conflict here between giving individual preferences full weight, even if it is known that they are 'wrong' and taking the relative frequencies in calculating the costs and benefits of environmental changes. Given the uncertainty attached to the relative frequencies as estimates of objective probability, it is appropriate to take the perceived probabilities and try to influence them as much as possible by providing the data on relative frequencies to the affected population.

The WTA risk at work may differ from the WTP for avoiding environmental risks for a number of reasons. First, WTA and WTP differ, for the reasons given earlier in this chapter. Second, the populations are not the same. In wage studies, the wage differential between low and high risk occupations may be reduced because the high risk occupations are chosen by individuals who have a low aversion to risk. Third, is there any analytical way in which the individual 'prices' for the two risks can be related? In response to the latter it has been shown that, as long as much of the risk in the two situations are similar, the WTP for the one and the WTA for the other should be approximately the same. However, as this is often not the case, the transfer of prices for risk cannot be made straightforwardly. All this suggests that hedonic wage studies have to be used with extreme care in arriving at the price to be attached to the environmental risk of mortality. The 'biases' do not necessarily work in the same direction and there is no easy was to assess the extent of the biases.

The use of data on safety goods to value life is much more limited[38]. However, information from this source can be valuable. If a person reduced the risks of death by a certain amount ß and undertakes an expenditure of \$X in doing so, the implied WTP for life is \$X/ß . Such a calculation can offer an *alternative* way of valuing risk. It would be useful to compare this valuation with the hedonic wage valuation but no single study has attempted that.

So far the discussion of WTP has ignored the time dimension. However, for many environmental impacts this can be important. Actions today can influence the probability of death many years from now. In order to analyse these impacts, Cropper and Sussman and Freeman (among others) have developed a life cycle model of the WTP at time for a change in the conditional probability of dying at age[39]. The model shows that, as expected, a latency period reduced WTP and the longer the latency period the smaller is WTP. The extent of the decline as a function of the length of period can be worked out in terms of a discount factor, which is itself a combination of the riskless rate of interest and the conditional probabilities of death.

The final issue is how should one take account of the impact of one individual's death on others. Should one add something for the pain and suffering caused to others? One way in which such impacts are allowed is through provision by bequest. If an individual makes such a provision then his WTP will reflect, in part, the value of his survival to his heirs. However, not all indirect efforts are captured by such a mechanism and there may well be other impacts that need to be accounted for. In general the current theoretical research argues against including such values, unless the context in which they are considered is fully specified. As Bergstrom has pointed out, an individual may attach some welfare to the life of another person, but he also attaches some value to the additional consumption he will obtain in the event of the former's death. Thus both effects should be allowed for[40]. Hence, in the absence of a satisfactory framework for looking at interpersonal effects it is recommended that they be excluded from any calculations.

CONCLUSIONS ON THE VALUATION OF MORTALITY EFFECTS

Valuing reductions in the risk of mortality is an important part of valuing environmental impacts. Doing so is not inhuman, but part of a process that individuals undertake all the time in their private lives. However, the processes for doing so are complicated. Ideally one should try and measure the WTP for the reductions, based on personal preferences. This can be approached via the hedonic wage method, a CVM method, or by looking at avertive expenditures. Of these, the first raises many problems of the transferability of the estimates to situations of environmental risk. Although such estimates have been used they must remain suspect on these grounds. In addition, the use of this method in developing countries, when labour markets are less well developed, is certain to be even less satisfactory.

Other methods of valuation can be used in developing countries. The easiest would be to take a forgone earnings approach. Its limitations are known and have been discussed, but it does provide a lower bound to the benefits. Imputed earnings can be used for non-waged groups and low discount rates can avoid biases against safety programs that benefit children. Alternatives such as CVM and averting expenditures may also be applicable, but each situation would need to be looked at in detail. In particular, with the CVM method a proper understanding of the risk involved is essential if the method is to yield sensible results.

VALUATION OF MORBIDITY IMPACTS

The valuation of morbidity changes caused by pollution is more difficult than the valuation of mortality changes, principally because morbidity manifests itself in more ways and has a time dimension. In addition, data on deaths and their causes are better than the data in illnesses. According to Freeman[41] morbidity is classified by duration (chronic or acute), degree of impairment or symptom. Impairment can be measured in terms of restricted activity days (RAD), bed disability days or work days lost. Symptoms can be measured in symptom days, when the individual exhibits certain symptoms. It is also important to remember that a person may show none of these measures but may still be bearing a health cost from the pollution. This is because he or she undertakes avertive action and uses medication to suppress the effects.

As with mortality, morbidity effects can be valued in terms of individual preferences or in terms of resource costs. Hence the comments regarding these methods made earlier also apply in this case. Measures based on individual preferences are preferable but more difficult to obtain. If resource cost measures are used, it is important to allow for changes in avertive behavior. One may observe little or no change in measures of health status as pollution falls: for example, if the population simply reduces its expenditures on avertive actions. The main categories of expenditure that need to be examined are:

- medical expenses arising from the pollution
- loss of earnings
- avertive expenditure
- the value of disutility arising from the associated symptoms.

In principle all should be measured. A basic step in the valuation is the estimation of a 'health production function'. The following exposition is based on Harrington and Portney, and taken from Freeman. Define the following variables:

159

s = no. of side days
d = level of exposure to pollution
a = level of avoidance or avertive activity
b = level of medical treatment
c = level of pollution

The model can be generalized to the case of many avoidance activities or forms of treatment, but for ease of presentation only one of each is assumed. The following relationships are postulated.

Sick days are a function of exposure level d and medical treatment b:

$$s = f(d,b)$$

exposure level d is a function of pollution level d and level of avoidance a

$$d = g(c,a)$$

Substituting for d in the first equation gives the health production function[42]

$$s = s(c,a,b)$$

An individual is assumed to choose levels of a and b to maximize his ability, which is a function of sick days s and other variables, such as the amount of non-sick leisure time and his total income.

From this maximization one can measure the value of reduced pollution in terms of the amount of income an individual can have taken away to keep him as well off as before. If all choices are optimal the individual will equate the marginal costs of reducing the impact of pollution by averting activities or by medication and *either* of those costs are equal to the aforesaid measure[43] from changes in illness. These could be compared using CVM techniques, but great care could have to be taken to ensure that the respondent separated medication and avertive expenditures from residual changes in utility.

In developing countries this 'second best' alternative approach is feasible and worth carrying out, given access to adequate data. In some cases estimates of the relationship between days lost, medication and avertive expenditures; and the level of pollution could be imported from 'similar' countries. However, the effort required to achieve acceptable results could be quite high, at least for the first few studies for which a data base would need to be assembled[44].

CONCLUSIONS

This paper has discussed in some detail the different methods for valuing environmental impacts in money terms. For each technique it has listed the difficulties as well as the strengths, indicating in which applications it is most likely to be effective and what are the prospects of its use in developing countries. It is concluded that there is some scope for the use of each of the market-based techniques in the valuation of environmental benefits in developing countries, but this has yet to be substantially exploited. Particular promise holds for contingent valuation methods and travel cost approaches. Hedonic models are better suited to valuing sites and services and for urban pollution problems. It is essential to note that such models often only provide 'orders of magnitude' to the size of the benefits, and that some inaccuracy is inherent in the nature of the task being attempted. Nevertheless, the values obtained are useful in reaching rational decisions with regard to investments involving such benefits.

It is not essential to be persuaded that the monetary valuations illustrated in this section are completely accurate before recommending their use. Economics is not, and cannot be, a precise science. Its laboratory, after all, is human society itself. What does matter is that the implications of the valuation procedures outlined here are understood. These are:

(i) By at least trying to put money values on some aspects of environmental quality one is underlining the fact that environmental services are not free. They do have values in the same sense as marketed goods and services have values. The absence of markets must not be allowed to disguise this important fact;

(ii) By trying to value environmental services one is forced into a rational decision-making frame of mind. Quite simply, the gains and losses, the benefits and costs, of actions have to be thought about. If nothing else, economic valuation has made a great advance in that respect;

(iii) Dose-response based methods are of great relevance and value in developing countries where market-based methods dependent on revealed preferences are not feasible. In these cases a careful study of the linkages between the environmental and the polluting activity, as well as the impact of the changes in the environment on economic and social activities of value is necessary. Once this has been done, the valuation task becomes relatively straightforward. The main difficulties that practitioners face and that they have to be aware of are:

- the quality of the dose-response relationship. If it is poor, this should be stated and a range of estimates provided;
- the fact that some effects cannot be valued. All these should be listed;
- the need to recognize that, as a result of changes in the environment human beings often adjust their behavior. They do so to minimize its adverse effects on their welfare, or maximize its positive effects. Where possible these should be allowed for, but if they are not then the direction of the bias is known and this should be stated;

(iv) Because of the relative uncertainty of the responses and the measures, it is especially important to carry out *sensitivity analysis* on project appraisals where there are significant environmental costs and benefits.

NOTES

1. The seminal paper on the hedonic method is Rosen [1974]. For a detailed survey of its theoretical aspects see McConnell et al. [1985] and Vaughan [1987].
2. The slopes of the bid and offer curves in Figure 1 need not be as they are shown, but the requirement that the system be an equilibrium ensures that the bid curve AB is more concave than the offer curve OF. This analysis is based on McConnell *et al.* [1985], but essentially the same argument can be found in Brookshire *et al.* [1982].
3. See Bartik [1985].
4. See Vaughan (op.cit.) [1987].
5. The study showing higher figure for the hedonic approach is Brookshire *et al.* [1982], and the one showing the lower estimate was Brookshire *et al.* [1984]. For studies comparing hedonic and other methods see also Smith *et al.* [1986], and Kealey *et al.* [1988].

A. Markandya

6. As an example of the two stage estimation procedure see Nelson [1978].
7. See McConnell *et al.* [1985] and Vaughan [1987]. One approach that might be interesting to develop is the one where the second stage estimation is carried out using a specific utility function with the parameters estimated from the marginal hedonic prices. This entails complex non-linear estimation procedures, and the choice of the utility function is uncomfortably arbitrary, but the results can be interesting and useful as a comparison with the marginal hedonic prices themselves. See Kaufmann and Quigley [1987] for one example of such a study on data from a sites and services project in El Salvador.
8. For a detailed discussion of this point see Abelson and Markandya [1985].
9. Formulae for the estimation of the transformation bias are given in Duan [1983] and Miller [1984].
10. For a discussion of the methods see Halvorsen and Palmquist [1980] and Blaycock and Smallwood [1983].
11. See for example Bishop and Heberlein [1979], or Randall *et al.* [1985]. The latter also makes some use of a computer assisted format to describe the impacts to be evaluated.
12. For a recent survey of the contingent valuation method and the biases described, see Cummings *et al.* [1986], or Mitchell and Carson [1989]. These books identify many more 'biases' but the ones listed in the text are the main ones raising methodological issues.
13. See Bishop and Heberlein [1990] and Mitchell and Carson [1989].
14. See Pommerehne et al. [1982] and Coursey *et al.* [1987].
15. See the EPA study, Randall *et al.* [1985].
16. There are many studies that attest to the fact that strategic bias is not a serious problem in practice. See, for example, Schnedier and Pommerehne [1981]. For the use of incentives for truth-telling in contingent valuation, see Smith [1980].
17. Experiments on iterated bidding with WTP and WTA are analyzed in Coursey *et al.* [1987]. Discussion of the alternative approach may be found in Gregory [1986].
18. For details see Markandya and Pearce [1989], Smith *et al.* [1986] and Kealey *et al.* [1988].
19. For a review of the World Bank's recent experience with CVM see Brisco *et al.* [1990].
20. The theory of travel cost models was initially set out by Hoteling [1949]. One of the first studies using the method was that of Clawson and Knetch [1966].
21. Studies showing the sensitivity of the results to the value of time include Bockstael, Strand and Hanemann [1987] and Kerry Smith and Kaoru [1990].
22. See Desvousges, Smith and McGivney [1983].
23. The most common method used to correct truncation bias is that of Heckmann (see Madalla [1984]), which only involves estimating the equation with non-zero observations. An alternative method, which has been suggested as being more appealing for recreation behavior, is that of Cragg [1971]. However, this does require a probit estimation of the participation decision. See also Bockstael, *et al.* [1991].
24. The method was developed by Smith and Desvousges [1985] and subsequently has been used in estimating benefits of site improvements in the US.
25. For a description of the multinomial logit in its simple or nested form see McFadden [1978]. For applications in the recreational literature see Bockstael, Strand and Hanemann [1987]. Note that in either form the household characteristics can only enter the equations as interaction terms with the site characteristics.
26. For a discussion of exact and approximate welfare measures see Willig [1976]. For a discussion of the issue in the context of quality changes see Maler [1974], Freeman [1979] and Bockstael, *et al.* [1991].
27. The seminal papers on welfare estimation with random utility models are Small and Rosen [1981] and Hanemann [1982]. The compensating income measure described in the text refers to the welfare benefits of a single choice. To get the overall benefits, this would have to be multiplied by the number of visits to all sites. However, this raises the question of how that number would change in response to the change in quality and that too has to be estimated.

162

28. See for example, Gerking and Stanley [1986] for health impacts and Adams, *et al.* [1982] for vegetation damage.
29. See Landefild and Seskin, [1977] who claim that this approach can be tracked back as far as the late 17th century.
30. The relevant measure of earning is an issue in this method. Should one include or exclude taxes? Should one include the direct consumption of the individuals concerned? Although there is no full consensus, the general opinion seems to be that gross earning should be taken to reflect society's interest in the individuals earning, and that own consumption should be included. Finally there are individuals with little or no earnings. Where they perform non-waged services (e.g. housewives) an imputed earnings system can be derived.
31. The discount rate plays an important part here. Using rates of around 10% (as are typical at the Bank) would render the present value of a child's future earning very small. For example, a child of two, who would have started early at the age of 18 would have a present value of his earning stream of only 20% of that of an 18 year old.
32. See Freeman [1991]. As long as the utility function is concave, and consumption is above subsistence this result will hold.
33. For a further discussion of the applications see Pearce and Markandya [1989].
34. For an example of the use of CVM to measure the value of life see Jones Lee *et al.* [1985].
35. Viscusi and O'Connor [1984] and Gerking, De Haan and Schulze [1988].
36. Slovic, Fischoff and Lichtensten [1979].
37. Fischoff et al. [1981].
38. On the use of data from smoke detectors see Dardis [1980] and from seatbelts see Blomquist [1979].
39. See Cropper & Sussman [1990] and the extension of that model by Freeman [1991]. The models are limited by the fact that they do not incorporate a utility from being alive *per se*. Lifetime utility increases with the lifespan only because consumption can be spread over more time periods.
40. See Bergstrom [1982], and Jones-Lee [1989].
41. Freeman [1991].
42. For more details see Harrington and Portney [1987].
43. This assumes that the individual has non zero levels of a and b, and that neither is restricted to its maximum level. In technical terms, it assumes there is no corner solution.
44. Another issue of importance is the distinction between private and public medication and avertive expenditures. In the individual choice model such expenditure would be excluded from the private calculation described in the text. Hence they would need to be added back in. However in the alternative approach both private and public expenditures can be included as part of the response to changes in pollution.

REFERENCES

Abelson, P.W. and A. Markandya (1985), 'The Interpretation of Capitalized Hedonic Prices in a Dynamic Environment', *Journal of Environmental Economics and Management,* Vol. 12, pp. 195–206.

Adams, R.M. et al. (1982), 'An Economic assessment of Air Pollution Damages to Selected Annual Crops in Southern California', *Journal of Environmental Economics and Management,* Vol. 9, pp. 42–58.

Aylward B. and E. B. Barbier (1990), *Valuing Environmental Functions in Developing Countries – A Challenge for Economics and Ecology,* London Environmental Economics Centre, London.

Bartik, T. (1985), *Measuring the Benefits of Amenity Improvements in Hedonic Models,* Paper 85-W18, Department of Economics, Vanderbilt University, Nashville.

Bergstrom, T.C. (1982), 'When is a Man's Life Worth More Than His Human Capital?' in M.W. Jones-Lee (ed.), *The Value of Life and Safety,* North Holland, Amsterdam.

Bishop, R. (1982), 'Option Value: An Exposition and Extension', *Land Economics*, Vol. 58, pp. 1–15.

Bishop R. and T.A. Heberlein (1979), 'Measuring Values of Extramarket Goods: Are Indirect Measures Biased', *American Journal of Agricultural Economics*, Vol. 64, pp. 927–930.

Bishop R. and T. A. Heberlein (1990), 'The Contingent Valuation Method', in L. and G.V. Johnson (eds.) *Economic Valuation of Natural Resources: Issues, Theory and Applications*, Westview Press, Boulder.

Blaycock, J.R. and D.M. Smallwood (1983), 'Interpreting the Effects of Binary Variables in Transformed Models', *Economic Letters*, Vol. 12, pp. 255–259.

Blomquist G. (1979), 'Value of Life Savings: Implications of Consumption Activity', *Journal of Political Economy*, Vol. 87, No. 3, pp. 540–558.

Bockstael, N.E. *et al.* (1987), *Measuring the Benefits of Water Quality Improvements Using Recreation Demand Models*, Environmental Protection Agency, Washington DC.

Bockstael, N.E. *et al.* (1991), 'Recreation', in J. Branden and C. Kolsstad, *Measuring the Demand for Environmental Quality*, North Holland, New York.

Brisco, R. et al. (1990), 'Toward Equitable and Sustainable Water Supplies: A Contingent Valuation Study in Brazil', *The World Bank Economic Review*, Vol. 4 pp. 115–143.

Brookshire, E. *et al.* (1982), 'Valuing Public Goods: A Comparison of Survey and Hedonic Approaches', *American Economic Review*, Vol. 72, pp. 165–172. D. Brookshire et al. (1984), 'A Test of the Expected Utility Model: Evidence from Earthquake Risk', *Journal of Political Economy*.

Clawson, M. and J. L. Knetch (1966), *Economics of Outdoor Recreation*, Resources for the future, Washington DC.

Coursey, D.L. *et al.* (1987), 'On the Supposed Disparity Between Willingness to Pay and Willingness to Accept Measures of Value', *Quarterly Journal of Economics*, Vol. 102, pp. 679–690.

Cragg, J.G. (1971), 'Some Statistical Models for Limited Dependent Variables with Application to the Demand for Durable Goods', *Econometrica*, Vol. 39, pp. 829–844.

Cropper, M.L. and F.G. Sussman (1990), 'Valuing Future Risks to Life', *Journal of Environmental Economics and Management*, forthcoming.

Dardis, R. (1980), 'The Value of a Life: New Evidence from a Marketplace', *American Economic Review*, Vol. 70, No.5, pp. 1077–1082.

Cummings, R.G. *et al.* (1986), *Valuing Environmental Goods: An Assessment of the Contingent Valuation Method*, Rowman and Alanheld, Totowa, New Jersey.

Desousvges, W.H. *et al.* (1983), *A Comparison of Alternative Approaches for Estimating Recreation and Related Benefits of Water Quality Improvements*, Environmental Protection Agency, Washington DC.

Duan, N. (1983), 'Smearing Estimate: A Nonparametric Retransformation Method', *Journal of the American Statistical Association*, Vol. 78, pp. 605–610.

Fisher, A.C. and W. M.Hanneman (1986), 'Environmental Damages and Option Values', *Natural Resources Modelling*, Vol. 1, pp 111–124.

Fischoff, B. *et al.* (1981), *Acceptable Risk*, Cambridge University Press, New York.

Freeman, A.M. (1985), 'Supply Uncertainty, Option price, and Option Value in Project Evaluation', *Land Economics*, Vol. 61, pp. 176–181.

Freeman, A.M. (1979), *The Benefits of Environmental Improvement: Theory and Practice*, Johns Hopkins University Press, Baltimore.

Freeman, A.M. (1991), *The Measurement of Environmental Resource Values*, forthcoming.

Gerking, S. and L. Stanley (1986), 'An Economic Analysis of Air Pollution and Health: The Case of St. Louis', *Review of Economics and Statistics*, Vol. 68, pp. 115–121.

Gerking, S. *et al.* (1988), 'The Marginal Valuation of Job Safety: A Contingent Valuation Study', *Journal of Risk and Uncertainty*, Vol. 1, No. 2, pp. 185–199. R. Gregory (1986), 'Interpreting Measures of Economic Loss: Evidence from Contingent Valuation Studies', *Journal of Environmental Economics and Management*, Vol. 13, pp. 325–337.

Halvorsen, R. and R. Palmquist (1980), 'The Interpretation of Dummy Variables in Semi-Logarithmic Equations', *American Economic Review*, Vol. 70, pp. 474–475.

Value of the environment

Hanemann, W.M. (1984), 'Welfare Evaluations in Contingent Valuation Experiments with Discrete Responses', *American Journal of Agricultural Economics*, Vol. 66, pp. 332–341.

Harrington, W. and P.R. Portney (1987), 'Valuing the Benefits of health and Safety Regulations', *Journal of Urban Economics*, Vol. 22, No. 1, pp. 101–112.

Hodgson, G. and J. A. Dixon (1988), 'Logging Versus Fisheries and Tourism in Palawan', *East-West Environment and Policy Institute Occasional Paper No. 7*, Hawaii.

Hoen, J.P. and A. Randall (1989), 'Too Many Proposals Pass the Benefit Cost Test', *American Economic Review*, Vol. 79, pp. 544–551.

Hotelling H. (1949), *The Economics of Public Recreation – An Economic Survey of the Monetary Valuation of Recreation in the National Parks*, (The Prewitt Report), National Parks Service, Washington DC.

IDB (1988), *Empirical Issues in the Estimation of Hedonic Rent or Property Value Equations and their Use in Prediction*, OEO/WP-02/88, Washington DC.

Johansson, P-O. (1987), *The Economic Theory and Measurement of Environmental Benefits*, Cambridge University Press, Cambridge.

Jones-Lee, M.W. *et al.* (1985), 'The Value of Safety: The Results of a National Sample Survey', *Economic Journal*, Vol. 95, No. 377, pp. 49–72.

Jones-Lee M.W. *et al.* (1989), *The Economics of Safety and Physical Risk*, Blackwell, Oxford.

Kaufmann, D. and J.M. Quigley (1987), 'The Consumption Benefits of Investment in Infrastructure', *Journal of Development Economics*, Vol. 25, pp. 263–284.

Kealey, M.J. *et al.* (1988), 'Accuracy in Valuation is a Matter of Degree', *Land Economics*, Vol. 64, pp. 158–171.

Krutilla, J.V. (1967), 'Conservation Reconsidered', *American Economic Review*, Vol. 57, pp. 777–786.

Krutilla, J.V. and A.C. Fisher (1975), *The Economics of Natural Environments*, Resources for the Future, Washington DC.

Landefeld, J.S. and E.P. Seskin (1982), 'The Economic Value of Life: Linking Theory to Practice', *American Journal of Public Health*, Vol. 72, No. 6, pp. 555–566.

Madalla, G.S. (1984), *Limited Dependent and Qualitative Variables in Econometrics*, Cambridge University Press, New York.

Maler, K-G. (1974), *Environmental Economics: A Theoretical Inquiry*, Johns Hopkins University Press, Baltimore.

Markandya, A. and D.W. Pearce (1989) (see Pearce D.W. and Markandya A. (1989)).

McConnell, K.E. et al. (1985), *Identification of Preferences in Hedonic Models*, Vol. 1 of *Benefit Analysis Using Indirect of Imputed Market Methods*, Environmental Protection Agency Contract No. CR-811043-01-0, Washington DC.

McFadden, D. (1974), 'Modelling the Choice of Residential Location' in Karlquist et al. (eds), *Spatial Interaction Theory and Planning Models*, North Holland, New York.

Miller, D.M. (1984), 'Reducing Transformation Bias in Curve Fitting', *The American Statistician*, Vol. 38, pp. 126–126.

Nelson, J.P. (1978), 'Residential Choice, Hedonic Prices and the Demand for Urban Air Quality', *Journal of Urban Economics*, Vol. 5 pp. 357–369.

Mitchell, R.C. and R.T. Carson (1989), *Using Survey Methods to Value Public Goods: The Contingent Valuation Method*, Resources for the Future, Washington DC.

Norton, G. (1984), *Resource Economics*, Arnold, London.

Pearce, D.W., E. Barbier and A. Markandya (1989), *Sustainable Development: Economics and Environment in the Third World*, Elgar Publishing, London.

Pearce, D.W. and A.Markandya (1987), 'Marginal Opportunity Cost as a Planning Concept in Natural Resource Managment' *Annals of Regional Science*, Vol. 21, pp. 18–32.

Pearce, D.W. and A. Markandya (1989), *Environmental Benefit Estimation: Monetary Evaluation*, OECD, Paris.

Pigou, A.C. (1932), *The Economics of Welfare*, Macmillan, London.

Pommerehne, W.W. *et al.* (1982), 'Economic Theory of Choice and the Preference Reversal Phenomenon: A Reexamination', *American Ecoomic Review*, Vol. 72, pp. 569–574.

Porter, P. (1982), 'The New Approach to Wilderness Preservation through Benefit-Cost Analysis', *Journal of Environmental Economics and Management*, Vol. 9, pp. 59–80.

Plummer, M.L. and R.C. Hartman, 'Option Value: A General Approach', *Economic Inquiry*, Vol. 24, pp. 455–471.

Randall, A. *et al.* (1985), *National Aggregate Benefits of Air and Water Pollution Control*, University of Kentucky, EPA Contract CR881-056-01-0, Washington DC.

Regan, T. (1981), 'The Nature and Possibility of an Environmental Ethic', *Environmental Ethics*, Vol. 3, pp. 19–34.

Rosen, S. 'Hedonic Prices and Implicit Markets: Product Differentiation in Price Competition', *Journal of Political Economy*, Vol. 82, pp. 34–55.

Schneider, F. and W. W. Pommerehne (1981), 'Free Riding and Collective Action: An experiment in Public Microeconomics' *Quarterly Journal of Economics*, Vol. 95, pp. 689–704.

Slovic, P. *et al.* (1979), 'Rating the Risks', *Environment*, Vol. 21, pp. 14–20.

Small, K.A. and H.S. Rosen (1981), 'Applied Welfare Economics with Discrete Choice Models', *Econometrica*, Vol. 49, pp. 105–130.

Smith, V.L. (1980), 'Experiments with a Decentralized Mechanism for Public Goods Decisions', *American Economic Review*, Vol. 70, pp. 584–599.

Smith, V.K. and W.H. Desvousges (1985), 'The Generalized Travel Cost Model and Water Quality Benefits: A Reconsideration', *Southern Economic Journal*, Vol. 50, pp. 371–381.

Smith, V.K. (1987), 'Nonuse Values in Benefit Cost Analysis', *Southern Economic Journal*, Vol. 54, pp. 19–26.

Smith, V.K. *et al.* (1986), 'A Comparison of Direct and Indirect Methods for Estimating Environmental Benefits', *American Journal of Agricultural Economics*, Vol. 68, pp. 280–290.

Smith, V.K. and Y. Kaoru (1990), 'Signals or Noise? Explaining the Variation in Recreation Benefit Estimates', *American Journal of Agricultural Economics*, Vol. 72, pp. 419–433.

Turner, R.K. (1988), 'Wetland Conservation: Economics and Ethics', in D. Collard, D.W. Pearce and D. Ulph, *Economics, Growth and Sustainable Environments*, Macmillan, London.

USEPA (1987), *EPA's Use of Cost-Benefit Analysis, 1981–86*, EPA-230-05-87-028, Washington DC.

Vaughan, J. (1987), *Hedonic Methodology and Project Benefit Measurement*, IDB, CON/OEO-218-87, Washington DC.

Viscusi, K.W. and C.J. O'Connor (1984), 'Adaptive Responses to Chemical Labelling: Are Workers Bayesian Decision-Makers?, *American Economic Review*, Vol. 74, No. 5, pp. 942–956.

Willig, R.D. (1976), 'Consumer's Surplus without Apology', *American Economic Review*, Vol. 66, pp. 589–597.

Chapter 12
Hedonic price estimation of variable urban air quality

James C. Murdoch and Mark A. Thayer

This paper investigates the hypothesis, used in numerous hedonic property value studies [3, pp. 156–60], that the appropriate specification of the hedonic function should use mean levels of environmental quality. Unlike characteristics such as the number of bathrooms and square feet of living area, the environmental quality for a particular house varies from day to day. This implies that the mean is just one parameter of the *distribution* of environmental quality. As a test of the validity of the mean model, hedonic price equations using visibility to measure environmental quality are estimated for the California South Coast Air Basin. The estimated equations using mean visibility are compared to a model using the probabilities of various levels of visibility occurring as independent variables.[1] The probabilities more accurately measure the distributional nature of visibility. Statistical tests indicate that the probability model outperforms the mean model. Hedonic prices are calculated to illustrate the magnitude of the specification error which can occur from using the mean model.

EMPIRICAL FINDINGS
A test of the mean specification is performed by estimating an equation with the probabilities of various levels of environmental quality entered as independent variables. Let

$$r = \sum_j \beta_j a_j + \sum_i \xi_i p_i e_i \tag{1}$$

be an estimated hedonic equation where r is the housing price, a_j is the jth housing attribute, p_i is the probability of the ith level of environmental quality (e_i) occurring, and the β_j's and ξ_i's are estimated coefficients. The traditional mean specification is a restricted form of Eq. (1) since the mean environmental quality ($\bar{e}$) is equal to $\Sigma_i p_i e_i$. The mean model,

$$r = \sum_j \beta_j a_j + \gamma \bar{e}, \tag{2}$$

is correct under the null hypothesis that $\xi_i = \gamma$ for all i. This hypothesis can be tested by comparing the sum of squared residuals in each model using a standard F test.[2]

Log-linear estimates of Eqs. (1) and (2) are presented in Table 12.1. The housing market represented is the California South Coast Air Basin in 1979. This region includes Los Angeles County and a portion of Orange County. Most of the independent variables are self-explanatory and correspond to other urban property value studies. Visibility in miles is used as the surrogate for environmental quality. The variability of the visibility is captured by using four

Table 12.1 Estimated coefficients and standard errors in parentheses for the hedonic price equations: the dependent variable is the natural logarithm of sales price of the home.

Variable:	Probability model	Mean model
Age of home[a]	−0.01	−0.008
	(0.005)	(0.005)
Square feet of interior living area[a]	0.51	0.512
	(0.025)	(0.02)
Number of bathrooms	0.06	0.057
	(0.013)	(0.013)
Number of fireplaces	0.054	0.054
	(0.01)	(0.01)
Pool	0.04	0.036
	(0.015)	(0.015)
View	0.12	0.133
	(0.022)	(0.02)
Percentage of population older than 64[a]	0.12	0.136
	(0.011)	(0.01)
Percentage of population white[a]	0.09	0.075
	(0.03)	(0.03)
Mean income[a]	0.42	0.42
	(0.02)	(0.02)
School quality[a]	0.01	0.01
	(0.05)	(0.05)
Housing density[a]	−0.05	−0.074
	(0.015)	(0.02)
Crime rate[a]	−0.06	−0.081
	(0.02)	(0.02)
Distance to central business district	−0.004	−0.004
	(0.001)	(0.001)
Distance to nearest beach[a]	−0.11	−0.094
	(0.008)	(0.007)
Visibility:		
Pr visibility 0–1 miles	−9.91	
	(2.09)	
Pr visibility 1–10 miles	−1.97	
	(0.33)	
Pr visibility 10–25 miles	−1.61	
	(0.33)	
Pr visibility > 25 miles	−0.69	
	(0.39)	
Mean visibility[b]		0.422
		(0.04)
Constant		−2.79
		(0.33)
Degrees of freedom	1337	1339
Sum of squared residuals	48.46	49.37

[a] Entered as natural logarithm.   [b] $p_1\text{in}(0.5) + p_2\text{in}(5) + p_3\text{in}(17.5) + p_4\text{in}(45)$.

levels: 0–1, 1–10, 10–25, and greater than 25 miles. The estimates for the likelihood of each level occurring were obtained by coding the visibility data at airports in the study area for all days in 1978 and 1979. The data set employed here is completely described in [7].

With the exception of the school quality measure, all estimated coefficients are statistically significant at the 5% level and have the expected influence on home sales price. Notice that the probability model excludes the constant term since the probabilities sum to one. The F statistic comparing the probability model to its mean counterpart is 12.71 while the critical value, with two degrees of freedom in the numerator and infinity in the denominator, equals 4.61 at the 0.01 level. Therefore, we reject the hypothesis implied by the mean model ($\xi_i = \gamma$ for all i), implying that the market does not weight the probability of various visibility levels occurring equally.

The specification error associated with the traditional mean model is examined by predicting price differentials from each equation that are based on a change in the distribution of the visibility at each location. Holding all other independent variables at their mean, price differentials are computed for a 0.01 change in probability from one visibility level to the next best level. Changing the probabilities in this fashion is not mean preserving, so we can evaluate predictions from the mean model and compare them to the probability model. Smith [6] shows that these price differentials correspond to the marginal willingness to pay (or marginal option price) for a change in probability.

Table 12.2 Predicted hedonic price differentials for changing probability by 0.01[a].

	Change in probability		
Model	From Level 1 to Level 2	From Level 2 to Level 3	From Level 3 to Level 4
Traditional mean model	785	595	473
Probability model	7346	336	863

[a] The other variables in the equations are assigned their mean values, which are age of house = 22.8, living area = 1532, number of bathrooms = 1.89, school quality = 62.46, density = 6.3, percentage of the population white = 85.4, percentage of the population older than 64 = 10.3, view = 0.07, pool = 0.16, average income = 27,974, number of fireplaces = 0.76, distance to central business district = 6.79, distance to beach = 11.52, and crime rate index = 0.05.

The predicted price differentials for each model are presented in Table 12.2. Interestingly, the probability model predicts a greater differential than the mean model for movements in the distribution below the mean and above the mean, but less for movements around the mean. (The mean visibility is approximately 13.) The difference between the differentials is quite substantial below the mean. These results suggest that the hedonic prices for air quality and the benefit estimates potentially derived from them are biased if based on average air quality measures.[3]

CONCLUSIONS
This paper implies that benefit estimates based on the traditional mean model are likely to be biased and that efforts to improve the accuracy of hedonic methods should consider more complete measures of environmental quality. Other studies, such as those designed to understand population migration and/or dose–response relationships, using average environmental quality indicators also may be biased. At the very least, further research into the variable nature of environmental quality measures should be performed before benefit estimates based on hedonic price method are used for environmental policy decisions.

NOTES
1. Hedonic price equations based on other summary statistics such as the median, the variance, and the natural logarithm of the mean also were estimated. None performed as well as the probability model.
2. Several issues surrounding the estimation of equations similar to (2) have been addressed

in the literature [1, 4]. Our test remains robust under several different functional forms and alternative specifications of the independent variable set.
3. The focus of this paper is on price differentials not benefit estimates. However, in the Freeman [2]-Rosen [5] procedure the price differentials provide the data for demand curve estimation. Several problems have been noted [1] in applying the Freeman-Rosen procedure.

REFERENCES

1. Bartik, J.J. and V.K. Smith, 'Urban Amenities and Public Policy,' Working Paper No. 84-W18, Vanderbilt University, Nashville, TN (1984).
2. Freeman, A.M., On estimating air pollution control benefits from land value studies, *J. Environ. Econom. Management,* **1,** 74–83 (1974).
3. Freeman, A.M., 'The Benefits of Environmental Improvement: Theory and Practice,' Johns Hopkins Press, Baltimore (1979).
4. Graves, P., J.C. Murdoch, M.A. Thayer, and D. Waldman, The Robustness of Hedonic Prices: Urban Air Quality, *Land Econom.* (in preparation).
5. Rosen, S., Hedonic prices and implicit markets: Product differentiation in pure competition, *J. Polit. Econom.* **82,** 34–55 (1974).
6. Smith, V.K., Supply uncertainty, option price, and indirect benefit estimation, *Land Econom.* **61,** 303–07 (1985).
7. Trijonis, J. *et al.* 'Air Quality Benefit Analysis for Los Angeles and San Francisco Based on Housing Values and Visibility,' report to California Air Resources Board (1984).

Chapter 13

Time and the recreational demand model

Nancy E. Bockstael, Ivar E. Strand and W. Michael Hanemann

Economists, especially those interested in recreation demand, have long recognized that time spent in consuming a commodity may in some cases be an important determinant of the demand for that commodity. Recreationalists cite time much more than money as the constraining element in their recreation consumption (e.g., U.S. Dep. of Interior). Although the potential importance of time has been discussed at some length in the literature, only recently has the problem of explicitly incorporating time into the behavioral framework of the consumer been addressed.

Even when the treatment of time is critical, a consensus as to a proper approach remains elusive. A number of approaches (e.g., Smith, Desvousges, and McGivney; McConnell and Strand; Cesario and Knetsch) to valuing time are currently in vogue; but no method is dominant, and researchers often improvise. Unfortunately, the benefit estimates associated with changes in public recreation policy are extremely sensitive to these improvisations. Cesario, for example, found that annual benefits from park visits nearly doubled depending on whether time was valued at some function of the wage rate or treated independently in a manner suggested by Cesario and Knetsch. More recently, Bishop and Herberlein presented travel cost estimates of hunting permit values which differed fourfold when time was valued at one-half the median income and when time was omitted altogether from the model.

In applications, researchers have often incorporated travel time in an arbitrary fashion as an adjustment in a demand function or, alternatively, by asking people what they would be willing to pay to reduce travel time. Ad hoc econometric specifications or general willingness-to-pay questions are particularly problematic, however, because time is such a complex concept. Time, like money, is a scarce resource. Anything which uses time as an input consumes a resource for which there are utility-generating alternatives. Because time is an essential input into the production of any commodity which we might call an "activity," time is frequently used as a measure of that activity as well. Thus, while time is formally an input into the production of the commodity, it may also serve as the unit of measure of output. Hence, direct questioning or poorly conceived econometric estimation may yield confusing results because the distinction between these two concepts is not carefully made.

This paper focuses on time as a scarce resource. Both travel time and on-site time are uses of the scarce resource and must appear in a time constraint to be properly accounted for by the model. The exclusion of either will bias results. The recreational commodity is defined in terms of fixed units of on-site time, and it is assumed that travel does not in itself influence utility levels.

The paper develops a general framework for incorporating time, drawing on recent advances in the labor literature. After discussing the wide range of complex labor constraints which the general model can handle, it is made operational. This task is more difficult than it might appear since the utility-maximizing framework now includes two constraints. The approach developed below not only incorporates a defensible method for treating the value of time but also addresses sample selection bias inherent in recreational survey design and derives exact measures of welfare. Finally, the approach is illustrated with a sample of recreationalists.

TIME AS A COMPONENT OF RECREATIONAL DEMAND: A REVIEW

The problems which arise when time is left out of the demand for recreation were first discussed by Clawson and Knetsch. Cesario and Knetsch later argued that the estimation of a demand curve which ignored time costs would overstate the effect of the price change and thus understate the consumer surplus associated with a price increase.

In practical applications, both travel cost and travel time variables have usually been calculated as functions of distance. As a result, including time as a separate variable in the demand function tended to cause multicollinearity. Brown and Nawas, and Gum and Martin responded to the multicollinearity issue by suggesting the use of individual trip observations rather than zonal averages. In contrast, Cesario and Knetch proposed combining all time costs and travel costs into one cost variable to eliminate the problem of multicollinearity.

Johnson and McConnell were the first to consider the role of time in the context of the recreationalist's utility maximization problem (although others had considered time in other consumer decision problems). In the context of the classical labor–leisure decision, the individual maximizes utility subject to a constraint on both income and time. When work time is not fixed, that is, when it is freely chosen by the individual, then the time constraint can be solved for work time and substituted into the budget constraint. As a result time cost is transformed into a money cost at the implicit wage rate.

However, when individuals are unable to choose the number of hours worked, the direct substitution of the time constraint into the budget constraint is not possible. McConnell suggested that in this case one should still value time in terms of money before incorporating it in the demand function. This is conceptually possible, since at any given solution there would be an amount of money which the individual would be willing to exchange for an extra unit of time so as to keep his utility-level constant. Unfortunately, this rate of trade-off between money and time, unlike the wage rate, is both endogenous and unobservable.

Much of the recent recreation demand literature follows the line of reasoning which relates the opportunity cost of time in some way to the wage rate. McConnell and Strand (see also Cesario; Smith and Kavanaugh; Nichols, Bowes, and Dwyer) demonstrated a methodology for estimating a factor of proportionality between the wage rate and the unit cost of time within the traditional travel cost model. More recently, Smith, Desvousges, and McGivney attempted to modify the traditional recreational demand model so that more general constraints on individual use of time are imposed. They considered two time constraints, one for work/nonrecreational goods and another for recreational goods; the available recreation time could not be traded for work time. The implications for their model suggest that when time and income constraints cannot be reduced to one constraint, the marginal effect of travel and on-site time on recreational demand is related to the wage rate only through an income effect and in the most indirect manner. Unfortunately, their model "does not suggest an empirically feasible approach for treating these time costs" (p. 264). For estimation, these authors confined themselves to a modification of a traditional demand specification which is not necessarily consistent with utility maximization.

Researchers are thus left with considerable confusion about the role of the wage rate in specifying an individual's value of time. But an important body of economic literature, somewhat better developed, has attempted to deal with similar issues. Just as the early literature on the labor–leisure decision provided initial insights into the modeling of time in recreational demand, more recent literature on labor supply behavior provides further refinement.

LABOR SUPPLY LITERATURE: A REVIEW
The first generation of labor supply models resembled the traditional recreational demand literature in a number of ways. These models either treated work time as a continuous choice variable allowing a continuous trade-off between income and leisure time at the wage rate or they treated work time as a fixed parameter with individuals being "rationed" with respect to labor supply in a "take-it-or-leave-it" fashion.

While useful in characterizing the general nature of a time allocation problem, first generation labor supply models were criticized on both theoretical and econometric grounds. The second generation of labor supply literature (see for example Ashenfelter, Ham, Burtless and Hausman) generalized the budget line to reflect more realistic assumptions about employment opportunities. As Killingsworth states in his survey, "the budget line may not be a straight line: Its slope may change (for example, the wage a moonlighter gets when he moonlights may differ from the wage he gets at his 'first' job), and it may also have 'holes' (for example, it may not be possible to work between zero and four hours)" (p. 18). This more general view of the problem is useful for recreation demand modeling for it argues that only those individuals who choose to work jobs with flexible work hours (e.g., self-employed professionals and individuals working second jobs or part-time jobs, etc.) can adjust their marginal rates of substitution of goods for leisure to the wage rate. All others can be found at corner solutions where no such equimarginal conditions hold and the wage rate cannot serve as the value of leisure time.

Two further aspects of the second generation labor supply models are noteworthy. The first generation studies estimated functions which were specified in a relatively ad hoc manner, but second generation labor supply functions were derived from direct or indirect utility functions (Heckman, Killingsworth, and MacCurdy; Burtless and Hausmann; Wales and Woodland). Such utility-theoretic models have particular appeal for recreational benefit estimation because they allow estimation of exact welfare measures.

Finally, first generation research was concerned either with the discrete work/nonwork decision or with the continuous hours-of-work decision. Second generation empirical studies recognized the potential bias and inefficiency of estimating the two problems independently and employed estimation techniques to correct for this. An analogous problem arises in recreation demand studies; both the discrete participation decision and the continuous demand for recreational trips are important.

N.E. Bockstael, I.E. Strand, W.M. Hanemann

A PROPOSED RECREATION DEMAND MODEL

The nature of an individual's labor supply decision determines whether his wage rate will yield information about the marginal value of his time. In the recreational literature, researchers have conventionally viewed only two polar cases: either individuals face perfect substitutability between work and leisure time or work time is assumed fixed. Yet, few people have absolutely fixed work time, since part-time secondary jobs are always possible, and only some professions allow free choice of work hours at a constant wage rate. A workable recreation demand model must reflect the implications which labor decisions have on time valuation and allow these decisions to vary over individuals.

In developing a behavioral model that includes time as an input, we begin with a household production model. The individual maximizes utility by choosing a flow of recreational services, x_R, and a vector of other commodities, x_N, each of which may be produced by combining purchased inputs with time.

The technology is assumed to be fixed-proportion so that the x's have fixed time and money costs per unit given by t and p, respectively. For the recreation good, x_R, it implies that a unit of x_R (e.g., a visit) has a constant marginal cost (p_R) and fixed travel and on-site time requirements (t_R). All other commodities are subject to unit money or time costs and the general problem becomes

$$(1) \qquad \max_{x_R, x_N} U(x_R, x_N),$$

subject to

$$E + F(T_w) - p'_R x_R - p'_N x_N = 0, \text{ and}$$

$$T - T_w - t'_R x_R - t'_N x_N = 0,$$

where $U(...)$ is a quasi-concave, twice-differentiable utility function, $E + F(T_w)$ is the sum of the individual's nonwage and wage income, T_w is labor time supplied, and T is the total time available.

In order to characterize an individual's solution to (1), the nature of the labor market constraints must be known. Figure 13.1 depicts one of many possible labor market scenarios where the individual has the opportunity of taking a primary job (at wage w_p) which requires a fixed work week of forty hours. Depending on the shape of the individual's indifference curve between work and leisure, this individual may choose not to work at all (at B), to work the primary job only (at A), or to work some additional hours at a secondary job which pays $w_s < w_p$ (some point along CA). At an interior solution, such as along line segment AC, the individual adjusts work time such that his marginal rate of substitution between leisure and goods equals his effective (marginal) wage rate. Alternatively, an individual may be at a corner solution of unemployment (point B), or a fixed work week (point A). At both these points no relationship exists between the individual's wage rate and his time valuation.[1]

Strictly speaking, the problem in (1) requires the simultaneous choice of both the x's and the individual position in the labor market (i.e., interior of corner solution). However, modeling the entire labor decision is beyond the scope of most recreation demand studies. Labor market decisions may be affected by individuals' recreational preferences and by the recreational opportunities available. However, the daily and seasonal recreational choices about which we collect data and develop models can reasonably be treated as short-run decisions

174

Recreational demand model

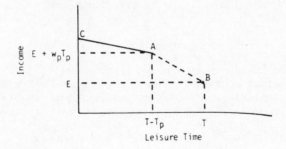

Figure 13.1 Second generation budget constraints.

conditioned on longer-run labor choices. Because changing jobs is costly, labor market adjustments are not made continually. Thus, we consider that recreational choices depend on the type of employment which the individual has chosen. If the individual chooses employment with flexible work hours, then time spent working is endogenous to the model.

Let us rewrite the problem in (1) so as to allow treatment of both interior and corner labor market solutions. Define t_F as hours spent working at a job with a fixed work week and t_D as hours of discretionary employment, i.e., hours freely chosen by the individual. The variable w_F is wage associated with t_F, and w_D is the wage received in discretionary employment. Additionally, define $\bar{T}$ as $T - t_F$ or the time available for discretionary activities. Now the tie constraint can be expressed as

$$(2a) \qquad T - t_F - t_D - t'_R x_R - t'_N x_N = 0, \text{ or}$$

$$(2b) \qquad \bar{T} - t_D - t'_R x_R - t'_N x_R = 0.$$

Given the distinction between discretionary and nondiscretionary time, it makes sense to define the budget constraint in a general way as well:

$$(3a) \qquad E + w_F t_F + w_D t_D - p'_R x_R - p'_N x_N = 0, \text{ or}$$

$$(3b) \qquad \bar{Y} + w_D t_D - p'_R x_R - p\, p'_N x_N = 0$$

where $\bar{Y}$ is nonwage income and income from nondiscretionary employment.

For any given individual t_D or t_F or both may be zero. Specifically, an individual with $t_D > 0$ will be at an interior solution in the labor market and one with $t_D = 0$ will be at a corner. The lagrangian problem for individuals with $t_D = 0$ can be written as

$$(4) \qquad \max L = U(x_R, x_N) + \lambda(\bar{Y} - p'_R x_R - p'_N x_N) + \mu(\bar{T} - t'_R x_R - t'_N x_N).$$

First-order conditions for these individuals are

$$(4a) \qquad \partial U/\partial x_i - \lambda p_i - \mu t_i = 0 \text{ for all } i,$$

$$\bar{Y} - p'_R x_R - p'_N x_N = 0,$$

$$\bar{T} - t'_R x_R - t'_N x_N = 0.$$

175

Since these individuals cannot marginally adjust work time, the two constraints are not collapsible. Solving (2a) for the demand for x_i yields a demand function of the general form

$$(4b) \qquad x_i = h^C(p_i, t_i, p^0, t^0, \bar{Y}, \bar{T})$$

where p^0 and t^0 are the vectors of money and time costs of all goods other than i.

For individuals at interior solutions in the labor market, at least some component of work time is discretionary, and time can be traded for money at the margin. In this case t_D is endogenous. Because of this, the lagrangian

$$\max L = U(x_R, x_N) + \lambda(\bar{Y} + w_D t_D - p'_R x_R - p'_N x_N) + \mu(\bar{T} - t_D - t'_R x_R - t'_N x_N)$$

can be rewritten as

$$(5) \quad \max L = U(x_R, x_N) + \delta(\bar{Y} + w_D \bar{T} - (p_R + w_D t_R)' x_R - (p_N + w_D t_N)' x_N),$$

where the time constraint has been substituted into the income constraint. This reflects the fact that when (at least a portion of) work time is endogenous, money can be traded for time and time for money at the margin. First-order conditions for the individual at an interior solution are

$$(5a) \quad \partial U / \partial x_i - \delta(p_i + w_D t_i) = 0 \text{ for all } i,$$

$$\bar{Y} + w_D \bar{T} - (p_R + w_D t_R)' x_R - (p_N + w_D t_N)' x_N = 0.$$

Solving for the general form of a recreational demand function for an interior solution yields

$$(5b) \qquad x_i = h^I(p_i + w_D t_i, p^0 + w_D t^0, \bar{Y} + w_D \bar{T}).$$

Consideration of demand functions (4b) and (5b) suggests that the data requirements for estimation are not overly burdensome. In addition to the usual questions about income and the time and money costs of the recreational activity, one need only ask (a) the individual's total work time and (b) whether or not he has the discretion to work during recreational time. If he does, his discretionary wage must be elicited.

In problem (5) the recreational demand function is conditioned on the individual having chosen an interior solution in the labor market. The wage rate (w_D) reflects the individual's value of time because work and leisure can be traded at the margin. When this is not the case, as in problem (4), the marginal value of the individual's time in other uses is not equal to the wage rate he faces. This does not imply that the opportunity cost of time is zero for this individual. Rather his opportunity cost is not equal to an observable parameter.

CONSIDERATIONS FOR ESTIMATING RECREATIONAL BENEFITS

At this point one would like to estimate demand functions such as (4b) and (5b) and relate the estimated parameters to welfare measures. The recent literature in benefit measurement emphasizes the use of "exact" welfare measures. The procedures for integrating back from a Marshallian demand function to utility and expenditure functions are now well established (Hausman, Hanemann), and techniques for approximating compensating variation using numerical methods (when "exact" measures have no closed form solutions) are well developed (e.g., Vartia). However, by formulating the problem above with two constraints (money and time), we open the door to a new set of problems in welfare measurement. It has been demonstrated (Smith) that the utility maximization problem with two linear constraints has two duals, one which minimizes money costs subject to utility and time constraints and the other which minimizes time costs subject to utility and income constraints. Associated with each dual is an expenditure function and a compensated demand. As discussed elsewhere (Bockstael and Strand), compensation can be measured in terms of time or money or any combination of the two.

We can choose the traditional money measure for welfare evaluation, but this does not solve all problems. The conventional wisdom on integrating back to expenditure functions or obtaining exact welfare measures does not apply in the two-constraint case. This means that the procedure of estimating a Marshallian demand function which fits the data well and deriving the associated expenditure function using the parameter estimates is not a feasible alternative at this juncture. If one wants exact measures, one needs to start with the preference structure and explore those demand functions which can be derived from alternative utility functions. One clear difficulty – a symptom of the integrability problem – is that the utility function considered must be a function of at least three goods because it will be maximized with respect to two constraints. It is no longer possible to use the single Hicksian bundle concept. These difficulties are not artificial constructs which follow from the specific formulation of the problem. They characterize any micro decision problem where the individual faces two constraints.

All is not lost, however. An alternative is to start with a plausible utility function and derive the corresponding demand function for the recreational good. An array of such utility functions and demand functions could be explored. Here we select a utility function which is somewhat restrictive in nature but which generates linear demand functions which ease illustration. Nonetheless, the theoretical development in the previous sections and the subsequent general empirical procedures are applicable to any preference function chosen.

Because our empirical illustration has a quality variable involved with the choice of recreational use, the utility function also has quality as an element. This is a straightforward adaption of a quantity/quality model discussed in Hanemann.

The utility function used for illustration has the form,

$$(6) \quad U(x) = \frac{(\gamma_1 + \gamma_2)x_1 + \beta}{(\gamma_1 + \gamma_2)^2} \exp\left[\frac{(\gamma_1 + \gamma_2)(\alpha + \gamma_1 x_2 + \gamma_2 x_3 - x_1 + \gamma_3 q + \epsilon)}{(\gamma_1 + \gamma_2)x_1 + \beta}\right]$$

As is the usual procedure, the parameters α, β, γ_1, γ_2, and γ_3 are assumed common to all individuals for estimation purposes. The random variable, ϵ, reflects the distribution of preferences over the population and is assumed to be distributed normally with mean zero and constant variance, σ^2.

The recreational good is designed as x_1, and q is some quality dimension associated with it. In the two-constraint case, it is useful to partition the set of other goods such that x_2 is a Hicksian bundle of goods with money but no significant time costs. The bundle, x_2, is a numeraire such that the money price of recreation is normalized with respect to p_2. Hicksian bundle x_3 is a bundle of goods with time but no significant money costs and serves as a numeraire such that time prices are normalized with respect to t_3. Thus, the general constraint set is

$$\bar{Y} - p_1 x_1 - p_2 x_2 = 0, \text{ and}$$
$$\bar{T} - t_1 x_1 - t_3 x_3 = 0,$$

where p_2 and t_3 are assumed to be equal to one.

The restrictive form of the utility function chosen has two undesirable properties. For an interior solution, when the two constraints collapse into one, this form implies that either x_2 or x_3 is chosen (but not both). When the two constraints are not collapsible, the functional form implies a constant trade-off between time and money. While restrictive with regard to the Hicksian goods, the utility function does have the advantage of producing easily estimated demand functions for the recreational good.

Solving the system for the optimum value of x_1, and denoting $\beta/(\gamma_1 + \gamma_2)$ as β', yields ordinary recreational demand functions, conditioned on each labor supply decision, of the form

(7) $$x_1 = \alpha + \gamma_1 \bar{Y} + \gamma_2 \bar{T} + \beta' \gamma_1 p_1 + \beta' \gamma^2 t_1 + \gamma_3 q + \epsilon$$

for individuals at corner solutions in the labor market and

(8) $$x_1 = \alpha + \gamma_1 (\bar{Y} + w_D \bar{T}) + \beta' \gamma_1 (p_1 + w_D t_1) + \gamma_3 q + \epsilon$$

for individuals at interior solutions in the labor market. Since equations (7) and (8) are linear in the respective variables, they might easily have been specified and estimated as ad hoc demand functions, without reference to utility theory, but the theoretical development provides a basis for interpreting the parameters and understanding the inherent restrictions of the model.

By first substituting demand functions into (6) to obtain the indirect utility function and inverting to obtain the money expenditure function, the compensating variation for each of the above cases can be derived. Compensating variation in money terms is[2]

(9) $$CV_I^Y =$$
$$\exp[\gamma_1(\bar{p}_1 - p_1^0)] \left(\frac{x_1^0 + \beta'}{\gamma_1} \right) - \frac{\beta'}{\gamma_1}$$

for the interior solution, where (p_1^0, x_1^0) is the initial observed point and $\bar{p}_1$ is the price which drives the individual out of the market for x_1. The money compensating variation for a loss of the recreation good conditioned on a corner solution in the labour market is then

(10) $$CV_C^Y =$$
$$\exp[\gamma_1(\bar{p}_1 - p_1^0)] \left(\frac{x_2^1 + \beta'}{\gamma_1} \right) - \frac{\beta'}{\gamma_1}$$

THE EMPIRICAL ILLUSTRATION

In this section, a specific application of the model is offered. Parameters of the recreational demand model are estimated for a group of Southern California sportfishermen who fished during 1983. All individuals in the group owned at least one boat and took at least one private boat trip during that year. About one-third

Recreational demand model

of the respondents claimed they could have worked in lieu of fishing and provided information on the wage rate from working. The others were assumed to face fixed work hours and thus were at corner solutions in the labor market. Individuals facing both types of labor market situations, represented by demand equations (4b) and (5b), could be found in the sample.

A more complete description of the questionnaire and data is given elsewhere (i.e. Wegge, Hanemann, and Strand), but the following description of the variables will serve our purposes: x_1 is annual private boat trips in Southern California during 1983; p_1 is the average transportation cost per trip (\$/trip); q is the average number of the principal species caught per trip (fish/trip); t_1 is the average round-trip travel time (hours/trip); $\bar{Y}$ is annual household income (in \$ × 10^{-3}); $\bar{T}$ is annual hours of paid vacation plus hours available after work (in hours × 10^{-3}); and w_D is hourly wage for discretionary work time (\$/hours).

Following the theoretical development, an individual's demand for trips is given by some systematic function of money and time price, income, discretionary time, and fish catch. The estimation procedure must take account of the different demand functions applicable for people in different labor market situations. Additionally, because the sample contained only recreational participants, a method which corrects for the implied truncation bias (Maddala, p. 165) must be used. One such method (the tobit) assumes the individual's behavior has the following pattern

$x_i = h_i(\cdot) + \epsilon_i$ if and only if $h_i(\cdot) + \epsilon_i > 0$
$x_i = 0$ otherwise,

where $h_i(\cdot)$ is the systematic portion of the appropriate demand function evaluated for individual i [equation (4b) and (5b)] and ϵ_i is the random disturbance associated with individual i.

Given this model of behavior, the likelihood function for the sample is

$$(11) \quad L = \prod_{j \in M_C} \frac{f(\epsilon_j^C/\sigma)/\sigma}{F(h_j^C(\cdot)/\sigma)} \prod_{j \in M_I} \frac{f(\epsilon_j^I/\sigma)/\sigma}{F(h_j^I(\cdot)/\sigma)}$$

where $f(\cdot)$ and $F(\cdot)$ are the density and cumulative distribution functions of the normal distribution respectively, h^C and h^I denote functions (4b) and (5b), respectively, $\epsilon_j^C = x_j - h_j^C(\cdot)$, and $\epsilon_j^I = x_j - h_j^I(\cdot)$. Finally, M_C is the subset of individuals who are found at corner solutions in the labor market, and M_I is the subset found at interior solutions. Estimates of the parameters of the demand functions in (4b) and (5b) are obtained by maximizing the log-likelihood function in (11).

The estimated parameters are shown in Table 13.1. Although it is difficult to predict signs for the coefficients, the estimates do not contradict a few expectations. One expects increased catch to increase utility and to influence demand positively ($\gamma_3 > 0$). Also, one would normally expect positive income and time effects, especially the time effects given frequent expressions by recreationalists that time is the limiting factor on recreation consumption. Thus both γ_1 and γ_2 are likely to be positive. If γ_1 and γ_2 are positive, and one expects the coefficient on the travel cost and travel time variables to be negative ($\beta'\gamma_1$, $\beta'\gamma_2 < 0$), then β' should also be negative. All of the above conditions were consistent with the results, although income's effect was statistically insignificant.

N.E. Bockstael, I.E. Strand, W.M. Hanemann

Table 13.1 Maximum likelihood estimates for recreation demand parameters.

Parameters	α	β'	γ_1	γ_2	γ_3	σ
Estimate	−3.838	−1.019	.024	2.982	.712	15.543
(t-ratio)	(−.743)	(−2.563)	(.899)	(3.715)	(3.208)	(12.486)

Note: Observations number 391; the log likelihood ratio = 45.23.

Much information of interest can be obtained from estimation of the type of model developed earlier in the paper. On the whole, the recreational decisions modeled here appear very sensitive to time considerations. This is an important result and likely characterizes many related recreational activities. To demonstrate this point, relevant elasticities (calculated at the mean) are reported for both groups of individuals in Table 13.2. For individuals at corner solutions, distinguishable elasticities exist for money price, time price, income and time. The elasticities of demand with respect to time variables are much larger than those with respect to money variables. Individuals at interior solutions presumably have equated their value of time and money at the margin by adjusting their work hours. For these individuals, elasticities of demand with respect to "full price" ($p + w_D t$) and "full income" ($\bar{Y} + w_D \bar{T}$) are appropriate. The "full price" elasticities and "full income" elasticities fall in the range between the money and time price elasticities and the income and time elasticities, respectively, of individuals with fixed work weeks.

Table 13.2 Recreational demand elasticities for individuals at corner solutions and interior solutions in the labor market.

	Corner solution individuals (fixed work week)	Interior solution individuals (flexible hours)
Money-price elasticity	.01	.
Time-price elasticity	.23	.
"Full price" elasticity	.	.10
Income elasticity	.06	.
Discretionary time elasticity	.77	.
"Full income" elasticity	.	.36

Estimates of the welfare losses associated with a hypothetical elimination of the fishing resource are reported in Table 13.3.[3] In the two-constraint case, welfare measures can be assessed either in money or in time compensation. Whether money or time measures are used, compensating and equivalent variations deviate from ordinary surplus by only a few percentage points. The average money compensation varies between $2,700 and $4,280 per year. These magnitudes are quite reasonable because the individuals in the data set spend on average $4,800 in 1983 for fixed items for their boats (items such as insurance, mortgage payments, and slippage fees not included in trip costs and thus not netted out of consumer surplus).

The average money compensation necessary to compensate individuals with flexible work hours for loss of the resource was about $2,700 per year. The average time compensation for this group was about 160 hours. This result suggests a money–time trade-off of about $17/hour, which is approximately the mean hourly wage reported for these individuals. By contrast, the average individual with a fixed work week would require more income compensation (about $4,200/year) but less discretionary time compensation (about 68 hours). Thus individuals with fixed work weeks would trade time for money at about $60 per hour, a much higher rate than the individuals with flexible work hours and a much higher rate than the labor market is likely to offer.

These specific results may be sensitive to the restrictions imposed by the choice of utility function, but nonetheless they are consistent with the following theoretical arguments. Individuals with fixed working hours appear to value time much more highly than the wage rate and would be willing to trade work for leisure. However, they have fixed work weeks and probably face all-or-nothing decisions in the labor market (i.e., if they want the job, they must work at least some fixed number of hours). Referring to Figure 13.1, these individuals would like to be at a point between A and B, but must choose either A or B. Applications of the general model using more generally underlying utility functions could provide more information about the time valuation of people at corner solutions in the labor market.

The numbers in Table 13.3 illustrate an additional point. Had only the money compensation measure been calculated, we would have been tempted to conclude that the group with fixed work hours would be hurt more by the elimination of this resource. However, focusing solely on time compensation, the reverse would appear to be true. Theory offers little guidance here for, as Samuelson recognized in his discussion of rationing coupons, any resource endowment which constrains the individual's consumption can be used as a standard. The ambiguities which arise in such cases are discussed at length in Bockstael and Strand.

Table 13.3 Average welfare measures associated with resource elimination.

	Individuals with fixed work hours	Individuals with flexible work hours
Money measures ($/year):		
Ordinary surplus	4192	2727
Compensating variation	4281	2776
Equivalent variation	4148	2703
Time measures (hours/year):		
Ordinary surplus	68	159
Compensating variation	69	162
Equivalent variation	67	157

CONCLUDING COMMENTS

The major contribution of this work lies in the explicit treatment of recreationalists' labour market situations. For individuals with fixed work hours, the arguments of demand functions and the computation of welfare are different from people whose labor/leisure choice is at an "interior" and whose opportunity cost of time is reflected by the wage rate. Arguments in the demand function for the corner solution include total discretionary time and the hours cost of the trip. An explicit linear model was developed to demonstrate that the general model could be made operational. While the properties of the linear model are somewhat restrictive, the theoretical development is applicable independent of the choice of preference structure. The example provides an illustration and suggests the difficulties encountered when empirical problems involve utility maximization subject to constraints.

NOTES

1. The wage rate is neither an upper nor a lower bound on the individual's marginal valuation of time when labor time is institutionally restricted. An individual may choose unemployment because he values a marginal leisure hour more than the wage rate. Alternatively, he may value marginal leisure hours less than the wage rate but not be better off accepting a job requiring 40 hours of work per week. An individual at point A in Figure 13.1, for example, may value the marginal leisure hour at more than w_p but more than a potentially lower wage which could be earned at a secondary job.

2. The compensating variation in terms of time rather than money could also be computed. For individuals at interior solutions the time-compensating variation is given by

$$CV_I^T = \exp[\gamma_1(\tilde{p}_1 - p_1^0)]\left[\frac{x_1^0 + \beta'}{\gamma_1 w_D}\right] - \frac{\beta'}{\gamma_1 w_D}$$

The time compensation for the loss of the recreational good, conditioned on a corner solution in the labor market is given by

$$CV_I^T = \exp[\gamma_1(\tilde{p}_1 - p_1^0)]\left[\frac{x_1^0 + \beta'}{\gamma_2}\right] - \frac{\beta'}{\gamma_2}$$

3. These numbers represent "adjusted" estimates of compensating variation (CV), equivalent variation (EV), and ordinary surplus (OS). The usual procedure for obtaining estimates of CV, EV, and OS has been to substitute econometric estimates of parameters in the formulas (9) and (10) to derive estimates of welfare measures. As Strand and Bockstael show, this procedure in general yields biased estimates of the welfare measures even when the parameter estimates are unbiased. This is because CV, EV, and OS are typically nonlinear functions of the estimated parameters. Based on results of Zellner and Park, Strand and Bockstael demonstrate how consistent estimates of welfare measures can be obtained. The correction formulas are in part functions of the variance of the estimated parameters, which can be approximated by the squared standard errors of the coefficients. They are based on the result of Zellner and Park that if the function of interest is of the form A/B, then the expected value of the function is approximately

$$E(A/B) \approx \frac{E(A)}{E(B)}\left(1 + \frac{\operatorname{var} B}{E(B)^2}\right)$$

REFERENCES

Ashenfelter, O. "Unemployment as Disequilibrium in a Model of Aggregate Labour Supply." *Econometrica* 48(1980):547–64.

Bishop, R.C., and T.A. Heberlein. "Measuring Values of Extra-Market Goods: Are Indirect Measures Biased?" *Amer. J. Agr. Econ.* 61(1979):926–30.

Bockstael, N.E., and I.E. Strand. "Distribution Issues and Non-market Benefit Measurement." *West. J. Agr. Econ.* 10(1985):162–69.

Brown, N.G., and F. Nawas. "Impact of Aggregation on the Estimation of Outdoor Recreation Demand Function." *Amer. J. Agr. Econ.* 55(1975):246–49.

Burtless, G., and J. Hausman. "The Effect of Taxation on Labour Supply." *J. Polit. Econ.* 86(1978):1103–30.

Cesario, F.J. "Value of Time in Recreation Benefit Studies." *Land Econ.* 52(1976):32–41.

Cesario, F.J., and J.L. Knetsch. "Time Bias in Recreation Benefit Estimates." *Water Resourc. Res.* 6(1970):700–704.

Clawson, M., and J.L. Knetsch. *Economics of Outdoor Recreation.* Washington DC: Resources for the Future, 1966.

Gum, R.L., and W.E. Martin. "Problems and Solutions in Estimating the Demand for and Value of Rural Outdoor Recreation." *Amer. J. Agr. Econ.* 57(1975):558–66.

Ham, J.C. "Estimation of a Labour Supply Model with Censoring Due to Unemployment." *Rev. Econ. Stud.* 49(1982):333–54.

Recreational demand model

Hanemann, W.M. "Some Further Results on Exact Consumer's Surplus." *Dep. Agr. and Resour. Econ.* Work. Pap., University of California, Berkeley, 1981.

Hausman, J.A. "Exact Consumer's Surplus and Deadweight Loss." *Amer. Econ. Rev.* 71(1981):662–76.

Heckman, J.J., M.R. Killingsworth, and T.E. McCurdy. "Empirical Evidence on Static Labour Supply Models: A Survey of Recent Developments." *The Economics of the Labour Market,* ed. Hornstein, Grace and Webb, pp. 75-122. London: Her Majesty's Stationery Office. 1981.

Johnson, B.M. "Travel Time and the Price of Leisure." *West. Econ. J.* 4(1966):135–45.

Killingsworth, M.R. *Labour Supply.* Cambridge: Cambridge University Press, 1983.

Maddala, G.S. *Limited-Dependent and Qualitative Variables in Econometrics.* New York: Cambridge University Press, 1983.

McConnell, K.E. "Some Problems in Estimating the Demand for Outdoor Recreation." *Amer. J. Agr. Econ.* 57(1975):330–39.

McConnell, K.E., and I.E. Strand. "Measuring the Cost of Time in Recreation Demand Analysis: An Application to Sportfishing." *Amer. J. Agr. Econ.* 63(1981): 153–56.

Nichols, L.M., M. Bowes, and J.F. Dwyer. "Reflecting Travel Time in Travel-Cost-Based Estimates of Recreation Use and Value." Dep. Forestry Res. Rep. No. 78–12, University of Illinois, 1978.

Samuelson, P.A. *Foundations of Economic Analysis.* Cambridge, MA: Harvard University Press. 1947.

Smith, R.J., and N.J. Kavanaugh. "The Measurement of Benefits of Trout Fishing: Preliminary Results of a Study at Grafham Water, Great Use Water Authority, Huntingdonshire." *J. Leisure Res.* 1(1969):316–32.

Smith, T.P. "A Comparative Static Analysis of the Two Constraint Case." Appendix 4.1 *Benefit Analysis Using Indirect or Imputed Market MEthods,* vol. 2, ed. N.E. Bockstael, W.M. Hanemann, and I.E. Strand. Washington, DC: Report to the Environmental Protection Agency, 1986.

Smith, V.K., W.H. Desvousges, and M.P. McGivney. "The Opportunity Cost of Travel Time in Recreation Demand Models." *Land Econ.* 59(1983):259–77.

Strand, I.E., and N.E. Brockstael. *MELO Estimates for Calculating Consumer Surplus. Dep. Agr. and Resour. Econ.* Work. Pap., University of Maryland, 1985.

U.S. Department of Interior, National Park Service. The 1982–1983 Nationwide Recreation Survey: Summary of Selected Findings." Washington DC, April 1984.

Vartia, Y.O. "Efficient Methods of Measuring Welfare Change and Compensated Income in Terms of Ordinary Demand Functions." *Econometrica* 51(1983):79–98.

Wales, T.J., and A.D. Woodland. "Labor Supply and Progressive Taxes." *Rev. Econ. Stud.* 46(1979):83–95.

Wegge, T.C., W.M. Hanemann, and I.E. Strand. "An Economic Assessment of Marine Recreational Fishing in Southern California. Terminal Island CA: U.S. Commerce Department NOAA Tech. Memo. NMFS-SWR-015, 1986."

Zellner, A., and Soo-Bin Park. "Minimum Expected Loss (MELO) Estimators for Functions of Parameters and Structural Coefficients of Econometric Models." *J. Amer. Statist. Assoc.* 74(1979):185–93.

Chapter 14

The generalized travel cost model and water quality benefits: a reconsideration

V. Kerry Smith and William H. Desvousges

INTRODUCTION

In earlier research [12] we proposed and estimated a generalized travel cost demand model that used recreation site characteristics to explain variations in the demand functions for recreation sites. This model was based on varying parameter framework, introduced by Vaughan and Russell [15]. It offered a flexible yet pragmatic basis for taking account of both site and individual characteristics in the estimation of the benefits associated with changes in site attributes (e.g., water quality). The purpose of this paper is to report a revised, second generation version of our model and to illustrate the importance of these revisions for the model's estimates of the benefits of improved water quality. Although the magnitude of the difference in benefit estimates between the original and new versions of the model varies with the specific recreation site selected, our findings indicate that the original model generally implied estimated benefits from three to over thirty times as large as the revised model.[1] Consequently, it is important to consider the plausibility of estimates provided by each version of the model and use this evaluation to judge the appropriate role for either version for benefit estimates associated with public policy decisions.

Section II reports the rationale for our revision to the model and the new estimates. Section III compares the two models' benefit estimates for water quality improvements and relates them to those available from other studies. The last summarizes the paper.

THE REVISED MODEL

The first version of our model used ordinary least squares (OLS) to estimate demand functions for 33 water based recreation sites and a weighted least squares estimator for the second stage demand parameter models. There are several problems with this strategy.[2] First, the demand models were estimated based on surveys of users conducted at each of the recreation sites. Although this type of survey is commonly used in recreation demand studies, it provides no information on individuals who chose not to use the site. Indeed it implies that the measure of the quantity demanded, the reported use of a site during the season (i.e., trips), will be truncated at one.

A second problem also arises from the data. In particular, the available measure of the quantity demanded censored the number of visits at the highest levels of use, with six or more trips reported in a single class. These two problems involving features of the dependent variable imply that the model's error will have a non-null expectation. In such cases, the OLS parameter estimates can be expected to be biased. To mitigate the potential effects of this bias, our earlier analysis used Olsen's [11] diagnostic index to evaluate the effects of truncation (and to a more limited extent censoring) on the OLS estimates. After this screening, a subset of the sample (22 of the original 33 sites), where the effects were judged to be small, formed the basis for our second stage model. This approach was admittedly an ad hoc attempt to mitigate the effects of bias that might be present in the first stage demand estimates for the second stage models involving the demand parameters and site characteristics. However, the selection of an alternative strategy that recognizes these problems in estimating the site demand functions is not clearcut. There are a number of alternatives and none of them can be considered to be ideally suited to our problems. For example, we could, again on ad hoc grounds, choose to ignore the truncation and apply a tobit estimator that would reflect the censoring. However, the estimates will not be consistent when the data are not from a censored normal. Alternatively, a model based on a discrete probability structure such as the Poisson [7] might be considered. This framework requires that we assume equality of the expected value of the dependent variable and its variance. To the extent this assumption is violated we can expect that the parameter estimates will not be consistent and inference based on asymptotic normality will be a misleading basis for judging hypotheses.

Other possibilities would include Stewart's [13] interval maximum likelihood method and Cragg's [2] early proposal to separate the process describing the dependent variable. To the extent the decision involves an independent judgment as to whether or not to use a site, and then a separate decision as to the level of use,[3] then the problem reduces only to one requiring an estimator to take account of the censoring and could be accomodated within the tobit framework mentioned earlier.

Since our objective is to illustrate the potential importance of decisions on the selection of an estimator, and with it often an implicit view of the decision process, we have selected a maximum likelihood estimator that attempts to take explicit account of aspects of both of the problems we noted. That is, it reflects the effects of the truncation in visits at low levels of use and of the censoring in the upper levels of use. Under the assumption of normality for the error structure, with truncation at zero[4] and censoring at k the likelihood function is given in equation (1).

$$L(\bar{\beta},\sigma^2,\overline{\ln V}) = \prod_{i\in S} [((1/\sigma)\ \phi((\ln V_1 - \bar{\beta}\overline{X_i})/\sigma))/(1 - \Phi(-\bar{\beta}\overline{X_i}/\sigma))]$$

$$\times \prod_{i\in S} [(1 - \Phi((k - \bar{\beta}\overline{X_i}))/(1 - \Phi(-\bar{\beta}\overline{X_i}/\sigma)))] \tag{1}$$

where:

$\ln V_i$ = natural log of the number of visits to the site by the ith individual
$\bar{\beta}$ = parameter vector $(1 \times K)$
$\overline{X_i}$ = vector of independent variables describing ith individual $(K \times 1)$
σ^2 = variance in the error associated with each site's demand function
S_1 = set of observations with $0 \le \ln V_t < k$
S_2 = set of observations with $\ln V_1 \ge k$

185

$\phi(.)$ = density function for the standard normal variate
$\Phi(.)$ = distribution function for the standard normal variate

Table 14.1 reports the demand estimates using OLS and the maximum likelihood (ML) methods for each of 22 sites used in the development of our original model. The ML estimates were derived using the Davidon-Fletcher-Powell [4] algorithm in GQOPT. The asymptotic variance-covariance matrix, calculated with numerical derivatives, was used to derive the test statistics (for the null hypothesis of no association) reported below the ML coefficients in the table. The demand functions were specified to be consistent with the first version. Equally important, the second stage demand parameter-site characteristics models were also specified to be comparable. The quantity demanded (the log of visits) was treated as a function of travel costs (including the round trip vehicle related costs and the time costs of travel) and the household income.[5]

Generally, the ML results differ substantially from the original OLS estimates. For example, the ML estimates of the travel cost parameter are larger in absolute magnitude, implying more elastic site demands. One simple way to gauge the implications of these differences for benefits analysis is to use a rule of thumb suggested for evaluating the site valuations implied by semi-log recreation demand models. The reciprocal of the travel cost parameter (in absolute magnitude) can serve as a measure of the consumer surplus generated by each site per trip.[6] Based on this standard, the new estimates imply substantially smaller site values per unit of use; ranging from $3.58 to $105.26 for the ML estimates in comparison to $39.00 to $400.00 for the OLS models (both in 1977 dollars). As described in more detail in section III, the per trip consumer surplus associated with ML estimates would generally be regarded as more consistent with the benefit estimates available in the literature for these types of recreation sites.

Table 14.2 reports the generalized least squares estimates for the second stage demand parameters using the ML estimates. While the specification corresponds to what was used in the first generation framework, there are substantial differences in the results. Water quality (as measured using dissolved oxygen) has a positive and statistically significant effect on the intercept but not the other two estimated demand parameters. Moreover, the record with respect to the other site characteristics is not as good as was reported for the first generation version of the model. Few characteristics would be judged to be significant determinants of these site demand parameters. Thus, these results taken alone do not provide a compelling case for accepting the revised model based on the ML estimates of site demand parameters. Of course, we should note that the sample size is relatively small and degree of discrimination required of these models is quite demanding. This problem is further compounded by the limited nature of the information available on site characteristics, especially water quality. Nonetheless, we must conclude that our attempt to improve the site demand estimates has led to more instead of fewer questions about the plausibility of the second stage equations for the generalized travel cost model.

GAUGING THE PLAUSIBILITY OF THE SECOND GENERATION MODEL

To evaluate the implications of this revision to the generalized travel cost model, two sets of comparisons were undertaken. The first is reported in Table 14.3. For each of 21 sites and each version of the model estimates of the increments to

Travel cost model

Table 14.1 Maximum likelihood and OLS estimates of general model by site, in visits $= \alpha_0 + \alpha_1 (T + M)$ costs $+ \alpha_2$ income.

Site name	Site No.	Estimator	Intercept	$T+M$ cost	Income	Function value	R^2	df
Arkabutla Lake, MS	301	ML	2.33 (8.21)	−0.0473 (−6.20)	1.9×10^{-6} (0.11)	−24.00	–	–
		OLS	1.58 (9.99)	−0.0093 (−3.09)	6.2×10^{-6} (0.67)	–	0.15	58
Lock and Dam No. 2 (Arkansas River Navigation System), AR	302	ML	2.31 (2.31)	−0.0125 (−0.28)	1.6×10^{-5} (64.95)	−17.67		
		OLS	2.31 (9.76)	−0.0125 (−2.30)	-1.8×10^{-5} (−1.08)	–	0.14	38
Belton Lake, TX	304	ML	2.94 (4.62)	−0.0727 (−2.70)	1.2×10^{-5} (0.42)	−23.61	–	–
		OLS	1.69 (9.38)	−0.0052 (−2.47)	2.6×10^{-6} (0.29)	–	0.12	50
Benbrook Lake, TX	305	ML	2.45 (1.54)	−0.0472 (−1.09)	8.3×10^{-5} (0.60)	−16.01	–	–
		OLS	1.83 (10.70)	−0.0054 (−4.11)	6.0×10^{-6} (0.80)	–	0.30	43
Blakely Mt. Dam. Lake Ouachita, AR	307	ML	2.44 (24.03)	−0.0374 (−13.63)	-9.6×10^{-6} (−0.88)	−18.17	–	–
		OLS	1.70 (10.08)	−0.0079 (−5.14)	-7.6×10^{-6} (−0.98)	–	0.24	88
Canton Lake, OK	308	ML	3.96 (8.94)	−0.2788 (−12.50)	1.4×10^{-4} (11.23)	−12.51	–	–
		OLS	1.77 (8.61)	−0.0206 (−5.28)	7.1×10^{-6} (0.86)	–	0.28	71
Cordell Hull Dam and Reservoir, TN	310	ML	2.91 (87.61)	−0.0657 (−22.02)	3.8×10^{-6} (0.90)	−29.26	–	–
		OLS	1.86 (14.13)	−0.0139 (−6.00)	-1.2×10^{-8} (−0.01)	–	0.34	101
DeGray Lake, AR	311	ML	2.36 (3.55)	−0.0267 (−1.57)	-1.5×10^{-5} (0.56)	−17.81	–	–
		OLS	1.79 (7.71)	−0.0070 (−3.00)	-6.9×10^{-5} (0.73)	–	0.17	46
Grapevine Lake, TX	314	ML	2.71 (6.41)	−0.0311 (−3.43)	1.8×10^{-5} (1.42)	−26.92	–	–
		OLS	1.80 (16.12)	−0.0073 (−8.80)	8.5×10^{-6} (1.70)	–	0.47	89
Greers Ferry Lake, AR	315	ML	2.10 (15.91)	−0.0287 (−9.84)	2.8×10^{-5} (3.20)	−51.84	–	–
		OLS	1.48 (14.08)	−0.0065 (−9.02)	8.4×10^{-6} (1.42)	–	0.28	214
Grenada Lake, MS	316	ML	4.92 (8.97)	−0.0924 (−4.58)	-3.5×10^{-5} (−0.58)	−29.47	–	–
		OLS	2.04 (12.61)	−0.0095 (−4.36)	-1.0×10^{-5} (−0.68)	–	0.22	73
Hords Creek Lake, TX	317	ML	2.77 (5.07)	−0.0502 (−2.38)	-6.5×10^{-5} (−2.22)	−13.49	–	–
		OLS	1.73 (8.22)	−0.0050 (−2.11)	-2.1×10^{-5} (−1.76)	–	0.19	51
Melvern Lake, KS	322	ML	−2.42 (−2.91)	−0.1797 (−20.00)	7.4×10^{-5} (2.56)	−14.17	–	–
		OLS-I	1.30 (4.47)	−0.0079 (−1.66)	4.1×10^{-6} (0.32)	–	0.06	42
Millwood Lake, AR	323	ML	1.43 (2.97)	−0.0331 (−6.51)	7.4×10^{-5} (2.97)	−20.14	–	–
		OLS	1.43 (7.94)	−0.0081 (−3.99)	1.8×10^{-5} (2.14)	–	0.25	50
Mississippi River Pool No. 6, MN	325	ML	1.49 (2.67)	−0.0565 (−1.75)	5.8×10^{-5} (1.41)	−22.21	–	–
		OLS	1.41 (7.45)	−0.0074 (−4.39)	1.3×10^{-5} (1.53)	–	0.22	68
New Savannah Bluff Lock & Dam, GA	329	ML	3.28 (2.24)	−0.0538 (−0.68)	-5.6×10^{-5} (0.59)	−19.51	–	–

Table 14.1 (continued).

Site name	Site No.	Estimator	Intercept	$T+M$ cost	Income	Function value	R^2	df
		OLS	1.88 (8.39)	−0.0067 (−1.44)	−9.8×10⁻⁶ (−0.70)	–	0.06	36
Ozark Lake, AR	331	ML	1.98 (3.70)	−0.0230 (−14.25)	1.2×10⁻⁵ (0.36)	−8.27	–	–
		OLS	1.66 (8.52)	−0.0046 (−4.44)	−8.8×10⁻⁶ (0.66)	–	0.31	49
Philpott Lake, VA	333	ML	2.21 (4.77)	−0.0335 (−22.71)	2.2×10⁻⁵ (0.80)	−8.80	–	–
		OLS	1.90 (9.28)	−0.0087 (−4.40)	−1.7×10⁻⁶ (−0.13)	–	0.36	35
Proctor Lake, TN	337	ML	4.09 (6.59)	−0.0643 (−2.14)	5.0×10⁻⁶ (0.27)	−6.63	–	–
		OLS	2.06 (13.61)	−0.0134 (−7.50)	1.2×10⁻⁶ (0.19)	–	0.54	49
Sam Rayburn Dam & Reservoir, TX	339	ML	1.60 (1.64)	−0.0744 (−2.52)	1.0×10⁻⁵ (0.23)	−14.41	–	–
		OLS	1.46 (7.06)	−0.0094 (−2.83)	1.0×10⁻⁶ (0.13)	–	0.11	64
Sardis Lake, MS	340	ML	2.48 (7.01)	−0.0095 (−2.05)	1.5×10⁻⁵ (0.64)	−100.97	–	–
		OLS	1.81 (20.73)	−0.0030 (−3.17)	4.3×10⁻⁶ (0.78)	–	0.05	202
Whitney Lake, TX	344	ML	−0.378 (−0.71)	−0.0166 (−1.04)	3.0×10⁻⁵ (0.83)	−98.95	–	–
		OLS	1.41 (13.07)	−0.0025 (−1.80)	3.2×10⁻⁶ (0.72)	–	0.02	201

Table 14.2 Generalized least squares estimates using maximum likelihood site demand estimates.

Independent variables[a]	Model[b]		
	Intercept	Travel cost parameter	Income parameter
Intercept	−.044 (−0.024)	−.022 (−0.431)	.17×10⁻⁴ (0.657)
Shore	.001 (0.782)	−.11×10⁻⁴ (−0.382)	−.60×10⁻⁷ (−1.449)
Access	−.039 (−1.071)	.27×10⁻² (1.301)	.14×10⁻⁶ (0.074)
Water pool	1.461 (1.030)	−.089 (−1.522)	.86×10⁻⁴ (2.731)
DO	.020 (2.076)	−.10×10⁻³ (−0.286)	−.24×10⁻⁶ (−0.766)
VDO	−6.47×10⁻⁵ (−2.077)	1.48×10⁻⁷ (0.127)	5.28×10⁻¹⁰ (0.573)
R^2	.475	.196	.455
F	2.89	2.50	2.68

a. The definitions for the site characteristics are:
Shore: total shore miles at site during the peak visitation period.
Access: number of multi-purpose recreational and developed access areas at the site.
Water Pool: size of the pool surface relative to total site area.
DO: dissolved oxygen (percent saturation).
VDO: variance in dissolved oxygen.
b. These designate the estimated demand parameters that served as the dependent variables for the second stage models.

Travel cost model

Marshallian consumer surplus associated with two levels of improvement in water quality were calculated. These benefits relate to a "representative" user of each site who is defined to have the average travel cost as his price, the maximum travel cost as the choke price, and the average household income of users of each site. In the three columns of Table 14.3 following the site number code the specific values for each of these variables are reported. The remaining four columns report the estimated benefits per season (in 1977 dollars) for two water quality improvements – boatable to fishable and boatable to swimmable conditions. Both changes are measured using dissolved oxygen and the standards defined by Vaughan [14].[7] The estimates based on the first generation model are substantially larger than those of the ML based model. Improvements from boatable to fishable range from $39.97 for site 302 to $155.73 for site 323. By contrast, the ML estimates are as low as $0.39 for site 325 and provide their largest estimate for site 323 of $33.63. These second generation estimates are uniformly smaller than the first. As a percent of the first generation results, the estimates based on the ML demand functions range from 0.4% to 72%. However, most sites fall within a somewhat narrower range of 3% to 33%. Thus, these results imply a substantial difference in the valuations derived from each of the two models.

Our second comparison attempts to gauge the plausibility of each set of estimates based on what has been found in earlier studies of the recreation values of water quality improvements. Table 14.4 presents the first water quality change – boatable to fishable – and compares our estimates with the second generation framework to earlier reported estimates (including our own earlier work [12]). Estimates derived from the travel cost models are reported on both a per trip and a per day basis in 1982 dollars.[8]

Two aspects of these results are especially important. First, our first model's benefit estimates for the Corps' sites are substantially outside the range of estimates provided by past studies for these types of recreation areas.[9] However, when the model was used to estimate the benefits for water quality improvements on the Monongahela sites, its estimates clearly fall within the range anticipated by past experience. This discrepancy in performance for the two types of sites would seem to be related to the characteristics of the Monongahela sites relative to the Corps sites. The Monongahela are substantially smaller, have fewer access points, and a larger fraction of each site's total area is associated with water in comparison to the Corps sites. Thus, use of the first generation version of the model to predict demand for the Monongahela River sites was a projection substantially outside the range of values for the site characteristic variables.

By contrast, the second generation model provides benefit estimates for the Corps sites that are more consistent with the valuations for water quality improvements obtained with earlier studies. Thus, we have an unusual example of a situation where the parameter estimates do not provide an especially strong case for a model but the end use of its estimates seems to offer somewhat more support.[10]

IMPLICATIONS

Improved recreational opportunities are the principal source of benefits for water quality improvements (Freeman [5]). Under Executive Order 12291, federal agencies are required to conduct benefit–cost analyses for each new major regulation as an important dimension of the activities and information designed

189

Table 14.3 A comparison of benefits estimates for water quality improvements for the first and second generation models[a].

Site	Site no.	Average income	Average travel cost	Maximum travel cost	Boatable to fishable		Boatable to swimmable	
					First	Second	First	Second
Arkabutla Lake, MS	301	13,184	20.04	209.35	104.57	29.37	274.20	66.13
Lock & Dam No. 2 Arkansas River, AR	302	10,409	3.04	70.01	39.97	29.01	89.45	67.42
Belton Lake, TX	304	17,279	33.18	302.86	115.84	9.62	331.45	21.34
Benbrook Lake, TX	305	19,135	30.23	344.44	124.64	6.53	366.68	14.52
Blakely Mt. Dam, Lake Ouachita, AR	307	17,144	45.39	286.03	49.54	3.38	131.73	7.41
Canton Lake, OK	308	17,392	32.30	106.16	42.83	4.90	101.59	10.94
Cordell Hull Resevoir, TX	310	15,491	29.65	184.35	68.75	14.21	173.75	31.52
DeGray Lake, AR	311	19,235	42.04	210.48	82.72	10.37	218.39	22.59
Grapevine Lake, TX	314	19,309	38.45	307.28	114.12	3.86	329.63	8.51
Grenada Lake, MS	316	9,199	24.57	207.05	99.16	19.17	262.04	43.53
Hords Creek Lake, TX	317	16,263	39.46	304.01	112.35	3.11	321.87	6.89
Melvern Lake, KS	322	18,087	31.48	130.50	56.21	5.46	136.35	12.14
Millwood Lake, AR	323	18,630	37.62	309.24	155.73	33.62	461.81	74.15
Mississippi River Pool No. 6, MN	325	19,589	52.23	843.86	100.17	0.39	300.51	0.84
New Savannah Bluff Lock & Dam, GA	329	12,609	18.65	157.36	84.92	13.07	209.64	29.53
Ozark Lake, AR	331	12,654	58.71	457.44	94.66	6.34	291.05	14.07
Philpott Lake, VA	333	14,268	26.09	268.76	117.99	16.79	328.58	37.54
Proctor Lake, TN	337	17,510	46.08	172.41	68.93	0.82	178.22	1.80
Sam Rayburn Dam & Reservoir, TX	339	19,515	40.23	155.30	49.30	9.35	122.62	20.46
Sardis Lake, MS	340	13,141	36.08	429.20	128.98	9.19	398.58	20.46
Whitney Lake, TX	344	18,688	35.40	303.62	109.78	6.79	315.02	15.03

a. These are the Marshallian consumer surplus estimates for each site using the maximum travel cost in each case as a finite choke price. See Note 7 for the definition of the water quality conditions.

Travel cost model

Table 14.4 A comparison of alternative estimates of the benefits of water quality improvements from boatable to fishable conditions in 1982 dollars.*

Study	Original estimate	1982 Dollars
Vaughan-Russell [15]	$4.00 to $8.00 per person per day was the range over the models used (1980 dollars)	$4.68 to $9.37
Loomis-Sorg [8]	$1.00 to $3.00 per person per day over regions considered; based on increment to value of recreation day for coldwater game fishing (1982 dollars)	$1.00 to $3.00
Smith, Desvousges, and McGivney [12]	$0.98 to $2.03 per trip using first generation generalized travel cost model with Monongahela sites, boatable to fishable water quality (1981 dollars)	$1.04 to $2.15
First generation generalized travel cost model	$5.87 to $54.20^a per trip ($2.24 to $122.00 per visitor day^b) for Corps sites, change from boatable to fishable water quality (1977 dollars)	$9.35 to $86.34 ($3.57 to $194.35)^c
Second generation generalized travel cost model	$0.08 to $5.43 per trip ($0.04 to $18.78 per visitor day) for Corps sites, change from boatable to fishable water quality (1977 dollars)	$0.13 to $8.65 ($0.06 to $29.92)^c

* The Consumer Price Index was used in converting to 1982 dollars. The scaling factor for the conversion from 1977 to 1982 was 1.593.
a. These estimates relate only to the Marshallian consumer surplus (M2).
b. The reason for the increase in the range for benefits per day is that some trips were reported as less than a day. The appropriate fractions were used in developing these estimates.
c. The numbers in parentheses are the per day consumer surplus, while those above them are the per trip estimates.

to evaluate it. Consequently, benefit–cost analyses of water quality changes can be expected to be an increasingly important part of the policymaking process.

Our progressive refinement in the generalized travel cost model illustrates how sensitive the benefit estimates can be to the modeling and estimation judgments made in deriving them. This finding, in turn, implies that the transfer of recreation benefit estimates that have been derived for a specific site under one set of conditions to a new site under a different set of conditions must be done cautiously. Judgment can play an exceptionally important role in the definition and use of economic models. Our re-evaluation of the generalized travel cost model indicates how important one class of decisions associated with estimation can be. As part of the process of estimating the first generation model we thought our screening approach mitigated any distortion to the site demand. However, our findings indicate that this was not the case. As a consequence, they reinforce the need for both better information on households' recreation decisions and more complete descriptions of recreation site characteristics that are hypothesized to affect those decisions.

NOTES

1. These comparative judgments relate to valuing water quality improvements from boatable to fishable conditions.
2. While the problem discussed below was acknowledged in the earlier paper, we assumed our screening of site demand functions provided the basis for limiting the potential effects of

any bias in the demand estimates. Most of these remaining assumptions stem from the available data. Thus, the information in the Federal Estate Survey, one of the more comprehensive surveys, limits the generality of the recreation demand models that can be considered.

3. The distinction parallels the separation often used in the early literature modeling recreation participation behavior [1]. A more complete discussion of the "hurdle models" fashioned after Cragg's suggestions is given by Mullahy [10].

4. The truncation at zero arises because the dependent variable for the demand function was the logarithm of visits.

5. We estimated vehicle related travel costs using round trip mileage and eight cents a mile as the cost in 1977 of operating an automobile. Time costs were valued at the full wage rate which was predicted for each individual using a hedonic wage model based on the 1978 Current Population Survey. See [12] for more details.

6. This result is readily established by considering the indefinite integral for the semi-log demand function:

$$B = \int f(P)dP = \int \exp(\alpha_0 - \alpha_1 P)dP = -(1/\alpha_1)\exp(\alpha_0 - a_1 P).$$

Defining the consumer surplus, CS, as the difference in B evaluated at the choke price P^* and actual price P^a we have:

$$CS = (-1 \; \alpha_1)\exp(\alpha_0 - \alpha_1 P^*) - (-1/\alpha_1)\exp(\alpha_0 - \alpha_1 P^a).$$

Allowing P^* to be arbitrarily large (since there is no finite choke price for the semi-log function) the first term approaches zero and the second term the consumer's surplus. Since also defines the quantity demanded at P^a, we have

$$(CS/Q) = (1/\alpha).$$

7. The values for dissolved oxygen are given as follows:
   (a) Improvement from boatable to fishable is assumed to be associated with a change from 45 to 64 percent saturation.
   (b) Improvement from boatable to swimmable is assumed to be associated with and change from 45 to 83 percent saturation.

8. These are based on the average number of trips for each site and the average number of days reported for the trip in which the respondents to the survey were interviewed. Actual trips were selected rather than predicted trips because the latter will be a biased estimate from a semi-log function. Moreover, there are additional problems in selecting the predicted number of trips for normalization. There are predictions available at each level of water quality that might be used as the base in evaluating each water quality change. Since the actual water quality conditions at these sites often were closer to or exceeded fishable conditions, actual use was judged to provide a better normalizing factor than the available estimates.

9. Of course, it should be noted that Vaughan-Russell [15] and most of the other studies also ignored similar problems and may be subject to the same limitations as our first generation model. Nonetheless, the range of benefit estimates they have implied has had independent confirmation with contingent valuation analysis. For a discussion of comparisons of travel cost and contingent valuation estimates see [3].

10. See [6] for a general discussion of these issues as they relate to selecting an objective function for selecting statistical estimators of the parameters of economic relationships.

REFERENCES

1. Cicchetti, Charles J., Joseph J. Seneca and Paul Davidson. *The Demand and Supply of Outdoor Recreation*. New Brunswick, New Jersey: Bureau of Economic Research, Rutgers University, 1969.
2. Cragg, John G., "Some Statistical Models for Limited Dependent Variables With Application to the Demand for Durable Goods." *Econometrica*, September 1971, 829–44.

Travel cost model

3. Cummings, Ronald G., David S. Brookshire and William D. Schulze. *Valuing Public Goods: The Contingent Valuation Method.* Totowa, NJ: Rowman and Allanheld Publishers, forthcoming, 1986.
4. Davidon, S., R. Fletcher and M. Powell, "A Rapidly Convergent Descent Method for Minimization." *The Computer Journal,* July 1963, 163–68.
5. Freeman, A. Myrick. *Air and Water Pollution Control: A Benefit Cost Assessment,* New York: John Wiley and Sons, 1982.
6. Klein, R.W., L.G. Rafsky, D.F. Sibley, and R.D. Willig, "Decisions with Estimation Uncertainty." *Econometrica,* November 1978, 1363–88.
7. Hausman, Jerry, Bronwyn Hall and Zvi Griliches, "Econometric Models for Count Data With an Application to the Patents-R&D Relationship." *Econometrica,* July 1984, 909–38.
8. Loomis, John and Cindy Sorg. "A Critical Summary of Empirical Estimates of the Values of Wildlife, Wilderness and General Recreation Related to National Forest Regions." Unpublished paper, U.S. Forest Service, 1982.
9. Maddala, G.S. *Limited Dependent and Qualitative Variables in Econometrics.* New York: Cambridge University Press, 1983.
10. Mullahy, John. "Hurdle Models for Discrete and Grouped Dependent Variables." Discussion paper No. QE84-03, Resources for the Future, 1984.
11. Olsen, Randall J., "Approximating a Truncated Normal Regression with the Method of Moments." *Econometrica.* July 1980, 1099–1106.
12. Smith, V. Kerry, William H. Desvousges and Matthew P. McGivney, "Estimating Water Quality Benefits: An Econometric Analysis." *Southern Economic Journal,* October 1983, 422–37.
13. Stewart, M.B., "On Least Squares Estimation When the Dependent Variable is Grouped." *Review of Economic Studies,* October 1983, 737–53.
14. Vaughan, William J. "The Water Quality Ladder," Appendix II in Robert Cameron Mitchell and Richard T. Carson, *An Experiment in Determining to Pay for National Water Quality Improvements.* Draft report, Resources for the Future, 1981.
15. Vaughan, William J. and Clifford S. Russell, "Valuing a Fishing Day: An Application of a Systematic Varying Parameter Model." *Land Economics,* November 1982, 450–63.

Chapter 15

An economic analysis of air pollution and health: the case of St. Louis

Shelby Gerking and Linda R. Stanley

INTRODUCTION

One cornerstone of the Clean Air Act and its subsequent amendments is that improved air quality leads to better human health. This policy link has inspired a considerable volume of research, including the pioneering work of Lave and Seskin (1973, 1977), aimed at measuring the strength of association between measures of mortality and morbidity and specific air pollutants. The overwhelming majority of the empirical results obtained, however, are not based on models of consumer choice.[1] As a consequence, the dollar value of health benefits stemming from improved air quality generally are estimated on an ad hoc basis and are therefore difficult to interpret. Moreover, the absence of a theoretically justifiable health benefits estimation method recently has become a more serious policy problem in light of Executive Order No. 12291, issued by President Reagan on February 17, 1981. This order directs federal agencies in the executive branch to assess both the costs and benefits of all proposed and final "major" rules and regulations.

This paper presents and empirically estimates a simple model from which an intuitively appealing measure of health benefits can be derived. In this model, individuals produce health capital in a utility maximizing framework and are able to adjust their behavior in order to defend against reductions in air quality. Those adjustments, which involve substituting medical care or other health producing activities for reduced air quality, form the basis for the method used in making the benefit or willingness to pay calculations. This method is empirically implemented using cross-sectional survey data on adult workers drawn from households in St Louis, Missouri. From a policy standpoint, the empirical results are of interest because they support the notion that individuals are willing to pay for better health resulting from air quality improvements. In particular, illustrative estimates are presented showing that St. Louis workers may bid as much as $24.48 annually in order to enjoy a 30% reduction in outdoor ozone exposures.

The remainder of this paper is divided into four sections. Section II describes the health model and the method derived for estimating willingness to pay for improved air quality. Section III outlines the empirical estimation strategy used, discusses certain features of the data, and presents the empirical results. Implications and conclusions are drawn out in section IV.

A SIMPLE HEALTH MODEL

The model to be applied has close parallels with the work of Grossman (1972), Cropper (1981), Rosenzweig and Schultz (1982) and Harrington and Portney (1982). As shown in equation (1), individuals derive utility from the consumption of two classes of goods: (1) their own stock of health capital (H) and (2) goods that yield direct satisfaction, but do not affect health (X).

$$U = U(X, H). \tag{1}$$

The stock of health capital is determined by the production function

$$H = H(M; \alpha, \delta) \tag{2}$$

where M denotes medical care (from which the individual derives no *direct* utility), α denotes air quality, and δ denotes a set of other exogenous variables, such as education, that affect $H(H_M > 0, H_\alpha > 0, H_\delta \gtrless 0)$. Utility is maximized subject to equation (2) and the full income budget constraint shown in equation (3):

$$Xq_x + Mq_M + WT_L = WT + A \tag{3}$$

where $q_i = (P_i + WT_i)$, $i = X, M$. P_i is the money price of commodity i, W is the wage rate, T_i is the time required to consume one unit of commodity i, T_L is the time lost from market and nonmarket activities due to illness, and A is an exogenously determined amount of asset income. T_L is related to the health stock according to

$$T_L = G(H) \tag{4}$$

where $G_H < 0$.

This model can be manipulated in order to derive a compensating variation (CV) type expression for the marginal willingness to pay for improved air quality.[2] Totally differentiate the utility function and set $dU = 0$ as shown in equation (5).

$$dU = 0 = U_x dX + U_H H_M dM + U_H H \alpha d\alpha + U_H H_\delta d\delta. \tag{5}$$

Then, totally differentiate the full income budget constraint, as shown in equation (6), holding $dq_i = dW = dT = 0$ for $i = X, M$.

$$d(WT) = 0 = q_x dX + (q_M + WG_H H_M)\, dM - dA + WG_H H_\alpha H_\alpha d\alpha + WG_H H_\delta d\delta. \tag{6}$$

Using the first order conditions from the model,

$$U_x - \lambda q_x = 0 \tag{7}$$
$$U_H H_M - \lambda(q_M + WG_H H_M) = 0, \tag{8}$$

equation (5) can be solved for dX and substituted into equation (6) to yield

$$\partial A/\partial \alpha = -H_\alpha q_M/H_M. \tag{9}$$

Six features of equation (9) and the underlying model warrant further comment. First, this equation indicates that the individual is willing to pay more (i.e., give up more asset income) for a given air quality improvement, the greater the associated improvement in health. Also, that bid is higher, the lower the productivity of medical services and the higher their cost. Therefore, if medical services are an expensive but ineffective means of improving health, the individual is willing to pay more for increased air quality. Second, equation (9) is relatively straightforward to implement empirically since utility terms have been eliminated. Third, the expression for $\partial A/\partial\alpha$ involves partial derivatives of the health production function rather than parameters from a reduced form "dose-response" model. A key difference between these two approaches lies in the treatment of M. The present model treats M as a choice variable while in the "dose-response" approach, H is specified as a function of a variety of variables (possibly including medical care, air quality, socioeconomic, and demographic measures), all of which are treated as exogenous. This distinction is important since most previous estimates of benefits of improved air quality are based on the "dose-response" approach.[3]

Fourth, equation (9) should be interpreted as the marginal bid to avoid the illness effects of reduced air quality in a one-period, perfectly certain world. Epidemiological evidence suggests that air pollutants can initiate and/or exacerbate a wide range of respiratory illnesses including chronic bronchitis, emphysema, asthma, and possibly lung cancer, which medical care can at least partially ameliorate. However, a bid to avoid illness alone may not include the willingness to pay to avoid minor symptomatic discomforts of pollution exposure such as watering eyes, chest pain, and general malaise. Equation (9) may, therefore, understate the total health related bid for improved air quality. Additionally, a different marginal bid may emerge from a multiperiod model in which health outcomes are treated as probabilistic. A multiperiod framework would allow for a more complete description of air pollution's long-term or cumulative physiological damage and probabilistic outcomes would capture the scientific uncertainties concerning the exact health consequences of air pollution. Nevertheless, the main ideas reflected in equation (9) almost certainly would be included in the marginal bid derived from a richer formulation of the model. Moreover, more complex versions of the model may prove difficult to test in light of the shortage of micro data sets containing detailed health and economic information.

Fifth, if attention is restricted to one period models with perfect certainty, there are several variants of the model presented that yield a marginal bid expression identical to equation (9). As one example, the existing model could be expanded to include a good Y, representing lifestyle factors including cigarette smoking, alcohol consumption, diet, or exercise, which directly affect both utility and health. As a second example, an exposure function of the form: $\alpha^* = \alpha^* (V, \alpha)$ could be added to the existing model. The variable still denotes ambient air quality levels, α^* denotes actual exposure levels, and V denotes the quantity of an averting activity (i.e., leaving town on weekends when air quality is poor) that has full price q_V.[4] One consequence of incorporating this equation into the model is to make α^* an endogenous variable. In both of these examples, however, equation (9) still contains the marginal bid to avoid ambient air quality reductions. The reasoning here lies in the model's optimization framework in which marginal conditions are equated.[5]

Sixth, the marginal air quality bid shown in equation (9) can be compared to the bid that would result if health was treated as a pure investment commodity, i.e., if H was eliminated from the utility function. In that event, the bid would be $WG_H H_\alpha$, which simply values the reduction in time lost from market and nonmarket activities caused by the improvement in air quality at the wage rate. This bid is similar to the damage function approach used by Lave and Seskin (1977) and is smaller than the marginal bid shown in equation (9). That result concerning the size of the bids should be expected since the model underlying equation (9) treats health as a commodity with both consumption and investment attributes.

EMPIRICAL ESTIMATES OF WILLINGNESS TO PAY
This section presents empirical estimates of willingness to pay for improved air quality in St. Louis. As shown in equation (9), the magnitude of the willingness to pay term hinges critically on the estimation of the health production function. The approach taken to estimate this function is considered in part A. Part B highlights certain features of the data and part C presents the empirical estimates.

Estimation approach
In estimating the health production function, H is treated as a multidimensional, rather than a unidimensional variable. More specifically, the St. Louis health survey contains three types of variables measuring H for adults. These variables are defined as: (1) subjectively reported health status (whether health is considered *EXCELLENT, GOOD, FAIR, POOR*), (2) existence of chronic illness (*CHRO*), and (3) years of suffering from those chronic conditions (*LENGTH*). Taken separately, each of these variables may measure a different dimension of the health stock. For example, the Pearson correlation between *POOR* and *CHRO* is 0.325. *CHRO* may measure the existence of health conditions that show up in a clinical setting while POOR may measure how the respondent "feels." In any case, the perspective that the health stock is better treated as a multidimensional, rather than a unidimensional, variable underlies the approach taken to estimate $\partial A/\partial \alpha$.

This approach can be illustrated by expressing equation (2) as

$$F(H, M; \alpha, \delta) = 0, \tag{10}$$

Assuming that the conditions of the implicit function theorem hold, i.e., that (1) the function F has continuous partial derivatives F_H, F_M, F_α, and F_δ and (2) $F_M \neq 0$; equation (10) can be rewritten as

$$M = M(H; \alpha, \delta). \tag{11}$$

This alternative specification of the production function has three features that are worth elaborating. First, in the empirical work described below, it allows for the possibility that H may be best measured as a set of health indicators rather than as a single variable since H now appears on the right hand side.[6] Second,

$$M_\alpha = -(F_\alpha/F_M) = -(F_\alpha/F_H)(F_H/F_M) = -H_\alpha/H_M.$$

Therefore, in order to obtain the marginal willingness to pay, $\partial A/\partial \alpha$, from equation (11), M_α need only be multiplied by q_M, the full price of medical care. Third, in the subsequent empirical analysis, equation (11) is over-identified by exclusion restrictions since one jointly dependent variable appears as a regressor and three predetermined variables, q_M, W, and A, have been excluded.[7]

Sample characteristics

The St. Louis survey, which was conducted over the period 1977–1980, provides information on the health, activity patterns and lifestyles of members of 2,594 households. For those households, the 2,197 individuals whose major activity was recorded as employed were used in this study. Non-workers were excluded because no wage data were available to assess their value of time, a necessary ingredient in computing the full prices.

The variables used in the empirical analysis can be divided into six categories measuring: (1) air quality, (2) consumption of medical services, (3) the price of medical services, (4) the wage rate and asset income, (5) socio-demographic characteristics, and (6) health stock measures (previously discussed). Each of these measures now will be considered.

With regard to the first category, air quality data are available from four sources for the St. Louis area: (1) the Regional Air Pollution Study (RAPS) (Strothman et al., 1979), (2) the county of St. Louis, (3) the city of St. Louis, and (4) the Illinois Environmental Protection Agency. The last three sources maintained air monitoring systems in the St. Louis area over the entire decade of the 1970s, while the RAPS air monitoring system only operated between 1974 and 1977. However, the air quality data obtained from the RAPS were of substantially better quality as compared with those from the other three monitoring systems.[8] As a consequence, they are used exclusively in this study in spite of the fact that they pertain to a time period earlier than the health survey data.

Data from 19 RAPS air monitoring stations are used in the estimations. Averages over the period 1975–77 were computed for each station for the following pollutants: (1) ozone (OZ), (2) Sulfur dioxide ($SULD$), (3) total inhalable suspended particulates (TSP), and (4) oxides of nitrogen ($OXNIT$). Those exposure estimates were matched to the individuals in the health survey according to which station was closest to their residence. If these average exposure measures are "typical," then they can be used as a measure of air quality for the time in which the health survey took place.[9]

The measure of medical care consumption (MED) comes from a yes/no question asking if a doctor usually was seen at least once per year. The measure was chosen since it indicates whether the respondent has received regular medical attention over time. That historical perspective is relevant since the air quality data are taken from a time period preceding the health survey. However, MED should be viewed only as a proxy for the continuous variable M in the theoretical model.

The price of medical care ($PMED$) was constructed to take into account direct dollar outlays for medical care, the time cost involved in commuting to and from the source of medical care, and the waiting time at the source of medical care. Direct dollar outlays were measured as the doctor's usual charge for an office visit and time was valued using the wage rate. Thus, $PMED$ = office visit charge + [$WAGE$ × (commuting time + office waiting time)] where commuting time + office waiting time were measured in hours.

The wage rate ($WAGE$) is defined as take home pay divided by average weekly hours computed over an eight week survey period. Unfortunately, data on take home pay were missing for 1,373 out of 2,197 workers. This situation resulted in giving separate consideration to a 2,197 worker data set and a $2,197 - 1,373 = 824$ worker data set. Results based on 824 observations are presented here, even though this culling of the original data may produce a selection bias problem. Results based on the 2,197 observation data set, which do not differ greatly from those in the smaller data set, are available from the authors on request[10]. Asset income (A) is defined as total family combined income multiplied by the portion of total income that comes from interest, dividends, rent, estates, trusts, or capital gains. Since information on these two variables was provided categorically (under $2000, $2000 to $2999, $3000 to $5999, etc. and less than 2%, 2% to 10%, etc.), the midpoint value of the category chosen was used in the computation. Finally, the variables in δ are: (1) years of age (AGE), (2) years of formal education completed $(SCHOOL)$, (3) $RACE$, and (4) SEX.

Empirical results
In this part, estimates of the willingness to pay for improved air quality are presented based on the 824 person sample of St. Louis adult workers. The basic equation to be estimated is

$$MED_i = MED(OZ_i, SULD_i, TSP_i, OXNIT_i,$$
$$AGE_i, SCHOOL_i, SEX_i$$
$$RACE_i, CHRO_i, LENGTH_i). \tag{12}$$

In equation (12), the aerometric variables measure air pollution rather than air quality. Hence, expected signs on the coefficients of these variables are positive, implying that they must be multiplied by minus one in computing $\partial A/\partial \alpha$. Moreover, the expected signs of $CHRO$, and $LENGTH_i$, should be negative since increases in these variables are associated with decreases in the health stock[11]. The expected signs on the four socioeconomic-demographic variables are as follows: (1) the coefficient of AGE would be positive if the ageing process reduces the efficiency with which the health stock is produced, (2) the coefficient of $SCHOOL$ would be negative if years of schooling increase the efficiency with which health is produced and (3) the coefficients of SEX and $RACE$ should be positive if males and blacks tend to have lower health stocks.

Equation (12) initially was specified as a translog function (Christensen, Jorgenson, and Lau, 1971). That general functional form, however, was discarded in favor of the more restrictive Cobb–Douglas because all of the quadratic and interaction terms were statistically insignificant at the 10% level. Additionally, because of the discrete nature of the dependent variable, MED, and the inclusion of the health stock (a choice variable) as a covariate, a simultaneous logit model was developed. Predicted values for $CHRO$ and $LENGTH$, denoted by "⌢", were obtained from reduced form regressions that use $PMED_i$, $WAGE_i$, SEX_i, $RACE_i$, AGE_i, $SCHOOL_i$, and the air pollution variables as covariates. The reduced form equation for $CHRO$ is estimated in a logit framework and the corresponding equation for $LENGTH$ is estimated as a tobit. The frequency distribution of the $LENGTH$ variable is characterized by a large number of zeros (more than half of the values are zero) and then integer values ranging as high as 27.

From an econometric viewpoint, the simultaneous system described above is atypical since the dependent variables either are discrete or truncated. Nelson and Olson (1978), however, have shown that the procedure used here produces estimated coefficients which are consistent and asymptotically normally distributed. Furthermore, on the basis of a small sample simulation experiment, those authors conclude that tests for whether those coefficients are statistically significant are conservative.

Estimates of six variants of equation (12) are presented in Table 15.1. The first column of this table shows the explanatory variables used and the prefix *LN* denotes those transformed to natural logarithms. As shown, the explanatory variables in some equations included interactions between *OZ* and *SULD* (*OZSULD*) and *OZ* and *OXNIT* (*OZOXNIT*). These interaction variables were included to detect synergistic effects between ozone and other pollutants. *t*-statistics are given in parentheses beneath each coefficient estimate. Below each equation is a X^2 statistic used to test the null hypothesis of no relationship between the dependent and all independent variables.

With respect to the air pollution variables, the coefficient of *LNOZ* is positive and significant at the 1% level in all equations. Moreover, the values of these coefficients are stable regardless of which other air pollution measures are included. None of the other pollution variables were significantly different from zero at the 10% level.[12] Using the 2,197 observation data set, however, *OZSULD* and *OZOXNIT* were significant at the 10% level in some of the equations estimated. The coefficients of *LNCHRO* and *LNLENGTH* also are not significantly different from zero at the 10% level.

Among the socioeconomic-demographic variables, *LNAGE* significantly entered each equation but with the wrong sign (negative). That result may seem surprising; however, in a sample composed only of employed workers, there may not be sufficient variation in years of age to capture the effect of the variable on the health stock. The coefficient of *LNSCHOOL* always had the correct sign (negative); but was never significant at the 10% level. The coefficients of *SEX* and *RACE* indicate that in the sample considered females and blacks tend to have lower health stocks than males and whites, respectively. In both sets of regressions, the coefficients of *SEX* and *RACE* are significantly different from zero, and significant at the 1% or 5% level.

With caution, the results from Table 15.1 can be used to make some illustrative willingness to pay estimates for a reduction in ozone levels. These benefit estimates are offered advisedly because of the caveats enumerated concerning the model as well as the data problems outlined above. Since ozone was the only air quality variable that performed consistently well, only reductions in that pollutant are used in making the benefit calculations. Because St. Louis experiences only a comparatively small number of days each year when the hourly average ozone level exceeds the national primary and secondary standards, only small reductions in ambient concentrations are necessary to meet the standard. Therefore, reductions in the ozone level of 30% of the mean ozone level (0.019) have been used to calculate benefits.

Illustrative willingness to pay estimates are calculated based on equations (1) and (5) in Table 15.1. For a 30% reduction in ambient mean ozone concentrations, the annual willingness to pay estimates range from $18.45 to $24.48. Since the *MED* variable reflects whether a doctor usually is seen at least once per year, the willingness to pay estimates are also annual figures. Moreover, the willingness to pay estimates reported are computed using the means of the independent variables. The willingness to pay estimates appear to be small. In

Table 15.1 Estimates of the health production function (824 cases).

CONSTANT	60.42[d]	57.26[d]	54.06[d]	57.45[d]	54.11[d]	32.24[d]
	(3.96)	(3.56)	(3.22)	(3.59)	(3.32)	(3.40)
LNOZ	10.24[d]	10.36[d]	10.04[d]	10.42[d]	9.95[d]	5.40[d]
	(4.75)	(4.78)	(4.60)	(4.78)	(4.50)	(3.08)
LNOXNIT						−0.337
						(−0.652)
LNSULD		−0.059				
		(−0.255)				
LNTSP		1.01	1.17	1.02	1.07	
		(0.0600)	(0.715)	(0.604)	(0.632)	
LNOZSULD				0.016	−0.016	
				(0.272)	(−0.242)	
LNOZOXNIT			0.153		0.169	
			(1.13)		(1.12)	
LNAGE	−3.49[d]	−3.46[d]	−3.53[d]	−3.46[d]	−3.53[d]	−1.98[d]
	(−2.86)	(−2.84)	(−2.88)	(−2.84)	(−2.88)	(−3.72)
LNSCHOOL	−0.164	−0.161	−0.155	−0.160	−0.160	−0.393
	(−0.331)	(−0.326)	(−0.315)	(−0.325)	(−0.324)	(−1.11)
SEX[a]	−1.93[d]	−1.93[d]	−1.95[d]	−1.93[d]	−1.95[d]	−1.66[d]
	(−5.35)	(−5.34)	(−5.38)	(−5.34)	(−5.38)	(−6.68)
RACE[b]	0.653[e]	0.659[e]	0.723[d]	0.659[e]	0.730[d]	0.681[d]
	(2.49)	(2.51)	(2.69)	(2.51)	(2.71)	(2.69)
LNCHRO[c]	2.01	1.97	2.00	1.97	2.01	0.931[e]
	(1.17)	(1.15)	(1.17)	(1.15)	(1.17)	(2.37)
LNLENGTH	1.28	1.29	1.30	1.29	1.31	0.783[f]
	(1.38)	(1.40)	(1.41)	(1.40)	(1.41)	(1.67)
x^2 (d.f.)	69.63 (7)	70.00 (9)	71.20 (9)	70.00 (9)	71.26 (10)	62.80 (8)

[a] 1 = male.
[b] 1 = black.
[c] 1 = presence of one or more chronic conditions.
[d] Denotes significance at 1% level.
[e] Denotes significance at 5% level.
[f] Denotes significance at 10% level.

fact, the highest value placed on a 30% reduction in ozone concentrations only is about 60% of the average full cost of one doctor's visit. However, the contemplated reductions in mean ozone levels are not large either. As previously indicated, the mean of the variable OZ was 0.019 ppm, reflecting the fact that ozone levels in St. Louis are lower than those found elsewhere in the United States. In the Los Angeles area, for example, average ozone concentrations would exceed that figure by a factor of five and peak ozone concentrations can be as high as 0.35 ppm. Additionally, the willingness to pay estimates account only for the effects of the improvement in air quality on illness. A total benefit estimate might also account for reduced materials damage, minor symptomatic discomforts, and improved visibility.

CONCLUSION

This paper has presented a health oriented choice model for the purpose of determining an individual's marginal willingness to pay for improved air quality. The marginal willingness to pay expression is quite simple in that it involves only one price (that of medical care) and two partial derivatives from the health production function (those for air pollution and medical care). Moreover, this expression does not involve any utility terms so that empirical estimation of it is relatively straightforward. The willingness to pay expression was estimated using health and air pollution exposure data on 824 adult workers in St. Louis, Missouri. These estimates range from $18.45 to $24.48 annually for a 30% reduction in ambient mean ozone concentrations. This comparatively low figure, which is about 60% of the average full or time inclusive cost of one doctor's visit, may be due to the low levels of ozone in St. Louis and the fact that estimates consider only illness effects of air quality improvements.

In order to more effectively implement this willingness to pay measure, better data must be collected. The St. Louis data measuring the consumption of medical care, for example, were a weak link in computing the estimates reported. In addition, with a more comprehensive data set, the theoretical model could be extended to include other inputs into the health production function and actions taken by individuals to avoid air pollution exposure.

NOTES

1. A notable exception is the work of Cropper (1981).
2. The CV method usually is defined in terms of the maximum amount of income that an individual would forgo or require in order to consume at a new set of relative prices, holding utility constant. The comparative static properties of the model presented, however, reveal that a change in air quality (α) is equivalent to a change in the ratio q_M/q_x.
3. Examples of the dose-response approach to estimating benefits of reduced morbidity include Ostro (1983), Portney and Mullahy (1983), and Seskin (1979).
4. Residential relocation represents another means by which air pollution exposure may be altered. However, relocation also may result in money price and wage changes and therefore may not be a good example of the commodity.
5. Even though the marginal bid expressions are unchanged, the econometric estimation strategy would have to be altered in order to reflect the changes in model specification.
6. Another approach might involve estimating separate equations for each health dimension measured. Any computation of total willingness to pay based on this approach, however, would have to allow for double counting benefits.
7. Two other exogenous variables are excluded from the entire empirical model. T is excluded on the grounds that it is the same for all sample members. The variable q_x can also be excluded as the variation in q_x will be proportional to the variation in the wage rate (assuming T_x and P_x are constant across all individuals).
8. This point is discussed more fully in Gerking, Stanley, and Weirick (1983). See chapter 5.
9. Even though the aerometric data pertain to one metropolitan area for one time period, there is still considerable variation in the pollution measures between the 19 monitoring stations. Mean values for the four pollutants had the following ranges and standard deviations: (1) OZ (.015 ppm – .025 ppm, .0019 ppm), (2) $SULD$ (.012 ppm – .034 ppm, .0088 ppm), (3) $OXNIT$ (.019 ppm – .059 ppm, .0095 ppm), and (4) TSP (21.84 mg/m^3 – 27.56 mg/m^3, 1.331 mg/m^3).
10. Also available on request are results from both data sets in which the health production function is estimated in a single equation framework. In these sets of results, willingness to pay to avoid ozone is up to 50% lower than the figures reported here.
11. Preliminary estimates using the subjectively reported health status variable produced results similar to those presented in this subsection; hence this variable was dropped from further consideration.
12. This same conclusion also applies to regressions (not reported) similar to those in Table 15.1 in which each pollution variable was entered by itself.

REFERENCES

Christensen, Laurits, Dale Jorgenson, and Lawrence Lau, "Conjugate Duality and the Transcendental Logarithmic Production Function," *Econometrica* 39 (July 1971), 255–256.

Cropper, Maureen L., "Measuring the Benefits from Reduced Morbidity," *American Economic Review* 71 (May 1981), 235–240.

Gerking, Shelby D., Linda R. Stanley, and William N Weirick, "An Economic Analysis of Air Pollution and Health: The Case of St. Louis," Office of Policy and Resource Management, United States Environmental Protection Agency, July 1983.

Grossman, Michael, "On the Concept of Health Capital and the Demand for Health," *Journal of Political Economy* 80 (Mar. 1972), 223–255.

Harrington, Winston, and Paul R. Portney, "Valuing the Benefits of Improved Human Health," mimeo, Resources for the Future, Washington, D.C., 1982.

Lave, Lester B., and Eugene P. Seskin, "An Analysis of the Association between U.S. Mortality and Air Pollution," *Journal of the American Statistical Associations* 68 (June 1973), 284–290.

——, *Air Pollution and Human Health* (Baltimore: Johns Hopkins University Press, 1977).

Nelson, Forrest, and Lawrence Olson, "Specification and Estimation of a Simultaneous Equation Model with Limited Dependent Variables," *International Economic Review* 19 (Oct. 1978), 695–710.

Portney, Paul, and John Mullahy, *Ambient Ozone and Human Health: An Epidemiological Analysis* (Washington, D.C.: Resources for the Future, 1983).

Ostro, Bart D., "The Effects of Air Pollution on Work Loss and Morbidity," *Journal of Environmental Economics and Management* 10 (Dec. 1983), 371–382.

Rosenzweig, Mark, and T. Paul Schultz, "The Behavior of Mothers as Inputs to Child Health: The Determinants of Birthweight, Gestation, and Rate of Fetal Growth," in V. Fuchs (ed.), *Economic Aspects of Health* (Chicago: National Bureau of Economic Research, 1982).

Seskin, Eugene, "Pollution and Health in Washington, D.C.," *Journal of Urban Economics* 6 (July 1979), 275–291.

Strothman, J.A., *et al.*, "Documentation of the Regional Air Pollution Study (RAPS) and Related Investigations in the St. Louis Air Quality Control Region," Research Triangle Park, Environmental Sciences Research Laboratory, 1979.

Chapter 16

Valuing public goods:
a comparison of survey and
hedonic approaches

David S. Brookshire, Mark A. Thayer, William D. Schulze and Ralph C. D'Arge

Although the theory of public goods has progressed rapidly since Paul Samuelson's seminal article, the empirical measurement of the value of (demand for) public goods only recently has received increased attention. Perhaps the best known and most widely accepted empirical approach has been the use of hedonic prices wherein, for example, it is assumed that either wages or housing values reflect spatial variation in public good characteristics of different communities. This indirect approach, based on theoretical work of Charles Tiebout, Kelvin Lancaster, Sherwin Rosen, and others, has proven quite successful. Among public goods or bads which have been valued using the hedonic approach are climate (I. Hoch), air pollution (Robert Anderson and Thomas Crocker; D. Harrison and D. Rubinfeld), social infrastructure (R. Cummings *et al.*) and other community characteristics such as noise level (J. Nelson), and ethnic composition (Ann Schnare).

An alternative approach is to directly ask households or individuals to state their willingness to pay for public goods using survey techniques. Despite arguments that strategic bias will invalidate survey results, there exists the need for an alternative to the hedonic approach. As an example, consider the case of a remote and unique scenic vista, valuable to recreators, which is threatened by air pollution from a proposed coal fired plant – a typical situation in the western United States. Although it is possible, in principle, to impute the value of clean air and visibility from the relative decline in local visitation which might follow construction of a power plant, information on the value of visibility at the site is needed prior to construction for socially optimal decision making on plant location and pollution control equipment. The hedonic approach is unavailable both because the scarcity of local population – as opposed to recreators – makes use of wage or property value data impossible and because scenic vistas may themselves be unique. For these reasons, A. Randall *et al.* first applied survey methods for valuing visibility and other environmental effects of large coal fired power plants in the Four Corners region of New Mexico. Since this initial application, the survey approach has been widely used to value environmental commodities where market data for hedonic analysis is difficult to acquire (see, for example, Brookshire, Ives, and Schulze; Rowe *et al.*; Brookshire, *et al.*). Other early attempts to value public goods using the survey approach include R. Davis, Peter Bohm, and J. Hammack and G. Brown.

Although results of using the survey approach for estimating the value of public goods appear to be internally consistent, replicable and consistent with demand theory (see Schulze *et al.*), little work on external validation has been reported. Thus, the purpose of this paper is to report on an experiment designed to validate the survey approach by direct comparison to a hedonic property value study.

The Los Angeles metropolitan area was chosen for the experiment because of the well-defined air pollution problem and because of the existence of detailed property value data. Twelve census tracts were chosen for sampling wherein 290 household interviews were conducted during March 1978. Respondents were asked to provide their willingness to pay for an improvement in air quality at their current location. Air quality was defined as poor, fair, or good based both on maps of the region (the pollution gradient across the Los Angeles metropolitan area is both well defined and well understood by local residents) and on photographs of a distant vista representative of the differing air quality levels. Households in poor air quality areas were asked to value an improvement to fair air quality while those in fair areas were asked to value an improvement to good air quality. Households in good air quality areas were asked their willingness to pay for a region-wide improvement in air quality. The region-wide responses are reported elsewhere (Brookshire *et al.*).

For comparison to the survey responses, data was obtained on 634 single family home sales which occurred between January 1977 and March 1978 exclusively in the twelve communities used for the survey analysis. As we show in the next section, households, in theory, will choose to locate along a pollution rent gradient, paying more for homes in clean air areas based on income and tastes. However, *ceteris paribus,* we show that the annualized cost difference between homes in two different air quality areas (the rent differential for pollution) will in theory exceed the annual willingness to pay for an equivalent improvement in air quality for a household in the lower air quality area. Thus, the rent differential associated with air quality improvement from hedonic analysis of the property value data must exceed estimates of household willingness to pay for the survey responses, if the survey responses are a valid measure of the value of air quality improvements. Section II describes the data analysis and experimental design in more detail.

We also conjecture that the willingness to pay for air quality improvements is greater than zero for residents in our sample communities based on statewide political support for air quality regulation. The state of California, principally in response to the air pollution problem in the Los Angeles metropolitan areas, has led the nation in imposing automobile emissions standards. The automobile industry, under pressure from the California Legislature, installed the first pollution control devices on California cars in 1961. This initial step was followed nationally in 1963. Again, California imposed the first exhaust emission control regulations in 1966, leading the nation by two years. Over the decade of the 1970s, California has had more stringent automotive emission standards than federal levels, resulting in higher initial costs and sacrifices in both performance and fuel economy. In spite of these difficulties, political support, as reflected both in the State Legislature and in several administrations, has remained strong for auto emission controls.

In Section III the results of the hypotheses tests are presented. As Table 16.2 illustrates, results of the experiment can be summarized as follows: In the nine census tracts where air quality improvements are possible (poor and fair communities), we cannot reject our dual hypotheses that, in each census tract, household willingness to pay for air quality improvements, as estimated by surveying households, falls below equivalent property value rent differentials and lies above zero. We view these results as a qualified verification of the survey approach for estimating the value of public goods. Further interpretation of the results is contained in the concluding remarks offered in Section IV.

A THEORETICAL BASIS
The property value and the survey approaches for valuing public goods have received considerable theoretical scrutiny. Property value studies are conceptually based on hedonic price theory as developed by Rosen and recently summarized by A. Myrick Freeman. The survey approach has been modeled using standard concepts of consumers' surplus by Randall *et al.*, Bohm, and Brookshire, Ives, and Schulze, where the latter two analyses also focus on the possibility of strategic behavior. The considerable empirical evidence now available suggests that strategic bias may be of little consequence both in survey work (see R.C. Bishop and T.A. Heberlein; Brookshire *et al.*; Rowe *et al.*; and Schulze *et al.*) and in experimental economics (see David Grether and Charles Plott; B. Scherr and E. Babb; and Vernon Smith). The hypothetical nature of the questions used in survey analysis may substantially reduce incentives for strategic behavior. However, respondents also may have little incentive to provide accurate answers concerning willingness to pay for public goods. Thus, it has even been suggested that the survey approach produces "noise" since responses are purely hypothetical and have no necessary connection to actual budgetary decisions.

In this section, a theoretical model is developed for comparison of survey responses to a property value study for valuing air quality improvements in the Los Angeles region in order to determine if valid public good measures can be obtained from survey data.

We use the following notation: Let P = the level of air pollution; X = consumption of a composite commodity excluding housing; C = unit cost or price of the composite commodity X; R = rent or periodic cost of housing; Y = household income; and $U(P, X)$ = household utility, a decreasing function of pollution $U_P < 0$ an increasing function of consumption $U_x < 0$.[1]

Each household maximizes utility, $U(P, X)$, subject to the budget constraint

$$Y - CX - R(P) = 0,$$

where we assume the existence of a continuous differentiable rent gradient $R(P)$. (See Rosen for a complete discussion of the generation and existence of rent gradients. Our model is a simple adaptation of Rosen's, so we will not elaborate here.) Two distinct choices are modeled: consumption of the composite commodity, X, and that of housing location by pollution level, P. Presumably, lower rents will be paid for homes in more polluted areas, so $R'(P)<0$.[2] The first-order conditions for choice of P and X imply that

$$C(U_P/U_X)=R'(P),$$

or that the marginal rate of substitution between pollution P, and the composite commodity X, valued at the cost of the composite commodity C, equals the slope of the rent gradient $R'(P)$ at equilibrium location and consumption levels.

Valuing public goods

Figure 16.1 illustrates the solution graphically and allows us to structure hypotheses for testing the validity of survey results in comparison to the property value approach. The vertical axis measures the quantity of the composite commodity, X, where we assume that the cost C of the composite commodity is unity; that is, the vertical axis measures dollars as well. Pollution is on the horizontal axis. Given household income Y^0, the budget constraint, shown as $Y^0 - R(P)$ in Figure 16.1, is obtained by vertically subtracting the rent gradient $R(P)$. Thus, household A with preferences shown by indifference curve 1_A^0 would maximize utility at point a, choosing to locate at pollution level P^0, consume X^0, and pay rent R^0. If household A's income were to increase to Y^1, the budget constraint would shift vertically to $Y^1 - R(P)$ and the same household would relocate, choosing point b, at a lower pollution level P^1 with higher consumption X^1, given tastes as represented by indifference curve I_A^1. Alternatively, another household B, with income Y^0 but tastes as shown by I_B^3, would choose point d, locating at P^1 as well but choosing lower consumption X^3. Thus, both tastes and income enter location decisions over pollution levels.

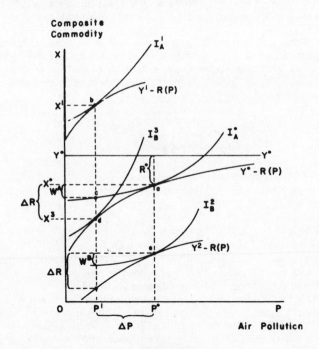

Figure 16.1
Note: With identical housing attributes, the identical rent differential ΔR exceeds individual willingness to pay, W^A and W^B.

The survey approach used in the Los Angeles metropolitan area to obtain an estimate of the value of air quality asked households how much, at most, they would be willing to pay for an improvement in air quality at the site where they presently live. Thus, the household in equilibrium at point a in Figure 16.1 asked how much X it would forego to experience P^1 rather than P^0 while maintaining the same utility level. Presumably, household A would be indifferent between points a and c and be willing to pay W^A dollars (or units of X) to achieve a reduction in air pollution of ΔP. Unfortunately, as is illustrated in Figure 16.1, the budget constraint $Y^0 - R(P)$, obtainable by estimating the rent gradient function $R(P)$, does not provide information on the bid for improved air quality W^A. Rather, the change in rent between locations with air quality levels P^0 and P^1, ΔR in Figure 16.1, must, for any household located at a, equal or exceed the bid W^A, if the second-order conditions for the household optimization problem are generally satisfied. Note that the rent gradient $R(P)$ need not be strictly concave or convex, but must lie "below" the relevant indifference curves. In fact, no a priori theoretical arguments on the shape of the rent gradient can be made. However, we can establish an upper bound on the willingness to pay for air quality improvement by examining the rent gradient. For example, if household B had a lower income, Y^2, it would locate at point e. Even though household B is now located at pollution level P^0 like household A, its bid for an air quality improvement ΔP would be W^B, smaller than W^A yet still less than ΔR. Thus, if survey bids are a valid measure of willingness to pay for air quality improvements, then $\Delta R \geqslant W$.

This hypothesis holds for each household even if we consider the case of multiple housing attributes. Including other multiple housing attributes. Including other attributes such as square footage of the home, bathrooms, fireplaces, neighborhood characteristics, etc., denoted by the vector $\vec{Z}$, the model is revised as follows:

$$max \ U(\vec{Z}, P, X);$$

subject to $Y - CX - R(\vec{Z}, P) = 0,$

with first-order conditions[3]

$$C \frac{U_P}{U_X} = R_P(\vec{Z}, P); \ C \frac{UU_{\vec{Z}}}{U_X} = R_{\vec{Z}}(\vec{Z}, P).$$

These first-order conditions constitute, along with frequency distributions for housing characteristics and household preferences, a system of partial differential equations which solve for $R(\vec{Z}, P)$.[4] Thus, a hedonic rent gradient is defined for pollution P, and other household characteristics $\vec{Z}$, as well.

As illustrated in Figure 16.1, in which housing characteristics other than pollution are not incorporated, budget constraints for different households are obtained by vertically shifting the same rent gradient. Thus, all households face the same rent differential ΔR for a change in pollution ΔP even though willingness to pay for that change may differ, that is, $W^A \neq W^B$. However, turning to Figure 16.2, household A, located at P^0, may occupy a house with attributes $\vec{Z}^A$ while household B also located at P^0 may occupy a house with a different set of attributes $\vec{Z}^B$. Household A, with income Y^A, would then face a rent gradient like that shown in Figure 16.2 defined by $R(\vec{Z}, P)$ and choose point a, but household B with income Y^B, would now face a different rent gradient of $R(\vec{Z}^B, P)$ and choose to locate at point b. Therefore, households with different housing characteristics may face different rent gradients over pollution when projected in the (X, P) plane. In general, ΔR, unlike the case shown in Figure 16.1, will no longer be constant across households at the same location. However, for each household $i(i=A, B$ in Figure 16.2), it is still true that the rent differential ΔR^i, for a change in pollution ΔP, calculated for the fixed vector of housing characteristics $\vec{Z}^i$, will exceed that household's willingness to pay, W^i, for the same change in pollution level at the same location. Note that households were asked their willingness to pay with the specific assumption that they remained in the same house and location. Thus, $\vec{Z}^i$ for a particular household was truly fixed – allowing the simple analysis in the (X, P) plane as shown in Figure 16.2.

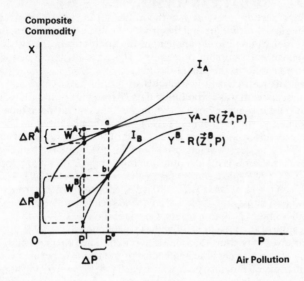

Figure 16.2
Note: With differing housing attributes across households, each rent differential exceeds that household's willingness to pay.

The first hypothesis for testing the validity of the survey approach can be constructed as follows: *for each household i in a community,* $\Delta R^i \geqslant W^i$. It then follows that in each community the average rent differential across households, $\overline{\Delta R}$, must equal or exceed the average willingness to pay $\overline{W}$ for an improvement in air quality. In other words, if survey bids are a valid measure of willingness to pay, then for each community in our sample, $\overline{\Delta R} \geqslant \overline{W}$, that is, average willingness to pay cannot exceed the average rent differential. Our second hypothesis is that, given the political history of air pollution control in the state of California as described in the introduction, *mean bids in each community are nonnegative,* $\overline{W} > 0$.

Our dual test of the validity of survey measures must remain somewhat imprecise because hedonic rent gradients themselves only provide point estimates of the marginal rates of substitution (slopes of indifference curves) between pollution and other goods (money) for individuals with possible differing tastes and income. One does not have information necessary to estimate, for example, the shape of I_A^0 in Figure 16.1 solely on the basis of the slope of the budget constraint, $R'(P^0)$, at point a. Attempts to estimate individual willingness to pay (W^A in Figure 16.1) from hedonic rent gradients must thus introduce strong assumptions about the nature of preferences. (See Harrison and Rubinfeld for an example of an hedonic approach which derives willingness to pay by implicitly making such assumptions.)

Finally, it should be noted that households were asked to hypothetically give up money for better air quality in this study, and not asked about hypothetical compensation to accept worse air quality. The latter type of question has consistently evoked biased responses (see, for example, Rowe *et al.*; Bishop and Heberlein).

SAMPLING AND DATA ANALYSIS

The previous section presented a theoretical framework for a comparison between the survey technique and the property value approach for valuing public goods. In order to empirically implement the comparison, the two approaches require a consistent sampling procedure. This section describes the sampling procedure and results of the separate studies.

Sampling was restricted to households within the Los Angeles metropolitan area. The first concern was air pollution data. Air monitoring stations are located throughout the Los Angeles area providing readings on nitrogen dioxide (NO_2), total suspended particulate matter (TSP), and other pollutants. The objective was to relate as closely as possible the readings of two constituents of air pollution (NO_2 and TSP) to census tracts used both for the property value and survey studies. The air shed was divided into the following air quality regions: "good" ($NO_2 < 9\ pphm$) ($TSP < 90\ \mu g/m^3$); "fair" ($NO_2\ 9$–$11\ pphm$) ($TSP\ 90$–$110\ \mu g/m^3$); and "poor" ($NO_2 > 11\ pphm$) ($TSP > 110\ \mu g/m^3$). Improvements from poor to fair and fair to good across the region are each associated with about a 30 percent reduction in ambient pollution levels. Consideration was given to wind patterns and topography of the area in making these distinctions.

Many variables may affect the value households place on air quality. To control for as many of these as possible in advance of the actual experiment, the sample plan identified six community pairs where each pair was relatively homogeneous with respect to socioeconomic, housing, and community characteristics, yet allowed for a significant variation in air quality.[5]

The property value analysis attempts to provide external validation for the survey approach. The absence of such validation explains, in our view, the lack of general acceptance of survey techniques. The objective then, is to estimate the hedonic rent gradient $R(\vec{Z}, P)$ and calculate rent differentials associated with the poor–fair and fair–good air quality improvements for sample census tracts. These results are then utilized for comparison to the survey results.

An hedonic rent gradient was estimated in accordance with literature as recently summarized by Freeman.[6] Housing sale price is assumed to be a function of housing structure variables (living area, bathrooms, fireplaces, etc.), neighborhood variables (crime rate, school quality, population density, etc.), accessibility variables (distance employment to centers and beach), and air quality as measured by total suspended particulates (TSP) or nitrogen dioxide (NO_2).[7] The primary assumption of the analysis is that variations in air pollution levels as well as other household, neighborhood, and accessibility attributes are capitalized into home sale price. Implicit or hedonic prices for each attribute are then determined by examining housing prices and attribute levels.

The property value analysis was conducted at the household level in order to provide an appropriate comparison to the survey instrument. Thus, the household data used were at the micro level of aggregation and include a large number of characteristics.[8] Data were obtained for 634 sales of single family homes which occurred between January 1977 and March 1978 in the communities used for the survey analysis. In addition to the immediate attributes of the household, variables which reflected the neighborhood and community were included to isolate the independent influence of air quality differentials on home sale price.

As indicated by Mäler, even under the presumption of correct model specification, estimation of a single equation hedonic rent gradient may be hindered by severe empirical difficulties, primarily multicollinearity. With respect to this problem, in each of three data categories – household, neighborhood, and air quality – multicollinearity forced the exclusion of variables and the usage of proxy variables. For instance, collinearity between number of rooms, number of bedrooms, and living area as quantitative measures of house size allowed the use of only one – living area, which serves as a proxy for all. Further, since housing density and population density measure essentially the same phenomenon, only the former is used in the estimated equations. The estimation procedure was not able to separate out the independent influence of each air pollutant. Thus, only one pollution measure, either NO_2 or TSP, was utilized to describe the level of air quality. In order to provide information concerning the sensitivity of our analysis, results are presented for each of these pollutants. Finally, contrary to expectation, a collinearity problem did not exist between distance from beach and air pollution. This can be attributed, in part, to the success of the sample plan in isolating the effects of air quality.

Two alternative nonlinear hedonic equations are presented in Table 16.1, alternatively using NO_2 or TSP to represent pollution level. A number of aspects of the equations are worth noting. First, approximately 90 percent of the variation in home sale price is explained by the variation in the independent variable set. Second, with only a minor exception, all coefficients possess the expected relationship to the dependent variable and are statistically significant at the one percent level. The exception is the crime rate in both the NO_2 and TSP equations. Third, in their respective equations, the pollution variables have the expected negative influence on sale price and are highly significant. The estimated relationship between house sale price and pollution is also consistent with the graphical analysis of Section I; that is, the rent gradient is convex from below in the pollution/dollars plane. Finally, the stability or relative insensitivity of the regression coefficients to the particular pollution variable indicates that individuals have an aversion to pollution in general rather than to any one pollutant.

Estimation of the rent gradient was also completed using other functional forms with respect to the pollution variable.[9] The functional forms which gave the best fit are presented in Table 16.1. Rent differentials were calculated both from these and from the other estimated forms with results nearly identical to those presented here.

The next step was to estimate the rent differential ΔR_i for each individual household for each census tract. The rent differential specifies the premium an individual household would have to pay to obtain an identical home in the next cleaner air region (poor to fair for six communities, fair to good for three communities). Due to the estimated functional form of the rent gradient, the calculated rent differential is dependent upon the value of all other variables.[10]

211

Table 16.1 Estimated hedonic rent gradient equations[a] dependent variable = *log* (home sale price in $1,000).

Independent variable	NO$_2$ equation	*TSP* equation
Housing structure variables		
Sale date	.018591	.018654
	(9.7577)	(9.7727)
Age	−.018171	−.021411
	(−2.3385)	(−2.8147)
Living Area	.00017568	.00017507
	(12.126)	(12.069)
Bathrooms	.15602	.15703
	(9.609)	(9.6636)
Pool	.058063	.058397
	(4.6301)	(4.6518)
Fireplaces	.099577	.099927
	(7.1705)	(7.1866)
Neighborhood variables		
Log (Crime)	−.08381	−.10401
	(−1.5766)	(−1.9974)
School quality	.0019826	.001771
	(3.9450)	(3.5769)
Ethnic composition	.027031	.043472
(percent white)	(4.3915)	(6.2583)
Housing density	−.000066926	−.000067613
	(−9.1277)	(−9.2359)
Public safety expenditures	.000026192	.00026143
	(4.7602)	(4.7418)
Accessibility variables		
Distance to beach	−.011586	−.011612
	(−7.8321)	(−7.7822)
Distance to employment	−.28514	−.26232
	(−14.786)	(−14.158)
Air pollution variables		
log (*TSP*)		−.22183
		(−3.8324)
log (NO$_2$)	−.22407	
	(−4.0324)	
Constant	2.2325	1.0527
	(2.9296)	(1.4537)
R^2	.89	.89
Sum of squared residuals	18.92	18.97
Degrees of freedom	619	619

[a]*t*-statistics in parentheses.

The average home sale price change based on individual data in each census tract associated with an improvement in air quality, *ceteris paribus,* is shown in column (2) of Table 16.2. Column (1) of Table 16.2 lists communities by air quality level. The table only shows results for the *log*-linear NO$_2$ equation since, as noted above, other specifications give nearly identical results. The numbers shown are derived by evaluating the hedonic housing expression, given the household's characteristics, for a pollution change from poor or fair to good as the case may be. The resulting sale price differential is then converted to an equivalent monthly payment through the standard annualization procedure and division by twelve.[11] Since our hypothesis test is posed in terms of the average rent differential in the relevant communities, a community mean and standard deviation are then calculated. Column (3) of Table 16.2 shows the number of homes for which data was available to calculate average rent differentials and standard deviations for each community. Monthly rent differentials ranged from $15.44 to $45.92 for an improvement from poor to fair air quality and $33.17 to $128.46 for an improvement from fair to good air quality. The higher figures in each case are associated with higher income communities. Again, these average differentials should provide an upper bound for the survey results.

The survey approach followed the work of Davis and Bohm in gathering the information necessary for estimating a David Bradford bid curve. The approach involves the establishment of a hypothetical market via a survey instrument. Through the work of Randall *et al.* and Brookshire, Ives, and Schulze, the necessary structure for constructing a hypothetical market for the direct determination of economic values within the Hicksian consumers' surplus framework has been developed. The survey reported on here is consistent with this previous literature.

The hypothetical market was defined and described both in technical and institutional detail. The public good (air quality) was described by the survey instrument to the respondent in terms of easily perceived levels of provision such as visual range through photographs[12] and maps depicting good, fair, and poor air quality levels over the region. Respondents had little difficulty understanding the levels of air quality represented to them because of the sharp pollution gradient across the region.

Payment mechanisms[13] were specified within the survey instrument and the respondent was asked to react to alternative price levels posited for different air quality levels. In every case the basis for the bid for better air quality was the existing pollution situation as determined by location of their home shown on a map of the Los Angeles metropolitan area which depicted regional air quality levels. Various starting points for the bidding prices and differing information structures were included in the survey format. Biases from alternative starting points and information structures were not present in the results (see Brookshire *et al.*).[14]

The survey was conducted over the period of March 1978. A total of 290 completed surveys were obtained for the above mentioned areas. Sampling was random within each paired area.[15]

Table 16.2 presents the mean bids and standard deviations and number of observations in columns (4) and (5), respectively, for each community for an improvement in air quality. Two types of bids are presented: proposed improvements from poor to fair air quality and from fair to good air quality. In poor communities – El Monte, Montebello, and La Canada – the mean bids ranged from $11.00 to $22.06 per month. For the fair communities – Canoga Park, Huntington Beach, Irvine, Culver City, Encino, and Newport Beach – the mean monthly amounts range from $5.55 to $28.18 to obtain good air quality.

TEST OF HYPOTHESES

The previous sections have described a theoretical structure and two different empirical estimation techniques for determining the value of urban air quality improvements in the Los Angeles metropolitan area. The theoretical relationship

Table 16.2 Tests of hypotheses.

Community (1)	Property value results[a]		Survey results		Tests of hypotheses	
	$\overline{\Delta R}$ (Standard deviation) (2)	Number of observations (3)	$\overline{W}$ (Standard deviation) (4)	Number of observations (5)	t-Statistics $\mu_{\overline{W}} > 0$[b] (6)	t-Statistics $\mu_{\overline{\Delta R}} \geq \mu_{\overline{W}}$[c] (7)
POOR–FAIR						
El Monte	15.44 (2.88)	22	11.10 (13.13)	20	3.78	1.51
Montebello	30.62 (7.26)	49	11.42 (15.15)	19	3.28	7.07
La Canada	73.78 (48.25)	51	22.06 (33.24)	17	2.74	4.10
Sample population	45.92 (36.69)	122	14.54 (21.93)	56	4.96	5.54
FAIR–GOOD						
Canoga Park	33.17 (3.88)	22	16.08 (15.46)	34	6.07	5.07
Huntington Beach	47.26 (10.66)	44	24.34 (25.46)	38	5.92	5.47
Irvine	48.22 (8.90)	196	22.37 (19.13)	27	6.08	5.08
Culver City	54.44 (16.09)	64	28.18 (34.17)	30	5.42	11.85
Encino	128.46 (51.95)	45	16.51 (13.38)	37	7.31	12.75
Newport Beach	77.02 (41.25)	22	5.55 (6.83)	20	3.63	7.65
Sample population	59.09 (34.28)	393	20.31 (23.0)	186	12.02	14.00

[a] Rent differentials for the hedonic housing equation in which $log(NO_2)$ is the relevant pollution variable are presented here.
[b] The hypotheses to be tested were $H_0: \mu_{\overline{W}} = 0$; $H_1: \mu_{\overline{W}} > 0$. All test statistics indicate rejection of the null hypothesis at the 1 percent significance level.
[c] The hypotheses to be tested were $H_0: \mu_{\overline{\Delta R}} \geq \mu_{\overline{W}}$; $H_1: \mu_{\overline{\Delta R}} < \mu_{\overline{W}}$. All test statistics indicate that the null hypothesis could not be

between the valuation procedures $(\overline{\Delta R} \geq \overline{W})$ and the hypothesis that survey bids are nonzero $(\overline{W} > 0)$ are tested in this section.

Table 16.2 presents the community average survey bids (col. (4)) and corresponding rent differentials (col. (2)). As is indicated, in each community the sample survey bids are nonzero and less than the calculated rent differentials in absolute magnitude. This establishes that the survey bid bounds are consistent with our theoretical arguments but does not indicate statistical significance, which is provided below.

With respect to the test of equality of mean survey bids to zero, Table 16.2 (col. (6)) presents the experimental results. The calculated t-statistics indicate rejection of the null hypothesis (that the population mean $\mu_{\overline{W}}$ equals zero) at the 1 percent level in every community sampled. These results are in accordance with the political history of the region and indicate that individual households are willing to pay amounts significantly greater than zero for an approximate 30 percent improvement in air quality.

The comparison of the survey bids to the estimated rent differentials is presented in Table 16.2 (col. (7)). In this instance the compound hypothesis that population average rent differential $(\mu_{\overline{\Delta R}})$ equals or exceeds the population average survey bid $(\mu_{\overline{W}})$ is again tested using the t-statistic. Rejection of the null hypothesis requires that the calculated t-statistics be negative and of sufficient magnitude.[16] The standard t-test calculations (col. (7)) imply that the hypothesis $\mu_{\overline{\Delta R}} \geq \mu_{\overline{W}}$ cannot be rejected for the population means $\mu_{\overline{R}}$ and $\mu_{\overline{W}}$ even at the 10 percent critical level. Although we present only the results for the hedonic housing equation in which log (NO$_2$) is the pollution measure, these results remain essentially unchanged for all communities, for all estimated hedonic rent gradients, regardless of the variable (NO$_2$ or TSP) utilized as a proxy for the general state of air quality. The results then are quite insensitive to the particular hedonic model specification, providing a degree of generality to the results.

The hypotheses tests indicate that the empirical analysis is entirely consistent with the theoretical structure outlined above. This conclusion, when combined with the absence of any identified biases (see Brookshire et al.) suggests that survey responses yield estimates of willingness to pay for environmental improvements in an urban context consistent with a hedonic-market analysis. A further implication is that individual households demonstrated a nonzero willingness to pay for air quality improvements rather than free riding. This conforms to the previous survey results of Brookshire, Ives, and Schulze, and Rowe et al., as well as the experimental work of Scherr and Babb, Smith, and Grether and Plott, concerning the role of strategic behavior. This seems to indicate that the substantive effort to devise a payment mechanism free of strategic incentives for consumers (see Theodore Groves and John Ledyard) has been directed towards solving a problem not yet empirically observed.

Another important question is the accuracy of willingness to pay estimates based on surveys. Bishop and Heberlein conclude – based on a survey approach quite different from that cited throughout this study – that survey estimates of willingness to pay might be biased downward by 55 percent for goose hunting permits. Interestingly, the more traditional travel cost approach gave a downward bias of 67 percent. The basis for calculating both biases was actual repurchase of goose hunting permits. For purposes of comparison, if survey estimates of willingness to pay for air quality improvement are increased by 50 percent over those shown in Table 16.2, then, for eight out of nine communities, average willingness to pay still lies below estimated average rent gradients. Thus, our results are consistent with the possibility of errors of about 50 percent in estimating willingness to pay, just as in the Bishop and Heberlein study. Although better accuracy would be highly desirable, in many cases where no other technique is available for valuing public goods, this level of accuracy is certainly preferable to no information for the decision-making process.

The conclusions of this experiment are not without further qualifications. In the next section, possible limitations of survey analysis and conclusions concerning the efficacy of employing surveys to value a wide range of nonmarket commodities are discussed.

CONCLUSION

There are a number of limitations in generalizing our results to all survey work. First, this experiment was conducted in the South Coast Air Basin where individuals have both an exceptionally well-defined regional pollution situation and a well-developed housing value market for clean air. The effect of clean air on housing values appears to be exceptionally well understood in the Los Angeles metropolitan area. Thus, the Los Angeles experiment may be a special case in which an informed populace with market experience for a particular public good allowed the successful application of the survey approach. In particular, situations where no well-developed hedonic market exists may not be amenable to survey valuation. Biases due to lack of experience must then be considered a possibility. However, existing studies by Randall *et al.* and Brookshire, Ives, and Schulze, and Rowe *et al.* of remote recreation areas certainly suggest that survey approaches provide replicable estimates of consumers' willingness to pay to prevent environmental deterioration, without prior valuation experience.

In summary, this paper set out to both theoretically and empirically examine the survey approach and to provide external validation for survey analysis. The theoretical model described in Section I predicts that survey responses will be bounded below by zero and above by rent differentials derived from the estimated hedonic rent gradient. In order to test the dual hypothesis a survey and a traditional analysis of the housing market were undertaken. Each was based upon a consistent sampling procedure in the Los Angeles metropolitan area. The empirical results do not allow the rejection of either of the two hypotheses, thereby providing evidence towards the validity of survey methods as a means of determining the value of public goods.

NOTES

1. Alternatively we could define the utility function $U(-P, X)$ which would be an increasing quasi-concave function of both arguments.
2. Primes or subscripts, denote derivatives or partial derivatives, respectively, throughout the paper.
3. The second expression is, of course, a vector of conditions, one for each attribute.
4. For a continuous model, one could specify a taste parameter in the utility function and specify a distribution of households over that parameter. To complete a closed model, one also needs the distribution of housing units over characteristics.
5. The paired areas with associated census tract marker and air quality level are, respectively: 1) Canoga Park, #1345, fair/El Monte, #4334, poor; 2) Culver City, #2026, fair/Montebello, #4301.02, and part of #5300.02, poor; 3) Newport Beach, central #630.00, fair/Pacific, northeast portion of #2627.02 and southwest intersection, good; 4) Irvine, part of #525, fair/Palos Verdes, portion of good; 5) Encino, portion of # 1326, fair/La Canada, south-central portion of #4607, poor; 6) Huntington Beach, central portion of #993.03 poor/Redondo Beach, eastern portion of #6205.01 and #6205.02, good. For a map showing the monitoring station locations in relation to the paired sample areas and the air quality isopleths, see Brookshire *et al.*

6. The estimation of a hedonic rent gradient requires that rather restrictive assumptions are satisfied. For example, K. Mäler has raised a number of objections to the hedonic property value approach for valuing environmental goods. These include the possibility that transaction costs (moving expenses and real estate commissions) might restrict transactions leaving real estate markets in near constant disequilibrium; and that markets other than those for property alone might capture part of the value of an environmental commodity. The first of these criticisms is mitigated by the extremely fluid and mobile real estate market of the late 1970s in Los Angeles, where rapidly excalating real property values increased homeowner equity so quickly that "housejumping" became financially feasible. The second of Mäler's concerns, that other prices, for example, golf club fees and wages, capture part of the willingness to pay can be addressed empirically. For example, attempts to test if wages from our survey data across the Los Angeles area reflected differences in pollution level produced negative results.

7. Note that we use sale price or the discounted present value of the flow of rents rather than actual rent as the dependent variable. Given the appropriate discount rate, the two are interchangeable.

8. Housing characteristic data were obtained from the Market Data Center, a computerized appraisal service with central headquarters in Los Angeles.

9. Since the calculated individual values of the rent differentials, ΔR_i, could be sensitive to the estimated functional form of the rent gradient with respect to the pollution variable, four alternative functional forms were tried. Where R indicates sale price, P the pollution variable, and $\Sigma_j \hat{b}_j X_j$ stands for the estimated coefficients ($\hat{b}_j$) and the other independent variables (X_j) exactly as specified in Table 16.1, the estimated equations for four alternative functional forms, where NO_2 is used as the pollution variable, are as follows (t-statistics are presented in parenthesis under the estimated coefficients):

(a) $\log R = \Sigma_j \hat{b}_j Z_j$ $-.224 \log P$ $R^2 = .8884$
(-4.03) $SSR = 18.92$;

(b) $\log R = \Sigma_j \hat{b}_j Z_j$ $-.0197 P$ $R^2 = .8874$
(-3.29) $SSR = 19.08$;

(c) $\log R = \Sigma_j \hat{b}_j Z_j$ $-.00297 P^2$ $R^2 = .8866$
(-2.56) $SSR = 19.21$;

(d) $\log R = \Sigma_j \hat{b}_j Z_j$ $-.0000391 P^3$ $R^2 = .8861$
(-1.88) $SSR = 19.31$.

Clearly, form (a), which is the same as that presented in Table 16.1, gives the best fit. The *log*-linear (a) and semi-*log* (b) forms imply a curvature for the hedonic rent function similar to that shown in Figures 16.1 and 16.2, while the semi-*log* exponential forms, (c) and (d), allow for either a concave or convex rent function in the rent–pollution plane depending on the estimated coefficient. If TSP is used as the pollution variable, precisely the same pattern emerges, with functional form (a) giving the best fit. However, rent differentials calculated from any of the functional forms, using either of the pollutants, give results almost identical to those presented in Table 16.2 which used the *log*-linear NO_2 equation.

10. It should be noted that nonlinear estimated equations will give biased but consistent forecasts of rent differentials. However, if a linear estimated equation is used for either NO_2 or TSP, forecast rent differentials are larger than the results from the nonlinear estimated equations presented here.

11. A capital recovery factor equal to .0995 which corresponds to the prevailing .0925 mortgage rate in the January 1979–March 1978 period is used.

12. In developing photographs, two observational paths from Griffith Observatory in Los Angeles were chosen: toward downtown Los Angeles; and looking down Western Avenue. The approximate visibility (discernable objects in the distance, not visual range) for poor visibility was 2 miles, for fair visibility 12 miles, and for good visibility 28 miles.

13. Payment mechanisms are either of the lump sum variety, or well-specified schemes such as tax increments or utility bill additions. The choice in the experimental setting varies according to the structure of the contingent market.

14. Questions have been raised as to problems of biases in the survey approach. Strategic bias (i.e., free-rider problems), hypothetical bias, instrument bias; all have been explored. Generally speaking, problems of bias within the survey approach have not been prevalent. For a general review of the definition of various biases and results of different experiments see Schulze *et al.*, and for investigations of strategic bias utilizing other demand revealing techniques, see Scherr and Babb, and Smith.

15. Interviewer bias was not present. No records were kept that would enable the testing for nonrespondent bias.

16. For instance, rejection of the null hypothesis ($\mu_{\overline{AR}} \geq \mu_{\overline{W}}$) at the 1 percent level would require a calculated *t*-statistic less than -2.326, given a large number of observations. Since none of the calculated *t*-statistics are negative, the null hypothesis cannot be rejected (see W. Guenther).

REFERENCES

Anderson, Robert and Crocker, Thomas, "Air Pollution and Residential Property Values," *Urban Studies,* October 1971, **8,** 171–80.

Bishop, R.C. and Heberlein, T.A. "Measuring Values of Extra-Market Goods: Are Indirect Measures Biased?," *American Journal of Agricultural Economics,* December 1979, **61,** 926–30.

Bohm, Peter, "Estimating Demand for Public Goods: An Experiment," *European Economic Review,* 1972, **3,** 11–130.

Brookshire, David *et al.*, "Experiments in Valuing Public Goods," in V. Kerry Smith, ed., *Advances in Applied Microeconomics,* Greenwich: JAI Press, 1980.

Brookshire, D., Ives, B., and Schulze, W. "The Valuation of Aesthetic Preferences," *Journal of Environmental Economics and Management,* December 1976, **3,** 325–46.

Bradford, David, "Benefit Cost Analysis and Demand Curves for Public Goods," *Kyklos,* November 1972, **23,** 775–82.

Cummings, R., Schulze, W., and Meyer, A. "Optimal Municipal Investment in Boomtowns: An Empirical Analysis," *Journal of Environmental Economics and Management,* September 1978, **5,** 252–67.

Davis, R., "Recreation Planning as an Economic Problem," *Natural Resources Journal,* October 1963, **3,** 239–49.

Freeman III, A. Myrick, "Hedonic Prices, Property Values and Measuring Environmental Benefits: A Survey of the Issues," *Scandinavian Journal of Economics,* 1979, **81,** 154–173.

Grether David and Plott, Charles "Economic Theory and the Preference Reversal Phenomenon," *American Economic Review,* September 1979, **69,** 623–38.

Groves, Theodore and Ledyard, John "Optimal Allocation of Public Goods: A Solution to the 'Free Rider' Problem," *Econometrica,* May 1977, **45,** 783–809.

Guenther, W., *Concepts of Statistical Inference,* New York: McGraw-Hill, 1973.

Hammack, J. and Brown, G., *Waterfowl and Wetlands: Toward Bioeconomic Analysis,* Baltimore: Johns Hopkins University Press 1974.

Harrison, D., Jr. and Rubinfeld, D., "Hedonic Housing Prices and the Demand for Clean Air," *Journal of Environmental Economics and Management,* March 1978, **5,** 81–102.

Hoch, I. with Drake, T., "Wages, Climate, and the Quality of Life," *Journal of Environmental Economics and Management,* December 1974, **1,** 268–95.

Lancaster, Kelvin, "A New Approach to Consumer Theory," *Journal of Political Economy,* April 1966, **74,** 132–57.

Mäler, K., "A Note on the Use of Property Values in Estimating Marginal Willingness to Pay for Environmental Quality," *Journal of Environmental Economics and Management,* December 1977, **4,** 355–69.

Nelson, J., "Airport Noise, Location Rent, and the Market for Residential Amenities,"

Valuing public goods

Journal of Environmental Economics and Management, December 1979, **6,** 320–31.

Randall, A., Ives, B., and Eastman, C., "Bidding Games for Valuation of Aesthetic Environmental Improvements," *Journal of Environmental Economics and Management,* August 1974, **1,** 132–49.

Rosen, Sherwin, "Hedonic Prices and Implicit Markets: Product Differentiation in Pure Competition," *Journal of Political Economy,* January/February 1974, **82,** 34–55.

Rowe, R., d'Arge, R., and Brookshire, D.S., "An Experiment in the Value of Visibility," *Journal of Environmental Economics and Management,* March 1980, **7,** 1–19.

Samuelson, Paul, "The Pure Theory of Public Expenditures," *Review of Economics and Statistics,* November 1954, **36,** 387–89.

Scherr, B., and Babb, E., "Pricing Public Goods: An Experiment with Two Proposed Pricing Systems," *Public Choice,* Fall 1975, **23,** 35–48.

Schnare, Ann, "Racial and Ethnic Price Differentials in an Urban Housing Market," *Urban Studies,* June 1976, **13,** 107–20.

Schulze, W., d'Arge R., and Brookshire, D.S., "Valuing Environmental Commodities: Some Recent Experiments," *Land Economics,* May 1981, forthcoming.

Smith, Vernon, "The Principal of Unanimity and Voluntary Consent in Social Choice," *Journal of Political Economy,* December 1977, **85,** 1125–40.

Tiebout, Charles, "A Pure Theory of Local Expenditures," *Journal of Political Economy,* October 1956, **65,** 416–24.

Chapter 17

Measuring values of extramarket goods: are indirect measures biased?

Richard C. Bishop and Thomas A. Heberlein

The well-known travel cost method (TC) has been widely applied to outdoor recreation. A second approach has been referred to in the past as the Davis method, the questionnaire approach, and contingent valuation. It will here be termed hypothetical valuation (HV), because it involves creating a hypothetical situation designed to elicit willingness to pay for or willingness to accept compensation for a recreational or other extramarket good (or bad). TC and HV are termed "indirect methods," because they do not depend on the direct information about prices and quantities that economists would prefer to use where available to value goods and services.

A number of potential sources of bias in HV and TC have been discussed in the literature and we shall summarize these in the first section of the paper. When summed together, these potential problems are sufficient to justify considerable skepticism about the accuracy of resulting value estimates. Still, the question remains: How large an impact do these supposed sources of bias have in actual practice? In the second section of the paper we report the results of an experiment where TC and HV values were compared to values based on actual cash transactions. Though preliminary, the results of this experiment indicate that substantial biases exist in both TC and HV estimates.

POTENTIAL SOURCES OF BIAS

In TC, differences in travel and possibly other costs to recreationists at varying distances from the recreation site are used to infer how recreationists would behave if prices higher than the actual admission fee were charged. Thus, potential sources of bias exist if there are substantial differences in the recreationists' tastes and preferences, access to substitutes, and income levels at varying distances from the recreation site. It is fairly straightforward to control statistically for differences in income. Potential problems relating to tastes and substitute availability are much more difficult.

A particularly thorny problem in developing TC value estimates relates to time costs. It is clear that those who live farther from the recreations site in question not only incur larger transportation costs, but also expend more time in travel. What sort of price should be attached to this time? Several factors make this a complicated issue. Clearly the wage rate of adults overestimates what they could earn from second jobs. Furthermore, in opportunity cost terms, if people were not traveling to the recreation site most would probably be engaged in other leisure time activities rather than working. What is leisure time in the next best recreational activity worth? Also, how to value time of children and adolescent participants is not well understood. To make matters even more complex it is not inconceivable that travel to some recreation sites may actually add to the benefits rather than the costs, as when the route is a scenic one. Cesario has suggested that time be valued at between one-fourth and one-half the wage rate. While this is a beginning, it must be considered as a very crude adjustment since it is based on urban transportation studies and offers little guidance as to the exact figure to be used. As we shall see below, whether a factor of one-fourth or one-half is used can make a substantial difference in the value estimates.

TC requires that recreationists treat travel expenditures as equivalent to admission costs yet this is a questionable assumption which no-one has examined empirically. Travel costs represent an aggregation of many smaller costs, some of which (e.g. tire wear) may not be obvious to the recreationist and which are not actually imposed on the recreationists at the time when the recreation is demanded. Admission fees are paid immediately, usually in cash. Particularly in a world of satisficing, travel costs may not be perceived as equivalent to admission fees.

Still other potential problems with TC techniques need to be noted. One stems from the fact that increases in density which recreationists label as crowding may affect quality. A travel cost demand curve implicitly assumes that recreational quality remains constant over the range from zero use to full use at the going admission fee. Thus, it may completely neglect changes in quality as quantity declines along the demand curve. Also, no satisfactory method has yet been devised to handle multiple-purpose trips (e.g., recreation plus work) or multiple-site trips (e.g., vacations involving several stops).

Because of these potential biases and because TC techniques are not applicable to recreational activities involving limited travel (e.g., backyard birdwatching) and many non-recreational extramarket goods (e.g., air quality; public health programs), HV has evolved as a major alternative method of valuing extramarket commodities. Unfortunately, HV also has major potential sources of bias.

Hypothetical valuation
Perhaps the source of bias that has most dominated the literature is gamesmanship. People who are asked hypothetically what they would be willing to pay for extramarket goods may recognize two different incentives to distort their responses. Perceiving that they will not actually have to pay and that their responses may influence the supply of an extramarket good or bad, people may respond in ways that are more indicative of what they would like to see done than how they would behave in an actual market. On the other hand, if people believe (correctly or incorrectly) that their responses will influence actual fees they may be more concerned about keeping their fees low than revealing their true values to the investigator. Similar thoughts apply if the HV measure is willingness to accept compensation (willingness to sell) rather than willingness to pay.

Furthermore, the hypothetical nature of the transactions may not be at all indicative of how people would behave in an actual market even if gamesmanship is not a major problem. When people buy things in a market, they may go through weeks or months of considering the alternatives. The process will often involve consultations with friends and may also involve professionals such as lawyers or bankers. It may also entail shopping around for the best deal on the product in question. And, for the majority of items in the consumer's budget, there is a whole history of past experience in the market to base the decision on. All this is markedly different than spending an hour or two at most with a mail survey or a personal interviewer attempting to discern how one might behave in a market for a commodity for which one has never actually paid more than a nominal fee.

Numerous other potential problems exist. Like TC, HV measures relate only to the status quo of the good whereas quality may change along the demand curve as the impact of density on recreational quality is felt. All the problems associated with surveys and interviews also may arise including the necessity of obtaining an adequate response rate, interviewer bias, and variations in response depending on the construction of individual questions and the overall survey instrument.

Furthermore, while economists have been more or less cognizant of the potential pitfalls of HV discussed so far, they have not given much attention to a whole literature in social psychology which is also rather discouraging about HV's prospects for success. In a classic study from that field completed in the early 1930s, La Piere wrote to 251 restaurants, cafés, hotels, autocamps, and tourist homes asking the hypothetical question: "Will you accept members of the Chinese race as guests in your establishment?" Of the 128 that replied, 91% said no, 9% said they were uncertain or that it depended on the circumstances, and only one said yes. However, prior to mailing the letter, all 251 of the establishments had been visited by a Chinese guest and at only one was service refused. La Piere's study was followed by a host of others examining the relationships between attitudes and behavior. In a review published in 1976 of 150 such studies, Schuman and Johnson (p.168) concluded that the correlations between attitudes and actual behavior are usually so low that they will not " . . . support the *substitution* of meåsured attitude for behavior . . . ". In other words, it may not be safe to assume, as economists applying HV techniques do, that what people say is what they would actually do.

As a matter of fact, there is some evidence that people do not even report their past behavior very well. For example, out of 131 people surveyed in one study who had been hospitalized during the preceding twelve months, 42% did not report it when interviewed (Cannell, Fisher, and Bakker). Parry and Crossley found that people over-report contributions to the Community Chest by 40% and voter registration by 25%. If people sometimes fail to report accurately what they have done in the recent past, it is a big step to assume, as we do in HV, that they can adequately predict and report how they would behave if a market for an extramarket commodity were created.

Our intention is not to argue that all answers to hypothetical questions will be inaccurate. Success in predicting many election results would be a counter example. Still, research on both attitude–behavior relationships and recall raise very serious questions about the validity of HV results.

But how serious are the biases?
While all these potential sources of bias in both TC and HV exist, by themselves they are not conclusive. Perhaps their impact is negligible or in total they counterbalance each other. What is needed is empirical research to assess the extent of the biases in practice.

Previously published empirical results are for the most part encouraging. Studies by Bohm, Scherr and Babb, and Smith tend to indicate that fears among economists relating to gamesmanship are exaggerated. Furthermore, Bohm's results indicate that HV measures of willingness to pay may not be far from the mark. In the next section we will report the results of our own experiment, results which are not nearly so encouraging.

RESULTS OF THE EXPERIMENT

Space constraints will not permit a thorough description of the experiment and how the results were arrived at. Only a summary will be presented here and the reader interested in a more thorough treatment is referred to an additional paper by Bishop and Heberlein.

The extramarket commodity that served as the subject of our study was 1978 early season goose hunting permits for the Horicon Zone of East Central Wisconsin. Nearly 14,000 such permits were issued and each entitled a hunter to take at most one goose from a well-defined area during the period 1 October through 15 October 1978. The hunters who were issued these permits fell into two groups. One group had applied for the early season as its first choice and automatically received a permit. The other hunters were allocated to the early season as their second choice, having lost in a lottery for middle season permits or applied for a middle season permit after the deadline.

Three entirely separate samples of goose hunters were drawn at random. The first consisted of 237 hunters who received actual cash offers for their permits. The offers were conveyed by mail along with checks ranging between $1 and $200 with instructions that each hunter should return either the check or his or her early season permit. A second sample (containing 353 hunters) received mail questionnaires specifically designed to develop HV measures of the value of its permits. A third (300 hunters) received questionnaires designed to estimate a travel cost demand curve for early season hunting.

The experiment itself was completed with response rates to all three surveys (recipients of the actual cash offers were surveyed after the early season) in the acceptable range of at least 80%. Comparison of the three samples using a one-tailed difference of proportions test on socioeconomic characteristics, commitment to hunting, past goose hunting experience and the like showed no intersample differences sufficient to interfere with comparison of the results across the samples.

Analysis of the results is still in progress, but our preliminary estimates are summarized in Table 17.1. While our final results may vary somewhat in terms of absolute magnitudes, the data are sufficiently clear to justify confidence in our qualitative conclusions.

Responses to our actual cash offers yielded total consumer surplus associated with 1978 early season goose hunting permits of $800,000 for all hunters combined or $63 per permit. This estimate is a bit conservative since it assumes a maximum value per permit of $200 while both the econometric model and the data indicate that 10 to 12% of the hunters would not have sold at $200.

The actual willingness to sell figure is most easily compared with the HV measure of willingness to sell which turns out to be 60% larger at $101 per permit. This estimate is also based on a maximum value of $200 per permit. In this case, the model predicted that 35% of the hunters would require offers of more than $200 before they would agree to sell their permits in hypothetical transactions. Thus, had the models been truncated at a higher figure the difference between willingness to sell measured using actual money and measured using hypothetical dollars would have been even more pronounced.

223

Table 17.1 Summary of results.

	Total consumer surplus	Surplus per permit
	$	
Actual cash offers	880,000	63
Hypothetical offers		
Willingness to sell	1,411,000	101
Willingness to pay	293,000	21
Travel cost estimates		
Model 1 (time value = 0)	159,000	11
Model 2 (time value = ¼ median income rate)	387,000	28
Model 3 (time value = ½ median income rate)	636,000	45

Comparisons of actual willingness to sell with hypothetical willingness to pay and the travel cost values are clouded by the well-known theoretical arguments relating to various measures of consumer surplus. However, following Willig, we would argue that for the range of values we are discussing here ($1–$200) and given any reasonable value for the income elasticity of demand for goose hunting permits, willingness to pay, and willingness to accept compensation should be quite close together. If so, then we could take $63 as being roughly the average willingness to pay of goose hunters for early season permits.

Referring again to Table 17.1, it turns out that our HV measure of willingness to pay falls far short of $63 at only $21 per permit. The table also gives three TC values of willingness to pay based on three different assumptions about the value of time. Even using what the literature would indicate is a relatively liberal time value of one-half the income rate, the travel cost estimate averages only $45, 29% below the benchmark figure of $63.

CONCLUSIONS

We must be careful at this point to avoid sweeping conclusions based on a single experiment. Our results may not be able to be generalized to other situations. Furthermore, although the market we created for goose permits used real money, it was still highly artificial and may include biases of its own. Still, the results summarized here must be interpreted as supporting the hypothesis that the sources of bias listed above do have significant impacts on HV and TC values for recreation and other extramarket goods. Had we attempted to value goose hunting permits using an HV measure of willingness to sell, a substantial overestimate would have been obtained. If we had used HV willingness to pay or a TC measure of demand we would have apparently fallen substantially short of the true value of willingness to pay.

While a full set of conclusions from our study must come after additional analysis, some tentative conclusions are evolving for future recreation economic studies. First, there has been a tendency to view HV willingness to pay as more or less accurate and HV willingness to sell as badly distorted. Our results suggest that both measures are biased, but in opposite directions. It appears that HV willingness to pay should be considered a lower bound and HV willingness to sell, an upper bound. Secondly, our results support those who have voiced concerns about adequately accounting for time costs in TC studies. Differences in tastes and the availability of substitutes may also be a significant source of bias here.

Finally, and on a more general level, we would suggest that recreation economics has a long way to go before it can claim accuracy comparable to analyses of market phenomena. Much more research is needed to further develop and refine both TC and HV measures. To the extent possible, this should involve experiments like the one reported here. Furthermore, we hope that our results will encourage the discovery of new, improved approaches to valuing extramarket goods of all kinds. Such research is essential if economists are to help society recognize the contribution of extramarket goods to the overall level of economic well-being and facilitate sound assessments of the trade-offs between market and extramarket goods and services.

REFERENCES

Bishop, R.C., and T.A. Heberlein. "Travel cost and Hypothetical Valuation of Outdoor Recreation: Comparisons with an Artificial Market." Mimeographed. Madison: University of Wisconsin, 1979.

Bohm, P. "Estimating the Demand for Public Goods: An Experiment." *Europ. Econ. Rev.* 3(1972):111–30.

Cannell, C.F., G. Fisher, and T. Bakker. "Comparison of Hospitalization Reporting in Three Survey Procedures." *Vital and Health Statistics.* Washington D.C.: U.S. Dep. of Health, Education, and Welfare, Public Health Service Ser. 2. no. 8, 1961.

Cesario, F.J. "Value of Time in Recreation Studies." *Land Econ.* 52(1976):32–41.

La Piere, R.T. "Attitudes vs Actions." *Social Forces* 13(1934):230–37.

Parry, Hugh J., and Helen M. Crossley. "Validity of Responses to Survey Questions." *Public Opinion Quart.* 14(1950):61–80.

Schuman, H., and M.P. Johnson. "Attitudes and Behavior." *Ann. Rev. Social.* 2(1976):161–207.

Scherr, B.A., and E.M. Babb. "Pricing Public Goods. An Experiment with Two Proposed pricing Systems." *Public Choice* 23(1975):35–53.

Smith, V.L. "The Principle of Unanimity and Voluntary Consent in Social Choice." *J. Polit. Econ.* (1977): 1125–29.

Willig, R.D. "Consumer's Surplus without Apology." *Amer. Econ. Rev.* 66(1976):589–97.

PART 3

*Instruments for environmental control
and applications*

Chapter 18

The use of standards and prices for protection of the environment

William J. Baumol and Wallace E. Oates

In the technicalities of the theoretical discussion of the tax–subsidy approach to the regulation of externalities, one of the issues most critical for this application tends to get the short end of the discussion. Virtually every author points out that we do not know how to calculate the ideal Pigouvian tax or subsidy levels in practice, but because the point is rather obvious rarely is much made of it.

This paper reviews the nature of the difficulties and then proposes a substitute approach to the externalities problem. This alternative, which we shall call the environmental pricing and standards procedure, represents what we consider to be as close an approximation as one can generally achieve in practice to the spirit of the Pigouvian tradition. Moreover, while this method does not aspire to anything like an optimal allocation of resources, it will be shown to possess some important optimality properties.

DIFFICULTIES IN DETERMINING THE OPTIMAL STRUCTURE OF TAXES AND SUBSIDIES

The proper level of the Pigouvian tax (subsidy) upon the activities of the generator of an externality is equal to the marginal net damage (benefit) produced by that activity.[1] The difficulty is that it is usually not easy to obtain a reasonable estimate of the money value of this marginal damage. Kneese & Bower report some extremely promising work constituting a first step toward the estimation of the damage caused by pollution of waterways including even some quantitative evaluation of the loss in recreational benefits. However, it is hard to be sanguine about the availability in the foreseeable future of a comprehensive body of statistics reporting the marginal net damage of the various externality-generating activities in the economy. The number of activities involved and the number of persons affected by them are so great that on this score alone the task assumes Herculean proportions. Add to this the intangible nature of many of the most important consequences – the damage to health, the aesthetic costs – and the difficulty of determining a money equivalent for marginal net damage becomes even more apparent.

This, however, is not the end of the story. The optimal tax level on an externality generating activity is not equal to the marginal net damage it generates *initially*, but rather to the damage it would cause if the level of the activity had been adjusted to its *optimal* level. To make the point more specifically, suppose that each additional unit of output of a factory now causes 50 cents worth of damage, but that after the installation of the appropriate smoke-control devices

229

and other optimal adjustments, the marginal social damage would be reduced to 20 cents. Then a little thought will confirm what the appropriate mathematics show: the correct value of the Pigouvian tax is 20 cents per unit of output, that is, the marginal cost of the smoke damage *corresponding to an optimal situation*. A tax of 50 cents per unit of output corresponding to the current smoke damage cost would lead to an excessive reduction in the smoke-producing activity, a reduction beyond the range over which the marginal benefit of decreasing smoke emission exceeds its marginal cost.

The relevance of this point for our present discussion is that it compounds enormously the difficulty of determining the optimal tax and benefit levels. If there is little hope of estimating the damage that is currently generated, how much less likely it is that we can evaluate the damage that would occur in an optimal world which we have never experienced or even described in quantitative terms.

There is an alternative possibility. Instead of trying to go directly to the optimal tax policy, one could instead, as a first approximation, base a set of taxes and subsidies on the current net damage (benefit) levels. Then as outputs and damage levels were modified in response to the present level of taxes, the taxes themselves would in turn be readjusted to correspond to the new damage levels. It can be hoped that this will constitute a convergent, iterative process with tax levels affecting outputs and damages, these in turn leading to modifications in taxes, and so on. It is not clear, however, even in theory, whether this sequence will in fact converge toward the optimal taxes and resource allocation patterns. An extension of the argument underlying some of Coase's illustrations can be used to show that convergence cannot always be expected. But even if the iterative process were stable and were in principle capable of yielding an optimal result, its practicality is clearly limited. The notion that tax and subsidy rates can be readjusted quickly and easily on the basis of a fairly esoteric marginal net damage calculation does not seem very plausible. The difficulty of these calculations has already been suggested, and it is not easy to look forward with equanimity to their periodic revision, as an iterative process would require.

In sum, the basic trouble with the Pigouvian cure for the externalities problem does not lie primarily in the technicalities that have been raised against it in the theoretical literature but in the fact that we do not know how to determine the dosages that it calls for. Though there may be some special cases in which one will be able to form reasonable estimates of the social damages, in general we simply do not know how to set the required levels of taxes and subsidies.

THE ENVIRONMENTAL PRICING AND STANDARDS APPROACH

The economist's predilection for the use of the price mechanism makes him reluctant to give up the Pigouvian solution without a struggle. The inefficiencies of a system of direct controls, including the high real enforcement costs that generally accompany it, have been discussed often enough; they require no repetition here.

There is a fairly obvious way, however, in which one can avoid recourse to direct controls and retain the use of the price system as a means to control externalities. Simply speaking, it involves the selection of a set of somewhat arbitrary standards for an acceptable environment. On the basis of evidence concerning the effects of unclean air on health or of polluted water on fish life, one may, for example, decide that the sulfur-dioxide content of the atmosphere in the city should not exceed x percent, or that the oxygen demand of the foreign matter contained in a waterway should not exceed level y, or that the decibel (noise) level in residential neighborhoods should not exceed z at least 99% of the time. These acceptability standards, x, y and z, then amount to a set of constraints that society places on its activities. They represent the decision-maker's subjective evaluation of the minimum standards that must be met in order to achieve what may be described in persuasive terms as "a reasonable quality of life". The defects of the concept will immediately be clear to the reader, and, since we do not want to minimize them, we shall examine this problem explicitly in a later section of the paper.

For the moment, however, we want to emphasize the role of the price system in the implementation of these standards. The point here is simply that the public authority can levy a uniform set of taxes which would in effect constitute a set of prices for the private use of social resources such as air and water. The taxes (or prices) would be selected so as to achieve specific acceptability standards rather than attempting to base them on the unknown value of marginal net damages. Thus, one might tax all installations emitting wastes into a river at a rate of $t(b)$ cents per gallon, where the tax rate, t, paid by a particular polluter, would, for example, depend on b, the BOD value of the effluent, according to some fixed schedule.[2] Each polluter would then be given a financial incentive to reduce the amount of effluent he discharges and to improve the quality of the discharge (i.e., reduce its BOD value). By setting the tax rates sufficiently high, the community would presumably be able to achieve whatever level of purification of the river it desired. It might even be able to eliminate at least some types of industrial pollution altogether.[3]

Here, if necessary, the information needed for iterative adjustments in tax rates would be easy to obtain: if the initial taxes did not reduce the pollution of the river sufficiently to satisfy the preset acceptability standards, one would simply raise the tax rates. Experience would soon permit the authorities to estimate the tax levels appropriate for the achievement of a target reduction in pollution.

One might even be able to extend such adjustments beyond the setting of the tax rates to the determination of the acceptability standards themselves. If, for example, attainment of the initial targets were to prove unexpectedly inexpensive, the community might well wish to consider making the standards stricter.[4] Of course, such an iterative process is not costless. It means that at least some of the polluting firms and municipalities will have to adapt their operations as tax rates are readjusted. At the very least they should be warned in advance of the likelihood of such changes so that they can build flexibility into their plant design, something which is not costless (see Hart). But, at any rate, it is clear that, through the adjustment of tax rates, the public authority can realize whatever standards of environmental quality it has selected.

OPTIMALITY PROPERTIES OF THE PRICING AND STANDARDS TECHNIQUE

While the pricing and standards procedure will not, in general, lead to Pareto-efficient levels of the relevant activities, it is nevertheless true that the use of unit taxes (or subsidies) to achieve the specified quality standards does possess one important optimality property: it is the least-cost method to realize these targets.[5] A simple example may serve to clarify this point. Suppose that it is decided in some metropolitan area that the sulfur-dioxide content of the atmosphere should be reduced by 50%. An obvious approach to this matter, and the one that often recommends itself to the regulator, is to require each smoke-producer in the area to reduce his emissions of sulfur dioxide by the same 50%. However, a moment's thought suggests that this may constitute a very expensive way to achieve the desired result. If, at existing levels of output, the marginal cost of reducing sulfur-dioxide emissions for Factory A is only one-tenth of the marginal cost for Factory B, we would expect that it would be much cheaper for the economy as a whole to assign A a much greater decrease in smoke emissions than B. Just how the least-cost set of relative quotas could be arrived at in practice by the regulator is not clear, since this obviously would require calculations involving simultaneous relationships and extensive information on each polluter's marginal-cost function.

It is easy to see, however, that the unit-tax approach can *automatically* produce the least-cost assignment of smoke-reduction quotas without the need for any complicated calculations by the enforcement authority. In terms of our preceding example, suppose that the public authority placed a unit tax on smoke emissions and raised the level of the tax until sulfur-dioxide emissions were in fact reduced by 50%. In response to a tax on its smoke emissions, a cost-minimizing firm will cut back on such emissions until the marginal cost of further reductions in smoke output is equal to the tax. But, since all economic units in the area are subject to the same tax, it follows that the marginal cost of reducing smoke output will be equalized across all activities. This implies that it is impossible to reduce the aggregate cost of the specified decrease in smoke emissions by rearranging smoke-reduction quotas: any alteration in this pattern of smoke emissions would involve an increase in smoke output by one firm the value of which to the firm would be less than the cost of the corresponding reduction in smoke emissions by some other firm. For the interested reader, a formal proof of this least-cost property of unit taxes for the realization of a specified target level of environmental quality is provided in an appendix to this paper. We might point out that the validity of this least-cost theorem does not require the assumption that firms are profit-maximizers. All that is necessary is that they minimize costs for whatever output levels they should select, as would be done, for example, by a firm that seeks to maximize its growth or its sales.

The cost saving that can be achieved through the use of taxes and subsidies in the attainment of acceptability standards may by no means be negligible. In one case for which comparable cost figures have been calculated, Kneese & Bower (p. 162) report that, with a system of uniform unit taxes, the cost of achieving a specified level of water quality would have been only about half as high as that resulting from a system of direct controls. If these figures are at all representative, then the potential waste of resources in the choice between tax measures and direct controls may obviously be of a large order. Unit taxes thus appear to represent a very attractive method for the realization of specified standards of environmental quality. Not only do they require relatively little in the way of detailed information on the cost structures of different industries, but they lead automatically to the least-cost pattern of modification of externality-generating activities.

WHERE THE PRICING AND STANDARDS APPROACH IS APPROPRIATE

As we have emphasized, the most disturbing aspect of the pricing and standards procedure is the somewhat arbitrary character of the criteria selected. There does presumably exist some optimal level of pollution (i.e., quality of the air or a waterway), but in the absence of a pricing mechanism to indicate the value of the damages generated by polluting activities, one knows no way to determine accurately the set of taxes necessary to induce the optimal activity levels.

While this difficulty certainly should not be minimized, it is important at the outset to recognize that the problem is by no means unique to the selection of acceptability standards. In fact, as is well known, it is a difficulty common to the provision of nearly all public goods. In general, the market will not generate appropriate levels of outputs where market prices fail to reflect the social damages (or benefits) associated with particular activities. As a result, in the absence of the proper set of signals from the market, it is typically necessary to utilize a political process (i.e., a method of collective choice) to determine the level of the activity.[6] From this perspective, the selection of environmental standards can be viewed as a particular device utilized in a process of collective decision-making to determine the appropriate level of an activity involving external effects.

Since methods of collective choice, such as simple-majority rule or decisions by an elected representative, can at best be expected to provide only very rough approximations to optimal results, the general problem becomes one of deciding whether or not the malfunction of the market in a certain case is sufficiently serious to warrant public intervention. In particular, it would seem to us that such a blunt instrument as acceptability standards should be used only sparingly, because the very ignorance that serves as the rationale for the adoption of such standards implies that we can hardly be sure of their consequences.

In general, it would seem that intervention in the form of acceptability standards can be utilized with any degree of confidence only where there is clear reason to believe that the existing situation imposes a high level of social costs *and* that these costs can be significantly reduced by feasible decreases in the levels of certain externality-generating activities. If, for example, we were to examine the functional relationship between the level of social welfare and the levels of particular activities which impose marginal net damages, the argument would be that the use of acceptability standards is justified only in those cases where the curve, over the bulk of the relevant range, is both decreasing and steep. Such a case is illustrated in Figure 18.1 by the curve PQR. In a case of this kind, although we obviously will not have an accurate knowledge of the relevant position of the curve, we can at least have some assurance that the selection of an acceptability standard and the imposition of a unit tax sufficient to realize that standard will lead to an increase in social welfare. For example, in terms of the curve PQR in Figure 18.1, the levying of a tax sufficient to reduce smoke outputs from level OC to OA to ensure that the quality of the air meets the specified environmental standards would obviously increase social welfare.[7]

On the other hand, if the relationship between social welfare and the level of the externality-generating activity is not monotonically decreasing, the changes resulting from the imposition of an acceptability standard (e.g., a move from S to Q in Figure 18.1) clearly may lead to a reduction in welfare. Moreover, even if the function were monotonic but fairly flat, the benefits achieved might not be worth the cost of additional intervention machinery that new legislation requires, and it would almost certainly not be worth the risk of acting with highly imperfect, inconclusive information.

In some cases, notably in the field of public utility regulation, some economists

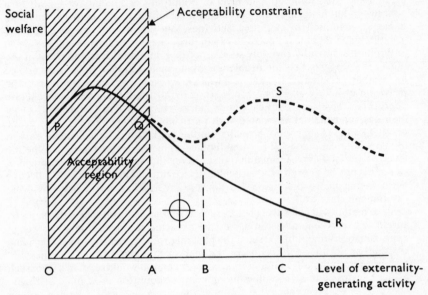

Figure 18.1

have criticized the employment of acceptability standards on both these grounds; they have asserted that the social costs of monopolistic misallocation of resources are probably not very high (i.e., the relevant portion of the social-welfare curve in Figure 18.1 is not steep) and that the regulation can itself introduce inefficiencies in the operations of the regulated industries.

Advocacy of environmental pricing and standards procedures for the control of externalities must therefore rest on the belief that in this area we do have a clear notion of the general shape of the social-welfare curve. This will presumably hold true where the evidence indicates, first that a particular externality really does have a substantial and unambiguous effect on the quality of life, if, for example, it makes existence very unpleasant for everyone or constitutes a serious hazard to health; and second that reductions in the levels of these activities do not themselves entail huge resource costs. On the first point, there is growing evidence that various types of pollutants do in fact have such unfortunate consequences, particularly in areas where they are highly concentrated. (On this see, for instance, Lave & Seskin). Second, what experience we have had with, for example, the reduction of waste discharges into waterways suggests that processes involving the recycling and reuse of waste materials can frequently be achieved at surprisingly modest cost.[8] In such cases the rationale for the imposition of environmental standards is clear, and it seems to us that the rejection of such crude measures on the grounds that they will probably violate the requirements of optimality may well be considered a kind of perverse perfectionism.

It is interesting in this connection that the pricing and standards approach is not too different in spirit from a number of economic policy measures that are already in operation in other areas. This is significant for our discussion, because it suggests that regulators know how to work with this sort of approach and have managed to live with it elsewhere. Probably the most noteworthy example is the use of fiscal and monetary policy for the realization of macro-economic objectives. Here,the regulation of the stock of money and the availability of credit along with the adjustments in public expenditure and tax rates are often aimed at the achievement of a selected target level of employment or rate of inflation. Wherever prices rise too rapidly or unemployment exceeds an "acceptable" level, monetary and fiscal variables are readjusted in an attempt to "correct" the difficulty. It is noteworthy that this procedure is also similar to the pricing and standards approach in its avoidance of direct controls.

Other examples of this general approach to policy are not hard to find. Policies for the regulation of public-utilities, for instance, typically utilize a variety of standards such as profit-rate ceilings (i.e., "fair rates of return") to judge the acceptability of the behavior of the regulated firm. In the area of public education, one frequently encounters state-imposed standards (e.g., subjects to be taught) for local school districts which are often accompanied by grants of funds to the localities to help insure that public-school programs meet the designated standards. What this suggests is that public administrators are familiar with this general approach to policy and that the implementation of the pricing and standards technique should not involve insurmountable administrative difficulties. For these reasons, the achievement of specified environmental standards through the use of unit taxes (or subsidies) seems to us to possess great promise as a workable method for the control of the quality of the environment.

CONCLUDING REMARKS

It may be useful in concluding our discussion simply to review the ways in which the pricing and standards approach differs from the standard Pigouvian-prescription for the control of externalities.

(1) Under the Pigouvian technique, unit taxes (or subsidies) are placed on externality-generating activities, with the level of the tax on a particular activity being set equal to the marginal net damage it generates. Such taxes (if they could be determined) would, it is presumed, lead to Pareto-efficient levels of the activities.

(2) In contrast, the pricing and standard approach begins with a predetermined set of standards for environmental quality and then imposes unit taxes (or subsidies) sufficient to achieve these standards. This will not, in general, result in an optimal allocation of resources, but (as is proved formally in the appendix) the procedure does at least represent the least-cost method of realizing the specified standards.

(3) The basic appeal of the pricing and standards approach relative to the Pigouvian prescription lies in its workability. We simply do not, in general, have the information needed to determine the appropriate set of Pigouvian taxes and subsidies. Such information is not, however, necessary for our suggested procedure.

(4) While it makes not pretense of promising anything like an optimal allocation of resources, the pricing and standards technique can, in cases where external effects impose high costs (or benefits), at least offer some assurance of reducing the level of these damages. Moreover, the administrative procedures – the selection of standards and the use of fiscal incentives to realize these standards

– implied by this approach are in many ways quite similar to those used in a number of current public programs. This, we think, offers some grounds for optimism as to the practicality of the pricing and standards technique for the control of the quality of the environment.

NOTES

1. We will use the term marginal *net* damage to mean the difference between marginal social and private damage (or cost).
2. BOD, biochemical oxygen demand, is a measure of the organic waste load of an emission. It measures the amount of oxygen used during decomposition of the waste materials. BOD is used widely as an index of the quality of effluents. However, it is only an approximation at best. Discharges whose BOD value is low may nevertheless be considered serious pollutants because they contain inorganic chemical poisons whose oxygen requirement is nil because the poisons do not decompose. See Kneese and Bower on this matter.
3. Here it is appropriate to recall the words of Chief Justice Marshall, when he wrote that, "The power to tax involves the power to destroy" (McCulloch vs. Maryland, 1819). In terms of reversing the process of environmental decay, we can see, however, that the power to tax can also be the power to restore.
4. In this way the pricing and standards approach might be adapted to approximate the Pigouvian ideal. If the standards were revised upward whenever there was reason to believe that the marginal benefits exceeded the marginal costs, and if these judgments were reasonably accurate, the two would arrive at the same end product, at least if the optimal solution were unique.
5. This proposition is not new. While we have been unable to find an explicit statement of this result anywhere in the literature, it or a very similar proposition has been suggested in a number of places. See, for example, Kneese & Bower, Chapter 6, and Ruff, p. 79.
6. As Coase and others have argued, voluntary bargains struck among the interested parties may in some instances yield an efficient set of activity levels in the presence of externalities. However, such coordinated, voluntary action is typically possible only in small groups. One can hardly imagine, for example, a voluntary bargaining process involving all the persons in a metropolitan area and resulting in a set of payments that would generate efficient levels of activities affecting the smog content of the atmosphere.
7. The relationship depicted in Figure 18.1 is to be regarded as an intuitive device employed for pedagogical purposes, not in any sense as rigorous analysis. However, some further explanation may be helpful. The curve itself is not a social-welfare function in the usual sense; rather it measures in terms of a numeraire (kronor or dollars) the value, summed over all individuals, of the benefits from the output of the activity minus the private and net social costs. Thus, for each level of the activity, the height of the curve indicates the net benefits (possibly negative) that the activity confers on society. The acceptability constraint indicates that level of the activity which is consistent with the specified minimum standard of environmental quality (e.g., that level of smoke emissions from factories which is sufficiently low to maintain the quality of the air in a particular metropolitan area). There is an ambiguity here in that the levels of several different activities may jointly determine a particular dimension of environmental quality, e.g., the smoke emissions of a number of different industries will determine the quality of the air. In this case, the acceptable level of pollutive emissions for the firm or industry will clearly depend on the levels of emissions of others. If, as we discussed earlier, unit taxes are used to realize the acceptability standards, there will result a least-cost pattern of levels of the relevant externality-generating activities. If we understand the constraint in Figure 18.1 to refer to the activity level indicated by this particular solution, then this ambiguity disappears.
8. Some interesting discussions of the feasibility of the control of waste emissions into waterways often at low cost are contained in Kneese & Bower. In particular, see their description of the control of water quality in the Ruhr River in Germany.

REFERENCES

1. Bohm, P.: Pollution, Purification, and the Theory of External Effects. *Swedish Journal of Economics 72*, no. 2, 153–66, 1970.
2. Coase, R.: The Problem of Social Cost. *Journal of Law and Economics 3*, 1–44, 1960.
3. Hart, A.: Anticipations, Business Planning, and the Cycle. *Quarterly Journal of Economics 51*, 273–97, Feb. 1937.
4. Kneese, A. & Bower, B.: *Managing Water Quality: Economics, Technology, Institutions*. Baltimore, 1968.
5. Lave, L. & Seskin, E.: Air Pollution and Human Health. *Science 21*, 723–33 Aug. 1970.
6. Portes, R.: The Search for Efficiency in the Presence of Externalities. *Unfashionable Economics: Essays in Honor of Lord Balogh* (ed. P. Streeten), pp. 348–61. London, 1970.
7. Ruff. L.: The Economic Common Sense of Pollution. *The Public Interest*, Spring 1970, 69–85.

APPENDIX

In the text, we argued on a somewhat intuitive level that the appropriate use of unit taxes and subsidies represents the least-cost method of achieving a set of specified standards for environmental quality. In the case of smoke-abatement, for instance, the tax–subsidy approach will automatically generate the cost-minimizing assignment of "reduction quotas" without recourse to involved calculations or enforcement.

The purpose of this appendix is to provide a formal proof of this proposition. More precisely, we will show that, to achieve any given vector of final outputs along with the attainment of the specified quality of the environment, the use of unit taxes (or, where appropriate, subsidies) to induce the necessary modification in the market-determined pattern of output will permit the realization of the specified output vector at minimum cost to society.

While this theorem may seem rather obvious (as the intuitive discussion in the text suggests), its proof does point up several interesting properties which are noteworthy. In particular, unlike many of the propositions about prices in welfare analysis, the theorem does not require a world of perfect competition. It applies to pure competitors, monopolists, or oligopolists alike so long as each of the firms involved seeks to minimize the private cost of producing whatever vector of outputs it selects and has no monopsony power (i.e., no influence on the prices of inputs). The firms need not be simple profit-maximizers; they may choose to maximize growth, sales (total revenues), their share of the market, or any combination of these goals (or a variety of other objectives). Since the effective pursuit of these goals typically entails minimizing the cost of whatever outputs are produced, the theorem is still applicable. Finally, we want simply to emphasize that the theorem applies to whatever set of final outputs society should select (either by direction or through the operation of the market). It does not judge the desirability of that particular vector of outputs; it only tells us how to make the necessary adjustments at minimum cost.

We shall proceed initially to derive the first-order conditions for the minimization of the cost of a specified overall reduction in the emission of wastes. We will then show that the independent decisions of cost-minimizing firms subject to the appropriate unit tax on waste emissions will, in fact, satisfy the first-order conditions for overall cost minimization.

Let

x_{iv} represent the quantity of input i used by plant $v(i=1, ..., n), (v=1, ..., m)$,

237

z_v be the quantities of waste it discharges,
y_v be its output level,
$f_v(x_{1v}, ..., x_{nv}, z_v, y_v) = 0$ be its production function,
p_i be the price of input i, and
k the desired level of $\sum z_v$, the maximum permitted daily discharge of waste.

In this formulation, the value of k is determined by the administrative authority in a manner designed to hold waste emissions in the aggregate to a level consistent with the specified environmental standard (e.g., the sulphuric content of the atmosphere). Note that the level of the firm's waste emissions is treated here as an argument in its production function; to reduce waste discharges while maintaining its level of output, the firm will presumably require the use of additional units of some other inputs (e.g., more labor or capital to recycle the wastes or to dispose of them in an alternative manner).

The problem now becomes that of determining the value of the x's and z's that minimize input cost

$$c = \sum_i \sum_v p_i(x_{iv})$$

subject to the output constraints

$$y_v = y_v^* = \text{constant} \qquad (v = 1, ..., m)$$

and the constraint on the total output of pollutants

$$\sum_v z_v = k.$$

It may appear odd to include as a constraint a vector of given outputs of the firms, since the firms will presumably adjust output levels as well as the pattern of inputs in response to taxes or other restrictions on waste discharges. This vector, however, can be any vector of outputs (including that which emerges as a result of independent decisions by the firms). What we determine are first-order conditions for cost-minimization which apply to any given vector of outputs no matter how they are arrived at. Using $\lambda_v(v=1, ..., m)$ and λ as our $(m+1)$ Lagrange multipliers, we obtain the first-order conditions:

$$
\begin{aligned}
\lambda_v f_{vz} + \lambda = 0 & \qquad (v = 1, ..., m) \\
p_i + \lambda_v f_{vi} = 0 & \qquad (v = 1, ..., m) \ (i = 1, ..., n) \\
y_v = y_v^* & \qquad (v = 1, ..., m)
\end{aligned}
\qquad (1)
$$

where we use the notation $f_{vz} = \partial f_v / \partial z_v$, $f_{vi} = \partial f_v / \partial x_{iv}$.

Now let us see what will happen if the m plants are run by independent managements whose objective is to minimize the cost of whatever outputs their firm produces, and if, instead of the imposition of a fixed ceiling on the emission of pollutants, this emission is taxed at a fixed rate per unit, t. So long as its input prices are fixed, firm v will wish to minimize

$$c = tz_v + \sum_i p_i x_{iv}$$

subject to

$$y_v = y_v^*.$$

Direct differentiation of the m Lagrangian functions for our m firms immediately yields the first-order conditions (1) – the same conditions as before, provided t is set equal to λ. Thus, if we impose a tax rate that achieves the desired reduction in the total emission of pollutants, we have proved that this reduction will satisfy the necessary conditions for the minimization of the program's cost to society.[1]

NOTES
1. In this case, λ (and hence t) is the shadow price of the pollution constraint. In addition to satisfying these necessary first-order conditions, cost-minimization requires that the production functions possess the usual second-order properties. An interesting treatment of this issue is available in Portes. We should also point out that our proof assumes that the firm takes t as given and beyond its control. Bohm discusses some of the problems that can arise where the firm takes into account the effects of its behavior on the value of t.

Chapter 19

Effluent charges and licenses under uncertainty

Marc J. Roberts and Michael Spence

INTRODUCTION

The purpose of this paper is to explore, in the context of a simple model, what kind of policy might be used to control pollution, when the regulatory authority is uncertain what the actual costs of pollution control will be. In posing the problem as we do, we are rejecting the idea that the government can iteratively 'feel out' the 'optimum' by successively announcing and revising its policies in light of the responses of waste sources. Much of the investment that will be made in any pollution control program will take several years to plan and complete and will be largely irreversible once in place. Thus the response to all subsequent policies will be heavily dependent on previous history. Indeed the cycle time may be so great as to prevent convergence, since the 'correct' solution will be constantly changing. Given these circumstances, we have chosen to explore the once-and-for-all problem, where the government seeks to achieve a comparative static maximum in expected utility terms.

The principal point of the paper is that a mixed system, involving effluent charges and restrictions on the total quantity of emissions via marketable licenses, is preferable to either effluent fees or the licenses used separately.[1] This follows because a mixed system permits the implicit penalty function imposed upon the private sector to more closely approximate the expected damage function for pollution at each level of total waste output.

In setting up this model, we are fully conscious of the differences between the formal structures we will use and real situations, and we will call attention to some of them as we proposed. The point of this exercise is not to 'prove' one or another approach 'better.' Rather, by exploring and manipulating some simplified conceptualizations, we hope to develop some insights and formulations which will prove to be useful in formulating policy.

The problem is posed as one of choosing a control scheme so as to minimize expected total social costs, these being the sum of (1) expected damages from pollution and (2) cleanup costs. In order to actually implement any policy, the regulatory authority must quantify its uncertainty about cleanup costs in the form of subjective probabilities. Given these probabilities, the calculation of the optimal parameters for the sort of mixed scheme we will develop is sufficiently straightforward that we believe it could be made even with limited analytical resources.

Effluent charges and marketable licenses have the virtue of inducing the private sector to minimize the costs of cleanup. But in the presence of uncertainty, they differ in the manner in which the ex post achieved results differ from the socially optimal outcome. Effluent charges bring about too little cleanup when cleanup costs turn out to be higher than expected, and they induce excessive cleanup when the costs of cleanup turn out to be low. Licenses have the opposite failing. Since the level of cleanup is predetermined, it will be too high when cleanup costs are high and too low when costs are low.

Given that effluent charges and license outcomes deviate from the optimum in opposite ways, which kind of imperfection is preferable? It turns out, plausibly enough, that the answer depends upon the curvature of the damage function. When the expected damage function is linear, an effluent charge equal to the slope of the damage function always leads to optimal results, regardless of what costs turn out to be, while licenses do not. On the other hand, if *marginal* damages increase sharply with effluents, licenses are relatively more attractive and yield lower expected total costs than the fee system.

Licenses and effluent charges can be used together further to reduce expected total costs. Each can protect against the failings of the other. Licenses can be used to guard against extremely high levels of pollution while, simultaneously, effluent charges can provide a residual incentive to clean up more than the licenses required, should costs be low.

In what follows, the model is described and the mixed effluent fee license scheme set forth and analyzed. In an appendix, we argue that one can come arbitrarily close to minimum expected total costs with the use of multiple licenses supplemented by a carefully constructed schedule of effluent fees.

NOTATION
To simplify the exposition we assume all waste dischargers have the same impact on ambient conditions at the point we monitor. We will not consider multiple monitoring points, or substances, though the analysis could be generalized in that direction.[2] Thus we can use a single variable, x, to indicate both the total pollution discharges and the resulting quality of the environment. Damages from pollution are measured in dollars. Expected total damages are denoted by $D(x)$. There are, of course, significant uncertainties associated with damages. And if risk aversion were assumed, the monetary equivalents of the damages associated with various policies would rise. The analysis to follow, which focuses upon costs and cleanup, could be amended to account for risk aversion. For expositional clarity, we will deal only with expected damages.

The current level of output of the pollutant of firm i is $\bar{x}_i$. The costs of cleanup for firm i are uncertain from the point of view of the regulators. This uncertainty is summarized by a random variable, ϕ. The costs of cleanup for firm i are stated as a function of its output of pollution, x_i, and the random variable ϕ, and are denoted by $c^i(x_i, \phi)$. These costs represent reductions in total profits. Adjustment in cleanup may be accompanied by changes in the levels of outputs and inputs of the firm. Our assumption here is that this reduction in profits accurately reflects the social cost of cleanup, which can be shown to be correct if markets are competitive.[3] By definition, when there is no cleanup, $x_i = \bar{x}_i$ and $c^i(\bar{x}_i, \phi) = 0$.

Total cleanup costs, $c(x, \phi)$, are simply the sum of the individual firm costs. Again we can simply use ϕ to parameterize our uncertainty. However, in what follows, whenever we write, c, we do so only to refer to circumstances where the cleanup is distributed among firms in a cost minimizing manner, so that by definition,

$$c(x, \phi) = \sum_i c^i(x_i, \phi),$$

where $x = \sum_i x_i$, and for all i and j,

$$c_x^i(x_i, \phi) = c_x^j(x_j, \phi).$$

The following assumptions are carried throughout: $D''(x)>0$, so that $D(x)$ is convex, and $c_x<0$, $c_{xx}>0$; marginal cleanup costs increase at an increasing rate. The random variable ϕ represents 'states of the world.' It simply captures all the relevant uncertainty about cleanup costs. It can be thought of as an exhaustive labeling of the possible cleanup cost functions for all polluters. The reader may find it easier to think in terms of a large, but finite, exhaustive list. However, to facilitate the following analysis, we will assume that $c_\phi>0$ and that $c_{x\phi}<0$. This means that as ϕ shifts, both absolute and marginal costs shift in the same directions for all values of x. In particular, members of the family of aggregate costs do not cross.

The regulatory authority's decision problem is to choose a pollution control scheme to minimize expected total costs. Their subjective distribution for ϕ is represented by $f(\phi)$. Expected total costs are

$$T = \int[D(x)+c(x,\phi)]f(\phi)\mathrm{d}\phi = E[D(x)+c(x,\phi)].$$

In general, x will be a function of ϕ. The function will vary with the scheme being used for controlling pollution. It is assumed that firms know or can find out their cleanup cost functions. The uncertainty therefore attaches to the regulatory authority.

CONTROLLING VIA MIXED EFFLUENT CHARGES AND LICENSES

The control mechanism we want to put forward has three components. First there is a finite set of transferable licenses that are issued by the regulatory authority, and are bought and sold in a market. The quantity of licenses is l. The number of licenses held by firm i is denoted by l_i. Second, there is a unit effluent subsidy, denoted by s. It is paid to any firm whose license holdings, l_i, exceed its emissions, x_i. Thus if l_i, the firm receives $s(l_i - x_i)$. Finally, if a firm's emissions exceed its holdings of licenses, so that $x_i>l_i$, then it is assessed a per unit penalty of p, or a total penalty of $p(x_i-l_i)$. The three components then are licences, l, an efficient subsidy, s, and an effluent penalty, p.

We want to demonstrate that this approach has several properties. First, it allocates cleanup among polluting firms efficiently.[4] Second, it is preferable to either a pure effluent fee or a pure license scheme. Expected total costs (cleanup and damages from pollution) are lower. Third, the system operates as if there were just one polluting firm confronted with a piecewise linear penalty function with one kink in it. This is demonstrated below.

The economic rational for this scheme is the following. One wants to limit effluents; this is done by issuing marketable licenses. But if cleanup costs have been significantly overestimated, one wants a residual incentive to clean up. This is provided by the subsidy, s. On the other hand, if cleanup costs turn out to be very high, one wants an escape valve from the restriction imposed by the licenses. This escape valve is provided by having a finite penalty, p, for exceeding levels of effluents permitted by licenses. It is assumed that $p \geqq s$.

Formally, the functioning of the system is represented as follows. Let q be the market price of the licenses. It is determined as part of the equilibrium in the market for licenses. The total costs for firm i consist of (1) cleanup costs, (2) license costs, and (3) penalties or subsidies when applicable. These costs are

$$c^i(x_i,\phi)+ql_i-s(l_i-x_i) \text{ if } x_i \leqq l_i, \tag{1}$$

and

$$c^i(x_i, \phi)+ql_i+p(x_i-l_i) \text{ if } x_i \geqq l_i. \tag{2}$$

The firm minimizes these by selecting x_i and l_i appropriately. In addition, in an equilibrium,

$$\sum_{i=1}^{N} l_i = l.$$

We turn now to the properties of the equilibrium. Suppose first that $q<s$. Then from (1) every firm could reduce costs indefinitely by buying licenses. This is clearly inconsistent with equilibrium in the license market. Thus q cannot be less than s. Now suppose that $q > p$. Then from (2), every firm would set $l_i=0$, and this is inconsistent with equilibrium in the license market. Therefore, q cannot exceed p. The subsidy s and the penalty p place bounds on the equilibrium value of q: $s \leqq q \leqq p$.

The next step is to show that $c_x^i(x_i, \phi)$ is always equal to $-q$. Suppose first that $s = q$. Then the firm will set $l_i \geqq x_i$ (in fact it is indifferent about the level); and then set $c_x^i(x_i,\phi) = -s = -q$. Next suppose $s < q < p$. Then from (1) and (2) firm i will set $x_i = l_i$. Thus its costs are

$$c^i(x_i,\phi)+qx_i.$$

These are minimized when $c_x^i(x_i,\phi)+q = 0$. Finally if $q = p$, the firm will set $l_i \leqq x_i$, and then minimize with respect to x_i by setting $c_x^i(x_i,\phi)+q = 0$. Thus in all possible cases, $c_x^i(x_i,\phi)+q = 0$. This fact has the immediate implication that $c_x^i(x_i,\phi) = c_x^j(x_j,\phi)$ for all i and j, so that cleanup is efficiently distributed among polluters.[5] In addition q is bounded by the effluent subsidy s and the penalty p.

Since marginal cleanup costs are minimized, the condition

$$c_x(x,\phi)+ q = 0 \tag{3}$$

is always satisfied.

The remaining question is what determines the levels of q and x? If $s<q<p$, then $x_i = l_i$ for all i, and hence $x = l$. Condition (3) will be satisfied if

$$s< -c_x(l,\phi) < p. \tag{4}$$

Inequality (4) will hold for some intermediate range of costs of cleanup. If cleanup costs are very high, then q will be driven up to the level of the penalty p. At that point, effluents will exceed licenses: $x > l$. The equilibrium condition is

$$c_x(x,\phi)+ p = 0 \tag{5}$$

243

Finally if costs are low, so that $c_x(l,\phi)+s < 0$, then $x < l$ and $q = s$. The level of effluents actually achieved will be given by

$$c_x(x,\phi)+ S = 0 \qquad (6)$$

In summary: (1) if $c_x(l,\phi)+s>0$, then $c_x(x,\phi)+s=0$ and $q=s$; (2) if $s<-c_x(l,\phi)<p$, then $x = l$ and $q = -c_x(l,\phi)$; and (3) if $c_x(l,\phi)+p<0$, then $c_x(x,\phi)+p=0$ and $q=p$.

The interesting feature of the mixed effluent-license is that it produces levels of the effluents, conditional on costs, that reproduce exactly the effluents that would occur if (1) the polluting firms were merged (and made cleanup decisions centrally) and (2) they faced a piecewise linear penalty function of the form,

$$P(x) = sx+p \, \text{Max} \, (x-l, 0).$$

If the firms collectively were to minimize the sum of penalties and cleanup costs, $P(x)+c(x,\phi)$, they would act as follows: if $s < -c_x(l, \phi) < p$, they would set $x = l$; if $-c_x(l, \phi) < s$, they would set $c_x(x, \phi)+s = 0$; and if $-c_x(l, \phi) > p$, they would set $c_x(x, \phi)+p = 0$. But this is exactly what the decentralized system does.

The pure efficient fee and pure license systems are special cases of the mixed system. The pure effluent fee is obtained by setting $s=p$, at which point the level of l becomes irrelevant. The implicit penalty function is then linear. If $s=0$ and $p= +\infty$, then we have a pure license system. It is not therefore surprising that the more flexible mixed system can achieve lower expected total costs.

The mixed system implicitly approximates the expected damage function by a piecewise linear penalty (see Figure 19.1). The same point can be seen in the context of the marginal damages (see Figure 19.2). The mixed effluent-license system approximates the marginal damage function with a step function.

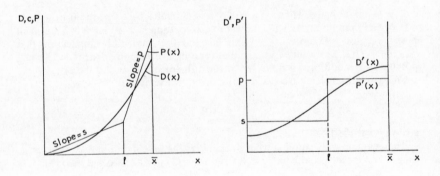

Figure 19.1   Figure 19.2

It is worth noting that the implicit penalty function $P(x)$, does *not* correspond exactly to the payments by firms for licenses, plus or minus penalties and subsidies. The actual payments depend upon the parameter ϕ that determines costs, and not just upon x, the final level of effluents. But if we plot ex post payments as a function of effluents, the result is as in Figure 19.3.

Effluent charges

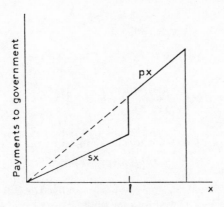

Figure 19.3

THE REGULATORY AUTHORITY'S OPTIMIZING PROBLEM

The decision variables for the regulators are s, p, and l. The objective is to minimize total costs, consisting of damages from pollution and cleanup costs. For given levels of s, p, and l, there will be two critical levels of the cost determining parameter ϕ. The first, ϕ_1, is the level of cost such that

$$c_x(l, \phi_1) = s = 0. \tag{7}$$

Here the marginal cleanup costs are just equal to the effluent subsidy when $x = l$. The second value, $\phi_2 > \phi_1$, is defined by

$$c_x(l, \phi_1) + p = 0. \tag{8}$$

Here costs are almost high enough to cause the system to have effluents exceed licenses.

Let $[0, b]$ be the support of the distribution $f(\phi)$. We define $x_1(\phi, s)$ and $x_2(\phi, p)$ by

$$c_x(x_1(\phi, s), \phi) + s = 0,$$

and

$$c_x(x_1(\phi, s), \phi) + p = 0.$$

Expected total costs are

$$T(s, p, l) = \int_0^{\phi_1} [D(x_1, (\phi, s)) + c(x_1(\phi, s), \phi)] f(\phi) \, d\phi$$
$$+ \int_{\phi_1}^{\phi_2} [D(l) + c(l, \phi)] f(\phi) \, d\phi$$
$$+ \int_{\phi_2}^{b} [D(x_2(\phi, p) + c(x_2(\phi, p), \phi] f(\phi) \, d\phi.$$

These expected total costs are minimized when the partial derivatives, T_s, T_p and T_l, are zero, or when the following conditional expectations hold:

245

$$E\left(\frac{D'(x_1)-s}{c_{xx}(x_1, \phi)} \,\middle|\, \phi \leq \phi_1 \right) = 0, \tag{9}$$

$$E(D'(l)+c_x(l, \phi)|\phi_1 \leq \phi \leq \phi_2) = 0, \tag{10}$$

$$E\left(\frac{D'(x_2)-p}{c_{xx}(x_2, \phi)} \,\middle|\, \phi \geq \phi_2 \right) = 0. \tag{11}$$

With perfect information about costs, the authority would set

$$D'(x)+c_x(x, \phi) = 0, \tag{12}$$

for all ϕ. Let the optimal schedule of effluents, defined by (12), be $x^*(\phi)$. Let $\hat{x}(\phi)$ be the effluent levels achieved with the optimal mixed system described above. The relationship between $x^*(\phi)$ and $\hat{x}(\phi)$ is depicted in Figure 19.4. The schedule $\hat{x}(\phi)$ crosses $x^*(\phi)$ three times, once in each interval.

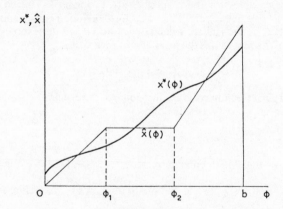

Figure 19.4

The optimizing conditions, (9) through (11), are simply conditions for optimal pure effluent fees or licenses on each of the three intervals. For example, equation (9) is the condition for s to be the optimal pure effluent fee assuming costs vary only on the interval $[0, \phi_1]$. A pure effluent fee schedule crosses the optimal schedule once. Hence, the mixed schedule crosses $x^*(\phi)$ once in each of three intervals. Notice that pure effluent fees induce excessive cleanup when costs are low and too little cleanup when costs are high. This occurs because at low levels of pollution the effluent fee exceeds marginal damages, and conversely. The pure license scheme has the opposite property. It is insensitive to variations in cleanup costs.

The superiority of the mixed scheme is simply a result of its ability to better approximate the optimal relationship between pollution levels and damages. The exception occurs when the damage function is linear. In that case, $\phi_1 = 0$, $\phi_2 = b$ and $p = s$. The pure effluent fee system is optimal.

246

EXPECTED GAINS FROM USING A MIXED SYSTEM
It is not possible in a short paper to comment extensively on the quantitative benefits of the mixed scheme. However, one can isolate the circumstances under which it is likely to yield significant gains. There are two conditions which make the mixed scheme attractive. First, the marginal damages must vary considerably with total effluents. Otherwise the pure effluent fee performs quite well. Second, there must be significant uncertainty about the cleanup costs. Otherwise, the pure license scheme performs well. It is perhaps worth noting that when marginal cleanup costs do not vary greatly with quantity, an effluent fee system performs poorly even with small amounts of uncertainty. The reason is that actual levels of cleanup may vary wildly with small shifts in the cost function.

The following numerical example illustrates the potential benefits of the mixed system. It assumes there is a threshold level of pollution, l, below which marginal damages are one, and above which they are six. Costs are assumed to have the form $(\phi/2)(\bar{x} - x)^2$, where ϕ takes on the values 0.12 and 2.0 with probabilities of one half. A mixed system yields the optimum for this kind of damage function. Table 19.1 summarizes the results for the various control schemes.

Table 19.1

Control scheme	Expected total costs	Percentage above the optimum
Optimum (also mixed system)	12.416	0
Pure effluent fee	20.6	66
Pure licenses	18.25	46

CONCLUSIONS
When the regulatory authority is uncertain about pollution control costs, the usefulness of monetary incentives to decentralize pollution control decisions is limited by our inability to pick the correct price. That price should be equal to marginal damages and thus depends upon the level of pollution. But it is not known exactly what pollution will be as a function of price because control costs are known only imperfectly. With a nonlinear damage function, and uncertain irreversible costs, we would like to find some way of confronting each firm with incentives to clean up that in fact depend upon marginal damages, and hence on total waste output. The combination of the license scheme with subsidies and penalties permits one simultaneously to ensure that all firms face the same marginal costs, but to have that cost vary (within limits) depending on what the aggregate costs of cleanup actually turn out to be. The level of pollution also varies with the aggregate cleanup costs.

The authority has three parameters to manipulate: the subsidy, the penalty and the stock of licenses. The authority knows that pollution will equal the stock of licenses provided the market price turns out to be between the subsidy and the penalty. The subsidy provides a residual incentive for firms to clean up even more when costs are low. The finite penalty provides an escape valve in case costs are very high. The aggregate damage function is approximated by a piecewise penalty function. But once the equilibrium in license prices is established, each firm effectively faces a linear penalty function whose slope is the price of the license. As a result, marginal cleanup costs are equalized and total cleanup costs are minimized.

How useful is this formulation in the real world? First, we do not believe that limiting our attention to regions of increasing marginal damages is a major

247

practical limitation. There are real cases in which marginal damages may decline – adding more waste to a river which is already an open sewer may have few environmental costs. But in general, even damage functions which exhibit such regions also often appear to be characterized by other regions in which marginal costs are increasing. For example, as the organic material in a river increases, and dissolved oxygen levels decline, we appear to move successively through several thresholds as we lose additional species and human uses. And, intuition suggests that output controls are more likely to be favorable in a region of increasing, rather than decreasing, marginal damages.

In practice, the scheme amounts to setting an ambient target (similar to the ambient standards widely used today) and working back to the magnitude of the discharges allowed by that constraint. Then the regulatory authority has to develop some notion about marginal damages in the regions above and below that point in order to set the subsidy and the penalty fee. Even if the regulatory authority does not quantify its uncertainty and compute an optimal schedule, the rough and ready approach should lead to a reasonable set of policies. After all, in a second-best world with imperfectly maximizing waste sources, the formal optimality of a policy scheme is not necessarily proof of what its actual impact will be.

Like any decentralized approach to pollution control, our scheme has certain serious limitations. It will not provide for efforts to act directly on the environment as opposed to on a waste source. Nor does it ensure that all economies of scale in treatment will be exhausted unless waste sources agree to appropriate joint ventures among themselves. We have also not discussed what should be done in the face of natural variations in climate which make it uncertain what damages will in fact result from any waste discharge.[6] All this suggests that a good deal of detailed work would be required to develop a viable set of policies and institutions for any specific circumstances. For example, could we vary policy seasonally or with actual natural conditions?

In theory, we would want a separate system of licenses to control each polluting substance we are concerned with at each geographic point of interest. Since administrative costs will rise with the complexity of the entire scheme, at some point we will need to make a (perhaps crude) compromise between the costs and benefits of additional elaboration and fine-tuning of the system. Note too that we have to construct our markets such that each has enough participants to ensure relatively competitive functioning. Nevertheless, even viewed as a practical measure designed to move us into a better, if not the best, position, we believe the mixed scheme we have proposed has significant merit. Perhaps the next important step is to consider how to set the penalty function in the presence of risk-aversion relative to damages.

APPENDIX: A GENERALIZED DECENTRALIZATION PROPOSITION

In the body of the paper, it was argued that expected total costs could be reduced by the use of both licenses and effluent fees, while maintaining the property of efficiently distributing cleanup among polluters. It was pointed out that the system operated as if the firms made a centralized decision against a penalty function with two facets and one kink. We want to argue now that if one is prepared to introduce more than one kind of license, the penalty function can be made to approximate any convex damage function arbitrarily closely. More precisely, by the use of multiple licenses, the system can be made to efficiently distribute costs and implicitly respond to a penalty function with as many kinks as there are types of licences.

Let $\bar{l}^j$ be the number of licenses of type j. Assume that $\bar{l}^0 \leq \bar{l}^1 \leq \bar{l}^2 \leq \ldots \leq \bar{l}^n$ and that $\bar{l}^0 = 0$. Let $s_0, s_1, \ldots, s_n+1$, be an increasing sequence of numbers with $s_0 = 0$. Define a penalty function $P(x)$, in the following way:

$$P(x) = \sum_{j=0}^{n} (s_{j+1} - s_j) \operatorname{Max} (x - \bar{l}^j, 0). \tag{A.1}$$

The function $P(x)$ is depicted in Figure 19.5. It is piecewise linear with kinks at $\bar{l}^1, \ldots, \bar{l}^n$. The slopes of the facets are $s_1, \ldots, s_{n+1}$, respectively.

The question then, is whether a system of licenses and effluent subsidies and penalties can induce the firms to act collectively as if the penalty function $P(x)$ had been imposed. Let $q_j(j = 1, \ldots, n)$ be the market price of the jth type of license. Let x_i be the ith firm's effluents, let l_i^j be the holdings of the jth type of license by the ith firm, and let $c_i(x_i)$ be the cleanup cost function for the ith firm. Having identified the ith firm's variables, we shall suppress the subscript i in what follows. It should be remembered that the following formulae apply to single firms.

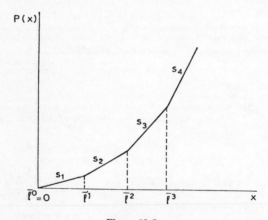

Figure 19.5

The required technique is to confront each firm with the following total cost function:

$$c(x) + \sum_{j=1}^{n} (q_{j-s_j}) l_j + \sum_{j=0}^{n} (s_{j+1} - s_j) \operatorname{Max} (x - \bar{l}^j, 0). \tag{A.2}$$

The last term looks very much like the earlier penalty function. The first term represents cleanup costs. The second term is special. The cost function can be interpreted as follows. The firm pays for cleanup. It also pays for the licenses it purchases, but it receives a rebate of s_j per license of type j that it holds. Then, having selected the licenses, the firm pays a penalty given by the piecewise linear function,

$$\hat{P}(x) = \sum_{j=0}^{n} (s_{j+1} - s_i) \, \mathrm{Max}\,(x - l_j, 0).$$

The locations of the kinks in this function are determined by the firm, through its license purchases. It is the second term in (A.2) that is crucial, for as we shall see, it has the effect of placing bounds on the license prices, q_j.

It remains to show that firms, in maximizing (A.2), efficiently distribute costs and act as if they were one firm facing the penalty function (A.1).

The first step is to show that

$$s_j \leqq q_j \leqq s_{j+1} \tag{A.3}$$

for all j. Suppose first that $q_j < s_j$. Then expand l^j so that $l^j > x$. It follows that the term in (A.2) involving l^j is

$$(q_j - s_j)l_j.$$

By allowing l_j to increase without limit, costs are reduced indefinitely. But that is inconsistent with equilibrium. Now suppose $q_j > s_{j+1}$. Reduce l^j so that $l^j < x$ and the term involving l^j becomes

$$(q_j - s_j)l^j - (s_{j+1} - s_j)l^j = (q_j - s_{j+1})l^j.$$

Hence costs are minimized when $l^j = 0$. If all firms do this, there cannot be an equilibrium in the market of j-type licenses. Therefore

$$s_j \leqq q_j \leqq s_{j+1},$$

for all $j = 1, \ldots, n$.

The next step is to show that if $q_j < s_{j+}1 = s_{j+1}$, then $q_{j+1} = s_{j+1}$. Suppose that $q_j < s_{j+1}$. We show that $l^j \leqq x$. Suppose to the contrary that $l^j > x$. Then the part of costs involving l^j is, from (A.2),

$$(q_j - s_{j+1})l^j.$$

Hence l^j should be contracted. Therefore if $q_j < s_{j+1}$, then $l^j \geqq x$, and $l^{j+1} > l^j \geqq x$, so that x is less than l^{j+1}. But if $l^{j+1} > x$, then q_{j+1} must equal s_{j+1}. For if $q_{j+1} > s_{j+1}$, then the part of costs involving l^{j+1} is

$$(q_{j+1} - s_{j+1})l^{j+1},$$

and l^{j+1} would be reduced. Hence if $l^{j+1} > x$, then $q_{j+1} = s_{j+1}$. This proves the assertion that if $q_j < s_{j+1}$, then $q_{j+1} = s_{j+1}$.

These arguments tell us a considerable amount about the equilbrium. Only one license price q^j can be in the interior of $[s_j, s_{j+1}]$. The remainder are on the boundaries – upper or lower depending upon whether the corresponding license has a lower or higher index than j, respectively.

We now take a typical interval $[s_j, s_{j+1}]$ and assume q_j is the interior of $[s_j, s_{j+1}]$. From the preceding argument, we know that $l^j = x$, that $q_k = s_{k+1}$ for $k < j$, and that $q_k = s_k$ for $k > j$. Thus the costs for the firm are, from (A.2),

$$c(x) + \sum_{k=0}^{j-1} (s_{k+1} - s_k)l^k + \sum_{k=j+1}^{n} (s_{k+1} - s_k)l^k$$

$$+\sum_{k=0}^{j-1}(s_{k+1}-s_k)(x-l^k)+(q_j-s_j)x+(q_j-s_j)x+(s_{j+1}-s_j)(0)$$

$$= c(x) + q_j x.$$

Similarly, if $q_j = s_j$, or $q_j = s_{j+1}$, and if $q_k = s_{k+1}$ for $k < j$ and $q_k = s_k$ for $k > j$, then (A.2) implies that the firm's costs (with licenses optimized out) are

$$c(x) + q_j x.$$

In an equilibrium, the costs for every firm will be

$$c(x) + q_j x,$$

for some j and some equilibrium value q_j. Thus when firms minimize, with respect to x, they set

$$c'(x) + q_j = 0. \tag{A.4}$$

In particular, marginal cleanup costs, $c'(x)$, are the same for every firm. Therefore cleanup costs are efficiently distributed in an equilibrium. Let $C(x)$ be the aggregate cost function, where x is now the sum of the effluents from all firms. In an equilibrium, (A.4) implies that

$$C'(x) + q_j = 0.$$

Moreover, if $s_j < q_j < s_{j+1}$, then $x = \bar{l}^j$, where $\bar{l}^j$ is the fixed total number of j-type licenses. If $q_j = s_j$, then $\bar{l}^{j-1} < x \leq$, and if $q_j = s_{j+1}$, then $\bar{l}^j < x \leq \bar{l}^{j+1}$. The equilibrium level of x is therefore determined by the level of costs. If

$$s_j < -C'(\bar{l}^j) < s_{j+1}, \tag{A.5}$$

then $x = \bar{l}^j$ in an equilibrium. If $-C'(\bar{l}^j) < s_j$ and $-C'(l^{j-1}) > s_j$, then $C'(x) = s_j$ in the equilibrium.[7]

The system therefore simply acts so as to minimize

$$C(x) + \sum_{j=1}^{n}(s_{j+1} - s_j)\,\text{Max}\,(x - \bar{l}^j, 0).$$

This is what we set out to show.

The implication of the preceding argument is that any convex damage function can be approximated to any desired degree of accuracy through the introduction of markets for different kinds of licenses. The private sector can be confronted with a nonlinear damage function without sacrificing efficiency in the distribution of cleanup.

As a practical matter, in the pollution context, the cost of the additional license markets may not be justified by the reduction in expected total cost. But it is perhaps a matter of some intellectual interest, both here and in other decentralization problems, that a carefully designed set of markets for options to buy or sell commodities at various prices can solve the problem of reconciling the competing demands of efficiency and decentralization. This subject is probably worthy of further investigation.

NOTES

1. Some of the previous treatments of effluent fees and marketable licenses include Kneese and Bower (1968), Jacoby, Schaumberg, and Gramlech (1972) and Montgomery (1972).
2. Montgomery (1972) considers the problem of multiple points of concern.
3. The argument is as follows. Let $P(q)$ be the inverse demand for the firm, and $d(q, x)$ its costs. The effluent charge is e. The surplus generated by the market is

$$T = \int_p^q P(s) \, ds - d(q, x) - ex.$$

Differentiating with respect to x, we have

$$\frac{dT}{dx} = (P - d_q) \frac{dq}{dx} - (d_x + e).$$

A profit maximizing firm will set $d_x + e = 0$. At that point $dT/dx = 0$ only if either $P = d_q$ (price equals marginal cost – the industry is competitive) or $dq/dx = 0$. The latter occurs when $d_{xq} = 0$. Therefore, when a competitive industry maximizes profits or costs or profit losses, the social optimum is achieved. But if the firm has market power $p > d_q$, there will be too much or too little cleanup depending on the sign of dq/dx.

4. If there is just one polluter, one could set a nonlinear effluent charge equal to marginal damages, $D'(x)$. This would lead to the optimum. But when there is more than one polluter, a nonlinear effluent charge is inconsistent with either decentralization or cost minimization, and possibly both.
5. Note that $c_x(x, \phi) = c^i_x(x_i, \phi)$, for all i, when x is distributed among polluters in a cost minimizing manner.
6. For a discussion of some of those issues, see Roberts (1975).
7. Note that (A.5) can only hold for one type of license because as j increases, and $-C'(l^j)$ falls, s_{j+1} rises.

REFERENCES

Jacoby, H., G. Schaumberg and F. Gramlech (1972), *Marketable pollution rights* (M.I.T., Cambridge, MA) unpublished.

Kneese, A.V. and B. Bower (1968), *Managing water quality* (Resources for the Future, Johns Hopkins Press, Baltimore).

Montgomery, W.C. (1972), Markets in licenses and efficient pollution control programs, *Journal of Economic Theory* 5, no. 3, 395–418.

Roberts, M.J. (1975), Environmental protection: The complexities of real policy choice, in: Fox and Swainson, eds., *Water quality management: The design of institutional arrangements* (University of British Columbia Press, Vancouver).

Chapter 20

Treating external diseconomies – markets or taxes?

David Starrett and Richard Zeckhauser

Sometimes the parties to an economic transaction do not reap all of the benefits and costs involved: there are externalities. Handling an externalities problem is like fighting an undiagnosed illness. At some times it will yield to any of a number of familiar treatments. At others, it will be resistant to any that are known. In this paper, we first consider those pathologies that can be adequately treated by standard remedies. Then we turn to examine some more resistant cases, cases that may require new diagnoses and unconventional methods of treatment.

TRACTABLE EXTERNALITY PROBLEMS

Thrust a price theorist into a world with externalities and he will pray for second best – many firms producing and many firms and/or consumers consuming each externality, with full convexity everywhere. No problem for the price theorist. He will just establish a set of artificial markets for externalities, commodities for which property rights were not previously defined.[1] Decision units, being small relative to the market, will take price as given. The resulting allocation will be a competitive outcome of the classical type. If artificial markets do not appeal, an equally efficient taxing procedure is available.

Where the externalities are beneficial, the price theorist's life is particularly easy; the more intractable aspects of externality problems do not appear. We concentrate here on external diseconomies, the more interesting case, and the case of greater empirical import.

For either artificial-market or taxing procedures it is essential to determine who has initial rights. Our common-law upbringings would lead us to expect that rights should go to the sufferers. It turns out, however, that it is just as efficient to give the rights instead to those who dump the sewage and soil the air.

Upton Paper Mills and Downley Baths are representative producer and recipient of an externality. Upton dumps organic residue into the very river that provides the water for Downley's swimmers. Downley of course screens and purifies, but not without cost.

Artificial markets[2]

Consider first the working of an artificial-markets scheme. If Downley has rights, he sells Upton the right to pollute. Upton, being but one of many polluters, can have no effect on the total pollution level, and hence no effect on its price. He takes price as given and continues polluting up to the point where his marginal gain from polluting (what is in effect his marginal cleanup cost) just equals the going price. Downley will sell rights to pollute up to the point where his marginal loss in profits from the pollutant equals the going price. The equilibrium level of production for the externality, the pollutant, is established where the marginal loss to the recipient equals the marginal cost to the producer of not providing the externality, these equal marginal amounts being the equilibrium price of the pollutant. This price times the amount of pollutant Upton dumps is the competitive charge Upton must pay Downley.

Give Upton the right to dump, and Downley must pay him a competitive charge equal to marginal cleanup cost times the amount of cleanup he provides. At the equilibrium, the equation of the marginals is the same as before. This second scheme presents a difficulty, however; it requires a benchmark for original filth in order to determine just how much cleanup has been provided. One possible benchmark is the amount Upton would dump if there were no Downleys, if there were no affected parties. For now we merely assume that the benchmark, N, can be established.[3]

A key question is whether shifting property rights here can drive either Upton or Downley out of business. If not, the marginal efficiency conditions will define a unique equilibrium, and the level of pollution will be the same whether Upton or Downley has rights.[4]

But the optimal allocations are quite different if one or the other of the firms ceases to function. If we given Upton rights, might Downley not decide to go out of business to avoid paying the charge for Upton's cleanup? Alternatively, might not a potential polluter who previously could not turn a profit because of high effluent charges now find it advantageous to go into business? When you consider that the size of N is arbitrary, it is evident that the answer to these important questions is yes. What is surprising, however, is that neither answer can be affirmative so long as the traditional convexity assumptions are satisfied.[5] For those interested we provide a mathematical demonstration of this assertion; others may wish to skip the next four paragraphs.

The assessment or payment of a competitive charge for an externality (as determined on an artificial market) to a firm with a convex production set can never determine whether it operates at a profit or at a loss. To see this, consider a simple case with a recipient firm (Downley in our model) that produces one output, b, using a single input, a, and that suffers from a single pollutant, z. The firm's production function may be written

$$b = f(a, -z),$$

with $f_1 > 0$, and $f_2 > 0$, where the subscripts refer to partial derivatives with respect to the first and second arguments. This function is assumed to satisfy the traditional convexity assumptions, i.e., it is concave throughout. We can measure the level of pollutant from the benchmark N so that the arguments of the production function are nonnegative. The translated production function,

$$b = g(a, N-z),$$

is clearly concave if f is.

The price of the output is normalized to unity. If p_a and p_z are the prices to the firm of the input and pollutant, respectively, then (regardless of whether it is an Upton- or a Downley-rights scheme) the marginal conditions

$p_a = f_1(a, -z) = g_1(a, N-z)$, and

$p_z = f_2(a, -z) = g_2(a, N-z)$

must be satisfied. In what follows, we suppress the arguments of f_1, g_1, f_2, and g_2. The properties of concave functions imply that

$$g(a, N-z) - g(0, 0) \geq g_1 a + g_2 (N-z) = p_a a + p_z (N-z).$$

If recipients have rights, Downley's profits, π, will be

$$\pi = g(a, N-z) - p_a a \geq p_z (N-z) + g(0, 0).$$

To achieve the outcome of the producers'-rights case, we need merely transfer $p_z (N-z)$ from recipient to producer. After the transfer the recipient firm, Downley, makes $g(a, N-z) - p_a a - p_z (N-z)$, a still greater profit than he would make if he went out of business and got $g(0, 0)$. Indeed, Downley has no incentive to change his behavior in any way.

The amount $p_z (N-z)$ of the transfer that shuttles back and forth depending on who has rights is a pure rent that returns to the fortunate party. As such it cannot reverse either a profitable or unprofitable status for the externality recipient. A completely parallel argument establishes this same result for a firm, such as Upton, which is an externality producer.

Note that as N becomes larger, this result becomes increasingly counterintuitive. Surely the amount of rent that can be passed back and forth without forcing a shutdown decision of either the externality recipient or producer is finite. It would hardly seem possible that it could depend on an arbitrarily chosen benchmark N. The apparent paradox is explained in the second half of the paper, where we show that for sufficiently large N, full convexity is logically impossible; without convexity the preceding analysis is not relevant.

Taxes

It is sometimes proposed that a taxing scheme be employed to overcome externality difficulties. With taxing schemes, the party with rights quotes its marginal loss to the government, which then makes the appropriate collection, the level of the externality times the marginal loss inflicted.[7] Given the conditions of (1) many-participant markets (assuring "honest" preference revelation), and (2) full convexity, the only difference between the artificial-markets scheme just described and a taxing scheme is that the latter does not provide positive payment for the party that has rights; the government makes a profit. A simple transfer from the government to the party with rights is all that is necessary to turn the taxing-scheme outcome to the one that would have resulted had an artificial market been established. The allocation of resources, following the argument of the previous subsection, is clearly the same. Furthermore, shutdown or operate decisions are not affected. Whether a firm is or is not paid the appropriate tax (the value on a competitive market of the loss it suffers) cannot reverse the profitability or unprofitability of its operation.

The most familiar proposal in the pollution world for this sort of tax scheme involves the imposition of effluent charges, the charge being a specific example of a unit tax on externality producers. It is sometimes proposed that instead of setting a per unit charge on effluent, a certain number of pollution rights should be auctioned among the potential polluters. Except for the mechanical way the equilibrium is reached, the two schemes are identical. The results they produce will be indistinguishable if the quantity of rights auctioned under the latter scheme is just equal to the amount of pollutant dumped given the particular effluent charge established for the former scheme. They are both, in effect, unit-tax schemes.[8] We conclude, then, that the four schemes, artificial market or tax, recipient or producer having rights, all produce identical allocations of resources, assuming many participants and full convexity.[9]

In the discussion that follows, we detail some frequently occurring situations in which the assumption system that supported the foregoing analysis is not applicable. The equivalences we just developed will no longer hold, and, for the most part, the schemes we have presented will not lead to efficient outcomes.

RESISTANT EXTERNALITY PROBLEMS
Sometimes, alas, we find ourselves in third- and fourth-best worlds, where the externalities problems are not of the convenient type treated thus far, and new, more resistant externality problems arise. First we discuss briefly the problem of noncompetitive behavior, a problem which has been noted elsewhere by Arrow [2], due to thinness of markets and the public bad nature of the externality. Then we analyze difficulties involving nonconvexities. Finally we discuss parallel aspects of these difficulties when consumers are externality recipients.

Thinness of markets
We have treated Upton and Downley, our representatives of the many producers and recipients, as buyers and sellers of the same externality. For this treatment to be meaningful on the selling side, it must be possible to have specific amounts of the externality conveyed privately to individual buyers. This would be the case, for example, with solid waste which could be disposed at any of a number of dumping grounds.

More commonly, unfortunately, any quantity of an externality received by one recipient is received by all. Thus, in the Upton–Downley example, Upton's effluent serves as a public bad for all downstream firms. The functioning of a market requires that the sellers compete with each other on the supply side. When the externality is a public bad, what is supplied by one (dumping rights in this instance) must be supplied by all. A traditional competitive market cannot exist.[10]

To achieve the equivalent of a competitive outcome, we would have to set up a separate competitive market for pollution rights between Upton and each one of the downstream firms. If each seller–recipient would take price as given in his particular market, and if Upton would act competitively and take as his given price the sum of these individual market prices, Upton would wind up paying a price per unit of externality equal to the sum of marginal downstream losses. To have such a price at the margin is the appropriate efficiency condition for the production of this public good (reduction in the level of externality). Given the public nature of the externality, the amount contracted on each market must be the same (the prices will differ in general). The simplest way to reach the efficient point may be to vary quantity on every market simultaneously and to ask each downstream firm to announce its going price, its marginal losses. Obviously, any scheme of this sort would require a substantial amount of centralized administration.

This scheme, as well as the tax proposals, will run into further difficulties given that there are not many producers and recipients dealing in the same commodity.

256

Participants will find it in their interests to behave strategically. If recipients have rights, they will each be empowered to block any producer's production of the externality. A producer will be permitted to produce the minimum amount of the externality for which he buys rights from all sellers. Individual buyer–seller negotiations will probably result. Each seller will be responsible for but a small portion of the total price a producer (or all producers should they band together) must pay for increasing externality production. He will thus have little effect on the total amount the producer demands, and will have an incentive to sell at an extortionary price, a price well above his marginal losses. The likely outcome is that much less than an optimal amount of externality rights will be sold, less than an optimal amount of externality production will take place.[11]

If producers have rights, the strategic shoe is on the other foot. A reduction in the amount of externality produced will benefit all recipients. The usual public goods, free-rider problem arises. Unless the recipients are capable of coordinating their activities, they will purchase less than an optimal amount of the public good (reduction of the externality).

Participants also have incentives to act noncompetitively in the tax schemes. If there are many downstream firms, they have an incentive to overstate their marginal losses to the government, since this may lead to a lower pollution level and there is nothing to lose. (Recall that recipients are not compensated in the tax scheme.)

Nonconvexities

Let us return to the river and assume that thinness-of-markets difficulties do not arise, or that the government can enforce the equilibrium through an administered planning process. Upton is still our representative producer. If property rights can be established for externalities, Downley is our representative recipient. Otherwise he is a single recipient whose losses from any level of externality production are the sum of the losses of all recipients. Both Upton and Downley act as price takers.

Our problems, alas, are not over. If Upton and his fellow polluters dump enough, it is absurd to expect that Downley will remain in the business of providing swimming facilities. Perhaps, if he had rights, he might stand around idle in order to collect his due from Upton. But from a resource allocation standpoint he would be out of business. This possibility was ruled out in Section 1 of this paper, where full convexity was assumed. Downley's quite appropriate shutdown decision must be associated with a nonconvexity in his production set.

To see that there is indeed such a nonconvexity, consider a single-product competitive firm that suffers from an external diseconomy. In the absence of externality markets or taxes, it could make a short-run, profit-maximizing decision for each potential level of externality. Plot its level of maximum profits as a function of the level of externality it receives. We know a lot about the shape of this function. It must be downward sloping since z is a diseconomy. If, as assumed, the firm's production function is concave, this curve must be concave as well. This implies that it must reach any arbitrarily great negative value, since z is unbounded.[12] But the firm could always choose to produce nothing and thus incur at most fixed costs. This implies that the maximum-profits vs. externality curve must be bounded below. The maximum loss floor that is established by the shutdown possibility rules out global concavity of the production function.

Figure 20.1 shows two possible shapes for the profits function when there is a nonconvexity in the production set.

A nonconvexity will obviously have no effect on any outcomes so long as N, the

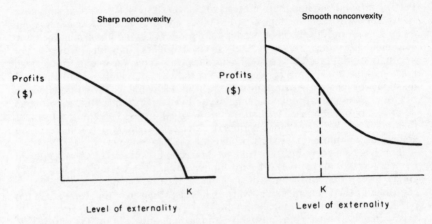

Figure 20.1 Externality recipient's profits.

level at which the externality would be produced in the absence of any compensation arrangements, is less than K, the point at which the nonconvexity begins.

In the analysis that follows, we are worried about cases where nonconvexities matter, where N > K. Such a location reflects a situation where the potential harm is serious enough that it may induce a firm to shut down operations.

Drawing on historical precedent, we turn from swimming to agriculture and consider as our example the classic farmer-cowman illustration developed by Coase [4]. Coase observes that wandering cattle trample the neighbor farmer's crops. Consider two possible schedules of damage, representing, respectively, a sharp and a smooth nonconvexity (Table 20.1).

For full convexity the cows must do increasing marginal damage; something like Schedule A must apply. The difficulty is that the addition of a fifth cow to the herd induces the farmer to discontinue operations. Beyond four cows profits are identically zero,[13] and the profit function is not convex.

Table 20.1 Two schedules of damage to farmer.

	Schedule A: sharp nonconvexity		Schedule B: smooth nonconvexity	
Size of herd	Total profits	Marginal loss	Total profits	Marginal loss
0	8		8	
1	7½	½	6	2
2	6	1½	5	1
3	3½	2½	4½	½
4	0	3½	4¼	¼
5	−4½	4½	4⅛	⅛
	0[a]	0[a]		

[a] This figure applies if the farmer stops farming.

Schedule B presents what we call a smooth nonconvexity. It illustrates a situation in which the marginal damage per cow is decreasing. Casual consideration of technological factors might lead us to suspect that this would be the case, that two cows would trample less apiece than one, and that a dozen would not multiply by six the damage done by but a pair.

Decreasing marginal damage over some range is not the only cause of the types of nonconvexities we have been considering. Nonconvexities will crop up if there are economies of scale in treating external diseconomies. For twice the price of a fence that keeps out one cow, the farmer could probably construct one that could keep out eight. Even if there were increasing marginal trampling damage over the one-to-eight range, once there are enough cows to make a fence worthwhile, a nonconvexity presents itself; extra cows will impose decreasing marginal costs (losses of profit) on the farmer. If, as seems not unlikely, the fence can keep out ten or one hundred, the nonconvexity will be of the sharp variety.

The results we are about to discuss hold equally whether nonconvexities are smooth or sharp. However, the exposition is somewhat easier when non-convexities are of the sharp type; therefore that is the case we shall discuss.[14]

Artificial markets

Consider Schedule A and the operation of an artificial market. Give the farmer, the recipient, rights. Say that the price, p^*, of the externality (cows that trample) is \$2. The farmer, adopting traditional marginal optimization procedures, decides to accept two cows, the number for which his marginal loss does not exceed the price. Assume that the cowman's profit schedule leads him to demand rights to graze two cows at this price. Do we have an equilibrium? No! Surely, with the present price, this position is not optimal for the farmer. He would make greater total profits (infinite) if he accepted an infinite number of trampling cows at this price, or indeed at any positive price.

Thus, unless there is some artificial restriction on the number of rights which can be sold, equilibrium cannot exist for this artificial-market scheme. The farmer who is offered a positive price for accepting cows which can cause him at most a finite amount of damage (his farming profit), will surely want to supply an unlimited number of rights; but if he is offered a zero price, he supplies no rights, so equilibrium is impossible. Nonexistence is somewhat surprising, since the presence of arbitrary nonconvexities does not ordinarily rule out the possibility of equilibrium.

There may still exist equilibria if we modify the rules by introducing an upper limit on the number of rights which can be sold. Indeed, an equilibrium will surely exist if we set the upper limit at the level K in Figure 20.1, since then the problem is convex and we can appeal to a standard existence theorem. However, such an equilibrium no longer has any efficiency properties; for example, if it happens that the best solution is to have the farmer out of business and pollution levels above K, any equilibrium which excludes this possibility is surely inefficient. To be sure that the upper limit does not exclude the best outcome, we would have to set that limit outside the "feasibility" region. In our example, we would set the limit at N, the maximum number of cows our rancher would put on the land if the farmer were absent.

Having taken this precaution, special circumstances are required in order that an equilibrium exist. Let us return to our example. When the externality market is introduced, the farmer receives an externality payment, p^*c, where c gives the number of cows grazed. His aggregate profits, π^a, are equal to his profits from farming, π, plus the externality payment. The line through the point (2, 6) in Figure 20.2 is an iso-aggregate-profits line; it offers a value of 10. The point (2, 6) is a local optimum for the farmer, but he could increase his profits by stopping all production and selling N externality rights. In the case shown, where N = 8, the farmer could secure aggregate profits of 16 at the present externality price by ceasing farming operations. This means that (2, 6) cannot be a global equilibrium; there is no price that would lead the farmer to choose to operate at that point.

No other price can be an equilibrium either. At prices above $\hat{p}$, the farmer will always want to sell N externality rights, while the cowman will not want to have as many as N cows.[15] At prices below $\hat{p}$, the farmer will want fewer than two cows (the number he would choose when the price is p^*), while the cowman would want at least the two he had when the price was higher. In terms of supply-and-demand analysis, the farmer's supply curve of cattle externalities is discontinuous and the cowman's demand curve passes through the gap of the discontinuity. Equilibrium will exist only if N is below 5 (so that at price p^* our farmer cannot offer enough rights to improve on the position of (2, 6)).

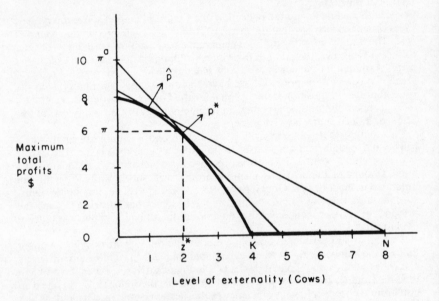

Figure 20.2 Externality recipient's profits – sharp nonconvexity. The p's in the diagram represent the gradients of the total profits function for their respective price vectors.

The instability in any proposed equilibrium which derives from the farmer's threat to quit may seem somewhat silly, but, as we shall see below, it is a signal that an efficient allocation of resources may require that the farmer get out of farming.[16] We conclude that in cases where externalities are potentially strong enough to drive out firms, situations where N is large, the artificial-markets scheme will not work at all.[17]

Taxes

Can we expect a tax scheme to lead to the optimum equilibrium? Returning to our diagram, it appears that not one, but two distinct points are candidates for such an equilibrium. The point (2, 6) is a possibility. If the government tells the farmer that there are going to be two cows, the farmer's quoted marginal losses will be $2, and at a tax (price) of $2, the cowman will want to have exactly two cows. But the point (N, 0) is also a contender. At that point, with the former out of business, marginal losses (and hence taxes) are zero and the cowman will want to have N cows, his profit-maximizing number of cows assuming zero externality payments.

The presence of multiple equilibria should not surprise us. Pigou [8] points out that nonconvexities will lead to multiple tax equilibria. The point that we want to make sure here is that since external diseconomies logically imply nonconvexities, multiple equilibria are going to be the rule rather than the exception.

Should the farmer operate or not? To find out, we need to know whether society is a net gainer or loser from having the farmer operate at this location. Assuming that prices of private goods correctly reflect social opportunity costs, the best point is the point of maximum combined profit.[18] In Figure 20.3, we plot the marginal profit loss of the farmer, ss, and the marginal profit gain, dd, for the cowman (derived from figures not given here), as functions of the number of cows.

Note that there are two points, A and N, where the marginal gain is equal to the marginal loss. These naturally correspond to the two potential tax equilibria. Whether we would prefer A or N depends on whether the total area under the ss curve between A and N (the farmer's profit loss moving from A to N) is greater or less than the total area under the dd curve over that range (the cowman's gain for the corresponding move).

We can conceive of situations in which the balance might be tipped either way. For example, if the soil is particularly rich, so that the farmer could earn considerable differential rent on it, and if it is the case that if the cowman intensified operations he would not secure much of a profits gain, then the situation would probably be reversed, and the farmer should cease operations.

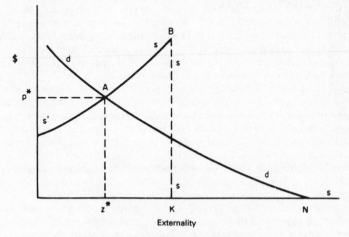

Figure 20.3 Marginal profit and loss curves.

Unfortunately, if we set up the adjustment mechanism for taxes described earlier, there can be no assurance that the preferred equilibrium will be found. Assuming that we follow the conventional marginal prescriptions, we will end up at A or N depending on whether we start with externality levels less than or greater than K. Where we start, not the merits of the situation, will determine the outcome. The only sure way to find the optimum when there is the possibility that it will be appropriate for the externality recipient to cease operation, is to engage in the type of macro cost–benefit analysis described above. And in a general equilibrium framework with a highly interdependent externality structure, the required analysis would be incredibly complicated. Searching for shortcuts in such a procedure will provide an important, and hopefully productive, area for future research.

The above analysis suggests at least one important implication for current policy far beyond the narrow example on which it was based. Until recently, externality producers have not been forced to bear many of the costs they impose on others. Thus, current pollution levels are probably beyond optimal levels. What taxes should be charged? The above analysis suggests that using marginal losses may understate the relevant costs and lead to less than desirable adjustments. Firms, or households (see below), which have quit or moved will not be counted at all, even though they would benefit from substantially lower pollution levels. Furthermore, agents who have already absorbed the bulk of their potential damage from pollution (whose loss-of-profit functions show a smooth nonconvexity) may have small marginal losses now. Under these circumstances a nonoptimal equilibrium may be established with relatively low taxes and relatively high pollution levels.

Consumers as externality recipients

What about consumers? They too suffer from external diseconomies. In fact, many would argue that the most important externalities are in consumption. There would seem to be two significant ways in which consumers as externality recipients are unlike firms. First, consumers do not present a convenient cardinal measure of their welfare which would correspond to profits for a firm. In a variety of capacities, the consumer's willingness to pay to reduce the level of an externality may play a parallel role to the marginal loss in profits concept when the externality recipient is a firm. But if we are interested, as many economists may be, in the question of whether an artificial-markets scheme can be counted on to lead to an efficient equilibrium, we must look deeper and see whether the consumer's indifference surfaces display nonconvexities.

Second, consumers, unlike producers, cannot shut themselves down. For them, going out of business is not an approved enterprise. But the consumer does have an equivalent to the shutdown option; he can cease consuming a particular good. Such an action would merely indicate a situation where an indifference curve met an axis. If the increased presence of an externality induces a consumer to stop consuming an affected good, we might expect to find a nonconvexity in the consumer's indifference map. We will find one if the consumer does not care about the level of externality once he ceases consumption, if in this sense his after-shutdown feelings about the externality parallel those of a firm.

That a nonconvexity will be present in such an instance can best be illustrated with reference to our polluted-river example. Consider, for instance, a consumer who swims not in the Downley Baths, but directly in the river. Beyond a certain level of filth, the consumer will swim elsewhere or take up another form of recreation. He will cease consuming a particular commodity.

A full geometric representation of the nonconvexity involved would require a complex three-dimensional diagram displaying the three arguments: pollution, swimming, and other goods (money). Fortunately, there is a simpler, though indirect, way in which we can demonstrate the presence of the nonconvexity. Look at a typical consumer's indifference curve on one swimming–pollution plane (Figure 20.4). Every point on the curve represents some positive level of swimming and offers satisfaction level I. We assume that by giving the consumer a sufficiently large increment in his consumption of other goods we could just compensate him for a loss of all his swimming; that is, we can find a point (in general, there will be many) in commodity space that has zero swimming and offers satisfaction level I.

We will argue that, given these assumptions, there is no point (such as Q) on the indifference curve displayed that can be a competitive equilibrium in the sense that there are prices (on real and artificial markets) for which this point is the least-cost way of achieving satisfaction level I. Since the consumer prefers less pollution, its price must be negative.

Now find the point in commodity space mentioned above, one that has zero swimming and offers satisfaction level I. Call it P. To purchase the goods bundle represented by P would cost a finite amount. But with zero swimming, the consumer no longer cares about the pollution level. With a negative price on pollution, the consumer would demand an arbitrarily large amount of it and would attain point P and satisfaction level I at as low a total cost as he wished. Thus, no point such as Q can represent a competitive equilibrium. This means that the consumer's indifference curves must present a nonconvexity; with full convexity of preferences, every commodity bundle is the least-cost way of achieving its own satisfaction level for an appropriate choice of prices.

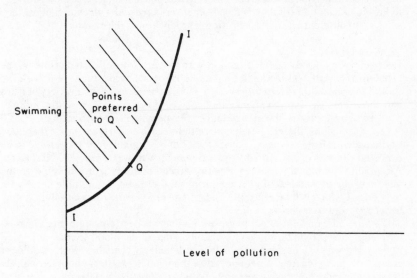

Figure 20.4 Swimming–pollution indifference curve.

With the consumer an externality recipient, there is no more assurance that an artificial-markets scheme will lead to an equilibrium than there is when the recipient is a firm. In effect, the two types of recipients display the same pathologies in these circumstances. It can be shown equivalently that if a tax scheme were employed in a consumer–recipient situation, the same form of macro cost–benefit analysis required with firms as recipients would be needed to find the efficient equilibrium among the multiple contenders.

To summarize, a consumer externality recipient may cease consuming a commodity and thus like a firm may present a nonconvexity that renders irrelevant conventional analyses about the existence and efficiency of competitive equilibria.

Despite these similarities, the consumer nonconvexity is less general than that for the firm. A consumer cannot always escape the effects of an externality. Suppose in our example that the consumer felt badly about river pollution even if he were not swimming in it. Then, although it is still likely that there will be a nonconvexity (since his dislike for pollution probably diminishes when he quits swimming), we can no longer demonstrate it logically. Furthermore, if an externality affects an individual through his consumption of an essential commodity, there will be no shutdown possibility and hence no essential nonconvexity. Air over New York City would not be such an essential commodity; one could always move away. But one cannot escape from radioactive contamination of our atmosphere. For this type of consumer externality there may not be a nonconvexity.

Even if full convexity is assured, the results for consumers differ from those for producers. With producers, the shuttling of rents that results from transfers of rights or switches from tax to market schemes do not affect resource allocations. But with consumers, these rents will exert income effects; these in turn will alter the efficient allocation of resources. Although tax and market schemes will both lead to Pareto-efficient outcomes when consumers are involved with externalities, they will lead to different efficient levels for the production of the externality.[19]

CONCLUSION

Ever since we left our opening section with its very restrictive assumptions, the problem of external diseconomies has looked more complex. In the real world we should expect to find externalities functioning as public bads for a variety of firms and consumers all of whom might exercise a shutdown option. The entire array of problems considered in the second half of this paper will be encountered.

Our conclusions, therefore, must be rather negative. We have shown that none of the decentralized schemes, even if they can be administered properly, can be expected to work in any straightforward manner when externalities are serious. An equilibrium may not even exist with artificial-markets setups. Even with tax schemes, our procedures of greatest promise, there may be multiple equilibria, only one of which will be efficient. To find and enforce the optimal solution may be a costly and complex procedure.

Despite these pessimistic findings, it would be wrong to conclude that a laissez-faire approach should be chosen by default. That mode of non-treatment has led to very serious present symptoms. Even rudimentary remedies, such as effluent charges or quota schemes, might be better than leaving matters untended. Surely we should conduct extensive research, both experimental and theoretical, to find positive treatments that might ameliorate existing conditions.

ACKNOWLEDGEMENTS

An earlier version of this paper was presented at the Second World Econometrics Congress, September, 1970. This research was supported by NSF Grant GS-2797 (Starrett) and NSF Grant GR-88 to the Analytic Methods in Public Policy Faculty Seminar (Zeckhauser). That paper was distributed as Starrett and Zeckhauser [12].

NOTES

1. Due to their elusive physical natures, most externalities have not developed property rights. Markets for externality rights are artificial in the sense that natural forces have been insufficient to foster their existence.
2. Allocation schemes of this type were first proposed by Lindahl [6]. They have since been discussed by Coase [4] and Arrow [2], among others.
3. There is a third possibility that also leads to the same result. The government can have rights. It will sell these rights, say N of them, on the open market to both producers and recipients. Any right purchased by a recipient is not available to a producer, and thus reduces externality production by one unit.
4. There is a more general way to look at this process of transferring rights and shuttling rents. An equivalent procedure is one where a standard level of externality production is set. Everything above that level requires a payment from producer to recipient and conversely. The case we call producers'-rights sets that standard level at N. The recipients'-rights case sets it at 0.

   The argument given here that a change in property rights will not alter resource allocations only holds if *final demand prices do not change*. They might change if individuals with divergent tastes own the firms involved in the transfers, and if these firms are large relative to the rest of the economy. See Dolbear [5] for a discussion of the distributional effects of property rights transfers.
5. This issue has a long but inconclusive literature. See, for example, Buchanan [3].
6. The first general discussion of tax schemes in this context was given by Pigou [8]. Further discussion can be found in Meade [7] and Coase [4].
7. For a discussion of the mechanics of such a scheme, see Aoki [1].
8. There are (unfortunately) many frequently proposed schemes that do not achieve equivalent or efficient results even under our ideal conditions. For example, the oft-heard proposal that total costs of damage should be divided in proportion among the externality producers responsible for it, a scheme which is essentially average-damage taxation, is inefficient for the same reason that average-cost pricing is inefficient.
9. We have demonstrated these results only for a particularly simple case. Starrett [11] has shown elsewhere that these results hold in a very general, abstract framework.
10. There can still be competition on the demand site, all producers competing with each other to dump, the total amount dumped being the sum of what is dumped by each.
11. If the recipients were acting in concert, they would act as a monopolist and sell an amount which equates marginal revenue (derived in the usual manner) and marginal cost (the sum of their marginal cost curves). In the strategic situation described, unless the sellers can achieve some degree of coordination they will sell even less than they would if they were acting in this monopolistic fashion.
12. A concave function always lies below its tangent line. If the tangent is ever downward sloping, it must cross the z axis, and so, therefore, would the profit function if it were everywhere concave.
13. Profit here should be thought of as return above and beyond variable cost, since in the short run the firm will quit only when it cannot cover variable cost. Returns to the fixed factor (land) are ignored in making short-run decisions.
14. The two types of nonconvexities may be combined in a single instance if the total profits curve of a smooth nonconvexity cuts the horizontal axis, the axis on which the externality is measured. But either nonconvexity, by itself, is sufficient to hinder the effectiveness of the corrective measures outlined above.

15. In the numerical example, the externality level can only take on integer values; $\hat{p}$ turns out to be 1 1/14, the price that makes the farmer's profits equal whether he accepts eight cows or one, the latter being his optimal inferior point.
16. Note that instability is even more likely in the long run, since then the farmer will quit whenever he cannot cover his fixed as well as his variable cost.
17. Our conclusion that equilibria will generally fail to exist seems to be related to some results of Shapley and Shubik [9]. They showed that in games with external diseconomies, the core frequently fails to exist. However, Starrett [10] has shown elsewhere that the two results are unrelated. The Shapley–Shubik result depends on a particular definition of property right, whereas ours does not.
18. We are assuming that our firms are small enough that their behavior does not affect final demand prices. Furthermore, the statement that everyone is better off at the point of maximum combined profit may require transfers among owners of the farm and the ranch.
19. The income effect on the purchase of externality production may well be negative. Rich people can swim in their own pools and will not have river pollution affect their natatory pleasures.

REFERENCES

1. Aoki, M. 'Two planning processes for an economy with production externalities', Harvard Institute of Economic Research Discussion Paper No. 157, Harvard University, Cambridge, Mass., 1970.
2. Arrow, K.J. 'The organization of economic activity: issues pertinent to the choice of market versus non-market allocation', in *The Analysis and Evaluation of Public Expenditures: The PPB System,* U.S. Congress, Joint Economic Committee, U.S. Government Printing Office, Washington, 1969, pp. 47–64.
3. Buchanan, J. 'External diseconomies, corrective taxes and market structure', *Amer. Econ. Rev., 59,* 174–177 (1969).
4. Coase, R.H. 'The problem of social cost', *J. Law Econ., 3,* 1–44 (1960).
5. Dolbear, F. 'On the theory of optimum externality', *Amer. Econ. Rev., 57,* 90–103 (1967).
6. Lindahl, E. 'Just taxation – a possible solution', in *Classics in the Theory of Public Finance* (R.A. Musgrave and A.T. Peacock, eds.), Macmillan, London, 1958, pp. 168–176.
7. Meade, J. 'External economies and diseconomies in a competitive situation', *Econ. J., 62,* 54–67 (1952); reprinted in *Readings in Welfare Economics* (K.J. Arrow and T. Scitovsky, eds.), Irwin, Homewood, Illinois, 1969, pp. 185–198.
8. Pigou, A.C. *The Economics of Welfare,* Macmillan, New York, 1920 (1st ed.) and 1932 (4th ed.).
9. Shapley, L. and M. Shubik, 'On the core of an economic system with externalities', *Amer. Econ. Rev., 59,* 678–684 (1969).
10. Starrett, D. 'A note on externalities and the core', Harvard Institute of Economic Research Discussion Paper No. 198, Harvard University, Cambridge, Mass., 1971.
11. Starrett, D. 'Fundamental non-convexities in the theory of externalities', *J. Econ. Theory, 4,* 180–196 (1972.
12. Starrett, D. and R. Zeckhauser, 'Treating external diseconomies – markets or taxes?' Public Policy Program Discussion Paper No. 3, Harvard University, Cambridge, Mass., 1971.

Chapter 21

Economic instruments for environmental regulation

T.H. Tietenberg

INTRODUCTION

As recently as a decade ago environmental regulators and lobbying groups with a special interest in environmental protection looked upon the market system as a powerful adversary. That the market unleashed powerful forces was widely recognized and that those forces clearly acted to degrade the environment was widely lamented. Conflict and confrontation became the battle cry for those groups seeking to protect the environment as they set out to block market forces whenever possible.

Among the more enlightened participants in the environmental policy process, the air of confrontation and conflict has now begun to recede in many parts of the world. Leading environmental groups and regulators have come to realize that the power of the market can be harnessed and channelled toward the achievement of environmental goals, through an economic incentives approach to regulation. Forward-looking business people have come to appreciate the fact that cost-effective regulation can make them more competitive in the global market-place than regulations which impose higher-than-necessary control costs.

The change in attitude has been triggered by a recognition that this former adversary, the market, can be turned into a powerful ally. In contrast to the traditional regulatory approach, which makes mandatory particular forms of behaviour or specific technological choices, the economic incentive approach allows more flexibility in how the environmental goal is reached. By changing the incentives an individual agent faces, the best private choice can be made to coincide with the best social choice. Rather than relying on the regulatory authority to identify the best course of action, the individual agent can use his or her typically superior information to select the best means of meeting an assigned emission reduction responsibility. This flexibility achieves environmental goals at lower cost, which, in turn, makes the goals easier to achieve and easier to establish.

One indicator of the growing support for the use of economic incentive approaches for environmental control in the United States is the favourable treatment it has recently received both in the popular business[1] and environmental[2] press. Some public interest environmental organizations have now even adopted economic incentive approaches as a core part of their strategy for protecting the environment.[3]

In response to this support the emissions trading concept has recently been applied to reducing the lead content in gasoline, to controlling both ozone depletion and non-point sources of water pollution, and was also prominently featured in the Bush administration proposals for reducing acid rain and smog unveiled in June 1989.

Our knowledge about economic incentive approaches has grown rapidly in the two decades in which they have received serious analytical attention. Not only have the theoretical models become more focused and the empirical work more detailed, but we have now had over a decade of experience with emissions trading in the US and emission charges in Europe.

As the world community becomes increasingly conscious of both the need to tighten environmental controls and the local economic perils associated with tighter controls in a highly competitive global market-place, it seems a propitious time to stand back and to organize what we have learned about this practical and promising approach to pollution control that may be especially relevant to current circumstances. In this paper I will draw upon economic theory, empirical studies, and actual experience with implementation to provide a brief overview of some of the major lessons we have learned about two economic incentive approaches – emissions trading and emission charges – as well as their relationships to the more traditional regulatory policy.[4]

THE POLICY CONTEXT

Emissions trading

Stripped to its bare essentials, the US Clean Air Act[5] relies upon a *command-and-control* approach to controlling pollution. Ambient standards establish the highest allowable concentration of the pollutant in the ambient air for each conventional pollutant. To reach these prescribed ambient standards, emission standards (legal emission ceilings) are imposed on a large number of specific emission points such as stacks, vents, or storage tanks. Following a survey of the technological options of control, the control authority selects a favoured control technology and calculates the amount of emission reduction achievable by that technology as the basis for setting the emission standard. Technologies yielding larger amounts of control (and, hence, supporting more stringent emission standards) are selected for new emitters and for existing emitters in areas where it is very difficult to meet the ambient standard. The responsibility for defining and enforcing these standards is shared in legislatively specified ways between the national government and the various state governments.

The emissions trading programme attempts to inject more flexibility into the manner in which the objectives of the Clean Air Act are met by allowing sources a much wider range of choice in how they satisfy their legal pollution control responsibilities than possible in the command-and-control approach. Any source choosing to reduce emissions at any discharge point more than required by its emission standard can apply to the control authority for certification of the excess control as an 'emission reduction credit' (ERC). Defined in terms of a specific amount of a particular pollutant, the certified emissions reduction credit can be used to satisfy emission standards at other (presumably more expensive to control) discharge points controlled by the creating source or it can be sold to other sources. By making these credits transferable, the US Environmental Protection Agency (EPA) has allowed sources to find the cheapest means of satisfying their requirements, even if the cheapest means are under the control of another firm. The ERC is the currency used in emissions trading, while the offset, bubble, emissions banking and netting policies govern how this currency can be stored and spent.[6]

The *offset policy* requires major new or expanding sources in 'non-attainment' areas (those areas with air quality worse than the ambient standards) to secure sufficient offsetting emission reductions (by acquiring ERCs) from existing firms so that the air is cleaner after their entry or expansion than before.[7] Prior to this policy no new firms were allowed to enter non-attainment areas on the grounds they would interfere with attaining the ambient standards. By introducing the offset policy EPA allowed economic growth to continue while assuring progress toward attainment.

The *bubble policy* receives its unusual name from the fact that it treats multiple emission points controlled by existing emitters (as opposed to those expanding or entering an area for the first time) as if they were enclosed in a bubble. Under this policy only the total emissions of each pollutant leaving the bubble are regulated. While the total leaving the bubble must be not larger than the total permitted by adding up all the corresponding emission standards within the bubble (and in some cases the total must be 20 per cent lower), emitters are free to control some discharge points less than dictated by the corresponding emission standards as long as sufficient compensating ERCs are obtained from other discharge points within the bubble. In essence sources are free to choose the mix of control among the discharge points as long as the overall emission reduction requirements are satisfied. Multi-plant bubbles are allowed, opening the possibility for trading ERCs among very different kinds of emitters.

Netting allows modifying or expanding sources (but not new sources) to escape from the need to meet the requirements of the rather stringent new source review process (including the need to acquire offsets) so long as any net increase in emissions (counting any ERCs earned elsewhere in the plant) is below an established threshold. In so far as it allows firms to escape particular regulatory requirements by using ERCs to remain under the threshold which triggers applicability, netting is more properly considered regulatory relief than regulatory reform.

Emissions banking allows firms to store certified ERCs for subsequent use in the offset, bubble, or netting programmes or for sale to others.

Although comprehensive data on the effects of the programme do not exist because substantial proportions of it are administered by local areas and no one collects information in a systematic way, some of the major aspects of the experience are clear.[8]

- The programme has unquestionably and substantially reduced the costs of complying with the requirements of the Clean Air Act. Most estimates place the accumulated capital savings for all components of the programme at over $10 billion. This does not include the recurring savings in operating cost. On the other hand the programme has not produced the magnitude of cost savings that was anticipated by its strongest proponents at its inception.
- The level of compliance with the basic provisions of the Clean Air Act has increased. The emissions trading programme increased the possible means for compliance and sources have responded.
- Somewhere between 7,000 and 12,000 trading transactions have been consummated. Each of these transactions was voluntary and for the participants represented an improvement over the traditional regulatory approach. Several of these transactions involved the introduction of innovative control technologies.
- The vast majority of emissions trading transactions have involved large

pollution sources trading emissions reduction credits either created by excess control of uniformly mixed pollutants (those for which the location of emission is not an important policy concern) or involving facilities in close proximity to one another.

- Though air quality has certainly improved for most of the covered pollutants, it is virtually impossible to say how much of the improvement can be attributed to the emissions trading programme. The emissions trading programme complements the traditional regulatory approach, rather than replaces it. Therefore, while it can claim to have hastened compliance with the basic provisions of the act and in some cases to have encouraged improvements beyond the act, improved air quality resulted from the package taken together, rather than from any specific component.

Emissions charges

Emission charges are used in both Europe and Japan, though more commonly to control water pollution than air pollution.[9] Currently effluent charges are being used to control water pollution in France, Italy, Germany, and the Netherlands. In both France and the Netherlands the charges are designed to raise revenue for the purpose of funding activities specifically designed to improve water quality.

In Germany dischargers are required to meet minimum standards of waste water treatment for a number of defined pollutants. Simultaneously a fee is levied on every unit of discharge depending on the quantity and noxiousness of the effluent. Dischargers meeting or exceeding state-of-the-art effluent standards have to pay only half the normal rate.

The Italian effluent charge system was mainly designed to encourage polluters to achieve provisional effluent standards as soon as possible. The charge is nine times higher for firms that do not meet the prescribed standards than for firms that do meet them. This charge system was designed only to facilitate the transition to the prescribed standards so it is scheduled to expire once full compliance has been achieved.[10]

Air pollution emission charges have been implemented by France and Japan. The French air pollution charge was designed to encourage the early adoption of pollution control equipment with the revenues returned to those paying the charge as a subsidy for installing the equipment. In Japan the emission charge is designed to raise revenue to compensate victims of air pollution. The charge rate is determined primarily by the cost of the compensation programme in the previous year and the amount of remaining emissions over which this cost can be applied *pro rata*.

Charges have also been used in Sweden to increase the rate at which consumers would purchase cars equipped with a catalytic converter. Cars not equipped with a catalytic converter were taxed, while new cars equipped with a catalytic converter were subsidized.

While data are limited a few highlights seem clear:

- Economists typically envisage two types of effluent or emissions charges. The first, an efficiency charge, is designed to produce an efficient outcome by forcing the polluter to compensate completely for all damage caused. The second, a cost-effective charge, is designed to achieve a predefined ambient standard at the lowest possible control cost. In practice, few, if any, implemented programmes fit either of these designs.

- Despite being designed mainly to raise revenue, effluent charges have typically improved water quality. Though the improvements in most cases have been small, apparently due to the low level at which the effluent charge rate is set, the Netherlands, with its higher effective rates, reports rather large improvements. Air pollution charges typically have not had much effect on air quality because the rates are too low and, in the case of France, most of the revenue is returned to the polluting sources.
- The revenue from charges is typically earmarked for specific environmental purposes rather than contributed to the general revenue as a means of reducing the reliance on taxes that produce more distortions in resource allocation.
- The Swedish tax on heavily polluting vehicles and subsidy for new low polluting vehicles was very successful in introducing low polluting vehicles into the automobile population at a much faster than normal rate. The policy was not revenue neutral, however, owing to the success of the programme in altering vehicle choices, the subsidy payments greatly exceeded the tax revenue.

FIRST PRINCIPLES

Theory can help us understand the characteristics of these economic approaches in the most favourable circumstances for their use and assist in the process of designing the instruments for maximum effectiveness. Because of the dualistic nature of emission charges and emission reduction credits,[11] implications about emission charges and emissions trading flow from the same body of theory.

Drawing conclusions about either of these approaches from this type of analysis, however, must be done with care because operational versions typically differ considerably from the idealized versions modelled by the theory. For example, not all trades that would be allowed in an ideal emissions trading programme are allowed in the current US emissions trading programme. Similarly the types of emissions charges actually imposed differ considerably from their ideal versions, particularly in the design of the rate structure and the process for adjusting rates over time.

Assuming all participants are cost-minimizers, a 'well-defined' emissions trading or emission charge system could cost-effectively allocate the control responsibility for meeting a predefined pollution target among the various pollution sources despite incomplete information on the control possibilities by the regulatory authorities.[12]

The intuition behind this powerful proposition is not difficult to grasp. Cost-minimizing firms seek to minimize the sum of (a) either ERC acquisition costs or payments of emission charges and (b) control costs. Minimization will occur when the marginal cost of control is set equal to the emission reduction credit price or the emission charge. Since all cost-minimizing sources would choose to control until their marginal control costs were equal to the same price or charge, marginal control costs would be equalized across all discharge points, precisely the condition required for cost-effectiveness.[13]

Emission charges could also sustain a cost effective allocation of the control responsibility for meeting a predefined pollution target, but only if the control authority knew the correct level of the charge to impose or was willing to engage in an iterative trial-and-error process over time to find the correct level. Emissions trading does not face this problem because the price level is established by the market, not the control authority.[14]

Though derived in the rarified world of theory, the practical importance of this theorem should not be underestimated. Economic incentive approaches offer a unique opportunity for regulators to solve a fundamental dilemma. The control authorities' desire to allocate the responsibility for control cost-effectively is inevitably frustrated by a lack of information sufficient to achieve this objective. Economic incentive approaches create a system of incentives in which those who have the best knowledge about control opportunities, the environmental managers for the industries, are encouraged to use that knowledge to achieve environmental objectives at minimum cost. Information barriers do not preclude effective regulation.

What constitutes a 'well-defined' emissions trading or emission charge system depends crucially on the attributes of the pollutant being controlled.[15]

To be consistent with a cost-effective allocation of the control responsibility, the policy instruments would have to be defined in different ways for different types of pollutants. Two differentiating characteristics are of particular relevance. Approaches designed to control pollutants which are uniformly mixed in the atmosphere (such as volatile organic compounds, one type of precursor for ozone information) can be defined simply in terms of a rate of emissions flow per unit time. Economic incentive approaches sharing this design characteristic are called *emission trades* or *emission charges*.

Instrument design is somewhat more difficult when the pollution target being pursued is defined in terms of concentrations measured at a number of specific receptor locations (such as particulates). In this case the cost-effective trade or charge design must take into account the *location* of the emissions (including injection height) as well as the *magnitude* of emissions. As long as the control authorities can define for each emitter a vector of transfer coefficients, which translate the effect of a unit increase of emissions by that emitter into an increase in concentration at each of the affected receptors, receptor-specific trades or charges can be defined which will allocate the responsibility cost-effectively. The design which is consistent with cost-effectiveness in this context is called an *ambient trade* or an *ambient charge*.

Unfortunately, while the design of the ambient ERC is not very complicated,[16] implementing the markets within which these ERCs would be traded is rather complicated. In particular for each unit of planned emissions an emitter would have to acquire separate ERCs for each affected receptor. When the number of receptors is large, the result is a rather complicated set of transactions. Similarly, establishing the correct rate structure for the charges in this context is particularly difficult because the set of charges which will satisfy the ambient air quality constraints is not unique; even a trial-and-error system would not necessarily result in the correct matrix of ambient charges being put into effect.

As long as markets are competitive and transactions costs are low, the trading benchmark in an emissions trading approach does not affect the ultimate cost-effective allocation of control responsibility. When markets are non-competitive or transactions costs are high, however, the final allocation of control responsibility is affected.[17] Emission charge approaches do not face this problem.

Once the control authority has decided how much pollution of each type will be allowed, it must then decide how to allocate the operating permits among the sources. In theory emission reduction credits could either be auctioned off, with the sources purchasing them from the control authority at the market-clearing price, or (as in the US programme) created by the sources as surplus reductions over and above a predetermined set of emission standards. (Because this latter approach favours older sources over newer sources, it is known as 'grandfathering'.) The proposition suggests that either approach will ultimately result in a cost-effective allocation of the control responsibility among the various polluters as long as they are all price-takers, transactions costs are low, and ERCs are fully transferable. Any allocation of emission standards in a grandfathered approach is compatible with cost-effectiveness because the after-market in which firms can buy or sell ERCs corrects any problems with the initial allocation. This is a significant finding because it implies that under the right conditions the control authority can use this initial allocation of emission standards to pursue distributional goals without interfering with cost-effectiveness.

When firms are price-setters rather than price-takers, however, cost-effectiveness will only be achieved if the control authority initially allocates the emission standards so a cost-effective allocation would be achieved even in the absence of any trading. (Implementing this particular allocation would, of course, require regulators to have complete information on control costs for all sources, an unlikely prospect). In this special case cost-effectiveness would be achieved even in the presence of one or more price-setting firms because no trading would take place, eliminating the possibility of exploiting any market power.

For all other emission standard assignments an active market would exist, offering the opportunity for price-setting behaviour. The larger is the deviation of the price setting source's emission standard from its cost-effective allocation, the larger is the deviation of ultimate control costs from the least-cost allocation. When the price-setting source is initially allocated an insufficiently stringent emission standard, it can inflict higher control costs on others by withholding some ERCs from the market. When an excessively stringent emission standard is imposed on a price-setting source, however, it necessarily bears a higher control cost as the means of reducing demand (and, hence, prices) for the ERCs.

Similar problems exist when transactions costs are high. High transactions costs preclude or reduce trading activity by diminishing the gains from trade. When the cost of consummating a transaction exceed its potential gains, the incentive to participate in emissions trading is lost.

LESSONS FROM EMPIRICAL RESEARCH

A vast majority, though not all, of the relevant empirical studies have found the control costs to be substantially higher with the regulatory command-and-control system than the least cost means of allocating the control responsibility.

While theory tells us unambiguously that the command-and-control system will not be cost-effective except by coincidence, it cannot tell us the magnitude of the excess costs. The empirical work cited in Table 21.1 adds the important information that the excess costs are typically very large.[18] This is an important finding because it provides the motivation for introducing a reform programme; the potential social gains (in terms of reduced control cost) from breaking away from the status quo are sufficient to justify the trouble. Although the estimates of the excess costs attributable to a command-and-control system presented in Table 21.1 overstate the cost savings that would be achieved by even an ideal economic incentive approach (a point discussed in more detail below), the general conclusion that the potential cost savings from adopting economic incentive approaches are large seems accurate even after correcting for overstatement.

Economic incentive approaches which raise revenue (charges or auction ERC markets) offer an additional benefit - they allow the revenue raised from these policies to substitute for revenue raised in more traditional ways. Whereas it is well known that traditional revenue-raising approaches distort resource allocation, producing inefficiency, economic incentive approaches enhance efficiency. Some empirical work based on the US economy suggests that substituting economic incentive means of raising revenue for more traditional means could produce significant efficiency gains.[19]

When high degrees of control are necessary, ERC prices or charge levels would be correspondingly high. The financial outlays associated with acquiring ERCs in an auction market or paying charges on uncontrolled emissions would be sufficiently large that sources would typically have lower financial burdens with the traditional command-and-control approach than with these particular economic incentive approaches. Only a 'grandfathered' trading system would guarantee that sources would be no worse off than under the command-and-control system.[20]

Financial burden is a significant concern in a highly competitive global marketplace. Firms bearing large financial burdens would be placed at a competitive disadvantage when forced to compete with firms not bearing those burdens. Their costs would be higher.

From the point of view of the source required to control its emissions, two components of financial burden are significant: *(a)* control costs and *(b)* expenditures on permits or emission charges. While only the former represent real resource costs to society as a whole (the latter are merely transferred from one group in society to another), both represent a financial burden to the source. The empirical evidence suggests that when an auction market is used to distribute ERCs (or, equivalently, when all uncontrolled emissions are subject to an emissions charge), the ERC expenditures (charge outlays) would frequently be larger in magnitude than the control costs; the sources would spend more on ERCs (or pay more in charges) than they would on the control equipment. Under the traditional command-and-control system firms make no financial outlays to the government. Although control costs are necessarily higher with the command-and-control system than with an economic incentive approach, they are not so high as to outweigh the additional financial outlays required in an auction market permit system (or an emissions tax system). For this reason existing sources could be expected vehemently to oppose an auction market or emission charges despite their social appeal, unless the revenue derived is used in a manner which is approved by the sources, and the sources with which it competes are required to absorb similar expenses. When environmental policies are not coordinated across national boundaries, this latter condition would be particularly difficult to meet.

In the absence of either a politically popular way to use the revenue or assurances that competitors will face similar financial burdens, this political opposition could be substantially reduced by grandfathering. Under grandfathering, sources have only to purchase any additional ERCs they may need to meet their assigned emission standard (as opposed to purchasing sufficient ERCs or paying charges to cover all uncontrolled emissions in an auction market). Grandfathering is *de facto* the approach taken in the US emissions trading programme.

Grandfathering has its disadvantages. Because ERCs become very valuable, especially in the face of stringent air quality regulations, sources selling emission

Economic instruments

Table 21.1 Empirical studies of air pollution control.

Study	Pollutants covered	Geographic area	CAC benchmark	Ratio of CAC cost to least cost
Atkinson and Lewis	Particulates	St Louis	SIP regulations	6.00[a]
Roach *et al.*	Sulphur dioxide	Four corners in Utah	SIP regulations Colorado, Arizona, and New Mexico	4.25
Hahn and Noll	Sulphates	Los Angeles	California emission standards	1.07
Krupnick	Nitrogen dioxide	Baltimore	Proposed RACT	5.96[b]
Seskin *et al.*	Nitrogen dioxide regulations	Chicago	Proposed RACT	14.40[b]
McGartland	Particulates	Baltimore	SIP regulations	4.18
Spofford	Sulphur Dioxide	Lower Delaware Valley	Uniform percentage regulations	1.78
	Particulates	Lower Delaware Valley	Uniform percentage regulations	22.0
Harrison	Airport noise	United States	Mandatory retrofit	1.72[c]
Maloney and Yandle	Hydrocarbons	All domestic DuPont plants	Uniform percentage reduction	4.15[d]
Palmer *et al.*	CFC emissions from non-aerosol applications	United States	Proposed standards	1.96

Notes:

CAC = command and control, the traditional regulatory approach.

SIP = state implementation plan.

RACT = reasonably available control technologies, a set of standards imposed on existing sources in non-attainment areas.

[a] Based on a 40 μg/m^3 at worst receptor.

[b] Based on a short-term, one-hour average of 250 μg/m^3.

[c] Because it is a benefit–cost study instead of a cost-effectiveness study, the Harrison comparison of the command-and-control approach with the least-cost allocation involves different benefit levels. Specifically, the benefit levels associated with the least-cost allocation are only 82 per cent of those associated with the command-and-control allocation. To produce cost estimates based on more comparable benefits, as a first approximation the least-cost allocation was divided by 0.82 and the resulting number was compared with the command-and-control cost.

[d] Based on 85 per cent reduction of emissions from all sources.

reduction credits would be able to command very high prices. By placing heavy restrictions on the amount of emissions, the control authority is creating wealth for existing firms *vis-à-vis* new firms.

Although reserving some ERCs for new firms is possible (by assigning more stringent emission standards than needed to reach attainment and using the 'surplus' air quality to create government-held ERCs), this option is rarely exercised in practice. In the United States under the offset policy firms typically have to purchase sufficient ERCs to more than cover all uncontrolled emissions, while existing firms only have to purchase enough to comply with their assigned emission standard. Thus grandfathering imposes a bias against new sources in the sense that their financial burden is greater than that of an otherwise identical existing source, even if the two sources install exactly the same emission control devices. This new source bias could retard the introduction of new facilities and new technologies by reducing the cost advantage of building new facilities which embody the latest innovations.

While it is clear from theory that larger trading areas offer the opportunities for larger potential cost savings in an emissions trading programme, some empirical work suggests that substantial savings can be achieved in emissions trading even when the trading areas are rather small.

The point of this finding is *not* that small trading areas are fine; they do retard progress toward the standard. Rather, when political considerations allow only small trading areas or nothing, emissions trading still can play a significant role.

Sometimes political considerations demand a trading area which is smaller than the ideal design. Whether large trading areas are essential for the effective use of this policy is therefore of some relevance. In general, the larger the trading areas, the larger would be the potential cost savings due to a wider set of cost reduction opportunities that would become available. The empirical question is how sensitive the cost estimates are to the size of the trading areas.

One study of utilities found that even allowing a plant to trade among discharge points within that plant could save from 30 to 60 per cent of the costs of complying with new sulphur oxide reduction regulations, compared to a situation where no trading whatsoever was permitted.[21] Expanding the trading possibilities to other utilities within the same state permitted a further reduction of 20 per cent, while allowing interstate trading permitted another 15 per cent reduction in costs. If this study is replicated in other circumstances, it would appear that even small trading areas offer the opportunity for significant cost reduction.[22]

Although only a few studies of the empirical impact of market power on emissions trading have been accomplished, their results are consistent with a finding that market power does not seem to have a large effect on regional control costs in most realistic situations.[23]

Even in areas having especially stringent controls, the available evidence suggests that price manipulation is not a serious problem. In an auction market the price-setting source reduces its financial burden by purchasing fewer ERCs in order to drive the price down. To compensate for the smaller number of ERCs purchased, the price-setting source must spend more on controlling its own pollution, limiting the gains from price manipulation. Although these actions could have a rather large impact on *regional financial burden,* they would under normal circumstances have a rather small effect on *regional control costs.* Estimates typically suggest that control costs would rise by less than 1 per cent if market power were exercised by one or more firms.

It should not be surprising that price manipulation could have rather dramatic effects on regional financial burden in an auction market, since the cost of *all* ERCs is affected, not merely those purchased by the price-setting source. The perhaps more surprising result is that control costs are quite insensitive to price-setting behaviour. This is due to the fact that the only control cost change is the net difference between the new larger control burden borne by the price searcher and the correspondingly smaller burden borne by the sources having larger-than-normal allocations of permits. Only the costs of the marginal units are affected.

Within the class of grandfathered distribution rules, some emission standard allocations create a larger potential for strategic price behaviour than others. In general the larger the divergence between the control responsibility assigned to the price-searching source by the emission standards and the cost-effective allocation of control responsibility, the larger the potential for market power. When allocated too little responsibility by the control authority, price-searching firms can exercise power on the selling side of the market, and when allocated too much, they can exercise power on the buying side of the market.

According to the existing studies it takes a rather considerable divergence from the cost-effective allocation of control responsibility to produce much difference in regional control costs. In practice the deviations from the least cost allocation caused by market power pale in comparison to the much larger potential cost reductions achievable by implementing emissions trading.[24]

LESSONS FROM IMPLEMENTATION

Though the number of transactions consummated under the Emissions Trading Program has been large, it has been smaller than expected. Part of this failure to fulfill expectations can be explained as the result of unrealistically inflated expectations. More restrictive regulatory decisions than expected and higher than expected transaction costs also bear some responsibility.

The models used to calculate the potential cost savings were not (and are not) completely adequate guides to reality. The cost functions in these models are invariably *ex ante* cost functions. They implicitly assume that the modelled plant can be built from scratch and can incorporate the best technology. In practice, of course, many existing sources cannot retrofit these technologies and therefore their *ex post* control options are much more limited than implied by the models.

The models also assume all trades are multilateral and are simultaneously consummated, whereas actual trades are usually bilateral and sequential. The distinction is important for non-uniformly mixed pollutants;[25] bilateral trades frequently are constrained by regulatory concerns about decreasing air quality at the site of the acquiring source. Because multilateral trades would typically incorporate compensating reductions coming from other nearby sources, these concerns normally do not arise when trades are multilateral and simultaneous. In essence the models implicitly assume an idealized market process, which is only remotely approximated by actual transactions.

In addition some non-negligible proportion of the expected cost savings recorded by the models for non-uniformly mixed pollutants is attributable to the substantially larger amounts of emissions allowed by the modelled permit equilibrium.[26] For example, the cost estimates imply that the control authority is allowed to arrange the control responsibility in any fashion that satisfies the ambient air quality standards. In practice the models allocate more uncontrolled emissions to sources with tall stacks because those emissions can be exported. Exported emissions avoid control costs without affecting the readings at the local monitors. That portion of the cost savings estimated by the models in Table 21.1 which is due to allowing increased emissions is not acceptable to regulators. Some recent work has suggested that the benefits received from the additional emission control required by the command-and-control approach may be justified by the net benefits received.[27] The regulatory refusal to allow emission increases was apparently consistent with efficiency,[28] but it was not consistent with the magnitude of cost savings anticipated by the models.

277

Certain types of trades assumed permissible by the models are prohibited by actual trading rules. New sources, for example, are not allowed to satisfy the New Source Performance Standards (which imply a particular control technology) by choosing some less stringent control option and making up the difference with acquired emission reduction credits; they must install the degree of technological control necessary to meet the standard. Typically this is the same technology used by EPA to define the standard in the first place.

A lot of uncertainty is associated with emission reduction credit transactions since they depend so heavily on administrative action. All trades must be approved by the control authorities. If the authorities are not co-operative or at least consistent, the value of the created emission reduction credits could be diminished or even destroyed.

For non-uniformly mixed pollutants, trades between geographically separated sources will only be approved after dispersion modelling has been accomplished by the applicants. Not only is this modelling expensive, it frequently ends up raising questions which ultimately lead to the transaction being denied. Few trades requiring this modelling have been consummated.

Trading activity has also been inhibited by the paucity of emission banks. The US system allows states to establish emission banks, but does not require them to do so. As of 1986 only seven of the fifty states had established these banks. For sources in the rest of the states the act of creating emission credits is undervalued because the credits cannot be legally held for future use. The supply of emission reduction credits is hence less than would be estimated by the models.

The Emissions Trading Program seems to have worked particularly well for trades involving uniformly mixed pollutants and for trades of non-uniformly mixed pollutants involving contiguous discharge points.

It is not surprising that most consummated trades have been internal (where the buyer and sellers share a common corporate parent) rather than external. Not only are the uncertainties associated with inter-firm transfers avoided, but most internal trades involve contiguous facilities. Trades between contiguous facilities do not trigger a requirement for dispersion modelling.[29]

It is also not surprising that the plurality of consummated trades involves volatile organic compounds which are uniformly mixed pollutants. Since dispersion modelling is not required for uniformly mixed pollutants even when the trading sources are somewhat distant from one another, trades involving these pollutants are cheaper to consummate. Additionally emissions trades involving uniformly mixed pollutants do not jeopardize local air quality since the location of the emissions is not a matter of policy consequence.

The establishment of the Emissions Trading Program has encouraged technological progress in pollution control. Although generally the degree of progress has been modest, it has been more dramatic in areas where emission reductions have been sufficiently stringent as to restrict the availability of emission reduction credits created by more traditional means.[30]

Theory would lead us to expect more technological progress with emissions trading than with a command-and-control policy because it changes the incentives so drastically. Under a command-and-control approach technological changes discovered by the control authority typically lead to more stringent standards (and higher costs) for the sources. Sources have little incentive to innovate and a good deal of incentive to hide potential innovations from the control authority. With emissions trading, on the other hand, innovations allowing excess reductions create saleable emission reduction credits.

The evidence suggests that the expectations based on this theory have been borne out to a limited degree in the operating programme. The most prominent example of technological change has been the substitution of water-based solvents for solvents containing volatile organic compounds. Though somewhat more expensive, this substitution made economic sense once the programme was introduced.

It should probably not be surprising that the number of new innovations stimulated by the programme is rather small. As long as cheaper ways of creating credits within existing processes (fuel substitution, for example) are available, it would be unreasonable to expect large investments in new technologies with unproven reliabilities. On the other hand, as the degree of control rises and the supply of readily available credits dries up, the demand for new technologies would be expected to rise as well. This expectation seems to have been borne out in those areas where unusually low air quality or stringent regulatory rules have served to limit the available credits.[31]

This is an important point. Those who fail to consider the dynamic advantages of an economic incentive approach sometimes suggest that if few credits would be traded, implementing a system of this type has no purpose. In fact it has a substantial purpose – the encouragement of new technologies to meet the increasingly stringent standards.

Introducing the Emissions Trading Program has provided an opportunity to control sources which can reduce emissions relatively cheaply, but which under the traditional policy were under-regulated due either to their financially precarious position or the fact that they were not subject to regulation.[32] Due to the social distress caused by any resulting unemployment, the control authorities and the courts are understandably reluctant to enforce stringent emission standards against firms which would not be able to pass higher costs on to customers without considerable loss of production. Since many of these sources could control emissions at a lower marginal cost than other sources, their political immunity from control makes regional control costs higher than necessary; other sources have to control their own emissions to a higher degree (at a higher marginal cost) to compensate.

Due to its ability to separate the issue of who pays for the reduction from the issue of which discharge points are to be controlled, the emissions trading programme provides a way to secure those low cost reductions. The command-and-control policy would assign, as normal, a very low (perhaps zero) emission reduction to any previously unregulated firm. Once emissions trading had been established, however, it would be in the interest of this firm to control emissions further, selling the resulting emission reduction credits. As long as the revenues from the sale at least covered the cost, this transaction could profit, or at least not hurt, the seller. Because these reductions could be achieved at a lower cost than ratcheting up the degree of control on already heavily controlled sources, non-immune sources would find purchasing the credits cheaper than controlling their own emissions to a higher degree. Everyone benefits from controlling these previously under-regulated sources. Another unique attribute of an emissions trading approach is the capability it offers sources for leasing credits.[33]

Leasing offers an enormously useful degree of flexibility which is not available with other policy approaches to pollution control. The usefulness of leasing derives from the fact that some sources, utilities in particular, have patterns of

279

emission that vary over time while allowable emissions remain constant. In a typical situation, for example, suppose an older utility would, in the absence of control, be emitting heavily. In the normal course of a utility expansion cycle the older plant would subsequently experience substantially reduced emissions when the utility constructed a new plant and shifted a major part of the load away from the older plant to the new plant. Ultimately growth in demand on the system would increase the emissions again for the older plant as its capacity would once again be needed. The implication of this temporal pattern is that during the middle period, as its own emissions fell well below allowable emissions, this utility could lease excess emission credits to another facility, recalling them as its own need rose with demand growth. Indeed one empirical study of the pattern of the utility demand for and supply of acid rain reduction credits over time suggests that leasing is a critical component of any cost-effective control strategy, a component that neither the traditional approach nor emission charges can offer.[34]

Leasing also provides a way for about-to-be-retired sources to participate in the reduction programme. Under the traditional approach, once the deadline for compliance had been reached the utility would either have to retire the unit early or to install expensive control equipment which would be rendered useless once the unit was retired. By leasing credits for the short period to retirement, the unit could remain in compliance without taking either of those drastic steps; it would, however, be sharing in the cost of installing the extra equipment in the leasing utility. Leased credits facilitate an efficient transition into the new regime of more stringent controls.

Unless the process to determine the level of an effluent or emissions charge includes some automatic means of temporal adjustment, the tendency is for the real rate (adjusted for inflation) to decline over time.[35] This problem is particularly serious in areas with economic growth where increasing real rates would be the desired outcome.

In contrast to emissions trading where ERC prices respond automatically to changing market conditions, emission charges have to be determined by an administrative process. When the function of the charge is to raise revenue for a particular purpose, charge rates will be determined by the costs of achieving that purpose; when the costs of achieving the purpose rise, the level of the charge must rise to secure the additional revenue.[36]

Sometimes that process produces an unintended dynamic. In Japan, for example, the charge is calculated on the basis of the amount of compensation paid to victims of air pollution in the previous year. While the amount of compensation has been increasing, the amount of emissions (the base to which the charge is applied) has been decreasing. As a result, unexpectedly high charge rates are necessary in order to raise sufficient revenue for the compensation system.

In countries where the tax revenue feeds into the general budget, increases in the level of the charge require a specific administrative act. Evidently it is difficult to raise these rates in practice, since charges have commonly even failed to keep pace with inflation, much less growth in the number of sources. The unintended result is eventual environmental deterioration.

CONCLUDING COMMENTS
Our experience with economic incentive programmes has demonstrated that they have had, and can continue to have, a positive role in environmental policy in the future. I would submit the issue is no longer *whether* they have a role to play, but

rather *what kind* of role they should play. The available experience with operating versions of these programmes allows us to draw some specific conclusions which facilitate defining the boundaries for the optimal use of economic incentive approaches in general and for distinguishing the emissions trading and emission charges approaches in particular.

Emissions trading integrates particularly smoothly into any policy structure which is based either directly (through emission standards) or indirectly (through mandated technology or input limitations) on regulating emissions. In this case emission limitations embedded in the operating licences can serve as the trading benchmark if grandfathering is adopted.

Emissions charges work particularly well when transactions costs associated with bargaining are high. It appears that much of the trading activity in the United States has involved large corporations. Emissions trading is probably not equally applicable to large and small pollution sources. The transaction costs are sufficiently high that only large trades can absorb them without jeopardizing the gains from trade. For this reason charges seem a more appropriate instrument when sources are individually small, but numerous (such as residences or automobiles). Charges also work well as a device for increasing the rate of adoption of new technologies and for raising revenue to subsidize environmentally benign projects.

Emissions trading seems to work especially well for uniformly mixed pollutants. No diffusion modelling is necessary and regulators do not have to worry about trades creating 'hot spots' or localized areas of high pollution concentration. Trades can be on a one-to-one basis.

Because emissions trading allows the issue of who will pay for the control to be separated from who will install the control, it introduces an additional degree of flexibility. This flexibility is particularly important in non-attainment areas since marginal control costs are so high. Sources which would not normally be controlled because they could not afford to implement the controls without going out of business, can be controlled with emissions trading. The revenue derived from the sale of emission reduction credits can be used to finance the controls effectively preventing bankruptcy.

Because it is quantity based, emissions trading also offers a unique possibility for leasing. Leasing is particularly valuable when the temporal pattern of emissions varies across sources. As discussed above, this appears generally to be the case with utilities. When a firm plans to shut down one plant in the near future and to build a new one, leasing credits is a vastly superior alternative to the temporary installation of equipment in the old plant which would be useless when the plant was retired. The useful life of this temporary control equipment would be wastefully short.

We have also learned that ERC transactions have higher transactions costs than we previously understood. Regulators must validate every trade. When non-uniformly mixed pollutants are involved, the transactions costs associated with estimating the air quality effects are particularly high. Delegating responsibility for trade approval to lower levels of government may in principle speed up the approval process, but unless the bureaucrats in the lower level of government support the programme the gain may be negligible.

Emissions trading places more importance on the operating permits and emissions inventories than other approaches. To the extent those are deficient the potential for trades that protect air quality may be lost. Firms which have actual levels of emissions substantially below allowable emissions find themselves with a trading opportunity which, if exploited, could degrade air quality. The trading benchmark has to be defined carefully.

There can be little doubt that the emissions trading programme in the US has improved upon the command-and-control programme that preceded it. The documented cost savings are large and the flexibility provided has been important. Similarly emissions charges have achieved their own measure of success in Europe. To be sure the programmes are far from perfect, but the flaws should be kept in perspective. In no way should they overshadow the impressive accomplishments. Although economic incentive approaches lose their Utopian lustre upon closer inspection, they have nonetheless made a lasting contribution to environmental policy.

The role for economic incentive approaches should grow in the future if for no other reason than the fact that the international pollution problems which are currently commanding centre-stage fall within the domains where economic incentive policies have been most successful. Significantly many of the problems of the future, such as reducing tropospheric ozone, preventing stratospheric ozone depletion, moderating global warming, and increasing acid rain control, involve pollutants that can be treated as uniformly mixed, facilitating the use of economic incentives. In addition, larger trading areas facilitate greater cost reductions than smaller trading areas. This also augers well for the use of emissions trading as part of the strategy to control many future pollution problems because the natural trading areas are all very large indeed. Acid rain, stratospheric ozone depletion, and greenhouse gases could (indeed should!) involve trading areas that transcend national boundaries. For greenhouse and ozone depletion gases, the trading areas should be global in scope. Finally, it seems clear that the pivotal role of carbon dioxide in global warming may require some fairly drastic changes in energy use, including changes in personal transportation, and ultimately land use patterns. Some form of charges could play an important role in facilitating this transformation.

We live in an age when the call for tighter environmental controls intensifies with each new discovery of yet another injury modern society is inflicting on the planet. But resistance to additional controls is also growing with the recognition that compliance with each new set of controls is more expensive than the last. While economic incentive approaches to environmental control offer no panacea, they frequently do offer a practical way to achieve environmental goals more flexibly and at lower cost than more traditional regulatory approaches. That is a compelling virtue.

NOTES

1. See, for example, Main (1988).
2. See, for example, Stavins (1989).
3. See the various issues in Volume XX of the EDF Letter, a report to members of the Environmental Defense Fund.
4. In the limited space permitted by this paper only a few highlights can be illustrated. All of the details of the proofs and the empirical work can be found in the references listed at the end of the paper. For a comprehensive summary of this work see Tietenberg (1980), Liroff (1980), Bohm and Russell (1985), Tietenberg (1985), Liroff (1986) Dudek and Palmisano (1988), Hahn (1989), Hahn and Hester (1989a and 1989b), and Tietenberg (1989b).
5. The US Clean Air Act (42 U.S.C. 7401–642) was first passed in 1955. The central thrust

of the approach described in this paragraph was initiated by the Clean Air Act Amendments of 1970 with mid-course corrections provided by the Clean Air Act Amendments of 1977.

6. The details of this policy can be found in 'Emissions Trading Policy Statement' 51 *Federal Register* 43829 (4 December 1986).

7. Offsets are also required for major modifications in areas which have attained the standards if the modifications jeopardize attainment.

8. See, for example, Tietenberg (1985), Hahan and Hester (1989a and 1989b), and Dudek and Palmisano (1988).

9. See Anderson (1977), Brown and Johnson (1984), Bressers (1988), Vos (1989), Opschoor and Vos (1989), and Sprenger (1989).

10. The initial deadline for expiration was 1986, but it has since been postponed.

11. Under fairly general conditions any allocation of control responsibility achieved by an emissions trading programme could also be achieved by a suitably designed system of emission charges and vice versa.

12. For the formal demonstration of this proposition see Baumol and Oates (1975), Montgomery (1972), and Tietenberg (1985).

13. It should be noted that while the allocation is cost-effective, it is not necessarily efficient (the amount of pollution indicated by a benefit–cost comparison). It would only be efficient if the predetermined target happened to coincide with the efficient amount of pollution. Nothing guarantees this outcome.

14. See Tietenberg (1988) for a more detailed explanation of this point.

15. For the technical details supporting this proposition see Montgomery (1972), and Tietenberg (1985).

16. Each permit allows the holder to degrade the concentration level at the corresponding receptor by one unit.

17. See Hahn (1984) for the mathematical treatment of this point. Further discussions can be found in Tietenberg (1985) and Misiolek and Elder (1989).

18. A value of 1.0 in the last column of Table 21.1 would indicate that the traditional regulatory approach was cost-effective. A value of 4.0 would indicate that the traditional regulatory approach results in an allocation of the control responsibility which is four times as expensive as necessary to reach the stipulated pollution target.

19. See Terkla (1984).

20. See Atkinson and Tietenberg (1982, 1984), Hahn (1984), Harrison (1983), Krupnick (1986), Lyon (1982), Palmer *et al.* (1980), Roach *et al.* (1981), Seskin *et al.* (1983), and Shapiro and Warhit (1983) for the individual studies, and Tietenberg (1985) for a summary of the evidence.

21. ICF, Inc. (1989).

22. As indicated below, the fact that so many emissions trades have actually taken place within the same plant or among contiguous plants provides some confirmation for this result.

23. For individual studies see de Lucia (1974), Hahn (1984), Stahl, Bergman and Mäler (1988), and Maloney and Yandle (1984). For a survey of the evidence see Tietenberg (1985).

24. Strategic price behaviour is not the only potential source of market power problems. Firms could conceivably use permit markets to drive competitors out of business. See Misiolek and Elder (1989). For an analysis which concludes that this problem is relatively rare and can be dealt with on a case-by-case basis should it arise, see Tietenberg (1985).

25. See Tietenberg and Atkinson (1989) for a demonstration that is an empirically significant point.

26. This is demonstrated in Atkinson and Tietenberg (1987).

27. See Oates, Portney, and McGartland (1988).

28. Not all of the cost savings, of course, are due to the capability to increase emissions. The remaining portion of the savings, which is due to taking advantage of opportunities to

control a given level of emissions at a lower cost, is still substantial and can be captured by a well-designed permit system which does not allow emissions to increase beyond the command-and-control benchmark. See the calculations in Atkinson and Tietenberg (1987).

29. The fact that so many trades have taken place between contiguous discharge points serves as confirmation that substantial savings can be achieved even if the geographic boundaries of the trading area are quite restricted.
30. For more details see Tietenberg (1985), Maleug (1989) and Dudek and Palmisano (1988).
31. For the experience in California see Dudek and Plamisano (1988).
32. See Tietenberg (1985).
33. See Feldman and Raufer (1987) and Tietenberg (1989a).
34. Feldman and Raufer (1987).
35. For further information see Vos (1989) and Sprenger (1989).
36. While it is theoretically possible (depending on the elasticity of demand for pollution abatement) for a rise in the tax to produce less revenue, this has typically not been the case.

REFERENCES

Anderson, F. R. et al. (1977), *Environmental Improvement Through Economic Incentives,* Baltimore, The Johns Hopkins University Press for Resources for the Future, Inc.

Atkinson, S. E. and Lewis D. H. (1974), 'A Cost-Effectiveness Analysis of Alternative Air Quality Control Strategies', *Journal of Environmental Economics and Management,* 1, 237–50.

—— and Tietenberg, T. H. (1982), 'The Empirical Properties of Two Classes of Designs for Transferable Discharge Permit Markets', *Journal of Environmental Economics and Management,* 9, 101–21.

—— (1984), 'Approaches for Reaching Ambient Standards in Non-Attainment Areas: Financial Burden and Efficiency Considerations', *Land Economics,* 60, 148–59.

—— (1987), 'Economic Implications of Emission Trading Rules for Local and Regional Pollutants', *Canadian Journal of Economics,* 20, 370–86.

Baumol, W. J., and Oates, W. E. (1975), *The Theory of Environmental Policy,* Englewood Clifs, N.J., Prentice Hall.

Bohm, P. and Russel, C. (1985), 'Comparative Analysis of Alternative Policy Instruments', in A. V. Knesse and J. L. Sweeney (eds.), *Handbook of Natural Resources and Energy Economics,* Vol. 1, 395–460, Amsterdam, North-Holland.

Bressers, H. T. A. (1988), 'A Comparison of the Effectiveness of Incentives and Directives: The Case of Dutch Water Quality Policy', *Policy Studies Review,* 7, 500–18.

Brown, G. M., Jr. and Johnson, R. W. (1984), 'Pollution Control by Effluent Charges: It Works in the Federal Republic of Germany, Why Not in the United States?', *Natural Resources Journal,* 24, 929–66.

de Lucia, R. J. (1974), *An Evaluation of Marketable Effluent Permit Systems,* Report No. EPA-600/5-74-030 to the US Environmental Protection Agency (September).

Dudek, D. J. and Palmisano, J. (1988), 'Emission Trading: Why is this Throughbred Hobbled?', *Columbia Journal of Environmental Law,* 13, 217–56.

Feldman, S. L. and Raufer, R. K. (1987), *Emissions Trading and Acid Rain Implementing a Market Approach to Pollution Control,* Totowa, N.J., Rowman & Littlefield.

Hahn, R. W. (1984), 'Market Power and Transferable Property Rights', *Quarterly Journal of Economics,* 99, 753–65.

—— (1989), 'Economic Prescriptions for Environmental Problems: How the Patient Followed the Doctor's Orders', *The Journal of Economic Perspectives,* 3, 95–114.

—— and Noll, R. G. (1982), 'Designing a Market for Tradeable Emission Permits', in W. A. Magat (ed.), *Reform of Environmental Regulation,* Cambridge, Mass., Ballinger.

—— and Hester, G. L. (1989a), 'Where Did All the Markets Go? An Analysis of EPA's Emission Trading Program', *Yale Journal of Regulation,* 6, 109–53.

Economic instruments

—— (1989b), 'Marketable Permits: Lessons from Theory and Practice', *Ecology Law Quarterly*, 16, 361–406.

Harrison, D. Jr. (1983), 'Case Study 1: the Regulation of Aircraft Noise', in Thomas C. Schelling (ed.), *Incentives for Environmental Protection*, Cambridge, Mass, MIT Press.

ICF Resources, Inc. (1989), 'Economic, Environmental, and Coal Market Impacts of SO2 Emissions Trading Under Alternative Acid Rain Control Proposals', a report prepared for the Regulatory Innovation Staff, USEPA (March).

Krupnick, A.J. (1986), 'Costs of Alternative Policies for the Control of Nitrogen Dioxide in Baltimore', *Journal of Environmental Economics and Management*, 13, 189–97.

Liroff, R.A. (1980), *Air Pollution Offsets: Trading, Selling and Banking*, Washington, D.C., Conservation Foundation.

—— (1986), *Reforming Air Pollution Regulation: The Toil and Trouble of EPA's Bubble*, Washington D.C., Conservation Foundation.

Lyon, R.M. (1982). 'Auctions and Alternative Procedures for Allocating Pollution Rights', *Land Economics*, 58, 16–32.

McGartland, A.M. (1984), 'Marketable Permit Systems for Air Pollution Control: an Empirical Study', Ph.D. dissertation, University of Maryland.

Main, J. (1988), 'Here Comes the Big Cleanup', *Fortune*, 21 November, 102.

Maleug, David A. (1989), 'Emission Trading and the Incentive to Adopt New Pollution Abatement Technology', *Journal of Environmental Economics and Management*, 16, 52–7.

Maloney, M.T. and Yandle, B. (1984), 'Estimation of the Cost of Air Pollution Control Regulation', *Journal of Environmental Economics and Management*, 11, 244–63.

Misioleck, W.S. and Elder, H.W. (1989), 'Exclusionary Manipulation of Markets for Pollution Rights', *Journal of Environmental Economics and Management*, 16, 156–66.

Montgomery, W. D. (1972), 'Markets in Licences and Efficient Pollution Control Programs', *Journal of Economic Theory*, 5, 395–418.

Oates, W.E., Portney, P.R. and McGartland, A.M. (1988), 'The Net Benefits of Incentive-Based Regulation: The Case of Environmental Standard Setting in the Real World', Resources for the Future Working Paper, December.

Opschoor, J.B. and Vos, H.B. (1989), *The Application of Economic Instruments for Environmental Protection in OECD Countries*, Paris, OECD.

Palmer, A.R. Mooz, W.E. Quinn, T.H. and Wolf, K.A. (1980), *Economic Implications of Regulating Chlorofluorocarbon Emissions from Nonaerosol Applications*, Report No. R-2524-EPA prepared for the US Environmental Protection Agency by the Rand Corporation, June.

Roach F., Kolstad, C., Kneese, A.V., Tobin, R., and Williams, M. (1981), 'Alternative Air Quality Policy Options in the Four Corners Region', *Southwestern Review*, 1, 29–58.

Seskin, E.P., Andeson, R. Jr., and Reid, R.O. (1983), 'An Empirical Analysis of Economic Strategies for Controlling Air Pollution', *Journal of Environmental Economics and Management*, 10, 112–24.

Shapiro, M. and Warhit, E. (1983) 'Marketable Permits: The Case of Chlorofluorocarbons', *Natural Resource Journal*, 23, 577–91.

Spofford, W. O., Jr. (1984), 'Efficiency Properties of Alternative Source Control Policies for Meeting Ambient Air Quality Standards: An Empirical Application to the Lower Delaware Valley', Discussion paper D-118, Washington D.C., Resources for the Future, November.

Sprenger, R. U. (1989), 'Economic Incentives in Environmental Policies: The Case of West Germany', a paper presented at the Symposium on Economic Instruments in Environmental Protection Polices, Stockholm, Sweden (June).

Stahl, I., Bergman, L, and Mäler, K. G. (1988), 'An Experimental Game on Marketable Emission Permits for Hydro-carbons in the Gothenburg Area', Research Paper No. 6359, Stockholm School of Economics (December).

Stavins, R. N. (1989), 'Harnessing Market Forces to Protect the Environment', *Environment*, 31, 4–7, 28–35.

Terkla, D. (1984), 'The Efficiency Value of Effluent Tax Revenues', *Journal of Environmental Economics and Management,* 11, 107–23.

Tietenberg, T. H. (1980), 'Transferable Discharge Permits and the Control of Stationary Source Air Pollution: A Survey and Synthesis', *Land Economics,* 56, 391–416.

—— (1985), *Emissions Trading: An Exercise in Reforming Pollution Policy,* Washington, D.C., Resources for the Future.

—— (1988), *Environmental and Natural Resource Economics,* 2nd edn., Glenview Illinois, Scott, Foresman and Company.

—— (1989*a*), 'Acid Rain Reduction Credits', *Challenge,* 32, 25–9.

—— (1989*b*), 'Marketable Permits in the US: A Decade of Experience', in Karl W. Roskamp (ed.), *Public Finance and the Performance of Enterprises,* Detroit, MI, Wayne State University Press.

—— and Atkinson, S. E. (1989), ' Bilateral, Sequential Trading and the Cost-Effectiveness of the Bubble Policy', Colby College Working Paper (August).

Vos, H. B. (1989), 'The Application and Efficiency of Economic Instruments: Experiences in OECD Member Countries', a paper presented at the Symposium on Economic Instruments in Environmental Protection Policies, Stockholm, Sweden (June).

PART 4

Environment and sustainable development

Chapter 22

Criteria for sustainable agricultural development

A. Markandya

This paper is drawn from a longer paper entitled, 'Criteria, Instruments and Tools for Sustainable Agricultural Development' which was prepared by the author for the FAO/Netherlands Conference on Agriculture and the Environment, in 's-Hertogenbosch, The Netherlands, 15-19 April, 1991. Particular thanks are due to the Legal Department, to the Policy Analysis Division and to the Nutrition Division of FAO, and to the participants of a preparatory seminar for useful comments and written contributions that have improved the final version. Needless to say none of them are responsible for any errors that remain.

INTRODUCTION
As its title indicates, this paper is concerned with providing a consistent analysis of what constitutes sustainable agricultural development and how it can be brought about by appropriate economic, legal and social policies. It is *not* a detailed evaluation of the economic and environmental impacts of agricultural policy in developing countries. Nor does it provide a comprehensive review of all instruments that impact on the agricultural sector – taxes, land reform policies, pricing policies, macroeconomic policies and so on. Instead it concentrates on the notion of *sustainability* and *sustainable development* and how they relate to the agricultural sector. From the concept of sustainability one can identify some key general policy reforms and actions that are necessary to achieve that goal. These relate to *how* decisions are made and the framework within which they are made, rather than to detailed prescriptions for policy in each sector.

Sustainability and sustainable development
The World Commission on Environment and Development defined Sustainable Development as 'development that meets the needs for the present without compromising the ability of future generations to meet their own needs'.[1] This 'definition', which incidentally leaves the meaning of the word 'development' undefined, brings out the notion that the process of improving present living standards should not be at the expense of the living standards of the future. At one level this must be regarded as a universally acceptable proposition – who would be willing to recommend a development path that guaranteed lower living standards to future generations? However, at a deeper level it is the trade-off of present against future welfare that is being debated here. Should a society be willing to accept lower welfare now, so that future generations can enjoy a permanently higher welfare and what exactly is the trade-off? Or how does one trade-off the possibility of a slightly lower welfare in the future against the certainty of higher welfare now? Growth models in economics have long been concerned with such questions. What the concept of sustainable development

does is to place a limit on that kind of 'trading-off'. It states that society should never be willing to countenance a policy which implies a decline in living standards in the future. In that sense it is a non-trivial proposition.

As with most concepts, it is not the broad term that is most informative or useful but its *operational content*. Although definitions of sustainability abound[2], there are very few operational ones that would help guide policy in the direction of sustainable development. If living standards are not to decline over time, future generations must have access to as effective a resource base as present generations. But the 'effectiveness' of a resource base depends on technology and that is an unknown as far as the future is concerned. It also depends on how the components of the resource base complement each other in providing the needs and wants of future generations. These components include man-made capital, exhaustible resources and renewable resources. If future generations are left with a total capital stock that is valued, in money terms, as much as the present one, is that enough, independent of how that stock is made up?

These issues are at the heart of deriving an operational definition of sustainable development. There are problems associated with uncertainty and with the complementarity of man-made and environmental capital. Many environmental economists would be unhappy with a working definition of sustainable development that translated itself as saying only that the *total* value of the capital stock must not decline over time. Their main concerns would be that the valuation of the environmental capital would be inadequate to ensure it sufficient importance in the make up of the total. Furthermore, they would argue that many components of the environmental capital stock have a natural limited capacity *which must not be exceeded.* If it is, the damage done would be very large, as ecosystems fall apart and habitats are destroyed. One way in which these concerns might be incorporated into an operational definition is to derive, in addition to a value of the capital stock a set of indicators of environmental resources, the use of which must not be exceeded at any time. Such indicators could be developed using notions of discontinuity in the impacts of resource use and economic activity on the environment. No formal definition exists of such a notion but many of the ideas expressed in recent work are consistent with such a definition. They are discussed later in this report.

It is true to say that there is no agreed operational definition of sustainable development at present. Apart from indicating a preference for conservation, and being against the destruction of natural habitats, it would appear then to have little to offer. However, individuals have proposed a number of *working rules* or policies that they argue are essential if such development is to be achieved. Of these, three are singled out as being important in the context of this discussion. One is to do with *equity*. It is argued that a declining and degraded natural resource base is more likely to result if the interests and needs of the poorest sections of poor societies are not satisfied. Hence sustainable development requires, 'help for the very poor because they are left with no option other than to destroy their environment'.[3] The linkage between poverty and the environment, however, is not as clear as is implied by that statement and there is some evidence to indicate that the role of equity as a *means* of achieving sustainability might be an inappropriate focus of policy. This question is taken up later when policies for sustainable development are discussed.

A second working rule for sustainable development is that of *resilience,* or the capacity of a system to maintain its structure and patterns of behaviour in the face of external disturbance. This requires an ability to adapt and is distinguished from ecological stability, which refers to the capacity of a system to maintain its equilibrium in response to normal fluctuations in the environment. The concept is of particular relevance to agriculture where it is used to define the sustainability of an agricultural system as its ability to maintain its productivity in the face of stress or shock. As Conway and Barbier state: 'stress may be growing salinity, or erosion . . . A major event such as a new pest or a rare drought or a sudden massive increase in input prices would constitute a shock'[4]. If such systems lose their resilience they are rendered more susceptible to other shocks, and hence it is considered a necessary requirement of sustainable development that agro–eco-systems maintain their resilience.

A third working rule is based on the notion of *efficiency* in the use of resources. Although many definitions of sustainable development do not directly address this issue, it follows from the fact that what is being pursued is sustainable *development*.[5] Development implies rising living standards, and the policies that are to be pursued have to be consistent with achieving the greatest improvements in living standards, subject to whatever constraints the sustainability criterion imposes. There are a number of models of great sophistication that define various criteria an economy should seek to maximise over time, and that characterise the path that an economy would take if it were to achieve those objectives.[6] They operate at a high level of abstraction and do not have any direct *policy guidelines* that can be used in the context of this study but it is clear that, whatever the objective function, the pursuit of sustainable development will require an efficient use of existing natural resources. By efficient is meant that the greatest value must be obtained from any given input. To achieve this objective policy-makers will have to use a variety of quite complex allocative mechanisms, including prices, taxes and other fiscal controls. They will also have to regulate resource use with a greater appreciation of the benefits and costs of the regulations.

In order to achieve these three working definitions of sustainable agricultural development, three broad areas of action can be identified – those of *valuation, regulation and monitoring*. The first is to value natural resources correctly. Such valuations should include all the services performed by them, including those that do not have any cash flows associated with them or that do not pass through any organised market. Doing this provides the basis of ensuring that key elements in the natural resource and environmental makeup are at least given due weight in the kinds of agricultural practices that are carried out. The valuation process draws on an agricultural, scientific and socioeconomic database, and in turn feeds into two regulatory activities that constitute the second broad area: pricing and investment analysis. On the pricing side it allows decisions on pricing, taxation and subsidies and other instruments to be taken in a more rational manner. On the investment side it feeds into the project appraisal activities that determine how capital funds are allocated between development activities, and between development activities and others related to environmental protection and conservation.

The right economic valuations are necessary, but they are not sufficient to ensure sustainable development. In addition, the appropriate legal and social framework has to be in place. This third broad area or regulation requires a careful evaluation of how and why existing systems have evolved and what the direct and indirect impacts of attempting them might be. The economic and the social and legal policies need to act together to ensure a more sustainable resource use.

A third area, related to the first, is that of environmental accounting or monitoring. As was pointed out earlier, at least one definition of sustainable development required that the future should not be left with a smaller resource base than the present. Following on from that is the notion that per capita consumption (as a measure of living standards) should not decline over time. This can be measured using a notion of net sustainable income but requires the national accounting framework to be adapted to take account of environmental and natural resources that are not normally valued in the national accounting framework. But national accounting systems are not only based on monetary values. They also look at the *physical* stocks of resources and their movement over time. In this respect they can be used as part of a set of sustainability indicators, picking up the issues that valuations of resources do not (and cannot) always address.

Figure 22.1 shows these broad policy areas and their relationships to each other and to the pursuit of a policy of sustainable development. Much of the discussion on this subject can be viewed in terms of these components, and in the way in which they are linked together.

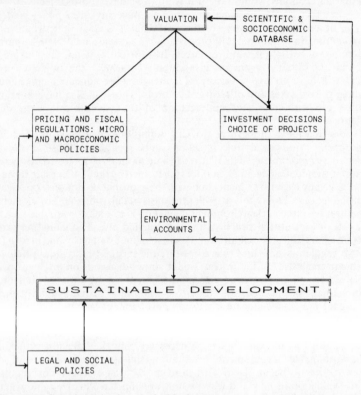

Figure 22.1 Broad policies for sustainable development: a schematic representation.

NOTES

1. World Commission on Environment and Development, *Our Common Future* (London, Oxford University Press, 1987). This document goes on to offer an 'operational definition' of sustainable development that is much along the lines developed in this paper (see p. 46 of that report and note 2 below).
2. In Pearce, Markandya and Barbier there is a survey of definitions of sustainable development, and about twenty-four are judged as worthy of inclusion. Of course there is some overlap, and they operate in different contexts, but it does indicate a proliferation that needs to be reduced. Pearce, D., A Markandya and E. Barbier, *Blueprint for a Green Economy* (London, Earthscan Publications, 1989).
3. Tolba, M., *Sustainable Development – Constraints and Opportunities* (London, Butterworth, 1987). What is at issue is not so much equity in its broadest sense, but poverty, more narrowly defined.
4. Conway, G. R. and E. B Barbier, *After the Green Revolution: Sustainable Agriculture for Development* (London, Earthscan, 1989).
5. In fact it is included in the definition of sustainable development by Goodland and Ledec which states, 'Sustainable Development is a pattern of social and structural economic transformations (i.e. development) which *optimizes* the economic and other societal benefits available in the present without jeopardizing the likely potential for similar benefits in the future', from FAO, *'The State of Food and Agriculture 1989'*, Rome. (author's emphasis).
6. Such models have been surveyed by R. Solow, 'On the Intergenerational Allocation of Natural Resources', *Scandinavian Journal of Economics,* 88, pp. 141–149 (1986). The arguments have recently been taken further in K-G. Maler, 'Sustainable Development', mimeo., The World Bank (1989) and E. Barbier and A. Markandya, 'The Conditions for Achieving Environmentally Sustainable Development', *European Economic Review,* 34, pp. 659–669 (1990). The term 'development' here incidentally is more general than just economic growth and should not be confused with the latter. For details on the distinction as it applies in this case see Pearce, Markandya and Barbier (1989 op. cit.)
7. The term 'pricing' is used here to cover all fiscal instruments that might be employed to influence the pattern and level of use of a particular resource. These could include taxes, subsidies, permits, etc.

Chapter 23

Allocation, distribution and scale as determinants of environmental degradation: case studies of Haiti, El Salvador and Costa Rica

George Foy and Herman Daly

CONCEPTS AND THEORY

INTRODUCTION

This study identifies, classifies, and evaluates critical environmental problems in selected Latin American countries (Haiti, El Salvador and Cost Rica) in order to promote sustainable development strategies. The selection of three small countries as the initial set was purposeful. Small countries reach certain ecological limits sooner than the large ones and offer an early warning system for dangers to come. In particular, Haiti and El Salvador stand as warnings both to large countries (such as Brazil) and to relatively successful small countries such as Costa Rica.

The classification of environmental problems will be in terms of three related, but conceptually distinct causes. First, environmental problems may be caused by a misallocation of resources due to government policy or market failure. Second, environmental problems may be caused by maldistribution of resources such as arable land. Unequal distributions limit individual options and have consequences for political participation which in turn affects the state of the environment. Third, environmental problems may be caused by too great a total human load on the regenerative and assimilative capacities of a country's environment. This is a macro level problem of total human resource use relative to the carrying capacity of the environment, which we refer to as "scale".

Scale and carrying capacity are closely related in that scale is the measure of the load that is being carried, and is judged large or small in relation to carrying capacity. Carrying capacity is not static. It can be increased by investment and technology, and decreased by consumption of capital. Prudent policy seeks to expand carrying capacity *before* expanding scale. Too often, however, scale expands ahead of carrying capacity thereby diminishing it in the next period. For a single nation carrying capacity may be defined to include the ability to import vital goods and services from other countries, as long as these goods and services can be paid for by current exports. Trade may loosen, but cannot remove the constraints of carrying capacity. It also imposes some conditions of complementarity on the trading partners – conditions that must be consistent with the technical complementarity between natural and manmade capital.

Our classification is based on the following considerations. The satisfaction of human wants derives ultimately from the environment, either indirectly by the transformation of raw materials into commodities, or directly as a source of life-support services and enjoyments unmediated by production and exchange of commodities. Historically economic development has been characterized by increasing the share of the environment devoted to indirect use, and consequently diminishing the share remaining for direct use. In the light of our findings we are led to conclude that future development must be characterized more by enhancing and restoring direct uses, while intensifying the quality (rather than expanding the quantity) of indirect uses. In our terminology scale expansion implies more indirect uses and less direct uses of the environment; more manmade capital and less natural capital, an expansion of the human presence within the overall ecosystem.

Natural capital
Natural capital can be divided into three types:

(a) marketable nonrenewable natural capital (e.g. petroleum)
(b) marketable renewable natural capital (e.g. farmland)
(c) nonmarketable renewable natural capital (e.g. wildlands, watersheds).

Due to the importance of renewable resources in Latin American countries, this study will consider category (a) only in so far as it affects the renewable resources. Exhaustible capital is not sustainable by definition, but the other types are if managed properly. In addition to primary products such as food and lumber, natural capital yields a flow of services such as watershed stabilization, soil protection, climate maintenance, chemical cycling, breakdown of pollutants, and recycling of waste. Some types of natural capital such as undiscovered species have potential for many future economic services.

A further reason for focusing on renewable natural capital is that it offers the only long run basis for sustainable development. Nonrenewable natural capital can over the long run be converted into renewable natural capital ("sembrar el petroleo"), but only if the renewable resource base itself is not being mined. An ingenious method for calculating the proper division of receipts from a nonrenewable resource into an income component (available for consumption) and a capital component (to be invested ultimately in renewables so as to sustain the income component indefinitely) has been worked out by Salah El Serafy of the World Bank (see reference 147).

Environmental problems
Environmental problem is defined as a degradation of natural capital and consequent decrease or loss of its service flows due to abuse/reduction of either the assimilative capacity or the regenerative capacity of the environment. Environmental problems vary in the degree of urgency depending on the tradeoffs involved and the reversibility of action as new knowledge becomes available. Some natural capital losses may be more than compensated in terms of new manmade capital. However, other natural capital losses may be much larger than the corresponding gains in manmade capital. Critical environmental problems involve large losses of natural capital with accompanying losses in vital nonmarket service flows and in the value of complementary manmade capital.

Sustainable development and environmental problems

Development is a process which raises income flows through quantitative increases or qualitative improvements in the capital stock; in the past, the emphasis has been on the manmade capital stock. The present emphasis on "sustainable development"[1] is due to the realization that the long term viability of development is not an automatic by-product of attempts to increase the manmade capital stock of a country. What appears to be development may be illusory short term gains derived from depletion of natural capital. A policy of maintaining intact the sum of natural and manmade capital might be referred to as "weak sustainability". It assumes a high degree of substitutability between the two classes of capital. "Strong sustainability" requires that both manmade and natural capital be maintained intact separately, on the assumption that they are more complements than substitutes. If they are complements then the one in shortest supply will be the effective limit on development. In the past manmade capital was the limitative factor; in the future natural capital may be limitative. This shift seems to be well advanced in the countries studied.

The Brundtland Commission defines sustainable development as a process which "meets the needs of the present without compromising the ability of future generations to meet their own needs".[2] The time horizon of sustainable development is on the order of many human generations, e.g. hundreds of years. Given this long run concern and the necessity of some level of natural capital for economic systems, sustainable development implies that human economic activity must continuously respect "certain rules of the game, notably the physical requirements for the perpetual use of resources such as land, water, biomass and the assimilative capacity of the environment".[3] The Brundtland definition of sustainable development and its consequences for the preservation of renewable natural capital are in agreement with environmental policies of the World Bank.[4]

Allocation, distribution and scale further defined

Allocation refers to the division of a given flow of resources among alternative uses. Allocations are efficient or inefficient. An optimal (most efficient) allocation is one in which returns per dollar are equal in all sectors (alternative uses) when prices reflect full marginal opportunity costs.

Distribution refers to the division of income and wealth among individuals or families. Distributions are by ethical criteria just or unjust, or by statistical criteria skewed or even. Resource inputs are *allocated* among alternative uses; product output is *distributed* among different people.

Scale refers to the physical dimensions of the economy relative to the ecosystem of which it is a part – not the scale of a single enterprise, but of the set of all enterprises and households in the economy. Scale is measured by population times per capita resource use, which is equal to the total flow of resources through the economic subsystem, beginning with depletion and ending with pollution. A given scale is ecologically sustainable or unsustainable. An optimal scale is one at which (falling) marginal benefits of further expansion are equal to (rising) marginal costs. Since we do not measure the costs and benefits of aggregate expansion the concept of optimum scale of the whole economy is for now a formalism. One attribute of an optimal scale is that it be sustainable, and that is what is most in focus here.

These categories are not at all novel. To emphasize their historical roots we may think of allocation as the neoclassical criterion; distribution as the neomarxist criterion; and scale as the neomalthusian criterion. Our point is not to show that one is right and the others are mistaken. Rather it is to argue that the relative emphasis among these three important categories as causes of environmental degradation needs reconsideration. The political economy explaining the relative emphases on these three criteria is not developed thematically, but is commented upon briefly in the contexts of the three case studies.

Each of the three criteria has both intra-and inter-generational aspects. The scale criterion in its intergenerational aspect involves population growth and resource consumption growth, its intragenerational aspect involves migration and spatial concentration of resource use. Standard economics distinguishes inter- and intra-generational distribution. The distinction between inter-and intra-generational allocation is problematic. Different generations are *different people*, so strictly speaking there is only distribution between generations. Yet individuals allocate over different stages of a lifespan that lasts two or three generations. The latter should perhaps be called intertemporal allocation and limited to a single generation (25 years). For allocation within a generation discounting the future is reasonable. For intergenerational division of resources we are in the domain of distribution rather than allocation and consequently discounting makes little sense. Efficient allocation over stages in the lifetimes of a given set of people is one thing; just distribution between different sets of people (generations) is something else.

Misallocation as a cause of environmental problems
Efficient resource allocation means that returns per dollar are equal in all sectors when all discounted benefits and costs are accounted for in monetary terms. Market failures and government policy can distort allocation and cause environmental degradation. For example, coal subsidies in some developing countries have caused a greater flow of resources into mining and thus more pollution than is justified in terms of allocative efficiency.[5] The remedy for such problems is to promote policies that encourage full cost pricing and competition rather than rent seeking, and to provide institutions that define property rights in public good settings.

The allocation category emphasizes the incentives of private economic agents in response to government fiscal rules and property rights structures. It implicitly assumes a public interest theory of government. Misallocation in this sense implies that the government made a technical mistake in attempting to reach a social goal such as greater growth. Misallocation does not include cases where the government was intentionally subsidizing private groups at the expense of the general social welfare. Such cases are considered in the distribution category. Separating technical mistakes from rent seeking is difficult. The original passage of legislation embodying perverse incentives we generally attribute to technical mistakes. The failure to eliminate such legislation once its perverse incentives are well demonstrated we attribute to rent seeking.

Inequitable distribution as a cause of environmental problems
Environmental problems may be caused by unjust resource distributions; even efficient resource allocation when coupled with a skewed land distribution may result in the colonization of lands unsuitable for agriculture by poor farmers with no land. The distribution category includes cases where government policymakers chose instruments which were rational in light of the goal of

subsidizing private interest groups regardless of social concerns of efficiency, equity, or sustainability. The probability of policy makers abandoning the general welfare in favor of private interests is positively linked to the degree of economic inequality in the country.

Excessive scale as a cause of environmental problems

Environmental problems may be caused by too great a total physical resource load, or scale of the economy, on the regenerative and assimilative capacities of a country's environment. For example, continual population growth will expand the scale of total resource use and eventually cause serious degradation of natural capital even if allocation is efficient and distribution is just. Scale is a macro-level concept which can be applied at different levels of ecosystems. We will consider scale as a country's resource use relative to critical natural capital. Physical and biological principles indicate that, at any point in time, there is a maximum scale of human resource use which an environment can withstand without widespread degradation of environmental capital. The maximum scale is dynamic; it will change as human technology and environmental conditions change. The ultimate determinant of sustainability is the relation between the total physical scale of the economy and the physical capacities of environmental capital. Technology is viewed here as a means of making better or worse adaptations to these fundamental environmental limits, not as a way of abolishing them. Note that a maximum sustainable scale does not imply a welfare maximum. There remains the possibility of squeezing more welfare from each unit of physical resources. Possible limits to such improvements are not addressed here.

The practical use of the scale concept requires estimates of major categories of natural resource use and pollution generation, and estimates of the human carrying capacity of major ecosystems in a country. Due to lack of comprehensive data, we will interpret scale in terms of population and dominant land uses. If the mix of natural systems (direct uses) and human economic activities (indirect uses) appears to be unsustainable, even with improved allocation and distribution, then we infer that there is a problem of excessive scale. Although such an analysis is crude, it is justified by the great need to explicitly recognize the scale issue. In fact, one of the main points of this paper is the need for better estimates of carrying capacity and total resource use in a national accounting framework in order to make sustainability an operational policy goal.

The distinction between allocation and scale issues

Scale issues may be confused with allocative issues because the scale decision may be thought of as an allocation of resources to the human economy and away from nature (the environment). But we would then have two very different kinds of allocation: (1) the allocation of a fixed flow from nature among alternative indirect uses within the economy, and (2) the allocation between nature and the economy as a whole, i.e., between direct and indirect uses. These two "allocations" are so different that it is best to call them by different names: allocation for the former (or micro-allocation), and scale for the latter (or macro-allocation).

The scale category is not a subset of the allocation category. Ideally, increases in scale due to new resources (lumber versus forests) coming into the economy could be handled as an allocation problem; the decision rule is to increase scale if the net present value of benefits is greater than the costs. However, allocative criteria in the market, and even in cost–benefit analysis without physical safe minimum standards, do not fully consider important influences on the scale decision. First, human population is one of the most important determinants of total scale, particularly in less developed countries. But human population decisions are unresponsive to allocative signals at least in the short run. Hence resource allocation operates virtually independent of differences in population levels, which implies significant differences in scale. Second, since many environmental resources are public goods, private allocative decisions rarely reflect the full costs and benefits of increasing scale. For example, the mining firm does not consider the incremental effect of its activity on the present total scale of the economy and present environmental capacity. Thus new resources come into the economy daily without full consideration of their effects on total environmental capacity. We can determine another efficient allocation after more resources have entered the economy, but it is at a greater scale. The allocation of all resources within the economy at any one time takes place semi-independently of the absolute physical load that the economy puts on the ecosystem by extracting those resources and later injecting their degraded wastes.

Allocation using monetary cost–benefit analysis to correct for market failure is not the same thing as judging the appropriate scale of the economy based on physical resource loads and physical carrying capacities. First, the monetization of all costs and benefits in the face of pervasive Knightian uncertainty of the true value of natural capital tends to focus on the more measurable benefits and costs which may not be the most important ones. This tendency is made more serious by potential irreversibilities and the fact that some minimum level of natural system services is needed for long term economic welfare. Second, the use of discounting means that any long term costs will count as virtually zero even if they are included in the monetary framework.[6] The goal of present value maximization is simply not a sustainable scale; efficient allocation may dictate scale expansions that guarantee an environmental catastrophe 100 years from now.[7] In contrast, the scale decision requires ecological criteria to determine whether the ecosystem can physically withstand the total human resource use. Scale is measured relative to the ecosystem rather than to the prevailing market prices and monetary rate of return within the economy. The primary reason for the scale criterion is the long term sustainability of the human economy within environmental limits; the primary reason for allocative efficiency is the maximization of the present value of wealth in an economy. A sustainable scale should be viewed as a constraint on the maximization of present value, not as a consequence of it.

The fact that efficient allocation does not guarantee a sustainable scale is important in light of the recent tendency to argue for ecologically sound policies using conventional economic arguments. For example, Robert Repetto has noted that many ecologically destructive cattle ranching operations in the Amazon are not economically viable without government subsidies.[8] This is true, but it does not imply that the correction of all microeconomic inefficiencies using present value maximization will in fact add up to a sustainable scale. In fact, arguments such as Repetto's concerning the inefficiency of ecological destruction only make sense due to an intuitive feeling that the economy is at or nearing scale limits. If ecological services are superabundant at the existing scale then their proper allocative price is zero and their destruction is not a misallocation. Hence the arguments that ecologically destructive policies are 'inefficient' must in the end rely as much on the scale criterion as on the allocative criterion.

The inadequacies of conventional economic criteria (maximizing discounted monetary present value) for situations involving intergenerational equity and irreversible effects have been considered by many individuals and organizations such as Cooper,[9] Ciriacy-Wantrup,[10] Warford,[11] and the World Bank.[12] Hence, our classification of scale and allocation problems is merely attempting to identify which problems can be solved by conventional allocative criteria alone and which need to be solved by scale limitations, possibly using allocative criteria for reaching the ecologically set goal as opposed to determining the goal itself. If there is no presumption that we are near an unsustainable scale of resource use, then there is a case for efficient allocation as the governing rule.

An optimal allocation (given distribution and scale) is efficient; an optimal distribution (given allocation and scale) is fair; an optimal scale (given allocation and distribution) is at least sustainable for a long future. Beyond that the notion of optimal scale is not well defined, except in very general terms as that scale which equates marginal cost of further growth with marginal benefit. Until we have better measures of the marginal costs and benefits of aggregate growth the concept of optimum scale remains a formalism, and we must think mainly in terms of sustainability. Of course advocating sustainability involves a value judgment, but so does advocacy of fairness, and for that matter so does efficiency. The issue is not whether these are value judgments, but whether they are sound value judgments. We submit that they are, and that policy, which must always be guided by some value judgments, needs to pay attention to fairness (distribution) and sustainability (scale), as well as to the traditional norm of efficiency (allocation).

In the following country studies these somewhat abstract concepts and categories are given concrete content and are shown to have specific policy implications in each of our three case studies.

CASE STUDY

COUNTRY STUDY I: HAITI

Key environmental problems

Haiti's primary environmental problem is massive deforestation and soil erosion. Haiti was completely forested upon its discovery by Europeans in 1492, but only 7 to 9 per cent of the forest cover remained in 1979.[13] If current trends continue, there will be no forests left by 2010. Due to mountains covering over 67 per cent of the land area, only 29 per cent of Haiti is suitable for planting, but 43 per cent is under cultivation.[14] The loss of forest cover on steep slopes for annual cultivation leads quickly to soil erosion. Deforestation and erosion are causing long term declines in agricultural productivity, silting of irrigation canals and hydroelectric reservoirs (including Peligre Dam, Haiti's largest hydro facility), increases in flooding of urban areas, possible changes in local rainfall patterns, increased rural to urban migration, and loss of Haiti's main energy source, wood and charcoal derived from wood. Although precise data on deforestation and soil erosion is lacking in Haiti, there is no doubt that this environmental problem is a serious threat to present and future development prospects.

Scale of resource use as a cause of environmental problems

The primary cause of erosion is a large and growing population pushing against a mountainous land in search of food and fuel. Population increases have caused a drastic shortening of the fallow period used to allow regeneration of secondary vegetation and soil.[15] The result is a long term degradation of the environment's carrying capacity. The 1985 population was 6 million people with a density of 214 persons per square kilometer, one of the highest in Latin America. Environmental pressure is greater than this high figure indicates as there are 739 people per square kilometer of arable land. Given a current population growth rate of approximately 1.9, Haiti is projected to have a population of 7.8 to 9.8 million by the year 2000.[16]

Haiti is not feeding its current population; over 25 per cent of children suffer from second or third degree malnutrition. A 1975 FAO study of 117 developing nations compared present and projected population sizes with food producing capacities for three scenarios corresponding to low, intermediate, and high input strategies. It was estimated that Haiti could support 4.0, 7.3, and 11.4 million people in the year 2000 as opposed to the actual population projection of 7.8–9.8 million.[17] Since the high input option is not realistic for Haiti, this data points toward increased soil erosion, hunger, and food imports for Haiti in the near future.

Haiti's problem of excessive scale resulted in official encouragement of emigration in the late 1970s in order to reduce domestic population pressure and to gain remittances from Haitians living abroad.[18] Both these factors allowed Haiti to alleviate its scale problem by the use of other countries' ecosystems. Obviously all countries cannot undertake such a policy. Recently, Haiti has considered emigration to be too high due to changes in the policies of receiving countries. The government has moved slowly on the population issue as a family planning program was not started until 1982. The 1981–1986 Five Year Plan called for measures to reduce fertility through family planning and greater participation of women in development activities.[19]

Haiti does not have a high level of per capita resource use, so their scale problem is primarily one of a relatively large and growing human population on a fixed land area of limited and declining resources. Although efficient allocation and distributional changes can lessen environmental problems in Haiti, sustainable development is not a possibility without population control.

Allocative causes of environmental problems

First, the primary government department concerned with preserving agricultural productivity and forestry, the Department of Agriculture, Natural Resources, and Rural Development (MARNDR), has inadequate expertise and personnel in soil and water conservation or forestry.[20] There is no systematic forestland management effort, and over 50 laws, decrees, and administrative decisions on forest protection have not slowed the rate of deforestation and land degradation.[21]

Second, certain government policies have created unintended incentives which worsen soil erosion. Until 1985, high export taxes on coffee and artificially high prices on some food staples (maize, beans, sorghum) through import restrictions caused farmers to grow more food staples to sell in nearby urban areas. Since perennial coffee trees hold soil better than these annual staples, an uncounted cost of the import restrictions has been an increase in soil erosion.[22] There was recognition of these problems in the development plans for 1987 which included improved technical support for the agriculture sector, and a reduction in the export tax on coffee from 22 to 10 per cent.[23]

Third, until recently the Haitian Gourde has been overvalued relative to the dollar. Setting official exchange rates above market exchange rates has the same effect as export taxes discussed above.

Fourth, there is a divergence in benefits and costs between uphill farmers directly causing soil erosion, and the lowland farmers and urban dwellers. The latter would benefit greatly from erosion control programs, but there is no market to arrange mutually advantageous trades. This is less of a problem to the extent that the direct short-term benefits and costs to uphill farmers present an urgent case for erosion control.

Fifth, there is a poor to non-existent credit market in rural areas. Only 10–15 per cent of the rural population has access to institutional credit.[24] Hence it is difficult to undertake investments which would increase agricultural productivity.

Sixth, widespread tenant farming hurts incentives of farmers for long term improvements through reforestation and soil conservation.[25]

Seventh, fuelwood is a public good in most rural areas that still have forests; the only private cost is a nominal tax. Hence there is a strong disincentive to forestry management and the establishment of plantations.[26]

Eighth, the price controls and taxes on competing cooking fuels (fuelwood, charcoal, kerosene, and LPG) are not designed with the goal of minimizing environmental degradation. Although kerosene and LPG prices are competitive with wood prices in deforested areas, most of the poor cannot afford kerosene or LPG stoves. Substitution of kerosene for fuelwood would lessen pressure on forests, but it would also require imports and may discourage incentives for reforestation. Haiti's energy policy does not consider such environmental impacts and tradeoffs.

Distributional causes of environmental problems

First, there is corruption in many departments including MARNDR which has paid a significant percentage of its salaries to professional working staff who do not work there. These giveaways hurt the morale of the working employees, and siphon badly needed money from departments with herculean development tasks even under the best of circumstances.[27] The two government agricultural credit agencies, the Agricultural Credit Bureau (BCA) and the National Bank for Agricultural and Industrial Development (BNDAI), were in a nonviable financial position in 1986 primarily because they did not fire nonperforming staff and did not collect payment from borrowers with political connections.[28] Public resources have also been transferred to a privileged minority through lease of productive state lands at prices far below fair market value.[29] In 1987, the Haitian government was planning to establish new agricultural credit bureaus and start leasing state lands at market prices. However, new bureaus will not change anything without a concerted effort to reduce corruption in the government.

Second, fear of expropriation of land by the state or private powerful individuals hurts incentives of farmers for long term improvements through reforestation and soil conservation. This problem is not due to uncertain land tenure arrangements in Haiti because both farmers with and without deeds feared expropriation. Rather, it stems from a basic distrust of the state's motives in the development process.[30] Of course, this fear and the first distribution problem above are intimately linked.

Third, inequitable land distribution results in more poor people being crowded onto marginal lands where the soil erosion cycle begins. However, Haiti's extensive agricultural use of highlands unsuited for farming is primarily a scale rather than a distribution problem. Unlike some other Latin American countries such as Brazil, there is relatively little scope in Haiti for redistribution of large landholdings to small farmers or landless rural laborers. Even if the available private and state owned lands were redistributed, the average increase in the arable land available to small farmers would be small.[31] Furthermore, such small increases would be quickly negated by population growth. Hence, maldistribution is a smaller factor than scale in causing the farming of steep slopes and consequent environmental degradation in Haiti. Nevertheless, some land in the plains is still undercultivated by absentee landlords, and this distributional factor contributes to overexploitation of marginal lands on hillsides.

Recommendations

First, population control is primary in order to reduce the scale of human demands on Haiti's limited natural systems. Given the evidence on current environmental trends and population growth rates, any comprehensive resource policy that does not emphasize population control is only postponing disaster. Inadequate effort has been placed in family planning in Haiti, given the magnitude of the problem.

Second, a national map of land capabilities and current land uses and degradation is critically needed in order to assess options for sustainable development. Such a map should follow the general outline of the *$206,000* Environmental Studies component of a proposed $3,000,000 Development Credit for Haiti in 1987. This component of the project would assess the extent of land degradation, and recommend remedial steps using an approach which integrates land management directly into economic and social policy.[32] Such a project is a prerequisite for a national accounting framework for Haiti's natural resources. More funding may be necessary for the proper follow-up of the above project, as a 1981 World Bank recommendation for a national inventory and mapping program of land cover and use was estimated to cost *$500,000.*[33] In any case, such a study followed by action as soon as possible is a first order priority for Haiti.

Third, there is a great need to integrate watershed reforestation and hydroelectric planning. At present, stop-gap solutions for the serious problem of sedimentation of hydroelectric facilities are being proposed. There are plans for two dams upstream of the Peligre Dam which are expected to significantly reduce the siltation problem at Peligre in addition to producing more electricity.[34] The feasibility of raising the height of the Peligre Dam is also being considered. The recent *Haiti Public Expenditure Review* recognizes the severity of the erosion problem, but recommends pilot projects rather than major investments because of no sound existing strategy which integrates hillside farming, economic incentives, and watershed management.[35]

Pilot projects may not be the best choice given the magnitude of the erosion problem and the large amount of experience garnered over the last twenty-five years in erosion control in Haiti.[36] The 1981 USAID Agroforestry Outreach Project in Haiti is a potential model for major watershed reforestation efforts. This program attempted to integrate reforestation into the peasant's agricultural/economic setting rather than as a separate tree plantation program. It worked through private voluntary organizations in its distribution of free seedlings and technical advice. Fast growing trees were presented as a means of increasing farm income (through sale of wood for poles, charcoal making, etc.) rather than as a means of preventing soil erosion. The project allowed farmers themselves to determine where the trees were planted; this helped to reduce the tree/

agricultural crop tradeoff and lessened the suspicion of peasants toward the aid agencies' motives. Between 1982 and 1986, the project distributed over 27 million seedlings to 110,000 farmers.[37] This has been by far the most successful public or private reforestation scheme in Haiti. A significant part of its success has been attributed to the use of NGOs which in the past have shown themselves to be more interested in development than the Haitian government.[38]

Fourth, the government's ability to allocate resources for sustainable development and poverty alleviation was severely constrained following the drastic cuts in bilateral aid flows after the aborted elections on November 29 1987.[39] In addition the frequent changes in government since then adversely affected the level of assistance provided by multilateral agencies. It might also have been responsible for delaying the implementation of environmentally relevant reforms, for instance, increasing the rentals on state lands, on which work had started following the departure of Jean-Claude Duvalier in 1986. Since November 1987 many bilateral donors, especially USAID, have increasingly channeled their aid through NGOs.[40] Even though several multilateral agencies have expressed concern that the increased utilization of NGOs would weaken the institutional capabilities of the public sector, the utilization of NGOs is definitely preferable to the alternatives of reduced or even nonexistent aid flows.[41] Besides it is only by channeling their assistance through NGOs that several bilateral agencies have been able to maintain their present, if limited, levels of assistance to Haiti. However, it is important to realize that arriving at a long term sustainable solution to Haiti's environmental problems would require a well coordinated effort among the government, NGOs, and the donor agencies. The World Bank should continue to play a catalytic role, initiated through financing of the environmental studies component under the technical assistance project, in involving the NGOs and other donors in the effort to address Haiti's daunting environmental problems.

The question of allocative incentives is minor relative to the scale and distribution issues in Haiti. If the population is within the carrying capacity of the environment and the policymakers indeed have a just distribution as a goal, then and only then would the allocative tools be the critical or limiting factor in development. The environmental situation in Haiti is primarily a result of pure scale effects combined with a history of maldistribution resulting in large part from internal corruption.

COUNTRY STUDY II: EL SALVADOR

Key environmental problems

El Salvador's primary environmental problem is massive deforestation and soil erosion. El Salvador was once over 90 per cent forested, but now less than 3 per cent remains, and 90 per cent of wood used domestically is imported. Although some relatively flat land is not intensively used, much land on mountainous slopes is under cultivation.[42] The conversion of increasingly marginal land from forest to farmland has resulted in high levels of erosion. As is the case with Haiti, deforestation and consequent soil erosion is leading to long term declines in agricultural productivity, silting of hydroelectric and irrigation facilities, increased urban flooding, and extinction of native flora and fauna. Of 32 mammal species listed in the 1979 IUCN Data Book, 8 are believed extinct in El Salvador, 9 are considered endangered, and 8 are listed as rare or very rare and local.[43]

After deforestation, the most serious environmental problem in El Salvador is poisoning of people, land, rivers and groundwater due to the increasing use of pesticides in export sector agriculture. El Salvador has far higher levels of pesticide poisoning than other Central American countries, which have far higher levels than the United States.[44] The high incidence of pesticide poisoning of El Salvador's agricultural workers is particularly alarming in view of the fact that many less acute cases probably go unreported, and nothing is known about chronic low level effects of pesticide use on workers and their children. Dangerously high pesticide levels have been found in fish, shrimp, meat and milk of livestock and human mother's milk.[45] Extensive pesticide use has resulted in increased resistance of the malaria vector (*Anopheles albimanus*) to DDT in cotton areas. This means either more expensive pest controls or extra costs in the form of higher malaria incidence.[46]

Scale of resource use as a cause of environmental problems

A primary cause of deforestation and consequent soil erosion in El Salvador is a large and growing population in a land of limited resources. The 1985 population was approximately 6 million people with a density of 249 persons per square kilometer, one of the highest in Latin America. Due to much mountainous land, there were 382 persons per square kilometer of arable land in 1983.[47] Given a current population growth rate of approximately 1.9 per cent, El Salvador is projected to have a population of 6.4 to 8.7 million by the year 2000.[48]

El Salvador is not feeding its current population as 75 per cent of children under 5 suffer from protein calorie malnutrition.[49] A 1975 FAO study of 117 developing nations compared present and projected population sizes with food producing capacities for three scenarios corresponding to low, intermediate, and high input strategies. It was estimated that El Salvador could support 3.1, 5.6, and 14.8 million people in the year 2000 as opposed to the actual FAO population projection of 8.7 million.[50] Since the high input option is not realistic, this data points toward increased soil erosion, hunger, and food imports for El Salvador in the near future. The government's family planning program had reached 21 per cent of the fertile female population by 1978.[51] Official effort is lacking relative to the magnitude of the task, particularly in rural areas where it is needed most.

Like Haiti, El Salvador officially encouraged emigration as a means of reducing internal population pressure in the late 1970s.[52] In 1985, El Salvador's active support of emigration was abandoned, and the government agreed to discuss projects with the United Nations High Commissioner for Refugees to alleviate the situation of over 700,00 Salvadoran migrants in Central America and the United States.[53]

El Salvador does not have a high level of per capita resource use, so their scale problem is primarily one of a growing human population on a land of limited resources. As long as the human population exceeds the carrying capacity of the land, people will deplete natural capital such as forests on steep slopes, thus foreclosing the future in order to survive in the present. The ongoing extinction of native flora and fauna is also a logical consequence of the expanding scale of the human economy; there simply is no room left for these species and their natural habitats. Although more equitable land distribution could ease the erosion problem by more intensive farming of lowlands, sustainable development in El Salvador is not a possibility without population control.

305

Allocative causes of El Salvador's environmental problems

First, until recently the El Salvadoran Colon has been overvalued relative to the dollar. Setting official exchange rates above market exchange rates discourages the production of agricultural exports such as coffee.[54] This only leads to greater soil erosion to the extent that crops which hold less soil such as maize and beans are substituted for coffee which protects the soil better. Coffee has been taxed in order to provide government revenue; this will have similar effects as the overvalued exchange rate.

Second, widespread tenant farming hurts incentives of farmers for long term improvements through reforestation and soil conservation, since there is at present no mechanism for compensating tenants for improvements.

Third, El Salvador has no comprehensive national environmental laws and no dominant institution for environmental management or land use planning.[55] Even if they had laws on paper, the money, technical expertise, and enforcement capabilities are lacking. There are no afforestation programs of any significance. The institutional response to the deforestation and soil erosion problem has been grossly inadequate.

Fourth, there is the strong possibility that pesticide use in export agriculture has been subsidized. Robert Repetto has found that neighboring Honduras has pesticide subsidies of approximately 35 per cent of the full retail costs.[56] Whether subsidized or not, there is evidence of inefficiency in pesticide use in El Salvador. A demonstration of integrated pest control on four principal cotton growing countries of Central America (El Salvador, Guatemala, Honduras, Nicaragua) indicated that it is possible to increase yields while reducing the number of pesticide applications by about 39 per cent.[57]

Distributional causes of El Salvador's environment problems

First, a primary reason for the colonization of land unsuited for farming was an extreme maldistribution of land in more fertile areas. Starting in the late 1800s, there was a consolidation of former subsistence and communally owned land for large private holdings dedicated to the production of coffee, sugar, and cotton for export. This consolidation created a large class of landless peasants and migrant workers.[58] In 1971, the top 10 per cent of the landowners owned 78 per cent of the land while the bottom 10 per cent owned 0.4 per cent.[59] In 1979, 80 per cent of rural households in El Salvador were landless or near landless.[60] The consolidation of land holdings acted (in the absence of other agricultural opportunities) as a factor independent of population growth in sending the poor with no clear title to their land up to deforest mountains unsuited for agriculture.

In 1979, a new government came to power in El Salvador and promised land reform. There were three stages: Stage I was for the expropriation of all farms over 500 hectares and creation of production cooperatives on this land. Stage II was for the expropriation of all farms over 245 hectares, while Stage III, to be carried out with Stage I, involved the transfer of land ownership to those who were cultivating it with a maximum of 7 hectares per family.[61] Stages I and III have been partially implemented, while it is uncertain whether Stage II will ever be implemented. With civil strife still in progress and a change of leadership coming soon, it is uncertain what the effects of this land reform will be for deforestation and soil erosion. A serious cost of delays in dealing with fundamental scale and distribution issues is the increased potential for civil unrest.[62]

A second serious environmental problem in part caused by maldistribution is

306

pesticide abuse. Both governments subsidizing pesticides and firms selling pesticides are not ignorant of the dangers; the harmful effects of chemicals such as DDT and parathion have been known for years. The primary reason for pesticide overuse is the great difference in market power between El Salvadoran agricultural workers and the large landowners who buy the pesticides and hire the help. Due to lack of regulations, illiteracy, virtually no job alternatives, and repressive working conditions, even pesticides considered 'safe' in the United States can be deadly in Third World countries.[63] Labor has no bargaining position, and producers would only lower short term profits by spending money on safety measures. Hence we have the high level of poisonings in El Salvador which is likely to be much lower than the actual chronic and acute poisonings due to poor reporting. The negative environmental effects of pesticide abuse of course extend well beyond agricultural workers.

Recommendations

First, the most obvious recommendation is for increased priority of family planning and population control.

Second, there is a need for a mapping of land potential with current land uses in order to promote macro-level sustainable development strategies. This would require investments similar to those proposed for Haiti.

Third, the deforestation/soil erosion problem must be linked to El Salvador's agricultural export strategies. Soil erosion will lower returns eventually in irrigated areas, and productivity loss in the hills implies more food imports which worsens the balance of payments. Although conservation can be justified even if it is not allocatively efficient, soil conservation in many areas of El Salvador may be a good investment. A 1979 study of the Acelhaute River Basin which covers 733 square kilometers and includes the capital city concluded that soil conservation had positive net benefits at a 10 per cent discount rate.[64] Since conditions of agriculture and erosion are similar in many other watershed areas of El Salvador, this study points to the cost effectiveness of a national effort to conserve farmland. Thus the funding of Agroforestry projects such as the one in Haiti by USAID may have positive effects in the balance of payments and the environment.

Fourth, the pesticide problem should be linked with the export agriculture plans. It may be that allocative efficiency and sustainability can both be served by a reduction in pesticide use. A specific analysis of pesticide subsidies in El Salvador would reveal the degree of misallocation. World Bank guidelines declare that, "Use of pesticides as well as other control measures should always be the result of a considered evaluation that the benefits to be gained outweigh the direct and indirect costs, insofar as they can be assessed". An evaluation of the benefits and costs of pesticide use in El Salvador is necessary to carry out this policy. Repetto has noted the World Bank's lack of systematic investigation of pesticide subsidies and their consequences.[65] This lack of knowledge is reflected in the recent *El Salvador Country Economic Memorandum* which does not integrate the pesticide problem (or deforestation problem) into the agricultural sector plans.[66] This underlines the need for the recent World Bank policy change toward the integration of key environmental problems into country economic and sector work.[67]

COUNTRY STUDY III: COSTA RICA

Key environmental problems

Costa Rica's most critical environmental problem is extensive deforestation and land degradation. Although Costa Rica was originally completely forested, only 31 per cent of the nation was forested in 1977.[68] One half of the deforestation has occurred since 1950. At the 1983 deforestation rate of 600 square kilometers per year, all forested areas (including national parks and reserves) will be gone by 2010.[69] The continuing deforestation is causing serious environmental damages because 32 per cent of the nation is only suitable for production forestry with another 24 per cent only suitable for absolute protection of critical watersheds.[70] Approximately 17 per cent of Costa Rica's land is severely eroded[71] while 24 per cent is moderately eroded. Virtually every watershed area in Costa Rica is threatened by land degradation and erosion which is leading to similar problems as in Haiti and El Salvador although they are not yet as serious on a national scale.

The deforestation/land degradation problem is linked to a second major environmental problem, the threats to the internationally famous national park and wildland system. Costa Rica, with a land area roughly the size of West Virginia, has five per cent of all biological diversity on earth. This is the largest wealth of diversity of any similar size land area in the world. Costa Rica has also shown more awareness in protecting this heritage than any Latin American country as legal established wildlands occupy about 19 per cent of the land area.[72] However, all of these reserved areas are threatened by illegal deforestation and infringement by settlers with no economic alternatives.

Scale of resource use as a cause of environmental problems

A steadily increasing scale of resource use is an important cause of deforestation/land degradation and consequent threats to the park system. At present, Costa Rica's total resource use is probably within the carrying capacity of the environment, but the present population of 2.6 million is young and growing at a relatively rapid rate of 2.3 per cent. Although the growth rate is expected to fall to 1.6 per cent in the next 12 years, the year 2000 population is projected to be 3.5 million people.[73] The low population density of 43 people per square kilometer is less meaningful for assessing scale limitations than the arable land density of 225 people per square kilometer.[74] A population of 3.5 million in the year 2000 would mean approximately 335 people per square kilometer of arable land; a density comparable to heavily populated countries in the present such as India. This trend toward increasing population density is a particularly serious problem for Costa Rica because 67 per cent of the population is already concentrated in the fertile Central Valley (6 per cent of national land area), and the nation's economic health in the foreseeable future is heavily dependent on its agricultural sector. If current rural to urban expansion continues, there will be 1.8 million people in this area by the year 2000 which means that much of the best farmland will be taken out of production.[75]

There has been direct government support for access to contraceptive devices since 1968, and the National Commission on Population Policy was established in 1978 to integrate population control into development planning.[76] The government attempts to provide people with the means of birth control (except abortion). Family planning efforts have reached far more people in Costa Rica than in Haiti or El Salvador.[77] Relatively high levels of social services and education have increased Costa Rica's ability to carry out successful family planning.

Allocation, distribution and scale

In addition to population increases, a significant cause of increased scale in Costa Rica has been the expansion of the cattle industry. From 1960 to 1980, land in permanent pasture increased from 19 to 13 per cent of the land area, while forests dropped form 56 to 31 per cent.[78] Since only 9 per cent (4656 square kilometers) of Costa Rican land is suitable for permanent pasture, most of the extensions of pasture have been on lands better suited for production or protection forestry, or farmland. This means either waste of good farmland or loss of natural capital through inappropriate use of forestland for cattle. An estimated 80 per cent of soil loss in Costa Rica is due to overgrazing of pasture lands.[79]

It may appear that bananas and coffee, Costa Rica's two biggest export crops, are greater factors in the increase of the scale of human resource use in the last three decades. However, cattle raising uses far more land than any other agricultural activity. In 1974 only 6.3 per cent of total land area in production was devoted to coffee and bananas while 82 per cent was devoted to cattle.[80] In 1980, beef cattle occupied 76 per cent of the total area in pasture and cultivation.[81] Increases in economic value due to cattle raising have come from extensive use of new land rather than from more intensive use of lands already in the economy. In addition to high land requirements, the economic gains from cattle production are usually brought at the expense of natural capital. Much pasture land is abandoned within a few years due to weed invasion, loss of nutrients, and soil compaction. Current trends in the scale of economic activity relative to Costa Rica's environmental limits cannot continue without serious ecological, social, and economic costs. Continuing scale increases in a relatively fragile environment will place Costa Rica within 20 to 25 years in an ecological position similar to present day Haiti and El Salvador.

Allocative causes of environmental problems

First, Costa Rica has no national environmental land use database and corresponding plan that integrates all sectors.[82] This makes the development and execution of national land use guidelines very difficult. There is little coordination among the many government agencies concerned with natural resource use. This lack of coordination in environmental affairs is part of a serious coordination problem throughout the Costa Rican public sector. Since 1948, the historical response to problems is to establish another autonomous government institution or committee or law. Environmental degradation has proceeded virtually unabated despite the stream of new laws and government agencies.

Second, the Forest Service (DGF) cannot manage existing forest laws or protected areas. According to Forestry Law, all tree cutting must be authorized by the DGF, and permits are only given when use capability justifies deforestation for agricultural use. However, in practice, there is pervasive uncontrolled deforestation. In 1980, the DGF gave permits for only 35 per cent of the area deforested that year.[83] Furthermore, the DGF regards forest reserves as sources of timber, yet many of them occupy critical catchment areas and deserve absolute protection in order to avoid débâcles such as that going on in Haiti. The DGF has not analyzed forest reserves in terms of what type of production or land use value they can sustainably support.

Third, much of Costa Rica is public land, but there is virtually no organized surveying, titling, or public control. Costa Rican common law encourages deforestation by recognizing squatters' (*precaristas*) rights on land which they have 'improved' through land clearing and agricultural usage. As in other areas of

309

Latin America, the trend is for squatters to invade the forest, farm it for a few years, and then sell the 'improved' land to cattle ranchers.[84]

Fourth, there may be net government subsidization of cattle ranching. It is difficult to determine the exact impact of the government on the cattle industry because there are incentives and disincentives to cattle production.[85] Export taxes, domestic price controls on beef, and overvalued exchange rates cause less cattle production. However, the banking system continues to provide low interest loans for cattle ranching with no regard for the type of land the cattle will be placed on.[86] This results in overexpansion of cattle and either depletion of natural capital or poor utilization of good farmland with resulting effects on food imports. We hypothesize that a closer review of the tax/subsidy data and the 'informal' policies of the government would show a definite allocative bias toward cattle pasture expansion.

Part of the reason for the expansion of cattle in Costa Rica (and for government low interest loans) is due to the pressure for exports. Exports have comprised 44 per cent of total beef production form 1961 to 1986.[87] The important question is whether Costa Rica actually has comparative advantage in cattle raising once the ecological costs are counted in the decision. Given the poor ecological record of cattle ranching all over Latin America including Costa Rica, it is remarkable that once-forested Costa Rica is rapidly becoming a net importer of wood while most of the agricultural credit and three-quarters of the land in agricultural production is devoted to livestock. The most alarming fact is not the static inefficiency of this resource allocation but the loss of natural capital due to grazing on lands that cannot sustain cattle.

Distributional causes of environmental problems

First, a highly skewed income and land distribution acts as a separate factor from population increases in causing deforestation and land degradation. The top twenty per cent of the population receives 54.8 per cent of the national income, while the bottom twenty per cent received 3.3 per cent.[88] In 1973, 58 per cent of landholders owned 4 per cent of the arable land while 1 per cent of the landowners held 25 per cent of the arable land. People without the resources necessary to survive in the market economy have nowhere to go but the remaining natural lands whether they are appropriate for farming or not. This distributional link to environmental problems was exemplified by an invasion of settlers in Corcovado National Park in 1985. Between 1000 and 3000 people started mining for gold there after banana plantations moved out of the area nearby.[90] They were evicted within the year, but Costa Rica does not have the manpower to keep people with no other economic opportunities from attempting to subsist in the parks.

Second, the disproportionate influence of the ranching lobby on government has enabled cattle operations to receive the bulk of the agricultural credit regardless of allocative efficiency concerns.[91] This lessens the credit available for small farmer tree crop systems which may have positive distributional and environmental effects. Furthermore, such unequal legislative influence allows the blocking of land taxes which encourages intensive use.

Recommendations

First, it is critical that the government attempt to maintain its population planning efforts despite the current economic problems. Even at current rates of fertility reduction, Costa Rica faces serious future problems due to its population structure and rate of increase.

Second, Costa Rica desperately needs a more detailed national land capabilities map with information on present land uses. This must be the basis for sustainable natural resource based economic activities. Allocative incentives can then be used to steer economic activities toward sustainable uses providing that special interests do not sabotage this clear national interest. It should also be cheaper to graze cattle on natural pastureland, plant crops on fertile land, forests on slopes, etc. than the current haphazard nonplanning.

Third, funding for environmental education is important in helping society to determine the path to sustainable development. A beginning is the Environmental Education Program started in the 1980s which has attempted to integrate environmental education into the formal education curricula. The program is gradually expanding across the entire country.[92] A complementary activity to this education program is the preparation of a *State of the Environment* report for Costa Rica in 1986. This report is meant to demonstrate the links between land management practices outside Costa Rica's parks and the government's ability to protect the parks.[93] We recommend the expansion of the above educational efforts into a Global 2010 Report for Costa Rica which focuses on environmental issues and economic development. This would show the public that current trends place Costa Rica 20 to 30 years behind Haiti in ecological conditions despite the proliferation of environmental laws. The report could also indicate what needs to be done (aligning economic activities in terms of ecological land supporting capability, policies for the landless, population control, control of special interest groups, etc.) to change these trends. Public awareness and discussion of serious scale and distributional issues should help required changes become political realities sooner with less degradation of natural capital.

Fourth, the deforestation/land degradation problem must be integrated into Costa Rica's export agriculture plans. An encouraging sign of the times is the significant increase in importance given to environmental issues in the 1988 Country Economic Memorandum[94] as compared to the 1985 Memorandum. The 1985 World Bank Country Memo on Costa Rica does not link the need for more agro-exports with the country's serious environmental problems even though long term agricultural productivity is not possible if current deforestation and land degradation rates continue. Such an integration of environmental factors would also address the issue of whether cattle at the present scale (or greater) is in fact a good economic investment for Costa Rica. The 1985 World Bank Report recommends closure of some inefficient government run facilities such as the oil refinery, but does not seriously address the efficiency of cattle raising. Instead, it recommends relief of export taxes, lifting domestic price controls, and more technical support for cattle production. Although the Report does recommend better pasture management, the real question is whether Costa Rica has comparative advantage in cattle versus other agricultural activities such as agroforestry when both activities have 'good management'.[95] The critical environmental problems must be integrated into country and sector work to keep policies from working at cross purposes as when cattle are recommended for export to reduce economic debts although they create widespread ecological debts.

The 1988 Country Economic Memorandum clearly analyzes the allocation problem arising from the misleading calculation of comparative advantage based on prices that omit environmental costs, and even states that "the country may therefore be impoverishing itself by exporting goods at less than their full cost of

311

production" (p.47). Distribution and scale factors are also given consideration, although emphasis is on allocation. The environmental section of the 1988 Country Economic Memorandum is the nearest thing we have found to a model of the kind of analysis we are advocating.

Fifth, Costa Rica must streamline its bureaucracy and fiscal machinery as the World Bank has noted. Fiscal responsibility is needed for the environmental problems as well as the conventional debt problems. International funds without a better government structure to implement them may just allow a country to lengthen the time until difficult decisions must be faced.

REFERENCES

1. The term sustainable development is ambiguous as are many relevant concepts. For a discussion of the meaning of this term, see: Clem Tisdell, "Sustainable Development: Differing Perspectives of Ecologists and Economists, and Relevance to LDCs," *World Development* Vol. 16, No. 3 (1988), pp. 373–384. See also H. E.Daly, Sustainable Development: From Concept and Theory Towards Operational Principles, *Population and Development Review,* (in press).
2. World Commission on Environment and Development, *Our Common Future,* (Great Britain: Oxford University Press, 1987), p. 8.
3. Pearce, David and Anil Markandya, "Marginal Opportunity Cost as a Planning Concept in Natural Resource Management," *The annals of Regional Science,* Vol. 21, No. 3, (November, 1987), p. 22.
4. Lee, James A., *The Environment, Public Health, and Human Ecology* (1985), The World Bank, Washington, D.C., p. 5.
5. *World Development Report 1988,* The World Bank, published by Oxford University Press, p. 53.
6. Although even a low discount rate means that environmental costs 1000 years from now count as virtually zero, we do not maintain that sustainability can be assured merely by lowering discount rates. As Pearce and Markandya have argued, low discount rates may increase or decrease environmental damage in different situations. Our main point is that the sustainability goal cannot be met by attempting to place it within the inherently short run framework of monetary present value maximization. Rather, sustainability must be a constraint on conventional economic reasoning. For a review of discount rates and the environment, see Anil Markandya and David Pearce, "Environmental Considerations and the Choice of the Discount Rate in Developing Countries," Environment Department Working Paper No. 3, The World Bank, May 1988.
7. Page, Talbot, *Conservation and Economic Efficiency: an approach to materials policy.* (Baltimore: John Hopkins University Press, 1977).
8. Repetto, Roberto, "Creating Incentives for Sustainable Forest Development," *Ambio,* Vol. 16, No. 2–3, 1987, pp. 94–99.
9. Cooper, Charles, *Economic Evaluation and the Environment.* (Great Britain: Hodder and Stoughton, 1981).
10. Ciriacy-Wantrup, S. V., *Resource Conservation: Economics and Policies,* 3rd edition. (Berkeley: University of California Division of Agriculture Science, 1968).
11. Warford, Jeremy, "Natural Resources and Economic Policy in Developing Countries," *The Annals of Regional Science,* Vol. 21, No. 3, November, 1987, pp. 3–17.
12. *Environment, Growth and Development,* Development Committee, Number Fourteen, December, 1987, pp. 8, 31–32.
13. *Draft Environmental Report on Haiti,* Science and Technology Division, Library of Congress, Washington, D.C., January, 1979, p. 33 (prepared for USAID).
14. Zimmerman, Thomas, "Agroforestry – a last hope for conservation in Haiti? *Agroforestry Systems,* Vol. 4, pp. 255–268, 1986.
15. Murray, Gerald F., *Terraces, Trees and the Haitian Peasant: An Assessment of Twenty-*

Five years of Erosion Control in Rural Haiti, October, 1979, p. 214. Prepared for USAID/Haiti.

16. Zacharian, K. C. and My, T. Vu, *World Population Projections,* 1987–88 edition, The World Bank.
17. *Potential Population Supporting Capacities of Lands in the Developing World,* Food and Agriculture Organization of the United Nations, Rome, 1982, p. 103.
18. *Population Policy Compendium Haiti.* Joint Publication of the Population Division of the United Nations Department of International Economic and Social Affairs and the United Nations Fund for Population Activities, 1980, p. 5. Haiti's encouragement of emigration extended primarily to unskilled workers rather than professionals.
19. *Inventory of Population Projects in Developing Countries Around the World 1985/86.* United Nations Fund for Population Activities, p. 217.
20. *Haiti Public Expenditure Review,* Volume 1, September, 1986, Report No. 6113-HA, The World Bank, pp. 28–30.
21. Cohen, Warren B., *Environmental Degradation in Haiti,* USAID, 1984, p. 27.
22. *Technical Assistance Report for Haiti,* April 7, 1987, Report No. P-4433-HA, The World Bank, p. 24.
23. *Technical Assistance Report for Haiti,* p. 48.
24. *Technical Assistance Report for Haiti,* p. 20.
25. Murray, Gerald, *Terraces, Trees and the Haitian Peasant: An Assessment of Twenty-Five Years of Erosion Control in Rural Haiti,* pp. 201–202.
26. *Haiti: Issues and Options in the Energy Sector,* Report No. 3672-HA, The World Bank, June 1982, p. 44.
27. *Haiti Public Expenditure Review,* Volume 1, pp. 30–32.
28. *Haiti Public Expenditure Review,* Volume 1, p. 33.
29. *Technical Assistance Report for Haiti,* p. 20.
30. Murray, Gerald, *Terraces, Trees and the Haitian Peasant: An Assessment of Twenty-Five years of Erosion Control in Rural Haiti,* p. 197.
31. Zuvekas, Clarence, *Agricultural Development in Haiti: an assessment of sector problems, policies and prospects under conditions of severe soil erosion.* Report prepared for USAID, 1978, pp. 100, 261.
32. *Haiti: Issues and Options in the Energy Sector,* p. 27.
33. *Haiti: Issues and Options in the Energy Sector,* p. 23.
34. *Haiti: Issues and Options in the Energy Sector,* p. 33.
35. *Haiti: Public Expenditure Review,* Volume 1, pp. 34, 57.
36. Murray, Gerald, *Terraces, Trees and the Haitian Peasant: An Assessment of Twenty-Five Years of Erosion Control in Rural Haiti.*
37. Winterbottom, Robert and Peter Hazelwood, "Agroforestry and Sustainable Development: Making the Connection," *Ambio,* vol. 16, No. 2–3, 1987, pp. 100–110.
38. *Politics, Projects, and People, Institutional Development in Haiti,* edited by Derick W. Brinkerhoff and Jean-Claude Garcia-Zamor. (New York: Praeger Publishers, 1986), pp. 223, 262–265.
39. After the recent Haiti coup, various foreign diplomats in Haiti viewed the coup as a return to massive political corruption, which they considered to be Haiti's biggest problem. *The Washington Post,* Saturday, June 25, 1988, p. A18.
40. *U.S. Assistance to Haiti: Progress Made, Challenges Remain,* U.S. General Accounting Office, 1985.
41. *U.S. Assistance to Haiti: Progress Made, Challenges Remain,* p. ii–111.
42. *Draft Environmental Profile of El Salvador,* prepared by Arid Lands Information Center, Office of Arid Land Studies, University of Arizona, Tuscon, Arizona, 1982, pp. 59, 79.
43. *Draft Environmental Profile of El Salvador,* p. 63.
44. Mendes, Rene, "Informe Sobre Salud Occupacional de Trabajadores Agricolas en Centro America y Panama," (Washington, D.C. Pan-American Health Organization, May 1977).

45. *Draft Environmental Profile of El Salvador,* p. 92.
46. *An Environmental and Economic Study of the Consequences of Pesticide Use in Central American Cotton Production,* pp. 126, 150. The report acknowledges that some resistance will develop among malaria carriers just due to the use of DDT as a control rather than for cotton. Thus not all of the extra costs of increased malaria resistance are due to applications of DDT on cotton. However, the indiscriminate use of DDT on cotton fields has led to statistically measurable increases in neighboring areas. From 1972 to 1975, the average resistance in Guatemala's cotton growing areas increased from 58 to 86 per cent.
47. *El Salvador Country Economic Memorandum,* Report No. 5939-ES, April 25, 1986, World Bank.
48. Zacharian, K. C. and My, T. Vu, *World Population Projections,* 1987–88 edition, The World Bank, p. 194.
49. *El Salvador: Demographic Issues and Prospects,* The World Bank, p. 23.
50. *Potential Population Supporting Capabilities of Lands in the Developing World,* Food and Agriculture Organization of the United Nations, Rome, 1982, p. 103.
51. *El Salvador: Demographic Issues and Prospects.*
52. *Population Policy Compendium El Salvador.* Joint Publication of the Population Division of the United Nations Department of International Economic and Social Affairs and the United Nations Fund for Population Activities, 1979.
53. *World Population Policies,* Vol. 1, United Nations, New York, 1987, pp. 198–201.
54. *El Salvador Country Economic Memorandum,* p. 16.
55. *Draft Environmental Profile of El Salvador,* p. 94.
56. Repetto,Robert, *Paying the Price: Pesticide Subsidies in Developing Countries,* World Resources Institute, Washington, D.C., December, 1985, p. 5.
57. *An Environmental and Economic Study of the Consequences of Pesticide Use in Central American Cotton Production* Instituto Centro Americano de Investigacion y Tecnologia Industrial (ICAITI), 1977, Guatemala, ICAITI Headquarters, p. 3.
58. *Draft Environmental Profile of El Salvador,* p. 34.
59. *El Salvador Country Economic Memorandum.*
60. Lassen, Cheryl A., *Landlessness and Rural Poverty in Latin America: Conditions, Trends and Policies Affecting Income and Employment.* Rural Development Committee, Cornell University, Ithaca, New York, 1980. The category of near landless includes marginal tenants and marginal farmers. The latter refers to cultivators who have title to or customary tenure of holdings that are of inadequate size or quality to provide a subsistence livelihood.
61. *El Salvador Country Economic Memorandum,* p. 22.
62. Durham, W. H., *Scarcity and Survival in Central America: Ecological Origins of the Soccer War* (Stanford: Stanford University Press, 1979).
63. Weir, David and Mark Schapiro, *Circle of Poison,* (San Francisco, California: Institute for Food and Development Policy, 1981), p. 3.
64. Wiggins, S. L., "The Economics of Soil Conservation in the Acelhuate River Basin," El Salvador, pp. 399–415 in *Soil Conservation Problems and Prospects,* edited by R.P.C. Morgan (New York: John Wiley & Sons, 1981).
65. Repetto, Robert, *Paying the Price: Pesticide Subsidies in Developing Countries,* p. 2.
66. *El Salvador Country Economic Memorandum.*
67. "Environmental Requirements of the World Bank," *The Environmental Profession,* Vol. 7, 1985, p. 207.
68. *Costa Rica Country Environmental Profile,* Gary Hartshorn, *et. al.,* Tropical Science Center, San Jose, Costa Rica, USAID, 1982, p. 28.
69. Nations, James D., and Daniel I. Komer, "Rainforests and the Hamburger Society," *The Ecologist,* Vol. 16, No. 4/5, 1987, p. 162.
70. *Costa Rica Country Environmental Profile,* p. 2.
71. *Costa Rica Country Environmental Profile,* p. 6.
72. *Costa Rica Country Environmental Profile,* p. 3.

73. Zacharian, K. C. and My, T. Vu, *World Population Projections,* 1987–88 edition, The World Bank, p. 184.
74. *Costa Rica Country Environmental Profile,* p. 2.
75. Leonard, H. Jeffrey, *Natural Resources and Economic Development in Central America.* International Institute for Environment and Development (New Brunswick, USA: Transaction Books, 1987), p. 223.
76. *Population Policy Compendium Costa Rica,* p. 1.
77. *Costa Rica Country Environmental Profile,* pp. 5–6.
80. Guess, George M., "Pasture Expansion, Forestry and Development Contradictions: The Case of Costa Rica," *Studies in Comparative International Development,* Vol. 14, No. 1, Spring, 1979, p. 46.
81. Leonard, H. Jeffrey, *Natural Resources and Economic Development in Central America.* International Institute for Environment and Development (New Brunswick, USA: Transaction Books, 1987), p. 223.
82. *Costa Rica Country Environmental Profile,* p. 8.
83. *Costa Rica Country Environmental Profile,* p. 30.
84. *Costa Rica Country Environmental Profile,* p. 28, 30.
85. *Costa Rica Main Economic Problems and Prospects,* Vol. II, Main Report, World Bank, June 24, 1985, Report No. 5759-CR, p. 63.
86. Nelson, Michael, "Renewable Resource Management in Latin American Countries," World Bank Working Paper, 1988.
87. Leonard, H. Jeffrey, *Natural Resources and Economic Development in Central America,* p. 216. From 1961 to 1986, beef exports were 308.6 out of the total production of 704.9 thousand metric tons.
88. *Costa Rica Main Economic Problems and Prospects,* Vol. II, Main Report, 1985.
89. *Costa Rica Country Environmental Profile,* p. 20.
90. Tangley, Laura, "Costa Rica – test case for the neotropics," *BioScience,* Vol. 36, No. 5, p. 296.
91. Guess, George M., "Pasture Expansion, Forestry and Development Contradictions: The Case of Costa Rica," *Studies in Comparative International Development,* Vol. 14, No. 1, Spring, 1979, p. 47.
92. Hall, Orlando, "Environmental Education in Costa Rica," *Prospects,* Vol. 15, No. 4, 1985, pp. 583–591.
93. Tangley, Laura, "Costa Rica – test case for the neotropics," *BioScience,* Vol. 36, No. 5, p. 299.
94. "Costa Rica: Country Economic Memorandum", World Bank, December 6, 1988.
95. *Costa Rica Main Economic Problems and Prospects,* Vol. II, Main Report, 1985, pp. 63–634, 102.
96. Ahmad, Yusuf J., Salah El Serafy, and Ernst Lutz, *Environmental Accounting for Sustainable Development,* World Bank, Washington, D.C., 1989. See also Roefie Heuting and Christian Leipert, "Economic Growth, National Income and the Blocked Choices for the Environment," Discussion Paper, Environmental Policy Research Unit, International Institute for Environment and Society, West Berlin.
97. Ibid.
98. Hansen, Stein, "Structural Adjustment Programs and Sustainable Development," Paper prepared for the annual session of the Committee of International Development Institutions (CIDIE) in Washington, D.C., June 13–17, 1988.

Chapter 24

The economics of environmental degradation: problems, causes and responses*

Theodore Panayotou
Harvard Institute for International Development, Harvard University

Environmental degradation is a more common and pervasive problem than rapid inflation, excessive foreign debt or economic stagnation. Rapid deforestation, watershed degradation, loss of biological diversity, fuelwood and water shortages, water contamination, excessive soil erosion, land degradation, overgrazing and overfishing, air pollution and urban congestion are as common to Asia as they are to Africa and Latin America. It is striking that rapidly growing Southeast Asia has similar environmental problems as stagnating sub-Saharan Africa or heavily indebted Latin America. And, while economic growth enables countries to better deal with environmental problems, there is an abundance of failures and a scarcity of success in dealing with environmental problems. These observations imply that (a) there are underlying causes of environmental degradation that are common to countries in different geographical locations with different cultures and at different levels of development, (b) economic growth by itself neither causes nor remedies environmental degradation, the connections being far more subtle and complex, and (c) environmental problems are insidious and refractory or at least poorly understood, resulting in either failure to deal with them or to interventions that tend to treat the symptoms rather than the underlying root causes with consequent failure.

The purpose of this paper is to analyse the economics of policy issues associated with environmental degradation, both from a causal and curative perspective. Special attention is paid to (a) the connection between economic growth, poverty, and environmental degradation, (b) the role that goverment policies play, often unwittingly, in causing and promoting environmental degradation, and (c) the role of market failures and the implications for public policy. The study deals with these theoretical issues in their practical manifestations by drawing heavily on illustrations of actual cases of policy and market failures as well as policy successes in dealing with environmental degradation. Alternative corrective mechanisms are discussed and guidelines for project design and policy dialogue are provided.

* An excerpt from Green Markets: The Economics of Sustainable Development (San Francisco: ICS Press for the International Center for Economic Growth, 1992). The assistance of Mona Yacoubias and Madeline Hirshland is gratefully acknowledged.

THE MAGNITUDE OF THE PROBLEM

There are few problems that are as common to all countries regardless of economic system and levels of development as environmental degradation. The underlying causes of environmental degradation, as we will discuss in the next section, are fundamentally similar. Yet, its manifestations, dimensions, and implications differ depending on history, geography and level of development, among others. Even within the same country, environmental degradation evolves over time with population growth, migration, urbanization, industrialization, structural change and economic growth. For example, with rural–urban migration, many of the rural environmental problems such as forest encroachment and degradation of marginal land resurface as urban problems in the form of slums, congestion and pollution.

Physical manifestations of environmental degradation.

The term "environment" covers both the quantity and quality of natural resources, renewable and non-renewable, as well as the ambient environment which is an essential element of the quality of life. As such, the environment is a critical determinant of the quantity, quality and sustainability of human activities and life in general. Environmental degradation then is the diminution of the environment in quantity and its deterioration in quality. Correspondingly, environmental problems have both a quantity and a quality dimension. Water-related problems include water shortages as well as deterioration of water quality through pollution and contamination. Forest-related problems include both deforestation in the sense of forest cover loss and forest degradation in the sense of reduction of forest productivity, loss of diversity and replacement of primary by secondary forest. Land-related problems include growing land and scarcity as well as soil erosion, nutrient leaching, waterlogging and salinization. Fishery-related problems include overfishing as well as changes in species composition to less valuable species, increasing share of trashfish in the catch and fish contamination. Urban environmental problems include congestion and thereby less open space available per person, as well as air, water, and noise pollution, and hence a lower-quality environment.

Quality problems at the extreme become quantity problems. For example, water may become completely unusable because of heavy pollution. Land may become unsuitable for cultivation because of severe erosion. A forest may completely lose its forest cover because of severe degradation as it happens when shortening of the fallow cycle in shifting cultivation results in replacement of forest by *imperata* grass. Certain urban areas (e.g. slum, residential areas near dumpsites, chemical or nuclear plants, etc.) may become unlivable because of excessive pollution and contamination. Quality problems also become quantity problems because quantity is defined for a given quality. For example, shortages of drinking water, or prime farmland, and of primary forests may coexist with abundance of low-quality water, marginal land and secondary forests.

Finally, diversity has value; expanding the supply of one resource or environment at the expense of another (known as substitution) may be beneficial up to a point, but as any given resource is driven to depletion or extinction, diversity is lost, and with it an option and an element of the quality of life. Diversity of species and environments is essential to long-term productivity and sustainability. Its preservation is a form of investment for the future or insurance against future uncertainties. Its diminution constitutes environmental

317

degradation even if its loss as a factor of production or a source of consumption has been fully compensated via substitution for an equally productive asset. In conclusion, when we speak of environmental degradation, we should keep in mind three dimensions, quantity, quality and diversity and their inter-dependence.

The economics of environmental degradation

A certain level of environmental degradation is an inevitable consequence of human activity. Any exploitation and use of non-renewable resources inevitably results in their partial or total depletion, as well as the degradation of the landscape and the generation of waste. Industrialization leads to increased consumption of minerals and energy and the generation of air, water and noise pollution and hazardous wastes. Agricultural extensification leads to deforestation, cultivation of marginal lands, and soil erosion while agricultural intensification leads to pesticide and fertilizer runoffs, waterlogging, soil salinity, etc. Even the use of renewable resources on a sustainable basis presupposes the mining of the stock down to a level that would generate a maximum annual growth (maximum sustainable yield). Virgin fisheries and undisturbed forests reach a natural equilibrium stock where net growth is zero; unless the stock is reduced and there is no sustainable yield to harvest. Therefore, some environmental degradation is inevitable.

The question is not how to prevent or eliminate environmental degradation altogether but how to minimize it or at least to keep it to a level consistent with society's objectives. When environmental degradation is seen in the context of the society's development objectives, not all deforestation, soil erosion or water pollution is bad or worth preventing. Some deforestation is necessary and beneficial when the forest land is put to a superior use which may be agricultural, industrial or residential. As long as all costs involved, including those arising from diminished quantity, deteriorated quality and lost diversity of forests have been accounted for; as long as both the productivity and the sustainability of the alternative uses have been considered with a due margin of error; and, as long as any side effects of the forest conversion have been internalized and paid for, deforestation should not be something we would like to prevent. The problem is that usually only the short-term benefits of forest conversion and none of its long-term costs are considered. As a result, too much conversion takes place in areas where no conversion should have been taking place because the present value of costs outweigh any short-term benefits. Even worse, forests are converted to wastelands with little current benefit and enormous current and future costs. It is unfortunate and renders a disservice to conservation when such wasteful forest destruction is lumped together with socially optimal forest conversion into a single deforestation figure. Considering, however, the rate at which tropical forests have been disappearing in recent years, it is understandable that all deforestation is considered undesirable, no matter what the economic justification. Nevertheless, this emphasis on the symptoms rather than the underlying causes, and the disgregard of the costs and benefits involved prevents the formulation of effective policies to deal with the problem while it antagonizes developing countries that depend on forest resources for development.

A similar case can be made for soil erosion and water pollution. Not all soil erosion is worth preventing. In deep fertile soils, erosion has little or no effect on land productivity, while it enhances considerably the productivity of downstream land where it is deposited. Still there may be other negative offsite effects such as sedimentation and eutrofication of waterways and reservoirs that should be taken into account in determining how much soil erosion to allow. In other areas, such as in much of the tropical rainforests, where the fertile soil is very superficial consisting basically of the humus formed by degrading matter, any soil loss may make the difference between lush growth and desertification. Again the tendency is to lump together all soil erosion and express it in tons per hectare without regard to the depth of soil, fertility, natural replenishment and deposition.

Similarly, air and water pollution are excessive not in any absolute sense, but in relation to the assimilative capacity of these media and in reference to their use and the society's constraints and objectives. To attempt to prevent all forms and levels of pollution in all water resources is to leave a flow resource of little opportunity cost unused with consequent reduction of social welfare or use of resources of higher opportunity cost for the same purpose. This does not imply that individuals should be allowed to use the assimilative capacity of the environment free of charge. If they do, not only will excessive pollution be generated but the resource itself, i.e., the assimilative capacity of the environment will be diminished as a result. Moreover, as the disposal of waste increases and the assimilative capacity is reduced, there is a definite opportunity cost that should be paid by individual users, consisting of two elements, (a) the use of a scarce resource to the exclusion of others, and (b) the damage to the productivity of the resource as waste disposal increases beyond a threshold. A charge for the use of the resource can be set at a high enough level to limit effluents to a level that can be assimilated without damage to its assimilative capacity.

Prevention is often far more cost-effective than rehabilitation ("an ounce of prevention is worth a pound of cure"). Once excessive environmental degradation takes place, it is not worthwhile to attempt to reduce it back to the level that would have been optimal with prevention because costs are higher, effectiveness is lower and vested interests stronger. Not only is a 100% abatement technically difficult and economically out of the question, but the optimal level of abatement would leave us with more pollution than we would have liked had we the option of a fresh start. Because of this economic irreversibility (which sets in much before the physical irreversibility), prompt internalization of environmental costs is both economically and environmentally preferable.

To sum up, physical manifestations of environmental degradation, such as rates of deforestation, rates of soil erosion, level of water pollution and densities of urban congestion tend to overstate the problem because they seem to suggest that all degradation is preventable or worth abating. Because they are based on observed symptoms rather than underlying causes, they tend to be devoid of analytical insight as to how to deal with the problem other than banning the activities that appear to be responsible. For example, if logging leads to deforestation, it is common sense that banning logging will solve the problem. As Thailand is gradually discovering, a logging "ban" does not stop logging (let alone deforestation), any more than Prohibition in the United States several decades ago stopped drinking.

Economic manifestations of environmental degradation
The first step for understanding the root causes of environmental degradation is to look for its economic manifestations, help define the true dimension of the

problem and suggest the scope and opportunity for cost-effective intervention. Economic manifestations are counterintuitive observations or contradictions (puzzles); their very identification calls for an analytical explanation (why?) and a policy implication (what and how?). The following is a representative list of such economic manifestations of environmental degradation:

1. Overuse, waste and inefficiency coexist with growing resource scarcity (shortages).
For example, increasingly scarce irrigation water in many parts of Asia is used wastefully and excessively by some farmers to the point of causing waterlogging and salinization of soils, while other farmers in the same irrigation system suffer from water shortages and unreliable supplies. This is true of most irrigation systems in Thailand, Indonesia, Philippines, India and Pakistan to mention only a few. The net loss consists of current production loss by those who receive inadequate water and future production loss by those who suffer from waterlogging as well as general degradation of the resource.

2. An increasingly scarce resource is put to inferior, low-return and unsustainable uses, when superior, high-return and sustainable uses exist.
For example, in Thailand, uplands suitable for fruit trees or other perennials are often planted with maize or cassava for a few years and abandoned as yields decline when perennials would yield both higher return (in present value terms) and be more sustainable. A second example comes from Morocco where scarce irrigation water is used to grow sugarcane in an arid environment when vegetables, orchards and other higher-value crops would have produced a higher return and fewer soil salinity problems. In Brazil, valuable forests have been converted to ranches that generate negative economic returns.

3. A renewable resource capable of sustainable management is exploited as an extractive resource (it is mined).
For example, tropical forests are being mined without concern for regeneration and future harvests as evidenced by the damage to the remaining stand, even when future harvests have a positive net present value at the market rate of interest. While some forest land conversion to other uses is economically justifiable, the fact that the rate of deforestation is 100 times the rate of reforestation alone suggests that tropical forests are mined not managed. There are indeed very few sustainable alternatives that would justify failure to regenerate a renewable resource capable of yielding a perpetual stream of income.

4. A resource is put to a single use when multiple uses would generate a larger net benefit.
For example, many tropical forests are managed for timber production alone when management for multiple uses such as non-timber goods, water and soil conservation, biological diversity and a host of other environmental services would generate a higher return. While not all uses are mutually compatible, the relevant question is which combination of uses would produce the highest net present value for a given forest.

5. Investments in the protection and enhancement of the resource base are not undertaken even though they would generate a positive net present value by increasing productivity and enhancing sustainability.
Examples include the failure of many farmers throughout Asia and Africa to invest in on-farm land development and soil conservation to reduce erosion and

320

improve irrigation. Another example is the failure of many forest concessionaires to regenerate or replant their concessions or even to protect them from encroachment. A third example is the failure of irrigation authorities to invest in watershed protection, to protect reservoirs from sedimentation and in maintenance and rehabilitation of deteriorating irrigation systems, to increase their efficiency and prolong their economic life.

6. A larger amount of effort and cost is incurred when a smaller amount of effort and cost would have generated a higher level of output, more profit and less damage to the resource.

Examples include capture fisheries and common pastures throughout the developing, and parts of the developed, world. Most fisheries employ twice as much labor and capital as needed to obtain less than the maximum sustainable yield and virtually no economic surplus. Any profit that the fishery is capable of generating is dissipated by excessive fishing cost. Fishermen tend to be among the lowest income groups in most countries.In the long run, overfishing results in decreased productivity of the stocks, lower output and a compositional change towards lower value species (see Panayotou, 1982). Nor is the excessive employment a benefit in itself since fishermen are earning no more than their opportunity costs (what they could earn in alternative employment). If they do, additional entry would nullify any income differential between the fishermen and comparable socioeconomic groups in the country. A reduction in fishing effort would reduce fishing costs and increase profits in the short run, and help the stock and catch recover over the long run leading to further increases in profits. The economic surplus so generated can be used to compensate, retrain and reemploy the surplus number of fishermen. Despite these obvious gains, no such reform takes place.

The situation with common (open access) pastures[1] is very similar. More animals are being grazed than the pastures can support with the result that total output is less than it could be, incomes are low and the pastures deteriorate. Incomes and output can be raised and pastures improved with a reduction of the numbers of animals but this does not happen, despite the obvious gains. It is as if the society is subsidizing the degradation of its resource base by raising and grazing an excessive number of animals. Of course, the problem arises from the fact that the sum of individual actions does not lead to socially desirable outcomes, under the prevailing institutional arrangements. Since the pasture is a common property, and livestock is viewed as a transformer of common property into private property, the more animals each individual has the larger his share of the common property, assuming that others do not also expand their herds. But since the other common owners would not sit and watch their share fall, they also increase their herds. The end result is neither efficient not equitable. The productivity of the pasture declines and the largest share goes to those that can afford the largest number of animals, that is, those who are initially better off. The poor suffer in what appears to be an equitable arrangement: property that is freely accessible to all.

7. Local communities and tribal and other groups such as women are displaced and deprived of their customary rights of access to resources regardless of the fact that by their very presence or specialized knowledge, tradition and self-interest, they may be the most cost-effective managers of the resource.

Many tropical resources, particularly the rainforests, are so complex and vulnerable that their sustainable management requires specialized knowledge of plants and animals and their interaction in such an environment. It also requires a physical presence to prevent encroachment or other interference by those less knowledgeable or less interested in the continued productivity and sustainability of the resource. Managers that combine such specialized knowledge with personal commitment to the long-term sustainability of the resource and willingness to live in the rainforest, far from the city lights, are hard to find. Even if they existed, employing an adequate number of them with all the necessary support would be prohibitively expensive.

Fortunately, there are people who do live in the forest, depend on it for survival, have the specialized knowledge of the ecosystem necessary for sustainable management and even have a tradition of doing so. By any criterion, such as cost effectiveness, present value maximization or equity, many local communities and tribal groups ought to be given the responsibility of managing the resource and vested with sufficient authority, protection and security of tenure to do so effectively. Yet, in most cases, central governments have assumed the ownership and management of tropical forests despite their lack of specialized knowledge and management skills, their absenteeism, and often their lack of interest in the sustainability of the resource. The rights of exploitation have been subsequently awarded to equally distant logging companies, with little knowledge of the rainforest environment and no interest or stake in its long-term productivity and sustainability. Short-term concessions and perverse taxation did not help either. In the meanwhile, local communities have been deprived of their customary rights of access or displaced altogether. Under these circumstances, it is no wonder that tropical forests are being destroyed by the combined actions of logging firms that seek short-term profits and local communities that seek a livelihood without a secure resource base. Neither group has an assurance of a share in the future of the resource. For example, African women who have the responsibility for managing resources but lack access to secure property rights, extension and credit, have no choice but to overuse land and to farm areas that should not be cultivated. The encroachment of the resource by farmers and ranchers in search of land for agriculture and cattle ranching further compounds the uncertainty and effectively reduces state ownership into open access land. Unlike most developing country governments that declared state ownership over all forest resources with little consideration of local customary rights, the government of Papua New Guinea recognizes and defends communal and tribal tenure over land and forest resources.

8. Public projects are undertaken that do not make adequate provisions or generate sufficient benefits to compensate all those affected (including the environment) to a level that they are decidedly better off with than without the project.

Public projects aim to increase total welfare or to promote economic development, not to effect a redistribution of income, although other things being equal, projects that benefit more the poor than the rich ought to be preferred. Therefore, public projects should fully compensate all those affected, including future generations. If indeed the project is as beneficial as its proponents maintain, the project ought to generate sufficient benefits to make all those involved or affected better off with the project than without the project through actual not hypothetical compensation. This should be especially so since those affected more severely are usually the poor that lack the political and economic power to avoid the damages. The analysis of who is affected by public projects should be broken down by location, income level, profession and gender. This will help ensure that the effects on disadvantaged segments of society are not neglected, as is often the case.

In addition, the expected benefits from the project ought to be sufficient to mitigate or compensate the project's environmental impacts to a level that the country's environment is not decidely worse off with the project than without the project. For example, if a forest area is inundated by the construction of a dam, an equivalent area of forest must be created elsewhere (e.g., by purchasing logging rights from concession companies or through extensive replanting with similar species).

Many irrigation projects fail to meet these conditions and thus create social tensions and long delays that result in cost overruns and forgone benefits, if indeed they are overall beneficial. Examples abound. The Narmada project in India which has been delayed for some thirty years, is a case in point. If such projects do go through without meeting these conditions, they run into problems of watershed encroachment by the displaced population, sedimentation and loss of capacity. A case in point is the Nam Pong reservoir in North East Thailand. The Dumoga irrigation system cum national park in Sulawesi, Indonesia is a counterexample that has met the conditions for a socially beneficial and sustainable project.

9. Failure to recycle resources and byproducts when recycling would generate both economic and environmental benefits.

With the exception of energy, the consumption of natural resource commodities such as minerals, wood products and other fibers generates recyclable materials. While not all recyclable materials can be economically recycled at the current levels of technology and costs, many could be profitably recycled except for the fact that material from primary sources is underpriced or subsidized and the fact that unrecycled waste can often be disposed of free of charge. Inadequate recycling means more exploitation of natural resources, more pollution and loss of salvageable economic value. Recycling is implicitly taxed by depletion allowances and exploration subsidies pertaining to primary resource extraction, but not to recycling. Even when recycling is more costly than primary production, the environmental benefits from recycling (less waste disposal, less degradation of the environment by primary production) could help tip the balance if appropriately internalized.

A good example is palm oil processing in Sumatra, Indonesia. The residuals from palm oil production could be economically converted into fertilizer if the averted damage to aquatic life and other uses of water were taken into account. However, because factories are free to dispose of their waste in the rivers free of charge, a profitable economic activity is foregone and, as a result, palm oil waste is today Sumatra's single most severe form of water pollution. Related losses include damage to the riverine and coastal fisheries and reduced water quality for household use.

10. Unique sites and habitats are lost and animal and plant species go extinct without compelling economic reasons which counter the value of uniqueness and diversity and the cost of irreversible loss.

As a resource becomes increasingly scarce, its social value rises regardless of whether it is traded in the market or not. The value of resources with no close substitutes, such as natural habitats and animal and plant species, approaches infinity as their numbers are reduced to levels that threaten their continued existence. Both uniqueness and the marginal contribution of threatened environments and species to diversity is of such "great" value that their irreversible loss and the associated loss of future options cannot be justified except in very special cases when survival is at stake, as in the case of famine or when enormous and indisputable economic benefits are expected. Yet unique sites and habitats and threatened species are often driven to extinction by public projects or with the help of government subsidies, without compelling economic reasons to counter such enormous loss. The burden of proof that such resources have a lower value than the proposed projects or policies ought to be with those who advocate these interventions.

The causes of environmental degradation

Unlike physical manifestations and symptoms that are devoid of analytical insight, the economic manifestations of environmental degradation raise analytical questions as to cause and effect. Why are increasingly scarce resources being inefficiently used and wasted instead of economized and conserved? Why are valuable resources being put to inferior uses when superior uses exist? Why are renewable resources being mined rather than managed for a perpetual stream of benefits when the latter would generate a higher net present value? Why are resources that generate a multitude of products and services being put to a single use when multiple use management would generate more benefits? Why are highly profitable investments that enhance both current productivity and future sustainability not being undertaken while scarce funds are being wasted on marginal investments? Why is a larger amount of effort and cost expended when a smaller amount would generate more profits and less damage to the resource? Why are resources and byproducts not recycled when recycling would generate both economic and environmental benefits? Why are local communities and tribal groups displaced and deprived of their customary rights to resources when by virtue of their physical presence and intimate knowledge they would be the most cost effective managers of the resource? Why are unique habitats and species going extinct without compelling economic reasons to counter the irreversible loss of uniqueness, diversity and future options?

The answers to these problems are to be found in the disassociation between scarcity and price, benefits and costs, rights and responsibilities, actions and consequences. This disassociation exists because of a combination of market and policy failures. The prevailing configuration of markets and policies leaves many resources outside the domain of markets, unowned, unpriced and unaccounted for and more often than not, it subsidizes their excessive use and destruction despite their growing scarcity and rising social cost. This results in an incentive structure that induces people to maximize their profits not by being efficient and innovative but by appropriating other peoples' resources and shifting their own costs on to others. Common and public property resources (e.g. forests, fisheries) are being appropriated without compensation; the cost of growing scarcity is diluted through subsidies paid by the general taxpayer and the cost of ultimate depletion is borne by the poor who lack alternatives and by future generations whose interests are sacrificed to short-term political expediency. Preventing prices from rising in line with growing scarcities and rising social costs distorts the signals that in a well-functioning market would have brought about increased efficiency, substitution, conservation and innovation to restore the balance between supply and demand.

324

Economics of environmental degradation

While policy and market failures are often intertwined and mutually reinforcing, for both analytical and policy reform purposes it is important to distinguish between them as clearly as possible. Policy failures or market distortions are cases of misguided intervention in a fairly well-functioning market or unsuccessful attempts to mitigate market failures that result in worse outcomes. Market failures are institutional failures partially attributable to the nature of certain resources and partially to a failure of the government to (a) establish the fundamental conditions (secure property rights, enforcement of contracts, etc.) for markets to function efficiently; and to (b) use instruments at its disposal (e.g., taxation, regulation, public investment and macropolicy) to bring into the domain of markets inputs and outputs (costs and benefits) that the institutional framework fails to internalize.

We will first review market failures not because they are more important, but because they outline a *potential* role for government policy against which current policies can be viewed to identify areas of policy failure and policy success. Policy failure, as used here, is defined as a government intervention that distorts a well-functioning market, exacerbates an existing market failure, or fails to establish the foundations for the market to function efficently. Policy success on the other hand is the successful mitigation of market failures; success is defined in terms of improvement in the allocation of resources among sectors and over time.

Before discussing market failures in detail, however, it is important to clarify a number of points that have often led to misunderstanding and advocacy of market replacement by government institutions. First of all, as we have seen, only a part of environmental degradation in developing countries is due to genuine market failure; much of it is due to misguided government interventions (such as tax distortions, subsidies, quota, interest rate ceilings, inefficient public enterprises, etc.), which distort an otherwise well-functioning market. Second, a good deal of genuine market failure, such as the failure arising from open access, insecure tenure, unpriced resources, and to some extent uncertainty and high transaction costs comes about because of government failure to establish the legal foundations of markets, such as secure property rights and enforcement of contracts.

Third, the mere existence of a market failure does not justify government intervention much less abandonment of the market as a mechanism for allocating resources; government intervention must lead to improved allocation outcomes over those of the free market and the ensuing benefits should exceed the cost of such intervention including those of enforcement and side effects (distortions). Fourth, experience suggests that the most cost effective intervention for mitigating market failures is the improvement of the functioning of the market through elimination of policy-induced distortions, the establishment of secure property rights over resources, the internalization of externalities through pricing and fiscal instruments, the encouragement of competition, the free flow of information and the reduction of uncertainty through more stable and predictable policies and politics.

Therefore, it is a misconception that the presence of market failures justifies the reduction in the role of the market resource allocation and an increase in the role of government. To the contrary, mitigation of market failures through secure property rights, internalization of externalities, increased competition and reduced uncertainty will enhance the role of markets in allocating resources such as water, land, fisheries, forests and environmental services and would make unnecessary the establishment of cumbersome and often inefficient public institutions for resource management and conservation. The government need only provide the initial institutional and policy reform necessary to allow the markets to function efficiently.

The first priority under the prevailing circumstances in developing countries is to eliminate policies that have significant environmental cost or which create perverse incentives that encourage the depletion of resources and environmental degradation beyond the free-market level. Reforming policies that distort incentives for efficient resource use is a priority because unless perverse incentives are removed, project investments aiming at improved utilization and conservation of resources are unlikley to succeed and when they do, their impact would be unsustainable, lasting only as long as the project lasts.

Reforming policies that are detrimental to both the economy and the environment is an easier point at which to start because no difficult development–environment tradeoffs or budget outlays are involved. If anything, eliminating policy distortions usually reduces government expenditures and may even generate additional budget revenues. The distributional implications are also in the right direction since many of these distortions (e.g., interest rate ceilings, capital subsidies, untaxed resource rents, monopolies, input subsidies, price supports, etc.) are not only sources of inefficiency but also of inequity and perpetuation of poverty. Finally, eliminating policy distortions can be done by adjusting prices, taxes, subsidies, interest rates, and exchange rates which is easier than introducing new instruments or developing new institutions to deal with market failures.

This is not to say that market failures need not be mitigated, but that both the priority and the acid test of successful policy interventions is the elimination of policy-induced market distortions. Only then can market failures be seen in the right perspective and cost-effective interventions for improving the functioning of the market be formulated and effectively implemented. For example, there is little rationale for trying to internalize the benefits from conserving biological diversity when the wholesale conversion of tropical forests into cattle ranches or pine plantations is heavily subsidized.

In what follows we analyze first market failures and their sources, then policy failures and their impacts, and finally policy successes and the need for further policy reforms.

MARKET FAILURES LEADING TO ENVIRONMENTAL DEGRADATION

Well-functioning markets are normally efficient mechanisms for allocating resources among uses and over time. Markets function efficiently when certain fundamental conditions are met. Property rights over all resources must be clear and secure: all scarce resources must enter active markets that price them according to supply and demand; there are no significant externalities; competition prevails; public goods are minor exceptions, and issues of myopia, uncertainty and irreversibility do not arise. If these conditions are not met, the free market fails to allocate resources efficiently among uses and over time. It wastes too many resources today and leaves too little for the future.

Much of the mismanagement and inefficient utilization of natural resources and the environment can be traced to such malfunctioning, distorted or totally absent markets. Prices generated by such markets do not reflect the true social costs and benefits from resource use. Such prices convey misleading information about resource scarcity and provide inadequate incentives for management, efficient utlization and enhancement of natural resources.

The most important market failures affecting resource use and management are:

1. Ill-defined or totally absent property rights which are essential for the efficient operation of markets.
2. Unpriced resources and absent or thin markets.
3. Pervasive yet unaccounted externalities, spillover effects or intersectoral linkages which are kept outside the domain of markets.
4. High transaction costs which discourage otherwise beneficial exchanges that would conserve resources and improve social welfare. Transaction costs include information negotiating, monitoring and enforcement costs.
5. Public goods which cannot and/or should not be provided by the private sector through the market because of either inability to exclude free-riders and recover the cost of provision of these goods because exclusion, though technically possible, reduces social welfare.
6. Market imperfections, particularly lack of competition in the form of local monopolies, oligopolies and segmented markets. Especially critical for resource conservation and management are the imperfections of the capital market.
7. Myopia in the sense of "too short" planning horizons or "too high" discount rates arising from poverty, impatience, and risk or uncertainty which affect individuals but not the society as a whole.
8. Uncertainty and risk aversion which may lead not only to high discount rates but also to unwillingness to undertake investments which are otherwise profitable but have a large variance of returns.
9. Irreversibility: when market decisions under uncertainty lead to irreversible results the market may fail to allocate resources prudently.

These market failures or rather sources of market failures are not unique either to natural resources or to developing countries. For instance, a good part of investment in education and human capital has public good aspects and so do investments in science and technology. Uncertainty and market imperfections permeate all sectors of the economy. However, no other sector can claim as many and as pervasive market failures as the natural resource sectors. Not only are these market failures intertwined with each other, but they are also intertwined with socioeconomic and sociocultural factors such as poverty, customs, and perceptions. For historical and sociocultural reasons, many of these market failures are more pervasive and refractory in some countries than in others. Below we discuss how each of these market failures contribute to the mismanagement of natural resources in general and the degradation of the environment.

Insecurity of ownership over resources

A fundamental condition for the efficient operation of markets is that there exist well-defined, exclusive, secure, transferable and enforceable property rights over all resources, goods and services. Property rights are a precondition to efficient use, trade, investment, conservation, and management of resources. No one in his right mind would economize on, pay for, invest in, or conserve a resource without an assurance that he has secure and exclusive rights over it, and that he can recover his costs through use, lease, or sale, and that such rights can and will be enforced. Property rights must be *well-defined*. Otherwise they give rise to competing claims that cause uncertainty of ownership and discourage investment, conservation, and management. The rights that accompany ownership must be fully specified along with restrictions that apply to owners and the corresponding rights of non-owners.

Property rights need also to be *exclusive* in the sense that others do not have similar or competing rights to the same piece of the resource. Multiple ownership, however secure, has detrimental effects on investment, conservation and management. No single joint owner has sufficient incentive in land improvements when he or she knows that all the other co-owners have a right to the benefits that accrue from this investment. Joint investment is a solution provided that the joint owners can agree on the type, scale, and financing of the investment (or conservation). The larger the numbers of owners and the higher the transaction (or negotiation) cost, the smaller the likelihood that they will reach a stable agreement. This has implications for communal management of resources, a subject which we will discuss later.

Property rights need to be *secure*. If there is a challenge to ownership, risk of expropriation (without adequte compensation), or extreme political or economic uncertainty, well-defined and exclusive property rights provide little security for long-term investments such as land improvements, tree planting, and resource conservation. If long-term investments are to be encouraged, property rights must not only be secure but also *indefinite*. Usufruct certificates or land titles for a specified period of time after which property rights expire do not provide the right incentives for investment and conservation. Only investments that can yield sufficient benefits within the given time framework of the right will be undertaken, and exploitative behavior will ensue as the expiration date approaches unless there is a high probability that the property right will be renewed or extended.

Property rights must be *enforceable*. Even if property rights are well defined, exclusive and secure, they will have little impact on resource use and management if they cannot (or will not) be enforced. An enforced right is effectively no right at all. This holds for both private and public property. For example, the declaration of forest as public or state property by most tropical countries, did little to prevent deforestation and, in fact, it may have accelerated it for the very reason that public ownership over vast areas has been proven unenforceable. Effective enforcement is the discovery of violations, the apprehension of violators, and the imposition of penalties. For penalties to be effective, their expected or certainty-equivalent value (fine multiplied by probability of apprehension) must exceed the benefit obtainable from violations. When it is difficult to enforce property rights through penalties because of sociocultural or other constraints, incentives for self-enforcement could be provided. For example, the government may rely on peer group pressure and community leadership to enforce communal and private property rights within a community that has a cohesive social organization.

Finally, property rights must be legally *transferable,* through lease, sale, or bequest. If they are not, the incentives for investment and conservation are considerably reduced and the efficiency of resource allocation is compromised. Owners of resources who are not allowed to transfer them are discouraged from making long-term investments because they cannot recover such investments were they to change occupation or residence. For example, a logging concessionaire has no incentive to invest in reforestation or conservation because his concession is not transferable and his investments accumulate no equity. Moreover, for markets to work efficiently in allocating scarce resources between competing uses, property rights must gravitate to the highest-value use. Restrictions on transferability of property rights are sources of inefficiency. Where there is a justification for such restrictions, it should be imposed on usage not on the transfer of ownership.

For historical and sociocultural reasons, property rights over many natural resources are ill-defined, insecure, and in a number of cases totally absent. Insecurely held resources include (a) private agricultural land, (b) public forest land and forest resources, (c) irrigation systems and water resources, (d) coastal zone and fishery resources, and (e) environmental resources. Resources over which property rights do not exist and therefore everybody has free access are known as open access or common property resources, or in layman's terms "no man's land". Common property must be distinguished from communal property, which is well-defined and enforceable.

Unpriced resources and thin markets

There is no market and therefore no price for open access resources since there is no secure and exclusive owner who should demand such a price and in its absence deny access. Moreover, prospective buyers would be unwilling to pay such a price as long as they have free access to the same resource elsewhere. With no sellers and no buyers, a market for open access resources does not develop and their price remains at zero even as they become increasingly scarce. True, there are markets for natural resource commodities such as fish, crops and fuelwood produced from open access resources, but the price that such commodities command reflects only the opportunity cost of labor and capital used in their production, not the opportunity cost of scarce natural resources used in their production. The implicit rent or user cost for the fishing ground, the newly opened forest land and the forest itself is still taken to be zero, regardless of scarcity and social opportunity cost.

With prices of zero (that is, available for free) and no market to register scarcity, that natural resources are depleted at rapid rates is not surprising, since demand is very high and supply (conservation) very low (zero) at a zero price. In a market economy, the only gauge of scarcity is price. Price is also the mechanism through which scarcity is managed and mitigated through demand and supply adjustments. In the case of natural resources, supply is limited by nature and adjustments can be made only through conservation and substitution: both are costly processes that need to be paid for by rising resource prices. Rising prices require working markets and working markets require secure property rights over resources.

However, the absence of markets and prices is not limited to open access resources such as fisheries and the environment. As we have seen earlier, even state property such as forests and forest lands are in effect open access resources since the state's ownership is unenforceable, or deliberately not enforced. For this reason, the market in forest properties is very thin, that is, one with very little competition, which is itself another market failure.

A more obvious case of an unpriced resource is irrigation water. Here, the state has made a deliberate decision to provide farmers with irrigation water free of charge or at a nominal fee. In this case, it is not only the water, a scarce natural resource of positive opportunity cost, which is left unpriced (or zero-priced), it is also the scarce capital invested in the irrigation systems that is left unpriced. The consequences are many and far reaching: (a) water is inefficiently and wastefully used without any attempt to conserve it even when its scarcity is obvious to the user; (b) the state is unable to recover capital, operation and maintenance costs with the result that watersheds remain unprotected and the irrigation system is poorly maintained; (c) serious environmental problems such as sedimentation, soil salinization and waterlogging result from watershed degradation and from overirrigation while other potentially irrigable areas receive insufficient quantities of water to grow dry season crops; and (d) better-off farmers near the irrigation canals are indirectly subsidized by worse-off farmers who pay taxes but have little or no access to irrigation water.

True, water pricing is neither technically nor politically easy to introduce especially in societies in which water has traditionally been regarded as a God-given and therefore free good, Yet, the potential gains justify some form of water pricing in the face of increasing scarcity. The alternatives range from volumetric pricing, to water rights, land taxation, contributions in kind and self-management through water users asociations.

Efficiency pricing is at the heart of natural resource policy and management. Almost all resource problems can be traced to discrepancies between private and social valuation of resource commodities and resource stocks. In the case of irrigation water the private cost of both the *commodity* water and the *resource* water is constant at zero, while the social cost of both is positive and rising. Similarly, the cost to the private sector of using the environment (waste, land, and air) for waste disposal is zero, while the cost to the society is positive and rising. Rapid deforestation and slow reforestation, even in securely owned forest land, is partly the consequence of the failure of the market to price forest products to capture the externalities of watershed and wildlife protection, and of other non-market services of the forest.

In general, the overexploitation, inefficient utilization, inadequate conservation and lack of investment in regeneration of natural resources can be attributed to undervaluation of resources arising from failure of either market or the government to efficiently price natural resources according to their social scarcity. The key to optimal pricing of natural resources is to identify and measure correctly the external social cost[2] and the intertemporal user cost[3] of resource exploitation and to internalize them or charge them to the current generation of consumers through appropriate pricing or taxation. This leads us to the discussion of external costs or externalities on spillover effects in the following section.

Externalities or spillover effects

A major factor that drives a wedge between private and social valuation of resources and leads to inefficient pricing is the presence of external costs or spillover effects known as externalities. An externality is an effect of one firm's or individual's actions on other firms or individuals who are not parties in those actions. Externalities might be positive or negative. An example of a positive externality is the benefit that upstream forest owners provide to downstream farmers in the form of a steady water supply made possible by a forested watershed. It is to the society's (and the farmer's) benefit that more of such positive externalities are provided, but since the forest owners receive no payment for their watershed service they have no incentive to provide more of this service by logging less and planting more. The result is that more logging and less planting than is socially optimal takes place. Looked at from another angle, logging has negative externalities (or spillover effects) on downstream activities such as farming, irrigation, transport and industry, in the form of flooding, sedimentation, and irregular water supply. These are real costs to downstream activities and to the society as a whole, but not to upstream loggers or shifting cultivators who have no cause or incentive to consider them as they do not affect the profitability of logging or shifting cultivation. In fact, taking such costs into account voluntarily amounts to a conscious decision to lower one's profit and price oneself out of the market. Unless every logger and every shifting cultivator takes such external costs into account, those who do are certain to lose to competitors who do not. This is exactly why government intervention is necessary to establish and enforce similar standards and incentives or disincentives for all competitors.

Another example of a negative externality is the damage that an upstream rice farmer's use of pesticides causes to a downstream fish farmer that uses the same water source. The society as a whole (not only the fish farmer) would be better off if less of this negative externality is produced, but again there is no market (or other) incentive for the upstream farmer to take the downstream farmers' interest into account. The government may react to this problem by banning the use of pesticides altogether. This however may reduce social welfare if the loss from rice production outweighs the gain from fish production (and if no other environmental effects are involved). The ideal solution would be for pesticide use to be reduced exactly to the level where the combined value of rice and fish is maximized. This level is obtained where the marginal benefit from pesticide use equals its marginal cost, where this cost is understood to include both the production costs of the pesticide and its environmental cost (effect of fish production). There are two ways in which this could happen: (a) the price of pesticide that the rice farmer pays includes a surcharge above production cost to account for the pesticide's environmental cost, or (b) if the same decision maker owns both the rice farm and the fish farm.

Will a free market produce either of these outcomes? The answer is no, except under very special circumstances. Environmental costs are outside the domain of markets because these costs arise from a technological rather than a market interdependence between economic activities. It is a fundamental premise for an efficiently functioning market that economic units interact only through their effect on prices; technological interdependence is ruled out. However, the market will stretch itself to handle technological interdependence if it is a private externality. If there is only one rice farmer and one fish farmer, one of the two (or both) will recognize that one could buy off the other, combine the two operations and end up with a profit because as we have seen, combined profits exceed the sum of individual profits. Alternatively, the fish farmer may offer to "bribe" the rice farmer to reduce the use of the pesticide if the latter has the right to pollute. Or, if the fish farmer has the right to clean water, the rice farmer may offer to bribe him to accept more water pollution. In either case the result will be an improvement in social welfare through internalization of the externality accomplished by a free market.

However, as the number of polluters and affected parties (say rice farmers, or upstream loggers and downstream farmers) increases, the market becomes less and less able to internalize externalities. First, the damage is spread over so many decision makers that it is not perceived as important enough by any individual decision maker to induce action although its aggregate effect might be enormous. Second, it is diffcult to unscramble the cause and effect or who damages whom and by how much. Third, and more detrimentally, another market failure comes into play: as the number of parties involved rises, so do information and transaction costs; bringing people together and obtaining an agreement becomes prohibitively expensive. A smooth functioning of markets assumes that information and transaction costs are zero or insignificant. In the case of public externalities, transaction costs may be so high that they will eat up all benefit from their internalization. Government intervention is justified provided that the government can bring about a more cost-effective internalization of externalities than the market. For example, a surcharge on the price of pesticides or wood to reflect respectively environmental costs of pesticide use and logging is a policy option which is likely to generate net social benefits if appropriately set and administered.

To sum up, the market mechanism may work out a solution as long as the externality is private or at least concentrated and important enough for the internalization of benefits to be apparent to all parties involved. Or, at least one of the parties involved should have such a high stake as to be induced to act despite the free-riding by other beneficiaries. When the external effects are too widely spread, as is usually the case, the correction of the externality is a *public good*, in which case, the market does not function effectively and government intervention might be necessary if the externality is worth rectifying. Not all externalities are worth correcting and few, if any, are worth eliminating entirely. The guiding principle should be that the gains in social welfare from correcting an externality should outweigh the costs of the intervention including any distortions in the rest of the economy that such an intervention might introduce.

It may be useful at this point to relate externalities to common property and insecurity of ownership. Common property or open access creates externalities, and externalities create insecurity of ownership. Common owners impose externalities on each other which they ignore to everybody's detriment. The larger the catch of one fisherman, the higher the fishing cost of all other fishermen. Since this cost is ignored, everybody's catch and costs are higher than necessary leading to economic and biological overfishing and ultimate social loss. In analogous fashion, pervasive externalities may lead to insecurity of ownership with the same devastating overexploitation results as those obtained under open access. A farmer with a secure and exclusive title to a piece of land subject to increasing erosion or flooding caused by upstream deforestation may decide to "mine" rather than farm his land before it is washed away ("make hay while the sun shines"), an outcome identical to that of common property or open access.

As we have already seen, the failure of the market to price externalities or to account for environmental costs is a major reason for the undervaluation of natural resources or alternatively for the discrepancy between private and social benefits and the costs of their exploitation. The market fails to deal with externalities for two related reasons, themselves major market failures. Correction of public externalities: (a) involves prohibitively high transaction costs, and (b) is by itself a public good. We now turn to these two market failures.

Transaction costs
Markets emerge to make possible beneficial exchanges or trade between parties

with different resource endowments and different preferences. However, establishment and operation of markets is not costless. Transaction costs in the form of information, coordination, bargaining, and enforcement of contracts are involved. Usually such costs are trivial compared to the benefits from trade that such markets make possible. Markets fail to emerge if there are very high set-up costs, if the costs per unit transacted exceed the difference between the supply and demand price, or if there are only a small number of buyers and sellers. Absence of well-defined property rights prevents markets from emerging, but well-defined property rights do not bring markets into existence if the coordination and marketing costs, necessary for the commodity in question to be traded voluntarily, are very high. Even if markets appear, they tend to be thin and inactive. The absence or paucity of futures markets and the high costs of rural credit market are usually attributed to high transaction costs.

Similarly, there are costs to establishing and enforcing property rights. If such transaction costs are high relative to the benefit from secure and exclusive ownership, property rights and the related markets will fail to be established. For example, the costs of parcelling out the sea to individual fishermen and enforcing property rights over a mobile resource are prohibitively high. Analogous is the case of externalities. There are costs to identifying the afflicted and generating parties and to negotiating a mutually agreeable solution. The more parties involved, the less likely that a bargaining solution will be arrived at voluntarily because the transactions cost tends to exceed the benefits from internalizing the externality. However, the government, either through its collective or coercive power, may be able to internalize externalities at a lower transaction cost than the free market. According to Stiglitz (1986, p.184), "The government may be looked upon as precisely the voluntary mechanism that individuals have set up to internalize externalities or to reduce the welfare losses from the externality in some other way." Another way to look at this is that the organizational services necessary to internalize the externality are public goods. Moreover, many externalities involve the provision of public goods such as clean air, clean water, watershed protection and biological diversity. Since it is very costly (and often detrimental to social welfare) to exclude anyone from enjoying the benefits from public goods, such goods cannot (or should not) be provided by the market. They can be best provided by the government and financed from general taxation. In some cases, public goods could be provided by non-governmental organizations (NGOs) through voluntary contributions by members or supplied by the private sector under contract with the government.

Public goods

When several originators and recipients are involved, externalities such as water and air pollution may be considered as public "bads" and their correction as a public good. In fact a public good may be thought of as an extreme case of a good that has only externalities, that is, no part of it is private to any individual. Each individual's consumption of such a good depends on the total quantity of the good supplied in the economy. Unlike the case with private goods, the consumption of a public good by an individual does not diminish its availability to other individuals. Although the production of public goods involves an opportunity cost in terms of foregone quantities of private or other public goods, a zero opportunity costs is associated with its consumption.

A public good is characterized by jointness in supply, in that to produce the good for one consumer it is necessary to produce it for all consumers. In many cases, no individuals can be excluded from the enjoyment of a public good (e.g., national defense) whether they pay for it or not. However, even if exclusion is possible (e.g., a bridge across a river), to do so violates pareto optimality, which requires that no opportunity of making one person better off without making anyone else worse off is left unutilized. Because nobody can or should be excluded from the benefits of a public good, consumers would not freely pay for it and, hence, no firm would be able to cover its production cost though the market; hence, the market mechanism would fail to supply a public good, although the good would contribute to social welfare. Thus, a free market will lead to underproduction of public goods and overproduction of private bads.

Because individual consumers cannot adjust the amount of public good they consume, a market for it cannot exist or, when it exists, it does not provide the public good in sufficient quantities. This provides a rationale for many government activities aimed at providing public goods. For the government to provide a public good, it is necessary to know each individual's marginal rate of substitution between the public and private goods, which would determine the optimal level of the public good and (perhaps) each individual's share of the cost. However, because consumers may not reveal their true preferences for fear that they may be taxed on the basis of their willingness to pay, public goods are usually produced or contracted out by public agencies on the basis of collective decisions and financed from general taxation. Thus, although consumers consume the same amount of the public good, they pay different "prices", whereas in the case of the private good, consumers pay the same price but consume different quantities of the good.

Natural resources and the environment involve many public goods ranging from environmental quality and watershed protection to ecological balance and biological diversity. Public goods range in geographical scope from local or regional to national or global. For example, biological diversity is an international public good since it is not possible (or desirable) to exclude other nations from benefiting from its conservation. Therefore, it is unreasonable to expect such a good to be provided in sufficient quantity by an individual country in a free market.

Certain goods are referred to as "publicly provided private goods" because of the large marginal cost associated with supplying additional individuals. The rationale for the public supply of such goods is their large set-up costs and the high (transaction) costs of running a market for these goods. When private goods are freely provided, they are overconsumed. Since the consumer does not pay for the good, he demands and uses it up to the point where the marginal benefit he receives from the good is zero, although the marginal cost to the society is positive and often substantial. The social loss from overconsumption is the difference between the individual's willingness to pay and the marginal cost.[4] A classic example of a publicly provided public good is irrigation water, whose overconsumption involves a double loss: a direct welfare loss from excessive consumption and an indirect loss from waterlogging resulting from overconsumption. There is a need for a rationing system to control consumption. Three possible rationing devices are (a) uniform provision, (b) queuing, and (c) user charges. The problem with uniform provision is that everyone gets the same amount regardless of his needs and desires. The problem with queuing is that it requires payment in waiting time and rewards those whose opportunity cost is lowest. User charges are particularly suited to publicly provided goods because users could be charged the marginal cost of providing the good which is often substantial though not suficient to cover the total cost of the public good. User charges result in both improved effciency of use and partial cost recovery. This is particularly relevant to irrigation water pricing. According to the World Bank (1985, p.456),

> True efficiency pricing requires accurate measurement of supplies by metering the volume of water delivered to individual users . . . Although true efficiency pricing may not be attainable, even a nominal charge for irrigation water would provide an incentive to use it more efficiently . . .

These complications notwithstanding, the pervasive shortage of public funds and the large income benefits derived from participants in irrigation schemes suggest that substantial cost recovery should be the goal in many instances. Most governments, however, have not attained anything like a full cost recovery from public irrigation schemes. A rule of thumb followed by some governments is to absorb the capital costs, but to establish water charges and benefit taxes at the level that in the aggregate will at least recover the operation and maintenance costs including repairs.

However, it must be noted that even when there is a marginal cost associated with each individual using a good, if the transaction costs of running a price system (that is the cost of collecting user charges) are very high, it may be more efficient for the government to provide the good and finance it from general taxation. However, raising revenues through taxes, such as the income tax, may introduce distortions (disincentives for work and investment) that raise the effective amount of private goods that individuals must give up to obtain an additional unit of the public good above the nominal cost.

Uncompetitive markets

Even when markets do exist and are very active, there may be market failures in the form of insufficient competition. For markets to be efficient there should be a large number of buyers and sellers of a more or less homogeneous commodity or, at least, a lack of barriers to entry, and a large number of potential entrants as an insurance against monopolistic practices by existing firms. In reality, we observe economies ridden with monopolistic elements. A market is imperfectly competitive if the actions of one or a few sellers or buyers have a perceptible influence on the price. Market imperfections may arise for a variety of reasons. A major source of monopolistic tendencies, affecting some resource related sectors such as water and energy supply, is the decreasing industry costs feature. Because of the indivisibility of the necessary investment, the average cost of the service falls continuously as more and more customers are served until the whole market is dominated by a single firm (known as natural monopoly). To prevent monopolistic practices, a government monopoly may be established as is often the case with utilities and the post service.

Other causes of limited competition may be institutional, legal, or political barriers to entry into certain professions or industries, high information costs; and the limited extent of the market, a common problem in developing countries which may result in oligopolies because only a few firms may supply the entire market. A usual monopolistic practice is to withhold supplies in order to raise prices. The monopolist's price is too high and his output too low for social optimality which requires marginal cost pricing rather than the monopolist's average cost pricing.

Monopoly is not altogether bad for conservation. For the wrong reason, the monopolist may approximate the social optimum rate of resource extraction. Even though a monopolist is equally likely to ignore the cost of his activities, his fear of depressing the price turns him into a conservationist. This is not to imply that monopoly is a solution to resource depletion: replacing one market failure by another does not usually improve welfare.

While monopolies are not uncommon, the natural resource sectors are not less competitive than other sectors of the economy. One market whose imperfections are likely to have more pronounced effects on natural resources than on the other sectors of the economy is the capital market. Ideally, economic activities and business ventures that promise to yield a net return higher than the going interest rate should be able to obtain funds for investment because they expect to earn enough to pay the cost of borrowed capital and still earn a profit. In reality, this does not always happen. Unless farmers already have sufficient property or capital assets to use as collateral, and unless they understand and are able to meet rigid repayment requirements, they cannot obtain institutional credit at the going rate of interest. Most farmers, being either subsistence or small-scale commercial farmers, have access only to non-institutional credit that comes with high interest rates, usually a multiple of the institutional rate and, more often than not, debilitating preemptive marketing arrangements. This means that even if a project is profitable at the institutional rate of interest (say 15%), it may be unprofitable at the much higher (usually above 50%) cost of informal credit, often the only source of funds for the small farmer. Thus, unless the government makes colateral-free credit available to small farmers at the institutional rate of interest, many privately and socially worthwhile projects would not be undertaken.

There are at least two reasons why farmers and other rural dwellers have no access to institutional credit. First, many farmers have no secure land title which they can use as collateral; semi-secure titles are not accepted for the long-term institutional credit required for long-term investments such as land improvement and tree planting. Second, interest rate ceilings intended to help rural borrowers result in the drying up of rural credit because banks are unwilling to lend at a loss (rural credit involves higher transaction costs than urban credit), leaving the far more costly informal credit as the only recourse for rural borrowers. Since informal credit is both costly and short-term, rural investments are biased against natural resource activities such as tree planting and soil conservation.

Myopic planning horizon and high discount rates

Natural resource conservation and sustainable development ultimately involve a sacrifice of present consumption for the promise of future benefits. Because of time preference, such an exchange appears unattractive unless one dollar of sacrifice today yields more than one dollar of benefits tomorrow. Future benefits are discounted, and the more heavily they are discounted the less attractive they are. A high rate of discount may discourage conservation altogether. Clark (1973) has shown that a sufficiently high market rate of interest combined with a low natural growth rate may lead to the extinction of species. If the market rate of interest accurately reflects the society's rate of time preference, such extinction should not be worrisome except for another market failure that results from the combination of irreversibility and uncertainty which we will discuss later. Here we are concerned with the possibilty that the market rate of interest (discount) fails to reflect the society's true rate of time preference. A combination of poverty, impatience, and risk, which either does not apply or applies to a smaller degree to the society as a whole than to individuals, drives a wedge between the private and social discount rate.

Environmental and market uncertainties (see below) coupled with a short and uncertain lifespan lead people to adopt myopic time horizons and discount rates which result in short-sighted decisions in pursuit of survival or quick profits at the expense of long-term sustainable benefits. At subsistence levels of living, when people's very survival is at stake, a "hand-to-mouth" economy prevails in which the future is infinitely discounted. The result of such "myopia" is over-exploitation of natural resources and underinvestment in their conservation and generation which ultimately leads to their depletion. The high cost of rural credit from informal sources, in the absence of institutional credit, also leads to high rates of discount. Conservation projects that would have been profitable at 10% or 15% interest rates are not profitable at the 50% or even 100% rates charged by informal credit sources.[5] Again, there is scope for government intervention to induce longer time horizons and lower discount rates (through increased savings), to regulate resource extraction and to invest in the conservation and regeneration of resources according to the society's true time preference. The society because of its continuity and risk pooling capacity tends to be less myopic than its indvidual members.

There is a clear relationship between this market failure and the ones discussed earlier. Common property or open access exploitation of resources is equivalent to the use of an infinite discount rate: that is, future benefits sacrificed by current resource use are infinitely discounted, effectively assigned a zero value by the common "owners", regardless of their value to society. This is understandable, since, under open access, no one is assured of the benefits of his investments and conservation efforts since others have free access to the same resource. Under open access, there is no future: common property is transformed into private property through prompt capture and use. From the individual's point of view, conservation is meaningless and irrational under open access conditions.

Public externalities or environmental costs and benefits are also infinitely discounted by an unregulated market regardless of whether they occur at present or in the future. Discounting also relates to undervaluation and transaction costs through the absence of organized futures markets.

Uncertainty and risk aversion

Natural resource management and conservation is about the future, a future which is beset with uncertainties and risks. A situation is said to involve uncertainty if more than one outcome is (or is perceived to be) possible from any given action. Two types of uncertainty may be distinguished: (1) environmental uncertainty arising from factors beyond the decision-maker's (farmer's) control, e.g., weather, epidemic disease, technological discoveries; and (2) market uncertainty arising from a market failure to provide information (prices) required for decisions affecting the future (absence of future markets). The longer the time horizon, the further into the future forecasts need to be made and the greater the uncertainties involved.

A distinction is sometimes made between uncertainty and risk. A situation is said to involve uncertainty if no objective probability of each of the many possible outcomes can be attached. In contrast, risk is a situation where the general level of probability of each outcome can be inferred, although known probabilities cannot be precisely assigned. In everyday use, a situation is said to be risky if one of the outcomes involves losses to the decision-maker. Thus, the risk of loss to a firm or a farm may be defined as the probability that profits will be less than zero, or the probability that returns will fall below some "disaster level" of income. Risks may be reduced through diversification of activities with negatively correlated outcomes, ("putting all one's eggs in one basket" is rarely a good policy). Risks in one activity may also be reduced by pooling them with risks from other independent activities. Where risks are of a given type (e.g. independent of the actions of the decision-maker), risk-pooling or insurance markets have often emerged to exploit these possibilities. Individuals transfer their risks to an insurance company by paying an insurance premium which in a perfect insurance market would equal the administrative costs of the company plus the cost of any remaining risk.

However, not all risks are insurable. Insurance markets fail to appear when the outcome is not external to the policyholder, the risk affects all policyholders in a similar way, or the probabilities of the various outcomes are difficult to assess. For example, a farm cannot insure itself against the risk of losses because profitability is as much a function of the farmer's actions as it is of environmental uncertainty (e.g., weather). Similarly, a fish farm cannot insure itself against the risk of an epidemic because such risk would affect all farms in a similar way, which reduces the benefits from risk-pooling.

Risks may be objective or subjective. Objective risks are calculated on the basis of the probability of occurrence of the adverse outcome. Attitudes towards risk differ among individuals based on sociocultural and economic factors. In general, risk aversion tends to be stronger among lower socioeconomic groups because survival is at stake.

While uncertainty affects all sectors of the economy, natural resource sectors are more seriously affected for a variety of reasons. First, there are more uncertainties about ownership and access to natural resources. Second, there are more potential spillovers from other activities. Third, natural resource investments such as tree planting tend to have much longer gestation periods than investments in agriculture or industry and, the longer the gestation the more the uncertainties and risks involved. Fourth, natural resource commodity prices are subject to more violent fluctuations than other commodities and as such they are difficult to forecast. Last, most resource commodities are under the constant threat of substitution from cheaper substitutes developed by continuous but unpredictable technological change.

Uncertainty about the future should make people more conservative in natural resource exploitation, and therefore it should work in favor of conservation of at least those resources, such as biological diversity, which are less likely to be substituted by technology. After all, one reason why people save is to provide themselves with a cushion against future uncertainty. However, insecurity of tenure and pervasive externalities create uncertainty about the benefits from conservation as compared to the benefits from current exploitation. For the individual, it makes good economic sense to cut down the forest and mine land to generate income which he can then consume or invest in more secure assets. From the society's point of view, it makes more sense to preserve the long-term productivity of the resource base both as a source of income in perpetuity and as insurance against uncertainty. Liquidating the resource base on the basis of short-term economics makes less sense in the face of uncertainty (than under certainty) if such action is also irreversible.

Irreversibility

Market decisions about the future (such as consumption vs. investment) are made with the best available, yet incomplete information about future developments, on the assumption that such decisions can be reversed if they are proved to be unwise in the light of new information. This assumption of irreversibility does not hold in many decisions involving natural resources. Consider the choice between preserving a tropical rainforest with some unique features and developing the site for logging and mining concessions. If the social benefits from development exceed the social benefits from conservation even marginally, we should choose logging and mining except for the fact that conservation is irreversible, while logging and mining are not. Choosing logging and mining forecloses our options, if we or future generations were to have a change of mind there would be no way to reproduce the uniqueness and authenticity of the original species that became extinct. In contrast, choosing conservation preserves our option to reverse our decision. Clearly, there is a social value or shadow price for the preservation of options, though it is difficult to estimate. However, there are reasons to favor "high" value. On the one hand, technical change is asymmetric: it expands our ability to produce ordinary goods, the products of development, but does little to improve our ability to produce natural environments, the products of conservation. On the other hand, consumer preferences tend to shift in favor of environmental services relative to ordinary goods. In conclusion, "Where economic decisions have an impact on the natural environment that is both uncertain and irreversible, there is a value to retaining an option to avoid the impact" (Fisher and Krutilla, 1985).

POLICY FAILURES LEADING TO ENVIRONMENTAL DEGRADATION

The tendency of free markets to fail in the allocation and efficient use of natural resources and the environment opens an opportunity and provides a rationale for government intervention. But it is a necessary condition, not a sufficient one. The sufficient conditions are that (a) the government intervention outperforms the market or improves its function, and (b) the benefits from such intervention exceed the costs of planning, implementation and enforcement as well as any indirect and unintended cost of distortions introduced to other sectors of the economy by such interventions.

Ideally, government intervention aims at correcting or, at least, mitigating market failures through taxation, regulation, private incentives, public projects, macroeconomic management and institutional reform. For example, if the market fails to allocate land to its best possible use because of insecurity of land ownership, the indicated government intervention ought to be the issuance of secure land titles through cadastral surveys, land registration, etc., provided the ensuing benefits exceed the costs. If on the other hand, the market fails to allocate land to its best possible use because of severe flooding due to upstream deforestation, the government ought to explore the costs and benefits of taxation on upstream logging and/or downstream agriculture and the use of the proceeds to subsidize upstream reforestation. If economic analysis that considers all costs and benefits involved concludes that such an intervention can make both upstream logger/shifting cultivators and downstream farmers better off, and no one else worse off (including the government treasury), it would be a policy failure not to act. Such an intervention is not a distortion, but a mitigation or correction of distortion introduced by a failing market.[6]

In practice, however, government policies tend to introduce additional distortions in the market for natural resources rather than correct existing ones. The reasons are many and varied. First, correction of market failure is rarely the sole or even the primary objective of government intervention; other objectives such as national security, social equity, macroeconomic management and political expediency may dominate. Second, government intervention often has unintended consequences and unforeseen or underestimated side effects. Third, policies such as subsidies and protection against imports or competition, often outlive their usefulness because they become capitalized into peoples' expectations and property values, creating vested interests that make their removal politically difficult. Fourth, policy interventions tend to accumulate and interact with each other in subtle but profound ways to distort private incentives away from socially beneficial activities. Finally, policies that are seemingly unrelated to natural resources and the environment may have more pronounced effects on the environment than environmental and resource policies; for example, capital subsidies, tax and tariff exemptions for equipment, and minimum wage laws that displace labor lead to increased pressures on forest, marginal lands, coastal areas and urban slums. For example, in Ghana, a grossly overvalued exchange rate resulting from macroeconomic mismanagement has a) nullified what otherwise was an efficient forest policy, b) accelerated deforestation by exacerbating poverty, and c) foiled reforestation by making reforestation incentives irrelevant.

Thus, environmental degradation results not only from overreliance on a free market that fails to function efficiently (*market failure*), but also from government policies that intentionally or unwittingly distort incentives in favor of overexploitation and against conservation of valuable and scarce resources (*policy failure*).

Policy failures may be classified into four basic types:

(a) Distortion of otherwise well-functioning markets through taxes, subsidies, quotas, regulations, inefficient state enterprises, and public projects of low economic return and high environmental impact. This is a case of "fixing what is not broken".

(b) Failures to consider and internalize significant environmental externalities (side effects) of otherwise warranted policy interventions. For example, fertilizer and pesticide subsidies may have a useful role to play in encouraging farmers to adopt new high-yielding crop varieties. In selecting the types of fertilizers and pesticides to subsidize and in setting the level and duration of the subsidy the effect on farmers' choice of other inputs (manure, soil conservation, weeding, irrigation, etc.) and on long-term productivity should be factored in. Moreover, the potential offsite damage from contamination and eutrophication of water resources from overuse and runoff should be considered and mitigated by setting a lower subsidy for a shorter period and promoting soil conservation, organic fertilizers and integrated pest mangagement (IPM). For example, Indonesia in its drive for rice self-sufficiency has provided generous subsidies (82% of the retail price) for a variety of pesticides. Subsidies led to overuse which, in turn, led to severe reduction of the predators of the brown planthopper which threatened the country's achieved self-sufficieny in rice. In a dramatic move, the government turned what was threatening to be a policy failure into a policy success by abolishing the subsidy and promoting IPM at lower cost.

(c) Policy interventions that aim to correct or mitigate market failure but end up generating a worse outcome than a free and failing market would have produced. It must be recognized that market failure does not mandate government interventions; it merely suggests the possibility that such intervention might prove beneficial. In some cases, doing nothing might be the best policy if intervening would make matters worse. However, in most cases the problem is not that no action is indicated, but that the wrong action is being taken. For example, if the free market fails to contain deforestation because the forests are open access resources and the negative externalities of deforestation are not internalized (paid by the parties responsible), a government intervention in the form of a logging ban is unlikely to be effective since (a) higher prices are likely to stimulate illegal logging, and (b) concessionaires may log illegally to recover sunk costs or they may abandon their conservation to encroachment and slash-and-burn activities, as Thailand is discovering following the January 1989 logging ban response to the catastrophic landslides of November 1988.

(d) Failures to intervene in failing markets when such interventions are clearly needed to improve the functioning of the market and could be made at costs fully justified by the expected benefits. For example, it would have been a policy failure for the government of Thailand not to undertake to issue secure land titles to its farmers, when it was established that the cost of titling was only a small percentage (less than 10%) of the potential benefits. By intervening in the land market to establish secure property rights, a precondition for well-functioning markets, the government has turned a market failure into a policy success. In contrast, the issuance of 25-year "usufruct" or "stewardship" rights to squatters on public lands in Thailand and the Philippines is a half measure that does not go to the root of the problem. It is unlikely to stimulate continued encroachment without significantly improving farmers' security of ownership, access to credit and incentives to invest. Such half measures risk turning a market failure into a policy failure of possibly greater dimensions.

To sum up, policy failures include both the failure to intervene when necessary and beneficial and the failure to refrain from intervention when unnecessary and detrimental. The policy failures which lead to environmental degradation range from poorly designed public projects that fail to account for their environmental impacts to structural adjustment programs that fail to internalize or at least cushion their environmental repercussions. Policy failures are not the exclusive domain of governments. Development assistance agencies, through their project and program lending and policy dialogue, may introduce or exacerbate a policy failure. For example, liberalization as part of a structural or sectoral adjustment loan, in the absence of secure property rights and other legal foundations of markets, may simply transform a policy failure into a market failure, an outcome not uncommon with African liberalization programs.

(a) Project-related policy failures, especially project selection on the basis of financial appraisal or narrow economic analysis that does not internalize environmental externalities.
(b) Sectoral policies that ignore long-term costs and intersectoral linkages and spillovers. Sectoral policies may in turn be divided into agricultural and industrial policies or even more narrowly into land policy, water resource policy, fisheries policy, urban development policy, industrial location policy, etc.
(c) Macroeconomic policies that lack either microfoundations (e.g., liberalization in the absence of functioning markets) or ignore significant environmental consequences (e.g., the effect of high interest rates, overvalued exchange rates or excessive borrowing on natural resource depletion).

Project-related policy failures

Project policies refer to both public and private projects. We will discuss public projects first. Public projects are a potent instrument of government intervention for mitigating market failures (e.g., provision of public goods such as roads, utilities, parks, etc.), but if used inappropriately, can become a major source of market distortion. First, since most public projects are financed directly or indirectly from general taxation, they tend to crowd out private investment as well as to redistribute resources. This is justified and beneficial only to the extent that public projects generate higher economic/social returns than private projects. Second, public projects, especially in developing countries, tend to be very large both by comparison to private projects and to the size of the economy. Because of their sheer size and their infrastructural nature, public projects tend to have non-marginal impacts on both the economy and the environment. Therefore, taking prices as given and ignoring environmental and social impacts is not appropriate.

Infrastructure projects such as roads and irrigation systems often have environmental impacts that extend far beyond the physical displacement of natural environments and any associated spillovers. For example, the environmental impact of road construction through an undisturbed forest is not simply the forest cut to make room for the road, or even the damage to the environment from road traffic and air pollution. The single largest environmental impact comes from the increased encroachment or colonization of the forest facilitated by the road, as the Trans-Amazon Highway through Accre and Rondonia amply demonstrated.

Two other examples come from Thailand. Only fifteen years ago the lower Northeast region of Thailand was covered with undisturbed forest. Then the area was made accessible by the construction of a major highway. According to Thailand's National Economic and Social Development Board (1982, p. 233): "Landless farmers . . . from around the area and elsewhere have moved in and cleared the land for cultivation, resulting in the destruction of forest land (and watersheds) of 5.28 million rai (one million ha) between 1973 and 1977. The sporadic immigration to clear new land for cultivation has given birth to 318 villages in the past nine years." Today, the area is totally devastated by salinization and soil erosion that make both forestry and agriculture unsustainable. Had private and communal property rights been issued before the opening up of the area, both agriculture and forestry could be sustainable.

Another example comes from the Nam Pong multipurpose reservoir–irrigation system constructed in 1966 in Northeast Thailand. In a strikingly similar fashion to the highway, the watershed area of the reservoir has been subjected to very high population increases both from people who were displaced from the reservoir area and from people attracted from other areas to the reservoir, which unexpectedly developed a productive fishery with more than 70 edible species. The influx of people into the area led to rapid deforestation of the open access watershed, increased soil erosion and sedimentation of the reservoir with adverse effects on the reservoir fishery and reduction in the outputs and benefits from power generation, irrigation and flood control.

It is easy to blame population growth, the proximate not the ultimate cause of deforestation, and prescribe population control. But this would amount to little more than treatment of symptoms, since in both the case of the dam and the case of the highway, the influx of population would have not taken place to the degree it did in the absence of the project. Prescribing population control as a remedy to a problem caused by poor project planning, by failure to establish secure property rights over agricultural and forest lands, and by failure to recognize externalities and internalize the environmental cost of the project is tantamount to arguing that no matter what the market and policy failures involved, without people there would have been no problem! In any case, Thailand over the past 20 years has undergone the most spectacular reduction in population growth of any country, from over 3% in the late 1960s to under 1.5% today through voluntary incentives, education, and economic growth. It is true that Northeast Thailand continues to be relatively densely populated and poor, but this is not because of high population growth but because of skewed economic growth (centered in the Central Region), barriers to mobility (insecure land ownership, inappropriate education policy) and distorted sector markets that favor capital intensity in industry at the expense of labor employment.

An econometric study of the causes of deforestation in Northeast Thailand has found that population density (as distinct from population growth), poverty, and infrastructure (both dams and roads) as well as economic incentives (wood and crop prices) played a significant role in deforestation (Panayotou and Sungsawan, 1989).

Public projects are usually justified economically through cost–benefit analysis, which in principle should consider all social benefits and costs, monetary or not, quantifiable or not. Project level distortions or biases against efficient resource use, environmental quality and sustainable development arise for one of the following reasons: (a) projects are selected based on financial appraisal (cash flows) or narrow economic analysis (shadow pricing some inputs and not others); (b) the social benefits and costs are too narrowly defined in space (excluding externalities) and in time (excluding long-term effects); (c) the environmental effects are unforeseen at the design stage of the project; (d) the environmental costs are foreseen and appreciated, but it is difficult to measure and evaluate them; (e) an unduly high social discount rate is used; and (f) the irreversibility of project-induced changes in the environment is ignored or not properly handled.

While difficulties remain, sophisticated evaluation techniques have been developed in recent years for evaluating environmental externalities and incorporating them into cost–benefit analysis. Similarly, methods, such as the "safe minimum standard" (SMS) approach, have been developed for dealing with irreversibility. As to the discount rate, two points need to be made here: (1) the discount rate does not discriminate against environmental benefits *per se* but against long-term benefits which may be development benefits; and (2) the discount rate is a public policy parameter which can be chosen to promote a long-term perspective as long as it is used consistently and with full appreciation of the fact that the lower the social discount rate, compared to the market discount rate, the more private investment will be crowded out by public projects.

A major policy distortion is the very emphasis on projects as opposed to policies and strategies. The emphasis is on choosing between projects rather than on asking whether anything needs to be done in a given resource area. Similarly, the emphasis is on designing and implementing new projects rather than on evaluating how well projects have fared in the past. Rogers (1986, p. 7) describes this bias in the case of water resource policies very aptly:

> In most countries the framework for interrelating national economic policies with water resources policies have been collapsed down to an accounting framework whereby the possible investments in the water sector are analyzed project by project. These projects are added together to make a portfolio of investments offered by the technical agencies to the planning commission as the investment policy. The planning commission then responds by checking to see if the overall resources demanded can be met from the available current, or projected, economic resources. The planning commission then either recommends changes or passes the portfolio on to the executive for approval. Depending upon the country, and the time and resources available to it, the planning commission may, or may not, check for consistency between the water sector and the other sectors of the economy.

Planning paradigms such as the above can be quite effective if the planners have sufficient time to go back and forth between the sectors two or three times before stopping the process. In practical planning situations, however, sufficient time is not available and one is left with a one-sided, one-directional analysis – the impacts of a sector (or parts of it) on the economic policies are assessed but the reverse is typically not done. Therefore, real assessments of the value of investments in the water sector are never effectively compared with those in other sectors. The enormous investments in irrigation systems were not seen in the context of a national development policy, or even an agricultural or water policy. Otherwise, the protection of the watersheds and the provision for system maintenance, water distribution, and drainage would not have been neglected. Similarly, seen in the context of a national or rural development policy, the construction of road infrastructure through forests without prior clarification of land rights should not have taken place.

The bias for or against projects as opposed to policies is not unique to government agencies. Environmental groups have focused on the environmental damage caused by projects such as Nam Choan Dam in Thailand, the Marmada project in India, and the Tucurui Dam in Brazil, rather than the massive market failures and policy distortions that lead to wholesale destruction of natural resources and degradation of the environment. When projects are seen as part of an overall development policy, many of what are now unaccounted externalities would be internalized and much of the development–environment conflict resolved. Many developing economies are far from their efficient production frontier. It is possible and feasible to produce more development and better environment at the same time by correcting market failures and eliminating policy distortions. It is in this context that public projects should be planned, designed, and evaluated.

Forest policy failures

Forest policy is an excellent example of a resource-specific policy that needs to be overhauled if the link between scarcity and prices is to be reestablished. If indeed we are facing a growing scarcity of forests, forest product prices should be rising to slow down deforestation and accelerate reforestation. At present, not only are most forest products and services not priced, but even timber which is an internationally tradeable commodity is priced below its true scarcity value due to implicit and explicit subsidies and institutional failures. Uncollected resource rents, subsidized logging on marginal and fragile forest lands, and volume-based taxes on timber removal encourage high grading and destructive logging. Forest concessions are typically too short to provide incentives for conservation and replanting. Failure to value non-timber goods and services results in excessive deforestation, conflicts with local communities, loss of economic value and environmmental damage. Promotion of local processing of timber often leads to inefficient plywood mills, excess capacity, waste of valuable tropical timber and loss of government revenues. Replanting subsidies often end up subsidizing the conversion of a valuable natural forest to inferior mono-species plantations, with the associated loss of the value of both tropical hardwoods and biological diversity.

Concerns over rapid rates of deforestation and slow rates of replanting have given rise to export bans on unprocessed timber by tropical timber producers such as Thailand, the Philippines and Indonesia. The primary motivation has been the conservation of forest resources and, in Indonesia, an increase in value added through domestic processing and, by implication, forest conservation. The log export bans have largely failed to slow deforestation in all three countries. In Thailand and the Philippines, illegal logging and clearing of land for permanent and shifting cultivation continued unabated. In Indonesia, the inefficient and excessive processing capacity stimulated by the log export ban has led to logging rates above the pre-ban levels.

Following the catastrophic landslides and floods of last November that have been attributed to deforestation, the Thai government introduced an indefinite logging ban. This is a well-meant and popular action. However, unless it is supplemented with effective enforcement and forest management, it is unlikely to succeed in stemming the rate of deforestation. Illegal logging, encroachment and shifting cultivation are likely to continue and even intensify in the absence of logging concessions, because population pressures, poverty and incentives for opening land for agriculture have not changed. Nor has the enforcement capability of the Department of Forestry, which is the legal owner of these forests. Already , there have been (controversial) reports in the local press that the rate of deforestation increased following the imposition of the ban last January.

Land policy failures

Insecurity of land ownership is the single most severe market cum policy failure in developing countries. It prevents the optimal use of land and leads to the degradation of the land, water and forest resources. Insecurity of land owner-ship takes many forms: (a) totally untitled land, the result of forest encroachment and squatting; (b) land under unclear, disputed or multiple ownership; (c) land under short-term lease or tenancy; (d) land under uncertainty of imminent or likely land reform or appropriation; (e) land under usufruct or stewardship certificates that are not indefinite and transferable; and (f) land ownership that is tied to compulsory state trading, price controls, and forced cooperatives through which the "owner" is forced to buy inputs at higher than market prices and to sell outputs at lower than market prices.

Untitled or insecurely-held land is commonly found in the Philippines and Thailand (the result of swidden cultivation), in Indonesia (the result of spontaneous migration), in Burma (in areas outside the control of the central government), in Nepal (as a result of migration from the hills to the Terrai) and in Africa (tribal lands). However, the quantitatively most significant form of insecurity of tenure in the Philippines and South Asia is tenancy. While owner and tenants with reasonable security do not seem to differ in their willigness to adopt innovations, such as new varieties, fertilizers and pesticides for annual crops, they may have different attitudes towards long-term investments that enhance land productivity and sustainability over the long-run such as irrigation and drainage structures, land terracing, tree crops, etc. (World Bank, 1985, p. 98).

A classic example of multiple or unclear ownership is provided by some 500,000 tanks and ponds covering 70,000 ha in land-secure Bangladesh that remain largely unused despite an apparent high potential for fish culture (Khan, 1989). Widespread multiple ownership aggravated by inheritance is suspected to be a major constraint (FAO/UNDP, 1977). Similarly, open acces pastures are clearly an extreme case of multiple ownership, but communally managed lands or pastures are not if the community has sufficient cohesion, social organization, and leadership to make decisions about optimal use. This is why communal and tribal land in Papua New Guinea and in parts of Africa does not suffer from insecurity of ownership while in other parts of Africa insecurity is pervasive. In fact, there are examples from Northern Thailand, India and Kenya and several other African countries where tribal land in one village is managed almost as if it is owned by a single individual, while in a neighboring village tribal land is exploited as no man's land, with the known consequences of the "tragedy of the commons."

The lack of security of ownership over land constitutes a serious obstacle to farm investments necessary for diversification, intensification, and increased productivity. Untitled land is not accepted by financial institutions as collateral for credit forcing farmers into the high interest rate informal credit market, which makes farm investments unprofitable (Feder et al. 1986). The risk of eviction, however small, adds an element of uncertainty that further discourages investments in land improvements and soil conservation. Uncertainty, lack of access to institutional credit, and easy access to public forest land combine to bias agricultural development against intensification on existing lands and in favor of expansion into new lands. This leads to encroachment of forest resources thereby depleting forest resources and increasing the amount of land under cultivation. Moreover, insecurity of land tenure and the consequent lack of access to credit biases the cropping system in favor of annual crops such as corn and cassava that generate a quick return at the expense of long-term productivity. Tree crops which may be more profitable over the long run and are certainly more protective of the soil and therefore more sustainable, are discouraged by insecurity of ownership, uncertainty and lack of credit because of their long gestation.

The importance of security of ownership for investment, long-term

346

productivity, and conservation cannot be overemphasized. The World Bank (1985), based on its 40 years of experience in lending for agricultural development around the world, has concluded that:

> How farmers use land is greatly affected by the degree of security of land-tenure – with respect to such matters as duration of user rights, clarity of land rights, ability to sell these rights or pass them on to succeeding generations, and ability to obtain compensation for investments. A farmer with unclear, insecure, or short-term tenure is more likely to "mine" the land, that is, to seek maximum short-run production gains through crop rotations and other practices that may degrade the biological and physical qualities of the soil.

The large percentage of agricultural land under insecure tenure in Thailand, the Philippines, Indonesia and parts of South Asia and Africa is partly due to the open access status of public forest lands. In the absence of enforcement of state ownership, forest land has been effectively made available for agricultural expansion free of charge. As an unpriced resource, forest land for agricultural expansion is in high demand and increasingly short supply as the limits of the land frontier are being approached. Yet, in the absence of secure and transferable titles, an efficient land market for encroached land failed to develop, and consequently, increasing land scarcity did not lead to higher prices and increased land conservation. Thus, we have a dual failure of the market to bring about the efficient allocation and use of land resources. First, an excessive acreage of forest land is being cleared even when its best use is in forestry rather than in agriculture. Second, cleared land is not used efficiently because of the insecurity of ownership discussed earlier. Moreover, the availability of free land discourages land investment even on securely owned lands because it biases relative prices in favor of extensification and against intensification.

Insecurity of land tenure and lack of access to credit have both on-farm and off-farm environmental consequences that result in further reduction of productivity. The on-farm environmental effects are soil erosion, nutrient leaching and waterlogging resulting from inadequate incentives (and funds) to invest in drainage and soil conservation practices. The off-farm effects are further encroachment of marginal lands and watersheds because of inability to maintain yields on existing agricultural lands. This results not only in loss of valuable forest resources but also in soil erosion and sedimentation of downstream irrigation systems.

Given these detrimental consequences of insecurity of land ownership on land productivity, on the owner's income and wealth, and the quality of the environment, governments have a critical role to play in improving security of ownership. Empirical evidence (see Feder et al.) suggests that the benefits of providing secure titles far exceed the costs. Unfortunately, well-intentioned governments have been exacerbating uncertainty and insecurity by talking about land reform rather than effectively carrying it out while ignoring other politically more acceptable and economically more efficient means of improving land distribution (e.g., land taxation). Graduated, progressive land taxation has been effectively used in Japan to effect a land reform without creating the kind of uncertainty that paralyzes long-term investments in the Philippines today. Moreover, since much of the wealth in developing countries is held in the form of land, and land value benefits from rural infrastructure, such as roads and irrigation, it is possible and appropriate to use land taxation as the principle source of financing of the operation and maintenance of rural infrastructure. At present, land taxes are nominal and little or no tax revenue is derived from land, partly because of the lack or inadequacy of land cadastre, lack of enforcement and very low tax rates.

Well-meant government policies that limit property rights to fixed-term use rights, and prohibit their transferability or tie the land granted through land reform to state trading, price controls or forced cooperatives create unnecessary uncertainty and diminish the value of these rights. Such land is not likely to be put to its best use. Concerns about land purchase and accumulation by land speculators can be dealt with through a land sales tax and a progressive property tax.

Water policy failures

A third example of a resource-specific policy that needs to be reformed to reestablish the broken link between scarcity and prices is water policy. Virtually all countries, regardless of the degree of scarcity of water, subsidize water for irrigation (and other uses) and, in many cases, they supply it free of charge. Take the example of Thailand. Both seasonally and spatially, Thailand experiences droughts and floods. Northeast Thailand suffers from perennial water shortages. The Central Region is inundated in the rainy season and imports water from the Northern Region in the dry season. Only 30 percent of the irrigable area covered by the Greater Chao Phraya Project has adequate irrigation in the dry season. Yet this profound and growing water scarcity does not register. According to the *National Resources Profile* (TDRI, 1987), "many farmers continue to think of water as a free, virtually unlimited resource whereas the facts increasingly suggest otherwise." Irrigation water is provided free of charge without any attempt to recover cost or to charge a price reflecting the scarcity value or opportunity cost of water. The result is overirrigation with consequent salinization and waterlogging in some areas and inadequate water in others. This gross waste of water limits the efficiency of irrigation systems to about 15 percent of a potential of 60 to 70 percent (ADB, 1984), while the failure to achieve any degree of cost recovery deprives the system of operation and maintenance funds.

Similar problems of growing water scarcity are also found in Indonesia which ranks second in the Asia/Near East (ANE) region in terms of freshwater endowment. Densely populated Java faces increasing water shortages that are being addressed through supply rather than demand management. But the area that is facing the most critical water scarcity is the Near East. According to Elias Saleh, a hydrologist with Jordan University, "In the mid 1990s farmers in the high plains and in the swelter of the Jordan Valley will face a crisis because the growing population will lay claim to water for drinking, and irrigation will be curtailed . . . Water is the future of the whole area . . . It is very critical" (*New York Times*, April 16, 1989 p. 1). Virtually all Near East countries but particularly Egypt, Yemen, Jordan and Tunisia face severe water shortages, yet water continues to be subsidized throughout the region, and water efficiency is unacceptably low. In Egypt, where 30 percent of the irrigated lands suffer from salinization and waterlogging due to overirrigation (FAO, 1980), "efficiency ratings will have to increase by 60 percent over the next 11 years to meet the needs of the population, projected to reach 70 million in the year 2000" (*New York*

Times, April 16, 1989, p. 1). According to the same source, "Jordan is expecting a water crisis within a decade and dearth of new water resources by the year 2005."

Urban–industrial environment: market cum policy failures

Industrial development and urbanization are highly correlated. Industries in many developing countries (and some developed ones) are often located in or near urban centers because of the skewed distribution of public infrastructure (roads, electricity, telephones, government offices, etc). About half of the industrial value added of countries as diverse as Brazil, Thailand, and Egypt comes from industries located in their largest urban centers. Correspondingly, industrial pollution is concentrated in and around urban centers such as Mexico City, Sao Paulo, Cairo, Bombay, Bangkok, and Manila. Thus, it is often difficult to determine what part of observed environmental degradation is caused by industrialization and what part by urbanization.

Increased urbanization (and industrialization) in the 1990s will exacerbate already serious problems of crowding and water and air pollution in cities such as Manila, Bangkok, Jakarta, Delhi, Calcutta, Cairo, Mexico City and Sao Paulo. This means that more emphasis and resources must be devoted to addressing urban environmental problems than have been the case in the past.

Regardless of urbanization, to employ the additional labor force in the 1990s more emphasis will be placed on industrial development, thus increasing the production and disposal of hazardous toxic chemicals and wastes. This is already a major problem in India, Thailand, the Philippines, Egypt, Mexico, and Brazil. Similarly, the intensification of agriculture to accommodate larger numbers on the same land will inevitably lead to increased use of toxic agricultural chemicals, which presents a new set of problems for policy makers. Indonesia has already had a dramatic experience with agricultural pesticides, as has India with industrial hazardous chemicals.

Industrialization is certain to have environmental implications not only for the urban centers but also for the rural areas. The impact of industrialization on the rural environment will depend on labor intensity, location and type of industry. Labor-intensive industry if combined with appropriate location and educational policy is likely to attract labor out of the marginal and fragile areas and thus reduce the pressure on natural resources. Capital-intensive industry would have little or negative impact on the rural environment.

Urban and industrial environmental quality is clearly an area of massive market failures. The urban environmment is an unpriced common property resource; environmental pollution is a public externality whose internalization involves prohibitively high transaction costs because of the millions of polluters and affected parties involved. Pollution abatement and its product, environmental quality, are public goods that cannot be provided by a free market because of inability to exclude and hence inability to finance.

While there is an increasing recognition of environmental problems in urban centers around the world as evidenced by increasing regulation of industrial pollution, the environment is still treated by both households and industries as an open access space for free disposal of wastes. In many countries, large industries are required to submit environmental impact studies before their establishment and meet certain emisssion standards during their operation, but effective enforcement is lacking. Moreover, the far more numerous small industries and millions of households continue to enjoy free disposal of waste into the environment. Urban centers in developing countries lack sewage treatment facilities. Unrestricted air and noise pollution from public and private automobiles is another example of the use of the environment as a free and open access resource. Similar is the perception and use of the environment by farmers who release water contaminated with toxic fertilizers and pesticides into the main water source. Free disposal of wastes is tantamount to a lack of property rights over the environment or use of the scarce assimilative capacity of the environment free of charge. Unpriced or open access resources are commonly overused, underconserved, and mismanaged.

Environmental pollution is a classic case of a public externality. It originates from a variety of sources including discharges of domestic wastewater, community solid wastes, industrial waste effluents and wastes from agricultural activities such as runoff of excess pesticides and fertilizers. It affects a variety of economic activities including industry, fisheries, tourism, and urban development, as well as the general quality of life. Thus, excessive environmental pollution constitutes both a misuse of an unpriced or open access resource and a negative externality on sectors and individuals who may or may not be parties to the pollution-generating activity. This is so because the environment serves both as the *recipient* of the residuals of economic activity and the *medium* which transmits offsite effects to second and third parties. Externalities created by economic activity in one area proliferate and become widespread via the environment. As countries become increasingly industrialized and urbanized, the environment is used beyond its assimilative capacity to dispose of the byproducts of economic activity, and, as a consequence, environmental quality deteriorates. Even agriculture, usually thought of as more benign to the environment than industry, is becoming a major source of pollution as it becomes more intensified through the use of mechanical and chemical inputs (toxic fertilizers, pesticides, fossil fuels, etc.). At the same time, as the supply of clean environment declines, the demand for environmental quality rises as a result of income growth. Thus, while the significance of forests, land, and water as inputs into the production process may decline somewhat with industrialization, urbanization, and agricultural intensification, their significance as assimilators of industrial, urban, and agricultural waste and as sources of environmental amenities is certain to rise.

Further industrialization and agricultural intensification, however, will not necessarily cause further environmental degradation. It depends on the type of the new or expanded industries, their spatial distribution, their input mix and technology and the incentive structure and environmental regulations introduced by the government.

Under the direct regulatory approach, the government sets maximum permissible levels of discharge of each pollutant from each source (effluent or emission standards) and relies on administrative agencies and the judicial system to enforce them. An alternative (or supplementary) type of standard is the ambient standard which sets the minimum acceptable level of environmental quality for a receiving watersource or airshed. In the US, both standards are used in water pollution in combination with heavy subsidies for construction of waste treatment facilities.

Incentives, such as tax writeoffs, accelerated depreciation, low interest loans or outright subsidies for the adoption of "clean" production technologies or the construction of waste treatment facilities are similarly inefficient and ineffective.

They do not make waste reduction or waste treatment any more profitable; they simply subsidize the producers and consumers of the products of these industries. Waste treatment is not always the most efficient means of reducing wastes; in many cases changing production processes, the type and quality of raw materials or the rate of output is more efficient. In some instances, rearrangement of the production process results in both reduction of waste and recovery of valuable by-products such as fertilizer from palm oil extraction and syrup from canning. Tax breaks, credits, depreciation allowances, and subsidies are a drain on the government budget and a disincentive to industries which might have otherwise developed more efficient methods for reducing emissions.

This direct regulation and subsidization suffers from many weaknesses: (a) it relies on centralized setting and enforcement of standards which is both costly and ineffective; (b) it promotes inefficiency since it requires similar reduction of pollution of all sources regardless of costs; (c) it emphasizes subsidized end-of-the-pipe, capital-intensive solutions (such as waste treatment plants); (d) it results in large bureaucracies and costly subsidies; (e) it requires that the environmental agency masters the technologies of both production and pollution control for hundreds of different types of industries and all their technological alternatives, a monumental task that detracts from the agency's principle monitoring functions; (g) compliance is very limited because the certainty-equivalent amount of the fine (fine times the probability of detection times the probability of conviction) for non-compliance is only a fraction of the cost of compliance in terms of expensive abatement equipment and loss of competitive position; (h) the environmental agency is engaged in endless negotiations with the polluters over the type of equipment to be installed resulting in long delays and compromise of the agency's standards; (i) the moral hazards of "regulatory capture" (the regulators are coopted by the regulated) and bribing of enforcement officials is higher than in any other pollution control system because of the protracted negotiations and ambiguity of compliance to the set standards; and (j) direct regulation provides ample opportunity for rent-seeking behavior.

Urban congestion and pollution increasingly dominates the life of large urban centers. Bangkok's commuters spent an average of 2.5 hours in crowded buses and congested roads, while school children in Mexico City start school late in the morning smog (*Economist*, February 18, 1989). Policy responses to congestion problems range from supply management (build more roads, introduce one way traffic, etc.) to rationing the use of scarce roads by doing nothing. Supply management works only temporarily: to the extent that congestion and traffic jams are relaxed by new roads, the benefits from driving increase inducing car-owners to drive more and non-owners tend to purchase cars. As long as open access to city roads prevails, any rents from using them will be driven to zero. And, this is the basis of rationing by doing nothing; delays are left to become long enough to discourage any further increase in driving. However, this is a very inefficient solution. Costs include: (a) loss of productive time, (b) increased use of fossil fuels, (c) increased air pollution (with all the associated health problems, medical bills, and cleaning costs), and (c) increased noise pollution, not to mention the frustration and psychological costs. Ultimately those who are left using the road are those who value least their time (low opportunity cost). A rough calculation of the lost time and increased use of gasoline for Bangkok produced an estimated loss of $1 billion a year. Medical bills and lost days of work due to pollution-related ailments, cleaning costs, damage to infrastructure and buildings from increased pollution and the extra cost that consumers incur for noise insulation, air conditioning of cars and houses that would not have taken place otherwise may double this figure. If we conservatively put the total annual costs of congestion at $1.5 billion and capitalized this figure at a 10% interest rate, we obtain a present value of congestion cum added pollution cost of $15 billion. Only a fraction of this amount would suffice to provide Bangkok with a clean and efficient public transport. Charges for the use of city center roads and surcharges on gasoline can be set high enough to hold traffic down to levels that permit it to move freely, and the proceeds can be used to improve public transportation. Singapore introduced a road pricing system whereby drivers purchase a permit to enter the city center during rush hours; buses and car pools are excluded, making the system not only efficient but also equitable.

Industrial and trade policy failures leading to environmental degradation

Industrial and trade policies may seem only remotely related to natural resource use and management, but they are in fact critical, because they affect: (a) the terms of trade between agriculture and industry and therefore the relative profitability of agriculture and other resource sectors; (b) the use of natural resources as an input in industry; (c) the level of industrial employment and hence the residual rural labor that exerts pressure on natural resources; and (d) the level of industrial pollution.

Agriculture's terms of trade in the ANE region have deteriorated over the years because of heavy protection of industry through import tariffs and investment incentives which reinforced the adverse effects of agriculture taxation. Adverse terms of trade for agriculture appear to be conducive to natural resource conservation since the less profitable agriculture is, the less intensively and extensively land and water resources are used and the less agricultural chemicals are applied. However, this may not be the case in labor-abundant economies, dependent on agriculture for employment of the majority of the labor force.

For the pressure on the agricultural resource base to be reduced, the number of people depending on agriculture must be reduced through labor movement into other sectors. Unfortunately, the increased relative profitability of industry often fails to attract much labor out of agriculture and other resource sectors because of the capital intensity and the urban bias of the promoted industries. Subsistence farmers and landless unskilled laborers faced with sliding real incomes, due to increasing land shortages (dimishing average holdings) and labor surpluses (low real wages), are in constant search for supplementary and/or alternative sources of income. Open access natural resources such as forests and forest land, inland and coastal fishing grounds, mineral-bearing lands and offshore areas, and the natural environment are the most conveniently accessible sources of supplementary or alternative employment and income. Additional income is earned through the gathering of fuelwood and other forest products, fishing and the collecting of minerals by underemployed members of the household. Illegal logging and poaching of logs or working for illegal loggers often yields substantially higher income than legal employment, if such can be found. The size of land holdings is maintained and sometimes increased by clearing additional forest land. Thus, the availability of open access resources helps halt the drop in incomes resulting from rapid population growth and slow rural development. When open-access resources in the vicinity of a rural community run out, migration to other areas where open access resources are found takes place. One of the major destinations of migration are the main urban centers where it results in squatting on public property, creation of slums, crowding, hawking and general environmental degradation.

The reduced profitability of agriculture as a result of industrial protection also results in reduced incentives for investment in farmland development and soil conservation both because of reduced returns to such investments and because of reduced savings. Moreover, the promotion of industry at the expense of agriculture does not necessarily reduce the use of natural resources. Many resources are indirectly resource-based, e.g., agroprocessing, furniture production, and mineral processing including cement, fertilizer, and gas separation. Industrialization certainly increases energy use both in absolute terms and relative to other inputs, as well as increasing the output of industrial waste. The type of urban-based, capital-intensive industry promoted by industrial and trade policies is more resource-intensive (creating more air, water, and noise pollution) *at the margin* than the low input agriculture that is being displaced (not considering forest land clearing which tends to be exacerbated rather than discouraged by industrial policies that limit industrial employment).

To date, environmental considerations have played little role in the formulation and implementation of industrial and trade policies partly because the connection has not been obvious and partly because policy changes are made in response to crises or immediate political pressures which do not afford consideration of long-term consequences. However, in the context of sustainable development, ignoring the impact of sectoral and trade policies on resource use and management can be self-defeating. For example, protection and credit subsidies for urban-based capital-intensive industries, combined with agricultural taxation to squeeze increasing surpluses out of agriculture and speed up industrialization, may backfire. Because the industry in its early stages depends heavily on agriculture for food, materials capital, foreign exchange and markets for its products, policies that promote industrialization too heavily, at the expense of agriculture, undermine the country's industrial base. Equally important, such policies promote inequality, underemployment and scarcity of rural credit, thereby discouraging investments in land conservation and encouraging encroachment of forest lands. Moreover, the consequent social tensions do not constitute a sound basis for sustainable development.

The most important industrial policy reform necessary is the restoration of the comparative advantage of labor-intensive industry *vis-a-vis* the highly protected and promoted urban based capital-intensive manufacturing. The best solution would be a sweeping reform of biased industrial and trade policies. For political reasons such reform may not always be feasible. Given the dimensions and urgency of the employment, poverty and resource mismanagement problems and the untapped potential of rural industry a pragmatic second-best policy would be development assistance to rural, labor-intensive industries to create off-farm employment opportunities as an alternative to encroachment and destructive resource exploitation.

To be successful the promotion of rural industries should build upon the basic features of the rural areas: availability of raw materials, seaonality of labor supply and dispersion of markets. The emphasis should be on restoring a competitive environment between the rural and urban areas by improving infrastructure, making credit available at competitive rates, providing technical assistance and market information, and assisting in skill development.

Three other industrial policies that need reconsideration in the light of their environmental costs are: (1) depreciation allowances, tax rebates and tariff exemptions on equipment and materials which might be a major source of pollution; (2) energy subsidies that may favor more polluting sources of energy over less polluting ones; and (3) the criteria for approving direct foreign investment (prior screening based on the record of particular firms or industries elsewhere may be more effective than after-the-fact environmental impact assessments).

The effects of macroeconomic policies on environmental degradation

Monetary, fiscal and foreign exchange policies seem even further removed from natural resource management than industrial and trade policies. Yet, they may have more powerful effects on how resources are being allocated and used than micro or sectoral policies. For example, other things constant, the higher the costs of inputs of capital and labor used in resource extraction or in polluting industries, relative to the price of outputs, the lower the rate of resource depletion and the amount of pollution. If capital-intensive technologies are more polluting than labor-intensive technologies, the lower the price of capital relative to labor the more pollution will result.

The rate of interest is an important macroeconomic parameter with microeconomic implications for resource allocation because it links the present with the future. The higher the interest rate (or discount rate) the higher the cost of waiting and, therefore, the faster the rate of resource depletion and the lower the investment in resource conservation. However, this effect may be mitigated somewhat by the fact that a higher interest rate means a higher cost of capital, which tends to reduce capital-intensive resource depletion and environmental degradation. Interest rate ceilings and implicit interest rate subsidies for promoted industries have been the main interest rate distortions affecting the agricultural sector and the rural economy in general. Credit policy has relied on mandates, quotes, interest rate ceilings and constrained use of loan proceeds. Yet, there is growing evidence that farmers would prefer more flexible terms and increased credit availability even if they had to pay higher interest rates. The liberalization of the capital market is critical to land improvements, reforestation investments, resource conservation, agricultural intensification and the growth of the rural industry.

As most of the resource-based commodities produced in developing countries are internationally tradable (e.g. copper, oil, jute, cotton, tin, fish, rice, beef, rubber, timber) or are substitutes for tradable commodities (e.g. natural gas, lignite, hydropower), an overvalued exchange rate would reduce their depletion by reducing their price relative to non-tradable goods (e.g. transport, services, construction). An overvalued exchange rate and export taxes have similar effects in that they discourage exports (and encourage imports) of resource-based commodities, thereby reducing the pressure on the domestic resource base.

Minimum wage laws (which also encourage capital intensity) reduce labor employment and depress real non-manufacturing wage rates. This, under conditions of labor abundance, leads to a) increased use of low-cost labor in depleting natural resources, and b) encroachment of resource sectors by unemployed or underemployed labor.

Therefore, even if the issues of open access and externalities are satisfactorily resolved, resource depletion and environmental deterioration may continue unless the macroeconomic policies responsible for price distortions in the economy are reformed. The unintended but pronounced effects of fiscal, monetary and trade policies on natural resources and the environment must enter the assessment and formulation of these policies. The effects of minimum wage rates, subsidized credit, interest rate ceilings, and exchange rate adjustments (along with those of export taxes, investment incentives, and import tariffs) on the rate of resource depletion in a resource-based economy cannot be ignored without endangering the long-term viability of the economy.

It would be unrealistic, however, to expect macroeconomic policies to be tailored to meet environmental objectives because of the many other overriding considerations, such as growth stabilization and macroeconomic management, which determine these policies. What can be expected, at best, is that environmental implications are somehow taken into account when these policies are being formulated and implemented. Consideration of the resource and environmental implications of macroeconomic policies could result in one of the following consequences: (a) environmental costs may tip the scale against marginal policies by raising their social costs above their social benefits; the reverse may happen with policies that have positive environmental effects; (b) macroeconomic policy interventions might be scaled up or down on account of their environmental implications; and, (c) provisions might be made for cushioning the negative environmental effect of policies when such policies cannot be scaled down sufficiently to reduce their environmental cost to acceptable levels.

On the other hand, macroeconomic mismanagement is as detrimental to natural resource management and environmental quality as it is to the other sectors of the economy. Mounting foreign debt, widening balance of trade deficits, hyperinflation, rising interest rates, low savings, negative growth of investments and growing budget deficits work their way through economic stagnation, increased poverty, structural reversal and shortening of the planning horizon (increase in the discount rate) to encourage environmental degradation. Environmental degradation arising from macroeconomic mismanagement is more common in Africa and Latin America than in Asia.

To help governments restructure their economies to better deal with the emerging problems, the World Bank, the International Monetary Fund (IMF) and other international development agencies have been financing structural adjustment loans (SALs) and sectoral adjustment loans (SECALs). For several reasons it is important to consider the impact of these structural and sectoral adjustment programs and loans on resource management and sustainable development: (a) these adjustment programs more or less define the macroeconomic and sectoral policies to be followed for a good part of the 1990s and, as we have seen, macroeconomic and sectoral policies affect resource allocation and use ; (b) since these programs aim to restructure the economies of the region, their impact will extend far beyond the expiration of the programs and loans; and (c) for the first time, environmental concerns have been raised by several countries and development assistance agencies in the context of macroeconomic and development policies and some provisions relating to natural resources and the environment have been included in the loan agreements. Regardless of the adequacy or effectiveness of these provisions, the mere recognition of the implications of macroeconomic, trade, and development policies on the resource base and the environment is a significant step in the right direction. Yet, questions have been raised as to the overall impact of structural adjustment policies on the environment.

The effects of structural adjustment programs on environmental degradation

The impact of sectoral and structural adjustment loans on environmental degradation is a substantial topic that cannot be addressed fully in this study. However, because of its importance we will consider for illustration the possible effects of trade, industrial and agricultural reforms on the environment.

Overall, trade and industrial policy reforms amount to promotion of exports, liberalization of imports and encouragement of foreign investment. This is done by reducing absolute and differential protection, lowering production and transactions costs of exports and imports and promoting competition through institutional reform.

The environmental effect of these policies operates at several different levels. To the extent that these policies generate economic growth, create additional employment and reduce poverty, they help improve environmental conditions in the country. Increased exports of primary commodities may have the reverse effect unless the prices of inputs and outputs involved fully reflect the true scarcity of resources being used and the environmental costs incurred. Similarly increased industrialization and foreign investments are not detrimental to the environment as long as all environmental costs have been accounted for (internalized) and no major irreversible changes to the environment take place. Countries could use tariff reform as an opportunity to favor import or manufacture of environmentally benign technologies and machinery and discriminate against highly polluting technologies. Similarly environmental conditions should be specified as part of any foreign investment project at the time of application and monitored as part of regular performance evaluation. Environmental conditions include industrial location, waste disposal, pollution control, accident prevention and site rehabilitation. Environmental regulations may also be supplemented by emission standards, effluent taxes, or pollution permits. However, there is a limit to how restrictive a developing country can be and still attract the desired level of foreign investment since foreign investment is likely to gravitate to where environmental controls are less restrictive.

To ensure that industrial and trade policy reforms result in relative if not absolute environmental improvement, the import tariff structure should be used to internalize environmental costs into the pricing of technologies and products.

The environmental effects of industrial and policy reforms taken by themselves are rather ambiguous. On the one hand, to the extent that these policies generate economic growth, create employment and alleviate poverty, they help improve the environmental conditions in the country. On the other hand, to the extent that they lead to intensified exploitation and export of natural resources at prices which do not reflect the true cost to the country, they lead to deterioration of environmental conditions (timber exports from Indonesia and cassava exports from Thailand are cases in point). Similarly the environmental effect of accelerated industrialization and foreign investment depends on the type of new industries, their capital and energy intensity, their location and the enforcement of environmental regulation in the country. In the absence of such regulations and effective enforcement, promotion of low-cost manuafctures and encouragement of foreign investment leads to increased industrial pollution. Examples abound but the cases of Bangkok, Manila and Cairo will suffice.

Acceptance of increased levels of pollution and other environmental costs in exchange for economic growth, employment, foreign exchange and government revenues is a legitimate tradeoff as long as all environmental costs are internalized. Where environmental costs cannot be adequately internalized into the economic costs and benefits of, for example, foreign investment there should be explicit determination of the relevant tradeoffs. We know of no structural adjustment program that attempts to either internalize environmental costs or determine these important tradeoffs.

Agricultural policy reforms involve: (a) increases in producer prices and reduction of taxes on agricultural exports to improve incentives for agricultural production; (b) changes in relative prices by reducing price support for certain crops (e.g., sugarcane in Morocco) or reducing taxes for others (rice and rubber in Thailand); and (c) reduction in agricultural input subsidies to reduce the drain on the budget, save foreign exchange (where inputs are imported) and improve the efficiency of resource use (e.g., Philippines, Nepal and Morocco). The environmental impact of such reforms depends on the crops and inputs that are promoted or discouraged by these policies, and the institutional context in which they are implemented. If land is securely owned and forests are effectively protected and managed better, prices for agricultural crops in general would lead to increased investment in land improvement, soil conservation and agricultural intensification. Otherwise, the very same policies may lead to increased forest land clearing, cultivation of marginal lands and agricultural extensification. On the other hand, changes in relative crop prices could benefit or damage the environment depending on the affected crops and the environmental conditions in which they are grown.

For example, the reduction of the price support for sugarcane in Morocco has a positive environmental impact because surgarcane is a soil-damaging and water-intensive crop in a water-scarce country. Thus, less price support for sugarcane stipulated by Morocco's SAL results not only in less drain on the budget, but also in less drain on soil and water resources. The market is, thus, more free to respond to market signals and shift resources (land and water) to more profitable crops, making a better use of limited natural resources with less damage to the environment.

Reduction of export taxes on certain crops such as tree crops helps diversify the economy away from soil-eroding crops such as maize, wheat or cassava and towards high value perennial export crops with positive environmental side effects. The irony in the case of Thailand is that high rubber prices and free forest land have encouraged overexpansion of rubber on to steep and fragile slopes contributing to the catastrophic landslides and floods of 1988 that claimed 350 lives and caused nearly half a billion US dollars in short and long-term damages. This case clearly demonstrates that economic incentives that have positive environmental effects under certain conditions, may be environmentally destructive under a different set of circumstances. Increased incentives for perennial crops (coffee, cocoa, rubber) vis-a-vis annual field crops such as cotton, ground nuts, or row crops such as maize and sorghum can help protect the soil on gentle slopes but are not a substitute for natural forest cover on steep or fragile slopes. Countries such as Nepal, Thailand and Morocco have introduced programs as part of (or parallel to) their structural adjustment programs.

Reduction of agricultural input subsidies, also an integral part of structural adjustment policies, generally has a positive impact on the environment. The Philippines, Nepal, Pakistan, Morocco and Tunisia have all agreed to substantially reduce pesticide and fertilizer subsidies. Judicial use of both pesticides and chemical fertilizers has helped countries increase their crop yield on existing land substantially (Pakistan, Indonesia, Philippines), thereby limiting encroachment of forest lands. However, the excessive and indiscriminate use of pesticides encouraged by generous subsidies has proved counterproductive by eliminating the pests' natural predators or promoting the emergence of pesticide-resistant strains of pests. Similarly, overapplication of chemical fertilizers over a prolonged period of time, to the total exclusion of organic fertilizers (manure), damages the structure of the soil. Heavy use of pesticides and chemical fertilizers also leads to water pollution and poisoning of aquatic life through runoff into the water systems. It does not matter that chemical subsidies have been cut to reduce the drain on the budget; their reduction also reduces the drain on the environment. Ideally, however, environmentally destructive inputs (pesticides, chemical fertilizers) should be taxed in proportion to their negative externalities, and environmentally beneficial inputs (IPM, organic fertilizers, soil conservation) should be subsidized in proportion to their positive externalities. However, there is no such provision in structural adjustment programs; any positive environmental effects of such policies are incidental rather than integral to these programs.

To the extent that structural adjustment programs require water pricing to improve efficiency in resource allocation or cost recovery to reduce budget deficits, water resources are being conserved and environmental costs are being reduced. Not only is salinization and waterlogging contained but more importantly the solution of water shortages through demand management averts the environmental problems of constructing new irrigation systems (supply management).

Structural adjustment programs also call for reductions in subsidies (or import duty exemptions) for farm equipment and land clearing machinery, again as part of their objective of reducing budget and trade deficits and eliminating policy-induced distortions. This policy reform has several positive effects on resource use and the state of the environment because subsidized land clearing machinery: (a) encourages deforestation and the clearing of marginal lands for agriculture; (b) compacts and damages the structure of fragile tropical soils; (c) increases the use of fossil fuels; and (d) distorts the farmer's labor-capital choice in favor of capital and against labor in countries with abundant labor. Aside from the economic inefficiency and misallocation of scarce capital that the latter entails, it also reduces agricultural employment thereby promoting encroachment of forest lands or undue urban migration.

Structural adjustment policies also require reduction of agricultural credit subsidies as in the case of the Philippines and Tunisia. The impact of this measure is somewhat ambiguous. If credit subsidies are benefiting large farmers and ranchers engaged in large scale land clearing (as is more the case in Latin America than in Asia or Africa) reduction of these subsidies clearly reduces environmental degradation. If, on the other hand, credit subsidies are benefiting small farmers who have inadequate funds for intensification on existing lands, and investment in land improvement and soil conservation, any reduction of these subsidies will induce more soil "mining" and forest land encroachment than is currently the case. However, even in the case of the small farmer, there are superior policies to outright credit subsidies, which are in any case fungible and can be used for other purposes. Removal of interest rate ceilings, issue of secure land titles that can be used as collateral, and increased credit availability at competitive rates are better for the farmer, the budget and the environment than credit subsidies, because they optimize the use of both capital and land. Credit subsidies are an incentive to borrow but not an incentive to invest in soil conservation or tree planting if the farmer has no security of land ownership.

POLICY SUCCESSES THAT CONTROL ENVIRONMENTAL DEGRADATION

Policy success is defined as a government intervention, or elimination of one, that improves the allocation of resources and reduces the degradation of the environment. Policy successes may be classified into three groups:

(a) Reduction and eventual elimination of policies (taxes, subsidies, quotas, public projects) that distort well-functioning markets or exacerbate market failures. Cases in point are the elimination of the pesticide subsidies in Indonesia and the ranching subsidies in Brazil.
(b) Correction or mitigation of market failures through interventions that improve the functioning of the market or result in outcomes superior to those of the free market. Examples include the introduction of water pricing in China and road pricing in Singapore.
(c) Consideration and internalization of environmental, social and other side effects of public projects and sectoral and macroeconomic policies. Examples include the Dumoga irrigation case cum national park project in Indonesia and the inclusion of environmental provisions in several structural adjustment programs.

Governments around the world are increasingly recognizing the growing threats to the sustainability of the growth process arising from environmental degradation. Concerns have been raised in international fora and structural adjustment negotations with development assistance agencies about environmental problems and the implications of macroeconomic policies for the environment.

Issues of deforestation, watershed destruction, soil erosion, insecure land use, excessive pesticide application, and inefficient water use have been raised in virtually every country. Issues of more localized interest include shifting cultivation in Southeast Asia, overgrazing in Africa and the Near East, waterlogging in South Asia (Pakistan) and the Near East (especially Egypt), cattle ranching subsidies in Latin America (Brazil) and desertification in the arid lands of India, the Middle East and Africa.

In response to these concerns, governments have introduced changes in existing policies as well as new policies and programs to deal with growing environmental problems. Particularly encouraging is a growing shift towards reduction and gradual elimination of pesticide and fertilizer subsidies that have been responsible for both misallocation of resources and environmental pollution. The radical change in Indonesian policy towards pesticides in recent years is a case in point. Following economic analysis that showed negative returns from insecticides and agroecological research that confirmed the link between insecticide use and the surge of brown planthopper that threatened 70 percent of

Java's rice, a Presidential degree (INPRES 3, 1986) banned 57 registered brands of broad spectrum insecticides, 20 of which were heavily subsidized by the government. The same decree declared integrated pest management as the national pest control strategy for rice.

More recently, there has been a shift towards reducing subsidies in the Philippines, Pakistan, Tunisia and Morocco. In many cases, the pressure comes more from a need to reduce the burden on the budget rather than the burden on the environment, although the latter is increasingly an added dimension as pesticide and fertilizer subsidies are brought out in macroeconomic and trade policy reform discussions and SAL negotiations. Sebastian and Alicbusan (1989) report that the Philippines, Nepal, Morocco and Tunisia have agreed to reduce their fertilizer subsidies as part of SAL packages.

In a parallel move, Brazil has recently reduced or eliminated most of the credit subsidies and tax breaks for the conversion of natural forests in the Amazon to privately lucrative but socially unprofitable ranches. Tunisia, Morocco, Nepal and Thailand have recently accelerated their land titling programs to improve security of land ownership.

Increasingly, policy successes, though still far fewer than policy failures, are easier to find. Papua New Guinea recognizes and protects customary communal tenure over land and forest resources. Indonesia, with assistance from the World Bank, uses water pricing to improve irrigation efficiency and to fund the management of a watershed area which has been declared a national park. Singapore uses marginal cost pricing to control urban congestion, while China has introduced water pricing to deal with water shortages.

NOTES

1. Common property and open access are used here interchangeably. Communal property is distinguished from common property by exclusion of other communities and by customary rules of access and management. Unlike common or open access resources, communal resources are often well managed.
2. Spillover effects damaging other activities which are ignored in private benefit–cost calculations.
3. The effect of current resource use on future resource availability: the more a resource is used today the less it is available for use in the future.
4. What it costs to supply one more unit of the good.
5. High discount rates cut both ways: they discourage both conservation and exploitation projects which require major investments with future streams of benefits, but on balance conservation is more adversely affected because its benefits are more distant to the future.
6. Here, as in all policy analysis, we assume away "second best" problems.

REFERENCES

1. Agency for International Development (AID), *Development and the National Interest: U.S. Economic Assistance into the 21st Century* (AID, Washington, D.C., February 1989).
2. Agency for International Development (AID), *Environmental and Natural Resource Management in Central America: Strategy for AID Assistance* (AID, Washington, D.C., 1988).
3. Agency for International Development (AID) "Safeguarding the Future: Restoration and Sustainable Development in the South of Thailand," USAID Team Report (AID, Bangkok, May 1989).

4. Agency for International Development (AID) Environmental and Natural Resource Management in the Asia and Near East Region: Strategies for AID in the 1990s (AID, Washington, D.C. September 22, 1989).
5. Ahmad, Yusuf J., Salah El Serafy and Ernst Lutz, *Environmental Accounting for Sustainable Development* (The World Bank, Washington, D.C., June 1989).
6. Anderson, Dennis, *The Economics of Afforestation, A Case Study in Africa* (John Hopkins University Press, Baltimore, 1987), p. 68.
7. Asian Development Bank and International Irrigation Management Institute, *Irrigation Service Fees Proceedings of the Regional Seminar on Irrigation Service Fees* (Asian Development Bank, Manila, 1986).
8. Australian UNESCO Committee for Man and the Biosphere, *Ecological Effects of Increasing Human Activities on Tropical and Sub-Tropical Forest Ecosystems* (Australian Government Publishing Services, Canberra, 1976).
9. Barbier, Edward B., *Economics, Natural Resource Scarcity and Development,* (Earthscan Publications, London, 1989).
10. Binswanger, Hans P., "Brazilian Policies that Encourage Deforestation in the Amazon" (World Bank, Washington, D.C., April 1989).
11. Booth, Anne, *Agricultural Development in Indonesia* (ASAA Southeast Asia Publications Series, Sydney, 1988).
12. "City Lights," *The Economist* (February 18, 1989).
13. Clark University Program for International Development, *Renewable Resource Trends in East Africa* (Clark University, Worcester, Massachusetts, 1984).
14. Conway, Gordon R., Ibrahim Manwan and David S. McCauley, *The Sustainability of Agricultural Intensification in Indonesia: A Report of Two Workshops of the Research Group on Agro-Ecosystems* (Ford Foundation and Agency for Agricultural Research and Development, Ministry of Agriculture, Indonesia, December 1984).
15. Cooter, Robert D,. "Inventing Property: Economic Theories of the Origins of Market Property Applied to Papua New Guinea."
16. Davis, Gloria, *Indonesia Forest, Land and Water: Issues in Sustainable Development* (World Bank, Washington, D.C., 1989).
17. Dhanansetthakarn, Apisak, "More Deforestation Since Logging Ban," *The Nation,* (June 29, 1989).
18. Dixon, John A. and Maynard M. Hufschmidt, eds., *Economic Valuation Techniques for the Environment* (Johns Hopkins University Press, Baltimore 1986).
19. Dunkerly, Harold B., Alan A. Walters and John M. Courtney, *Urban Land Policy Issues and Opportunities, Volume II,* World Bank Staff Working Paper No. 2833, (World Bank, Washington, D.C., 1987).
20. "The Environment Survey," *The Economist* (September 2, 1989).
21. Erlanger, Steven, "Indonesia Takes Steps to Protect Rain Forests," *New York Times* (September 26, 1989).
22. "The Extended Family – A Survey of Indonesia," *The Economist* (August 15, 1987).
23. Falloux F., "Land Information and Remote Sensing for Renewable Resource Management in Subsaharan Africa A Demand Driven Approach" (World Bank, Washington, D.C., June 26, 1989).
24. Feder, Gershon, Tongroj Onchan, Yongyuth Chalamwong and Chira Hongladrom, *Land Policies and Farm Productivity in Thailand* (Johns Hopkins University Press, Baltimore, 1988).
25. Food and Agriculture Organization (FAO) *Integrated Pest Management in Rice in Indonesia* (FAO, Jakarta, May 1988).
26. Gillis Malcolm, "West Africa: resource management policies and the tropical forest" in Robert Repetti and Malcolm Gillis, eds., *Public Policies and the Misuse of Forest Resources* (Cambridge University Press, New York, 1988).
27. Goodland, Robert and George Ledec, "Environmental Management in Sustainable Economic Development," *International Association of Impact Assessment* (Spring 1987).
28. Gorse, Jean Eugene and David R. Steeds, *Desertification in the Sahelian and Sudanian Zones of West Africa* (World Bank, Washington D.C. 1987).

29. "Government to Abolish Subsidy for Utilization of Pesticide" *The Jakarta Post,* (December 2, 1988).
30. Harvard Institute for International Development, "The Case for Multiple-Use Management of Tropical Hardwood Forests" (Harvard Institute for International Development, Cambridge, MA, January 1988).
31. Johnson III, Sam H. *Physical and Economic Impacts of Sedimentation on Fishing Activities: Nam Pong, Northeast Thailand* (University of Illinois, Urbana-Champaign, 1984).
32. Ledec, George and Robert Goodland, *Wildlands Their Protection and Management in Economic Development* (World Bank, Washington, D.C., 1988).
33. Leonard, H. Jeffrey, *Natural Resources and Economic Development in Central America* (Transaction Books, New Brunswick, 1987).
34. Mahar, Dennis J., *Government Policies Deforestation in Brazil's Amazon Region* (World Bank, Washington, D.C., 1989).
35. McCoy-Thompson, Meri, "Sliding Slopes Break Thai Logjam," *World Watch* (September/October 1989).
36. McNeely, Jeffrey A., *Economics and Biological Diversity: Developing and Using Economic Incentives to Conserve Biological Resources* (International Union for Conservation of Nature and Natural Resources, Gland, Switzerland, 1988).
37. McNeely, Jeffrey A., "How Dams and Wildlife Can Coexist: Natural Habitats Agriculture, and Major Water Resource Development Projects in Tropical Asia," *Journal of Conservation Biology,* Volume I, No. 3 (October 3, 1987).
38. McNeely, Jeffrey A., "Protected Areas and Human Ecology: How National Parks Can Contribute to Sustaining Societies of the Twenty-first Century" in David Western and Mary C. Pearl, eds., *Conservation for the Twenty-first Century* (Oxford University Press, Oxford, 1989).
39. Mirante, Edith, "A 'Teak War' Breaks Out in Burma," *Earth Island Journal* (Summer 1989).
40. National Research Council Panel on Common Property Resource Management Board on Science and Technology for International Development Office of International Affairs, *Proceedings of the Conference on Common Property Resource Management,* (National Academy Press, Washington, D.C., 1986).
41. Panayotou, Theodore, "An Econometric Study of the Causes of Tropical Deforestation: The Case of Northeast Thailand", Development Discussion Paper No. 284 (Harvard Institute for International Development, Cambridge, MA, March 1989).
42. Panayotou, Theodore, "Economics, Environment and Development," Development Discussion Paper No. 259 (Harvard Institute for International Development, Cambridge, MA, December 1987).
43. Panayotou, "The Economics of Man-Made Natural Disasters: The Case of the 1988 Landslides in South Thailand" (Agency for International Development, Washington, D.C., August 1989).
44. Panayotou, Theodore, "Natural Resources and the Environment in the Economies of Asia and the Near East: Growth, Structural Change and Policy Reform" (Harvard Institute for International Development, Cambridge, MA, July 1989).
45. Panayotou, Theodore, "Natural Resource Management: Strategies for Sustainable Asian Agriculture in the 1990's," (Harvard Institute for International Development, Cambridge, MA, September 1988).
46. Panayotou, Theodore, "Thailand Management of Natural Resources for Sustainable Development: Market Failures, Policy Distortions and Policy Options," (Harvard Institute for International Development, Cambridge, MA, May 1988).
47. Pezzey, John, "Economic Analysis of Sustainable Growth and Sustainable Development" (The World Bank, Washington, D.C. March 1989).
48. Program for International Development, Clark University in cooperation with National Environment Secretariat, Ministry of Environment and Natural Resources, Government of Kenya, *Resources, Management Population and Local Institutions in Katheka, A Case Study of Effective Natural Resources Management in Machakos, Kenya* (Clark University, Worcester, MA, October 1988).

49. Repetto, Robert, "Economic Policy Reform for Natural Resource Conservation" (World Bank, Washington, D.C., May 1988).
50. Repetto, Robert, *The Forest for the Trees? Government Policies and the Misuse of Forest Resources*, (World Resources Institute, Washington, D.C., May 1988).
51. Repetto, Robert, *Skimming the Water: Rent-seeking and the Performance of Public Irrigation Systems* (World Resources Institute, Washington, D.C., December 1986).
52. Rogers, Peter, "Fresh Water," in *The Global Possible: Development and the New Century,* Robert Repetto, ed. (Yale University Press, New Haven, 1985).
53. Ross, Lester. *Environmental Policy in China* (Indiana University Press, Bloomington, 1988).
54. Schramm, Gunter and Jeremy J. Warford, eds., *Environmental Management and Economic Development* (World Bank, Washington, D.C., 1989).
55. Southgate, David and David Pearce, "Agricultural Colonization and Environmental Degradation in Frontier Developing Economies" World Bank, Washington, D.C., October 1988).
56. Spears, John, "Containing Tropical Deforestation A Review of Priority Areas for Technological and Policy Research" (World Bank, Washington, D.C., October 1988).
57. Spears, John and Edward S. Ayensu, "Resources, Development and the New Century: Forestry" in *The Global Possible: Resources, Development and the New Century,* Robert Repetto, ed. (Yale University Press, New Haven, 1985).
58. Sirvardhana, Ruandoj, *The Nam Pong Case Study: Some Lessons to be Learned* (Environment and Policy Institute, East-West Center, Honolulu, 1982).
59. Szulc, Tad, "Brazil's Amazonian Frontier" in Andrew Maguire and Janet Welsh Brown, eds., *Bordering on Trouble Resources and Politics in Latin America* (Adler and Adler Publishers, Bethesda, Maryland 1986).
60. Thomas, Vinod, "Pollution Control in Sao Paulo, Brazil: Costs, Benefits and Effects on Industrial Location," World Bank Staff Working Paper No. 501 (World Bank, Washington, D.C., November 1981).
61. "Traffic Jams: The City, the Commuter and the Car," *The Economist* (February 1989).
62. Watson, Peter L. and Edward P. Holland, "Relieving Traffic Congestion: The Singapore Area License Scheme," World Bank Staff Working Paper No. 281 (World Bank, Washington, D.C., June 1978).
63. "Win Some, Lose Some," *Far Eastern Economic Review,* (October 27, 1988).
64. World Commission on Environment and Development, *Our Common Future* (Oxford University Press, New York, 1987).
65. World Resources Institute, The World Bank and The United Nations Development Programme, *Tropical Forests: A Call for Action, Parts I and II* (World Resources Institute, Washington, D.C., October 1985).
66. World Resources Institute and International Institute for Environment and Development, *World Resources 1986,* (Basic Books, New York, 1986).
67. World Resources Institute and International Institute for Environment and Development, *World Resources 1987,* (Basic Books, New York, 1987).
68. World Resources Institute and International Institute for Environment and Development, *World Resources 1988–89,* (Basic Books, New York, 1988).

Chapter 25

Wasting assets: natural resources in the national income accounts

Robert Repetto, William Magrath, Michael Wells, Christine Beer and Fabrizio Rossini

THE NEED FOR NATURAL RESOURCE ACCOUNTING

Overview and recommendations

Whatever their shortcomings, and however little their construction is understood by the general public, the national income accounts are undoubtedly one of the most significant social inventions of the twentieth century. Their political and economic impact can scarcely be overestimated. However inappropriately, they serve to divide the world into "developed" and "less developed" countries. In the "developed countries," whenever the quarterly gross national product (GNP) figures emerge, policy-makers stir. Should they be lower, even marginally, than those of the preceding three months, a recession is declared, the strategies and competence of the administration is impugned, and public political debate ensues. In the "developing" countries, the rate of growth of GNP is the principal measure of economic progress and transformation.

The national accounts have become so much a part of our life that it is hard to remember that they are scarcely fifty years old. They were first published in the United States in the year 1942. It is no coincidence that the period during which these measures have been available, with all their imperfections, has been the period within which governments in all developed and most developing countries have taken responsibility for the growth and stability of their economies, and during which enormous investments of talent and energy have been made in understanding how economies can be better managed. Forecasting the next few quarterly estimates of these statistics has become, with no exaggeration, a hundred million dollar industry.

The aim of national income accounting is to provide an information framework suitable for analyzing the performance of the economic system. The current system of national accounts reflects the Keynesian macroeconomic model that was dominant when the system was developed. The great aggregates of Keynesian analysis – consumption, savings, investment, and government expenditures – are carefully defined and measured. But Keynes and his contemporaries were preoccupied with the Great Depression and the business cycle; specifically, with explaining how an economy could remain for long periods of time at less than full employment. The least of their worries was a scarcity of natural resources. Unfortunately, as Keynesian analysis largely ignored the productive role of natural resources, so does the current system of national accounts.

In fact, natural resource scarcity played little part in 19th century neo-classical economics, from which traditional Keynesian and most contemporary economic theories are derived. Gone were the dismal predictions of Ricardo, Malthus, Marx, and other earlier classical economists that industrial economies would stagnate or collapse because of rising rents and subsistence wages. In 19th century Europe, steamships and railroads were markedly lowering transport costs while foodgrains and raw materials were flooding in from North and South America, Australia, Russia, and the imperial colonies. What mattered to England and other industrializing nations was the pace of investment and technological change. The classical economists had regarded income as the return on three kinds of assets: natural resources, human resources, and invested capital (land, labor, and capital, in their vocabulary). The neo-classical economists virtually dropped natural resources from their model and concentrated on labor and invested capital. When these theories were applied after World War II to problems of economic development in the Third World, human resources were also left out on the grounds that labor was always "surplus," and development was seen almost entirely as a matter of savings and investment in physical capital.

As a result, there is a dangerous asymmetry today in the way we measure, and hence, the way we think about, the value of natural resources. Man-made assets – buildings and equipment, for example – are valued as productive capital, and are written off against the value of production as they depreciate. This practice recognizes that a consumption level maintained by drawing down the stock of capital exceeds the sustainable level of income. Natural resource assets are not so valued, and their loss entails no debit charge against current income that would account for the decrease in potential future production. A country could exhaust its mineral resources, cut down its forests, erode its soils, pollute its aquifers, and hunt its wildlife and fisheries to extinction, but measured income would not be affected as these assets disappeared. Ironically, low-income countries, which are typically most dependent on natural resources for employment, revenues, and foreign exchange earnings are instructed to use a system for national accounting and macroeconomic analysis that almost completely ignores their principal assets.

Underlying this anomaly is the implicit and inappropriate assumption that natural resources are so abundant that they have no marginal value. This is a misunderstanding. Whether they enter the marketplace directly or not, natural resources make important contributions to long-term economic productivity and so are, strictly speaking, economic assets. Many are under increasing pressure from human activities and are deteriorating in quantity or quality.

Another misunderstanding underlies the contention that natural resources are "free gifts of nature," so that there are no investment costs to be "written off." The value of an asset is not its investment cost, but the present value of its income potential. Many companies valued by the stock market as worth many billions of dollars have as their principal assets the brilliant ideas and inventions of their founders: the Polaroid Camera, the Apple Computer, the Lotus Spreadsheet, for example. These inspired inventions are worth vastly more than any measurable costs to their inventors in developing them and could also be regarded as the products of genius – free gifts of nature.

Common formulas for calculating depreciation by "writing off" investment costs (e.g., straight line depreciation) are just convenient rules of thumb, or artifacts of tax legislation. The true measure of depreciation, which statisticians have tried to adopt for fixed capital in the national accounts, is the capitalized value of the decline in the future income stream because of an asset's decay or obsolescence. (Usher 1980, pp. 104–105) Thus, in the same sense that a machine depreciates, soils depreciate as their fertility is diminished since they can produce only at higher costs or lower yields.

Codified in the United Nations system of national accounts closely followed by most countries, this difference in the treatment of natural resources and other tangible assets provides false signals to policymakers. It reinforces the false dichotomy between economy and the "environment" that leads policymakers to ignore or destroy the latter in the name of economic development. It confuses the depreciation of valuable assets with the generation of income. Thus it promotes and seems to validate the idea that rapid rates of economic growth can be achieved and sustained by exploiting the resource base. The result can be illusory gains in income and permanent losses in wealth.

Indeed, natural resource assets are legitimately drawn upon to finance economic growth, especially in resource-dependent countries. The revenues derived from resource extraction finance investments in industrial capacity, infrastructure, and education. A reasonable accounting representation of the process, however, would recognize that one kind of asset has been exchanged for another, which is expected to yield a higher return. Should a farmer cut and sell the timber in his woods to raise money for a new barn, his private accounts would reflect the acquisition of a new asset, the barn, and the loss of an old asset, the timber. He thinks himself better off because the barn is worth more to him than the timber. In the national accounts, however, income and investment would rise as the barn is built, but income would also rise as the wood is cut. The value of the timber, less that of any intermediate purchases (e.g., gas and oil for the chainsaw) would be credited to value added in the logging industry. Nowhere is the loss of a valuable asset reflected. This can lead to serious miscalculation of the development potential of resource-dependent economies by confusing gross and net capital formation. Even worse, should the proceeds of resource depletion be used to finance current consumption, then the economic path is ultimately unsustainable, whatever the national accounts say. If the same farmer used the proceeds from his timber sale to finance a winter vacation, he would be poorer on his return and no longer able to afford the barn, but national income would only register a gain, not a loss in wealth.

Many countries now heavily burdened with debt are resource-dependent: Mexico, Venezuela, and Nigeria are oil exporters, for example. Their national balance sheets before the debt crisis deteriorated substantially as they drew down national resource assets and piled up external debt, using the proceeds of both to finance consumption and subsidize investments of little or no economic value. A national accounting system that drew attention to their deteriorating asset positions might have alerted policy-makers to the need for policy changes and international lenders to the growing risks of further exposure.

The fundamental definition of income encompasses the notion of sustainability. In accounting and in economics textbooks, income is defined as the maximum amount that the recipient could consume in a given period without reducing the amount of possible consumption in a future period (Edwards and Bell 1961; Hicks 1946). Business income is defined as the maximum amount the firm could pay out in current dividends without reducing net worth. This income concept encompasses not only current earnings but also changes in asset positions: capital gains are a source of income, and capital losses are a reduction in income. The depreciation accounts reflect the fact that unless the capital stock is maintained and replaced, future consumption possibilities will inevitably decline. In resource-dependent countries, failure to extend this depreciation concept to the capital stock embodied in natural resources, which are such a significant source of income and consumption, is a major omission and inconsistency.

This is not academic hairsplitting. For resource-based economies, evaluations of economic performance and estimates of macroeconomic relationships are seriously distorted by failure to account for natural resource depreciation. In this report, Indonesia is used as an example. Over the past 20 years, Indonesia has drawn heavily on its considerable natural resource endowment to finance development expenditures. Revenues from production of oil, gas, hard minerals, timber, and forest products have offset a large share of government development and routine expenditures. Primary production contributes more than 43 percent of gross domestic product, 83 percent of exports, and 55 percent of total employment. Indonesia's economic performance over this period is generally judged to have been successful: per capita GDP growth averaging 4.6 percent per year from 1965 to 1986 has been exceeded by only a handful of low and middle-income countries, and is far above the average for those groups. Gross domestic investment rose from 8 percent of GDP in 1965, at the end of the Sukarno era, to 26 percent of GDP (also well above average) in 1986, despite low oil prices and a difficult debt situation (World Bank 1988).

Estimates derived from the Indonesian country case study, presented in more detail in Part II of this report, illustrate how much this evaluation is affected by "keeping score" more correctly. Table 25.1 and Figure 25.1 compare the growth of gross domestic product at constant prices with the growth of net domestic product, derived by subtracting estimates of net natural resource depreciation for only three sectors, petroleum, timber, and soils. It is clear that conventionally measured gross domestic product substantially overstates net income and its growth after accounting for consumption of natural resource capital. In fact, while GDP increased at an average annual rate of 7.1 percent from 1971 to 1984, the period covered by this case study, our estimate of net domestic product rose by only 4.0 percent per year. If 1971, a year of significant additions to petroleum reserves, is excluded, the respective growth rates from 1972 to 1984 are 6.9 percent and 5.4 percent per year, for a gross and net domestic product.

The overstatement of income and its growth may actually be considerably more than these estimates indicate since only petroleum, timber, and soils in Java are covered. Other important exhaustible resources that have been exploited over the period, such as natural gas, coal, copper, tin, and nickel have not yet been included in the accounts. The depreciation of other renewable resources, such as non-timber forest products and fisheries, is also unaccounted for. When complete depreciation accounts are available, they will probably show a greater divergence between growth in gross output and net income.

Other important macroeconomic estimates are even more badly distorted. Table 25.2 and Figure 25.1 compare estimates of gross and net domestic investment, the latter reflecting depreciation of natural resource capital. This statistic is central to economic planning in resource-based economies. Countries such as Indonesia that are heavily dependent on exhaustible natural resources *must* diversify their asset base to preserve a sustainable long-term growth path. Extraction and sale of natural resources must finance investments in other productive capital. It is relevant, therefore, to compare gross domestic

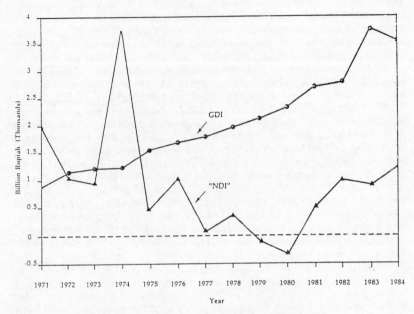

Figure 25.1 GDI and "NDI," in constant 1973 Rupiah.

Table 25.1 Comparison of GDP and "NDP" in 1973 Rupiah (billions).

| Year | GDP[a] | Net change in natural resource sectors[b] | | | | NDP |
		Petroleum	Forestry	Soil	Net change	
1971	5,545	1,527	−312	−89	1,126	6,671
1972	6,067	337	−354	−83	−100	5,967
1973	6,753	407	−591	−95	−279	6,474
1974	7,296	3,228	−533	−90	2,605	9,901
1975	7,631	−787	−249	−85	−1,121	6,510
1976	8,156	−187	−423	−74	−684	7,472
1977	8,882	−1,225	−405	−81	−1,711	7,171
1978	9,567	−1,117	−401	−89	−1,607	7,960
1979	10,165	−1,200	−946	−73	−2,219	7,946
1980	11,169	−1,633	−965	−65	−2,663	8,506
1981	12,055	−1,552	−595	−68	−2,215	9,840
1982	12,325	−1,158	−551	−55	−1,764	10,561
1983	12,842	−1,825	−974	−71	−2,870	9,972
1984	13,520	−1,765	−493	−76	−2,334	11,186
Average Annual Growth	7.1%					4.0%

a. In constant 1973 Rupiah, billions. From the Indonesian Central Bureau of Statistics.

b. The flow of resources in each sector is elaborated in the sections on the specific resource later in the text. Positive numbers imply a growth in the physical reserves of that resource during the year.

investment with the value of natural resource depletion. Should gross investment be less than resource depreciation, then, on balance, the country is drawing down, rather than building up, its asset base, and using its natural resources endowment to finance current consumption. Should net investment be positive but less than required to equip new labor force entrants with at least the capital per worker of the existing labor force, then increases in output per worker and income per capital are unlikely. In fact, the results from the Indonesian case study show that the adjustment for natural resource asset changes is large in many years relative to gross domestic investment. In 1971 and 1973, the adjustment is positive, due to additions to petroleum reserves.[1] In most years during the period, however, the depletion adjustment offsets a good part of gross capital formation. In some years, net investment was negative. A fuller accounting of natural resource depletion might conclude that in many years depletion exceeded gross investment, implying that natural resources were being depleted to finance current consumption expenditures.

Table 25.2 Comparison of GDI and "NDI".

Year	GDI[a]	Resource depletion[b]	NDI
1971	876	1,126	2,002
1972	1,139	− 100	1,039
1973	1,208	−279	929
1974	1,224	2,605	3,829
1975	1,552	−1,121	431
1976	1,690	−684	1,006
1977	1,785	−1,711	74
1978	1,965	−1,607	358
1979	2,128	−2,219	−91
1980	2,331	−2,663	−332
1981	2,704	−2,215	489
1982	2,783	−1,764	1,019
1983	3,776	−2,870	906
1984	3,551	−2,334	1,217

a. In constant 1973 Rupiah, billions. From the Indonesian Central Bureau of Statistics.
b. In constant 1973 Rupiah, billions. Includes depletion of forests, petroleum and the cost of erosion on the island of Java. These figures are explained fully in Part II.

Such an evaluation should flash an unmistakable warning signal to economic policy-makers that they were on an unsustainable course. An economic accounting system that does not generate and highlight such evaluations is deficient as a tool for analysis and policy in resource-based economies and should be amended.

The same holds true with respect to evaluation of performance in particular economic sectors, such as agriculture. Almost three-quarters of the Indonesian population live on the fertile but overcrowded "inner" islands of Java, Bali, and Madura, where lowland irrigated rice paddies are intensively farmed. In the highlands, population pressures have brought steep hillsides into use for cultivation of maize, cassava, and other annual crops. As hillsides have been cleared of trees, erosion has increased, now averaging over 60 tons per hectare per year, by our estimates.

Erosion's economic consequences include loss of nutrients and soil fertility from thin soils, and increased downstream sedimentation in reservoirs, harbors, and irrigation systems. Increased silt concentrations affect fisheries and downstream water users. Although crop yields have improved in the hills because farmers have used better seed and more fertilizers, the estimates imply that the annual depreciation of soil fertility, calculated as the value of the lost farm income, is about 4 percent of the value of crop production, which is as large as the annual production increase. In other words, these estimates suggest that current increases in farm output in Indonesia's uplands are being achieved almost wholly at the expense of potential *future* output. Since the upland population is unlikely to be smaller in the future than it is now, the process of soil erosion represents a transfer of wealth from the future to the present. By ignoring the future costs of soil erosion, the sectoral income accounts significantly overstate the growth of agricultural income in Indonesia's highlands.

A considerable and growing body of expert opinion has recognized the need to remove this anomaly from the accounting framework by accounting for depreciation of natural resource assets like depreciation of other physical capital. In the words of a recent treatise on the measurement of economic growth, "Policy-makers need, among other types of information, a set or sets of accounts which describe the significant dimensions of the system for which they are responsible . . . a cogent argument can be made for the view that the present set of national accounts provides an increasingly deficient representation of the substantive economic activities taking place within the system, and that many of these deficiencies are capable of being remedied by using available data" (Juster 1973, pp. 26–27).

In June 1985, the member governments of the OECD adopted a "Declaration on Environment: Resources for the Future." They declared that they will "ensure that environmental considerations are taken fully into account at an early stage in the development and implementation of economic and other policies by . . . [*inter alia*] . . . improving the management of natural resources, using an integrated approach, with a view to ensuring long-term environmental and economic sustainability. For this purpose, they will develop appropriate mechanisms and techniques, including more accurate resource accounts." (OECD, 1986)

Our Common Future, the 1987 report of the World Commission on Environment and Development, stated, "Thus, figuring profits from logging rarely takes full account of the losses in future revenue incurred through degradation of the forest. Similar incomplete accounting occurs in the exploitation of other resources, especially in the case of resources that are not capitalized in enterprise or national accounts: air, water, and soil. *In all countries, rich or poor, economic development must take full account in its measurements of growth of the improvement or deterioration in the stock of natural resources" (Our Common Future,* p. 52).

Similarly, academic experts (Stauffer, 1983) and such international agencies as the OECD have recommended that capital consumption allowances be extended to natural resource assets, such as mineral deposits (OECD, 1986). The World Bank and the United Nations Environment Programme have emphasized the deficiencies in the current accounting system and have sponsored work on improvements. According to a recent Bank publication, "GDP is essentially a short-term measure of economic activity for which exchange occurs in monetary terms. It is of limited usefulness to gauge long-term sustainable growth, partly because natural resource depletion and degradation are being ignored under current practices." (Lutz and El-Sarafy 1988)

A number of OECD member governments, including Canada, France, Netherlands, Australia, and Norway, have carried out substantial statistical work programs to compile accounts on natural resource stocks and stock changes. France and Norway have made perhaps the most extensive official estimates, France's patrimony accounts have emphasized the development of physical accounts (Weber 1983). Norway's resource accounts for energy and other significant economic resources have stressed integration with macroeconomic models and budgets (Alfsen, Bye and Lorentsen 1987). There is a detailed estimate of the national balance sheet of the United States that includes values for timber and subsoil assets, and an important study of national balance sheets covering twenty countries by the same scholar (Goldsmith, 1982, 1985).

Within the last few years, governments in developing countries, recognizing their natural resource dependence, have become interested in a more adequate accounting framework. The World Resources Institute is collaborating on pilot studies with government research institutes and statistical agencies in Indonesia, Costa Rica, and the People's Republic of China. Other governments considering new work programs in natural resources accounting include Thailand, the Ivory Coast, and Argentina. Policy-makers in these countries recognize the need for a planning tool that more effectively integrates economic and ecological considerations.

In filling this need, the United Nations Statistical Office has an important role to play. The U.N. System of National Accounts provides a standard and model that, at least in its core flow accounts, is closely followed by most countries. The U.N. Statistics Office is also a worldwide source of expertise and guidance in the development of national income and other statistical systems.

The system of national accounts (SNA) published by the United Nations Statistical Office (United Nations 1968) is more complete with respect to natural resource accounting than are the accounting systems actually implemented by most national governments. The SNA provides for balance sheets that record opening and closing stocks, and sources of increase and decrease. Such accounts are included for reproducible tangible assets, such as tree plantations, and non-reproducible tangible assets, such as agricultural land and subsoil minerals. The criterion for inclusion in the SNA is whether the assets are privately owned and used in the commercial production of goods and services so that economic values can be established. Natural resources in the public domain, such as surface water, atmosphere, and wilderness, are excluded on the grounds that the SNA deals with the market economy and that the economic values of natural resources outside the market system cannot readily be established.

For natural resource assets included in the SNA, the accounting framework provides for "reconciliation accounts" that link balance sheet and flow accounts. These revaluation accounts encompass changes in opening stocks due to changes in prices during the period, and due to physical changes such as growth, discoveries, depletion, extraction, and natural losses. The valuation principle endorsed by the United Nations for use in these accounts is market asset value, when possible. When direct asset value cannot be established, the U.N. guidelines endorse the economic asset-valuing principle discussed above: the present value of the expected future income stream obtainable from the resource is the measure of the resource's asset value.

The U.N. Statistical Commission, advised by a number of expert working groups, is currently considering changes in the SNA, as it does periodically. Dissatisfaction stems from many inconsistencies and omissions in the current system. For example, production of goods and services outside the enterprise sector, notably by households, is largely omitted. Also, along with natural resources, other kinds of capital assets, such as knowledge and the stock of skills possessed by the workforce are ignored. Furthermore, in the government sector, the goods and services produced are not directly measured, but are valued at their factor cost. These and many other deficiencies have led to a long agenda of suggested improvements.

Although deliberations will continue until 1991, the U.N. Statistical Commission has evidently already reached the decision that there should be no fundamental changes in the existing SNA. The existing accounting methodology is protected, in a sense, by its very inadequacy; wholesale reform is a large task, and improvement limited to just one aspect is hard to justify when so many other problems would still remain. Moreover, both at the national and international level, decisions regarding the accounting system are in the hands of the *producers* of statistics, not the users. The national income accounts are like sausages: there are many consumers, but few who want to know how they are put together. Partly for this reason, decisions are dominated by the concerns of national income statisticians, who are typically handicapped by shortages of staff, budgets, and raw data. These statisticians are resistant to recommending changes when so much work remains to be done before the *existing* SNA can be fully implemented.

With respect to depreciation accounts for natural resources, therefore, the expert committees of the U.N. Statistical Office have taken the position that countries should be encouraged to implement balance sheet accounts for reproducible and non-reproducible tangible assets and link those to conventional national income measures through "satellite accounts," as indicated in the present system. In other words, their position is that depletion accounts for natural resources should be calculated, but kept apart from the main tables. The measure of depreciation in the national income accounts should not be extended to include natural resources, and the present misleading indicators of economic performance should be maintained.

The rationale for this position is pragmatic: until more national statistical offices are capable of estimating depreciation accounts for natural resource assets, the core national income accounts should not be modified. Any estimates of natural resource balance sheets and depreciation should be displayed in ancillary tables, so that users can make their own evaluations.

Therefore, from the statistician's perspective, the amount of effort required to implement national resource accounts is important. The Indonesian country case study was implemented partly to obtain first-hand information about the level of effort needed to prepare numerical estimates. The accounts presented in this report were prepared almost entirely by pre-doctoral and master's level graduate students. Enough information to make reasonable estimates was found to be already available, so that compilation and reorganization of data were the main tasks. In this pilot study, without prior experience, working solely with existing data (no fresh field surveys were conducted), without the access to data a government statistical office would have, researchers spent approximately 12 person-months mostly in the United States. This modest input generated estimates that shed substantial new light on Indonesia's growth performance over more than a decade.

The importance of bringing such estimates into the main national income accounts, rather than relegating them to "satellite" or "reconciliation" accounts, is demonstrated by events of the past decade. While virtually all countries calculate national income accounts, few have implemented the United Nation's recommendations with respect to ancillary tables in the SNA because with limited resources they have had to "stick to the basics." Similarly, despite their recognized deficiencies, politicians, journalists, and even sophisticated economists in official agencies continue to use GDP growth as the prime measure of economic performance. (In the first statistical table of the World Bank's annual *World Development Report,* for example, entitled, "Basic Indicators," the economic indicators are GDP, GDP growth per capita, and the rate of inflation.) Only if the basic measures of economic performance, as codified by the official national accounting framework, are brought into conformity with a valid definition of income will economic policies be influenced toward sustainability.

There is ample time before the revisions to the SNA are announced for the U.N. Statistical Office to explore fully the implications of extending the concept of depreciation to natural resource assets. It should use this time to prepare for that change. At the same time, key international economic institutions, such as the World Bank, other multilateral development banks, the IMF, and the OECD, should begin to compile, use, and publish revised estimates of net national product and national income, as this report has done. All these institutions should ready themselves to provide technical assistance to the growing number of national statistical offices that wish to adopt these changes and make such estimates for themselves.

CURRENT NATIONAL INCOME ACCOUNTING

Imputations and the treatment of depreciation

The market economy – goods and services exchanged for financial consideration – broadly limits the scope of national income accounts. For this reason, intra-household production and exchanges are excluded, except for subsistence agricultural production. Nonetheless, the accounts often do impute values to important economic activities that take place without any market transaction. For example, the rental value of owner-occupied housing is treated as if the owner rented the premises to himself. The criteria used to judge whether nonmarket activities should be included in national accounts are (1) whether they are directly comparable to production taking place in the market, and (2) whether their value can be reliably measured, given the statistical resources.

An imputed value of particular concern here is for the consumption of capital stock. The value of capital goods, such as structures and equipment, declines over time with use because of physical wear and obsolescence. This gradual decrease in the future productive potential of capital goods is reflected in the national accounts by a depreciation allowance that amortizes the asset's value over its useful lifetime. There are markets for some used capital goods, such as vehicles, from which depreciation factors can be estimated. Otherwise, amortization is a surrogate measure for the loss of income-generating capacity of older assets. Straight-line depreciation and other formulas are imputations for the loss of value.

Depreciation of tangible producible capital is subtracted from gross national product (GNP) in calculating the net national product (NNP) and national income. A nation must invest enough in new capital goods to offset the depreciation of existing assets if the future income-producing ability of the entire capital stock is to be preserved. Therefore, according to the definition of income given above, this capital consumption allowance must be excluded from total production. However, this procedure is applied only to structures and equipment, not to natural resources or other types of assets. NNP should provide a more useful measure of economic performance than GNP but generally receives less attention in economic policy planning. As currently defined and estimated to include only buildings and equipment assumed to depreciate at fixed rates, gross and net product tend to move closely together. However, ignoring or underestimating the deterioration or depletion of the capital stock can lead to economic policy errors with serious, long-term consequences.

Income statements and balance sheets

A complete system of financial accounts consists of two parts, one (the *income statement*) dealing with transaction flows over a period of time, and the other (the *balance sheet*) with stocks of tangible and financial assets at different points in time. The concepts of production, consumption, revenues and costs relate to transaction flows within accounting periods. The national economic accounts in which they appear are comparable to income statements in business accounting. In contrast, balance sheets comprise stocks or levels of assets, liabilities and net worth at the end of accounting periods. Flows and stocks are linked, in that flows are equal to differences between stocks, and the stocks are equal to accumulated past flows.

National balance sheets provide a picture of a country's tangible and financial wealth at different points in time, facilitating intertemporal and international economic structural comparisons. The evaluation of a nation's future potential for sustained income generation can be enhanced by the detailed analyses of national assets and liabilities, through the preparation of national balance sheets. In the United Nations' SNA, the importance of balance sheets and wealth estimates for economic analysis are fully recognized, and the SNA includes models and an explicit recommendation to construct national balance sheets. However, while neither business firms nor households would ignore significant changes in their balance sheets, few national governments even calculate theirs.

At least in concept, the United Nations has endorsed accounting for certain natural resources. SNA specifically includes forests and subsoil assets (e.g., oil and gas reserves) in model national balance sheets. Two principal approaches to valuing assets have been endorsed for application to natural resources. These are (1) the use of values derived from market transactions in assets, and (2) the use of the discounted present value of estimated future income flows derived from the assets to be valued. For example, the SNA guidelines (United Nations 1977) suggest that the value of timber tracts should be based upon market data if available, taking account of timber type and the situation and character of the land. If there have been insufficient market transactions in timber to provide estimates, standing timber should be valued by discounting the future proceeds of selling the timber at current prices after deducting management and harvesting costs. An identical approach is suggested with respect to subsoil assets, using as a discount rate a rate of return "expected by investors in mining or quarrying enterprises."

Neither the United Nation's SNA nor the national income accounts of any country now integrates the treatment of natural resource between income and balance sheet accounts. Final sales to consumers are included on the product side; on the income side, the value added from resource extraction is included in wages and salaries, in rental incomes and in company profits. In other words, the *total* value of current production, net of purchased inputs, is imputed to current income.

There are no accounting entries in the flow accounts for depletion, growth (in the case of forests), discoveries (in the case of subsoil assets) or asset revaluation due to price changes. Only capital investments in durable structures and equipment used in the industry are subject to depreciation, not the resources themselves. There is no depreciation factor in the flow accounts to represent the loss of forests, the depletion of minerals, the erosion of soils, or the deterioration of water resources, even though these user costs impair the future income-generating capacity of those assets.

The U.N. recommends instead that these balance sheet valuation adjustments should flow through reconciliation accounts and not the current income accounts. The SNA guidelines suggest, for example, that reductions in the market value of land due to erosion be reflected in the reconciliation accounts (United Nations 1977). An expert group of the United Nations has expressed general support for a calculation of the change in the value of proven subsoil mineral reserves that would include allowances for both depletion and new finds, as well as the effects of price changes. This group recommended that the resulting adjustments also flow through the reconciliation accounts (United Nations 1980), leaving GNP and NNP unadjusted.

In arguing for keeping such asset revaluations in satellite accounts, the U.N. guidelines pointed out that large and sudden revaluations of subsoil asset values as a result of (1) extensive new discoveries; (2) changes in technology increasing the range of exploiting reserves; or (3) changes in market conditions could markedly affect estimates of current income if admitted into the flow accounts. This position ignores the fact that changes in technology or market conditions can equally affect the reproducible capital stock. Energy price shocks, for example, first made most older heavy industrial equipment economically worthless because at high energy prices those plants could not produce at a profit. The same fluctuations in energy markets led to drastic inflation, then deflation, in real estate values in oil-producing regions, such as Texas. The income accounts were insulated from these changes in asset values only because depreciation rates are estimated at constant "book" values, a procedure equally applicable to natural resource assets. The impact of capital consumption allowances for natural resources on the national income accounts would depend, as it should, entirely on the importance of natural resources to the particular economy.

In essence, reconciliation accounts provide a means of recording changes in the value of net assets between successive measurement dates *without having to show any effect on the income of the intervening period*. Recording these adjustments in reconciliation accounts is likely to minimize their consideration in national policy analysis. Therefore, while it is significant that the United Nations has specifically endorsed the principle of valuing natural resource assets and asset changes in the system of national accounts, the procedure they have recommended would still leave the income account seriously biased as an estimate of economic performance.

375

THE SCOPE OF NATURAL RESOURCE ACCOUNTING

A number of developed countries have proposed to set up systems of environmental accounts, including Norway, Canada, Japan, the Netherlands, the United States, and France. These systems have been reviewed in detail and evaluated for the United Nations Environment Programme by Weiller (1983) and Friend (1983). While natural resources take priority in Norway and France, pollution and environmental quality have been the focus in the United States and Japan. The approaches of Canada and the Netherlands combine elements of both approaches.

In both Norway and France, extensive systems of resource accounting have been established to supplement their economic accounts. The Norwegian system of natural resource accounting and the past decade's experience with it has recently been described (Alfsen, Bye, and Lorentsen, 1987; Garnasjordet and Saebo, 1986). Accounts have been compiled for "material" resources, such as fossil fuels and other minerals, such "biotic" resources as forests and fisheries, and such "environmental" resources as land, water, and air. The accounts are compiled in physical units of measurement, and not integrated with the national income accounts. However, resource accounts, especially those for petroleum and gas, have been expressed in value terms for use in macroeconomic planning and projection models maintained by the Central Bureau of Statistics.

The French natural patrimony accounts are intended as a comprehensive statistical framework to provide the authorities with the facts and data they need to monitor the state and changes in "that subsystem of the terrestrial ecosphere that can be quantitatively and qualitatively altered by human activity" (Corniere, 1986). They are conceptually broader than the national income accounts: material and energy flows to and from economic activites form only a subset of the accounts (Commission Interministerielle des Comptes du Patrimoine Naturel, 1983). Methodology and empirical estimates have been under development since 1971, and they now cover the same range of resources as Norway's: non-renewables, the physical environment, and living organisms. The basic accounting units are physical, with provision for monetary valuation of stocks and flows that are marketed or contribute directly to market production (Weber, 1983).

The construction of such frameworks for the compilation of environmental statistics may well encourage decision-makers to consider the impact of specific policies on the national stock of natural resources. However, a physical accounting approach *by itself* has considerable shortcomings. On the one hand, it does not lend itself to useful aggregation. Aggregating wood from various species of trees in physical units (cubic meters) obscures wide differences in the economic value of different species. Aggregating reserves of a mineral in physical units (tons) obscures vast differences in the value of different deposits, due to grade and recovery cost. On the other hand, maintaining physical accounts in disaggregated detail results in a mountain of statistics that are not easily summarized or used.

A further problem is that accounts maintained in physical units do not enable economic policy-makers and planners to understand the impact of economic policies on a nation's natural resource and environmental considerations into economic decisions – presumably, the main point of the exercise. While the information from the physical resource accounts undoubtedly facilitates the assignment of monetary values to balances and transaction flows (as will be described in this paper), from the perspective of *economic* policy, it is only an intermediate step (Theys, 1984). Yet, there is no conflict between accounting in physical economic units because, as the Indonesian study shows, physical accounts are necessary prerequisites to economic accounts. If the measurement of economic depreciation is extended to natural resources, physical accounts are inevitable by-products.

Notwithstanding these points, there are limits to monetary valuation, set mainly by remoteness of the resource in question from the market economy. Some resources, such as minerals, enter directly. Others, such as surface water, are extensively used as input market production, and although they are rarely bought and sold, values can be readily imputed. Others, however, such as noncommercial wild species, do not contribute directly to production and can be valued in monetary terms only through quite roundabout methods involving numerous, somewhat questionable assumptions. While methodological and empirical research into the economic value of resources that are remote from market processes is to be encouraged, common sense suggests that highly speculative values should not be included in official accounts.

In industrialized countries experiencing increasingly acute problems of pollution and congestion while becoming less dependent on agriculture, mining, and other forms of primary production, the focus of attention has been on "environmental" rather than natural resource accounting. Since Nordhaus & Tobin (1973) proposed their "measure of economic welfare" as an alternative to GNP, several different approaches to the development of more comprehensive systems of national income accounting have been described that go well beyond the scope of natural resource accounting described above. An excellent recent survey of these approaches is available (Eisner, 1988). Each reflects their authors' particular concerns (e.g., Daly, in press; Hueting 1980, 1984; Peskin 1980; Peskin & Peskin 1976, 1978). For example, Herfindahl & Kneese (1973) considered how GNP might be modified by the costs and benefits associated with pollution and its abatement. Others have proposed general systems to account for the impacts of economic activities on the quality of the environment more broadly defined.

Problems with the current framework are obvious since they lead to bizarre anomalies. If toxic substances leak from a dumpsite to pollute soils and aquifers, measured income does not go down, despite possible severe impairment of vital natural resources. If the government spends millions of dollars to clean up the mess, measured income rises, other things equal, because such government expenditures are considered to be purchases of final goods and services. If industry itself undertakes the cleanup, even if under court order, income does not rise because the same expenditures are considered to be intermediate production costs if carried out by enterprises. If the site is not cleaned up, and nearby households suffer increased medical expenses, measured income again rises because household medical expenses are also defined as final consumption expenditures in the national income accounts.

Although the system that gives rise to such results is widely regarded as faulty, there is little consensus on the remedy. Suggested approaches can initially be classified into those involving physical accounting and those that attempt to establish monetary values. The physical approach rests on a straightforward extension of input–output analysis to keep track of "deliveries" of various material from various resource stocks to producing and consuming sectors, and "deliveries" of materials from producing and consuming sectors to various receiving bodies in the environment (Leontief, 1970; Kneese, Ayres, & d'Arge, 1970). Thus, for example, each industrial sector's discharges of waste materials to water, land, and air are estimated, along with each sector's use of water, primary raw materials, land, and other natural resources.

This approach, conceptually straightforward and empirically feasible, has the virtue of bringing common economic models of "production" and "consumption" into approximate accord with the physical laws of nature. Moreover, the data thus organized provides an important intermediate step toward approaches that do involve estimation of monetary values. However, the plausible assumption of approximate linearity in the relation of waste generation to production and consumption activities cannot be carried over to the effects of emissions on environmental quality, or to the effects of environmental quality on human welfare. Both of these linkages are often highly non-linear, due to thresholds and chemical or biological interactions.

Establishing monetary accounts for changes in environmental quality is by no means so straightforward. While all would agree in principle that a good environment yields a continuing flow of beneficial goods and services, valuing those benefits is complex. For one thing, the existing accounts already reflect some of those values, but not others, so that there is the danger of double-counting along with that of omitting important elements of income. Agricultural output, yields, and income, for example, already reflect the environmental inputs of sunshine and precipitation, which make purchased inputs more productive. Increased concentrations of ozone and other air pollutants reduce agricultural yields and thus diminish measured income in the existing accounts. Environmental deterioration, insofar as it raises current production costs or reduces productivity, is already reflected in the accounts of the enterprise sector.

The glaring omission is the direct value of environmental quality or quality changes to the household. In principle, the damages to individuals from increasing pollution, congestion, and noise can be estimated by measuring willingness to pay, lost productivity, or needed defensive expenditures. Despite a large body of research literature on methodology and statistical problems, the task would be formidable if attempted on a national scale and remains in the realm of research rather than accounting.

On the other side of the ledger, there are problems – although perhaps not so serious – in improving the accounting of expenditures undertaken to prevent or remedy environmental damages. These problems can be brought into focus by assuming that households and enterprises are forced to spend more and more as the economy grows to maintain a constant level of environmental quality (Juster, 1973). One anomaly might be addressed by treating such expenditures as intermediate purchases when undertaken by households and governments, as they now are when undertaken by enterprises. However, this immediately raises the broader question of treating as intermediate expenses a wide range of outlays by governments and households that have the basic function of maintaining productivity (including, for example, traffic control, health maintenance, and so on). The notion of "defensive" expenditures is elusive, since spending on food can be considered a defence against hunger, clothing a defence against cold, and religion a defence against sin.

Another difficulty is in establishing the boundary between outlays to maintain environmental quality and those undertaken for other purposes. A household's purchase of a water filter, or a firm's installation of a water treatment plant, might be readily identified. However, a household's move to another region with a superior environment, or a firm's adoption of an intrinsically low-residuals process technology would probably not.

There has been little consensus on the principles or quantification of proposals for broader environmental quality accounting so far, though the discussion has helped highlight the importance of incorporating environmental protection and effective natural resource management in national economic planning. However, for most developing countries and other resource-based economies, it is more relevant to think of natural resources as productive assets than as consumer goods. The first priority is to account for those disappearing assets in a way that gives due emphasis to the costs.

SETTING UP NATURAL RESOURCE ACCOUNTS

Physical accounts

Natural resource physical stocks and any changes in those stocks during an accounting period can be recorded in physical units appropriate to the particular resource. The basic accounting identity is that opening stocks *plus* all growth, increase or addition less all extraction, destruction, or diminution *equals* closing stocks. Although the following discussion refers to oil and gas reserves and timber stocks as examples, the principles are applicable to many other resources.

Oil and natural gas resources, the former measured in barrels and the latter in barrel-equivalents, consist of identified reserves and other resources and identified reserves can be divided into proven reserves and probable reserves. Proven reserves are the estimated quantities of oil and gas that geological and engineering data indicate with reasonable certainty to be recoverable from known reservoirs under existing market and operating conditions – that is, prices and costs as of the date the estimate is made. Probable reserves are quantities of recoverable reserves that are less certain than proven reserves. Thus, one limit on the stock of reserves is informational. Additional proven reserves can usually be generated by drilling additional test wells or undertaking other exploratory investments to reduce uncertainty about the extent of known fields. The boundary between reserves and other resources is basically economic. Vast quantities of known hydrocarbon deposits cannot be extracted profitably under current conditions. They are thus known resources, but cannot be counted as current reserves, though price increases or technological improvements might transform them into reserves in the future.

For other mining industries, geological characteristics tend to be known with more certainty, so there is less distinction between proven and probable reserves but a sharp division between economic reserves and total resources. Many minerals are present at very low concentrations in the earth's crust in almost infinite total amounts (Goeller & Weinberg, 1984). Technological changes in mining and refining processes have markedly reduced the minimum ore concentrations that can profitably be mined, correspondingly expanding mineral reserves.

A similar framework is applicable to sub-soil deposits of water in available aquifers, except that accounting for changes in stocks must take into consideration the annual recharge. Accounting for water *quality* changes encounters problems that illustrate the limitations of physical accounting. Quality changes can be reflected in economic valuation rather readily, if they affect treatment costs or the economic uses to which water can be put. However, the numerous dimensions of quality, reflecting contamination by many other substances in varying concentrations and combinations, makes the construction of discrete physical categories difficult.

Changes in oil and gas stocks may be classified under various headings. Landefeld & Hines (1982) include under additions to reserves: "discoveries," the quantity of proven reserves that exploratory drilling finds in new oil and gas fields or in new reservoirs in oil fields; "extensions," increases in proven reserves because of subsequent drilling showing that discovered reservoirs are larger than originally estimated; and, "revisions," increases in proven reserves because oil and gas firms acquire new information on market conditions or new technology. Extensions of and revisions to oil and gas reserves have historically been significantly larger than new discoveries. Landefeld & Hines (1982) point out that reserve statistics generally produce very conservative estimates of the total resource stocks that will ultimately enter the economic system. Soladay (1980) estimated that actual production from new U.S. fields and reservoirs was over seven times the amount initially reported as discovered.

Reserve levels fall because of extraction and downward revisions. In the United States, oil and gas companies are required by the Securities and Exchange Commission to disclose net annual changes in estimated quantities of oil and gas reserves, showing separately opening and closing balances; revisions of previous estimates (from new information); improved recovery (resulting from improved techniques); purchases and sales of minerals in place; extensions and discoveries; and, production (FASB 1977).

The accounting framework for timber resources in physical units could be expressed in hectares, in tons of biomass, or in cubic meters of available wood (Weber 1983), though the last is probably the most important economic measure. As in the case of minerals, the total resource is larger than the economic reserve since a substantial part of the total stock of standing timber in any country cannot be profitably harvested and marketed with current technologies and market conditions.

Additions to the timber stock can originate from growth and regeneration of the initial stock, and from reforestation and afforestation. Reductions can be classified into production (harvesting); natural degradation (fire, insect infestations, etc); and, deforestation by man. Separate accounts might be established for different categories of forests – for example, virgin production forests, logged (secondary) forests, protected forests, and plantations. In temperate forests, where species diversity is limited, timber stocks are further disaggregated by species.

Physical accounts can be constructed along similar lines for agricultural land. Land and soil maps and classification systems are used to disaggregate land into productivity categories. Changes in stocks of each land category within a period reflect various phenomena: conversion to non-agricultural uses; conversion to lower productivity classes through physical deterioration by erosion, salinization, or waterlogging; and conversions to higher productivity classes through physical improvements by irrigation, drainage, and other investments. A set of physical accounts for agricultural land would record stocks of land at each accounting date by productivity class, and flows among classes and to other land uses according to cause.

Similarly, physical accounts can be set up for other biological resources, such as wildlife or fish populations. The principles are essentially those of demography. Additions to initial populations are attributed to fertility, estimated from reproduction rates and the size of the breeding population, and immigration. Subtractions from stocks are attributed to natural mortality, estimated from age-specific or general mortality rates, harvesting operations, other special sources of mortality, and outmigration.

Valuation principles

The concept of economic rent is central to natural resource valuation. Economic rent is defined as the return to any production input over the minimum amount required to retain it in its present use. It is broadly equivalent to the profit that can be derived or earned from a factor of production (for example, a natural resource stock) beyond its normal supply cost. For example, if a barrel of crude oil can be sold for $10 and costs a total of $6 to discover, extract, and bring to market, a rent of $4 can be assigned to each barrel.

Rents to natural resources arise from their scarcity and from locational and other cost advantages of particular stocks. These rents are distinct from monopoly rents, which increase returns to a factor of production beyond its opportunity cost by restricting supply through market power or government action. In principle, rents can be determined as the international resource commodity price less all factor costs incurred in extraction, including a normal return to capital but excluding taxes, duties and royalties. Thus, the economic rent is equivalent to the net price.

This is the same concept of rent that appears in a Ricardian-scarcity model, which assumes that resources from different "deposits" will be supplied at a rising incremental cost until profit on the marginal source of supply is completely exhausted. In this Ricardian model, rents arise on relatively low-cost, infra-marginal sources of supply.

It is also equivalent to a user cost in a Malthusian scarcity model, which assumes that a homogeneous exhaustible resource is exploited at an economically efficient rate, such that the profit on the marginal amount brought to market is equal to the expected return derived from holding the asset in stock for future capital gain (Hall & Hall 1984). In such a Malthusian model, if the resource is being extracted at an efficient rate, the current rent on the last unit of resources extracted is thus equal to the discounted present value of future returns from a unit remaining in stock.

As Ward (1982) has pointed out, the gross operating surplus of the extractive sector in the SNA, represented by the sum of the profits made by all the different enterprises involved in resource extraction activities, does not represent true rewards to factors of production alone but also reflects rents from a "one time only" irredeemable sale of a non-renewable natural asset. By failing to measure an appropriate depletion allowance, conventional national accounting procedures allocate a disproportionate share of current income flows to present generations at the expense of future generations. The basic definition of income as the amount that can be consumed without becoming worse off is clearly being infringed as the value of the asset base declines.

Ward presents the sad exemplary tale of Kiribati, the small atoll republic of the Solomon Islands, which depended throughout the 20th century on its phosphate mines for income and government revenues. While the mines ran, gross domestic product was high and rising, but the mining proceeds were treated as current income rather than as capital consumption. When the deposits were mined out in the 1970s, income and government revenues declined drastically because far too little had been set aside for investment in other assets that would replace the lost revenues.

It would seem reasonable to apply this argument, not only to all soil and subsoil assets, but also to tropical forests which, though theoretically renewable, are being removed without adequate provision being made for their replacement in many areas. In forest economics, the concept of "stumpage value" is very close to that of economic rent. Stumpage value represents timber sale proceeds, less the costs of logging, transportation, and processing. Better quality and more accessible timber stands will command a higher stumpage value.

Asset transactions in natural resources, such as competitive auction sales of rights to extract timber or minerals, closely follow estimated stumpage values or rents, with allowance for risk. Because holders of those rights can usually hold the resources in stock or bring them to market immediately, the current rent or stumpage value tends to reflect the present value of expected future net income that can be derived from them.

This principle is readily extended to other resources: agricultural land can be valued directly on the basis of its current market worth, or indirectly as the present value of the future stream of net income, or annual rent, that can be derived from it. The value of sub-surface irrigation water deposits can be estimated from market transactions in water rights, or by comparing the value of agricultural land overlaying a usable, known, aquifer with that of otherwise equivalent land without subsurface water. Alternatively, it can be estimated as the present value of future rents, calculated as the difference between the costs (per cubic meter) of supplying the water for irrigation and the incremental net farm income attributable to the use of the water for irrigation. The value of a fishery could be estimated, in principle, as the maximum amount of revenue that a government authority could collect in bids from potential fishermen for the rights to participate in the catch. Alternatively, it could be estimated as the present value of the net income fishermen could derive from the catch under optimal regulation. In a world of frictionless, competitive markets, these valuation methods would yield the same results.

If adjustments to national income accounts for natural resource stock changes are to attain broad acceptance, a credible standard technique for valuing natural resources must be adopted that can be applied to various resources by statisticians in different countries. That method must be as free as possible from speculative estimates (about future market prices, for example) and must depend on underlying data that is reasonably available to statistical agencies.

Landefeld & Hines (1985) have recently compared the three principal methods discussed above for estimating the value of natural resource stocks: 1) the present value of future net revenues; 2) the transaction value of market purchases and sales of the resource *in situ*; and 3) the net price, or unit rent, of the resource multiplied by the relevant quantity of the reserve.

The present value method requires that future prices, operating costs, production levels, and interest rates be forecast over the life of, for example, a given oil field, after its discovery. The present value of the stream of net revenue is then calculated, net revenue representing the total revenue from the resource less all extraction costs. Soladay (1980) extends the present value method by attempting to take into account the upward revisions in estimates of reserves that typically occur subsequent to the initial discovery. The United Nations Statistical Office has recommended use of the present value method when market values for transactions in resource stock are not available (United Nations 1979).

The net price method applies the prevailing average net price per unit of the resource (current revenues less current production costs) to the physical quantities of proved reserves and changes in the levels of proved reserves. Landefeld & Hines make the important point that while the net price method requires only current data on prices and costs, it will be equivalent to the other two methods if output prices behave in accordance with long-run competitive market equilibrium. "Equilibrium in natural resource markets (where the net price rises in accordance with the rate of return on alternative investments) produces the interesting result that depletion as measured by changes in the present value of the resource equals depletion as measured by the net price method" (Landefeld & Hines 1985, p.14). The assumption here is derived from the theory of optimal depletion of exhaustible resources, that resource owners will tend to arbitrage returns from holding the stock into future periods with returns from bringing it immediately to market, adjusting current and future supplies until price changes equate those returns. (Dasgupta, 1982) When expected future increases in the net price take place at a rate equal to the return on alternative investments, these increases would therefore be eliminated in the calculation of the net present value of future cash flows (Miller & Upton, 1985).

A number of recent studies (Boskin et al. 1985; Landefeld & Hines 1982, 1985; Soladay 1980; Ward 1982; Lutz and El-Sarafy 1988, Devarajan and Wiener 1988) have considered the issues associated with valuing the discovery and use of depletion of exhaustible natural resources in measures of national income and wealth.

In the private sector, financial accounting and reporting for petroleum- and mineral-producing companies has been debated for many years in the United States by the accounting profession, regulatory agencies, industry groups, and the companies themselves. The U.S. Securities and Exchange Commission (SEC) and Financial Accounting Standards Board (FASB) have given extensive consideration to the appropriate accounting and financial reporting for publicly traded corporations involved in extractive activities. The debate was initially focused on the two widely different methods of reserve valuation used by companies, the full cost method and the successful efforts method (FASB 1977). Each was based upon the costs of exploration and development actually incurred, but without reflecting the market value of reserves or annual changes in reserves to which the company has rights of ownership. Believing with ample justification that neither method provided sufficient information to stockholders, the SEC proposed a new method of reserve recognition accounting (SEC 1978) that valued proven oil and gas reserves according to the discounted present value of the stream of future income at current prices and costs. Following further debate on the issue, however, SEC abandoned this method of accounting since the burden of producing the information was considered to outweigh its usefulness to users of financial statements (SEC 1981).

The FASB recently considered means by which companies could provide information about future cash flows from oil and gas reserves as supplemental information, outside the financial statements (FASB 1982). They evaluated the alternatives of fair market value, discounted future net cash flows, and a "standardized measure" of discounted net cash flows. Fair market value was rejected on the basis that relatively few exchanges of oil and gas mineral interests take place, and the geological characteristics of each property are unique and thus incomparable. The use of discounted future net cash flows, based on estimated future prices and costs, production timing, and an enterprise-specific discount rate as a surrogate for fair market value, was also rejected since such subjectively based calculations could not provide sufficiently comparable and verifiable information for financial reporting. The Board settled on a standardized measure of discounted net cash flows. Future net cash flows result from subtracting future development and production costs (and tax expenses) from future cash inflows relating to proved oil and gas reserves, using prices and unit costs as of the end of the reporting year. A discount rate of 10 percent is specified. The FASB points out that the standardized measure cannot be considered an estimate of fair market value but should reflect some of the key variables that affect fair market value – such as changes in reserve quantities, selling prices, production rates, and tax rates. Thus, the private accounting profession, after lengthy consideration, has adopted a valuation method based on the net price approach.

INTEGRATING NATURAL RESOURCES INTO THE NATIONAL ACCOUNTS

Income accounts for natural resources can be developed directly from accounts expressed in physical units by assigning appropriate monetary values to stock levels and changes. Net changes in the value of stocks are attributed to current year additions (discoveries, net revisions, extensions, growth or reproduction) less deductions (degradation, deforestation, or depletion) plus any price changes of the resource during the year, as illustrated in Table 25.3. This framework is applicable with suitable specification to a wide variety of resources.

If the primary objective were only the national balance sheet presentation of natural resource accounts, the example shown in Table 25.3 would be relatively straightforward. The net value of the resource increased by $155 ($255–$100) during the year and net national wealth also increased by $155.

To adjust gross national product to a net basis, economists have a number of options. If the only desired adjustment to income were to reflect resource *depletion*, then net national product would be reduced by $32, using the average valuation rate of $1.60 per barrel. If *all* the physical changes in the resource base were netted, yielding a decrease of 15 physical units, NNP would be reduced by $24, at the same average valuation. However, if the gain in value of the opening stock due to price changes were also treated as current income, NNP would be increased by $155, the difference between the two balance sheets.

In other words, alternative adjustments are possible, depending on the objective. Treating unrealized capital gains and losses due to price changes as income is inconsistent with the definition of income given above, since the capital gain during the year could be consumed without reducing future potential consumption below what it would have been at the original price level. However, accounting conventions now in use for physical plant and equipment value assets at "book value" rather than replacement cost: they *do not* reflect changes in asset values in current income accounts.

The United Nations (1977, 1980) has suggested that all changes in the value of natural resource stocks due to new finds, price changes, and depletion should be excluded from the income accounts. At the opposite extreme, Eisner (1980, 1985) has argued that capital revaluations in excess of those generated by general price

Wasting assets

Table 25.3 Example of resource inclusive national accounting system.

	Physical units	Unit value	Value ($)	Basis of calculation
Opening Stock	100	1.00	100	
Additions:				
Discoveries	20	1.60	32	
Revisions (Net)	(30)	1.60	(48)	
Extensions	15	1.60	24	
Growth*	0	1.60	0	
Reproduction*	0	1.60	0	
Reductions:				
Production	(20)	1.60	(32)	
Deforestation*	0	1.60	0	
Degradation*	0	1.60	0	
Net Change	(15)	1.60	(24)	
Revaluations:				
Opening stock	–	–	200	$100 \times (3.00-1.00)$
Transactions	–	–	(21)	$15 \times (3.00-1.60)$
Closing stock	85	3.00	255	

Note: Example of a natural resource account as it might appear in national economic accounts. The resource unit value (based on international commodity prices less factor costs incurred in extraction or production) is assumed to be $1.00 at the beginning of the year, $3.00 at the end of the year, and to average $1.60 during the year.

The total increase in the value of the resource over the period shown is equal to $155 ($255–$100). The methodology recommended in this paper would result in a downward adjustment to net national product of ($24). The remaining net change in total value of $179 ($155 + $24 or $200 – $21) would be recorded in a revaluation reserve and have no impact on income of the current period.

Items marked * are specific to forest resources; all other categories are applicable to subsoil minerals, e.g., oil and gas.

rises should be included in measures of income and capital accumulation. Accordingly, the money value of all capital gains in excess of those necessary to keep the real value of capital intact should be included in income. Eisner (1980) extends this argument to propose the inclusion of capital gains arising from the discovery of new resources in income, and the exclusion of resource depletion from income.

International resource commodity prices are subject to dramatic fluctuations over comparatively short time periods because price elasticities of demand and supply are often small in the short run. Including unrealized capital gains from natural resource price changes in current income could lead to significant swings in income between successful periods in resource-dependent countries. However, natural resource price swings (such as the energy price shocks) also markedly affect the value of plant, equipment, and real estate that are specific to those natural resource sectors.

The procedures illustrated here, which incorporate the net price method (Landefeld & Hines 1982, 1985), include only the value of *physical* resource stock changes in national income. This procedure is consistent with current asset-accounting practices. In addition, it is more readily implemented since, for most natural resources, information on stock changes due to extraction or discovery is more accurate than information on the size and composition of the total stock. At the end of each accounting period, the physical units comprising the opening balance of natural resource stocks have been revalued at the net price prevailing at the end of the period. The revaluation adjustment (which, in the example shown in Table 25.3, equals $200) has been recorded in a revaluation reserve and therefore has no effect on the current period's income. The net physical change (15 units) is valued at the average net price prevailing during the period and is used to adjust NPP downwards by $24. The remaining revaluation adjustment, which arises from the difference between average and closing prices applied to the net physical change in resource stocks ($21) is recorded in the revaluation reserve as an unrealized capital gain, with no impact on income.

If national accounts are adjusted to show income at constant prices, thereby eliminating the effects of general inflation, the adjustment to income ($24) should be deflated by an appropriate price index. As a result, only real wealth increases or decreases will be reflected in measured national income.

Preliminary resource accounts in physical and value terms for tropical timber, petroleum, and soil resources in Indonesia from 1970 to 1984 illustrate this methodology. The net charges in resource values from physical sources (for example, excluding price revaluations) implied by these tables were reflected in the summary tables and figures presented earlier to illustrate the usefulness of such calculations in macroeconomic evaluation. The resource accounts are preliminary, in that they have not been endorsed by official Indonesian statistical or economic agencies, but represent a non-governmental research effort that drew on published and some unpublished statistical sources. Efforts are currently under way in cooperation with the Ministry for Environment and Population and a consortium of universities in Indonesia to revise these accounts and to extend the methodology to other resource sectors.

NOTE

1. It may seem anomalous that in 1971 and 1973 depreciation was a negative number, that is, net capital consumption was *added* to gross domestic product and investment. The reason for this is that the value of additions to petroleum reserves in these years were considerably larger than all categories of depletion combined, leading to "negative" depreciation.

   One way of resolving this apparent anomaly would be to account separately for additions and subtractions from natural resource assets. Real capital gains (as distinct from those resulting from price changes) can be accounted for as gross income and gross capital formation. This is consistent with our earlier definition of income, because additions to resources during the current year augment the amount that *could* be consumed currently without reducing potential consumption in future years. This is obvious in the case of forest growth, but less obvious for mineral discoveries, since current discoveries may leave less to be discovered later on. However, insofar as additions to mineral reserves reflect advances in the technology of exploration or extraction, the total potential resource base will have expanded.

REFERENCES

Alfsen, Knut H., Torstein Bye and Lorents Lorentsen, 1987. Natural Resource Accounting and Analysis: The Norwegian Experience 1978–1986. Oslo, Norway: Central Bureau of Statistics of Norway.

Boskin, Michael J., Marc S. Robinson, Terrance O'Reilly, and Praveen Kumar, 1985. New

Estimates of the Value of Federal Mineral Rights and Land. *American Economic Review* (December): 923–936.

Commission Interministerielle des Comptes du Patrimoine Naturel, (1983). *Les Comptes du Patrimoine Naturel.* Paris: Institut National de la Statistique et des Etudes Economiques.

Corniere, P., (1986). Natural Resource Accounts in France. An Example: Inland Water. In Organisation for Economic Cooperation and Development, *Information and Natural Resources.* Paris: OECD.

Dasgupta, Partha, (1982). *The Control of Resources.* Cambridge: Harvard University Press.

Devarajan, Shantayanan and Robert J. Weiner, (1988). Natural Resource Depletion and National Income Accounts. Unpublished. Harvard University, John F. Kennedy School of Government, Cambridge, Massachusetts.

Edwards, E.O. and P.W. Bell, (1961). The Theory and Measurement of Business Income. Berkeley: University of California Press.

Eisner, R., (1980). Capital gains and income: real changes in the value of capital in the United States, 1946–77. In Usher, D. (ed.), *The Measurement of Capital. Studies in Income and Wealth,* Vol. 45. Chicago: University of Chicago Press.

Eisner, R., (1985). The total incomes system of accounts. *Survey of Current Business.* Vol 65 (1): 24–28.

Financial Accounting Standards Board , (1977). Financial accounting and reporting by oil and gas companies. Statement of financial accounting standards no. 19. Accounting Standards Board. Stamford, California.

Friend, Anthony. Natural Resource Accounting: International Experience. Paper presented at Consultative Meeting of United Nations Environment Programme. Geneva, February 23–25, 1983.

Garnasjordet, P.A. and H. Viggo Saebo, (1986). A System of Natural Resource Accounts in Norway. In Organisation for Economic Cooperation and Development, *Information and natural resources.* Paris: OECD.

Goeller, H.E. and A. Zucker, (1984). Infinite resources: the ultimate strategy. *Science.* Vol. 223, (February): 456–62.

Goldsmith, R.W., (1982) *The national balance sheets of the United States,* 1952–1975. Chicago: University of Chicago Press.

Goldsmith, R.W., (1985). Comparative national balance sheets. A study of twenty countries, 1688–1978. Chicago: University of Chicago Press.

Hall, Darwin C. and Jane V. Hall, 1984. Concepts and Measures of Natural Resource Scarcity with a Summary of Recent Trends. *Journal of Environmental Economics and Management.* Vol 11: 363–379.

Hicks, John R., (1946). *Value and Capital: An Inquiry into Some Fundamental Principles of Economic Theory.* Oxford: Oxford University Press.

Hueting, R., (1980). *New Scarcity and Economic Growth.* Amsterdam: North-Holland Publishing Company.

Hueting, Roefie, (1984). Economic Aspects of Environmental Accounting. Paper prepared for the Environmental Accounting Workshop, organized by UNEP and hosted by the World Bank, Washington, D.C., 5-8 November, 1984.

Juster, F. Thomas, 1973. The framework for the measurement of economic and social performance. In: M. Moss (ed.), *The Measurement of Economic and Social Performance. Studies in Income and Wealth.* Vol. 38. National Bureau of Economic Research, New York.

Kneese, A. Ayres, R. & d'Arge, R., (1970). Economics and the Environment: A Materials Balance Approach. Resources for the Future, Washington, D.C.: Johns Hopkins Press.

Landefeld, J.S. & J.M. Hines (1982). Valuing non-renewable natural resources: the mining industries. In: *Measuring Nonmarket Economic Activity: BEA Working Papers,* Bureau of Economic Analysis.

Leontief, W., (1970). Environmental Repercussions and the Economic Structure. *Review of Economics and Statistics,* August.

Lutz, Ernst and Salah El Serafy. Environmental and Resource Accounting: An Overview. Environment Department Working Paper No. 6, World Bank, Washington, D.C.: June 1988.

Miller, Merton H. and Charles W. Upton, (1985). A Test of the Hotelling Valuation Principle. *Journal of Political Economy*. Vol. 93, No. 1: 1–25.

Organisation for Economic Cooperation and Development, (1986). Declaration on environment resources for the future. In OECD, *OECD and the Environment*. Paris: OECD.

Peskin, Henry M. and Janice Peskin, (1978). The Valuation of Nonmarket Activities in Income Accounting. *Review of Income and Wealth*. Vol. 24, March: 41–70.

Peskin, Henry M., (1980). Two papers on national accounting and the environment. Discussion Paper D-71, Resources for the Future, Washington, D.C., October.

Securities and Exchange Commission, (1981). Financial reporting by oil and gas producers. ASR No. 259, Securities and Exchange Commission, Washington, D.C.

Soladay, J., (1980). Measurement of Income and Product in the Oil and Gas Industry. In: D. Usher (ed.), *The Measurement of Capital Studies in Income and Wealth*. Vol. 45. University of Chicago Press.

Stauffer, Thomas R. Accounting for "wasting assets": Income Measurement for Oil and Mineral-Exporting Rentier States. Paper presented to Eighteenth General Conference International Association for Research in Income and Wealth, Luxembourg, 1983.

Theys, J., (1984). Environmental accounting and its use in development policy. Proposals based on the French experience. Unpublished manuscript.

United Nations, Department of Economic and Social Affairs, (1968). A System of National Accounts. Statistical Papers, Series F, No. 2, Rev. 3. United Nations, New York.

United Nations, Department of Economic and Social Affairs, (1977). Provisional international guidelines on the national and sectoral balance-sheet and reconciliation accounts of the system of national accounts. Statistical Papers, Series M, No. 60. United Nations, New York.

United Nations, Statistical Office (1979). Future Directions for Work on the System of National Accounts. United Nations, New York.

United Nations, Economic and Social Council, Statistical Commission, (1980). Future Directions for Work on System of National Accounts.

Usher, Dan, (1980). *The Measurement of Economic Growth*. New York: Columbia University Press.

Ward, Michael, (1982). Accounting for the Depletion of Natural Resources in the National Accounts of Developing Economies. Paris, France: Development Centre, Organisation for Economic Cooperation and Development, June.

Ward, Michael. The Impact of Resource Depletion on the National Accounts. Paper presented to Conference on "National Accounts and their Uses in Development Planning in the Arab Countries," Kuwait, May, 1984.

Weber, J.L., (1983). The French Natural Patrimony Accounts. *Statistical Journal of the United Nations*. ECI 1:419-444.

Weiller, Edward, (1983). The Use of Environmental Accounting for Development Planning. Report to the United Nations Environment Programme, New York, January.

World Bank, (1987). Indonesia, The Outer Islands: Issues in the Sustainable Use of Land and Forest Resources. Main Report. Unpublished paper.

World Bank, (1988). *World Development Report, 1988*. Oxford: Oxford University Press.

World Commission on Environment and Development, (1987). *Our Common Future*. Oxford: Oxford University Press.

PART 5

International and global environmental problems

Chapter 26
Economics and the global environmental challenge

David Pearce

INTRODUCTION: GLOBAL ENVIRONMENTAL MORALITY

For many people, the idea of promoting the greatest good is a moral intuition, something that cannot rationally be defended. The idea of caring for future generations and other sentient beings is perhaps in the same category. The environmental challenges of the last part of the twentieth century raise all the problems of 'future care', since so many of the costs of environmental degradation will be borne by future generations and by the natural world. In some recent work, my colleagues and I *assumed* the imperative of future concern, the source of the imperative was not discussed.[1] Interest centred on what such a moral principle would mean in practice. Following, but also departing from, the important writings of Solow, Page, Hartwick and Maler,[2] it was argued that concern for the future could be made operational by a rule that required each generation to pass on to the next one a stock of natural environmental assets ('natural capital') no less than the stock of assets already in existence. Simply put, we should not degrade our environment any further – we should not 'live off our capital'. By so doing, current generations could do what is feasible to compensate future generations for damage now being done; the costs of which would be largely borne in the future. This is the 'intergenerational externality' phenomenon, and the correction of this externality is required if intergenerational fairness is to be observed. In turn, intergenerational fairness is a critical constituent part of any definition of 'sustainable development'.[3]

This 'constant natural capital' rule is a variant of one that might have wider appeal to economic orthodoxy, namely, passing on a stock of natural and human-made capital. But the distinction between the two rules is fundamental. Leaving a constant stock of all kinds of capital is consistent with burning the Amazon forests and converting them to industrial forestry or agriculture. It would always be acceptable to run down nature's wealth provided we built up another form of wealth – roads or machinery, knowledge or technology. The arguments for narrowing the focus to nature's capital are not developed here – they are spelled out elsewhere[4] – but the rationale includes :

(1) The widespread public view that we have gone far enough, and often too far, in destroying natural environments;
(2) The high economic values that are often revealed when conservation is properly accounted for;
(3) The asymmetry between the types of capital, more specifically, human-made capital is reproducible from knowledge, while nature's is not. Human-made assets can be created or destroyed almost at will. However, once nature's capital is extinguished, much of it cannot be reproduced. Thus, there is *irreversibility*;

(4) The *uniqueness,* and hence non-substitutability, of much environmental capital – e.g., the ozone layer and tropical rainforests;
(5) The extensive *uncertainty* that surrounds our knowledge of how natural ecosystems function and serve as life-support agencies.

Conserving nature's capital is an instrumental rule for being fair to future generations. It is a means of implementing the moral intuition that we should serve the greatest good, where the good includes that of future generations, sentient non-humans and current generations – and especially the poor of the current generation who tend to suffer most when environments are degraded (e.g., the resource-dependent people of the Sahel or Nepal).

The constant capital concept needs a great deal of further thought.[5] But even at the superficial level, it appears inconsistent with a utilitarian approach, since it implies that reductions in natural capital cannot be contemplated regardless of the benefit of such reductions. Utilitarianism would compare the costs and benefits of actions and is thus consistent with degrading the environment provided the benefits of so doing exceed the costs. But even a utilitarian approach must account for the three features that tend to characterise modern global environmental challenges: uncertainty, irreversibility and uniqueness. Taken together, these features of the problem justify a very cautious approach to environmental capital, since the payoff from present destructive action could have extremely large negative consequences in the future. This is very much how the challenge of global warming is being characterised. The 'constant capital' approach implies high (but not infinite) values for the environment, but it does not require that as each tree is cut down, another identical one is replaced. It countenances a commitment to overall environmental conservation, not a commitment to conserve each environmental asset. In its most dilute form, the principle requires that we pay special attention to the conservation of 'critical' environmental capital – capital on which we depend for life support and spiritual well-being.

CONSERVING CAPITAL AND GLOBAL ENVIRONMENTAL CHANGE

The instrumental principle of conserving natural capital has secured a place in international negotiation on environmental change, although it is not necessarily articulated in this way. We would expect a constant capital rule to be applied most urgently to those natural resources that have the features of non-substitutability and irreversibility, and that are under the gravest threat. The resources which have these features and which are the subject of actual imminent or near-term global agreements are the ozone layer, the atmosphere and the last great wilderness – Antartica. The conspicuous resource which is non-substitutable and which is suffering effective irreversible damage, but which is not yet the subject of international agreement, is the tropical forest.

In the ozone layer case, the world has agreed to what is effectively a zero depletion policy, which is formally identical with constant natural capital. In the case of greenhouse gases and climate change, discussions are heading that way.

The ozone layer

International action on the ozone layer was taken with the drawing up of the United Nations Convention on the Protection of the Ozone Layer in Vienna in 1985. The Montreal Protocol on Substances that deplete the Ozone Layer, which came into force at the start of 1989, is the actual agreement to reduce the use of chlorofluorocarbons (CFCs). Under the initial agreement, *consumption* of five CFCs (11, 12, 113, 114, 115) was frozen at the 1986 levels by 1989 and had to be cut by 20 per cent of the 1986 levels by 1994, eventually to be lowered to 50 per cent by 1998-99. The cuts in *production* were slightly less severe in order to allow for the needs of the developing countries, with the aim being to allow 65 per cent of the 1986 level by 1999. Three halons (1211, 1301, 2402) were the subject of a 1986-based consumption freeze and a production level freeze of 110 per cent of the 1986 level by 1992. An agreement reached in London in June 1990 produced stricter controls still and revised the Montreal Protocol to achieve 50 per cent cuts by 1995 and 85 per cent by 1997. Some countries pressed for total phase-out by 1997. Halons will be cut by 50 per cent by 1995 and will be phased-out by the year 2000. Carbon tetrachloride and methyl chloroform were added to the agreement – the former to be phased-out by 2000, the latter by 2005. Developing countries have to achieve these targets within a grace period of ten years. Virtually all developed countries are now party to the Montreal Protocol, and these countries account for about 70 per cent of the global consumption of the relevant CFCs and halons. While 23 developing nations have signed the Protocol, India and China have not signed, but have announced their decision to do so in 1992. The London meeting also established a special fund of US$240 million to help developing countries adjust to the CFC phase-out.

Effectively then, the Montreal agreement and its modifications seek a virtual cessation of production of ozone-depleting CFCs. Although this will still result in increased chlorine releases in the atmosphere, due to the time lags between CFC production, consumption and release to the atmosphere, the Protcol is as near as we can get to the intent of treating the ozone layer in terms of the instrumental rule to maintain constant natural capital. 'Intent' is the operative word, because there are potentially formidable implications of the Protocol if developing countries do not accede and major implications even if they do accede, but increase their consumption of CFCs to the limit allowed under Article 5.[6]

Greenhouse Gases
CFCs are also greenhouse gases and are thus implicated in global warming. The other greenhouse gases are carbon dioxide, methane, nitrous oxides and tropospheric ozone arising from regions involving methane, carbon monoxide, nitrogen oxides and sunshine.[7]

SETTING TARGETS: EXISTING DISCUSSIONS
We do not yet have a convention on global warming, but national positions are being determined. The US has engaged in some retraction of earlier proactive positions on global warming, primarily because of concerns over the economic costs of emissions reductions and perhaps because of some scientific reservations.[8] Japan has also expressed doubts about the wisdom of positive action. In contrast, European countries, notably Germany and the Netherlands, are urging strong immediate action. Indeed, they have effectively adopted unilateral targets for carbon dioxide reduction: Germany is discussing a 25 per cent reduction of 1986 emissions by 2000 and the Netherlands endeavouring for constant 1990 emissions by 1995.

In November 1989, ministers from developed and developing countries met in Noordwijk, the Netherlands and agreed the following declaration:

[The conference] recognizes the need to stabilize, while ensuring stable development of the world economy, CO_2 [carbon dioxide] emissions and emissions of other greenhouse gases not controlled by the Montreal Protocol. Industrialized nations agree that such stabilization should be achieved by them as soon as possible, at levels to be considered by the IPCC (Intergovernmental Panel on Climate Change] and the Second World Climate Conference of November 1990. In the view of many industrialized nations such stabilization of CO_2 emissions should be achieved as a first step at the latest by the year 2000.

[The conference] urges all industrialized countries to support the process of IPCC through the investigation of the feasibility of achieving targets to limit or reduce CO_2 emissions including *e.g.* a 20 per cent reduction of CO_2 emission levels by the year 2005 as recommended by the scientific world conference on the Changing Atmosphere in Toronto 1988.[9]

Representatives from 67 counntries, including the US, the UK, China and India, agreed to this statement. The targets for greenhouse gas emissions are loosely worded, especially in respect of the omission of a base year for the 20 per cent reduction of carbon dioxide. However, the 1988 Toronto Conference recommendation referred to makes it quite clear that the base year for the 20 per cent reduction is the year of the conference, 1988.[10] That is, by 2005, the industrialised nations should be emitting 20 per cent less carbon dioxide than in 1988. Moreover, the Toronto conference indicated that this was only a first step: the 20 per cent has to be a global goal, not one for just the developed world, and 50 per cent cuts from 1988 carbon dioxide emission levels would be necessary to stabilize atmospheric concentrations. The State of Victoria, Australia, has officially adopted the target in its own greenhouse gas policy statement.

The Noordwijk declaration is thus ambiguous. It could mean one of three things:

(1) Stabilising carbon dioxide emissions at their level in 2000;
(2) Securing a 20 per cent cut on what the levels would otherwise be in 2005;
(3) Securing a 20 per cent cut on 1988 levels by 2005.

Each of these targets may be further varied according to what grace periods might be given to the developing world.

SETTING TARGETS: THE ACCEPTABLE LEVEL OF GLOBAL WARMING

The world is already committed to some global warming because of the thermal inertia of the oceans. Even if the emission of all greenhouse gases stopped tomorrow, some global warming would still occur. The Toronto Conference target of 20 per cent reduction in emissions from current levels was thought to be consistent with a rate of warming of 0.1°C each decade.[11] This rate has been advanced as an 'ecologically manageable' rate of increasing in warming – *i.e.,* it is the rate at which non-disruptive ecological change will take place. This idea of using 'ecological limits' is very much akin to the constant natural capital approach.[12] Within policy circles, this rate of change of warming is increasingly being regarded as an 'acceptable' level.

There is, however, an alternative way of deriving the acceptable level of warming. This would be to approach the issue from the standpoint of comparing costs and benefits in monetary terms – *i.e.*, by adopting a utilitarian approach in which sacrifices now are weighed against future gains.[13] One significant attempt to compute 'ballpark' figures for costs and benefits has been undertaken by Nordhaus.[14]

Nordhaus suggests that the cost and benefit picture appears as in Table 26.1. The table should be read so as to find the greatest *difference* between costs and benefits – *i.e.*, maximum net benefits from reduced emissions (and from afforestation as a means of 'fixing' carbon dioxide). Thus, a 5 per cent reduction in emissions is clearly worthwhile, since the world would gain about US$6 billion in avoided damages at a cost of only US$400 million. Reductions are worthwhile up to a maximum net benefit level corresponding to 17 per cent reductions, but beyond this the net benefit figure is reduced. For cuts of approximately 30 per cent, costs actually exceed benefits.

Nordhaus shows that this overall reduction should comprise a virtual phase-out of CFCs and a reduction of 6 per cent in carbon dioxide emission. The finding that CFCs should be phased out is wholly consistent with the existing international discussions, but this is the only correspondence. A probable interpretation of the Noordwijk Declaration and the follow-up is that carbon dioxide cuts should be around 20 per cent cuts on level of emissions in the year *2000*, whereas Nordhaus is referring to reductions of some 6 per cent of carbon dioxide levels that would otherwise exist in *2050*. The implication is that the 'optimal' level of warming is significantly higher (and hence, emission reduction requirements are substantially lower) than is countenanced in the current international discussions, which we characterized as a constant capital approach. Cost–benefit analysis would be telling us not to take such drastic action.

There are some reasons for supposing that Nordhaus's analysis understates the degree of control required. First, his damage costs could be conservative if the potential for catastrophic events is realized. Table 26.1 demonstrates that if the damages are higher (the benefits of emission reduction are the same as avoided damages), then the 'optimal' level of control will also be higher. This is the essence of the 'constant capital' approach, which puts the emphasis on the degree of uncertainty and hence the potential for irreversible losses. How far the potential for catastrophic damage is borne out by the scientific evidence is, however, open to question. Second, the control cost estimates used by Nordhaus appear to ignore energy conservation measures that are cost-effective now without the need to introduce measures to raise energy prices through, for example, carbon or gasoline taxes. If this is correct, then Table 26.1 shows that lower reduction costs will mean a higher level of optimal control.[15]

What can we conclude about the cost benefit approach to global warming? At the very least, we can say that it should be pursued vigorously as a check on the economic implications of targets like those presented in Toronto. If the two approaches result in very different outcomes, then attention needs to be focused on why this is so. There is another reason for pursuing the cost–benefit approach. The Toronto target and the Noordwijk Declaration focus on *emissions reduction* as the appropriate response to global warming, but it is very unlikely that it will be efficient for policy to be formulated solely in terms of emissions reduction. Adaptation to global warming, through economic adjustment and defences against sea level rise, will surely play a part. The 'ecological limits' approach tells us nothing about the optimal combination of prevention and adaptation. Cost–benefit analysis is expressly formulated for just such a purpose. What a more detailed analysis would show, however, remains open to question.

Table 26.1 Costs and benefits of greenhouse gas reductions.

Reductions in greenhouse gas emissions as percentage of base level	Total of reduction (US$ billion)	Total benefit of reduction (US$ billion)
0	0	0
5	0.4	5.9
10	1.6	11.8
15	4.1	17.7
17	5.6	19.6
20	11.9	23.6
30	46.7	35.4
40	107.0	47.2
50	200.6	59.0

Source: W. Nordhaus, *To Slow or Not to Slow: The Economics of the Greenhouse Effect* (New Haven, CT: Yale University, Department of Economics, mimeo, 1990). The benefit figures are from Nordhaus's 'medium damage' scenario, corresponding to damage of some $13 per tonne carbon dioxide equivalent (in 1989 US dollars).

ACHIEVING GLOBAL WARMING TARGETS

The minimum cost principle

The idea of *minimising the costs of compliance* is important. This principle directs negotiators to find the most cost-efficient way of achieving a given environmental target. It is easy to misunderstand the principle, because it could be confused with getting environmental quality 'on the cheap'. This is not so. The idea is not to sacrifice environmental quality, but to achieve a quality target at the lowest possible cost. This releases resources for other purposes, including other environmental purposes. The minimum cost principle is also important when considering the probable shape of environmental policy over the next two decades. It seems very likely that all nations will face a rising bill for securing environmental quality. This is very much a legacy of our failure to take action during the past two decades – a reminder that precaution is better than reaction. But if the bill is going to rise anyway, then it is essential to seek the most effective means of minimising the increased costs. In this way, the cost burden to be borne by industrialists and consumers can be contained. This is not just a matter of wise husbandry, it is of strategic importance for the environmentalist case. Inefficient expenditures will risk alienating industry and, for that matter, consumers. By keeping costs down, the risks of a 'polluter backlash' can be minimised.

ALTERNATIVE ROADS TO CONTROL

In order to achieve internationally agreed global environmental targets, there are only three possible routes: command and control, pollution taxes and tradeable permits.

The last two forms of regulation can be classified as *market-based incentives.* Their particular feature is that they make use of market signals. Pollution taxes involve: altering the prices faced by industry and, through these increases in industry's costs, the prices faced by consumers as well; or taxing consumers directly on the consumption of a polluting commodity. Tradeable permits operate through quantities, by allowing polluters to switch between sources of pollution provided they honour an overall target quality of the environment.[16] Command-

and-control approaches, on the other hand, do not make use of the market at all.

Command-and-control

The three forms of regulation are not exclusive. In general, a sensibly designed environmental policy will be a mix of all three. Currently, and with odd exceptions, environmental policy is based on command-and-control. Regulation involves setting targets for those responsible for the intial emission of pollutants; this is the 'command'. The 'control' involves monitoring, inspection and penalty. Countries vary according to the intensity with which they pursue control. Self-evidently, command-and-control will not work if the penalties for non-compliance are small and less than the net gain from exceeding the standard. Typically, polluters prefer regulation: regulation is certain; polluters know where they stand; the standards are usually in place for some period of time; and, depending on the degree of control, polluters can usually negotiate with the regulator over special difficulties. There is something to be said for a system which reduces the uncertainty associated with regulation. But regulation is also more expensive than the other means of control and therefore offends the principle of minimum cost. There are two basic reasons why regulation is more expensive:

(1) It requires that the regulator acquire information from the polluter, for example, about the costs of abatement technology;
(2) It leaves the polluter with no flexibility. The polluter has to abide by the standard regardless of the fact that his or her costs of abating pollution could be much higher than those of another polluter. Because both polluters face the same standard, there is no possibility of the polluter with the lower costs of abatement taking a larger share of the control.[17]

Compliance cost savings will be very important as the cost of protection rises. Expenditures on environmental protection in the Organization for Economic Cooperation and Development countries constitute between 1.5 and 2 per cent of their GDPs. To underline the prediction that these costs will rise, we may note that the Netherlands' National Environmental Protection Plan anticipates a rise in this share to 3, or even 4, per cent. The Netherlands is one country which has formulated a detailed strategy for marked improvement in its environment. Interestingly, it is based mainly on command-and-control policies. The percentage of GDP spent on environmental protection would almost certainly have been lower had they adopted market-based incentives, such as taxes and tradeable permits.

Some studies have begun to suggest that command-and-control may impose significant burdens on wealth creation in its more traditional form. Jorgensen and Wilcoxen estimate that the rate of growth of US GNP between 1973 and 1985 was 0.19 percentage points less than it otherwise would have been without environmental control.[18] Thus, a growth rate of, for example, 2.5 per cent per annum would have been reduced to 2.3 per cent per annum because of pollution control measures based almost entirely on command-and-control measures.

Taxation solutions

The principles underlying a pollution tax are readily understood. If the aim is to control, for example, carbon dioxide emissions, then emitters of carbon dioxide would be charged according to the carbon content of the fuels they burn. Coal would attract a higher charge than oil, which would attract a higher charge than natural gas. The effect of the tax would be to induce three things: substitution of lower carbon fuels for high carbon fuels, substitution of non-carbon energy for carbon energy (nuclear power and renewables) and energy conservation. The essence of the tax is to encourage tax avoiding behaviour. It is thus an incentive tax rather than a revenue raising tax. Nonetheless, revenues will be raised, and these can be used in a 'fiscally neutral' way to reduce income or other taxes. This softens any burden that may be believed to exist under the tax option, and it serves to reduce tax disincentives in the economy. Command-and-control procedures generate no revenue, so this option does not arise.

There are other virtues of a tax solution. For instance, because a pollution tax is a tax on all emissionns, there is a systematic, continuing incentive to search for new technologies that will reduce the tax burden by removing the basis on which the tax is assessed – *i.e.,* pollution. Again, the command-and-control approach tends to lack any 'technology-forcing' characteristic, because it is invariably based on some concept of 'best available technology', although , in principle, standards can be set so as to be technology-forcing.

Tradeable permits

As a final piece of evidence on the cost minimisation properties of market-based instruments, consider the limited experience there has been with tradeable emission permits under the Clean Air Acts in the US. A brief digression on the nature of tradeable permits is necessary, since their functioning is perhaps less straightforward than emission taxes.

Two broad sources of inefficiency arise in the command-and-control approach. First, command-and-control requires the regulator to use up resources to acquire information that polluters already possess. For example, polluters know far better than governments what it will cost to abate or clean-up waste emissions. Yet, under the command-and-control approach, governments must obtain this information. Second, polluters vary in the ease with which they can abate pollution; stated another way, their costs of control differ. Under the command-and-control system, each polluter has to achieve a given standard, subject usually to some consideration about 'excessive' cost. Control is not concentrated in the sources that find it cheapest to abate pollution. Yet, such a process of concentration would enable overall costs of compliance with the standard to be minimised.

The basic idea underlying tradeable permits is straightforward. First, an acceptable level of pollution is determined. This may be expressed as: some allowable concentration of, for example, lead in gasoline; a production or consumption target for chemicals, for example, CFCs; or an allowable national emission level, which is likely with carbon dioxide at some time in the future. Permits are then issued for the level of emissions up to the allowable amount. If, for instance, 100 units of pollution is allowable, then 100 permits (each with a value of one unit of emission) might be issued. There are various ways of determining the initial issue of the permits. Because of the disruption that might ensue by alternative allocations, a popular initial allocation is one based on historical emission levels. This is known as *grandfathering*: rights to pollute are based on past emission levels. However, this is not the only way to determine the initial allocation.

Once the initial allocation is made, polluters are then free to trade the pollution rights. It is this *tradeability* which is the hallmark of the permit system, since it is tradeability which helps to keep down the costs of complying with regulations; tradeability is the main attraction of the permit system. Basically, a firm that finds it comparatively easy to abate pollution will find it profitable to sell its permits to a firm that finds it expensive to abate pollution. Essentially, it will sell the permit if it receives a price higher than the cost it will have to bear of abating pollution now that it has no permit. The high cost polluter, on the other hand, will find it profitable to buy permits if the price is below what it will otherwise cost him or her to abate pollution. Both low and high cost polluter, therefore, stand to gain, and this provides the incentive for them to trade. Moreover, by trading, the control of pollution will tend to be concentrated among those polluters who find it cheap to pollute, and permit holding will tend to be concentrated among those who find it expensive to control pollution. Yet the overall environmental standard is safeguarded, because nothing has happened to alter the overall number of permits, and it is this that determines the level of pollution.

Clearly, such a description is simplistic, but it captures the essence of the tradeable permit system. One important point to note is that trade need not be between *different* polluters. It can be between different sources within a single firm. The result is the same, however, because the firm will gain by concentrating abatement in its low cost sources and concentrating permits in its high costs sources.

If the above description is broadly accurate, then we would expect the actual experience of permit trading to result in no decline in environmental standards and a reduction in the costs of compliance compared to what would have been incurred in a command-and-control system. By and large, this is the experience in the United States, where a tradeable permit system exists as part of the US Clean Air Act.

There is no evidence that US environmental standards have been sacrificed because of the trading system. Of course, it could be argued that without the permits system standards might have had to be made tougher still, but this is an untestable proposition. Nor would it follow that tougher standards would be cost-effective, if it were true. The second objection has to be countered by an education process. All regulatory systems 'permit' pollution if by pollution is meant waste. No economic process is waste free. Nor could it be, by the laws of thermodynamics. The issue has, therefore, to be one of whether a tradeable permits system somehow allows more waste than a command-and-control system. As we have seen, there is no reason at all for this to be the case. Objections to a tradeable permits system on the grounds of 'permitting' pollution are deficient, but the political reality is that such false arguments have influence. It is important, therefore, to secure well-informed debate on permit systems, as with other market-based incentives.

Regulators will naturally be sensitive to the concerns of both environmentalists and industry. Nonetheless, they will also have their own concerns, primarily arising from the costs of considering, formulating and implementing any departure from the established command-and-control approach. It is worth remembering that the command-and-control mode of thinking is ingrained in environmental regulation in Europe, reflecting as it does the experience of over 100 years of public health, workplace and environmental legislation. Anxiety also tends to increase as less is known about the new system.

MARKET-BASED INSTRUMENTS AND GLOBAL ENVIRONMENTAL CHANGE

What is the relevance of market-based instruments to global environmental issues? A protocol on greenhouse gases will set a target for greenhouse gas reduction; but, just as it is inefficient to set each polluter the same target reduction in emissions, so it is inefficient to set each country the same target. There is a real danger that negotiators of a global warming protocol will make this mistake. For example, it seems fair for each country to achieve the stable emissions target of the Toronto Conference or a laxer one of stabilising emissions at current levels of carbon dioxide; but the fairness is illusory, because the target is set regardless of the different costs of achieving it. The aim should be to bias the reductions towards those countries that can most easily achieve them. The logic of this requirement is fairly simple: if one country has lower costs of abatement than another, then it will be cheaper to require more control in that country than in the high abatement cost country. A protocol that requires equal emission reductions by country offends this principle and hence incurs an unnecessary aggregate cost burden. It is conceivable that a protocol based on regulation could take account of the minimum cost objective, but it would be complex and, as it happens, unnecessary, because use of the tax or tradeable permits solution avoids the problem. Additionally, the tax and permit solutions help solve the other dominant problem in international agreements, namely, how to devise incentives for co-operation.

Global warming affects different countries in different ways. A few states may conceivably gain from climate change; but even if all lose, some will lose far more than others. Under these circumstances, it is going to be difficult to secure agreement on appropriate targets and on the initial allocation of emission reduction targets among countries. More importantly, the avoidance or containment of global warming is an example of what economists call a 'public good'. If global warming is reduced, then it will generally be of benefit to all countries, and no country can be excluded from the benefit. Any one country could secure the benefit of a global agreement without sharing the cost. The United Kingdom, for example, could refuse to co-operate and wait for the rest of the world to solve the problem. After all, the UK contributes only 3 per cent of the world's emissions of greenhouse gases. By not co-operating, the UK could avoid the costs and reap the benefits and thus would be a 'free rider'.

The potential existence of free riders means that any protocol must have inbuilt incentives to encourage co-operation. We have already noted the problems of securing global co-operation on CFCs, and this is in the context of a comparatively straightforward agreement, since relatively few countries are involved. Barratt has drawn attention to the dissimilarity of the ozone layer case and global warming case, contrary to the widespread view that all we need to do for global warming is follow the example set by the Montreal Protocol.[19] Essentially, the Montreal Protocol is a game being played among very few players. Moreover, the costs of switching out of CFCs are comparatively modest. In order to persuade the potential free riders to co-operate, it is necessary to create incentives. This involves transferring resources – funds, technical assistance and technology – to these potential free riders. The scale of these transfers could be large, and it is far from clear that the world's leaders have understood the requirement to make transfers on the scale that is likely to be necessary.[20] But in the ozone layer case, the transfers are relatively modest.

Markandya has estimated that perhaps US $1.8 billion to US $2 billion is needed to assist developing countries to develop subsidies for CFCs.[21] Very much larger sums will be needed to assist with substitution for coal, energy efficiency, *etc*. In short, the critical feature of a global warming protocol has to be the design of incentives for co-operation, and that means resource transfers.

It is the twin features of cost minimisation and resource transfer which make the use of market-based instruments attractive for implementating a global warming protocol. Both the tax and tradeable permits solutions need to be considered.

The international tax solution

In discussing an international tax solution we focus on carbon dioxide, but as noted earlier, it will be more efficient if any protocol allows individual greenhouse gases to be traded off in ratios determined by their radiative properties. Hoel has shown that a tax internationally administered and collected by some central agency is too bureaucratic and would interfere with domestic sovereignty. A tax implemented by each government would run foul of the free rider problem, since governments could easily offset a carbon tax by reducing other fuel taxes.[22] The solution therefore has to be one in which a central agency taxes each country according to emission levels. The tax level set would be the same for each country. Tax revenues would then be reimbursed: handed back to countries, but according to some formula of allocation. Each individual country would then act to minimise the sum of its tax payments and abatement costs. It would prefer to pay the tax if the cost of abatement is higher than the tax, but would prefer to abate if that is cheaper than paying the tax. We would expect some combination of both actions.[23] The size of the tax would be determined by the agreed carbon dioxide emission reduction. Depending on the reimbursment rule chosen, some countries would then be net payers of tax to the central agency, while other countries would be net recipients of tax revenues. But the net payers of tax would still be better off under the agreement than they were without it, for they would have secured the benefits of the global warming damage that would have been avoided. Indeed, a condition of a successful agreement is that each country is better off with the agreement, taking into account net tax payments, abatement costs and environmental benefits.[24]

The rationale for reimbursement of tax revenues arises from the need to make resource transfers, as I have already demonstrated. Reimbursements should therefore relate to the costs of controlling carbon dioxide emissions and the damage likely to be experienced from global warming. The higher the cost of control, the higher will be the reimbursement required. Coal-based economies, for example, China and India, will tend to require large reimbursements. Countries that can switch easily from coal to gas-fired electricity production will have low reimbursement requirements. The United Kingdom might be such a country, but as noted earlier, the UK will have an incentive to focus a protocol on all greenhouse gases in order to minimise the extent that adjustments have to be made to carbon fuels and hence to the country's coal industry.

As far as damage is concerned, those countries that stand to lose most from warming, such as deltaic or island countries, are likely to co-operate because of their concern that the protocol should not fail. They will tend to require lower reimbursements from the tax revenues.

If, as in the ozone layer case, it is the developing countries which are most likely not to co-operate, then a formula that relates reimbursements to population would appear to be a prime candidate for the protocol. The resulting scale of transfers from rich to poor could be substantial and could arouse strong opposition, because some industrialised countries could be worse off after the tax than before it. Not only does Grubb doubt that an international fund with substantial carbon tax revenues would be acceptable,[25] but a team of New Zealand authors also questions its political acceptability and efficiency.[26] However, Hoel thinks that such a fund is feasible and that reimbursements should be based mainly on GNP (and only partially on the basis of population) in order to secure co-operation.[27] Recent work in Canada suggests that a global carbon tax designed to secure the Toronto Conference ultimate target of 50 per cent reduction in carbon dioxide could result in tax revenues of US$600 billion of which US$480 billion would be reimbursed to developing countries.[28] To gather some idea of the significance of these figures, US$600 billion is equal to: 51 per cent of the entire external debt of the developing world in 1989 or one-and-a-half times the entire external debt of Latin America or six times the total of all disbursements to the developing countries in 1989. It is scarcely credible that any single international agency would have the capability to manage such resource transfers.

If a tax solution could be implemented, how big would the tax have to be? Barratt estimates that the long run tax (*i.e.*, the tax that would prevail once people were able to adjust by switching technologies, *etc.*) would be approximately 54 per cent on the current price of coal, 43 per cent on the oil price (prior to the Gulf Crisis) and 32 per cent on the price of gas in the UK in order to achieve the Toronto aim of a 20 per cent reduction in the rate of 1988 emissions.[29] Short-run taxes (*i.e.*, not allowing for longer run adjustments) would be three times these levels. Another work by Ingham and Ulph suggests that any carbon tax would have to increase rapidly over time to substantial levels of over 100 per cent of average energy prices.[30] Whalley and Wigle suggest that a global tax rate of 90 per cent would secure 50 per cent reduction in carbon dioxide emissions.[31] There are also problems in setting the tax. It is well known that setting the initial tax may be a hit-and-miss affair. This may not matter much if there is scope for adjusting the tax at a later date. However, the problem with global warming is that delays in adjusting the tax will mean additional committed warming because of thermal inertia in the oceans. The adjustment process may therefore be quite complex.

An international carbon tax is not to be dismissed, but it is clear that, as with any solution, there will be formidable problems of design and implementation. The main reason for keeping such a tax on the agenda is that it is likely to be a more efficient instrument of control than country-by-country targets.

Internationally tradeable permits

The last option for implementing a protocol is through tradeable permits. The essence of the permit solution is that countries have an incentive to trade permits with each other and make net gains in the process. For example, suppose country A and country B receive the same level of quotas (i.e. permits to release greenhouse gases), but that country A finds it much cheaper to control emissions than country B. Country A has an incentive to sell its quota to country B, collecting money from country B in excess of the cost of abating carbon dioxide, which it must now do, because it has no permits. Country B secures the permits and gains financially, because the cost of buying the permits is less than the cost it would otherwise have incurred by reducing carbon dioxide emissions. Both countries gain, and the overall emission target has not been compromised. In general, countries have an incentive to trade their permits until the marginal costs of abatement are just equal to the price of the permits in the market place. If costs exceed the price, then it will pay to try to buy further permits. If abatement costs are lower than the price of permits, then it will pay to sell the permits, collect the revenue from their sale and use some of the proceeds to abate emissions. Recalling the earlier discussion of tradeable permits, this is entirely analogous to the company trading of emission credits in the US, but with companies replaced by countries. A number of other trading systems exist: for example, fisheries quotas in New Zealand and Iceland and milk quotas in the UK.

Once again, some agency to oversee the trade in permits would be needed. Three major problems arise from this requirement. First, some countries are large emitters of carbon dioxide, notably , the US, USSR and the European Community. This may have some undesirable consequences for the efficiency of the tradeable permit approach, because the price of the permits on the open market will be influenced by sales and purchases by 'big' countries.[32]

Second, the tax solution penalises countries that emit too much, but the permits system requires additional penalties if countries go over their permitted level. This is a particularly relevant problem in the global warming context, since it is not clear what sanctions can be applied if countries persistently exceed their permitted emissions.

Third, the overriding problem involves the initial allocation of permits. This is akin to determining reimbursements under the tax solution. Few writers have favoured the grandfathering of permits, whereby they are initially allocated according to the existing levels of emissions. This would appear to favour the industrialized countries and does little or nothing to create incentives for the developing world to co-operate. But, in fact, any allocation other than grandfathering is likely to be resisted strongly by the major emitting nations. Without grandfathering, an agreement would be unlikely to come about. This suggests that, initially, a grandfathering approach would be most appropriate, but then emission allowances should be modified by altering the 'value' of the quota over time. Thus, a developed country quota would have declining allowances over time, while developing countries could have rising allowances that less than offset the developed nations' reductions. The burden of international agreement would be thus shifted from the initial allocation as emission allowances change over time. Countries are more likely to agree to this formula, because it allows time for adjustment and reduces the uncertainty attached to buying permits in the international market at the outset of the agreement.

Some authors have favoured a system whereby the initial allocation is based on GNP, but this would again favour the industrialised countries (as would GNP per capita). Per capita allocations have found most favour, and an initial allocation based on such a rule would have the effect of providing developing countries with a large quantity of permits that could then be sold to other countries at a profit over the cost of abating greenhouse gas emissions.[33] Grubb has suggested that in order to avoid the implicit reward for overpopulation, only adult populations should be counted. Another suggestion involves allocating all permits to non-polluters (*i.e.,* the world's poor) and then allowing trade thereafter. To avoid the hoarding of permits by rich countries, permits could be subject to renewal – *i.e.,* be subject to lease rather than ownership.[34] Countries with a capacity to create carbon sinks, such as new forests, could secure credits under the system – they might be allowed to emit beyond the level in their permits, provided the carbon sinks offset the excess.

The reality of international political economy is likely to work against any allocation of permits based on population. It would require assurance at the outset that international trade in permits would take place, otherwise the burden of adjustment would fall heavily and rapidly on the countries with high per capita emissions (*e.g.*, the United States). In these circumstances, such countries are unlikely to agree at the outset. Gandfathering of some kind is, therefore, likely to be the only initial allocation that will meet with agreement. The sheer 'newness' of tradeable permits on the international scene may, in any event, militate against them totally. If so, one essential message for international negotiators is that they should 'mimic' as best they can the efficiency of market-based approaches. To this end, allocated emission reductions must bear some resemblance to the pattern that would emerge if they were allocated according to costs of abatement. Even that requirement is a formidable one in terms of international negotiation.[35]

CONCLUSION

The problems of designing international agreements to meet the global environmental challenge are formidable. This paper has offered only the briefest of overviews of what is a major set of issues for immediate and future debate. The basic questions posed are highly problematic, namely, what is an acceptable level and rate of global warming and how can we design an efficient structure of global incentives for co-operation. The answers will involve more imagination and vigour than the international community has shown so far. It is evident that many of the existing discussions are based on the belief that science alone can determine what is acceptable. This is false. Social scientists also have an important part to play as global warming impacts are measured and its costs are computed. However, assessing impacts is only one aspect of the decision-making problem, since the task of designing incentives is also pivotal. Humans are too rational in their self-interest. It is this self-interest which will threaten international agreement, unless of course, we can use and manipulate self-interest to global advantage. This is the real global challenge.

REFERENCES

This is a substantially revised version of the Henry Sidgwick Memorial Lecture which the author gave at the University of Cambridge, 23 February 1990. The author is indebted to Jonathan Fisher, David Fisk, Edward Barbier and Scott Barratt for comments on the earlier version. The author accepts responsibility for any remaining errors.

1. D.W. Pearce, A. Markandya and E. Barbier, *Blueprint for a Green Economy* (London Earthscan Publications, 1989).
2. R. Solow, 'On the Intergenerational Allocation of Natural Resources' *Scandinavian Journal of Economics* (Vol. 88, No. 1 1986) pp. 141–54; T. Page, *Conservation and Economic Efficiency*, (Baltimore, MD: Johns Hopkins University Press, 1977): J. Hartwick, 'Intergenerational Equity and the Investing of Rents from Exhaustible Resources' *American Economic Review* (Vol. 66. 1977), pp. 972–74; and K-G Maler, 'Theoretical Foundations of the Concept of Sustainable Development', Seminar on *The Economics of Environmental Issues* (Paris; OECD, October 1989, unpublished).
3. See World Commission on Environment and Development. *Our Common Future* (Oxford: Oxford University Press, 1987).
4. See, for example, D.W.Pearce, E. Barbier and A. Markandya. *Sustainable*

Development: Economics and Environment in the Third World (London: Edward Elgar, 1990).

5. One obvious issue is what measure of capital is being held constant: some 'physical' concept, real prices or real values.

6. See I Mintzer. 'Cooling Down a Warming World: Chlorofluorcarbons, The Greenhouse effect, and the Montreal Protocol', *International Environmental Affairs* (Vol. 1, No. 1, Winter 1989) pp. 12-25.

7. A very readable introduction to the global warming issue is S. Boyle and J. Ardill. *The Greenhouse Effect* (London: Hodder and Stoughton, 1989).

8. Thus, speaking at the White House Conference on Science and Economics Research Related to Global Change, April 1990, Michael Boskin, Chairman of the President's Council of Economic Advisers, compared the cost of greenhouse gas emission reduction to the economic disruption caused by oil price rises in the 1970s and early 1980s. He remarked that 'available studies suggest that it would cost at least 1 per cent of annual US GNP, or perhaps several times that amount, to meet widely-discussed CO_2 reduction targets and that economic growth could slow significantly'. The conference itself was clearly aimed at persuading other countries to adopt more cautious attitudes, coming as it did before the publication of the reports of the UN Intergovernmental Panel on Climate Change (IPCC) and the World Climate Conference of November 1990.

9. *The Noordwijk Declaration on Climate Change* (Leidschendam, the Netherlands: Climate Conference Secretariat, 6–7 November 1989).

10. *The Changing Atmosphere: Implications for Global Security, Conference Statement* (Toronto, 27–30 June 1988) Paragraph 22 states (emphasis added):
    An initial global goal should be to reduce CO_2 emissions by approximately 20 per cent of 1988 levels by the year 2005. Clearly, the *industrialized nations have a responsibility to lead the way,* both through their national energy policies and their bilateral and multilateral assistance agreements. About one-half of this reduction would be sought from energy efficiency and other conservation measures. The other half should be effected by modifications in supplies.

11. The limit of 0.1°C is suggested, for example, by International Project for Sustainable Energy Paths, *Energy Policy in the Greenhouse* (El Cerrito, CA: International Project for Sustainable Energy Paths, 1989).

12. In turn, the constant capital approach has similarities with the idea of adopting 'safe minimum standards' (SMSs). A SMS approach calls for a strong bias to conservation of natural capital unless the opportunity costs of the conservation – *i.e.,* the foregone benefits of developing the resource – are clearly very large. See R. Bishop, 'Endangered Species and Uncertainty: The Economics of a Safe Minimum Standard', *American Journal of Agricultural Economics* (February 1978), pp. 11–18.

13. See E. Barbier and D.W. Pearce, 'Thinking Economically About Climate Change', *Energy Policy* (January/February 1990), pp. 11–18.

14. W. Nordhaus, *To Slow or Not to Slow: The Economics of the Greenhouse Effect* (New Haven, CT: Yale University, Department of Economics, mimeo., February 1990). For some modifications of Nordhaus's estimates see J. Walter and R. Ayres, *Global Warming: Damages and Costs* (Laxenberg, Austria: International Institute for Applied Systems Analysis, mimeo., 1990); and R. Ayres and J. Walter, *Global warming: Abatement Policies and Costs* (Laxenberg, Austria: International Institute for Applied Systems Analysis, mimeo. 1990).

15. Various studies suggest that there are very low costs of control through energy conservation. See Ayres and Walter, *op. cit.,* in note 14. For the United Kingdom, see Department of Energy, *An Evaluation of Energy Related Greenhouse Gas Emissions and Measures to Ameliorate Them,* Energy Paper No. 58 (London: HMSO, 1989). How far this observation affects the Nordhaus study is not clear, however, since Nordhaus captures energy saving measures by simulating the effects of a carbon fuel tax.

16. There is a formal relationship between taxes and the prices of tradeable permits. Both the tax and the permit are aimed at securing a predetermined level of pollut ion. Under

conditions of certainty, it is then the case that the market price of a tradeable permit is equal (per unit of emission) to the tax.

17. The basic requirement for a minimum cost approach to regulation is that the different polluters' marginal costs of pollution abatement should be equalized. A tax that is the same for all polluters will achieve this result, because each polluter will prefer to abate than pay the tax if abatement costs are lower than the tax and will prefer to pay the tax if it is above abatement costs. A tradeable permit system has the same property. If marginal abatement costs differ, then there are gains to be obtained by having high abatement costs polluters buy permits from low abatement cost polluters.

18. See T. Tietenberg, 'Economic Instruments for Environmental Regulation' *Oxford Review of Economic Policy* (Vol. 6. No. 1, 1990).

19. D.W. Jorgensen and P.J. Wilcoxen, *Environmental Regulation and US Economic Growth* (Cambridge, MA: Harvard University, Department of Economics, mimeo., July 1989).

20. S. Barratt, *On the Nature and Significance of International Environmental Agreements,* (London: London Business School, mimeo., May 1989).

21. The transfer issue is emphasised in M. Grubb, *The Greenhouse Effect: Negotiating Targets* (London: Royal Institute of International Affairs, 1989).

22. See A. Markandya, *The Costs to Developing Countries of Joining the Montreal Protocol* (London: London Environmental Economics Centre, mimeo., 1990)

23. M. Hoel, *Efficient International Agreements for Reducing Emissions of CO_2* (Oslo: University of Oslo, Department of Economics, mimeo., 1990).

24. The minimum cost theorem occurs again here, since the result will be that each country will determine its combination of tax and abatement measures according to the rule that the tax rate, which is common to all countries, should equal the marginal cost of abatement. In this way, marginal costs are equated across countries, and this is the requirement for cost mimimisation.

25. Unfortunately, it is more complex than this. The assumption here is that the global warming target is set in such a way that global environmental benefits exceed total abatement costs, in other words, that a cost–benefit rule is used. Only then is there a global 'surplus' to be redistributed. As we have seen, this may well not be the case. This raises the prospect that some countries will be net payers of tax and that their individual avoided damage costs will be less than the net payment. In these circumstances they are unlikely to co-operate. For this reason, it is important that some sort of cost–benefit rule is used for setting global targets.

26. Grubb, *op. cit.,* in note 21.

27. I.G. Bertram, C. Wallace and R. Stephens, *Economic Instruments and the Greenhouse Effect* (Wellington, New Zealand: Victoria University of Wellington, Economics Department, mimeo., August 1989).

28. Hoel. *op. cit.,* in note 23.

29. J. Whalley and R. Wigle, *Cutting CO_2 Emissions: The Effects of Alternative Policy Approaches* (London, Ontario: University of Western Ontario, Department of Economics and Waterloo, Ontario: Wilfred Laurier University, Department of Economics, mimeo., December 1989).

30. S. Barratt, London Business School, personal communication.

31. A. Ingham and A. Ulph, *Carbon Taxes and the UK Manufacturing Sector* (Southampton: University of Southampton, Department of Economics, mimeo., 1990).

32. Whalley and Wigle, *op. cit.,* in note 29.

33. See Hoel, *op. cit.,* in note 23.

34. Bertram *et al., op. cit.,* in note 27; and Grubb, *op. cit.,* in note 21.

35. Grubb, *op. cit.,* in note 21.

36. For further discussion, see D.W. Pearce, *Greenhouse Gas Agreements: Part 1 – Internationally Tradeable Greenhouse Gas Permits* (London: London Environmental Economics Centre, mimeo., 1990).

Chapter 27
International environmental problems

Karl-Göran Mäler *Stockholm School of Economics*

INTRODUCTION

Man-made borders are completely arbitrary from the point of view of the biosphere. There is no reason that environmental disturbances should be confined by human definitions of areas of jurisdiction. But that means that the 'environmental problem area' will in general not be identical to the area of jurisdiction and control and there is as a result no single authority with the right to control and decide on a solution to the problem. One may therefore expect lack of co-ordination and inefficiency whenever the area of jurisdiction differs from the area of environmental concern. In no other field is this as apparent as in the field of international environmental problems. As there is no international or multinational 'government' that can enforce international environmental policy, these problems must be solved by voluntary agreements among the countries concerned, and as some countries may lose from an agreement, it is scarcely surprising that effective international co-operation is lacking. In spite of this, a number of international treaties have been agreed upon, treaties that perhaps do not aim to solve the environmental problems directly but have as their main objective the creation of an atmosphere conducive to further discussions and negotiations.

Building on the work of Landsberg and Russel (1971) the following taxonomy of international environmental relations is proposed. First, let us differentiate between the various kinds of environmental relations: there are physical relations, that is when a pollutant moves across a border through rivers, currents in seas, or by winds in the atmosphere. Second, there is the human transport of wastes across international borders. Even if a particular transport is accepted by both the sending and the receiving country, it may be that the transport is not compatible with sustainable development. Moreover, there is the hazard of accidental discharges. Third, there are non-physical relations that arise because individuals in one country may be concerned with environmental resources in another country. For example, there are many individuals in Europe and North America who are concerned with the preservation of the African elephants and are willing to sacrifice part of their present consumption in order to guarantee their survival. Fourth, there are the economic side-effects that arise because of environmental policies, in particular effects through the international trade. A second dimension which must be kept in mind in discussing international environmental problems is where the sources of pollution or resource loss are, and who are the sufferers of the damage done.

The classical case is the *unidirectional externality,* exemplified by upstream polluting countries and downstream suffering countries. This case can be divided into the many victim case, when many countries are affected negatively by the externality, and the one victim case, where only one country is damaged. This differentiation is important for the economic analysis, given the incentives to 'free ride'. Much of the analysis in this paper deals with this problem. Furthermore, there is the differentiation between the case with one sourse and the case with many sources. In the latter case, there is the important question on how abatement costs should be shared and how control measures should be allocated among countries in a cost efficient way.

The next main case is *regional reciprocal externalities,* in which a group of countries is both the source and victim of an environmental problem. Acid rain in Europe is one example of such a regional problem.

Finally, we have the case of *global environmental problems,* which affect most of the countries of the earth in one way or another. Here it is useful to separate out three sub-cases. The first deals with environmental problems in which one or a few countries are the sources of the problem but all or almost all countries are suffering from the problem. Excessive hunting of whales is carried out by only a couple of countries, but the threat of extinction of some of the species is a cost that will be carried by all mankind. It is quite similar to unidirectional externalities but with the difference that almost all countries will be hurt (including the countries causing the problem). The second case deals with the opposite situation, when almost all countries on earth contribute to the degradation of the environment but only a few countries are hurt. Finally, we have the case of global commons, when all countries are also victimized. This use of the term global commons is not the usual one. The established interpretation of global commons is in legal terms, covering resources such as the deep seas or the Antarctic or the radiation spectrum. This taxonomy is however based on the economic analysis of incentives to economize with resources, and from that point of view, biodiversity, global climate, the common biosphere are all very similar to the deep seas or the radiation spectrum.

We can display this taxonomy in the matrix shown in Table 27.1. This classification is founded in the economic analysis of incentive problems and not in the legal status of the various situations.

In this paper, we concentrate on physical relations and on unidirectional externalities and regional reciprocal externalities. However, from an analytical point of view, global commons have very much in common with regional reciprocal externalities. Two questions will be addressed: (i) what are the incentives to co-operate and (ii) how should institutions be designed in order to promote co-operation to achieve economic efficiency.

In the remaining sections of this article physical and non-physical transnational problems will be discussed. Although the two remaining issues in the matrix – waste transport and economic side-effects – are important as parts in the network of international environmental relations, they will not be dealt with further.

INTERNATIONAL TREATIES

International co-operation on environmental issues was in its early stage mainly concerned with the preservation of species. A few treaties on damage from oil spills and on the use of nuclear power were also signed. There were also some agreements on pollution of rivers. After the Stockholm Conference of 1972 the situation changed. At the conference decisions were made to establish the United

Table 27.1 A matrix of international environmental problems.

	Global externality			Regional reciprocal externality	Unidirectional externality	
	Many sources few victims	Many victims few victims	Common property		One victim	Several victims
Physical						
Non-physical						
Waste transport						
Economic side-effects						

Nations Environment Programme (UNEP), to ensure that different UN organizations (FAO, UNESCO, etc.) should include environmental considerations in their operations and to adopt a number of recommendations on international co-operation. In particular, paragraph 21 in the Stockholm Declaration dealt explicitly with transboundary pollution problems. That paragraph states that 'States have . . . responsibility to ensure that activities within their jurisdiction or control do not cause damage to the environment of other States or of areas beyond the limits of national jurisdiction'.

This paragraph has guided and will probably continue to guide international co-operation on environmental problems. It can be interpreted as a defence for the polluter pays principle, meaning that the one who is causing an environmental problem has the responsibility to take the necessary measures to eliminate the problem and bear the full cost of these measures.

The polluter pays principle or 'PPP' was adopted by the OECD countries in 1972 mainly as a guideline for domestic environmental policies. The main reasons for adopting PPP were the following. First, it was argued that PPP was a necessary condition for economic efficiency. Any attempt to subsidize pollution abatement would lead to biased incentives and therefore to distortions in the domestic economy. Thus, PPP can be defended on this account. Second, if we take the long-run technical development into account, it seems that the case for PPP is even stronger, as companies are rewarded by developing better and less expensive abatement technologies. Third, it was argued that the application of PPP would not create unintended distortions in foreign trade, as the exporter would have to absorb the total social cost for the product he is selling.

These arguments deal solely with the application of PPP to domestic environmental policy. It is, however, a very short step to extend the application of PPP to international environmental problems, i.e. that polluting countries should bear the cost of controlling the transboundary pollution emanating from them. This application also has a superficial mark of fairness, which probably lies at the bottom of the popularity of the polluter pays principle. On the basis of the Stockholm Declaration, a large number of conventions, protocols, and agreements (about 80) have been signed. Among these are such global treaties as the Law of the Sea (1982), the convention on trade in endangered species, and the Vienna convention on protection of the ozone layer (1985). A number of regional treaties have also been signed, for example conventions on the Baltic Sea and the

North Sea, which regulate the form of co-operation between the countries involved. There are also treaties on the use of rivers such as the Rhine (1986) and the Niger (1980). Within the European Community, there are several very specific agreements and directives.

Most of these conventions have the character of a framework, in which countries can agree on particular methods for co-operation. The Vienna convention on the protection of the ozone layer is of this nature, as is the 1979 Geneva convention on long-range transport of pollutants. Pursuant to these conventions, there are special protocols that regulate the obligations of the signatory countries, for example the 1987 Montreal protocol of the ozone convention, which regulates nations' responsibilities to reduce the use and emission of chlorofluorocarbons (CFCs). Another example is the protocol (1985) to reduce the emissions of sulphur by 30 per cent and a protocol on the control of nitrogen emissions. We will come back to a discussion of these two protocols later. Most of these conventions are not legally binding but should be seen as moral obligations on the part of the signatories.

All these conventions presume the polluter pays principle. However, OECD (1981) has recognized that the PPP may not be applicable in all cases of international environmental problems. In fact, in an analysis of the role of international financial transfers in solving transboundary pollution problems, OECD wrote, 'A willingness on the part of the countries to give and to accept such compensation is an extremely important aspect of transfrontier pollution problems, since it often will be difficult, particularly in existing situations, to negotiate an efficient solution without such payments.' Obviously, what OECD must have had in mind is that in some cases, PPP must be abandoned in favour of 'VPP' – the victim pays principle. We will analyse this concept in later sections. For the present it is important to recognize that the application of VPP in international agreements on transboundary pollution problems is not necessarily contradictory to the application of PPP in domestic environmental policy. It may then happen that the government of a downstream country finds it beneficial to pay the government of an upstream country to reduce the pollution of a river and that the upstream government accepts the payment, but applies PPP to the domestic companies that are polluting the river. It is in this sense that we will interpret PPP and VPP in the international context – as transfers between governments.

UNIDIRECTIONAL EXTERNALITIES

We will distinguish three cases of unidirectional externalities. The first is the classic case where there is an upstream country, 1, that pollutes a river running into a downstream country, 2. Here we have a standard case of bargaining between two parties. In the second case, there are many downstream countries that are harmed by the pollution dumped into the river. In the third case there are many polluting countries. The interesting difference between the three cases is that in the second, downstream countries have the incentive to be free-riders, hoping that the other downstream countries will solve the pollution problem for them. In the third, there is a problem of allocating abatement measures among the sources in a cost-efficient way. These two latter issues will, however, only be illustrated with respect to regional reciprocal externalities.

One upstream and one downstream country

Let E stand for the emission of a pollutant in the river in the upstream country. For concreteness, let us assume that E is the amount of degradable organic material discharged. The upstream country – country 1 – can reduce that discharge by applying sewage treatment, controlling pulp-mills, etc. Assume that the original discharge is E_o, so that the amount of discharge reduction is $R = E_o - E$. Let the cost of reducing the discharge be given by a cost function $C = C(R)$.

The cost will naturally increase with the amount of reduction, but it is also natural to assume that the *marginal cost* will increase, as it will in general be more expensive to control the discharge of one more unit when the waste stream is already much controlled.

The discharge of organic wastes will consume free oxygen in the river, with detrimental effects to the downstream country. The downstream country is experiencing environmental damage which can be expressed as a monetary damage function $D = D(E)$.

From this information it follows that the benefits to the downstream country from reducing the discharge with R is given by

$$B(R) = D(E_o) - D(E_o - R).$$

We assume that $B(R)$ is increasing in the amount of waste reduction but that the marginal benefit is decreasing. This corresponds to the case when a marginal improvement in the water quality has a higher value when the river is highly polluted than when it is quite clean. It should be noted that this assumption is not always satisfied. Let us assume that the river is so polluted that it is an open sewer. A marginal improvement of the river would not change the appearance of the river or bring back natural ecological systems, and in this case it seems natural to assume that the marginal benefits are zero. This corresponds to the case when there are non-convexities in the feasibility set.[1] For this discussion, we will, however, retain the assumption of convexity, that is that the marginal benefits decrease with pollution control. We can now draw the marginal reduction (or abatement) cost curve and the marginal benefit curve in a diagram (see Figure 27.1).

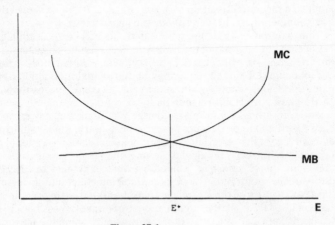

Figure 27.1

411

Let us now assume that (i) both countries know the abatement cost function and the damage cost function in each country, (ii) there are no transaction costs, (iii) the original distribution of property rights is well defined, (iv) the pollution of the river can be seen in isolation from other international relations, and (v) the change in the distribution of the rights between the countries will not change the abatement-cost or the damage-cost functions. Most often the original distribution of rights is not determined by any convention of binding international law, but is based on traditions giving the upstream country the right to pollute. Assumption (iv) is made in order to prevent the possibility that an agreement on the river can prejudice agreements with other countries or with the same country on other common problems. Assumption (v) is the standard assumption made in discussing the Coase theorem.[2]

In this situation, the Coase theorem guarantees that an agreement will be reached by which country 1 voluntarily restricts its discharges to E^*. If country 1 has the initial right to pollute the river, country 2 will cover the abatement costs to 1 and will bear the residual damage costs. If 2 has the initial right to a clean river, the agreement would mean that 1 covers the abatement costs and compensates 2 for the residual damage.

In order to understand this diagram better and to prepare for later analysis, let us formulate this result in terms of non co-operative game theory. As before, let $B(R)$ be the benefit function for the downstream country, and assume that the downstream country pays a side-payment, $\$S$, to the upstream country. The pay-off for the downstream country is therefore $NB_2 = B(R) - S$. The pay-off for the upstream country is then $NB_1 = S - C(R)$. Assume that the negotiations between the two countries take place in the following way: both countries make offers (R_1, S_1) and (R_2, S_2), meaning that the upstream country offers to reduce its discharges with R_1 if it is paid S_1, and the downstream country offers to pay S_2 if the upstream country reduces the discharges with R_2. If the two offers are such that either $S_2 - C(R_2) \geq S_1 - C(R_1)$ (that is the offer from the downstream country is as good for the upstream country as the upstream country's offer) or $B(R_1) - S_1 \geq B(R_2) - S_2$ (that is the offer from the upstream country is as good for the downstream country as its own offer), there will be an agreement. Otherwise both countries are left in the initial situation with pay-off zero. It can be shown that there are a large number of equilibria satisfying the above game.

Thus, given the five assumptions stated above, there exist equilibria that would entail efficient solutions of the transboundary pollution problem. The problem is the richness of equilibria. However, the assumptions made above are questionable. First of all, there may be substantial transaction costs involved in monitoring and enforcing an agreement. Second, the assumption that both parties have perfect information on the cost functions in both countries is hardly realistic. Insufficient information on the cost functions may create incentives to bluff in order to improve gains to the home country. Finally, the assumption that one can regard this environmental problem in isolation is generally wrong. If the upstream country has the right to pollute, then the Coase theorem would dictate the victim pays principle, something that may not be acceptable to the downstream country in view of its prejudicing effect on the negotiations with a third country. These three problems must be addressed in order to make a serious economic analysis of the unidirectional externality possible. It is possible to secure an efficient outcome to bargains when incomplete information prevails since incentives exist for both countries to tell the truth. However, the conditions necessary for this result to hold are very restrictive, and attention needs to be paid to the design of incentive structures for the avoidance of cheating. One such structure is the *mutual compensation principle*.[3]

The mutual compensation principle

The mutual compensation principle, as well as the other that will be reviewed here, is based on the existence of an international agency that has as its objective to create an environment fostering co-operation among the countries. We will here only look at the economic environment, although it is quite clear that other aspects may be equally or more important. The objective for the agency is thus to establish an economic environment through economic incentives for the involved countries to reveal correctly their abatement costs and their estimated benefits from pollution control and thereby encourage them to co-operate. However, one should note that we now have to some extent left the approach that characterized our previous analysis of the bargaining problem. There we looked at what could be accomplished with completely *voluntary* agreements, while we now assume the existence of an international agency and that countries are willing to endow this agency with some powers of taxing the member countries. We should of course have tried to establish this agency as an outcome of negotiations between the interested countries. We have selected the much simpler solution of assuming that countries already have agreed to establish co-operation in this field, and the problem we will address is what policies the agency should adopt in order to induce countries to behave in a certain way. Moreover, it may be argued that the case of unidirectional externality with only two countries involved is not the best area for the application of mechanisms that induce countries to reveal correct information. This is probably a correct criticism and the main reason why the mutual compensation principle is discussed here is the simplicity offered by the analysis of only two countries.

With this interpretation of the agency, the analysis of these economic incentives is an application of the theory of compatibility of different incentives. Groves's mechanism (Groves, 1973) is one of the earliest attempts rigorously to analyse incentives in public decision-making. We can interpret the international agency as a government (although with very limited power) and the two countries as the citizens. The problem for the government is to make a decision on the control of pollutants so that the resulting outcome is Pareto-efficient. In order to do that, the government (or the agency) needs information from the citizens on their valuation of the pollutants. The citizens (or the countries) send messages to the government and on the basis of these messages, the government pays or taxes the citizens and makes the decision on pollution abatement. It should be pointed out, however, that the existence of the international agency must be agreed upon, and one should enlarge the appropriate game so as to include agreements on the agency, its objectives, and its instruments. This has, however, not been done in the literature, and we will not pursue that question further. The discussion of different mechanisms which would make truth-telling profitable indicate that the problems of incomplete information may not be that severe, if they exist at all. We will come back to these issues when discussing reciprocal externalities. However, there is another information problem that should be addressed. We have tacitly assumed that both countries would agree on the amount of actual waste discharged into the river. This is patently not so in very many cases. In fact, many international treaties have their origin in the need to monitor the actual flow of wastes. The EMEP – Environmental Monitoring and Evaluation Program – was

413

set up by the ECE (the United Nations Economic Commission for Europe) as a protocol under the Geneva convention, to monitor the emissions of sulphur oxides and of other pollutants. Important though the monitoring problem is, we will leave it for now and come back to it in connection with the analysis of reciprocal externalities. When there are many source countries, special problems arise in connection with the question of how the reduction of waste discharges should be allocated among them. Similarly, if there are many downstream countries, the problem of cost-sharing will also arise. Moreover, in this case the downstream countries have strong incentives to be free-riders, hoping that other downstream countries will 'buy' a better environment for them. These problems will also be encountered in connection with the problems of regional reciprocal externalities and discussion is deferred until then.

The victim pays principle
It seems to be clear from the discussion that a necessary condition for an effective agreement between the two countries involved in a unidirectional externality is that the victim pays principle is upheld. However, the applications of this principle are very rare in reality. There may be several reasons for this, but two merit a more detailed discussion. The first has to do with the prejudicing effect of accepting the victim pays principle. If a country has to deal with two or more countries on transboundary pollution issues, or deal with the same country on several such issues, then too fast an acceptance of the victim pays principle in the negotiations on one of these issues, may give the country a reputation as a 'weak' negotiator. In view of this, it may pay for the country to insist rather stubbornly on the polluter pays principle in the negotiations on the first issues in order to gain the reputation of being a tough negotiator. This kind of situation has been illustrated in game theory by the so called chain store paradox.[4] It is also much discussed in the literature on time consistent macroeconomic planning. In a way, the situation reflects the situation where there is true uncertainty about the benefit function of waste reductions in the downstream country, and where an agreement will give information on the true nature of this function.

Another factor is that countries exist and develop in a web of international relations. Two countries with a transboundary pollution problem will have a large number of links other than the flow of pollutants from one of the countries to the other. They are probably trading with each other, they operate on the same international capital market, they have mutual or antagonistic goals in foreign policies, people from one country visit the other as tourists, etc. The negotiations on the transboundary pollution problem will obviously reflect all these other relations and the repercussion of the negotiations on environmental issues on these relations will of course be taken into account. One country may want to make concessions in order to improve friendly neighbourhood relations and thereby achieve advantages in other areas of mutual interest.

Krutilla (1966, 1968) studied the economics of the Columbia River Treaty. This treaty between the United States and Canada, although not on transfrontier pollution problems, illustrates these points. The Columbia river is a joint Canadian–American river and there were plans to develop that resource into hydro-power generation and flood protection. It was thought that the best way of accomplishing that would be through co-operation between the two countries. In 1961 this materialized in the Columbia Treaty.

Krutilla found that (a) 'there seems little to commend it in terms of realizing, through co-operation, economies unavailable to each riparian independently' and (*b*)' . . . there is a demonstrable gain to Canada from the Columbia River Treaty, but there is no similar net gain to the United States'. In fact, Krutilla's analysis suggested a gain of about $225 million to $275 million to Canada and a loss equal to about $250 million to $375 million to the US. Moreover, the treaty did not achieve an overall economically efficient outcome. Why did the United States accept the treaty? There were several reasons for this, but one of the more important is given in the following quotation from one of the American negotiators:

> . . . we were anxious that this agreement operate to progressively reduce power costs in British Columbia; firstly and obviously because if there was going to be an agreement it had to operate in that direction for the Canadians; secondly we regard Canada as a partner in the free world, and its growth, its economic growth, as being important to the United States.[5]

Thus, an important treaty on the use of an international river was accepted in spite of the fact that the downstream country subsidized the development in the upstream country, although there were no legal or purely economic reasons to do that. The most important motivation seems to have been that in the long run the downstream country would benefit from a strong economic development in the upstream country.

Kneese's study (1988) on US–Mexican rivers reaches the same conclusions. He looked in particular at the 1973 agreement (Minute 242 of the International Water and Boundary Commission) on desalinization of the Colorado river as it crosses the Mexican–American border.

Mainly through consumptive use of relatively pure water in the upper basins of the river, the salinity in the downstream areas has increased substantially. In the early 1960s the salinity grew dramatically because of increased use of the water for irrigation in Wellton-Mohawk district. Mexico complained about the bad quality of water delivered by the USA which resulted eventually in a pledge by the Nixon administration to undertake several measures among which the most important and most costly was the construction of a desalinization plant at Yuma, Arizona where the Colorado river crosses the border. The US Congress approved essentially the entire package.

There are several interesting features of this programme. First, the administration chose a very costly solution to reduce the salinity of the river. The main reasons for the increase in salinity in the 1960s was the expansion of irrigation in the Wellton-Mohawk district, an expansion that came about through large federal subsidies. According to Kneese, a reduction of the irrigated acreage in the Wellton-Mohawk district might even produce positive benefits besides the reduction of the salinity of the river. Thus it would have been possible to achieve the desired salinity reduction at a very small or even negative cost. Why did the administration choose a much more costly way? The answer is local politics and the way water politics had developed in the South West. Moreover, the international aspects of the salinity made it possible: ' . . . to argue successfully that reducing and controlling the salinity in the Colorado was a national obligation, the states were able to shift the cost to the national taxpayer.'

Second, why did the United States want to enter an agreement with Mexico in such a way that the visible benefits accrued to Mexico and the high costs were borne by the United States? The outcome was in accordance with the polluter pays principle, but as we have argued above, there is no direct role for PPP in this context. The answer, according to Kneese, is that there were non-visible benefits to the US from desalinization of the water in the Colorado river. Kneese goes on to say:

> Indeed, as long as all interested parties have something of value to trade, and as long as national self-interest is the primary motive force in international affairs, as I believe it is, this broad trading process seems to be the only sure path to international agreements. This may be especially true in the situation that characterizes the salinity problem.

Kneese illustrates this conclusion with the 1939–44 negotiations over the Colorado and the Rio Grande, in which the US agreed to deliver a large quantity of water in the Colorado to Mexico. One reason was that the US wanted to cultivate good relations with Mexico during the Second World War. Another reason was that the situation in the Rio Grande was the opposite of the previous case. Here most of the water in the lower parts originates in Mexico. Therefore, it was possible to make trade-offs between the two rivers in addition to trade-offs between water and other valuable services. The 1973 agreement on the Colorado can be seen in the same light. The US wanted to cultivate more favourable relations with Latin American countries. Moreover, there is the speculation that it had something to do with the discovery of Mexican oil.

Krutilla's and Kneese's studies reveal that at least along the US–Canada and the US–Mexico borders, agreements on water and water quality have involved 'trades' in areas other than the rather restricted area defined by the environmental resource. The important point is that there have been trades, although they may not be directly visible. One could therefore argue that, even if it seems superficially that the polluter pays principle has been adhered to, the victim pays principle has been applied, although the payment has not been in cash but in kind, and made in such a way that it may be difficult or impossible to register it.

What are the implications of these findings for the analysis of international environmental problems by using game theory? One first implication is that neither national nor local governments always behave rationally. The choice of a very costly scheme to reduce the salinity in Colorado shows this convincingly. Game theory, on the other hand, is based on extreme rationality of the players. One should therefore not expect game theory to produce realistic predictions of negotiation processes. However, game theory can identify incentives that the various countries have to agree. Even if it cannot predict accurately how the countries will react to these incentives, it is an important step by itself that such incentives are identified. This is probably the most important contribution we should expect from game theoretical analysis of international environmental problems. Furthermore, another implication is that side payments do not appear to be common, if by side payments we mean transferable utility. In the discussion in the previous section we have applied the assumption of transferable utility. We should model these negotiation games as games without transferable utility. However, much less is known about such games, which is also the reason that we will continue to make the apparently unrealistic but very simplifying assumption that utility is transferable.

REGIONAL RECIPROCAL EXTERNALITIES

Regional reciprocal externalities exist when there is a common property resource with free access for many countries. The North Sea as a fishery is such an example, the European atmosphere used for waste disposals is another example. Whenever there is a common property resource with free access, one should suspect that it is being over-used. The reason is simply that each user will extend his use as far as is beneficial for him, without regard for the consequences to other users. Suppose that the net benefit from using a common property resource to an individual country i is $NB_i = h_i(x_i, \Sigma x_j)$, where x_i is the i'th country's use of the resource (harvest of fish in the North Sea, emission of sulphur in the European atmosphere, etc.) while Σx_j, is the total use of the resource (the total harvest of fish, the total emission of sulphur, etc.). It is reasonable to assume h is increasing in its first argument but decreasing in its second argument. Each country will in its self-interest maximize NB_i, and a necessary condition for this is

$$\delta NB_i/\delta x_i = h_{i,1}' + h_{i,2}' = 0,$$

that is the sum of the partial derivatives should be equal to zero. When each country does this, the result will be a Nash equilibrium[6] x_i^*, $i = 1, \ldots, n$.

The Pareto efficient outcome (if we assume that countries can make side payments to each other) is defined by Maximize ΣNB_i.

The necessary conditions for a maximum of the sum of net benefits can be written

$$h_{i,1}' + \Sigma_j h_{j,2}' = 0.$$

If the h-function is concave in its first argument, it follows that each country will use more of the common property resource in the Nash equilibrium than in the Pareto efficient outcome. Thus, countries that are not bound by an agreement will tend to harvest more fish than is efficient and they tend to emit more pollutants to the atmosphere than is efficient.

Before illustrating these general points with a more detailed discussion of one particular case of reciprocal externalities, it is worthwhile pointing out that there are indeed two different problems that show up in connection with reciprocal externalities. The first is the problem of cost-efficiency. As all countries are contributing to the environmental problem, the measures necessary to reduce the problem must be allocated among the countries, and one way would be to look for the least expensive way of allocating the measures. Note that in the case of unidirectional externalities, the problem of cost-efficiency will be there as soon as two or more countries are polluting the environment of a downstream or downwind country or countries. To the extent that the following analysis deals with cost-effective approaches, it is also relevant for these unidirectional externality situations. The second is the problem of incentives to participate in agreements. All will gain from being free-riders, hoping that the other countries will undertake abatement measures. This problem will also arise in connection with unidirectional externalities whenever there is more than one country that is damaged from a transboundary problem. Therefore, the following analysis on the free-rider aspects will be relevant also for those cases of unidirectional externalities with many downstream or downwind countries.

The acid rain game – a short-run model

In order to illustrate these points, we will use the simulations in Mäler (1986*b*) on the use of the European atmosphere as a dump for sulphur oxides. It has been well known for at least twenty years that such emissions will contribute to acid rains with detrimental effects on ground and surface water and on forests. However, it is also known that nitrogen oxides contribute to acid rains. We will, for simplicity, leave nitrogen out of the discussion. The reader can easily imagine the qualitative changes that would be necessary to accommodate emissions of other substances.

Although it may seem that European problems of acid rain are rather special, the constructs and analysis that will be presented in this section have a much wider application. The problems of global warming and the emissions of greenhouse gases have essentially the same economic nature and the discussion on sulphur emissions will throw light on this larger issue.

Sulphur oxides are emitted when fossil fuels are burnt and in some industrial processes. In the atmosphere, the oxides are oxidized into sulphates, which can be transported by winds for very long distances. Ultimately, they are removed from the atmosphere by rain – wet deposition, and by contact with plants, surface water, etc. – dry deposition. In either case, the deposition of the sulphates will increase the acidity of the surface water, the top soil, etc. and will have detrimental environmental effects.

As the winds blow in various directions, this is a case of reciprocal externality, although because some winds are more prevailing than others, the situation is not completely symmetric. Some countries are more upwind than others and some are more downwind. The extent to which a country is a net receiver of sulphates is given by a transport model. In this case of sulphur, the annual transport between countries can be described in terms of a matrix A with co-efficients $a_{i,j}$ indicating the amount of sulphur deposited in country j from the emission of one ton of sulphur in country i. As most of the sulphur emitted in a country will be deposited in the same country, the diagonal elements of the transport matrix will in general be large compared with the non-diagonal elements.

Let us assume there is for each country a well-defined cost function for reducing sulphur emissions and a well-defined damage function from the deposition of sulphur. If a country is acting rationally, and if it is not bound by international agreements, it will emit sulphur to the point where the marginal abatement cost equals the marginal damage cost. The marginal damage cost from domestic emissions is equal to the marginal damage cost from sulphur depositions multiplied by the proportion of the deposition that originates from domestic sources. Thus, country i emits sulphur until

$$C_i'(E_i) = a_{i,i} \, D'_i(Q_i)$$

where E_i is the emission in country i, C' the marginal abatement cost, Q_i the deposition and D' the marginal damage cost from further deposition of sulphur.

This condition describes the Nash non-co-operative equilibrium that would be the outcome from the interplay of rational countries that are not bound to take into account the effects of their emissions on other countries. However, this Nash non-co-operative equilibrium will not correspond to a collectively rational outcome. A collectively rational outcome would be a situation where the total net gains to all countries is maximized and would correspond to the following necessary condition

$$C_i(E_i) = \sum_j a_{i,j} D'_j(Q_j).$$

This condition says that the marginal abatement cost in each country should be equal to the marginal damage in all countries that are affected by the emissions.

In order to use this model for illustrative purposes, the unknown cost and damage functions must be numerically specified and a relevant transport model must be found. Within the European Monitoring and Evaluation Programme (EMEP) a transport model has been estimated and used for producing 'sulphur budgets' for Europe.[7] The matrix A above has been estimated on the basis of the sulphur budgets for 1980–5. Cost of abatement functions have been estimated by IIASA,[8] and although these estimated abatement functions have some serious drawbacks, they have been used for this application. There are no available consistent estimates of damage functions from acid rain. In order to overcome this problem, the following procedure was followed.

We assume that 1984 was a year when the emissions of sulphur in Europe could be characterized as a Nash equilibrium. This assumption implies that if we know $a_{i,j}$ and the marginal abatement cost C'_i we would be able to calculate the marginal damage cost D'_i. Thus all required information for a calibration of the marginal damage cost D' in 1984 exists. If we finally make the assumption that the marginal damage costs are constant and independent of the amount of deposition, the whole model can be calibrated numerically. It should be stressed that the damage function estimate so obtained is quite different from the concept used previously. It may be interpreted as the revealed preferences of the governments for reductions in emissions of sulphur. Because of this procedure of calibrating the damage functions and the model, all numerical results should be interpreted with caution. The simulations do not purport to give numerical predictions but only qualitative insights into the problem of regional reciprocal externalities.

By using the calibrated model, different co-operative outcomes can be illustrated. One possible outcome is achieved if the sum of the net benefits over all European countries is maximized. This will be called the full co-operative solution. The consequences for some countries of this solution are summarized in Table 27.2.

Table 27.2 Net benefits from the full co-operative solution.

Country	Emission reduction (%)	Net benefit (million Deutschmarks)[9]
Czechoslovakia	75	152
Finland	14	-2
GDR	80	11
FRG	86	328
Poland	27	599
Sweden	4	606
Soviet Union	2	1,505
United Kingdom	81	-336
Europe	39	6,290

One can first note that substantial gains of over 6 billion Deutschmarks can be made from co-operation. Moreover, in view of the calibration procedure, it is certain that the gains are understated in Table 27.1. The full co-operative solution requires an average reduction of sulphur emissions in Europe of almost 40 per cent, more than that corresponding to the protocol of the convention on long-range pollutants on sulphur emission reductions, the so-called 'Thirty Per Cent Club'. More interestingly, the net benefits from co-operation are very unevenly distributed among the countries. Some countries will even experience losses from co-operation. This is mainly due to the geographical location of these countries, some are more upwind than others so that they will not have as big net benefits as those countries that are more downwind. An extreme case is provided by the United Kingdom, which is very much upwind, and therefore would have to abate its emissions quite a lot, while not benefiting from the abatement in other countries. Sweden is an example of a downwind country, having to reduce emissions by only 4 per cent, and making substantial net benefits. The USSR is a special case because it is large and very little of its substantial emissions affects other European countries.

Why should the United Kingdom be willing to sign an agreement by which it would lose more than 300 million Deutschmarks? We are obviously back to the earlier issue of the polluter pays principle versus victim pays principle. The only reason the UK would be willing to accept this burden is by expecting to gain something in some other arena. Let us stick to the assumption that it is possible to measure this other gain in Deutschmarks – that is, assume that the transferable utility can be measured in this currency. Then the UK needs a gain worth more than 300 million Deutschmarks in order to sign the full co-operative agreement. In fact, in the full solution, four countries (Finland, Italy, Spain and the UK) would experience losses that must be compensated in order to induce these countries to sign the agreement. However, the net benefits in the rest of Europe would be more than sufficient to cover their losses.

The situation is however more complicated, because if the United Kingdom does not sign the agreement, while the other countries do, the UK will benefit from the reduction of emissions in the rest of Europe, while not bearing any burden. It may pay the UK to become a free-rider. Let us assume that all the four countries that would experience losses decide not to sign an agreement but that the rest of Europe decides to go ahead and maximize their total net benefit. The result is shown in Table 27.3.

Not only have the losses for the four countries disappeared but they have even turned into substantial gains. These are the gains from being a free-rider – enjoying the benefits from the co-operation among other countries without having to make any sacrifices. However, these free-rider gains can be achieved by all countries. By defecting, Sweden, could achieve a gain, although only a very small one as Sweden does not have to abate much of its emissions in the full co-operative solution. Similarly for every other country – they all stand to gain by not signing the agreement hoping that the rest of Europe will co-operate. The outcome will obviously be that there will be no agreement that includes all European countries. The free-rider incentives in this model are so pervasive, that we should not expect a full co-operative solution to emerge. Why it is necessary to include the words 'in this model' we shall soon see.

Note that exactly the same mechanism will be working in the case of unidirectional externalities when there is more than one country receiving pollution from other countries and the downwind countries ave to compensate the upwind countries.

Table 27.3 Net benefit from coalition formation.

Country	Emission reduction (%)	Net benefit (million Deutschmarks)
Co-operating countries		
Czechoslovakia	75	125
GDR	80	−47
FRG	86	78
Poland	27	544
Sweden	3	478
Soviet Union		1,372
Total for co-operating Europe	37	4,933
Defecting countries		
Italy		150
United Kingdom		87
Total		247
Total for Europe	28	5,180

A long-run model

Before continuing, it is of some interest to note the rather simplifying assumptions that have implicitly been made on the acidification processes in the discussion of the short-run model. We have assumed that it is the *annual* deposition of sulphur that matters and that each year starts afresh. In reality, there is an accumulation of sulphur in surface waters, ground water, and soil, which will only slowly disappear because of leaching or because of the buffering capacity of the environment. Thus, current deposition will have detrimental environmental effects not only now but also far into the future. The speed at which sulphur is removed from the environment depends on the media. A stream with low pH[10] may recover quite fast because of the replenishment of the water. For a lake, it may take a much longer time and still longer for ground water and the soil. In order to simplify, let us assume that there is a fixed amount per hectare of sulphur that the environment can assimilate. This amount is known as the 'critical load', and is defined as 'a quantitative estimate of the exposure to one or more pollutants below which significant harmful effects on specified sensitive elements of the environment do not occur according to present knowledge' (Nilsson, 1986).

In order to take critical loads into account, one can construct a model[11] that makes the annual change in the accumulated sulphur in the environment equal to the annual deposition minus the assimilative capacity of the environment. In view of the definition of critical loads, it seems possible to interpret this assimilative capacity as the critical load. Thus, the stock of sulphur will change over time reflecting both the deposition and the removal of sulphur. It is then natural to assume that the annual damage from sulphur is a function of the stock of sulphur and not of the annual deposition. In this way, the situation can be modelled as a dynamic game, in which each country tries to minimize its present value of future abatement costs and damage costs.

In dynamic games of this type, it is important to differentiate between different kinds of strategies, depending on the information structure. If no country expects new information on what the other countries are doing in emission abatement or on the deposition in their own country, then each country will formulate an abatement policy that it will follow for ever. In this case we have 'open-loop' strategies. If each country expects to be able at each moment of time to get correct information on the deposition in its own country, then the country can formulate a strategy such that the actual emission abatement at any point of time depends on this deposition. In this case we have a 'closed-loop' or 'feedback' strategy.

One can show that if the strategies are restricted to open-loop strategies, there exists a unique Nash non-co-operative equilibrium. Moreover, the equilibrium strategies are such that the emissions will in the long run approach the levels that are compatible with the critical loads. Thus, if countries are not receiving more information than they have now, we should expect a long-run equilibrium such that the stock of sulphur in the environment will not grow further.

However, it is a rather strong assumption that countries will not get any more information on emissions and depositions. Therefore, a more realistic equilibrium should take as its base the use of closed-loop strategies. Countries could adjust their emissions according to the information available on the stock of sulphur in the environment. What kind of adjustments of the emissions would constitute an equilibrium in closed-loop strategies? There exist an infinite number of different equilibria in closed-loop strategies. However, one can show that there exists at least one perfect equilibrium that would correspond to countries choosing co-operating strategies if side-payments are allowed to compensate the countries that would lose from using such strategies. In principle, these equilibrium closed-loop strategies supporting co-operation are very close to the trigger strategies discussed in the theory of repeated games. If a country discovers that the stock of sulphur increases more than would correspond to co-operation, the country would break the co-operation with the result that all countries would be punished, including the defecting country. It can be shown that this threat is sufficient to make it unprofitable to break co-operative agreements.

Moreover, it can also be shown that, in the long run, these co-operative strategies imply emissions that would be compatible with the critical loads. Thus in the long run, the emissions in a co-operative equilibrium and in an open-loop non-co-operative equilibrium will be the same. However, the convergence toward the critical loan emissions are faster with the co-operative strategies and the resulting stock of sulphur will be smaller.

Thus, analysing the incentives from a dynamic point of view seems to change the conclusions reached earlier significantly. First of all, the conclusion that there is a need for international transfers remains. Unless countries that are losing from co-operation are compensated, no co-operation with them will be established. Second, given this compensation, there are in the long run incentives for the countries to co-operate, and even if there are incentives to be a free-rider, these incentives will gradually diminish when the horizon goes to infinity. Third, in the long run, emissions will be adjusted in such a way as to become compatible with the critical loads.

Cost efficiency

The previous discussion suggests that an optimal co-operative policy could be approximated by a policy that would see to it that the emissions are reduced fast to levels consistent with critical loads. These international negotiations on reducing sulphur emissions should proceed in such a way to ensure that the depositions eventually correspond to the critical loads. The question is how to design international institutions that can manage agreements on these issues.

International environmental problems

Before discussing this it may be a good time to take stock of the results reached so far. The numerical estimates that have been presented in Tables 27.1 and 27.2 are of course not worth more than the assumptions that were used to produce them. The numbers should therefore not be taken literally. However, together with the qualitative analysis on repeated games and dynamic games they do represent some real and valuable conclusions, namely:

(a) the net benefits from co-operation will in general be very unevenly distributed among the countries in a region with reciprocal environmental externalities. This implies that there is a need for a compensation system in order to redistribute the gains from co-operation in a way that is fair and gives countries incentives to co-operate;
(b) in the short run, countries will have strong incentives to be free-riders;
(c) in the long run, countries will try to maintain co-operation because they are expecting losses exceeding the short-run benefits from defecting from the agreement;
(d) in the long run, optimal co-operative solutions will tend towards a steady state in which the annual deposition will correspond to the critical loads; and
(e) monitoring the performance of the agreement can be made through monitoring of depositions, until reliable technologies for monitoring emissions are available.

Let us now see whether it would be possible to construct a concrete institution that would produce incentives to co-operate so as to reach approximately the full co-operation solution. We shall look at two different issues: (a) the cost efficiency of different ways of reducing the depositions, and (b) different institutional arrangements to induce countries to limit their sulphur emissions.

Suppose that there is an agreement among European countries to reduce the emissions of sulphur oxides and that the objective is ultimately to reduce the deposition of sulphur to levels corresponding to the critical loads. This can be done in many ways. A first, but unsatisfactory attempt, has been made through the protocol on 30 per cent uniform reduction of emissions. It is unsatisfactory in many ways, one being that not all countries (UK and Poland are the notable exceptions) have signed the protocol, another being that 30 per cent reduction is not enough (we saw in the simulations earlier that even in a static setting, an average reduction of about 40 per cent is warranted, although this is not enough to satisfy the critical load requirements). However, there is another way that is of concern here, namely the cost-effectiveness of such a solution.

Using the same notation as above, we can define cost-efficiency as the emissions reductions R_i necessary in each country i to reduce the depositions in each country to the critical load level in the least expensive way possible. Mathematically, this can be formulated as

$$\text{Minimize } \Sigma_i C_i(R_i) = C^1$$

subject to

$$\Sigma_j a_{ij} R_j \geq Q_{oi} - Q_i^c, i = 1, \ldots, n,$$

where the right hand side is the necessary deposition reductions to achieve the critical loads.

In contrast to this, the agreed reduction on sulphur emissions is formulated as an emission reduction uniform for all signatory states. This will henceforth be called the 'club solution'. If we are trying to reach the critical loads by a club solution, we would

$$\text{Minimize } \sum_i C(R_i) = C^2$$

subject to

$$\sum_j a_{ij}R_j \geq Q_{oi} - Q_i^c,$$
$$R_i/E_i = \theta, i = 1, \ldots, n$$

where θ is the variable representing the uniform emission reduction. The solution to this problem determines the proportional emission reduction k and the country reductions R_i necessary to meet the requirement that the depositions do not exceed the critical loads in the least expensive way.

Obviously, this solution will yield a higher total cost than the previous one, as we have restricted the reductions more in the second problem than in the first. Thus we know that $C^1 \leq C^2$.

It would be interesting to know whether the difference between C^1 and C^2 is 'big' or 'small'. If it is small, we might be satisfied with the club solution as it is easier to manage and gives a superficial sense of fairness.

By using the same transport model and the same cost functions as before,[12] the solutions to these two problems were computed. It turned out that the club solution would cost 76 per cent more than the cost-efficient solution. Furthermore, the club solution would reduce the total emissions in Europe by 88 per cent while the cost-efficient solution would reduce the emissions by 63 per cent. Thus, in order to reach the targets set by the critical loads, the club solution would require an 'Eighty-Eight Per Cent Club' to be formed. The computations indicate quite clearly that the club strategy with uniform emission reductions is very expensive.

However, it may happen that the cost of achieving the cost-effective solution is very unevenly distributed among the participating countries, which would necessitate transfers among the countries. In fact, this is not so and, moreover, if each country accepts the targets set by the critical loads, formal co-operation may not even be necessary! In order to see this, let us therefore assume that each individual country strives for a deposition in its own country that does not exceed the critical load. We can then define the Nash non-co-operative equilibrium as such a pattern of emission reductions, that no country would gain by deviating from its equilibrium emission reduction as long as the other countries follow their equilibrium strategies. More formally, the Nash equilibrium is defined by

$$\text{Minimize } C_j(R_j)$$

subject to

$$\sum a_{j,i} R^* + a_{j,jj}^{R} \geq Q_{oj} - Q_j^c, = 1, \ldots, n$$

where R_i^* is the equilibrium reduction for country i.

It follows that if the transport matrix A has an inverse, the Nash equilibrium is given by

$$E^* = A^{-1}(Q_o - Q^c).$$

However, if the maxtrix A has a non-negative inverse, the cost-effective soluition is

$$E = A^{-1}(Q_o - Q^c),$$

the same solution. In practice, A does not have a non-negative inverse and the Nash solution would yield a 1 per cent higher cost that the cost-effective solution. Thus, if countries accept the objective of reducing emissions so that the deposition in their own countries equals the critical load, they will accomplish this by themselves, without the need to have a formal agreement. Obviously, this result depends on the very peculiar shape of the marginal damage cost function underlying these models. We have, in fact, assumed that the marginal damage cost is infinite for depositions exceeding the critical load and zero below that load. It is hardly likely that countries believe such valuations. Also note that in the previous model of the acid rain problems as a differential game, we did not need such an extreme assumption.

The main conclusion to be drawn from this exercise is that substantial cost savings can be achieved if international agreements are suitably designed. We will therefore in the next sections look at two types of agreements that will achieve efficiency or near efficiency.

It should finally be stressed that the importance of cost efficiency is as relevant for unidirectional externalities with many upstream or upwind countries, and in fact the same kind of analysis carried out above could and should be performed as soon as gains can be expected from choosing a more cost-effective strategy.

Taxation of sulphur export

Suppose the countries involved agree on the following:

(a) To establish a European Acidification Fund (EAF) with the purpose of giving participating countries a platform for discussions and negotiations and to manage any agreement that will result, including the collection of taxes, redistribution of tax revenues, and responsibility for the necessary monitoring of emissions. As before, EAF could also be charged with the duty of finding and funding economically and environmentally viable projects which would otherwise not be undertaken.
(b) A transport model for sulphur oxides and nitrogen oxides in Europe.[13]
(c) A scheme for redistributing a proportion of the tax revenues in order to compensate countries that would otherwise lose and to achieve a fair distribution of the gains from the co-operation.
(d) A tax rate which will be applied on the airborne export of sulphur from one signatory country to all other signatory countries. The export of sulphur will be determined by the actual emissions and the transport model.
(e) Finance for mutually beneficial environmental projects. As market failures can be expected to be pervasive in East Europe, it may be desirable for EAF to fund some pollution abatement activities in this part of Europe, abatement that otherwise would not come about.

It is clear that a tax system such as the one proposed above will not achieve a first-best optimum, as it will not differentiate between exports to countries with high marginal damage cost and countries with low damage cost. In a first-best policy one should differentiate the tax rate between different exporters.

However, such a differentiation would create not only practical problems but also obstacles to reaching an agreement. Moreover, as we will soon see, the gains from going to the first-best optimum seem to be marginal. Therefore, the proposal is one of a uniform tax rate, independent of the exporting country.

By using the numerically calibrated short-run model discussed previously, it is possible to find the effects of different tax rates. In Table 27.4, the simulations with a tax rate of 4 Deutschmarks per kilogram sulphur exported are shown for a sample of countries.

It is extraordinary how close this second-best solution is to the first-best solution in Table 27.2. The total benefit from the full co-operative solution is 6,290 million Deutschmarks while the uniform tax solution would yield a total benefit only about 1 per cent lower. Not only the aggregate benefit but also the *distribution* of emission reductions and country specific net benefits are very similar between the full co-operative solution and the uniform tax solution. On the basis of these results, it is possible to feel comfortable with this second-best solution.

The total tax payments would be about 7 billion Deutschmarks (DM), exceeding the total net benefits by about 850 million DM. Thus, EAF needs to use this 850 million DM form the tax revenue to compensate the losing countries, but would still end up with a net revenue corresponding to the total net benefit from the emission reductions.

The difficult problems with the proposed scheme have to do with the distribution of the net tax revenues (net after compensating the losers) among the participating countries, the incentives to reveal the objective cost- and damage-

Table 27.4 Effects of a tax equal to 4 DM/kg sulphur exported.

Country	Emission reductions (%)	Net benefits	Tax payments	Net benefits–taxes
Czechoslovakia	75	147	585	− 438
GDR	80	− 11	374	−385
FRG	81	363	332	32
Poland	30	530	1,495	−965
Sweden	4	580	114	466
Soviet Union	2	1,508	234	1,274
United Kingdom	79	− 326	133	−546
Europe	38	6,213	7,067	−856

functions, and the problem of monitoring the emissions. Given that the latter problems can be solved, the first problem could be attacked by trying to reach an agreement in which the Nash bargaining solution is achieved. That would mean that with the Nash non-co-operative solution as a threat point, the total net benefits would be shared equally among the participating countries. One can doubt whether such a solution will be reached in reality as countries differ substantially in size and importance. It would be surprising if a small country with small emissions would be able to secure for itself as much as France, Poland, or the United Kingdom. However, we do not have to determine the outcome of this bargaining process here. The important point is that there will be a substantial gain that must be distributed.

The other problems are more demanding. Both have to do with the revelation of information necessary for a fruitful co-operation. Let us start by assuming that emissions can be monitored perfectly but countries can give false information on their true abatement and damage cost.

The first thing to note is that in contrast to the unidirectional externality with only one downstream and one upstream country, we can no longer expect that truth-telling to be an equilibrium strategy. In fact, because of the incentives to be a free-rider, there will be no equilibrium in which all countries are giving correct information.

Secondly, as long as countries agree to the tax solution, the information they supply is only used for calculating the tax rate. Irrespective of the rate, we can be quite sure that the resulting allocation of emission reduction is cost-effective. We therefore know that whatever the outcome will be, it will be cost-effective. The problem is, however, that the tax rate may be too high or too low to support emission reductions that would maximize the total net benefit. Moreover, incorrect information may distort the negotiations.

We could think of applying the mutual compensation principle in this situation in order to induce participating states to give correct relevation of abatement- and damage-cost. We have already seen that this principle will generate a surplus that must be disposed of. However, this is not a significant problem in this application, because as we will soon see, there are some investments that would not come about automatically and which would enhance the welfare of the European countries and which the EAF should finance. A more important objection is that the mutual compensation principle would destroy the simplicity, both of the export tax solution and the solution based on tradable permits, to be discussed in the next section.

The second problem is perhaps even more important, because if emissions cannot be monitored, countries would have strong incentives to violate the agreement. However, as has already been pointed out, technical development may eventually permit satellite monitoring of the transboundary flux of pollutants. Meanwhile, statistical analysis of the actual deposition, together with information on the transport model and the actual weather conditions, may give indications on violations of the agreement.

Tradable export permits

Instead of taxing the export of sulphur from one country to other signatory states, the agreement could establish export quotas for sulphur for each country and in order to make the scheme efficient, the quotas or export permits would be made transferable between countries. The export of sulphur would be determined exactly as in the tax solution by the use of a transport model. Assume that the countries involved agree on the following:

(a) To establish a European Acidification Fund (EAF) with the purpose of giving participating countries a platform for discussions and negotiations and to manage any agreement that will result, including the determination of export permits for each country, and the responsibility for the necessary monitoring of emissions. Moreover, EAF could also be charged with the duty of finding and funding economically and environmentally viable projects which would otherwise not have been undertaken;

(b) A transport model for sulphur oxides and nitrogen oxides in Europe;

(c) The rules for using funds available to EAF;

(d) The total amount of export of sulphur from one participating country to other co-operating countries;

(e) Calculations of the 'weights', i.e. the export shares of each country;

(f) Auction of initial permits, either to governments or to organizations in participating countries, or agreement in other ways of distributing the initial rights;

(g) If further reductions of sulphur are judged desirable, EAF buys permits at market prices;

(h) As before, finance for mutual beneficial environmental projects.

Obviously, this proposal is very similar to that for a sulphur export tax. In fact, given that the total amount of sulphur export between the participating states is set equal to the amount potentially achieved in the tax solution, the allocation of exports will be the same in the two proposals (assuming that informational and monitoring problems can be neglected). Moreover, the price on permits will in equilibrium be equal to the tax rate.

If the allocative properties are the same, what are then the differences between the two approaches? First, if costs and benefits are not known with certainty, there will be allocative differences. This follows from Weitzman's (1974) analysis of prices versus quantities as regulatory instruments. If a tax is chosen as a regulatory instrument, uncertainty in the cost of abatement functions may have as a consequence that the actual export will significantly exceed the optimal export. If the marginal benefit function is inelastic, it follows that the cost from too much sulphur being transported between countries would be large. This conclusion is strengthened if the marginal cost of abatement function is elastic as, in that case, small changes in the tax will cause large changes in abatement. Thus, with elastic marginal abatement cost functions and inelastic marginal benefit functions, a tax solution may cause large *ex post* costs. If, on the other hand, a permit system is chosen, the total amount of sulphur exported is fixed. However, if the marginal abatement cost functions are inelastic, a small error in determining the total amount controlled may cause large variations in abatement cost. Thus, the relative slopes of the marginal abatement cost curves and the marginal benefit curves are important for deciding which approach is to be preferred.

Second, the tax proposal has the advantage that it will generate revenues for EAF, revenues that are needed to compensate the losers and to finance other abatement measures that are deemed desirable. A permit system may be designed to raise the same amount of money, if the permits are valid only for a limited time, and if they are auctioned off regularly. Then the permit system will be identical to a tax system under full information. However, it is possible to design the permit system differently. If the initial distribution of rights is determined in some other way, for example as a proportion to the initial sulphur export, no revenues will be raised. In that case the compensation to the losers must be made through the distribution of initial rights. One possibility would be that countries that are expected to have negative expected net benefits would be given permits equal to their initial exports, while the other countries would be given permits as a fixed uniform proportion of their initial exports ('grandfathering'). In this case, no country would lose, and an efficient outcome could still be expected. Under these circumstances EAF would not raise any money, but it would not need any funds for compensation either. However, as we will come back to, such an EAF would need some financial means in order to increase cost efficiency.

Third, the two approaches differ with respect to incentives to cheat. With a tax system, it is in the interest of each country to understate the actual emissions, and with imperfect monitoring, countries will probably try to make gains by giving biased reports. With a tradable permit system, countries still have incentives to cheat. If cheating becomes pervasive, however, the demand for permits will go down and so will the equilibrium price on permits, thereby reducing the incentives to cheat.[14] Thus, the tradable permit system has a self-regulating mechanism that makes cheating less profitable than in a system with a tax as a regulatory instrument.

Cost efficiency and market failures

We have several times pointed to the need for taking into account various forms of market failures. In regional environmental problems, and perhaps much more so in global environmental problems, countries with different economic systems have to deal with each other. As the economic systems differ, there will be unexploited trades between different economic systems that can be of interest for an agreement on environmental issues. In Europe, the controls of the markets for capital and foreign exchange in Eastern Europe provide an example of this. Because of these controls the real cost of capital is higher in Eastern Europe than in the West and the cost of buying West European technology is higher because the exchange rate is lower in the West than in the East. Thus, pollution abatement in Eastern Europe may be less expensive if it is undertaken and financed by organizations in Western Europe. The European Acidification Fund can therefore potentially play an important role in initiating and financing pollution abatement projects in Eastern Europe. The reason why EAF should do this is not to 'help' the East Europeans, but to promote the interests of all EAF countries by exploiting less expensive measures to improve the environment.

One should be aware of some rather difficult problems that seem to be inherent in a scheme like this. These problems have to do with the possibility for the receiving country to react to the proposed measure. In Figure 27.2 the marginal cost of abatement is drawn together with the marginal benefit curve in the receiving country.

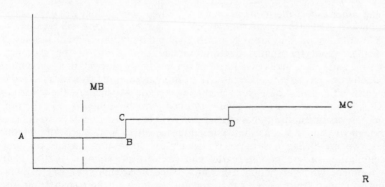

Figure 27.2 Marginal abatement cost and marginal damage cost in a country receiving environmental aid.

Here we have assumed that the MC-curve has a staircase shape with each step representing a particular abatement measure. We have also assumed that the marginal benefit curve is inelastic, so that the existing abatement is R^*. Let us assume now that Western countries decide to finance the measures represented by the step CD in the diagram. With the given marginal benefit function, it is profitable for the receiving country to stop abatement altogether, because the foreign financed abatement alone will reduce the emissions with more than R^*. Of course, this problem of perverse incentives can be solved, at least in the short run. The best way is probably to introduce conditions in the contracts that guarantee satisfactory monitoring. However, in the long run, when the country is developing its industry, it may become difficult and even impossible to keep track of which abatement measures that have not come about because of the measure CD.

GLOBAL ISSUES

Physical externalities

Global physical externalities are, from an analytical point of view, very similar to regional reciprocal externalities. The emissions of chlorofluorcarbons or CFCs is a good example. The CFCs will, irrespective of where they are released in the atmosphere, reduce the ozone in the troposphere, and thereby create health hazards through increased ultraviolet radiation. From an economic analytical point of view, this situation is almost identical to the situation with acid rain, discussed in the previous section. The Montreal convention shows that the same incentive problems to create effective co-operation exist for international control of CFC emission as do for managing sulphur emissions.

The increases in the emission of greenhouse gases, primarily carbon dioxide but also methane, CFCs and di-nitrogen oxide are, from an economic theoretical perspective, also very similar to the sulphur and nitrogen emissions in Europe.[15] However, one can suspect that the variation in net gains from any actions to reduce global warming will be much greater compared with the case of acid rains in Europe. Therefore, it seems necessary to develop the idea of side-payments into new institutional frameworks much further in order to get the much needed global co-operation on reducing the threats to global climate.

One other aspect merits mentioning. Although climatologists agree that the greenhouse effect is real and that global average temperature will rise over the next hundred years, they are very uncertain about quantitative predictions and in particular about the spatial distribution and the timing of the warming.[16] Moreover, the consequences in terms of sea-level rise, precipitation, agricultural productivity, etc. are very uncertain. Therefore, any action taken today to reduce the emission of greenhouse gases (including measures to increase the absorption of CO_2 by afforestation) will have very uncertain consequences. On the other hand, any change in the global temperature will have irreversible consequences, although we cannot predict these consequences with a high degree of precision. Thus, we are facing a situation in which the 'no-action' means continued accumulation of greenhouse gases and irreversible changes in the global environment, while any action in order to reduce the accumulation of greenhouse gases will have consequences that are not, at least in their spatial and time dimensions, well known. The description of this decision-making problem obviously calls for a 'Bayesian approach',[17] that is an approach by which we take into account both the irreversibility of the changes and the possible forthcoming of new information on the consequences from global warming. In the theory of 'quasi-option values', as developed by Arrow and Fisher (1974) and Henry (1974),[18] it has been shown that a rational decision-maker should be cautious, not committing himself to 'too many' irreversible changes. The loose phrase 'too many' can be made quite precise in the theory, but it is not necessary to go into any details here. The main point is that even if the expected future damage from global warming is quite small (i.e. less than the expected cost of reducing CO_2 emissions), it may still be desirable to take action to reduce the irreversible consequences from the change in the climate. Thus, even if there is considerable uncertainty about the future climate, one can argue convincingly that in spite of (or perhaps because of) this uncertainty, action should be taken today to reduce the release of greenhouse gases in order to prevent 'too many' irreversible changes.

NON-PHYSICAL EFFECTS

There are many good examples of global environmental interdependencies that are not based on physical interactions between different countries or regions of the world. The threat to some old Egyptian temples from the flooding of lake Nasser created a willingness on part of Europeans and North Americans to pay for the removal of the temples to non-flooded areas. The preservation of the cultural heritage is thus an example of an international externality that does not correspond to any physical flows between countries. Similarly, the general concern for preservation of biological diversity and in particular for whales, elephants, rhinos, etc., is an example of an externality that extends across national boundaries without any associated flows of materials from one country to another. In contrast to the pollution cases, discussed in previous sections, we here have cases of services that one country can but is not necessarily induced to provide to the rest of the world.

It is important to understand the nature of these services and we will therefore discuss one such service – that of *preserving biodiversity* – in some detail. As the tropical rainforests represent the greatest biological variation and as these forests are seriously threatened today, it is natural that the discussion focuses on the preservation of these forests. The values of biological diversity to mankind are of different kinds. First of all, many species are used for various purposes – food, clothing, transport, fuel, pets, medicine, hydrological control, etc. It is difficult to overestimate the importance of these *use-values*, not only for single species but also for complete ecological systems.[19] For many species and ecological systems, these use-values can only be attributed to the people using the corresponding resources. Thus, it is mainly the people of Amazonia that gain from the control of the hydrological cycle that the tropical forests in that area provide. Most of these use-values are therefore local or regional. The role for the global carbon cycle played by these forests is perhaps an example of use-values of a global nature.

Many of the species existing in a tropical rain-forest have no use value today, but may in the future become important p reconditions for new medicines, new hybrids of grains, or for other human activities. However, we do not know which species will generate use-values in the future. On the other hand, we do know that the extinction of a species today will for all future time be irreversible. Therefore the extinction of a species means that we have reduced our future options with respect to the use of environmental resources. The value of keeping these options

– the option value – may sometimes be quite important.[20] The option value may be interpreted as the conditional expected value of future information, given that the species is preserved. This value cannot in general be assumed to go to any particular group. As the value will be realized only in the future in activities unknown today, it will have the character of a global public good. Thus, the private incentives to preserve biological diversity will not in general reflect appropriately the option values.

In particular, it can be expected that people in countries outside the tropics may have great interest in preserving species. Moreover, this interest is strengthened by *existence values* or *preservation values*. These values represent the values that people associate with the preservation of biological diversity without expecting that they ever will be able to obtain direct use values. The total value from preservation of biological diversity is thus equal to the sum of use values, option values and preservation values. Of these terms, the use values are most often concentrated in the area where the species are to be found. Option values and preservation values can on the other hand arise all over the earth. They have the character of *global public goods*.

However, there are no institutional arrangements which would enable people to express their willingness to pay for preserving biodiversity at the present. In a way, the situation is similar to the situation of acid rains in Europe. The net gains from the preservation of biodiversity is very much dispersed among nations and there are strong incentives to behave as a free rider for some nations. However, because of the irreversibility of species extinction, these incentives are moderated. A country which does not co-operate in the preservation of a species knows that the result from its behaviour may be irrevocable, and that will reduce the incentives to act as a free rider. The problem is to design the international institutions that would encourage the needed co-operation.

One approach, which to some extent already has been tested, is the *debt for nature swaps*. Such swaps are defined as the purchase of developing country debt at a discounted value in the secondary debt market, and cancelling the debt in return for environment-related action on part of the debtor nation (Hansen, 1988). These measures can probably only make marginal contributions to the preservation of the tropical rain-forests. One reason is the incentive problems arising from the public good aspect of the preservation. Another, and perhaps more important is the problem of creating the right incentives in the debtor countries. We have here a similar problem to the one discussed in connection with the European Acidification Fund and its relation with Eastern Europe. Unless the swap is tied to some national measure of preservation which can be monitored, there is no reason to assume that the swap will make any contributions to the preservation of forests.

Other measures such as buying land in the developing world have the same problems. The scale will be too small because of the incentive problems and the result may not be satisfactory if the country can exploit other areas instead.

There seem to be two different but not necessarily mutually exclusive routes which can be followed. The first is to help those countries to make *policy reforms* including the institution of private property rights to land. It has been shown that much of the present destruction of tropical forests is due to badly designed property rights and to macroeconomic policy measures.[21] In general, policy reforms will improve the overall efficiency of the economies and should be desirable, even without positive environmental side-effects. Therefore, one can hope that the World Bank and various donor countries will be able to convince developing nations that it is in their interests to reform their main economic institutions.

The second route is to try to accomplish global agreements on the greenhouse effect. Such agreements may involve a *tradable emission permit,* similar to what was discussed for acid rains in Europe. Preservation of tropical forests should in such a system generate the right to increases in the initial allocation of permits. As such permits can be sold, the preservation of tropical forests therefore means export revenues, and investments in tropical forests may become quite profitable in some countries. Of course, to accomplish such agreements and to develop the necessary monitoring and enforcing organizations may prove to be very difficult.

CONCLUDING COMMENTS

We have seen that there are many different kinds of international environmental problem, and an attempt to classify them was given in section I. In the paper, only four problem types are analysed – the unidirectional externality case, the regional reciprocal externality case, the global physical externality case, and the global non-physical externality case. The following main conclusions emerge from the analysis:

(a) There will be many situations where the victim pays principle, or transfers from the country whose environment has been degraded to the country that causes the degradation, will be necessary in order to achieve an efficient solution.

(b) Quite often, these transfers will take the form of concessions in other areas in which the countries have common interests and not of financial transfers.

(c) In the case of several 'upstream' countries causing damage or regional reciprocal externalities, substantial gains can be made by searching for, and implementing, a cost efficient allocation of abatement among the upstream countries compared to agreements on uniform reductions.

(d) In the case of several 'downstream' countries or regional reciprocal externalities, there will in the short run be strong incentives for the countries experiencing environmental damage to be free-riders. In the long run, however, the incentives to be a free rider will diminish because the temporary gains from being a free-rider will not be sufficient to compensate for the long-run losses if co-operation breaks down.

(e) In the case of acid rain, the optimal strategy consists of reducing the emissions over time in such a way that they ultimately become compatible with the sulphur deposition pattern that would not lead to long-term damage, that is the critical loads.

(f) The emission reductions can be achieved by various economic instruments such as export taxes or tradable export quotas. In both these cases cost-efficiency will be achieved.

(g) The global problems discussed – mainly the greenhouse effect and the preservation of biological diversity – are very similar from an analytical point of view to the regional reciprocal externality case, and one should expect the same kind of incentive structures.

(h) Both the extinction of species and global warming involve irreversible changes. The possibility of more information forthcoming in the future should make us more cautious about accepting such irreversibilities.

(i) Much of the reduction in biological diversity is due to badly designed

(i) Much of the reduction in biological diversity is due to badly designed macroeconomic policies and to badly designed property rights. By policy reforms which would improve the overall efficiency of the economics, much can be accomplished to preserve species.

(j) Global agreements based on internationally tradable permits to emit greenhouse gases can make preservation of tropical forests profitable.

NOTES

1. For a discussion of the existence and importance of non-convexities in connection with negative externalities, see Starret (1972) and Baumol and Bradford (1972).
2. It is interesting to note that Coase himself does not think this assumption about the absence of income effects is necessary. See Coase (1988).
3. This principle is a special case of the Groves' mechanism (Groves, 1973), but was independently discovered by Smets (1973) in the OECD discussions on transboundary pollution problems.
4. The chain store paradox was discovered by Selten and discussed in Friedman (1986). It illustrates the choices available to a chain store in order to prevent newcomers from taking its business. A perfect equilibrium in the model would require that the chain store should play 'soft', letting the newcomers enter the market, a result which is counter-intuitive.
5. Statement made by Ivan B. White, Deputy Assistant Secretary of State, in Hearings before the Committee on Foreign Relations, United States Senate, 87th Cong., 1 Sess., 8 March 1964. The quotation is from Krutilla (1968).
6. Note that we have made no assumption that the h function is separable. Runge, in an often cited article (1981) argues that whenever costs (or benefits) are not separable, one has to use a quite different paradigm – the problem is to co-ordinate the actions of the agents and one has therefore to change the pay-offs. This is nonsense and it is disturbing that an article that demonstrates such loose thinking has been so much cited.
7. See The Norwegian Meteorological Institute (1987).
8. See Amann and Kornai (1987).
9. The IIASA cost functions are expressed in Deutschmarks, and we have kept that currency in these simulations.
10. pH is a measure of the acidity of a solution. The lower the pH-level is, the more acid is the solution. A neutral solution has pH-level of 7. Lakes in Scandinavia that have turned acid because of sulphur and nitrogen emissions may have levels as low as 4–5.
11. For details, see Mäler (1989b) where a model for a differential game is constructed and analysed.
12. In fact, a number of countries have been excluded from the simulations because of the unsatisfactory estimates of cost functions available. It turned out that if Albania, Ireland, Norway, Portugal, Turkey, and the Soviet Union were included, emission reductions far outside the domain of the cost functions were needed. For more details on the simulations see Mäler and Olsson (1990).
13. The EMEP model that has been used previously in this article, is an example of such a transport model. In light of recent finding on the emissions of sulphates from the North Sea due to decay of algae, it seems that existing models may need some revision.
14. Andreasson (1989) has rigorously studied these interesting characteristics of taxes and tradable permits.
15. For an overview of the current views on global warming and the greenhouse effect, see Houghton and Woodwell (1989).
16. See Beardsley (1989) for an illustration of the wide estimates of the warming rising from different assumptions on cloud formation and heat absorption in the oceans.
17. For an excellent introduction to Bayesian decision-making, see Raiffa (1968).
18. See Mäler (1989c) and (1989d) for an attempt to create a more general theory on these issues.
19. For a more precise definition of use values see Carson and Mitchell (1989) or Mäler

(1989d). For an interesting discussion of use values from preserved biodiversity see Wilson (1988) and McNeely *et al.* (1989, forthcoming).
20. See Fisher and Hanemann (1986) for an interesting study of the option value of keeping a special variety of Mexican rye.
21. See Warford and Schramm (1987) for a collection of studies that discusses the role of policy failures for environmental degradation and Binswanger (1989) for a discussion of land titles and taxes for deforestation in Brazil.

REFERENCES

Andreasson, I.-M. (1988), *Costs of Controls on Farmers' Use of Nitrogen*, Stockholm School of Economics, Stockholm.

Amann M. and Kornai, G. (1987), 'Cost Functions for Controlling SO_2 Emissions in Europe', Working Paper, May, WP-87-06,5 IIASA.

Arrow, K.I. and Fisher, A.C. (1974), 'Environmental Preservation, Uncertainty and Irreversibility', *Quarterly Journal of Economics*, 88.

Baumol, W.J. and Bradford, D.F. (1972), 'Detrimental Externalities and Non-Convexity of the Production Set', *Economica*, 39.

Beardsley, T. (1989), 'Not so Hot', *Scientific American*, November.

Binmore, K. (1987), 'Nash Bargaining and Incomplete Information', in K. Binmore and P. Dasgupta (eds.), *The Economics of Bargaining*, Oxford, Basil Blackwell.

Binswanger, H. (1989), 'Brazilian Policies that Encourage Deforestation in the Amazon', Environment Department Working Paper No. 16, The World Bank, Washington D.C.

Carson, R.T. and Mitchell, R.C. (1989), *Using Surveys to Value Public Goods: the Contingent Valuation Method*, Resources for the Future.

Coase, R.H. (1988), *The Firm, the Market and the Law*, Chicago, The University of Chicago Press.

Fisher, A.C. and Hanemann, W.M. (1986), 'Option Value and the Extinction of Species', *Advances in Applied Micro-Economics*, 4.

Friedman J. (1986), *Game Theory with Applications to Economics*, New York.

Green, J.R. and Laffont, J.-J. (1980), *Incentives in Public Decision-Making*, Amsterdam, North Holland.

Groves, T. (1973), 'Incentives in Teams', *Econometrica*, 41.

Hansen, S. (1988), 'Debt for Nature Swaps: Overview and Discussion of Key Issues', Environment Department Working Paper, Washington D.C., The World Bank.

Harsanyi, J.C. (1967–8), 'Games with Incomplete Information Played by 'Bayesian' Players', Parts I-III, *Management Science*, 14, 159–82, 320–34, 486–502.

—— Selten, R. (1972), 'A Generalised Nash Solution for Two Person Bargaining Games with Incomplete Information', *Management Science*, 18.

Henry, C. (1974), 'Investment Decision under Uncertainty: the Irreversibility Effect', *American Economic Review*, 64:6.

Houghton, R.A. and Woodwell, G.M. (1989), 'Global Climatic Change', *Scientific American*, April.

Kneese, A.V. (1988), 'Environmental Stress and Political Conflicts: Salinity in the Colorado River', paper presented at conference December 1988 at the Royal Swedish Academy of Sciences, Stockholm.

Krutilla, J. (1966), 'The International Columbia River Treaty: An Economic Evaluation', in A.V. Kneese and S. Smith (eds.), *Water Research*, Baltimore, The Johns Hopkins Press.

—— (1968), *The Columbia River Treaty: A Study in the Economics of International River Basin Development*, Baltimore, Johns Hopkins Press.

Laffont, J.-J. and Maskin, E. (1982), 'The Theory of Incentives: an Overview', in W. Hildenbrand (ed.), *Advances in Economic Theory*, Cambridge, Cambridge University Press.

Landsberg H.H. and Russel, C.S. (1971), 'International Environmental Problems – a

Taxonomy', *Science,* 172, 25 June.

McNeely, J.A., Miller, K.R., Reid, W.V., Mittermeier, R.A. (forthcoming), *Conserving the World's Biological Diversity,* IUCN, WRI and WWP–US, Washington D.C.

Mäler, K.-G. (1974), *Environmental Economics – A Theoretical Inquiry,* Baltimore, The Johns Hopkins Press.

—— (1989a), 'The Acid Rain Game', in H. Folmer and E. van Ierland (eds.), *Valuation Methods and Policy Making in Environmental Economics,* Amsterdam, Elsevier.

—— (1989b), 'The Acid Rain Game 2', paper presented at the workshop on Economic Analysis and Environmental Toxicology, Noordwijkerout, May.

—— (1989c), *Risk and Environment,* Research Paper 6390, Stockholm School of Economics.

—— (1989d), *Environmental Resources, Risk and Bayesian Decision Rules,* Research Paper 6391, Stockholm School of Economics.

—— C. Olsson (1989), 'The Cost-Effectiveness of Different Solutions to the European Sulphur Problem', forthcoming in *European Journal of Agriculture Economics.*

Nilsson, J. (ed.) (1986), 'Critical Loads for Nitrogen and Sulphur', The Nordic Council of Ministers, Report 1986: 11, Copenhagen.

The Norwegian Meteorological Institute (1987), Sulphur Budgets for Europe for 1979, 1980, 1981, 1982, 1983, 1984 and 1985 EMEP/MSC-W Not 4/87.

OECD (1981), *Transfrontier Pollution and the Role of States,* Paris.

Olsson, C. (1988), 'The Cost-Effectiveness of Different Strategies Aimed at Reducing the Amount of Sulphur Deposition in Europe', Research Report 261, EFI Stockholm School of Economics.

Raiffa, H. (1968), *Decision Analysis, Introductory Lectures on Choices under Uncertainty,* New York, Random House.

Runge, C.F. (1981), 'Common Property Externalities: Isolation, Assurance and Resource Depletion in a Traditional Grazing Context', *American Journal of Agricultural Economics.*

Smets, H. (1973), *The Mutual Compensation Principle,* Paris, OECD.

Starret, D. (1972), 'Fundamental Non-Convexities in the Theory of Externalities', *Journal of Economic Theory.*

Warford, J. and Schramm, G. (eds) (1987), *The Annals of Regional Science,* November 1987.

Weitzman, M. (1974), 'Prices vs Quantities', *Review of Economic Studies,* 90.

Chapter 28

Biological diversity and developing countries

Michael Flint

INTRODUCTION

Biodiversity refers to the variety and variability of all animals, plants and micro-organisms on earth. Some of this diversity is essential, in that mankind is dependent on other species for the maintenance of the biosphere and the supply of basic necessities, particularly food. A larger proportion of biodiversity is considered valuable because of the goods and services provided by other species, and because of the potential inherent in what has been described as the world's most fundamental capital stock.

Any description of biodiversity involves large and uncertain numbers. For example, there are variously estimated to be between 5 and 30 million living species, of which only 1.4 million have been described (Wilson, 1988). Each species contains up to 400,000 genes, and virtually no two members of the same species are genetically identical. But if the magnitude of the genetic resource is vast, so too is the current rate of genetic loss. Species extinction rates are estimated at approximately 10–20,000 per year, or between 1,000 and 10,000 times faster than the natural rate before human intervention (Wilson, 1988). Whereas rates of extinction and rates of speciation were roughly equal for most of the history of life on earth, contemporary extinction rates may be one million times faster than rates of speciation (May, 1988). Estimates vary, but it is unarguable that biodiversity is now being lost at an extremely rapid rate. Rates of loss are especially high in developing countries, and particularly in the humid tropics where terrestrial diversity is highest.

The rapid loss of biodiversity in developing countries has become the subject of increasing national and international concern. This is evidenced in the substantial increase in the interest accorded to biodiversity by governments, aid donors, and conservation organisations, and in the wide support for an international convention on biodiversity. However, it is clear that the level of interest in biodiversity as an abstract good far exceeds the level of understanding of biodiversity as an environmental and developmental problem which requires and justifies practical action. This will require a much improved critical appreciation of the precise nature and value of biodiversity, the rate and causes of its loss, and the specific priorities for action.

This paper represents a synthesis of the strategic work commissioned by ODA from scientists and consultants over the past year. The aim of the paper is to contribute to the international debate on biodiversity, and to the development of an informed strategy for biodiversity conservation in developing countries. Much of the recent interest in biodiversity has tended to focus on the humid tropics, and in particular on rainforests. While this is justified by the disproportionate amount of the world's diversity contained in rainforests, very substantial amounts of diversity occur in other habitats and areas. This fact has been reflected in the attention given in this paper to wetland, freshwater, marine, and other wildland habitats.

The paper is structured as follows. Section 2 examines the economic valuation of biodiversity. Section 3 discusses the general causes of biodiversity loss. Sections 4 and 5 describe and analyze the nature and threats to biodiversity in two main ecosystem types: forests and wetlands. Section 6 discusses the main issues in biodiversity conservation. The paper concludes with a discussion of the options for biodiversity conservation.

THE VALUE OF BIODIVERSITY

A definition of biodiversity

The value of biodiversity depends on how it is defined. Biodiversity refers to the variety and variability of all animals, plants and micro-organisms on earth, and can be considered at three levels – genetic diversity (variability within species), species diversity, and habitat diversity. The important point is that biodiversity is the degree of variety in nature. It is not nature itself. To the extent that most habitat modification or reduction entails an erosion of biodiversity (WRI, 1989), diversity and biological resources are identical at a local level. But at a larger scale of analysis, and when benefits are less local, diversity and resources are not identical, and trade-offs exist. Diversity is not evenly distributed in geographical space – some areas are much more rich in diversity than others. Conservation of 10% of the habitat area could, for example, conserve 50% of the species. Given that some reduction in biodiversity is both inevitable and acceptable, the non-equivalence of biodiversity and biological resources is a significant characteristic.

The failure to distinguish between biodiversity and biological resources at different scales has led some authors to attribute the value of all ecological services to biological diversity, and to equate biodiversity with all wild/natural products. This paper will argue that a distinction should be made between the value of biodiversity and the value of biological resources, and that the failure to make this distinction has tended to mean that the value of biodiversity *per se* has been exaggerated.

The value of biodiversity is the difference between the current or future value of a diverse range of genes/species/ecosystems, and the value of a less-diverse range. It is not the gross value of all naturally derived goods and services. There is a sense in which all natural products are the product of past biodiversity. Rubber would not be in use now if the Amazonian rain forest (and Royal Botanic Gardens at Kew) had not existed 100 years ago. But we are now benefiting from that past biodiversity only to the extent that synthetic rubber remains a more expensive substitute. The extreme case would entail comparison with a single habitat/species/gene, or substitute product, available to the end-user. This difference may be considerable, but it will be significantly less than the gross value of all the wild products.

Any species-diverse habitat also performs valuable ecological processes because of the interactions between species, and the interactions between species and the environment (WRI, 1989). Ecological processes include biogeochemical recycling, the maintenance of soil fertility and water quality, and climate regulation. The relationship between biodiversity and ecological processes is neither simple nor clear, and it is not known how far biodiversity can be reduced before crucial ecological processes are affected. A reduction in species diversity may or may not affect biological productivity, stability or ecological processes (WRI, 1989). The general conclusion is that there is no direct or obvious link between the importance of an ecosystem in maintaining essential global ecological processes and its diversity.

The conservation of biodiversity should thus be seen as an objective distinct from, but obviously related to, the conservation of biological resources, with distinct costs and benefits. The conservation of biological resources in general will assist in maintaining biodiversity – although it may not be the most effective way of doing so – but the conservation of some target level of biodiversity can be achieved without conserving the natural habitat in its entirety. Equally, the ecosystem services provided may or may not be sensitive to the level of biodiversity. It is therefore important, but not necessarily easy, to distinguish the value of diversity as a distinct characteristic of biological resources, and not as synonymous with biological resources in general. This distinction is not always made (IUCN *et al.*, 1990).

Economics, ethics and values

This section concentrates on the economic values of biodiversity. This should not be interpreted as implying that ethical, cultural, aesthetic, social values are not also important. The recognition that humankind is part of nature; that all species have an inherent right to exist regardless of their material value to humans; that human culture must be based on a respect for nature; and that present generations have a social responsibility to conserve nature for the welfare of future generations all provide a justification for biodiversity conservation (IUCN, 1990).

The reality nevertheless is that choices and trade-offs have to be made in the context of scarce resources. Powerful social and ethical arguments can also be mustered for programmes which are designed to improve the welfare of poor people in developing countries, but which involve some reduction in biodiversity. Conservation does not have a monopoly on ethics. Unless and until the social and economic implications are clearer, governments are likely to continue to give insufficient weight to biological degradation. Improving the economic case for biodiversity conservation is therefore an important goal.

There are two extreme views about the contribution of economics to the biodiversity debate. The first holds that economics has no place in what is fundamentally an ethical issue. However, as mentioned already, the consideration of economics need not imply that economic efficiency is the only or most important consideration. Other value judgements and ethical considerations may be equally important. Nevertheless, it is argued that an anthropocentric utilitarian framework (i.e. one in which biota count to the extent that people want and value them) is not only the dominant paradigm, but that it can encompass many of the more ecocentric concerns. Although ultimately expressed in money values, economic analysis can and should be expanded to take into account human preferences which are not revealed in organised markets. Existence values are, for example, a reasonable proxy for moral values, and the absence of economic value. Biodiversity does have positive economic value which needs to be taken into account.

The opposing view holds that economics has a major role to play, and that the conservation of biodiversity can be justified largely on economic grounds. The financial and economic benefits of conserving biodiversity are increasingly being cited by the conservation lobby as an argument for increased aid resources. As will be demonstrated, both the economic value of biodiversity, and the contribution of economics to conservation policy and practice, are significant. The particular problem presented by biodiversity is that its economic valuation is difficult in theory, and even more difficult in practice. Few environmental goods present such problems of definition, uncertainty, irreversibility, uniqueness and estimation.

Uncertainty and irreversibility

The understanding of biodiversity is fraught with uncertainty. Scientific knowledge is deficient to the extent that there is no way of knowing whether there are 5, 10, or 30 million species on Earth (Wilson, 1988). With only 1.4 million species described to date, this means that there is no information of any kind on the overwhelming majority of species. Biodiversity is much more than the number of species, but the extent of our ignorance is immense. Other aspects of scientific knowledge crucial for the determination of a sound biodiversity policy – such as biogeography, extinction ecology, and species interdependency – are weak. However, if the state of knowledge about the current status and value of biodiversity is limited, knowledge about the future is even more so.

There are two types of uncertainty – scientific uncertainty and economic uncertainty. Scientific uncertainty refers to the lack of knowledge about what genes, species, and habitats will exist in the future (i.e. supply uncertainty). Economic uncertainty refers to the lack of knowledge about future trends and patterns of income, preferences and technologies. These in turn will determine which aspects of biodiversity become useful (i.e. demand uncertainty). Given that there is near total uncertainty over the future existence and values of yet undiscovered species, the future costs of genetic/species/habitat impoverishment, or the preferences of future generations, the problems of valuation are considerable. The future value of biodiversity is thus in a very real sense the valuation of the unknown.

The effect of technological change on the value of biodiversity is one of the greater unknowns. It is not clear whether technological change will increase or reduce the demand for, and therefore value of, biodiverse products or services. Progress in biotechnology, for example, can either be judged as reducing or increasing the need for maintaining a natural stock of diversity. To the extent that biotechnology will make it easier to synthesise new material *ab initio,* the value of natural ecosystems will be reduced (Ehrenfeld in Wilson, 1988). Biotechnology as a substitute or bypass technology will reduce incentives to preserve biodiversity (Southgate, 1988). The counter-argument is that biotechnology will increase the scope of germplasm needs, and the economic potential from innovation based on natural compounds, hence increasing the value of natural diversity (Sedjo in Kloppenburg, 1988). Asymmetric technological change in general may also increase the value of the products of natural environments. Biotechnology aside, in the absence of opportunities for technological substitution of many natural products and services (eg. amenity and ecology), the value of these should increase relative to conventional commodities (Bishop, 1978).

These uncertainties have the effect of increasing the value of biodiversity. If the outcome is uncertain, and if the potential costs of genetic erosion are large, the sensible course of action for a risk-averse society is to "play-safe" (Pearce, 1989).

This argues for policies which place a premium on the uncertain values of biodiversity (Southgate, 1988).

The other important characteristic of biodiversity which affects valuation is irreversibility. Many development decisions can be reversed as and when new information becomes available, or circumstances change. Many aspects of biodiversity cannot be recreated once lost. Habitat restoration can reverse degradation at the local level, but species extinctions are effectively permanent and irreversible on the human timescale. Combined with uncertainty, irreversibility adds a further premium to valuations which preserve the option of acting in the context of better information (Hanemann in Wilson, 1988). If development is irreversible, the use of expected values unadjusted by uncertainty will lead to insufficient preservation (Barrett, 1989). The presence of irreversibility therefore generally favours both more preservation and the postponement of decisions which erode biodiversity.

Types of values

The value of biodiversity is difficult to define, and is often impossible to estimate. Some discussion of the various types of value is nevertheless instructive. This will indicate that although biodiversity rarely has a money price in local or international markets, its economic value is wide-ranging and significant. Economists recognise two main types of value: **use-values** and **non-use values.** Use values refer to the current or future utilitarian value of biodiversity to humankind, and can in turn be sub-divided into **direct, indirect,** and **option values**. Examples include the use of wild genes in crop breeding, the tourism value of a game reserve, or the ecosystem services of a unique wetland habitat. Non-use values refer to the intrinsic, vicarious values attached by individuals to, for example, the continued existence of a particularly "charismatic" species such as the African elephant. These various types of values are shown in Table 28.1 below.

The direct use-value of biodiversity can be further sub-divided into three categories: consumptive, productive and non-consumptive. The main difference between consumptive and productive value is that the former is consumed directly without being traded. This makes valuation more difficult, and may involve a wider range of goods, but is not otherwise of major significance. A common problem for both types is to identify that component of value which is attributable to diversity *per se.*

Table 28.1 Typology of biodiversity values.

Value Type	Sub-Type	Example
Use values:		
A) Direct	Consumptive	variety of home consumed forest fruits
	Productive	plant breeding
	Non-consumptive	tourism
B) Indirect		ecological processes
C) Option values		future values of drugs etc.
D) Quasi-option value		value of being able to ascertain option value
Non-use values:		existence value of elephants, turtles

Biodiversity confers direct use value in at least three areas: agriculture, medicine, and industry. The benefits of biodiversity in **agriculture** include new crops, diverse traditional farming systems, improved varieties of existing crops, and new pesticides. The introduction of new crops has had a massive economic impact in the past – 98% of US crop production is based on species originating outside its borders (Plotkin in Wilson, 1988). New products, such as the kiwi fruit from China, continue to be important. It is nevertheless instructive to note that less than 20 species of the thousands of edible plants known to exist produce most of the worlds food (op. cit.). Three species – wheat, maize and rice – account for 54% of the calorific consumption in developing countries (CGIAR, 1987). This demonstrates the important point that economic growth in agriculture is best served by concentrating on a **reduced** range of species (and a reduced range of varieties). Recent claims that multi-species extractive forest systems give higher financial returns than timber and agriculture need to be assessed critically in this light (Peters et al., 1989; Flint, 1990). The main reasons why diverse extractive systems and subsistence agricultural systems are replaced by more specialised agro-ecosystems is because they are inherently less productive. The important qualification to this is that even specialised agro-ecosystems benefit from local habitat diversity (wild pollinators, natural predators, etc.) and from management which maintains diversity, such as crop rotation.

While the exploitation of a diverse range of species may have a long-run economic cost, genetic diversity is more clearly beneficial. Whether bred into advanced agrosystems, or inherent in traditional ones, genetic diversity has considerable economic value. In controlled environments and with low technology levels, genetically diverse traditional agricultural systems exhibit greater stability in the face of climatic, pest and disease risks. Production in any one year might be higher if a smaller range of species and genes was utilised, but the long-run average production, and/or the minimum production in a particularly bad year, is higher if a wider range is utilised. This argument should not be taken too far. Traditional technologies are more stable and sustainable than, for example, genetically narrow Green Revolution technologies, but are also considerably less productive (Conway in Redclift, 1987). Few seriously question the value of replacing local varieties with high-yielding varieties (HYVs) provided the local germplasm is preserved elsewhere, and provided a level of diversity is maintained in the local farming system.

Genetic diversity will remain extremely important in the future because of the increasing genetic uniformity, and therefore vulnerability, of improved varieties. These have a finite life, and require periodic infusions of new genetic material if pest and disease resistance is to be maintained. New biotechnological techniques can be expected to increase the use of wild germplasm in breeding programmes. The threat presented by global climatic change also requires that the maximum biodiversity be retained, and also that access to important genetic resources in the transition zones be protected. Maintaining the flexibility to respond to climatic change will be an important benefit. With developing country agriculture increasingly vulnerable, the conservation of local landraces and wild relatives of economic crops and livestock is of overriding importance.

In addition to the 20 or so major food crops, between 5,000 and 10,000 plant species provide an important source of food and materials. Examples include timber and fuelwood; rattans; forage and pasture crops; rootcrops; beverage crops; spices; fruits; and fibres. Many of these may currently be only of local importance, but have wider potential. Much less is known about the diversity of these species compared with the major food crops, and very little is being done to conserve them, either *ex-situ* or *in situ*.

The value of plant germplasm derived by "gene-poor" developed countries from "gene-rich" developing countries has lead to demands for free access to all plant resources (including elite breeders' lines) and/or financial compensation. The fact that south-south germplasm flows are probably more important than south-north flows has not been fully appreciated (Frankel in Kloppenburg, 1988). A more telling point in this context is that the financial value of unresearched exotic landraces at source is very low, even if the potential value of one particular genetic trait is enormous (Harlan: op.cit.).

The consumptive and productive value of **medicines** directly or indirectly derived from wild species is often cited as one measure of the current, and particularly the future, value of biodiversity. In developing countries up to 80% of the people rely on traditional medicine for their primary health care, most of which involves the use of plant extracts (Farnsworth in Wilson, 1988). Around 20,000 plant species are believed to be used medicinally in the Third World. Some plant-derived drugs have also proved to be extremely valuable for advanced health care. One quarter of all prescriptions in developed countries are based on plants, including 21 indispensable mainstream drugs. In addition to current drugs, plants contain complex chemical structures which may never be synthesised in the laboratory, and which might provide important clues for new medicines. One of the more remarkable examples are the so-called vinca alkaloids used in the treatment of childhood leukaemia and Hodgkin's disease. These were developed from an extract of the Madagascan periwinkle (Catharanthus roseus) and had a market value to the drug company concerned of US$100 million in 1985 (op.cit.).

The value of medicinal diversity *per se* is less easy to determine. There are real costs which would follow from the reduction in the diversity of accessible medicinal plants. These would either be the costs of subsequent untreated disease, and/or the additional costs of commercial alternatives. These costs have not been estimated. However, the low current value of patented or unpatented novel chemical compounds – measured in terms of commercial companies' willingness to pay – is indicative of a low market value. Few naturally occurring compounds are marketable without an enormous input of costly research and testing. This accounts for most of the value added in drug development. Undeveloped and untested novel chemical compounds are readily available and very cheap for this reason (@ UK£50). Even patented discoveries are only worth around UK£5,000 (Ruitenbeek, 1988). This indicates that the value attached by the market to biodiversity at source is low, even though the potential economic value to society may be considerably higher.

Similar considerations will apply in the case of traded industrial raw materials. The market value of biodiversity for a developing country is not the total export value of natural products. It is the difference between the discounted present value of the export earnings of a diverse export portfolio over time, and the export earnings of a less diverse portfolio. This calculation is not easy to do. As in the case of agriculture, it is likely that the trend towards specialisation in line with comparative advantage means that the long-term export value of biodiversity is limited.

Diverse habitats and species can also have **non-consumptive** use-value, such as tourism and scientific research. Tourist revenues are clearly affected by the diversity of species that can be seen, and the range of habitats that can be visited. Species diversity, and particularly the presence of charismatic big game species, is a selling point. However, it is doubtful whether much tourism value can be attached to the vast majority of species, such as the 1 million species of invertebrates, except as part of special ecosystems. No overall valuation of wildlife diversity has ever been attempted.

Indirect use-values of biodiversity include ecosystem processes only to the extent that these are dependent on species diversity. While the total loss of a unique habitat involves the loss of the ecological processes dependent upon it, the precise effect of a partial reduction in species diversity will vary from site to site. There is, for example, no clear evidence of what effect, if any, the removal of a large percentage of the populations of large whales has had on oceanic ecosystems. Nevertheless, valuable ecological services are provided by certain ecosystems and attempts have been made to value these services in particular situations (McNeely, 1988; Pearce and Turner, 1990). An overall estimation of the value of ecosystem services attributable to biodiversity has never been attempted for obvious reasons. Other types of indirect use-value – such as the welfare gain from television and other media coverage of aspects of biodiversity – could conceivably be estimated.

The potential value of biodiversity in the future provides one of the main justifications for conservation. Given the immense uncertainty about future values, the **option value** represents the willingness to pay to retain the option of preserving access to a diverse range of habitats/species/genes. A **quasi-option value** is the economic value of choosing not to take irreversible steps if new information about alternative outcomes will become available in the future (Bishop, 1978). There will certainly be a need for new genetic material to offset new disease or pest threats to major food crops. Conservationists also point to the current value of a few naturally occurring compounds, and to the fact that only a fraction of the number of existing species have been assessed for their value to science, agriculture, medicine and industry. Most plant-derived drugs, for example, are obtained from less than 100 of the 250–750,000 species of higher plants in existence (Farnsworth in Wilson, 1988). However, the costs of accessing and realising this genetic potential are immense, and may be prohibitive. Only a small fraction of the number of species existing have ever been screened, and there is evidence that gene banks are already too large and poorly documented to be effectively used (Wilson, 1988; Kloppenburg, 1988; WRI, 1989).

There are reasons for believing that option values may not be as large as have been suggested. **First,** the current value which can be attributed to current or past biodiversity is considerably less than the current market values of the products or services, for reasons given above. **Second,** the past is a very uncertain guide of the future, not least because of technological change. **Third,** the market value at source of undiscovered chemical compounds or unresearched genes is relatively low (although the economic value may be higher). **Four,** it will be difficult to realise option values because of the costs of accessing the amount of material in existence. **Five**, most species are of no material value at all, and many could disappear without any significant ill-effects (Ehrenfeld in Wilson, 1988). Even if we lose 50% of all plant species, that will still leave 350,000 or so. The problem with the latter argument, of source, is that nobody knows **which** species are or will be valuable. Uncertainty is again the dominant feature. Thus, while there are good reasons for conserving tropical moist forests, option values are not necessarily a major one. Option values are undoubtedly positive, and the presence of uncertainty makes them even more so. This does not, however, make the estimation of option values any easier. In fact, there are no methods available to estimate either option values or quasi-option values (Bishop, 1978).

The final category of value is **existence value**. These are intrinsic values, unassociated with actual or potential use, which reflect the utility that people receive from simply knowing something exists (Pearce, 1989; Bishop, 1978). The fact that hundreds of thousands of people in developed countries are willing to pay conservation organisations to campaign on behalf of endangered species and habitats indicates that people do attach economic value to the existence of some species. There are reasons for thinking that the existence values attached to charismatic species such as whales, elephants and rhinos may not be indicative of existence values more generally. On the other hand, high existence values are attached to habitats even when most of the constituent species are neither known nor valued individually.

Methods exist to estimate existence values, and have been fairly widely used in the United States. Contingency valuation methods using a willingness-to-pay questionnaire approach suggest that American households were in theory willing to contribute US$28 to a preservation fund for Blue Whales (Hageman in Gregory, 1989). Average responses are approximately US$5-15 per endangered species. There are many problems with contingency valuation, and it is doubtful whether these methods have a major contribution to make to the valuation of biodiversity in less developed countries. The amount spent by non-governmental organisations (NGOs) on overseas biodiversity conservation would provide a more realistic measure of the existence value. In the absence of these figures existence value is best considered as (another) immeasurable, but not necessarily unimportant, benefit.

Conservation cost and willingness-to-pay

An alternative approach to the valuation of biodiversity is to estimate the cost of not proceeding with a project or policy in the interests of conservation. These costs are likely to be considerable in developing countries. The costs of conservation include the development benefits foregone, research costs, and management/policing costs (Bishop, 1978). It is generally easier to value these than it is to value externalities and/or unknowns. While not providing a direct estimate of the benefits of biodiversity, the costs of conservation provide a minimum value against which the largely qualitative benefits of biodiversity can be judged. An alternative method is to include the costs of a 'shadow project' designed to offset the erosion of biodiversity in the project by conserving it elsewhere. These and other methods for addressing the problem of biodiversity in project appraisal are covered in an ODA manual (Winpenny, HMSO, 1991).

The theory of willingness-to-pay is simple – biodiversity is worth what society is willing to pay for it. By evaluating the actual amount of money spent on conservation projects over time, and by knowing what it was spent on (e.g. no. of species/hectares), it is in theory possible to derive figures showing what society has been willing to pay (Ruitenbeek, 1988). The World Bank and other donors were, for example, willing to spend US$13/ha. on setting up a forest reserve in Madagascar (Grut, 1989). The problems with this approach are, firstly, that the necessary data covering a large number of projects are not available, and secondly, the suggestion that donors should base their valuations on what other donors have spent seems rather circular. Furthermore, as with existence values, the method is sensitive to the rarity value of certain "flagship" species or sites. Thus, while the method may provide a rough benchmark for particular projects, it has limited applicability to the valuation of biodiversity overall.

Value for whom?

The distribution of the various types of value has important implications for the loss of biodiversity and for biodiversity policy. At the aggregate level, there is an inverse relationship in terms of biodiversity, and national income as conventionally measured. Most of the world's biodiversity resides in "gene-rich" less developed countries. Equally important, the distribution of the various benefits of biodiversity, and the perception of those benefits, differs between groups. As a general rule, the direct use-value of diversity is most highly valued by local people, while option and existence values are of more value to developed countries. Local, developing country, developed country, and international values may not be congruent. This asymmetric valuation is one obstacle to the conservation of biodiversity.

Estimating value: conclusions

This section has concentrated on the economic value of biodiversity, in part because of its increasing profile in the conservation debate. Ethical, cultural and other non-economic values are central to any case for conservation, but tend to be less widely accepted (and even less amenable to estimation).

The basic requirement for informed policy is a better understanding of the economic value of environmental goods. In the case of biodiversity, the practical contribution of economic valuation is real but limited. The main reason for this is scientific and economic uncertainty, and explains why economists have made much more progress in identifying the types of value than they have in estimating those values. There are a lot of empty boxes, and few numbers. It is occasionally possible to indicate the order of magnitude, and in all cases it has been demonstrated that the economic value of biodiversity is significant, if not as large as some conservationists have suggested. However, the extent of ignorance surrounding biodiversity suggests that there is little point in attempting to do more that this, except possibly in the context of project appraisal. Many aspects of biodiversity cannot be quantified, let alone valued.

The economic case for biodiversity rests on five main types of value: the value of biodiverse economies, ecosystem services, crop and animal genetic resources, option values, and existence values. For the reasons given above, any economic assessments of these are highly general. It can be concluded that the economic values of biodiversity are positive but uncertain. The economic case for biodiversity conservation in developing countries is nevertheless strong. However, while economics can strengthen the general case for conserving biodiversity, it cannot at present provide answers to the following questions: how valuable is biodiversity relative to other resources, and how much should be spent on conserving biodiversity? It can, however, contribute to decision making by demonstrating that biodiversity has significant social and economic value. It can also be demonstrated that biodiversity is undervalued by markets and society. The implications of this for the loss of biodiversity, and for possible policy options to counteract this, are the subject of subsequent sections.

THE CAUSES OF BIODIVERSITY LOSS

The previous section has confirmed that biodiversity is of real social and economic value. This begs the question: if biodiversity is so valuable, why is it being lost at such a fast rate? Some loss of biodiversity is clearly inevitable and justifiable. However, even if this is the case, it can still be argued with some justification that the rate of biodiversity loss is socially excessive. The exact rate of loss is unknown. Few figures are available for documented species loss but it has to be assumed that many plant and animal species are being lost as a result of the massive habitat loss which has occurred during the past decades. Habitat loss will also have resulted in a contraction of species distribution, and many species will accordingly have suffered genetic erosion (i.e. the loss of a considerable part of the genetic variation and variability within the populations). This is particularly serious for species of current economic value – such as crop and pasture species – where genetic variation is important for breeding new strains and varieties.

The **immediate** causes of biodiversity loss – such as habitat loss and overexploitation – are reasonably well known and are discussed in more detail in following sections. However, the **underlying** causes are less clearcut, and certainly more difficult to address. The complex of underlying causes can be divided into three groups: **development pressure, market failure,** and **intervention failure.**

Immediate causes

The main causes of biodiversity loss are as follows: habitat loss, degradation, and fragmentation; resource over-exploitation; species/genetic introductions; ignorance; pollution; and climatic change. Of these, by far the most important is habitat loss. Tropical deforestation will be the single greatest cause of species extinction in the next fifty years. Depending on the assumptions used, tropical deforestation may eliminate between 5 and 15% of species by 2020 (WRI, 1989). The detailed causes of this and other aspects of biodiversity loss are well covered in other documents (WRI, 1989; Wilson, 1988). The social and economic factors underlying these proximate causes are the main subject of this section. Because of the lack of data on biodiversity, habitat loss and overexploitation are used as reasonable proxies.

Development pressure

The trade-offs between economic growth and environmental degradation have not been removed by the use of the term "sustainable development". It is entirely correct to stress the complementarities between economic growth and environment, the potential for income and employment generation from conservation-based activities, and the need for the full and proper valuation of the environmental costs (Pearce, 1989). The reality nevertheless is that there is an **inevitable** cost in terms of the erosion of biodiversity. This cost can be reduced, but the world cannot support 5 billion people, and will not support 10 billion, without serious degradation of the environment. Declining biodiversity will be both a symptom and a cause of this accelerating degradation of the global environment.

The simple growth of **population** is not the whole pattern. The pressure of production on biological resources is exacerbated by the unequal distribution of agricultural land, and by the replacement of traditional common property rights by open access regimes. Population growth is nevertheless a powerful force for biotic impoverishment. Projected high rates of population growth means that the pressure on existing land and undisturbed habitats will increase at an unprecedented rate. In the agricultural sector, both an increase in the area cultivated, and an increase in the yields per unit area, will lead to the loss of genetic diversity. Estimates of deforestation caused by agriculture vary, but were estimated at between 5.9 and 7.5 million hectares in the late 1970s, of which a minimum of 4.5 million ha. was transformed to permanently cleared land (Myers, 1989). The rate of habitat loss attributable to agricultural expansion accelerated during the 1980s, and can be expected to increase further as improved infrastructure increases the access to forest resources and encourages internal migration. Both non-agricultural species and the wild relatives of current crops and livestock will be lost as a result.

The intensification of agriculture will also lead to the further genetic simplification of agro-ecosystems as traditional cultivars are replaced by new varieties. Stability and diversity are traded for uniformity and productivity. This process is related to another major force for biodiversity loss, which is the rapid incorporation of semi-independent social and ecological systems into the global exchange economy (Norgaard in Wilson, 1988). Specialisation in accordance with comparative advantage inevitably leads to the simplification of agro-ecological systems, while improved linkages with international markets create the conditions for the unsustainable exploitation of natural resources. Tropical hardwood is the best-known example, but other so-called minor forest products, including rare flora and fauna, are also being overexploited. Other factors contributing to overexploitation and extinction are discussed below.

The final aspect of development pressure which impacts upon biodiversity are **discount rates.** These are simply a measure of the rate at which individuals or governments prefer the present over the future (i.e. the implicit reduction of costs and benefits which occur in the future). There is an extensive literature on discount rates in project appraisal (Markandya, 1987; ODA/Winpenny, forthcoming). However, most economic behaviour in developing countries takes place outside the context of projects, and is conditioned by a complex of social, economic and political factors. These factors, and particularly the short-term pressure to address chronic development problems at the household or national level, combine to decrease the value of the future relative to the present. In economic terminology, the real social rate of time preference is very high. Environmental goods such as biodiversity, the costs and benefits of which are both uncertain and concentrated in the future, are severely discounted as a result. The immediate costs of any development foregone in the interests of conservation will likewise be keenly felt.

The net effect of development pressure on biodiversity is well-known. However, it is equally important to appreciate that, even if biodiversity is correctly valued, these same development pressures mean that some loss of biodiversity is socially justified. This is an important perspective. Biodiversity will be lost even if development becomes more sustainable, and trade-offs will have to be made.

Market failure

Market failure occurs when markets do not maximise social welfare. Market prices are a valid indicator of value where the goods concerned are private, have no indirect effects (externalities), and are exchanged in small quantities in competitive markets. In these restrictive circumstances the free market results in socially optimal behaviour. Most of the issues involved with biodiversity violate

Biological diversity

this special case (Randall in Wilson, 1988). Many of the goods derived from biodiversity are public not private; considerable externalities are present; and such limited markets as exist are not competitive. The "market" in biodiversity is either non-existent, incomplete, or distorted. As a result, market prices do not reflect value. The particular reasons for market failure in the case of biodiversity can be discussed under the following headings:

i)   property rights;
ii) externalities;
iii) uncertainty and irreversibility;
iv) market imperfections;
v)   policy distortions.

Property rights theory provides much of the explanation for why biodiversity is lost despite its value. There are three types of property rights: private property, common property, and open-access common property. Private property is subject to exclusive use and individual possession. Many of the goods and services derived from biodiversity are open-access public goods in the sense that consumption is non-rival and non-exclusive. Wild plant germplasm, for example, is seen as the "common heritage of mankind". Deep sea resources such as whales are also open-access property. Unfortunately, because open-access resources belong to everybody, access is open to all and nobody has an individual incentive for conservation. This is the so-called "tragedy of the commons" (Hardin, 1968). Common property is in a sense midway between pure public goods and private goods. While it is subject to individual use, it is neither owned individually, nor is it open-access. Access to many local resources in developing countries is restricted to members of a particular community, and exploitation is frequently controlled by community rules and regulations. Common property does not inevitably lead to resource degradation. However, with increasing economic pressure, and the decay of common property regimes, many resources become effectively open-access.

Private and common property rights affect the rate of biodiversity loss in different ways. Open-access common property resources are at greater risk of overexploitation and species extinction. In some cases open-access resources have no market price. Wild genes, for example, are a zero-priced resource. Their unintended destruction incurs no financial costs to the individual, even when the economic value to society may be considerable. Because property rights for natural species are not recognised under international law, no individual, company or country has an incentive to invest in species preservation (Sedjo in Kloppenburg, 1988). But even with positive market prices, resources under ill-defined or open-access property regimes are much more likely to be overexploited. If the market price of a species exceeds its "harvesting" costs at very low stock levels, extinction is more likely under open-access conditions. When the discount rates of hunters/poachers is also high, and exceeds the rate of growth of the resource, it can be privately optimal to reduce stocks to zero (Pearce, 1990). The extinction of slow growing resources such as hardwoods and elephants can be optimal for this reason (Grut, 1989; Pearce, 1990). Because indirect values – such as externalities – and non-use values are not represented in the market, the overexploitation of resources may, perversely, be entirely rational behaviour.

449

The existence of more defined common or private property rights is no guarantee of sustainable exploitation for the same reasons, but the risk is reduced. Private property in particular avoids the problem of "free riding" by internalising more, but not necessarily all, of the costs and benefits of using that resource (see externalities below). The fact that nearly all the forest clearance in the Amazon has occurred either on privately owned land, or in order to establish private ownership, does, however, demonstrate that private property rights are not necessarily the solution (Hecht, 1990).

The question of property rights for genetic resources warrants further discussion. Under present open-access regimes, local people and developing countries have no way of capturing the benefits of conserving genetic/species diversity. The costs of habitat destruction are borne by society as a whole, while the benefits of new products or varieties are captured by a few. Where new commercial products and varieties are developed from wild genetic resources, only the company and consumers benefit. Under present institutional arrangements these beneficiaries are unlikely to include the source country or local people (i.e. the capturable production value is low). New crop varieties developed under the CGIAR or other international auspices are, of course, more widely available. The two contrasting proposals for addressing this problem – "farmers rights" and extending the concept of "common heritage" to cover all genes, not just wild unimproved stocks – are important.

While this answers the question as to why local people and developing countries have little incentive to conserve genetic resources, it does not answer the question as to why pharmaceutical or agro-chemical companies are not more active in the utilisation and/or protection of biodiversity. The gene pools of unique commercially valuable plant species are in fact protected to some degree by commercially motivated behaviour. Commercial plant breeders have some incentive to maintain stocks of germplasm for future use (Sedjo in Kloppenburg, 1988). Commercial companies are also involved in screening naturally occurring chemicals to a limited extent. Research into naturally occurring substances – particularly those known to be useful by indigenous people – can represent a cheaper route to some new products than chemical synthesis *ab initio*. There are nevertheless a large number of reasons why commercial companies are not more active in this area. The lack of solid patent protection for naturally occurring compounds is one reason (Farnsworth in Wilson, 1988), although the fact that most compounds are either too potent, ineffective or unsafe in the natural forms means that substantial, patentable, modification is required. More importantly, most sources of novel chemical compounds are open-access, and companies therefore have little incentive to do other than free-ride as long as some plant material is available somewhere. Other reasons why the new drug argument may have been overstated include the low value of untested novel compounds at source. The amount commercial companies are willing to pay is correspondingly low. There is also the problem of knowing where to start in screening naturally occurring chemicals. A single fig leaf, for example, contains some 20,000 unique chemicals. The costs of random screening are prohibitive, and for this reason it is often more cost-effective to start the search for new products from known chemical compounds.

The other relevant aspect of property rights is tenure insecurity and/or uncertainty. Insecure property rights may encourage behaviour which is detrimental to biodiversity. In the case of the Amazonia, the clearance of forest is a precondition for claiming defined rights. Other social and economic pressures also encourage deforestation, but the fact that migrants can obtain rights of possession simply by clearing the forest is an important factor (Mahar, 1989). More generally, the argument that secure and certain tenure encourages conservation rather than overexploitation is intuitively correct, even if the available evidence is limited.

The existence of **externalities** is a major reason why markets fail to deliver socially optimal outcomes. Habitat destruction, for example, can be a perfectly rational economic response to prevailing incentives as revealed in market prices. But those market prices will not include indirect values, option values, or non-use values, and market outcomes will therefore fail to take into account the real costs and benefits to society. In economic terms, the price of the resource will be less than its "marginal opportunity cost" – that is, the direct and indirect costs to the user, the benefits foregone by using the resource now rather than in the future (marginal user cost), and the marginal external cost (Pearce, 1989). The net result of ignoring the marginal external cost (benefit) is that too much (little) biodiversity will be lost (preserved). While this remains true even under private property, it is even more so under open-access regimes where no institutional restraints to individual behaviour apply.

The effect of **uncertainty** and **irreversibility** on the amount of biodiversity lost/ preserved has already been covered. It is sufficient here to repeat that uncertainty and irreversibility compound the problem of market failure, and provide additional reasons why unadjusted competitive markets discriminate against biodiversity. Uncompetitive **imperfect markets** may also have the same effect, although this is less clear. To the extent that information on the real costs and benefits is not freely available to producers and consumers, and the existence of barriers to entry which prevent, for example, the free participation of conservation organisations in developing country land markets, such imperfections worsen market failure. The political power and violence employed by land speculators in Brazil to usurp traditional or smallholder land rights similarly leads to an allocation of resources different from that under free market conditions (Hecht, 1989). Whether this is harmful or beneficial for biodiversity will vary from case to case.

Intervention failure

The effect of intervention failure – or government failure – on the loss of biodiversity has arguably been at least as important as that of market failure. There is now a large literature on the social and economic costs of poorly conceived and implemented government policies. Much government intervention has, largely unintentionally, added to those costs by increasing the loss of biodiversity. The lack of data on biodiversity makes this difficult to demonstrate directly, but habitat loss and overexploitation can be considered as reasonable proxies. Intervention failure can take two forms:

i) ineffective positive intervention;
ii) unintentional negative intervention.

Ineffective positive intervention mainly consists of the failure to implement existing conservation policies effectively. Examples include the failure to protect demarcated nature reserves, to implement land use policies, or to enforce land regulations and environmental legislation. In most instances these failures can be explained by reference to wider institutional, social, economic and political problems, rather than technical deficiencies. In some cases it reflects a simple lack of implementation capacity associated with a chronic shortage of recurrent funds for the responsible government departments. But in most cases it indicates that the real conflicts between development and preservation, between different sectors, and between different interest groups, have not been resolved by the drafting of legislation and plans. The result is that outcomes continue to be determined by the balance of immediate social, economic and political forces (Hall, 1989). As has been demonstrated above, the combination of market failure and development pressure will ensure that the rate of biodiversity loss will be socially excessive in the absence of effective government intervention.

Unintentional negative intervention has been a large cause of biodiversity loss, not least because positive interventions have been limited. The adverse effects of intervention can be analyzed under the following categories:

i) general development strategy;
ii) fiscal policy;
iii) monetary policy;
iv) market interventions;
v) land tenure.

The common feature of these interventions is that they were designed to meet other objectives without reference to the costs in terms of reduced biodiversity. Biodiversity has not so much been undervalued as effectively ignored in both policy and project contexts. Project appraisal has generally failed to consider the costs and benefits of biodiversity, and national income accounts compound the problem by counting the depletion of natural capital as income (Pearce, 1989; Schramm and Warford, 1989). It is only relatively recently that biodiversity has come to be recognised as valuable in its own right.

Fiscal policies have contributed to habitat loss and overexploitation. The role of tax credits and subsidised rural credit in the destruction of the Amazonian rainforest is well documented (Mahar, 1988). The massive increase in deforestation rates in the 1980s coinciding with a sharp decline in rural credit suggests that this is only a partial explanation (Hecht, 1990). That said, economic policies have exacerbated deforestation in a wide range of countries by creating perverse incentives for forest clearing industries such as plantations and livestock ranching (Repetto, 1988). In each case the effect of the tax and subsidy policies increase the private rate of return to investment, and thereby encourage activities which would not have been undertaken had prices been more competitively determined, let alone priced at their social opportunity cost. The failure to collect tax has also encouraged speculative and exploitative behaviour which, by increasing forest clearance and the destructive logging of a few timber species, has reduced biodiversity (Mahar, 1988; Pearce, 1990).

The effect of monetary policy and market interventions on biodiversity loss is less clear. Overvalued exchange rates and marketing controls have undoubtedly depressed agricultural product prices, but insufficient research has been carried out to determine the relationships between higher prices, conservation, and an expansion in cultivated area (Pearce, 1990). The effect of land tenure policies has been more clearly detrimental.

The overall negative effect of government intervention needs to be qualified in two ways. First, it cannot be presumed that efficiency distortions arising from government intervention necessarily contribute to biodiversity loss in all situations, or that the use of efficiency prices would necessarily improve the situation (Pearce, 1990). The widespread assumption that better economic policy will lead to better environmental outcomes is not proven, even if on balance it is probably correct (Schramm amd Warford, 1989). More importantly, it cannot be assumed that efficiency pricing will significantly alter the rate of biodiversity loss. Better, freer markets cannot include the majority of the values of biodiversity, nor can most of the obstacles to conservation presented by externalities and property rights be overcome by markets alone. Government intervention is still required. Second, it cannot be assumed that the more explicit and correct valuation of biodiversity would necessarily have altered government policies. Destructive environmental policies are not primarily the result of ignorance of the real environmental costs and benefits, although this is a contributory factor. Policy is part and parcel of the political economy, and those in Brazil are the product of a powerful coalition of state, foreign and domestic interests. Policy making may have been short-sighted but it has not, within its narrow terms of reference, been irrational (Hall, 1989; Hecht, 1989). This observation has important implications for the design of improved policy.

The overall conclusion is that, although biodiversity is valuable, there are powerful forces working against its conservation and which explain its loss. These forces are not generally the result of scientific ignorance or irrationality. The lack of information about the long-term costs and benefits of biodiversity may be significant in some circumstances, but so-called "information failure" is a lesser explanatory factor overall. Individuals and governments have, in the main, acted rationally in response to prevailing social, economic and political pressures. The challenge is to design a strategy for biodiversity conservation which takes account of these pressures, and which seeks to address the underlying causes of biodiversity loss.

FORESTS
Tropical forests cover 14% of the earth's land surface (8 million sq.km.) and are exceptional in the wealth of their biodiversity. Half of all vertebrates, 60% of known plant species, and possibly 90% of the world's total species are found in tropical forests. This section considers the two main types of tropical forest: **tropical moist forest** and **tropical dry forests.** The third main category – forested wetlands – is covered in the Wetlands section.

Tropical moist forests
The greatest diversity of species is found in tropical moist forests (TMF). Although covering only 5–7% of the land surface, these extraordinarily rich but fragile habitats contain more than half the species in the entire world biota. A single hectare of rainforest can contain up to 300 tree species. This compares with 700 species in the whole of continental north America.

Large areas of TMF are concentrated in a small number of countries. By far the largest area remaining in a single country is in Brazil. Indonesia and Cameroon contain approximately one third and one half of the remaining closed forest in Asia and Africa respectively. Cameroon, Gabon and the Congo together contain over 70% of the African total. However, area of forest alone is not an adequate indicator of diversity. Historical and environmental influences have led to the concentration of diversity in certain areas, so-called 'hot spots'. The level of information on species numbers and distributions is still limited, but there is nevertheless broad agreement on the regions, countries and sites of high diversity and/or exceptional degrees of endemism. An atlas of the current distribution of tropical forests is in preparation (IUCN/WCMC). This could be used to identify priority sites for conservation.

Tropical dry forests
Much larger areas of the tropics are covered with forests which experience a dry season and have a more open canopy. These tropical dry forests are considerably less important than TMF in terms of biodiversity. However, although they are less rich in species than comparable areas of TMF, they may contain genetic resources of populations with potentially valuable adaptations to withstand environmental stress, and to survive on degraded sites. Dry forests in some areas are particularly significant, such as Central America which is recognised as a centre of genetic diversity for many tree species as well as for the wild relatives of some crop plants. These forests have already been severely depleted because they are relatively accessible and easy to clear for agriculture. Two-thirds of the remaining dry forest is in Africa, approximately one-third in Latin America, and the remainder in the Asia-Pacific region.

The value of forest biodiversity
Tropical forests embody all the types of value discussed in Section 2 above. These include direct use-values in the form of the diverse range of products harvested from the forest, and the indirect use-values in the form of ecological services. As discussed earlier, the precise contribution of diversity *per se* is uncertain. However, the capability of tropical forests to grow productively on poor soils – and therefore to provide the level of ecological services – is due at least in part to the interactions between species.

The rich diversity of tropical forests has an option value. Tropical forests have already provided an enormous range of useful plant species for agriculture, medicine and industry. Examples of important crops include bananas, coffee, cocoa, citrus fruits, vanilla, and black pepper. Conservation of the wild relatives of these species is necessary to maintain their productivity. There is also the as yet unrealised potential of the thousands of under-exploited and/or unresearched species, although the value of these is uncertain.

The genetic resources of forests may also contribute to coping with the expected climatic changes associated with regional deforestation and global warming. The transition zones between closed forests and dry forests – such as between the Amazonian closed forest and the cerrados – are important for this reason.

Losses of forest biodiversity
Latest estimates suggest that tropical forests are being cleared at the rate of 140,000 sq.kms. per year, or approximately 1.8% of the remaining forest cover (Myers, 1989). Losses vary markedly both between and within countries. For example, 98% of the Atlantic forests of Brazil have been cleared, compared to 20% of the Amazonian forest. In general, a significantly higher percentage of dry forest has been cleared and degraded compared with moist forest.

Despite their high diversity, tropical forests are fragile ecosystems and are less able to recover from severe or repeated human disturbance than temperate forests. Many tropical forest species are extremely vulnerable to habitat change. This is partly because of the limited and/or scattered distribution of most species, their adaptation to specific ecological niches, and the interdependencies between species (WWF, 1989). Information on species extinctions and genetic erosion is limited, and estimates of loss can only be rough. One estimate is that the continuation of current deforestation rates will lead to the loss of approximately one quarter of the world's plant species in the next 20 years (IUCN, 1990).

The principal proximate cause of losses of forest biodiversity is the destruction of habitat, or its fragmentation and degradation. Most of the habitat clearance is carried out by smallscale agriculturalists, although commercial logging and livestock ranching are responsible for substantial deforestation and degradation in certain areas.

Underlying causes are discussed above.

Conservation status

Approximately 5% of tropical moist forests are in legally gazetted national parks or nature reserves. Systematic work on assessing the adequacy or otherwise of the siting of these protected areas, and on determining the minimum size of area to achieve specified conservation objectives, is in progress (IUCN, 1990). Previous work had suggested that a network of 500 protected and managed areas, with an average size of 200,000 ha., covering 10% of the area of remaining forest represented a minimum acceptable target (WWF, 1989). Some conservation biologists suggest that even this would be insufficient to maintain viable populations, but it is clear that the current network of protected areas is far from adequate.

Most of the important major tropical forest wilderness areas are relatively unthreatened. These include the Southern Guianas/Southern Venezuela/Northern Brazil Amazonia, the Zaire Basin, and New Guinea (IUCN, 1990). However, a number of the critical centres of tropical forest biodiversity ("hotspots") are seriously under threat, such as the Philippines, Western Ecuador, and the Atlantic forest in Brazil.

The management of protected areas is at least as important as their extent and siting. The poor management of many existing protected areas, and the lack of proven management systems which combine forest exploitation with biodiversity conservation, is a major constraint. Similar financial and staff constraints affect the 250 or so botanic gardens and arboreta located in the tropics. While the range of genetic material which can realistically be conserved *ex situ* is small, their potentially vital contribution to biodiversity conservation is not being fully realised.

Forest biodiversity issues

Tropical forests are without doubt the most important ecosystem type from the point of view of global biodiversity. The threat to this diversity is widespread and severe, and the action required is correspondingly urgent and broad in scope, and will require substantial and long-term commitments. This in turn means that the need for priorities is particularly pressing.

WETLANDS

Wetlands as defined by the Ramsar Convention include a diverse range of inland, coastal and marine habitats. For management and conservation purposes these can be reduced to seven landscape units where wetlands form the only or major component: estuaries (including mangroves); floodplains; freshwater marshes; peatlands; swamp forest; open coasts; and lakes. The latter two are covered in other sections.

Little systematic information exists on the extent and distribution of the world's wetland ecosystems. If the large areas of peatland in the polar regions is included, the total area of wetlands is 6% of the world's land surface. Mangrove forests are generally regarded as among the most important of wetland habitats. They dominate the tropical and subtropical coastal habitat, and constitute an important economic resource for local people.

Much of the available information on wetland biodiversity is anecdotal, except that relating to birds. Directories of wetlands of international importance are currently available for the Neotropics, Asia, and Africa, and an inventory of Oceania is underway. However, because these directories have mainly been compiled from a literature review rather than fieldwork, they do not provide a rigorous analysis of the most important wetlands for the conservation of biological diversity. Work is currently underway to rectify this and identify those wetlands of exceptional biological diversity (IUCN/WRI/USAID).

The value of wetland biodiversity

Wetlands in general are not high in species diversity or endemism. Most wetlands do not therefore have a significant option value. Wetlands are nevertheless complex ecosystems and many support vast concentrations of individual species of wildlife. Some old lakes display high degrees of diversity and endemism, and in many countries the inaccessibility of wetlands has made them important sanctuaries for threatened species, such as the Bengal Tiger and the Jaguar.

Wetlands are important as a genetic reservoir for certain plant species, notably rice. Wild relatives of rice continue to be an important source of new genetic material used in developing disease resistance and other traits. Important woody species are also found in wetlands. Even in a single location there are likely to be a range of families and genera, each representing a different adaptation to the changing conditions in the ecological succession. These adaptations may be of value in the context of global climatic change and rising sea levels.

The abundance of wetland plant and animal life produces substantial benefits for local people in developing countries. A particular role of mangrove forests is the production and maintenance of nearshore fisheries. Wetlands also perform important ecological functions such as flood control and storm protection. However, the extent to which the value of wetland products and functions can be attributed to biological diversity is open to question (see Section 2). Wetlands are extremely important habitats because of these products and functions. They are less important for diversity.

Losses of wetland biodiversity

Little detailed information is available on rates of wetland loss in developing countries. Even less is available on the loss of biodiversity associated with wetland loss and degradation. However, the limited information available suggests that entire ecosystems are now under threat. For example, in the Philippines, 67% of the country's mangrove resources were lost between 1920–80. As a general rule, estuarine wetlands and freshwater floodplains, especially in arid regions, are the most threatened habitat type.

The major direct cause of the loss of biodiversity is the conversion of wetland habitats. Dams, industrial and urban development, and conversion for irrigated agriculture and aquaculture have all contributed substantially to the loss of wetlands. Wetlands are also degraded by other factors, notably pollution. Road construction has had a major impact in some cases by disrupting critical hydrological flows.

Conservation status
Protected areas have been established to preserve wetland sites of unique or scarce resources, and as management areas for endangered fauna and flora. More protected areas need to be established to improve the protection of priority wetland ecosystems and sites. Equally important, many protected areas are poorly managed and suffer from pollution, poaching, and loss of habitat. In Asia, 69 (31%) of 191 wetland sites of international importance wholly within protected areas are reported to be under moderate to severe threat. A similar situation is reported to apply in Latin America.

Three features make protected wetlands particularly vulnerable. First, wetlands are open systems influenced by activities well beyond their boundaries. Second, wetlands are dynamic systems which change over time. Merely protecting them from external threats may not be sufficient to save them. Third, the intensive use of wetlands by local people requires more sensitive integrated systems of management if multiple objectives are to be met.

Wetland biodiversity issues
It is accepted that wetlands do not have the biological diversity characteristic of tropical forests or coral reefs. The main value of wetland biodiversity therefore lies in the ecosystem diversity represented by wetlands at the global level, and by products and ecological functions associated with wetlands at the more local level. The main categories of natural wetlands are reasonably covered by protected areas, but the majority of these are poorly managed. The most important priority is to improve the management of existing wetland protected areas.

BIODIVERSITY ISSUES
The previous sections confirm that biodiversity is being lost at a rapid rate in many ecosystems. The rates, causes, and impact of this loss varies between habitats and sites, although they have much in common. There are also a number of common issues which warrant discussion, and which have a major bearing on any biodiversity strategy. These include questions of objectives, information, measures of biodiversity, mechanisms for conserving biodiversity, and priorities. Of these, the issue of priorities is the most important, but also the most difficult.

Biodiversity objectives
The objectives of any biodiversity strategy need to be explicit, clear, and achievable. This is rarely the case at present, for three reasons. **First,** it reflects a genuine lack of agreement over what is valuable. The ethical objective of maintaining all existing biodiversity is very different from the anthropocentric objective of maintaining biodiversity to the extent that it is of actual or possible value to humankind. **Second,** there has been a failure to recognise that biodiversity objectives will vary according to who is the intended beneficiary and the scale of analysis. Global, regional, developed country, developing country, and local peoples' priorities are often different. **Third,** there has been the difficulty of making objectives precise enough to be useful. For example, the

objective "to maintain as much biodiversity as possible" is unhelpful in the absence of a precise definition and measure of biodiversity, and clear targets.

The wider objective of any biodiversity expenditure within aid programmes should be **to maximise the conservation and use of biodiversity in order to provide sustainable social and economic benefits to developing countries.** Where funds are provided outside aid budgets in order to benefit the world in general, or to support ethical objectives, the resultant priorities and activities may be different. For example, the most deserving habitat or botanical garden in one country might be a very low global priority. National prioritisation may therefore lead to a misallocation of resources from an international perspective, even if there is considerable overlap between the interests of the developed and developing world. However, it is also important to recognise the possibility of significant differences in objectives, and the implications these may have for priorities.

Information requirements

A persuasive case can be made for an increase in research and information processing, either to improve priority setting or to guide management. One of the main problems with biodiversity conservation is uncertainty both about the present state of the biosphere, and how that state will change. More precisely, there is for almost all habitat types a shortage of information about the extent, characteristics, status and management of habitats, species, and the genetic resource. Only in the case of tropical forests does there appear to be sufficient assimilated information to permit global priorities to be determined. But even in this case there is an identified need for a rapid expansion in taxonomy in order to interpret, manage, conserve and utilise forest biodiversity, and a need to pull together existing data from all sources. Without this and equivalent information for all the major biomes there is a risk that the limited resources available will not be allocated to the best possible effect.

The counter argument is that the enormity and urgency of the problem means that it is both impractical and misguided to spend scarce time and resources on improving the information base. Sufficient is often known about the priorities and problems for action to be taken now. Implementation, not information, is the primary constraint to conservation in many cases.

There is merit in both arguments, and there is clearly no general conclusion which will apply in all cases. The important point is that the relative priority to be attached to information gathering and/or processing on the one hand, and other biodiversity related actions on the other, is not self-evident. Given the competing demands for limited funds, and the destruction of habitats for known importance, the observation that there is incomplete knowledge does not mean that all or any research is justified. The unpalatable reality is that research and implementation are competitors for scarce resources. Research into biodiversity issues will accordingly need to be guided by the same set of criteria as other activities. The probable exception to this is the requirement for some research, or at least analysis of existing information, to guide the process of priority setting and project appraisal.

Measures of biodiversity

In addition to incomplete knowledge about the extent and state of biodiversity, comparative analysis is hampered by the lack of a single measure of diversity. Part of the problem is that all units of classification above the gene are artificial and inexact approximation to the real world, and there is therefore disagreement over how to take account of diversity at different taxonomic levels. New techniques for discrimination (e.g. DNA probes) should afford greater precision for within species taxonomy. It is clear, for example, that the number of species only provides a partial indication of diversity. Measures of diversity also need to take into account genetic diversity, habitat diversity, and the numbers of organisms within species. The extremely uneven knowledge of different taxa and ecosystems, with some having been much better researched than others, compounds the problem.

A variety of indices are in use or proposed for conservation planning. Most involve a weighted combination of some of the following: the number of species; the number of endemic species; evenness of abundance of species; the number of taxa higher than species level; spread of size classes and trophic levels; rarity; degree of uniqueness; and ecological importance (connectance and interaction). However, although the inclusion of most of these factors might be ideal, the fact is that there is unlikely to be any universal and comprehensive measure of diversity which is scientifically acceptable and/or workable. However, given the urgency of the task, and the limited information available, there is a need to agree a simple, workable index. Standardising on a weighted combination of the number of total species and endemic species, adjusted for area, would appear to have some merit. Species-area indices of this type are already in common use, and provide a rough but acceptable method of identifying the high diversity systems.

Biodiversity priorities
Given the limited availability of conservation funds, the competing uses for biological resources, and the variable utility of biodiversity, any policy which does not address the need for trade-offs and choices will be counterproductive. Some, possibly a large percentage, of genes/species/habitats will be lost if current trends continue. Approximately 5–10% of closed tropical forest species will become extinct per decade at current rates of forest loss and disturbance (WRI, 1989). To the extent that the international community can and should seek to minimise the cost of biodiversity loss, and maximise its contribution to human welfare in developing countries, priorities for action need to be set. This requires answers to the following four questions, the first three of which are covered in this section:

1) what values are important for developing countries?
2) which genes/species/habitats are a priority?
3) how much biodiversity should be conserved?
4) how should biodiversity be conserved?

What values are important for developing countries?
The problems of determining priorities both across and within ecosystems are formidable. Priorities and activities depend to a large extent on the values we are seeking to maximise, and on an assessment of the significance of those values. This, and the different priorities of different actors, needs to be taken into account in considering priorities. It is apparent that local, developing country, developed country and global values are unlikely to be congruent. The direct value of biodiverse livelihoods and the genetic improvement of locally important crops is likely to be a first order priority for the least developed countries. The potential value of unknown species for advanced industrial and medicinal uses, or the existence value of unique wilderness habitats, may be of less immediate

459

importance to least developed countries.

This has potentially major implications for biodiversity priorities within normal aid programmes. These must be responsive to, and determined by, government and non-government priorities in developing countries first and foremost, and not global priorities or domestic political pressures in developed countries. (The exception to this rule is where additional resources are made available for global biodiversity conservation or where, as in the case of the UK, there are some resources separate from aid programmes.) The problem with this approach is the now familiar one of valuation. Economics can assist in determining the types of value associated with biodiversity, the likely beneficiaries, and occasionally with the broad orders of magnitude, but is unlikely to generate usable figures. However, even a ranking of the different types of economic value for developing countries is instructive.

For example, if the directly productive use-value of biodiversity in the form of genetic resources for developing country agriculture is considered to be the most important value, the conservation of wild relatives of food crops will be a major priority. The priority accorded to tropical moist forest would, according to this criterion at least, be rather lower. The ultimate priority accorded to each broad category of biodiversity would need to be determined by a wider set of criteria than just value (see below). However, the important point to emphasise is that some consideration of the types and rank order of values for developing countries is an absolute necessity for priority setting.

Which genes/species/ecosystems?

A number of criteria and methods of determining priorities for biodiversity conservation have been proposed. IUCN and WRI suggested three rules of thumb: distinctiveness, threat, and utility (WRI, 1989; IUCN, 1990). The suggested list of criteria given below draws on these suggestions, but includes three additional criteria which should be taken into account in deriving priorities for action by any particular aid agency. The important point to emphasise is that priorities should not be determined by biological or ecological criteria alone, such as concentrating on centres of diversity.

1) Value for developing countries
2) Diversity and distinctiveness
3) Threat
4) Gaps in other programmes
5) Comparative advantage
6) Likelihood of success

1) **Value:** the case for including this criteria has been outlined above. The choice of priority genes/species/ecosystems must be guided by some judgement of the socio-economic value of different biological resources to developing countries and/or particular constituent groups. While these values are not known with any certainty, some general priorities can be identified, and should influence aid programmes. Cultural, ethical and aesthetic values may also be a factor in determining priorities.
2) **Diversity and distinctiveness:** this criterion is likely to remain a major determinant of conservation decisions. Other things being equal, priority should be accorded to those habitats and areas with the greatest number of

species, so called "centres of diversity." Areas under ecological stress, and the degree of endemism and distinctiveness will also be important considerations.

3) **Threat:** resources should be allocated first to the conservation of the most threatened genes, species and habitats (subject to criterion 6). The severity of threat will depend on the distribution of the aspect of biodiversity in question, its vulnerability, and the type of anthropogenic pressures.

4) **Gaps in other programmes:** decisions on priorities for action must take full account of the current and planned programmes of other countries, agencies and institutions, and the extent to which these will meet conservation and development needs.

5) **Comparative advantage:** each country, institution or agency has particular expertise or other resources to offer. UK expertise in taxonomy and tropical forestry is a case in point.

6) **Likelihood of success:** an informed assessment of the relative likelihood of a particular biodiversity project meeting its objectives will be an important consideration. This is related to the efficacy of different conservation strategies.

A combined analysis of these various criteria could provide the basis for any biodiversity strategy. The exact criteria to be employed would need to be decided by those involved in planning, implementing and affected by the strategy. Decisions will also need to be made on the relative weights to be attached to each criteria, and on a method for combining individual scores/ranks across criteria. This is likely to be a contentious exercise, but has been managed successfully in other circumstances, such as in determining the strategic priorities in natural resources research (CGIAR, 1987; ODA, 1989). The great virtue of the method is the way, by forcing value-judgements and trade-offs to be explicit rather than implicit, it can make the derivation of priorities a more transparent and objective process. The problem is that priority setting is inevitably a difficult and contentious process. It is often resisted by sectional interest, and will tend to be avoided as long as the solution to unpopular choices is seen to lie in increasing the total resources available. The simplest way to avoid contentious choices is to make almost everything a priority. This tendency is apparent in other strategic plans, such as some of the national Tropical Forestry Action Plans, and it remains to be seen whether the WRI/IUCN/UNEP Global Strategy for the Conservation of Biodiversity will be more successful.

The combination of these or other criteria could be used to set priorities at any level, whether global, national or local. An example of an ecosystem priority matrix is shown in Table 28.2. It should be emphasised that this is a subjective assessment based on the information contained in the background papers, and is included for illustrative purposes. It is not intended to indicate actual priorities, although it does show the effect of taking into account additional criteria apart from diversity. Tropical moist forests are the clear priority if species-richness in terrestrial ecosystems is the prime criteria. But this implicitly assumes that all species are equally valuable to developing countries. If, on the other hand, it is accepted that protecting and enhancing the productivity of species of **known** value in developing country agriculture is more important than conserving species of as yet **unknown** value to mankind in general, the source areas (and areas of cultivated plant diversity) for agricultural crops become at least as important a priority. Given that most economically valuable species originated in areas that

Table 28.2 Ecosystem priority matrix: Example.

Criteria[1]	Forest	Wetland	Freshwater	Other Wildland	Marine
1) VALUE[2]	high	low	low	medium	low
Direct values	medium	low	medium	medium	low
Indirect value	high	medium	low	medium	medium
Option values	medium	low	low	high	low
Non-use values	high	medium	medium	low	low
2) DIVERSITY	high	low	medium	low	low
3) THREAT	high	medium	medium	medium	low
4) GAPS IN OTHER PROGRAMMES	low	medium	high	medium	high
5) COMPARATIVE ADVANTAGE[3]	–	–	–	–	–
6) LIKELIHOOD OF SUCCESS[4]	–	–	–	–	–
OVERALL PRIORITY[5]	1	4	3	2	5

Notes:
1. Note that these are relative, not absolute assessments, and are included for illustrate purposes only.
2. Estimated value to developing countries. The direct value can be considered to be a function of the number of people supported by the system and its diversity. Indirect value is a function of the extent of the system and the importance of the indirect services performed. It is recognised that the local and regional value of some ecosystems (eg. marine) may be much higher.
3. Comparative advantage will vary with the countries involved. This matrix assumes that the international community has equal expertise in all ecosystems.
4. Likelihood of success has not been considered. This will be more relevant when choices need to be made between alternative actions in alternative sites or countries.
5. Overall priority ranks ecosystems in order of priority based on the criteria estimates given (with a higher weight attached to the value criterion).

are not particularly species rich (WRI, 1989; IBPGR, 1988), it can be argued that a concentration on the areas of greatest diversity will not necessarily be in the best interests of developing countries.

This paper cannot attempt to determine detailed priorities. However, some discussion of possible priorities for different aspects of biodiversity is possible on the basis of current knowledge. For example, the priority for **genetic conservation** (i.e. the maintenance of genetic diversity) is likely to be primarily determined with reference to two criteria: the current economic value of the plant/animal, and the adequacy of existing *in situ* or *ex situ* conservation (i.e. other programmes). Gaps in the latter are now well documented for certain habitats (WRI, 1989). There is broad agreement that, by these criteria, the wild relatives of plants of current economic importance are a first order priority, because of their role in increasing and maintaining the productivity of agricultural systems. Crop landraces are important for the same reason, but tend to be better represented in existing gene banks (Kloppenburg; WRI, 1989, p.64). Other important gaps in genetic conservation include many tropical species of regional importance (e.g. roots and tubers), species with recalcitrant seeds, and livestock (WRI, 1989).

Underutilised crops with wider potential should be a second order priority. Priorities attached at the local or regional level may again be different.

Priorities at the species and habitat level will be more difficult to determine. In setting **species** priorities it is important to distinguish between the following (Williams in Wilson, 1988):

i) domesticated species;
ii) wild relatives of domesticated species;
iii) species which are used but not domesticated;
iv) species (known or unknown) which might be useful.

Priorities for the first three categories have already largely been covered under genetic conservation. The conservation of species with tourist value are the obvious exception, but arguably this is already disproportionately well funded (Huntley in Wilson, 1988). Priority setting for the fourth category encounters the familiar problem of ignorance. Given such poor knowledge about which species occur where – let alone what their value might be – it is generally advocated that priorities be set on a habitat basis (Brady in Wilson, 1988). This is more tractable than a species approach – and is probably the best available approach – but still does not completely overcome the problem of ignorance, particularly in marine ecosystems.

Economic values are likely to be influential here. The relative importance of different domesticated/used species, other direct use-values (livelihood diversity or tourism), and/or indirect values (i.e. ecosystem services) should indicate broad ecosystem priorities. Option and existence values are unlikely to be large or quantifiable at a national level, or sufficiently differentiated between species or habitats. Except for those related to economic plants, they are likely to be a lower priority for assistance directed at developing countries.

These broad economic priorities then need to be combined with the other criteria listed above. Scientific decisions about habitat priorities have tended to use a form of "gap analysis". This classifies habitats, matches the classification with existing reserve coverage, and identifies poorly covered habitats as conservation priorities (Burley in Wilson, p. 228). The main shortcomings of this approach include a lack of biological information, and uncertainty about what constitutes adequate coverage (i.e. the minimum reserve size necessary to conserve biota over the long-term). These shortcomings can be overcome, and with a wider set of criteria employed, but the question of scale remains. In other words, how much biodiversity?

How much biodiverssity should be conserved?

Biogeographic theory indicates that there are approximate, if uncertain, relationships between area and species numbers. If it is assumed that species/habitat option and existence values are undifferentiated (i.e. that all species are equally valuable or useless, and intrinsic values are the same across the habitats), and given the uncertainty about the sensitivity of ecosystem services (indirect use-value) to loss of biodiversity, the most cost-effective option is to protect those areas with the highest concentration of species. A similar argument applies for the conservation of the genetic resources of economically important habitats. However, this still does not answer the question of how much biodiversity should be lost/conserved.

463

Economics cannot answer this question. Theoretical models to determine a socially optimal level of biodiversity conservation and/or habitat loss have ben proposed, but most of these are at a very early stage of development (Barrett, 1989; Southgate, 1988). This fact, together with the overriding problems of ignorance and uncertainty which characterise biodiversity, mean that they can only provide some general insights. The concept of a "safe minimum stock" (SMS) has been proposed as a possible solution (Bishop, 1978). This states that society should choose a strategy that minimises the maximum possible losses, or more exactly, that society should not deplete species beyond the critical population size (its SMS) unless the social costs are "unacceptably large". This immediately raises the questions – what is the SMS, and what is an "unacceptably large" social cost? Neither ecology nor economics can provide definite answers to these questions.

It is concluded that decisions on the scale of conservation can only be made on scientific and political grounds. This will incorporate consideration of ethical and aesthetic considerations. Economics can demonstrate that biodiversity is currently undervalued, that too little is being conserved, and that too much will be lost. This is true from the perspective of the world as a whole; from the perspective of any one developed country; and from the long-term perspective of developing countries which contain most of the biological diversity. Consideration of the various types of value can also yield general insights, but economics cannot determine the appropriate scale of activity. Whatever scale is chosen, the conservation of biodiversity in a situation of ever-increasing pressure requires rigorous prioritisation, and implementation of cost-effective conservation strategies.

CONCLUSIONS

The aim of this paper is to contribute to the development of an informed strategy for biodiversity conservation in developing countries. The work summarised has confirmed the value of biodiversity for developing countries, and the strong economic case for increased resources to be directed towards biodiversity conservation. Nevertheless, some of the economic arguments have been overstated by the conservation lobby. In part this reflects a confusion of biological resources with biological diversity. The value of the latter is difficult to ascertain, but is demonstrably distinct from, and less than, the value of biological resources as an entirety. The other reason why the value to developing countries may have been overstated is the failure to distinguish between types of value, and who stands to benefit. Local, developing country, developed country, regional and global values and priorities do not always coincide. These qualifications aside, the wider developmental and ethical case for biodiversity conservation remains strong.

There are three reasons why biodiversity is being lost in developing countries at such a dramtic rate despite its value: development pressure, market failure, and intervention failure. **First,** although biodiversity is valuable, other goods and services are often more immediately valuable. Some loss of biodiversity is thus an inevitable and justifiable cost of economic development and population growth. "Sustainable" development may reduce the rate of loss, but the influence of pressing economic problems, high discount rates and global markets will work against conservation. **Second,** because most of the value of biodiversity is not revealed in market prices, and the lack of clearly defined property rights, markets will fail to conserve sufficient biodiversity. Market failure is exacerbated by externalities, uncertainty, irreversibility, and market imperfections. **Third,** governments have not only been ineffective in intervening positively to correct market failure, but have also increased the loss of biodiversity with inappropriate policy interventions. In the absence of improved intervention, current policies and markets will result in the excessive loss of biodiversity.

Any strategy for addressing the problem of biodiversity loss must address these underlying causes. A strategy for biodiversity conservation must also confront three key issues: objectives, information, and priorities. This paper has argued that priorities will vary with the objectives, values and intended beneficiaries. The wide objective of any biodiversity expenditure within aid programmes should be to maximise the conservation and use of biodiversity in order to provide sustainable social and economic benefits to **developing countries.** Where funds are provided to meet global biodiversity objectives, the focus of programmes is likely to remain on developing countries, but with possibly significant differences in priorities. It follows from this that the priorities of aid agencies and conservation organisations are likely to differ in some respects.

The formulation of a strategy is hampered by the limited information on biological diversity. For many ecosystems there is a chronic shortage of information about the status, characteristics and management of habitats, species and the genetic resource. The degree of scientific uncertainty means that the scope for meaningful economic valuation is limited. This, and the lack of a single accepted measure of diversity, makes planning difficult. However, while the shortage of information is a real problem which warrants attention in its own right, there is arguably sufficient information to allow better priorities to be determined.

A major conclusion of this paper is that the need to determine priorities for biodiversity conservation is itself the first and major priority. For aid agencies this must extend beyond ecosystem-specific and country-specific priorities, important though these are, and consider biodiversity priorities for developing countries as a whole. Six main criteria are proposed: socio-economic value; diversity and distinctiveness; threat; gaps in other programmes; comparative advantage; and the likelihood of success. The exact criteria employed and the method of arriving at final priorities, is less important than a commitment to priority setting as a process.

The need for priorities is generally accepted. The problem lies in agreeing ranked priorities which take into account the resources likely to be available. Priority setting is a difficult and contentious process. However, the risk of continuing to avoid the need for real prioritisation is that scarce resources will not be used to best effect, and the key aspects of biodiversity of value to developing countries will be lost.

It is important that priorities for biodiversity conservation are not solely guided by biological or ecological criteria. The socio-economic value of biodiversity to developing countries, and to local groups within these, must be taken into account. Information is limited, but it is argued that all aspects of biodiversity are not equally valuable, and are not equally valued by different groups. One result of using a wider range of criteria is that conservation priorities may be less concentrated on tropical moist forests and other terrestrial centres of diversity. For example, the conservation of the wild relatives and diverse landraces of economic plants and animals, or of biodiversity in marginal areas under ecological stress, may be at least as important for the future of developing countries. Much of this type of biodiversity will be found in less diverse ecosystems.

Priorities for biodiversity conservation cannot be considered in isolation from the alternative means of achieving the objectives set. One strategy is to continue to try to improve the management of biological resources in general. The emphasis on sustainable economic development, the better valuation of renewable natural resources, strengthened national institutional capacity, and improved project appraisal methologies will all benefit the conservation and use of biodiversity. Arguably such a strategy does not go far enough. While it is clear that biodiversity will not be conserved without considering the broader context, improving the management of biological resources in general will not be sufficient. Biodiversity can and should be addressed as a distinct, but not separate issue.

A more positive response to the loss of biodiversity will require clear judgements to be made on the effectiveness of different conservation options. These fall into three broad groups: aid procedures, policy reforms and projects. Procedural improvements which give greater weight to biodiversity in project and programme design and appraisal are essential. These will not, however, address biodiversity loss outside the context of aid programmes. Policy reform, institutional strengthening and other wider approaches have a crucial role, but are still unlikely to be sufficiently effective on their own. The conservation of priority sites and aspects of biodiversity which are under serious threat require more immediate and targeted action. A project approach can provide this, provided long-term support is assured, and the wider policy and institutional environment is supportive. The general conclusion therefore is that combined procedural, policy and project action is required if the rate of biodiversity loss is to be slowed. The causes of biodiversity loss are too pervasive for there to be single or simple solutions. However, as with biodiversity objectives more generally, there is a more critical appraisal of the relative merits of alternative conservation activities.

The general case for biodiversity conservation in developing countries is now widely accepted. The greater awareness of the value of, and threats to, biodiversity has lead to a significant increase in the funding of conservation programmes. New funding sources, such as Global Environment Facility, will increase still further the resources available. However, while this trend is welcome and jusified, it is nevertheless the case that the financial resources available for biodiversity conservation are likely to remain limited in relation to the scale of problem. The pressure on natural habitats associated with increasing population and economic growth in developing countries will continue to lead to the loss of biological diversity. A recognition of the scale of the problem, the nature of the underlying causes, and the limited resources available to counteract powerful destructive trends means that there is an urgent need to set priorities. It is no longer sufficient to argue solely for an increase in funding, or to view any and all biodiversity initiatives as justified. There is now a need for a much more critical assessment of biodiversity projects and programmes. This will require a greater commitment to prioritisation between and within countries, ecosystems, species, and genetic resources, as well as improved monitoring of the effectiveness of different conservation activities.

REFERENCES

Barbier E.B. (1989). "Economics, natural resource scarcity and development: conventional and alternative views" Earthscan.

Barrett S. (1988). "Economic guidelines for the conservation of biological diversity". IUCN paper.

Barrett S. (1989). "Deforestation, biological conservation and the optimal provision of wildlife reserves" LEC paper 89–06.

Bishop R. (1978). "Endangered species and uncertainty: the economics of a safe minimum standard" *American J of Ag. Econ.* February 1978.

Brown G. & Goldstein J.H. (1984) "A model for valuing endangered species". *Journal of Environmental Economics and Management* 5 pp 292–300.

CGIAR (1987). "Priorities and future strategies" TAC Secretariat. FAO Rome.

Fisher A.C., Krutilla J.V. & Cichetti C.J. (1972). "The economics of environmental preservation: a theoretical and empirical analysis." *American Economic Review* 62 pp 605–19.

Flint M.E.S. (1990). "TFAP and non-wood products". Paper presented at the FOE/ODA conference on Sustainable Strategies for Saving Tropical Forests. London, May 1990.

Goodman G. & Hall A. (1988). "The future of Amazonia: destruction or sustainable development?" Macmillan.

Gregory R., Mendelsohn (1989). "Measuring the benefits of endangered species preservation – from research to policy". *J. of Environmental Management* 29 pp 399–407.

Grut M. (1989). "Economics of managing the African rainforest". Paper prepared for the Commonwealth Forestry Conference, September 1989.

Hecht S. & Cockburn (1989). "The fate of the forest – developers and destroyers of the Amazon". Verso.

Hall A.L. (1989). "Developing Amazonia: deforestation and social conflict in Brazil's Carajas programme". Manchester Unversity Press.

Hardin G. (1968). "The tragedy of the commons" *Science* Vol. 162.

Hyde W.F. (1983). "Development versus preservation in public resource management – a case study from the timber: wilderness controversy". *J. of Environmental Management* 16 pp 347–55.

IBPGR (1988). "Conserving the wild relatives of crops". IBPGR/IUCN/WWF.

IDS (1987). "The retreat of the state". IDS Bulletin XVIII July 3. Sussex.

IPCC (1989). "Biodiversity – a unifying theme paper". Working Group III paper.

IUCN *et al.* (1990). "Conserving the world's biodiversity". IUCN/WRI/CI/WWF-US/World Bank.

Ives J. & Pitt D.C. (1988). "Deforestation: social dynamics in watersheds and mountain ecosystems". Routledge.

Kloppenburg J.R. (1988). "Seeds and sovereignty: the use and control of plant genetic resources". Duke University Press.

Krautkraemer J.A. (1985). "Optimal growth, resource amenities and preservation of natural environments" *Review of Economic Studies* 52 pp 153–170.

Leach G. & Mearns R. (1988). "Beyond the woodfuel crisis: people, land and trees in Africa" Earthscan.

Ledec G. & Goodland R. (1988). "Wildlands: their protection and management in economic development" The World Bank.

Mahar D.J. (1989). "Government policies and deforestation in Brazil's Amazon region". World Bank.

Markandya A. & Pearce D. (1988). "Environmental considerations and the choice of discount rate in developing countries" Environment Department Working Paper No. 3 World Bank.

May R.M. (1988). "How many species are there on Earth?". *Science* Vol. 24 September 16 1988.

McNeely J.A. (1988). "Economics and biological diversity: developing and using economic incentives to conserve biological resources" IUCN.

McNeely J., Miller K. (1989). "Conserving the world's biological diversity". IUCN/WRI.

Melillo J. Palm C. (1985). "Comparisons of two recent estimates of disturbances in tropical forests". *Environmental Conservation* 12 (1).

Myers N. (1989). "Deforestation rates in tropical forests and their climatic implications" Friends of the Earth.

National Research (1986). "Proceedings of the conference on common property resource management" National Academy Press.

ODA (1988). "A strategy for research on renewable natural resources".

Pearce D. Markandya A. & Barbier E.B. (1989). "Blueprint for a green economy" Earthscan/IIED.

Pearce & Turner R. (1990). "Economics of natural resources and the environment"

Peters C.M., Gentry A. & Mendelsohn R.O. (1989). "Valuation of an Amazonian rainforest" *Nature* Vol. 339 June 1989 pp 655–6.

Poore D. (1989). "No timber without trees: sustainablility in the tropical forest" Earthscan.

Porter R. (1982). "The new approach to wilderness preservation through benefit-cost analysis". *Journal of Environmental Economics and Management* 9.

Prance G. (1990). "Fruits of the rainforest". *New Scientist* 13 January 1990.

Prescott-Allen R & C (1982). "What's wildlife worth" Earthscan.

Prescott-Allen R & C (1988). "Genes from the wild" Earthscan.

Redclift M. (1987). "Sustainable development: exploring contradictions".

Repetto R. (1986). "World enough and time: successful strategies for resource management" Yale University Press.

Repetto R. & Gillis M. (1988). "Public policies and the misuse of forest resources " World Resources Institute.

Ruitenbeek H.J. (1989). "Korup National Park social cost-benefit analysis" Appendix 13 in WWF/Republic of Cameroon "Korup Project: plan for developing the park and its support zone", WWF UK.

Schramm G. & Warford J. (1989) "Environmental management and economic development" World Bank.

Sedjo R. & Clawson M. (1983). "Tropical deforestation: how serious?" *Journal of Forestry* 81: 12 pp 792–94.

Southgate D. (1988). "Efficient management of biologically diverse tropical forests" LEEC paper no. 89–03.

Southgate D., Sierra R. & Brown L. (1989). "The causes of tropical deforestation in Ecuador: a statistical analysis" LEEC paper no. 89–09.

Schwartzman S. & Alegretti M.H. (1989). "Extractive production and the Brazilian Rubber tappers movement" *in* Hecht and Nations (eds).

Turner R.K. (ed.) (1988). "Sustainable environmental: principles and practice". Belhaven Press.

Wilson E.O. (ed.) (1988). "Biodiversity" National Academy Press.

World Resources Institute (1989). "Keeping options alive: the scientific basis for conserving biodiversity".

WWF (1984). "World Wildlife Fund yearbook 1983/84".

ACRONYMS

CGIAR	Consultative Group on International Agricultural Research
CI	Conservation International
FAO	Food and Agricultural Organisation
FOE	Friends of the Earth
LEEC	London Environmental Economics Centre
ODA	Overseas Development Administration
IBPGR	International Board for Plant Genetic Resources
IDS	Institute of Development Studies
IIED	International Institute for Environment and Development

Biological diversity

IPCC	Intergovernmental Panel Climate Change
IUCN	International Union for Conservation of Nature and Natural Resources
WCMC	World Conservation Monitoring Centre
WRI	World Resources Institute
WWF	World Wide Fund for Nature